THE INSPIRATION OF HOLY SCRIPTURE,

ITS NATURE AND PROOF:

EIGHT DISCOURSES,

PREACHED BEFORE THE UNIVERSITY OF DUBLIN.

BY

WILLIAM LEE, M.A.,

FELLOW AND TUTOR OF TRINITY COLLEGE.

Ἔστι γὰρ ἐν τοῖς τῶν Γραφῶν ῥήμασιν Ὁ ΚΥΡΙΟΣ.

S. ATHANASIUS, *Ad Marcellin.*

NEW YORK:

ROBERT CARTER & BROTHERS,

No. 530 BROADWAY.

1876.

PREFACE.

I DO not feel that any lengthened defence is necessary for having undertaken an inquiry into the subject with which the present work is occupied. Independently of the intrinsic importance of every question connected with the elucidation of Holy Scripture—the vagueness which too often characterizes the language employed by writers who, in modern times, have treated of its Inspiration seems to render a fundamental examination into the nature of this Divine influence daily more desirable.

So long, indeed, as the 'mechanical' theory of Inspiration was generally maintained, there was no want of distinctness or consistency in the views put forward. So long as it was believed that each word and phrase to be found in the Bible—nay, even the order and grammatical connection of such words and phrases—had been infused by the Holy Ghost into the minds of the sacred writers, or dictated to them by His immediate suggestion, so long must the opinion held respecting Inspiration have been clear, intelligible, and accurately defined. But such a theory could not stand the test of close examination. The strongest evidence against it has been supplied by the Bible itself; and each additional discovery in the criticism of the Greek or Hebrew text confirms anew the conclusion that the great doctrine of the infallibility of Holy Scripture can no longer rely upon such a principle for its defence.

The 'mechanical' theory having been tacitly abandoned—at least by all who are capable of appreciating the results of criticism—and no system altogether satisfactory having been proposed in its stead, there has gradually sprung up a want of definiteness and an absence of consistency in the language used when speaking of Inspiration, owing to which those who are most sincere in maintaining the Divine character of the Bible have, not unfrequently, been betrayed into concessions fatal to its supreme authority.

And not only is there a vagueness in the language which most writers employ when approaching this topic, there is also a want of completeness in the method usually adopted when discussing it. It is true that on one branch of the subject abundant and valuable information is to be found in various treatises; and so far as relates to the *direct* arguments which may be deduced from the expressions of the sacred penmen themselves in proof of their Inspiration, but little remains to be said that has not been forcibly said already. With reference, however, to the *nature* of Inspiration itself, and to the possibility of reconciling the unquestionable stamp of humanity impressed upon every page of the Bible with that undoubting belief in its perfection and infallibility which is the Christian's most precious inheritance—it may safely be maintained that in English theology almost nothing has been done; and that no effort has hitherto been made to grapple directly with the difficulties of the subject. At least I am unacquainted with any works in our language (with the exception of Mr. Westcott's "Gospel Harmony," where some valuable but brief remarks are thrown out incidentally, and the treatise of Mr. Morell, to which I shall presently revert,) that even profess to entertain the question.

There is one principle, too, which forms a chief element of the theory proposed in the following Discourses,—I mean the distinction between Revelation and Inspiration,—that has never, to my knowledge, been consistently applied to the contents of Holy Scripture, even by those writers who insist upon its importance. At all events, the principle has never hitherto been made use of to the extent of which it is obviously capable.

In advancing such assertions respecting the labors of others, I do not presume to lay claim to any amount of originality for my own. My object, throughout, has simply been to collect as many facts and results as my acquaintance with ancient or modern researches into the text or interpretation of Scripture could supply; and thence to deduce what appeared to be the necessary inference. In every inquiry so conducted, the safety of the inference must, of course, depend upon the extent of the induction: and, consequently, the success of the method which I have ventured to suggest is susceptible of being indefinitely increased, in proportion to the number of new facts and results which may hereafter be accumulated by those whose learning and attainments far surpass any that I can pretend to possess. At all events, there is one obvious, and by no means inconsiderable, advantage to be gained by pursuing this method. Valuable hints casting light upon the nature of Inspiration are being continually suggested; conclusive evidence in reply to the cavils of objectors is gradually accumulating; many positive arguments in support of the Church's belief in the Divine influence under which the Bible was composed repeatedly present themselves in the writings of theologians;—but the information thus existing is only to be discovered after diligent and patient toil. Such hints and arguments are, for the most part, confusedly scattered through the various "Introductions" to the Old and the New Testament; or they occur in the course of works which treat of 'Christian Evidences' in general; or they are to be occasionally found in some of those learned monographs with which the periodical literature of our time, and especially that of Germany, is enriched. To the ordinary inquirer, however, such information is practically inaccessible: and the labor must, therefore, be regarded as not destitute of utility that shall present, in a compact and intelligible form, elements so varied, and, in their original shape, so unconnected.

I have not scrupled, as I have said, to avail myself largely of the learning and researches of others: and among the works to which I owe the greatest obligations I may mention Olshausen's[1] "Commentary on the New

[1] It may not be unnecessary to add that, when I make use of the writings of others, it is by no means to be understood that I adopt any opinions put forward in the works referred to beyond those conveyed by the words which I have expressly quoted. E.g.: in Lecture vii. I have directly opposed certain views maintained by Olshausen; and, in Lecture i., the closing words of the former of the passages quoted in page 9, note [3]—viz: "und *nur zufällig* des Gesites nicht auch Erwähnung thut"—have been omitted, as conveying an idea altogether indefensible.

Testament;" Hävernick's "Introduction to the Old Testament;" Sack's "Christliche Apologetik;" Beck's "Propädeutische Entwicklung;" and, especially, Rudelbach's treatise on Inspiration, published in his and Guerike's "Zeitscrift." I have endeavored, in all cases, honestly to state how far I have thus borrowed, even at the risk of incurring the charge of pedantry. Should I be found, however, to have appropriated the labors of others without due acknowledgment, I trust that the manner in which I have treated the present subject will plead my excuse; since, in reproducing an extensive body of facts and results, it is occasionally impossible to trace to their source certain of the suggestions and ideas previously collected,—owing either to the loss of the original reference, or to some inadvertence in taking note of it.

There are two English treatises on the subject of Inspiration to which constant allusions will be found in the following pages:—Mr. Coleridge's "Confessions of an Inquiring Spirit;" and Mr. Morell's "Philosophy of Religion."

The former work has been thus alluded to by Dr. Arnold:—"Have you seen your uncle's 'Letters on Inspiration,' which I believe are to be published? They are well fitted to break ground in the approaches to that momentous question which involves in it so great a shock to existing notions; the greatest, probably, that has ever been given since the discovery of the falsehood of the doctrine of the Pope's infallibility."[1]

[1] "To Mr. Justice Coleridge, Jan. 24, 1835."—"Life and Correspondence," Letter xciv, 6th ed., p. 317.

It cannot be doubted, I apprehend, that Dr. Arnold's remark is, to a certain extent, well founded; and that this treatise of Mr. Coleridge has done more than any modern work to unsettle the public mind, in these countries, with respect to the authority due to the Bible *considered as a whole.* Independently of the high reputation and well-deserved influence of its author,—the peculiar charm of Mr. Coleridge's style and diction and the atmosphere of poetry with which his pen invests every subject on which it touches have gained for this posthumous work a celebrity which, I venture to think, is altogether disproportionate to its merits. Its leading features will be considered in the course of the following pages: for the present, therefore, I content myself with referring to Mr. Coleridge's statement of what he considered to be the strength of the argument with which he had to contend:—"It will, perhaps, appear a paradox," he observes, while repeating some of the popular objections to the infallibility of Scripture, "if, after all these reasons, I should avow that they weigh less in my mind against the Doctrine, *than the motives usually assigned for maintaining and enjoining it.* Such, for instance, are the arguments drawn from the anticipated loss and damage that would result from its abandonment; as that it would deprive the Christian world of its only infallible arbiter in questions of Faith and Duty; suppress the only common and inappellable tribunal; that the Bible is the only religious bond of union and ground of unity among Protestants, and the like."—*Letter* iv. Such having been his notion of the proofs which an upholder of the strict idea of Inspiration could allege in its behalf, it is not going too far to say that, of the many brilliant compositions with which he has enriched our literature, these "Letters" are the least worthy of Mr. Coleridge's genius; and that their subject was one upon which the extent of his information did not entitle him to pronounce an opinion.

The other treatise to which I have, in like manner, devoted considerable attention, is that of Mr. Morell; in which he professedly undertakes to recommend to English readers the theology of Schleiermacher (see *infra*, p. 11, note[3]). No stronger proof can be given of the unsettled state of opinion respecting Inspiration prevalent even with well-informed persons, than the manner in which the observations of Mr. Morell have been accepted by Dr. Peile. Dr. Peile, in his "Annotations on the Apostolical Epistles," when giving at length the passage of which I have cited a portion in Lecture i., page 21, introduces the quotation with the remark:—"To borrow the words of Mr. Morell, who, in his 'Philosophy of Religion,' has devoted two invaluable chapters to the elucidation of this deeply interesting subject."[1]

The extent to which the system of Schleiermacher strikes at the root of all objective Christianity, I have endeavored to exhibit in the following pages. I trust, however, that, while noticing Mr. Morell's adoption of Schleiermacher's views respecting Scripture, I have not expressed myself so as to appear insensible to the merits possessed by other portions of his remarks on the "Philosophy of Religion."

The form which the present work has, owing to special

[1] "Annotations on the Apostolical Epistles," vol. iii. p. 178.

circumstances,[1] assumed, is, perhaps, attended with some inconvenience; inasmuch as certain portions of the subject which might have been more fitly conjoined have been, of necessity, considered separately. I have endeavored, however, to remedy this inconvenience, such as it is, by the adoption of a system of cross references, whereby all that is said on any particular branch of the inquiry can be taken in at a single view. I may be permitted also to observe, that a reader who does not desire to enter minutely into the different questions discussed in the following pages, can obtain a full idea of the theory of Inspiration which I have proposed from Lectures i., iv., vi., and viii.

I cannot conclude without taking the opportunity of returning my warm thanks to the friends whose kindness and valuable assistance I have so repeatedly tasked during the progress of this volume through the press.

W. L.

DUBLIN, TRINITY COLLEGE,
June, 1854.

[1] This form has been imposed by the fact that the first six of the following Discourses were preached in the course of my duty as Donnellan Lecturer in this University for the year 1852.

CONTENTS.

LECTURE I.

THE QUESTION STATED.

LECTURE II.

THE IMMEMORIAL DOCTRINE OF THE CHURCH OF GOD.

LECTURE III.

THE OLD TESTAMENT AND THE NEW.—THE LOGOS THE REVEALER.

LECTURE IV.

REVELATION AND INSPIRATION.

LECTURE V.

REVELATION AND INSPIRATION.

(*Subject continued.*)

LECTURE VI.

SCRIPTURAL PROOF.

LECTURE VII.

THE COMMISSION TO WRITE.—THE FORM OF WHAT WAS WRITTEN.

LECTURE VIII.

RECAPITULATION.—OBJECTIONS CONSIDERED.

APPENDIX.

EDITIONS REFERRED TO IN THE FOLLOWING PAGES.

Novum Testamentum Græce,	Ed. Tischendorf, *Paris.* 1842
Vetus Test. Græce, juxta LXX. Interpretes,	Ed. Tischendorf, *Lips.* 1850.
Josephus,	Ed. Havercamp. *Amst.* 1726.
Philo Judæus,	Ed. Mangey, *Lond.* 1742.
"SS. Patres Apostolici,"	Ed. Coteler. *Amst.* 1724.
"Scriptor. Ecclesiast. Opusc." (rec. Routh),	Ed. altera, *Oxon.* 1840.
"Reliquiæ Sacræ" (rec. Routh),	Ed. altera, *Oxon.* 1846.
S. Ambrosius,	Ed. Ben. *Paris.* 1686.
S. Athanasius,	Ed. Ben. *Paris.* 1698.
Athenagoras (ap. Opp. S. Justin. Mart.),	Ed. Ben. *Paris.* 1742.
S. Augustinus,	Ed. Ben. *Paris.* 1679.
S. Basilius M.,	Ed. Ben. *Paris.* 1721.
Cassiodorus,	Ed. Ben. *Rothom.* 1679.
Clemens Alex.,	Ed. Potter, *Oxon.* 1715.
S. Cyprianus,	Ed. Ben. *Paris.* 1726.
S. Cyrill. Alex.,	Ed. Aubert. *Paris.* 1638.
S. Cyrill. Hieros.,	Ed. Ben. *Paris.* 1720.
S. Ephræm Syr.,	Ed. Asseman, *Romæ.* 1732.
S. Epiphanius,	Ed. Petav. *Paris.* 1622.
Eusebius Pamphili ("Hist. Eccl."),	Ed. Reading, *Cantab.* 1720.
S. Gregor. M.,	Ed. Ben. *Paris.* 1705.
S. Gregor. Nazianz.,	Ed. Ben. *Paris.* 1778, 1840.
S. Gregor. Neocæs.,	*Paris.* 1622.
S. Gregor. Nyssen.,	*Paris.* 1638.
S. Hieronymus,	Ed. Vallars. *Veron.* 1734.
S. Hilarius Pictav.,	Ed. Ben. alt. *Veron.* 1730.
S. Hippolytus,	Ed. Fabric. *Hamb.* 1716.
S. Irenæus,	Ed. Ben. *Paris.* 1710.
S. Isidorus Hispal.,	*Colon.* 1617.
S. Isidorus Pelus.,	*Paris.* 1638.
S. Johannes Chrysost.,	Ed. Ben. *Paris.* 1718.
S. Johannes Damascen.,	Ed. Le Quien, *Paris.* 1712.
S. Justin. Martyr,	Ed. Ben. *Paris.* 1742.
S. Macarius Ægypt. (ap. Opp. S. Gregor. Neocæs),	*Paris.* 1622.
Origenes,	Ed. Ben. *Paris.* 1733.
Tertullianus,	Ed. Rigalt. *Paris.* 1634.
Theodoretus,	Ed. Sirmond. *Paris.* 1642.
Theophilus Antioch. (ap. Opp. S. Justin. Mart.),	Ed. Ben. *Paris.* 1742.
Theophylact.,	Ed. De Rubeis, *Venet.* 1754.
S. Thomas Aquinas,	*Venet.* 1745.

LECTURE I.

THE QUESTION STATED.

"Quod colimus, Deus unus est, qui totam molem istam cum omni instrumento elementorum, corporum, spirituum, verbo quo jussit, ratione qua disposuit, virtute qua potuit, de nihilo expressit in ornamentum majestatis suæ, unde et Græci nomen mundo ΚΟΣΜΟΝ accommodaverunt. * * * Sed quo plenius et impressius tam Ipsum, quam dispositiones ejus et voluntates adiremus, instrumentum adjecit literaturæ, si qui velit de Deo inquirere, et inquisito invenire, et invento credere, et credito deservire."

TERTULL. *Apolog.* c. xvii. xviii.

"Scripturæ quidem perfectæ sunt, quippe a Verbo Dei et Spiritu ejus dictæ."

S. IRENÆUS, *Cont. Hær.* lib. ii. xxviii. 2.

Ὅσα ἡ θεία γραφὴ λέγει, τοῦ Πνεύματός εἰσι τοῦ Ἁγίου φωναί.

S. GREGOR. Nyssen. *Cont. Eunom.* Orat. vi.

LECTURE I.

THE QUESTION STATED.

WE ARE LABORERS TOGETHER WITH GOD.—1 *Cor.* iii. 9.

IN tracing the foundation of the Christian doctrine of Inspiration, all researches must arrive at one ultimate fact. Man, by his natural powers, can not attain to the knowledge of his Maker. "No man hath seen God at any time."[1] "Dwelling in the light which no man can approach unto, Him no man hath seen, nor can see."[2] Whence, then, is derived that knowledge on the degree of which depends the perfection of man's nature, and the ground of his hopes?

A philosopher of modern times, who makes no profession of any Christian sympathies, thus aptly states the question:—"It is a phenomenon which merits the attention, at least, of an observer, that among all nations, so far as they have raised themselves from the perfectly savage state to that of a community, there are to be found opinions of a communication between higher beings and men; traditions of supernatural inspirations and influences of the Deity upon mortals; in a word, although presented here more rudely, there under an aspect more refined, still, as a universal fact, the observer finds the notion of Revelation. This notion seems, of itself, were it only on account of its universality, to deserve some respect; and it appears more worthy of a fundamental philosophy to trace out its origin, to seek for its claims and its authority, and to pass sentence upon it according to the measure of these discoveries, rather than at once, and without a hearing, to class it among the inventions of deceivers, or to banish it to the land of dreams."[3] It is unnecessary here to state how far such

[1] John i. 18. [2] 1 Tim. vi. 16.

[3] "Versuch einer Kritik aller Offenbarung," von Johann Gottlieb Fichte.—s. 1 2te Auflage. Königsberg, 1793. See Appendix A.

a criticism has resulted in adding a further confirmation to the universal belief of mankind—a belief which has been expressed in every age and in every land. The fact, however, of such communications from the Supreme Being is one which may fairly be assumed; and with an examination of what is implied by a Divine Revelation, our inquiry must commence.

According to the usage of language, the word expressing this idea is employed in two different senses. It either denotes the Divine act of unveiling, or disclosing, or manifesting information to man—that is, the manner or form of the Revelation; or it signifies the very information thus imparted,—that is, the matter or contents. During the course of our inquiry we shall have occasion to consider each of these two significations, although the latter relates chiefly to the province of Bibilical exposition. As all knowledge of God is essentially connected with the idea of Religion, it may be well, in order to avoid ambiguity, to commence with the ordinary and real distinction conveyed by the phrases Natural and Revealed Religion; the former being founded upon such manifestations of the Divine Being, His will and acts, as are made by, or may be inferred from,—firstly, external nature, and, secondly, the inward constitution of man;[1] the latter having as its basis the revelation, strictly so-called, which rests upon facts,[2] and of which the record is the Bible, to which sense also it may be well to restrict the term "Revelation,"[3] (ἀποκάλυψις). The former class of Divine manifestations is implied and assumed in the Bible itself, which, as I have said, is the record of the latter; the term "manifestation" (φανέρωσις), too, being appropriated by St. Paul to this very idea.[4]

1 "So ist die natürliche Religion die Erkennbarkeit Gottes, das γνωστὸν τοῦ Θεοῦ (Röm. i. 19) aus den Werken, wofern diese nur mit Einschluss des Menschen als seines höchsten Werks gefasst werden * * * so ist auch die natürliche Religion ihrem Wesen nach Offenbarung."—Sack's *Christliche Apologetik*, s. 63.

2 I mean *facts*, as opposed to *phenomena*.

3 In the New Testament dialect ἀποκάλυψις has the fixed signification, "divine communication," "revelation." S. Jerome observes:

"Verbum quoque ipsum ἀποκαλύψεως, id est, *revelationis*, proprie Scripturarum est, et a nullo sapientum sæculi apud Græcos usurpatum. Unde mihi videntur quemadmodum in aliis verbis, quæ de Hebræo in Græcum Septuaginta Interpretes transtulerunt, ita et in hoc magnopere esse conatos, ut proprietatem peregrini sermonis exprimerent, nova novis rebus verba fingentes."—*Comment. in Ep. ad Gal.*, lib. i. cap. 1. tom. vii. p. 387.

In the LXX. the word ἀποκάλυψις is found but seldom; viz., 1 Sam. xx. 30; Ecclus. xi. 27; xxii. 22; xli. 23: but in none of these cases has it the sense of "divine communication."

4 Rom. i. 19, 20: "That which may be known of God is manifest (φανερόν) in

In the first place, in the world of sense, Nature[1] is represented in Scripture as disclosing the Being and the Agency of God. From it, as the organ of the Divine power, the *super*-natural shines forth: "The heavens declare the glory of God, and the firmament showeth his handywork."[2] The creation itself is an instance of God's coming forth from the mysterious and silent depths of his invisible Being; its pages present, as it were, a marvellous language in cipher, from which the Author permits some of His thoughts to be more or less distinctly inferred; "The invisible things of Him from the creation of the world are clearly seen, being understood by the things that are made, even His eternal power and Godhead."[3] Again, in the intimations afforded by the inward constitution of man, God manifests himself no less plainly in the world of thought; partly by the higher powers of knowledge, partly by the voice of conscience and the moral sense. In the depths of our souls we are conscious of feelings more sublime than can spring from our own finite and limited individuality.[4] "The Gentiles," writes the Apostle, "having not the Law, are a Law unto themselves, which show the work of the Law written in their hearts, their conscience also bearing witness."[5] These two sources of Divine knowledge imply each other, and belong to the province of philosophy. They are as universal as the human race; "there is no speech nor language where their voice is not heard."[6] God has never left Himself without a witness "in that He did good, and gave us rain from heaven, and fruitful seasons, filling our heart with food and gladness."[7] For, such "manifestations" of God's Being it is the duty of all to seek: "He hath made of one blood all nations of men, that they should seek the Lord, if haply they might feel after Him, and

them; for God hath showed it (ἐφανέρωσεν) unto them." Cf. Acts, xiv. 17. Bretschneider was, I believe, the first thus to employ the term "manifestation" as expressive of the peculiar sense in which the Apostle here applies the idea.—Cf. "Handbuch der Dogmatik," 1er Band. s. 155, 4te Auflage.

[1] Cf. Bockshammer's "Offenbarung und Theologie," s. 5.

[2] Ps. xix. 1.

[3] Rom. i. 20.

[4] Twesten, referring to the arguments which reason supplies for the existence of God, justly appeals to the results of modern investigations in proof of the proposition that reflecting upon the *finite* can never lead man beyond *the finite*, if he does not already bear within himself the consciousness of the *Infinite*.—Cf. "Vorlesungen über die Dogmatik," 1er Band. s. 345.

[5] Rom. ii. 14, 15.

[6] Ps. xix. 3.

[7] Acts, xiv. 17

find him, though He be not far from every one of us, for in Him we live, and move, and have our being."[1]

The particulars just considered form the groundwork of what is termed Natural Religion ; the conveyance of God's will by means of facts[2] is the foundation of what we term Revealed Religion. Natural and Revealed Religion can never be contrasted ; but there is a real, although it is but relative contrast between the channels through which they are conveyed, i. e., between Nature and Revelation.[3] How, then, are they related ; and where in nature can we recognise a Divine activity other than that exhibited in the order of the universe ?[4] Nature and Revelation alike proceed from God, and, consequently, if their relation to each other be correctly expressed, all semblance of absolute opposition must, of itself, disappear. We have, therefore, to seek for some point in which they both unite ; in which Nature assumes a religious aspect, as plainly as Revelation presents itself as a matter of fact.

We have assumed that the Divine influence over Nature did not cease at the act by which the world was called into being :—the perfection of creation, surely, does not suspend the vital impulse which it received from God, nor is the Creator's power to be restricted to the original imposition of purely mechanical laws. Now, if God speak by means of the phenomena of the universe to the spirit of man, such a result can never be ascribed to the purely natural element which pervades the world. This only points to some other element of the same kind, equally finite with itself ; and by virtue of the chain of causes reveals to us

[1] Alluding to the passage here cited (Acts, xvii. 26–28) Bretschneider (*loc. cit.*) observes: "Bei der Manifestation ist der Mensch activ, und muss Gott *suchen* und ergreifen." This writer goes on to confound the ideas of *Revelation* and *Inspiration*. Inspiration he defines to be that species of Revelation in which God acts without the intervention of any intermediate cause ("sine causarum externarum interventu ; and as man is *active* in the case of "Manifestation," so in "Inspiration" he is *passive* ("Bei der Inspiration verhält sich der Mensch leidend") ; in proof of which he quotes 2 Pet. i. 21. But see *infra*, p. 40.

To the class of Divine "Manifestations" some writers (e. g. C. F. Fritzsche, "De Revelationis notione Biblica, p. 13) add that effected by the course of history : "Our fathers understood not Thy wonders in Egypt. * * * Nevertheless He saved them for His name's sake, that He might make his mighty power to be known."—Ps. cvi. 7, 8, cf. Ps. cxxxvi.

[2] E. g. the giving of the Law from Sinai—the Incarnation, &c.

[3] "Differunt certe informationes oraculi et sensus et re et modo insinuandi : sed spiritus humanus unus est, ejusque arculæ et cellæ eædem. Fit itaque, ac si diversi liquores, atque per diversa infundibula, in unum atque idem vas recipiantur."—Bacon, *De Augment. Scient.* lib. ii. cap. i.

[4] This subject is discussed by Sack in his remarks, "Vom Begriffe der Offenbarung," *Apologetik*, ss. 114–147

nothing more than the mutual dependence of the particular existences in the world of Nature, but not the sovereignty of God. That which reveals the Supreme Being, and thus mediates between God and man, is the divine LOGOS, or Creating Word, which proceeds from the essence of Deity. Without this notion there is no religious view of Nature, nor can we recognize its Divine Author as revealed by it.[1] It is only the relationship of our spirit to this Original Intelligence (which is at once exalted above Nature, and really operative within it), which renders it even conceivable that Nature should thus influence us. Between this view of the world and Atheism (which banishes God from His universe), or Pantheism (which identifies Him with it), there is no alternative. Hence it is that the active revealing power in Nature, and the historically revealing element in Religion, have one and the same principle. In short, the true notion of all Revelation is expressed in a saying of S. Athanasius when speaking of the Incarnation:—"It was the office of the Divine Word, who by His peculiar providence, and setting in order of the universe, affords instruction concerning the Father, to renew that same instruction."[2] This renewed instruction effected by direct communications from above, as well as that "manifestation" of God effected through the medium of Nature, are alike to be traced to the same Eternal Word. No man hath seen God at any time, the only-begotten Son, which is in the bosom of the Father, He hath declared Him."[3] Now, Revelation, properly so called, is distinguished in Scripture into Revelation by Word, and Revelation by Act—the

[1] "So ist alle Offenbarung ein Thatwort des Logos an den Geist des Menschen; und dieses Thatwort auch in der Natur zu erkennen, ist die einzige Art, die Natur religiös und als Mittel der Offenbarung anzusehen."—Sack's *Apologetik*, s. 121.

[2] S. Athanasius, *De Incarn.* cap. 14, tom i. par. i. p. 59. The chapter begins by stating that when the features of a portrait have been effaced, it is necessary that the original should again be present, in order that the likeness may be restored. *Κατὰ τοῦτο καὶ ὁ πανάγιος τοῦ πατρὸς ὑιὸς, ἐικὼν ὢν τοῦ πατρὸς, παρεγένετο ἐπὶ τοὺς ἡμετέρους τόπους, ἵνα τὸν κατ' ἀυτὸν πεποιημένον ἄνθρωπον ἀνακαινίσῃ * * * τίνος ὂυν ἦν πάλιν χρεία, ἢ τοῦ θεοῦ λόγου τοῦ καὶ ψυχὴν καὶ νοῦν ὁρῶντος, τοῦ καὶ τὰ ὅλα ἐν τῇ κτίσει κινοῦντος, καὶ δι' ἀυτῶν γνωρίζοντος τὸν πατέρα; τοῦ γὰρ διὰ τῆς ἰδίας προνοίας καὶ διακοσμήσεως τῶν ὅλων διδάσκοντος περὶ τοῦ πατρὸς, ἀυτοῦ ἦν καὶ τὴν ἀυτὴν διδασκαλίαν ἀνανεῶσαι.*

In addition to this passage (the closing sentence of which is quoted by Sack, p. 132), I may adduce the expression of the same thought by S. Irenæus: "Per ipsam conditionem, revelat Verbum conditorem Deum, et per mundum fabrificatorem mundi Dominum, et per plasma eum qui plasmaverit artificem, et per Filium eum Patrem qui generaverit Filium * * * Sed per Legem et Prophetas similiter Verbum et Semetipsum et Patrem prædicabat."—*Cont. Hær.*, lib. iv. cap. vi. p. 234.

[3] John i. 18.

Act, or miracle, representing and expressing, in the world of sense, what the Word, or knowledge communicated, expresses in the world of thought: the former being to the ordinary law of Nature, what the latter is to the light of Reason.[1] In one point of time, and in one form of life, both these elements have found their perfect union. Both have been united in Him who is the subject of all Revelation.[2] The being to whom we must ascribe the words, although expressed by the messengers of God; He who, in like manner, performed the acts, although by the instrumentality of these same agents, was the LOGOS, God's eternal, personal, self-Revelation,—God, who as Word, spiritually, and yet really, maintains the world.[3] But now the fact of the Incarnation presents to our view both these forms of Revelation combined;—that entrance of the Eternal Word into the personal and historical limitations of a "Son of Man." In this great fact Revelation, on its historical side, has been closed, on its spiritual side has been rendered perfect and immortal. And thus we can not conceive (nor does Scripture record) that any Revelation was ever made *to* Christ. He was not only the *Revealer*,—"the true Light which lighteth every man that cometh into the world,"[4]—but also *the* Revelation, "God manifest in the flesh."

There are three epochs in which Divine Revelation gives to the history of religion the very condition of its existence:—The Primitive Revelation; the Covenant Revelation to Israel; Revelation in the appearance of Christ. It has pleased God that of this Revelation a record should be conveyed to after times. It could only be conveyed by the medium of language; and since Scripture appears, in history, as the acknowledged means of preserving this record, we here behold the transmission of Revelation by a written document. But whence the title Holy Scripture?

[1] Cf. "Twelve Sermons on Heb. i. 1, 2," delivered at the Boyle Lecture, A. D. 1708, by Bishop Williams (of Chichester), p. 17: a work which, notwithstanding some (as I conceive) erroneous statements as to Inspiration, is of much value.

[2] In God as Logos, Word and Act are ever united: "He spake, and it was done; He commanded, and it stood fast."—Ps. xxxiii. 9. "Wie sein Wort immer die allererfolgreichste That ist, schlechtin schaffend: so ist auch seine That immer im höchsten Grade redend und unendlich Gedanken erzeugend."—Sack, s. 136.

[3] Nature, observes S. Athanasius, is sustained and preserved by the Logos from that dissolution which its own fleeting and frail materials must have induced. For God who by His eternal Word gave existence to the Creation,—

Ὡς ἀγαθὸς τῷ ἑαυτοῦ λόγῳ καὶ ἀυτῷ ὄντι θεῷ τὴν σύμπασαν διακυβερνᾷ καὶ καθίστησιν, ἵνα τῇ τοῦ λόγου ἡγεμονίᾳ καὶ προνοίᾳ καὶ διακοσμήσει φωτιζομένη ἡ κτίσις, βεβαίως διαμένειν δυνηθῇ.—Orat. cont. Gentes. n. 41, tom. i. p. 40.

[4] John, i. 9, cf. Luke, ii. 32.

Traced to its true source, this notion depends upon the fact, that the ideas of the Eternal Word, and of the Divine Spirit, are here, to a certain degree, correlative.[1] The Word, as divine and eternally *creative*, has the Spirit as the divine and eternally *animating* principle, in and with Himself. By the agency of the Divine Spirit the meaning and the will of the Eternal Word are introduced into the real being of things.[2] All divine activity in the world is organic. So also the arrangements of God's Revelation form a system which comprehends all things ; which aids in bringing light into darkness ; whose centre is Christ, to whom every Revelation in earlier times must be referred, and from whom every Revelation, of a later period, has proceeded, by vir-

[1] Cf. Sack, "Von der heiligen Schrift," *Apologetik*, s. 418.

The topic here introduced is so essential to a just view of the present subject, that I am induced to quote in full the following passages. On Rom. xi. 36 (*ἐξ ἀυτοῦ καὶ δι' ἀυτοῦ καὶ ἐις ἀυτὸν τὰ πάντα*), Olshausen observes:—

"Paul at length closes his great dogmatic discussion with a doxology, in which God is described as embracing all things—as the Beginning, Middle, and End, of all things, and, consequently, of the believing Israel as a whole, and of every individual. That these references are what is intended by the prepositions *ἐξ*, *διά*, and *εἰς*, is no longer questioned by later expositors. But, on the other hand, they continue blind to the fact that these references also express the relation of Father, Son, and Spirit. In an exactly similar way it is said of God, Eph. iv. 6, *ὁ ἐπὶ πάντων καὶ διὰ πάντων, καὶ ἐν πᾶσιν*. Of the Father as the *source* of all being, *ἐκ* or *ὑπό* is always (*stets*) used in the New Testament, and *ἐπί* with respect to His absolute power; of the Son, always *διά*, as the Revealer of the Father, the organ of His agency (comp. on John i. 3); of the Spirit, *εἰς*. so far as He is the End to which the divine agency leads, or *ἐν*, so far as He is the element which penetrates and supports all things. 1 Cor. viii. 6, is decisive in favor of this interpretation; where Paul himself explains the *ἐξ οὗ* and *δι' οὗ* of the Father and the Son."—*Der Brief an die Röm.*, Comm. 3er Band. s. 420.

Again, on Col. i. 17, Olshausen, returning to this subject, writes as follows:—

"The various relations of the creature to the Eternal are expressed by the prepositions *διά*, *εἰς*, and *ἐν*. The *διά* refers to the *origin* of the creature, which proceeds from the Father *through* the Son; *εἰς* refers to the *end* of the creature, as all is created *to* or *for* Him, as the final aim of things (cf. verse 20); on the other hand *ἐν* points, as the *συνέστηκε* unmistakeably shows, to the present stability of the world, which is always *in* the Son, so far as He supports and upholds the world with His word (Heb. i. 3), and the upholding may also be considered as a continuation of the creation. There is but *one* difficult point in this description, which sets forth Christ's divine nature in the most distinct manner; namely, that elsewhere the relation of the Holy Ghost to the creature is usually expressed by the prepositions *εἰς* and *ἐν* (cf. on Rom. xi. 36); but here the Son is always the subject. In other passages, e. g. 1 Cor. viii. 6, *εἰς* is also used of the Father. However, this difficulty is satisfactorily explained by the fact, that to each of the three Divine Persons, by Himself, just because they are *real* Persons, and carry life in themselves, all relations of the Trinity can be attributed."—*Der Brief an die Coloss.*, Comm. 4er Band. s. 339.

This reference to the mystery of the Trinity, as denoted by the three prepositions, is noticed by Origen, Comm. in Epist. ad Rom. lib. VIII. tom. iv. p. 642. The passage is quoted by Mr. Alford *in loc.*

[2] It is well observed by Rudelbach, in his Essay "Die Lehre von der Inspiration der heil. Schrift," published in his Journal för 1840, that "the transition to a written document, composed according to God's will, can detract in no respect from the power and efficacy of His Word. On this assumption rests the whole notion of Inspiration."—1er Theil. s. 24.

tue of that Holy Spirit imparted, through Him, to the world.[1] This agency of the Holy Spirit, by the very force of the term, forms the essence of the idea of Inspiration ; and the two conceptions thus pointed out, of the Eternal Word as the Divine Person who reveals, and of the Holy Spirit as the Divine Person who inspires, are the pillars upon which must rest any theory respecting the Bible and its origin which can deserve serious notice.[2]

But, before entering upon the direct question of Inspiration, a matter of vital moment must be adverted to, any confusion of ideas respecting which must perforce mar and distort the whole aspect of the inquiry. It must first be settled, What is the Bible ? and In what light are we to regard it ? In reply to the former of these questions, with which the present investigation is not directly concerned, I point to that collection of writings, whether of the Old or New Testament, which our Church accepts as Canonical, and which she defines in her Sixth Article. The answer to the latter question, viz., "In what light is the Bible, as a collection of such and such books, to be regarded ?" demands some observation. There is an error growing up in our time, closely allied to that false spiritualism which in the second century formed the essence of the heresy of Marcion, which draws a sharp line of distinction between the Old Testament and the New. The leading representative of this opinion in modern times is the founder of a school which commands extensive influence on the Continent, and the principles of which have been recently advocated with no small ability among ourselves.[3] The

[1] Cf. Twesten's "Vorlesungen," 1er Band. p. 289.

[2] See on this question Lecture iii. *infra.*

[3] "The Philosophy of Religion, by J. D. Morell, A.M. London, 1849."

"If there be one mind whose personality may have impressed itself more than any other upon my own, in tracing out the whole course of the following treatise, it is assuredly that of the revered Schleiermacher; indeed the analysis of the idea of religion, and its reference to the absolute feeling of dependence, is taken substantially out of the introduction to his great work, the 'Glaubenslehre.' That God would send such a mind and such a heart to shed their influence upon ourselves, and guide us from the barren region of mere logical forms into the hallowed paths of a divine life, is the best wish I can breathe for the true welfare of every religious community in our land."—Pref. p. xxxiii.

Quinet, in his eloquent essay on Strauss in the "Revue des Deux Mondes" for 1838 (tom. 4me., p. 463, &c.), adverts with justice to the influence of Schleiermacher. He observes, that in the commotion of the German mind, and the daily increasing destruction of all belief, nothing causes him greater surprise than the calmness of those writers "qui, effaçant chaque jour un mot de la Bible, ne sont pas moins tranquilles sur l'avenir de leur croyance." Schleiermacher was the greatest of them all—

founder of this school, the celebrated Schleiermacher, maintains that while Christianity is no doubt connected historically with Judaism by the fact that Jesus was born among the Jewish people, still the reason of this merely was, that the universal Redeemer could not well appear except among a monotheistic people.[1] This whole system regards the Old and New Testament as factors of a perfectly heterogeneous nature: the Law is not inspired; nor even the historical parts of the Old Testament;[2] and Christianity, so far as its peculiar features are concerned, stands in precisely the same relation to Judaism as to Heathenism. But not to dwell upon sentiments so extreme, and from which even the followers of Schleiermacher seem to recoil,[3] I can refer to the views of a respectable English writer. Dr. Pye Smith thus expresses himself in some remarks upon the Old Testament contained in his work on "The Scripture Testimony to the Messiah:"—"Many of the facts thus recorded have not *directly* a religious interest, but they were valuable to the Israelites and Jews as fragments of national and family history; and in our times they have proved to be of great importance in casting light upon the almost lost history of several nations."[4]

"fait pour régner dans ce trouble universel si l'anarchie dés intelligences eût consenti à recevoir un maître."

[1] Cf. "Der Christliche Glaube von Dr. Friedrich Schleiermacher," 4te Aufgabe, Berlin, 1842. 1er Band. s. 77. And even this prerogative of the Jews must be received with qualifications: "Und so war auf der andern Seite auch das hellenische und römische Heidenthum auf mancherlei Weise monotheistisch vorbereitet, und dort die Erwartung auf eine neue Gestaltung aufs äusserste gespannt, so wie im Gegentheil unter den Juden die messianischen Verheissungen theils aufgegeben waren, theils missverstanden. So dass wenn man alle geschichtlichen Verhältnisse zusammenfasst, der Unterschied weit geringer ausfällt, als auf den ersten Anblick scheint."—s. 78.

[2] Nay more, as to the value of the Old Testament for Christians: "Werden wir gewiss eben so nahe und zusammenstimmende Anklänge auch in den Aeusserungen des edleren und reineren Heidenthums antreffen."—s. 80.

[3] E. g. Twesten, who, as Nitzsch justly observes ("Studien und Kritiken," 1828 s. 227), rather omits the consideration of this question, than treats it with the attention which its importance deserves. Nevertheless he follows in the footsteps of his master so far as to assert, "We cannot regard these writings as a rule for Christians, and, therefore, the question arises, how we are to regard them from the stand-point of Christian theology."—*Vorlesungen*, 1er Band. s. 322.

[4] "The Scripture Testimony to the Messiah." 2d Ed. vol. i., notes, p. 41. Of this "note" Mr. Morell observes, "So, also, to some extent that admirable scholar and theologian, Dr. J. P. Smith, in one of his notes to the Scripture Testimony to the Messiah; a note which had almost brought out the controversy [as to Inspiration] fairly into this country, but that its hour was not yet arrived."—*The Philosophy of Religion*, p. 189. I quote this observation as illustrating the extent to which the question has been fermenting in the public mind.

Mr. Morell himself observes, with respect to the books of the Old Testament from Joshua to Chronicles: "All that we can say is, that they were universally received,

All such views, according to the principles which it will be my endeavor to establish, are founded upon a fundamentally erroneous conception of the nature and structure of the Bible. This Divine record, comprising the two great divisions of Old and New Testament, presents itself to the acceptance of mankind as one organized whole: as an elaborate structure whose various parts conspire to the attainment of one definite end, the entire edifice being constructed according to one grand design. That one end is the Salvation of man,—that grand design is the economy of Redemption. The stage on which this great drama was to be enacted was the history of the human race; and in no other language than that of the Bible itself can be described the antithesis which this history affords: "God saw every thing that He had made, and behold it was very good,"[1] is the statement of the first chapter of the Old Testament;—the writer who closes the New Testament, on the other hand, proclaims, "We know that we are of God, and the whole world lieth in wickedness."[2] With the two ideas of Redemption and Salvation, the entire framework of Revelation is inseparably connected. To the first man was given a hope of the redemption of his race; and beyond this the last of the Prophets can not go.[3] The appearance of the Redeemer Himself did no more than give reality to these anticipations.

There is an inseparable bond of union connecting the two divisions of the inspired volume: "The law was our schoolmaster to bring us unto Christ."[4] The aim of each earlier Revelation of the Eternal Word was to restore, in their original purity, the lost truths of religion, and to build them up anew in the midst

both as veracious histories, and as containing correct religious sentiments, by the Jewish people."—*Ibid.* p. 161.

Of the Psalms, he concludes:—

"All we can say is, that they embodied the religious consciousness, or, if the term be preferred, the state of *inspiration* to which the mind of the writer was elevated."—P. 162. This view may be illustrated by what the author had just observed as to the Pentateuch: "All we mean is, that the inspiration here involved did not spring from any outward commission to write that particular book; but only from the Divine light which was granted to the age, and to the mind of the author—a gift which he was left to make use of as necessity or propriety might suggest."—*Ibid.* p. 161.

[1] Gen. i. 31. [2] 1 John, v. 19.

[3] See Davison, "Discourses on Prophecy," 5th Ed. p. 74. Twesten has received much praise for having similarly connected the ideas of Revelation and Redemption. "Unter Offenbarung verstehen wir hier die Aeusserung der göttlichen Gnade zum Heile (εἰς σωτηρίαν) des gefallenen Menschen in ihrer ursprünglichen Wirkung auf die menschliche Erkentniss."—*Vorlesungen*, 1er Band. s. 345.

[4] Gal. iii. 24.

of historical and positive false religions.[1] This latter circumstance, of necessity, stamped a character of separation upon the Revelation of the Old Testament; which Revelation, however, from its design of restoration, must be also characterized by a principle of development. The patriarchal Revelation elected and separated an individual and his family; the sanctions of its covenant were faith and hope.[2] When this became clouded by idolatry and unbelief, a new Revelation was annexed to and founded upon it; and which, while it imposed, in the Mosaic Law, a more positive or penal discipline,[3] held out in the field of prophecy a greater fulness of promise, and a brighter prospect of hope. In the legal element, Revelation develops more strongly its separating character; in the element of promise, its movement in advance is more apparent, removing more and more the barriers which confined the covenant people. Lastly, the Dispensation introduced by Christ includes and perfects all previous phases of Revelation, and combines them in itself into an organism complete on all sides. It perfects both the legal and promissory side of the Old Testament Revelation. The Law becomes real, living truth; the promise becomes actual grace: "The Law was given by Moses, but grace and truth came by Jesus Christ."[4] Its individuality is now stamped with universality: "Many shall come from the east and west, and shall sit down with Abraham, Isaac, and Jacob, in the kingdom of heaven."[5] Its character of separation at length expands into that of a kingdom of the elect, extending over all the people of the world. And thus, following the course and progress of Revelation, the several parts of the inspired volume sprang gradually into being: "The brook became a river, and the river became a sea."[6]

The immediate design, indeed, of each element of this collection of writings, or the precise end attained by its connection with the others, we may not as yet be able to discern—although the progress of knowledge, and the light afforded by the fulfilment of prophecy, have largely extended our information as to these

[1] Compare, on this point, the admirable remarks of Beck, pp. 120–143 of his "Propädeutische Entwicklung der Christlichen Lehr-Wissenschaft," Stuttgart, 1838.

[2] "Your father Abraham," said Christ to the Jews, "rejoiced to see my day, and he saw it and was glad."—John, viii. 56; cf. Heb. xi.

[3] "Wherefore then serveth the Law? It was added because of transgressions."—Gal. iii. 19; cf. Rom. vii. 7.

[4] John, i. 17.

[5] Matt. viii. 11.

[6] Ecclus. xxiv. 31.

matters.[1] But, the fact of such ignorance respecting the purpose of each portion, and the functions performed by it in the organized structure of the Holy Scriptures, is no reason for our denying that a purpose was designed; while, as in the case of every organized whole, each discovery of such or such a final cause but serves to illustrate the connection and mutual relation of all its parts, although our researches may fall very far short of perfection. Take, for example, the animal economy. The veins and arteries had performed their appointed functions, and diffused the vital current through the frame for thousands of years before their final cause was pointed out. To the present hour the nervous system remains a mystery; and yet, who will question its importance or its utility?[2] And, to carry the analogy one step farther,—as the various portions of the animal structure are called at different times and for different purposes into different degrees of activity, so the relative value and prominence of the various parts of Scripture alter according to the wants and interests of the age. In our day, certain portions of Holy Writ, which were of main importance in the early ages of the Church (and which will maintain to the last their vital, though relative, value), may not be of such immediate practical applicability; while, on the other hand, what is all essential now was not then so peculiarly called into action. The character of the inspired record itself, however, does not vary. The landscape remains

[1] Thus St. Jerome profoundly observes:—"Paralipomenon liber, id est, Instrumenti veteris ἐπιτομή, tantus ac talis est, ut absque illo si quis scientiam Scripturarum sibi voluerit arrogare, se ipsum irrideat. Per singula quippe nomina, juncturasque verborum, et prætermissæ in Regum libris tanguntur historiæ, et innumerabiles explicantur Evangelii quæstiones."—*Epist.* liii. *ad Paulinum*, tom. i. p. 277.

Thus it is that Ezra, i. 1, is inexplicable without the predictions of Isaiah and Jeremiah; which, in their turn would be altogether obscure without the record of their fulfilment preserved by Ezra and Nehemiah. Again, as Mr. Westcott justly remarks, "The relation of Christianity to the old dispensation, which is historically exhibited in St. Matthew, is argumentatively deduced and specially illustrated in the Epistle to the Hebrews, the authority of which can never be doubted by those who have any deep sense of the perfect providential instruction of the Church; for without it the types of the Old Testament are, in most cases, unexplained, and the full significance of the past unrecognized and undeclared."—*Elements of the Gospel Harmony*, p. 140. See Appendix B.

[2] Origen has well developed this same analogy:

* * * *ὁι γὰρ περὶ τὰς ἀνατομὰς πραγματευσάμενοι τῶν ἰατρῶν, δυνάνται λέγειν ἕκαστον καὶ τὸ ἐλάχιστον μόριον ἐις τὶ χρήσιμον ὑπὸ τῆς προνοίας γεγένηται· νόει μοι τοίνυν καὶ τὰς γραφὰς τοῦτον τὸν τρόπον πάσας βοτάνας, ἢ ἓν τέλειον λόγου σῶμα· ἐι δὲ σὺ μήτε βοτανικὸς ἐι γραφῶν, μήτε ἀνατομεὺς τῶν προφητικῶν λόγων, μὴ νόμιζε περι έλκειν τι τῶν γεγραμμένων ἀλλὰ σεαυτὸν μόνον ἢ τὰ ἱερὰ γράμματα ἀιτιῶ, ὅτε μὴ ἑυρίσκεις τὸν λόγον τῶν γεγραμμένων.*—*Homil.* xxxix. *in Jerem.* tom. iii. p. 286.

still the same, although the sun, as the storm-cloud floats along, may lend greater brilliancy to some features of the scene, and cast others for a moment into the shade.

The various parts of Holy Scripture, then, I would again repeat, in order to be rightly understood, or justly valued, must be regarded as the different members of one vitally organized structure; each performing its appropriate function, and each conveying its own portion of the truth. Consider the parts sustained by two of our four Gospels. A one-sided apprehension of Apostolic teaching had introduced in the early Church different phases of false doctrine. Had there been but one Gospel, the Church's teaching might have been, in like manner, one-sided. From the Gospel of St. Matthew the higher nature of Christ could not have been so clearly proved to the Ebionites, as from that of S. John; while the former was better calculated to oppose the dreams of the Gnostics.[1] But the four Gospels having been combined in the Canon, the Church has thus been defended on all sides. Hence the Gospels were well termed by an early Father[2] the four

[1] Of these heresies S. Irenæus observes:

"Ebionei eo Evangelio, quod est secundum Matthæum, solo utentes, ex illo ipso convincuntur, non recte præsumentes de Domino. * * * Hi autem qui a Valentino sunt, eo quod est secundum Joannem plenissime utentes ad ostensionem conjugationum suarum ex ipso detegentur," &c.—*Cont. Hær.*, lib. iii. 11, p 189.

[2] S. Irenæus. 'Επειδὴ * * * *στύλος δὲ καὶ στήριγμα ἐκκλησίας τὸ ἐυαγγέλιον, καὶ πνεῦμα ζωῆς, ἐικότως τέσσαρας ἔχειν ἀυτὴν στύλους.*—*Ibid.* p. 190. S. Irenæus adds the well-known comparisons of the four regions of the world, the four principal spirits, and, in fine, the four forms which made up the Cherubim, (Ezek. i. 10. Rev. iv. 7.); observing that the Divine Logos, who sits upon the Cherubim, "dedit nobis quadriforme (*τετράμορφον*) Evangelium, quod uno spiritu continetur." In like manner, S. Cyprian: "Ecclesia Paradisi instar exprimens, arbores fructiferas intra muros suos intus includit. * * * Has arbores rigat quatuor fluminibus, id est Evangeliis quatuor."—Ep. lxxiii. p. 132. On this passage Mr. Westcott aptly observes:—"An old Father compared our four Evangelists to the rivers which encircled the earthly Paradise: truly their streams spring from different lands, and flow in different ways: yet each protects some boundary of the Church, and conveys to it the waters of life."—*Elements of Gospel Harmony*, p. 73. To the same effect S. Jerome styles the four Evangelists "quadriga Domini, et verum Cherubim."—Ep. liii. *ad Paulinum*, tom. i. p. 278.

Gieseler, in his essay "On the origin of the written Gospels," p. 200, points out with his usual learning the source of such metaphorical language, which writers unacquainted with the questions agitated in the primitive Church are wont to regard as puerile or unmeaning. The heretics continually objected that the Church claimed *four* Gospels, while the Apostles taught but *one*. Thus, in the "Dialogus de recta in Deum fide," which is contained in the first volume of the works of Origen, the Marcionite argues:

'Εγὼ *ἐλέγχω ἑτέρωθεν, ὅτι φάλσα ἐστὶν τὰ ἐναγγέλια, λέγει γὰρ ὁ ἀπόστολος ἓν ἐναγγέλιον, ὑμεῖς δὲ τέσσαρα λέγετε.*—P. 807.

Hence, observes Gieseler, "the Fathers are at great pains to point out that their Gospel is always One; presented, nevertheless, under *four* forms, handed down by *four* witnesses, divided into *four* books." How well suited to the taste of the age

pillars of the Church, each supporting its own portion of the structure, and guarding it from subsiding into any of those forms of false doctrine to which partial views of the truth had given rise.

In seeking for the grounds of that peculiar authority which is claimed for the Bible, we are first of all met by the question as to the authorship and genuineness of the separate writings of which the volume is composed. With this portion of the subject our present inquiry has no immediate concern. The various points connected with it constitute a distinct branch of theological science, to which in recent times the title "Introduction" (Einleitung) has been appropriated;[1] and the results of which the present investigation must assume. Were we to content ourselves with such results, no small advantage would be attained. The Holy Scriptures would still be to us objects of the highest value were we merely to regard them as historical documents from which we might learn to know the doctrine of Christ, as we learn the opinions of Socrates from the pages of Xenophon and Plato. But we have too much depending on the certainty of these documents not to feel ourselves disquieted by the doubt, Is the original Revelation transmitted to us through them in its primitive purity?—a doubt which at once disappears if we firmly establish the Inspiration of the writers; and show how such Inspiration is reflected by and preserved in the pages of Scripture.

The Bible presents to us, in whatever light we regard it, two distinct elements,—the Divine and the Human. This is a matter of fact. On the one hand, God has granted a Revelation; on the other, human language has been made the channel to convey, and men have been chosen as the agents to record it. From this point all theories on the subject of Revelation take their rise; and all the varieties of opinion respecting it have sprung from the manner in which the fact referred to has been taken into account. There are two leading systems in this department of theology:

were the comparisons employed in the elucidation of this fact, appears from the general custom, founded upon the simile of the Cherubim, of ascribing to each Evangelist one of the forms of which the Cherubim consisted.

[1] Perhaps the earliest instance of the use of this term is to be found in the Preface to the treatise by Cassiodorus (A. D. 538), "De Institutione Divinarum Literarum," where he styles his work "introductorios libros." Ed. Bened. tom. ii. p. 537. He refers subsequently to previous "Introductores Scripturæ divinæ;" of whom he names Tichonius the Donatist, S. Augustine, in his work, "De doctrina Christiana," Hadrian, Eucherius, and Junilius. *Ibid.* c. x. p. 545.

the one suggested by the prominence assigned to the Divine element, the other resulting from the undue weight attached to the Human. The former of these systems practically ignores the Human element of the Bible, and fixes its exclusive attention upon the Divine agency exerted in its composition. This system admits and can admit of no degrees. It puts forward one consistent and intelligible theory, without subdivisions or gradations. According to it, each particular doctrine or fact contained in Scripture, whether in all respects naturally and necessarily unknown to the writers, or which, although it might have been ascertained by them in the ordinary course of things, they were not, in point of fact, acquainted with; or in fine, everything, whether actually known to them, or which might become so, by means of personal experience or otherwise,—each and every such point has not only been committed to writing under the infallible assistance and guidance of God, but is to be ascribed to the special and immediate suggestion, embreathment, and dictation of the Holy Ghost. Nor does this hold true merely with respect to the sense of Scripture and the facts and sentiments therein recorded, but each and every word, phrase, and expression, as well as the order and arrangement of such words, phrases, and expressions, has been separately supplied, breathed into (as it were) and dictated to the sacred writers, by the Spirit of God.[1] For the present, I shall merely observe, that, while I can by no means accept this system as correct, or as consistent with the facts to be explained, it will be my object in the present Discourses to establish in the broadest extent all that its supporters desire to maintain; namely, the infallible certainty, the indisputable authority, the perfect and entire truthfulness of all and every the parts of Holy Scripture.

The characteristic of the other system to which I have alluded, and to which the great majority of the modern theories of Inspi-

[1] "Omnia et singulæ res quæ in S. Scripturâ continentur, sive illæ fuerint S. Scriptoribus naturaliter prorsus incognitæ, sive naturaliter quidem cognoscibiles, actu tamen incognitæ, sive denique, non tantum naturaliter cognoscibiles, sed etiam actu ipso notæ, vel aliunde, vel per experientiam, et sensuum ministerium, non solum per assistentiam et directionem divinam infallibilem literis consignatæ sunt, sed singulari Spiritûs S. suggestioni, inspirationi, et dictamini acceptæ ferendæ sunt. Omnia enim, quæ scribenda erant a Spiritu S. sacris Scriptoribus in actu isto scribendi suggesta, et intellectui eorum quasi in calamum dictitata sunt, ut his et non aliis circumstantiis, hoc. et non alio modo, aut ordine scriberentur."—J. A. Quenstedt. *Theologia Didactico-Polemica*, cap. IV. sect. ii. p. 67.

ration are to be referred, is that of ascribing undue prominence to the Human element of the Bible. I must content myself here[1] with briefly stating the three heads to which, I conceive, all the varieties of opinion, which may be traced to this source, can, with more or less definiteness, be reduced.

I. To the first head may be referred those writers who have changed the formula 'The Bible *is* the Word of God,' into 'The Bible *contains* the word of God.' Writers of this class, while they generally shrink from absolutely drawing the line between what is and what is not inspired, yet broadly assert as well the possibility as the existence of imperfections in Scripture, whether resulting from limited knowledge, or inadvertence, or defective memory on the part of its authors.[2] Such imperfections are often restricted to what are termed 'unimportant matters.'

II. Under the second head may be placed the different hypotheses which assume various *Degrees* of Inspiration; the Divine influence by which the sacred writers were actuated having been universal, but unequally distributed. The tendency of all such hypotheses—for even their authors allow that as hypotheses alone can they be regarded—is to fine down to the minutest point, if not altogether to deny, the agency of the Holy Spirit in certain portions of the Bible. "What the extent of the Inspiration was in each case" (I quote the words of Bishop Daniel Wilson, who maintains this view of various "Degrees" of Inspiration)—"What the extent of the Inspiration was in each case, we need not, indeed we cannot, determine. We infer from the uniform language of the New Testament that in each case such assistance, and only such assistance, was afforded as the exigencies of it required. Where nature ended, and Inspiration began, it is not for man to say."[3]

III. The third head comprises Schleiermacher and his follow-

[1] For some account of the modern theories of Inspiration, see Appendix C.

[2] Cf. Ebrard. "Kritik der Evang. Geschichte." 1er Th. s. 63.

[3] "The Evidences of Christianity, by Daniel Wilson." London, 1828, vol. i. p. 506. The "Degrees" of Inspiration usually laid down are as follows: "By the Inspiration of *Suggestion*, is meant, such communications of the Holy Spirit as suggested and dictated minutely every part of the truths delivered. The Inspiration of *Direction*, is meant, of such assistance as left the writers to describe the matter revealed in their own way, directing only the mind in the exercise of its powers. The Inspiration of *Elevation* added a greater strength and vigor to the efforts of the mind, than the writers could otherwise have attained. The Inspiration of *Superintendency* was that watchful care which preserved generally from anything being put down derogatory to the revelation with which it was connected."—*Ibid.* p. 508.

ers; the Shibboleth of whose school, in brief, is this, 'The letter killeth, the spirit giveth life.'[1] The idea of Revelation, according to Schleiermacher, is confined to the *person* of Christ:—the notion of Inspiration he considers to be one of completely subordinate importance in Christianity;[2] the sole power which the Bible "possesses of conveying a Revelation to us, consisting in its aiding in the awakenment and elevation of our religious consciousness; in its presenting to us a mirror of the history of Christ; in its depicting the intense religious life of His first followers; and in giving us the letter through which the spirit of truth may be brought home in vital experience to the human heart."[3]

I now proceed to that view of Inspiration, to establish which will be the object of the present inquiry. In entering upon the task my first object will be to look steadily at the *facts* of the case, which, while it is our duty never to distort or exaggerate them, it is equally our duty to recognise, and estimate at their true value. The Bible, I have already observed, consists of both a Divine and a Human element. This leading fact may be regarded as the first of the two Conditions of our problem; a Condition which can only be satisfied by showing how the two elements may be combined. According to the former of the systems to which I have just referred, the Human element is entirely lost sight of. On its principles the sacred writers, on receiving the Divine impulse, resigned both mind and body to God, who influenced and guided both at His sole pleasure; the human agent contributing, the while, no more than the pen of the scribe: in a word, he was the *pen*, not the *penman*, of the Spirit.[4] Now, cer-

[1] Quinet, in the essay already referred to, well describes the result of this principle when so applied: "Mais qui ne voit qu' à son tour l'esprit en grandissant peut tuer, et remplacer la lettre?"

[2] "Was die Eingebung betrifft, so hat dieser Begriff im Christenthum eine durchaus untergeordnete Bedeutung. Denn eine Beziehung desselben auf Christum findet gar nicht statt, indem die göttliche Offenbarung durch ihn immer, wie sie auch gedacht werde, mit seiner ganzen Existenz identisch gedacht wird. und nicht als fragmentarisch in zerstreuten Augenblicken erscheinend."—*Der Christliche Glaube.* 1er Band. s. 97.

[3] This statement of Schleiermacher's system is taken from Mr. Morell's exposition of his views on Inspiration, "Philosophy of Religion," pp. 143–4.

[4] Cf. Westcott's "Gospel Harmony," p. 6. Thus, even Hooker in his first sermon on Jude, 17–21, having quoted 1 Cor. ii. 12, 13, gives expression to the following sentiment: "This is that which the Prophets mean by those books written full within and without; which books were so often delivered them to eat, not because God fed them with ink and paper, but to teach us, that, so often as He employed them in this heavenly work they neither spake nor wrote any word of their own, but uttered syllable by syllable as the Spirit put it into their mouths."—Vol. iii. p. 662, Keble's Ed.

tain phenomena, obvious of themselves, and brought still more prominently forward by the progress of criticism, demand explanation upon this, as upon every other, theory. The varieties in diction which meet the student as he examines the original text of Scripture, arising partly from the changes undergone by the Hebrew language during the lapse of ages,[1] partly from the natural genius and personal peculiarities of the writers of either Testament;[2] the differences in point of style which are so apparent between the prophetical and historical parts of Scripture[3] as well as between the different prophets and historians themselves; —all these are matters of which some account must be given. The maintainers of the theory of Inspiration which we are now considering, either offer no explanation at all of such phenomena —except by employing some rather general metaphors[4]—or are reduced to the necessity of putting forward another hypothesis, which, although in one point of view a real advance in the true direction, yet closely resembles the doctrine of the Docetæ of old.[5] It is asserted that the Holy Ghost merely "accommodated Himself" to the different peculiarities of the sacred writers.[6] An admission of the originator of this hypothesis exhibits its insufficiency. "The Holy Ghost," he observes, "inspired His amanuenses with those expressions which they would have employed had they been left to themselves."[7] It is, perhaps, unnecessary to remark,

But see the context for some profound remarks on one of the most obscure parts of this subject.

[1] Cf. Hävernick's "Einleitung." 1er. Theil, 1te Abtheil. 2er Kap., § 34, s. 225 ff.

[2] E. g. The use, by S. John alone, of the term *παροιμία*, the other Evangelists employing the word *παραβολή*.

[3] E. g. Compare Isa. xxxvi., and Jer. xxxvi., with other portions of these books.

[4] "Andr. Rivetus *Isag. ad Script. S.* cap. ii. T. ii. Opp. f. 858, simili a perito scriba petito illustrat, qui diversis calamis commode utitur, aliquando subtilioribus et magis acutis, aliquando crassioribus et obtusis, ubi literæ quidem et scriptura scribæ in solidum tribuenda, ductus autem vel subtilior vel crassior, indoli et habitui pennæ vel gracilioris, vel crassioris est adscribendus."—Carpzovius, *Critica Sacra Vet. Test.* p. 59.

[5] The Docetæ held that all relating to Christ's human appearance was a mere vision; and hence their name. The idea thus applied was of long standing among the Jews. Thus Raphael tells Tobit, "All these days I did appear unto you; but I did neither eat nor drink, but ye *did see a vision.*"—Tobit xii. 19.

Neander, in his remarks on the Docetæ, observes: "The opinion corresponding to the fantastic tendency of the East, and which had long obtained currency among the Jews, that a higher spirit has the power of representing himself to the eye of sense in various deceptive forms, which possess no reality, was transferred to Christ."—*Allgem. Geschichte der Kirche,* 2te Aufl. 1er Band. s. 667.

[6] "Fatendum est Spiritum S. in suggerendis verborum conceptibus *accommodasse* ad indolem et conditionem amanuensium."—Baier, Prol. ii. § 7, note g, quoted by Twesten, *Vorlesungen,* 1er Band, s. 418.

[7] "Ea verba Spiritus S. amanuensibus inspiravit, quibus alias usi fuissent, si sibi fuissent relicti."—Quenstedt, cap. iv. p. 76. Rudelbach, who states that Musäus first

that this wholly hypothetical statement assumes an exercise of the Divine agency for which no motive can be assigned, or end pointed out; while it seems impossible to reconcile this phase of the purely organic, or as it has, of late years, been termed, *Mechanical*, theory of Inspiration with the highest aim of religion—the elevation and enlightenment of the faculties of man.

Are we then compelled, by this failure of the theory before us, to solve the difficulties of the question, to accept as true that other system which ascribes undue influence to the Human element of the Scriptures? Assuredly not; our task is rather to make our own those portions of the truth which each system may contain.

In whatever manner we conceive the Bible to convey to us a Revelation, we must, from the nature of the case, recognise its two elements. Without the Divine element it would cease to be a Revelation; without the Human, the communication from God would have been confined to the individual to whom it was originally made. The whole analogy of nature, too, teaches us that God accomplishes all His ends by the intervention of certain means. Here, the end is the conveyance of Divine truth; while the means consist in exhibiting that truth in those aspects under which alone it can be grasped by man. That it should be possible for man to apprehend it, it must present itself allied to human conceptions, and clothed in human language.[1] To attain this object, the same power which gave the message selected the messenger; and the grounds of this selection we can clearly discern to have been the natural capacities and the opportunities, as well as the traits of individual character, which marked each sacred writer. Moses was skilled in all the wisdom of the Egyptians; and S. Paul, who had been the pagan scholar in the school of Tarsus, and the Jewish scholar in the schools of Jerusalem, while by his Jewish learning he could show from the Scripture that Jesus

started this idea, entertains a far more favorable view of it than I have been able to form. It is a conception, he remarks, "welche die tiefsten Blicke in den ganzen Organismus der Offenbarung verräth, und mit Recht die Theodicee der Inspiration genannt werden mag."—*Die Lehre von der Insp.* 4es Kap. s. 24.

[1] "The narrowness and imbecility of the human mind being such as scarcely to comprehend or attain a clear idea of any part of the Divine nature by its utmost exertions; God has condescended, in a manner, to contract the infinity of His glory, and to exhibit it to our understandings under such imagery as our feeble optics are capable of contemplating."—Lowth, *Lectures on the Sacred Poetry of the Hebrews*, Lect. xxxi. 2d ed. vol. ii. p. 312.

was Christ, could also appeal to the hearts of his Gentile hearers in the words of their own philosophers and poets. No less conducive to the successful communication of Divine truth was the calling into activity the individual peculiarities of the agents thus chosen. The unbending intellect of Paul; the practical temperament of James; the heart which throbbed alike with zeal and love in the bosom of John, were chosen, in their turn, to convey the message best suited to each;—while the principle which linked together the several parts of the chain of doctrine thus called into being was the one Divine Spirit which selected, and guided, and inspired each writer. What just reason indeed can possibly be assigned for supposing that the Divine power should have obliterated the peculiar characteristics of each before it qualified him for his task? Must we not rather assume that, when the individual was chosen, there were certain grounds existing in his nature, in consequence of which the lot fell upon him? Such peculiarities of character, therefore, are rather to be regarded as the *condition* of the particular form under which the Divine influence willed to exhibit itself in operation. And thus, the actuation of the Spirit will not consist in the exclusion of the Human element, but rather in illuminating and exalting it, according to its several varieties, for the attainment of the end proposed.[1] Shall we, then, in consequence of this variety of means, and diversity of agencies, refuse to recognise the power which stamps its unity and confers its vital energy upon the whole? On grounds equally appropriate here did the Christian Apologist maintain before the masters of the world the Personality and the Majesty of God. In opposition to the prevailing Pantheism of his age, he appeals to the structure and the harmony of the universe. "I adore," said Athenagoras, "the Being who harmonized the strains, and leads the melody, not the instrument which He plays. What umpires at the Games, omitting to crown the minstrel, place the garland upon his lyre?"[2]

[1] Cf. Steudel's excellent treatise, "Ueber Inspiration der Apostel." "*Tübinger Zeitschrift für Theologie.*" 1832. 2te Heft. s. 117.

[2] *'Ει τοίνυν ἐμμελὲς ὁ κόσμος ὄργανον καὶ κινοῦμενον ἐν ῥυθμῷ, τὸν ἁρμοσάμενον καὶ πλήσσοντα τοὺς φθόγγους, καὶ τὸ σύμφωνον ἐπᾴδοντα μέλος, οὐ τὸ ὄργανον, προσκυνῶ. 'Ουδὲ γὰρ ἐπὶ τῶν ἀγωνιστῶν, παραλιπόντες ὁι ἀθλοθέται τοὺς κιθαριστὰς, τὰς κιθάρας στεφανοῦσιν ἀυτῶν.*—*Legatio pro Christianis*, cap. xvi. p. 291.

This Apology was presented by Athenagoras (*circ.* A. D. 177) to the Emperor Marcus Aurelius and his son Commodus. Guericke ("De Schola Alexandriæ," p. 22)

According to the view here taken, and which has been termed the "Dynamical" theory of Inspiration,—or that which implies such a Divine influence as employs man's faculties according to their natural laws,—man is not considered as being in any sense the cause or the originator of the Revelation of which God alone is the source, but human agency is regarded as the condition under which the Revelation becomes known to others. Nature itself supplies a striking analogy to this species of co-operation. When the principle of life has been communicated to any portion of unorganized matter, the power which animates receives, indeed, its condition from the matter to be animated, but in no sense can we ascribe its source to the inorganic mass to which it is annexed. Nevertheless the further development of that which has once received the vital influence admits of no separation between the purely passive matter and the principle of life, which alone is active. Or, to take an illustration from the province of theology:—in Regeneration it is allowed by all that Divine Grace is the *sole* influence which *operates* at the instant when Regeneration takes place. Afterwards it is the *joint* influence which *co-operates* with the human powers and human will.[1] From this view, then, it results that that peculiar, natural type, according to which each sacred writer was moulded at his creation, was assimilated, as it were, by the power of Inspiration, and appropriated by the Spirit; while, at the same time, the Spiritual Influence is no more to be confounded with the tokens of individual character than it is to be identified with the essence of the natural life. In short, the Divine and Human elements, mutually interpenetrating and combined, form one vital, organic whole,—not mechanically, still less ideally, but, as it has been termed, Dynamically united.[2] So far as to the first Condition of our problem.

The second, and no less important Condition, is supplied by a fact which must have forced itself in some shape or other upon the attention of every reader of the Bible, and which presents another phase of its Human element. Certain portions of the Bible are, strictly speaking, *Revelations;* that is, such as, from

mentions that Philippus Sidetes alleges that this work was dedicated to the Emperors Hadrian and Antoninus Pius. At all events it was composed in the latter half of the second century.

[1] See Twesten, "Vorlesungen," 1er Band, s. 418.

[2] Cf. Beck's "Propädeutische Entwicklung," s. 240.

their supernatural character or the circumstances of the writer who records them, could not have been known to him without a special communication from heaven. Other portions, again, are not of this nature. The historical incidents, for example, recorded in both the Old and New Testament were such as must frequently have been familiar to the sacred writers, either from their own observation, or from sources which were at their command: and this very fact, like their individual peculiarities, is employed by the Holy Spirit as a vehicle of truth and a ground for conviction. This may be distinctly seen from the case of S. John, who thus opens his first Epistle: "That which was from the beginning, which we have heard, which we have seen with our eyes, which we have looked upon, and our hands have handled, of the Word of life, * * * that which we have seen and heard, declare we unto you." On this fact, which cannot be gainsayed, rests a distinction which claims particular attention, as it forms a leading idea of the theory adopted in the present inquiry. The distinction is that between Revelation and Inspiration.[1]

By Revelation I understand a direct communication from God to man, either of such knowledge as man could not of himself attain to, because its subject-matter transcends human sagacity or human reason (such, for example, were the prophetical announcements of the future, and the peculiar doctrines of Christianity), or which (although it might have been attained in the ordinary way) was not, in point of fact, from whatever cause, known to the person who received the Revelation.[2] By Inspira-

[1] Sontag ("Doctrina Inspirationis," p. 134), states that this distinction was first introduced by Quenstedt. This is an error. The earliest work in which I have noticed an express allusion to the subject is that of Melchior Canus (*obiit*, an. 1560). "De Locis Theologicis," Colon. 1605:—

"Non enim asserimus, per immediatam Spiritus Sancti *revelationem*, quæ quidem propriè revelatio dicenda sit, quamlibet Scripturæ Sacræ partem fuisse editam. Quin Lucas, quæ ab Apostolis accepit, ea scripto ipse mandavit, ut in Evangelii sui proœmio testatur. Et Marcum, quæ a Petro didicerat, rogatum a discipulis scripsisse. * * * Sive ergo Matthæus et Joannes, sive Marcus et Lucas, quamvis illi visa, hi audita referrent, non egebant quidem nova Spiritus Sancti *revelatione*, egebant tamen peculiari Spiritus Sancti *directione*."—Lib. ii. cap. xviii. p. 126.

I conceive that Origen has clearly noticed the distinction in question in a well-known passage in his commentary on S. John (Opp. tom. iv. p. 4). On this point see Appendix C. I may observe that I have not been able to procure or consult a work constantly referred to as fully discussing this subject, viz., Baumgarten's treatise "De discrimine Revelationis et Inspirationis." Hal. 1745.

[2] This latter point will be illustrated by an incident in the history of Elisha, stated in the fourth chapter of the second Book of Kings, as contrasted with what is told of the prophet Ahijah in the fourteenth chapter of the first Book of Kings:

"And when she came to the man of God to the hill she caught him by the feet:

tion, on the other hand, I understand that actuating energy of the Holy Spirit, in whatever degree or manner it may have been exercised, guided by which the human agents chosen by God have officially proclaimed His will by word of mouth, or have committed to writing the several portions of the Bible.[1] I repeat, in whatever degree or manner this actuation by the Holy Spirit may have been exercised: for it should never be forgotten that the real question with which our inquiry is concerned is the result of this Divine influence as presented to us in the Holy Scriptures, *not* the manner according to which it has pleased God that this result should be attained. Moses unquestionably received more abundant tokens of the Divine favor than Ezra, or

but Gehazi came near to thrust her away. And the man of God said, Let her alone, for her soul is vexed within her; and the Lord hath hid it from me, and hath not told me."—2 Kings, iv. 27.

"And Jeroboam's wife arose, and went to Shiloh, and came to the house of Ahijah. But Ahijah could not see, for his eyes were set by reason of his age. And the Lord said unto Ahijah, Behold the wife of Jeroboam cometh to ask a thing of thee for her son, for he is sick: thus and thus shalt thou say unto her: for it shall be, when she cometh in, that she shall feign herself to be another woman."—1 Kings, xiv. 4, 5.

[1] Understanding the several portions of the Bible, whether they consist of actual *Revelations*, in the strict sense of the term, or of moral teaching, or of mere historical details. Thus, the *Revelation* of the Law from Sinai, and the *facts* connected with the wanderings of the Israelites, were alike recorded under the influence of *Inspiration.* Or, again, the facts connected with the personal history of Job, the words of God Himself from "out of the whirlwind," the sayings of the Patriarch, and the reasoning of his friends. were all committed to writing under the actuation of the Holy Ghost,—although "the Lord said to Eliphaz the Temanite, My wrath is kindled against thee, and against thy two friends: for ye have not spoken of Me the thing that is right, as my servant Job hath."—Job, xlii. 7. Indeed, it is plain that neglecting to attend to this application of the term Inspiration is to overlook the design of the Scriptures as defined by S. Paul: "Whatsoever things were written aforetime were written for our learning that we through patience and comfort of the Scriptures might have hope."—Rom. xv. 4.

Mr. Coleridge's "Confessions of an Inquiring Spirit" afford a pregnant illustration of this neglect. He is throughout haunted by the belief that no other view of Inspiration is conceivable than the "mechanical" theory in its baldest form. His remarks, consequently, tend to subvert the entire authority of the Bible. If the reader will bear in mind the distinction which I have drawn between Revelation and Inspiration, and will also substitute for the phrase "dictated by" in the following extract, the words "committed to writing under the guidance of"—the objection which it expresses will appear absolutely pointless:—"Yet one other instance, and let this be the crucial test of the Doctrine. Say that the Book of Job was [dictated by] an infallible Intelligence. Then re-peruse the book, and still, as you proceed, try to apply the tenet: try if you can even attach any sense or semblance of meaning to the speeches which you are reading. What! were the hollow truisms, the unsufficing half-truths, the false assumptions and malignant insinuations of the supercilious bigots, who corruptly defended the truth:—were the impressive facts, the piercing outcries, the pathetic appeals, and the close and powerful reasoning with which the poor sufferer—smarting at once from his wounds, and from the oil of vitriol which the orthodox *liars for God* were dropping into them—impatiently, but uprightly and holily controverted this truth, while in will and in spirit he clung to it;—were both [dictated by] an infallible Intelligence?"—*Letter* iii. p. 38.

Nehemiah, or the author of the Books of Chronicles; but this does not render that element of the Bible, in composing which Moses was the agent, one whit more true or more accurrate in its details than the writings of the others.[1] The Disciple whom Jesus loved, and who reclined upon His bosom, enjoyed personally far higher privileges than S. Mark or S. Luke. But still this affection of his Divine Master does not render S. John's Gospel, in one single feature, a more trustworthy vehicle of that portion of Divine truth which it conveys than the records of those who were but the companions of the Apostles.

It has been already observed, that Revelation and Inspiration are also to be distinguished by the sources from which they proceed,—Revelation being the peculiar function of the Eternal Word; Inspiration the result of the agency of the Holy Spirit. Their difference, in short, is specific, and not merely one of degree:[2] a point which is amply confirmed by the consideration, that either of these Divine influences may be exerted, although the other be not called into action. The Patriarchs received Revelations, but they were not inspired to record them; the writer of the Acts of the Apostles was inspired for his task, but we are not told that he ever enjoyed a Revelation.[3] But although

[1] The importance of the distinction on which I am insisting will be further apparent from the following statement of Dr. Pye Smith: "Those who affirm in a general and indiscriminate manner, that all and every the parts of the Old Testament were immediately dictated by [see last note] the Holy Spirit, and that, to each the same kind of inspiration belongs, appear to me to go farther than the evidence warrants, and to lay the cause of *revealed* religion under the feet of its enemies."—*Scripture Testimony to the Messiah*, vol. i. Notes, p. 39.

[2] This view differs altogether from the popular employment of the terms, according to which their distinction is wholly lost sight of. Thus Mr. Morell writes:—

"All Revelation, as we showed, implies two conditions: it implies, namely, an intelligible *object* presented, and a given power of recipiency in the subject: and in popular language, when speaking of the manifestation of Christianity to the world, we confine the term *Revelation* to the former of these conditions, and appropriate the word *Inspiration* to designate the latter. According to this convenient distinction, therefore, we may say, that revelation, in the Christian sense, indicates that act of Divine power by which God presents the realities of the spiritual world immediately to the human mind; while inspiration denotes that especial influence wrought upon the faculties of the subject, by virtue of which he is able to grasp these realities in their perfect fulness and integrity. God made a revelation of Himself to the world in Jesus Christ; but it was the inspiration of the Apostles which enabled them clearly to discern it. Here, of course, the objective arrangements and the subjective influences perfectly blend in the production of the whole result; so that, whether we speak of Revelation or of Inspiration, we are, in fact, merely looking at two different sides of that same great act of Divine beneficence and mercy, by which the truths of Christianity have been brought home to the human consciousness. Revelation and Inspiration then indicate one united process."—*Philosophy of Religion*, p. 150.

[3] So again, we have no reason to suppose that when Samuel was composing the

thus specifically distinct, a fixed relation subsisting between the two ideas, as applied to the Bible, must be noticed. It is plain that, without Inspiration a Divine communication would have been, in a measure, useless as a guide and a rule; for without such Spiritual illumination how could we be assured that the Revelation would be correctly transmitted to others, or even rightly apprehended by the recipients themselves? Consider a single case, which exhibits the relation of the two ideas. Certain Tyrian prophets, mentioned in the twenty-first chapter of the Acts, "said to Paul, through the Spirit, that he should not go up to Jerusalem." To them had been *revealed* what the Holy Ghost was witnessing "in every city"[1] namely, that bonds and afflictions awaited S. Paul in Jerusalem. These prophets, however, enjoyed no *Inspiration;* they adulterated the Revelation which they had received with human wishes and human feelings, and thus directly contradicted the will of God, which the guidance of the Spirit enabled S. Paul himself to understand and to obey. "And now, behold! I go bound in the Spirit unto Jerusalem, not knowing the things that shall befall me there, save that the Holy Ghost witnesseth in every city that bonds and afflictions abide me."[2]

But whatever may be the result of this distinction between Revelation and Inspiration, as applied to the contents of the Bible; in whatever manner we can satisfy ourselves that certain portions convey to us a message direct from heaven, or that others simply record historical facts which were naturally known to the writers,—it must ever be borne in mind that the true idea of Inspiration is altogether *objective*, extending to every portion of every book; and that it stamps the Word of God, as such,

book which bears his name, he received a renewal of the Revelations which God had made to him in his youth.

Köppen ("Die Bibel ein Werk der Göttlichen Weisheit," 3te Aufl. 2er Band, s. 307) draws attention to a fallacious mode of reasoning often employed:—"In order to prove that the books of the Bible have been written under Divine *Inspiration*, appeal is sometimes made to the extraordinary *Revelations* which are here and there announced in the Bible; but this is plainly a false conclusion, and a weakness not to be concealed. Although God has revealed Himself to certain persons by means of a supernatural influence, the question, notwithstanding all this, still remains,—how has the Divine influence exerted itself in the composition of the Bible?" For an instance of an express *Revelation* being intermingled with *inspired* teaching, see 1 Tim. iv. 1.

[1] Acts, xx. 23.

[2] *Ibid.* See Olshausen, *in loc.* Also Storr and Flatt, "Biblical Theology," Part iii. § 11.

in the most profound sense of the term ; thereby distinguishing it from every thing which is merely human. Inspiration, in short, as the attestation of God's Spirit, *in*, *through*, and *for* man, belongs essentially to the organism of Scripture as the record of Revelation; and is at length unfolded to us in its full bearings in that department of it where God reveals Himself as the Spirit.

In theological language the *ordinary* operations of the Holy Ghost are divided into *preventing*, *operating*, *co-operating;* a division which may help to guide us in our conception of the manner in which the sacred writers were influenced: although *their* Inspiration (I would observe in passing) differs, not merely in *degree*, but absolutely in *kind*, from that *ordinary* operation of the Spirit usually called by the same name.[1] We may distinguish in the first place, the stage in which the Holy Spirit *prevents;* that is, prompts to the task of writing: the outward channel through which such suggestion was usually conveyed being the various occasions or motives which, in what men call the ordinary course of things, have led to the composition of most of the books of the Bible.[2] The task having been thus undertaken, in the second stage the Holy Spirit *operates ;* that is, selects from the mass of materials which were at the writer's command,—whatever may have been their character, whether naturally known, or supernaturally revealed—and so disposes the course of his labors, that S. Paul could say of certain parts of the Jewish history that "they were written for our admonition."[3] In the third stage, the Holy Spirit *co-operates* with the natural faculties of the mind, in the manner already dwelt upon when considering the first Condition of our problem ; the result of this co-operation being the different books which in their combination constitute the Bible, and which have been molded into unity by the power of the Spirit.

And here we shall most fitly advert to the language employed under the influence of Inspiration. In the common course of things men of ordinary capacity have the power of clothing their thoughts and feeling in appropriate words ; and from the very nature of the case we cannot but believe that the words adopted by the sacred writers must, in like manner, be

[1] See *infra*, Lecture v. [2] See *infra*, Lecture iv. [3] 1 Cor. x. 11.

the adequate expression of their inward conceptions, and, therefore, of that internal life produced by the Holy Spirit. But, furthermore, the same Divine power which breathed this life into the soul must be regarded as the vital principle of the language which represents it. To this utterance of that Spirit, Whose glance penetrates the universe, Whose intimations extend to every age, and apply to every circumstance with a fullness and definiteness which embrace time and eternity—to this utterance of the Spirit there is essentially appropriated that pregnant style which in a few syllables conveys such infinitude of meaning,[1] which is unexhausted by all commentators, and which possesses that marvellous "capacity of translation into any dialect which has a living and human quality."[2] The opinion, that the subject-matter alone of the Bible proceeded from the Holy Spirit, while its language was left to the unaided choice[3] of the various writers, amounts to that fantastic notion which is the grand fallacy of many theories of Inspiration; namely, that two different spiritual agencies were in operation, one of which produced the phraseology in its outward form, while the other created within the soul the conceptions and thoughts of which such phraseology was the expression. The Holy Spirit, on the contrary, as the productive *principle*, embraces the entire activity of those whom He inspires, rendering their language the word of God.[4] The entire substance and form of Scripture, whether resulting from Revelation or natural knowledge, are thus blended together into one harmonious whole: direct communications of religious truth, as well as the inferences which the sacred writers deduced therefrom; the lessons to be learned, whether from exhibitions of miraculous power, or from the facts of history; such matters, together with all the collateral details of Scripture, have been assimilated into one homogeneous organism by the vital energy of the Spirit.

[1] Ἀπὸ μιᾶς λέξεως ἔνεστιν ὁλόκληρον ἑυρεῖν νοῦν.—S. Chrysost. *Hom.* I. *in Joan.* tom. viii. p. 293.

[2] F. D. Maurice. "The Kingdom of Christ," vol. ii. p. 246.

[3] An opinion held by Seb. Castalio, Episcopius, Geo. Calixtus, &c., who assert "res inspiravit Deus, voces a scriptore sunt." But see the remarks of Beck, "Propädeutische Entwicklung," s. 240.

[4] "For this cause also thank we God without ceasing, because when ye received the word of God which ye heard of us, ye received it not as the word of men, but as it is in truth, the word of God."—1 Thess. ii. 13. Cf. iv. 1, 2, 8.

Such is the aspect under which I propose, in the present investigation, to consider the question of the inspiration of Holy Scripture. In order to establish this theory, it will be necessary to prove that the two Conditions of the problem which it involves have been satisfied; one of these Conditions being defined in that expression of S. Paul which forms the text of this Discourse, "We are laborers together with God;" the other being presented by that distinction pointed out between the ideas of Revelation and Inspiration. The proof must rest, as in all departments of knowledge, upon a patient examination and induction of facts; and such is the task which lies before us. Previously to entering upon that proof, however, I would refer, once for all, to a line of argument which has often been adopted, and which has been as unduly exalted on the one hand, as it has been the subject of unmerited ridicule on the other.[1] I allude to what

[1] Thus it is laid down in Art. IV. of the Gallican Confession of 1561:—

"Nous connoisons ces livres estre canoniques et reigle tres certaine de nostre Foy non tant par le commun accord et consentement de l'Eglise, que par le tesmoignage et intérieure persuasion du S. Esprit, qui les nous fait discerner d'avec les autres livres Ecclésiastiques."

So also in the "Westminster Confession," c. i. § 4, 5:

"The authority of the Holy Scripture, for which it ought to be believed and obeyed, dependeth not upon the testimony of any man or Church, but wholly upon God (who is Truth itself), the author thereof; and therefore it is to be received because it is the Word of God. * * * Our full persuasion and assurance of the infallible truth and divine authority thereof is from the inward work of the Holy Spirit bearing witness by and with the word in our hearts."

On the other hand, J. D. Michaelis writes as follows:—

"An inward sensation of the effects of the Holy Ghost, and the consciousness of the utility of these writings in improving the heart and purifying our morals, are criterions as uncertain as the foregoing. With respect to that inward sensation, I must confess that I have never experienced it in the whole course of my life; nor are those persons who have felt it either deserving of envy or nearer the truth, since the Muhammedan feels it as well as the Christian."—*Marsh's Michaelis*, vol. i. part i. p. 77.

Hofmann justly observes:—"Ob ein Wort der Wahrheit, zu welchem sich der Geist bekennt, kanonisch sey oder nicht, Wort der heiligen Schrift oder Wort der Ueberlieferung, darüber sagt jenes Zeugniss des Geistes nichts, und nicht blos einem J. D. Michaelis nichts, sondern auch einem Luther beim Briefe Jacobi und der Apokalypsis."—*Weissagung und Erfüllung*, i. s. 44. Hofmann's allusion to Luther suggests at once the great danger of this exclusive reliance on "the witness of the Spirit" as the foundation of our belief in the Bible. "Luther," observes Olshausen, in his treatise on the "Genuineness of the Writings of the New Testament," "shows himself a determined opponent of John's Revelation. He says, in his Preface to it: 'There are various and abundant reasons why I regard this book as neither apostolical nor prophetic. * * * But let every man think of it as his spirit prompts him. My spirit cannot adapt itself to the production, and this is reason enough for me why I should not esteem it very highly.'"—*Clarke's For. Theol. Lib.* p. cv. For a more detailed account of Luther's opinion on this subject, see Appendix C. The distinction which is to be made between erroneous views respecting the Canon of Scripture and erroneous views respecting Inspiration is one which deserves particular attention. See *infra*, Lecture ii. p. 71, note, the remarks as to Theodore of Mopsuestia.

is usually termed "the witness of the Spirit," or the testimony which the Holy Ghost Himself conveys to each reader of the Scriptures. The fundamental defect of this mode of upholding Inspiration appears to consist, not in the conception itself, but in the place assigned to it in the chain of Christian evidences, when employed to prove, and not to confirm,—when addressed to the judgment of the understanding, not to the affections of the heart. If offered as the sole, or even leading proof, we can scarcely feel surprise at its rejection by the sceptic or the unbeliever. To the intellect of such persons, the alleging such a fact, as *proof*, must be absolutely unintelligible. As well might any of us discourse with the blind upon the varieties of colours; or a being of some higher order offer to our minds some new idea for the reception of which the proper sense was wanting. The Bible must be recognised as Divine, before such a witness can be called in confirmation of previous evidence. But to the Christian, who, with willing mind and humble acquiescence, accepts the Scriptures as the word of God, this testimony of the Holy Spirit is a precious treasure. The proof is one which is even sealed with the promise of Christ. It results from no chain of elaborate argumentation; it rests upon that living and intuitive syllogism of the heart, "If any man is willing to do His will, he shall know of the doctrine, whether it be of God."[1] The Spirit which breathes the principle of Christian life into the being of man produces, as we read the words of the sacred writers, this recognition of His own former agency; and unconsciously, like the statue of ancient story, the soul makes symphony when the ray touches it from above.[2]

And here, if one might venture to be eclectic as to any part of Holy Scripture, and to point out any portion of it which most fitly illustrates this idea, we may, perhaps, safely refer to that discourse of the Lord, beginning at the fourteenth and ending with the seventeenth chapter of S. John's Gospel: that

[1] *'Εάν τις θέλῃ τὸ θέλ. αὐτ ποιεῖν.* S. John, vii. 17. Cf. Nitzsch, "System der Christl. Lehre," 1er Th. § 32, who justly observes that in this point of view Christianity can not be a matter of *demonstration.*

[2] "Why has the Holy Scripture its peculiar adaptation to man's nature, save because it is His *Word*, after whose image man was originally fashioned, and who is Himself the 'true light which lighteth every man?' Therefore, when we read it, we recognise the higher rule of our original composition."—Wilberforce, *On the Incarnation*, 2d ed. p. 481.

Holy of Holies, as it has been aptly termed, of Christ's history; that wonderful passage from every line of which shines forth the Divinity of Him who spake, though each syllable be tinged with the sadness of a soul which even now gazed full upon the agony in the Garden, and bore, in prospect, the crown of thorns—syllables, too, which were uttered from the very shadow of the tomb! Who is there that peruses those solemn words, whose heart does not burn within him as each expression of human affection—that sympathy with His earthly brethren which every tone conveys—becomes the point of contact through which those Revelations of the Eternal Word reach the spirit of man? Who is there that does not recognise the impress of the Divine nature in every sentence of that discourse, which, while it announces to the Disciples the sorrows of earth, at the same time pledges to them the aid and the joys of heaven: that discourse, so commanding, while shaded with the gloom of human anguish; so sublime in its tenderness; so majestic in its repose? From this source still streams forth a light which illumines the Christian's path, and cheers him on his pilgrimage; and hence, too, if his trust be shaken, can he draw conviction unclouded and serene. When difficulties embarrass the reason, and perplexities entangle the intellect,—and who is that man over whose understanding doubt has not at times cast its shadow, or whose faith the stern realities of life have not put to the trial?—the fainting soul will find its refuge in the words which introduce this series of promise and encouragement; words which still whisper to our ear the same assurance which once supported the Apostle sinking in the wind-tossed sea, "Let not your heart be troubled, ye believe in God, believe also in Me."

LECTURE II.

THE IMMEMORIAL DOCTRINE OF THE CHURCH OF GOD.

"Scripture teacheth us that saving truth which God hath discovered unto the world by Revelation, and it presumeth us taught otherwise that itself is Divine and Sacred."

HOOKER, *Eccl. Pol.* b. iii. c. 8.

Ἑρμηνεὺς γάρ ἐστιν ὁ Προφήτης, ἔνδοθεν ὑπηχοῦντος τὰ λεκτέα τοῦ Θεοῦ.

PHILO, *De Præm. et Pœn.*

Εἰ δ' ἀκριβῶς χρὴ ἡμᾶς λέγειν τὰ πρὸς τὸν Κέλσον, οἰόμενον τὰ αὐτὰ ἡμᾶς Ἰουδαίοις περὶ τῶν ἐγκειμένων δοξάζειν· φήσομεν ὅτι, τὰ μὲν βιβλία θείῳ γεγράφθαι Πνεύματι, ὁμολογοῦμεν ἀμφότεροι.

ORIGENES, *Cont. Cels.* v. 60.

"Quid est autem Scriptura Sacra nisi quædam Epistola omnipotentis Dei ad creaturam suam? * * * Imperator cœli, Dominus hominum et angelorum, pro vita tua tibi Suas Epistolas transmisit: et tamen, gloriose fili, easdem Epistolas ardenter legere negligis. Stude ergo, quæso, et quotidie Creatoris tui verba meditare. Disce cor Dei in verbis Dei, ut ardentius ad æterna suspires, ut mens vestra ad cœlestia gaudia majoribus desideriis accendatur."

S. GREGOR. M. Ep. xxxi. *Ad Theodorum Medicum.*

LECTURE II.

THE IMMEMORIAL DOCTRINE OF THE CHURCH OF GOD.

WHAT ADVANTAGE THEN HATH THE JEW? OR WHAT PROFIT IS THERE OF CIRCUMCISION? MUCH EVERY WAY: CHIEFLY, BECAUSE THAT UNTO THEM WERE COMMITTED THE ORACLES OF GOD.—*Rom.* iii. 1, 2.

WHEN intimating in this passage the leading prerogatives of the Jewish people, the Apostle employs a phrase,[1] correctly rendered in our version by the word "chiefly," but which, if we look merely to the form of the expression, points to other advantages which he had intended to name. His pausing, however, without pursuing the idea any further, proves how deeply S Paul felt that *all* was in reality contained in that one privilege which he had particularized. The entire history of the ancient Church of God tells how this treasure was revered; and that it had been guarded with the most scrupulous fidelity is evident, as well from the Apostle's allusion in this place, as from the whole tone and tenor of the New Testament.

To the Christian Church, in like manner, were confided, not only the new documents which were added to the Canon;—the Scriptures of the Old Testament also were transferred to its care. That it was the privilege of the Christian Church, as it had been of the Jewish, to be the "witness and keeper of Holy Writ,"[2] and that to the chief officer in each of its divisions was intrusted the fulfilment of this commission, is proved by the existence of a rite which has been retained in every branch of the Church Catholic since the second century. As our own Ordinal presents it, the words of Episcopal Consecration are immediately followed by the delivery of the Bible into the hand of the

[1] Πρῶτον μέν. Cf. Olshausen's remarks on this text.
[2] Art. xx. Eccles. Anglic. "De Ecclesiæ Auctoritate."

newly-made Bishop; the Church symbolizing thereby two aspects of the duty which he must discharge:—the maintenance of the doctrine, and the preservation of the record.[1]

When we consider, then, the fact, that to the Jewish and Christian Churches, respectively, and in their capacity of divinely instituted Societies, "the oracles of God" have been committed, no inquiry respecting the subject of Inspiration can possess greater importance, than that which will exhibit the degree and kind of estimation in which the writings which contain those "oracles," have been always held, as well as the spirit in which the trust thus reposed has been discharged. This inquiry is to be distinguished from the examination of that testimony which proves the genuineness and authenticity of the different parts of the Bible;—although the two questions are often confounded. Greater clearness will also be attained, if it be kept apart from what are usually termed Christian evidences; for these relate to the belief in the contents of the Scriptures, rather than to the nature of the agency employed in their composition. Its bearing, too, will be better understood when we reflect upon the manner in which opinions, such as we are about to consider, have influenced the actions of those who held them; as also when we picture to ourselves the impression which would have been produced upon our minds had the expression of those sentiments been less decided, or less peculiar. I propose in the present Discourse to give the leading outlines of the doctrine respecting the inspiration of the Bible held by the Jews who lived before the birth of Christ, or who were His contemporaries, as well as by the

[1] Immediately after the Imposition of Hands by the "Archbishops and Bishops present * * * upon the head of the elected Bishop," the Rubric of our Ordinal further directs—"Then the Archbishop shall deliver him the Bible, saying: 'Give heed unto reading, exhortation, and doctrine. Think upon the things contained in this Book,'" &c., &c.

The antiquity of this rite is proved by the words of the Apostolic Constitutions, lib. viii. cap. 4, *περὶ χειροτονιῶν*. The direction there given is as follows: *σιωπῆς γενομένης, εἷς τῶν πρώτων ἐπισκόπων ἅμα καὶ δυσὶν ἑτέροις, πλησίον τοῦ θυσιαστηρίου ἑστὼς, τῶν λοιπῶν ἐπισκόπων καὶ πρεσβυτέρων σιωπῇ προσευχομένων, τῶν δὲ διακόνων τὰ θεῖα εὐαγγέλια ἐπὶ τῆς τοῦ χειροτονουμένου κεφαλῆς ἀνεπτυγμένα κατεχόντων, λεγέτω πρὸς Θεόν· Ὁ Ὢν, δέσποτα, κύριε, κ. τ. λ.*—Cotelerius, t. i. p. 395.

Gieseler, to whom I am indebted for this remark and reference, observes: "Dieser Ritus scheint die Collation des Zeugnisses symbolisch dargestellt zu haben, und entstand wahrscheinlich, nachdem die schriftlichen Evangelien als heilige Schriften an die Stelle der Tradition gesetzt waren."—*Die Entstehung der schriftl. Evangelien*, s. 171. I may add, that Gieseler employs this and kindred facts in order to develop his ingenious argument in support of the genuineness of the Ignatian Epistles.

Christian Church from the earliest period.[1] The importance of such external evidence, before adducing that supplied by the nature and contents of the Scriptures themselves, is too obvious to permit us to pass it over without due consideration, or, as is too frequently the case, to assign it a subordinate place in our chain of proofs.

It has been already pointed out that the Bible must be regarded as no fortuitous compilation of scattered writings ; that the several books which make up the Old and New Testaments conspire to form one organized whole ; and that each member of the inspired volume performs its own part in completing the record of Revelation.[2] In short, the completion of this assemblage of writings may be compared to that of a pre-arranged structure, to which many laborers contribute their toil, of whom

[1] On this evidence Doddridge observes: "I greatly revere the testimony of the primitive Christian writers, not only to the real existence of the sacred books in those early ages, but also to their divine original: their persuasion of which most evidently appears from the veneration with which they speak of them, even while miraculous gifts remained in the Church; and consequently, an exact attendance to a written rule might seem less absolutely necessary, and the authority of inferior teachers might approach nearer to that of the Apostles."—*A Dissertation on the Inspiration of the New Testament: Works*, vol. v. p. 531. That miraculous gifts were continued for at least half a century after the death of the Evangelist John, we have the express testimony of S. Justin Martyr. *Παρ' ἡμῖν ἐστὶν ἰδεῖν καὶ θηλείας καὶ ἄρσενας, χαρισματα ἀπὸ τοῦ Πνεύματος τοῦ Θεοῦ ἔχοντας.*—*Dial. c. Tryph.*, c. 88, p. 185. Cf. *ibid.* c. 82. Alluding to the uncertainty which exists as to the authors of some portions of the Bible, whether didactic or historical—e. g. the Books of Kings, the Book of Job, &c.,—Sack observes, "that the recognition of any Book by the Church (of either Old or New Covenant) is a fact, at least, as important as its having been written by such or such a person. For the question does not so much relate to the author in his individual capacity, but to the circumstance that, as a matter of fact, he was acknowledged by the Church as a person divinely qualified or called to write of divine things for the Church."—*Apologetik*, s. 434.

[2] It could only have arisen from a complete ignoring of this idea, that Mr. Coleridge has given utterance to the following sentiment, with which he closes a denunciation of "indiscriminate Bibliolatry:" "And lastly, add to all these [evils] the strange—in all other writings unexampled—practice of bringing together into logical dependency detached sentences from books composed at the distance of centuries, nay, sometimes a *millennium*, from each other, under different dispensations, and for different objects. Accommodations of elder Scriptural phrases—that favorite ornament and garnish of Jewish eloquence—incidental allusions to popular notions, traditions, apologues—(for example, the dispute between the Devil and the Archangel Michael about the body of Moses, Jude, 9),—fancies and anachronisms imported from the synagogue of Alexandria into Palestine by, or together with, the Septuagint Version, and applied as mere *argumenta ad homines*—(for example, the delivery of the Law by the disposition of the Angels, Acts, vii. 53 ; Gal. iii. 19 ; Heb. ii. 2)—these, detached from their context, and, contrary to the intention of the sacred writer, first raised into independent *theses*, and then brought together to produce or sanction some new *credendum* for which neither separately could have furnished a pretence!"—*Confess. of an Inquiring Spirit*, letter iv. p. 50. As to Mr. Coleridge's assertion that the writers of the New Testament have cited the Old merely by way of "accommodation," "that favorite garnish of Jewish eloquence."—see *infra*, p. 71, &c.

none, perhaps, have any adequate notion of the Architect's design—some being occupied upon that portion of the building committed to their own workmanship; others overseeing sections of the plan, and perfecting its various parts as the work proceeds—the Master-builder alone overlooking the whole, distributing his orders to one immediately, to another mediately, and rejecting every addition inconsistent with his original conception. And so the structure grows to completion according to the original idea, but, in no part, without the Master-builder's care.[1]

It must be at once conceded that this theory, as to the design and compilation of the several elements of the Bible, cannot be proved by direct, historical evidence. The very nature of the case precludes such proof. But if it can be shown that such a theory supplies a full and satisfactory explanation of the facts to be accounted for, and that, unless we assume its truth, a series of remarkable phenomena in the history of human conduct must remain an inexplicable enigma, then, I submit, that evidence, as satisfactory as men are capable of attaining, *has* been adduced in proof of the position here laid down; and further, that if it be rejected as in itself insufficient, the rejection of such evidence cannot be restricted to the province of religion.

The facts to be explained are briefly as follows:—Firstly, from a multitude of writings extant among the ancient Jews and Christians, a selection of certain books was made, to the exclusion of others. Secondly, the several books thus selected were received as infallible and divine; those which were excluded being regarded as fallible and human. Thirdly, in defence, not merely of the doctrines and religious system contained in these books, but of the very books themselves, both Jews and Christians have submitted to persecution and to death.

To the first class of facts I can only advert in the most cursory manner. The selection of the writings acknowledged as sacred by the Jews cannot have been owing to their antiquity merely, for we learn from the fourteenth verse of the twenty-first chapter of the Book of Numbers, that even in the days of Moses there was extant a record entitled "the Book of the Wars of the Lord." Nor, in order to confer Divine authority upon any book, was the

[1] Cf. Köppen, "Die Bibel ein Werk der göttlichen Weisheit," Band. ii. s. 59.

fact sufficient that it had been written by a prophet known to have received revelations from heaven; for, if so, why do we not find in the Canon "the acts of Uzziah first and last" written by "Isaiah the Prophet, the son of Amoz?"[1] Nor, again, did the circumstance of a document having been composed in the Hebrew language secure its recognition as Divine; for the Jews never admitted among their sacred writings the book of Ecclesiasticus, which was undoubtedly drawn up in Hebrew, and whose author, moreover, assumes the prophetic tone, and lays no small claim to authority.[2] Add to all this, the astonishing fidelity and affection with which the Jews preserved the writings which they *did* receive into their Canon,—writings, too, which were not the memorial of their glory, but of their shame; and in which their Lawgiver, from the very first, calls heaven and earth to witness against them.[3]

[1] 2 Chron. xxvi. 22. For some account of this class of writings, see Appendix D. With respect to such books, Prof. Moses Stuart observes, that if any one should hesitate to acknowledge that the works of this class written by Nathan, Gad, Isaiah, and others, were counted of Divine authority by the Hebrews, "on the ground that prophets might write other books than those which were inspired, still the manner of appeal to the works in question which are now lost, both in Kings and Chronicles, shows beyond all reasonable doubt that they were regarded as authoritative and sacred."—*The Old Testament Canon*. p. 163. That these "lost" writings were regarded as *veracious annals* is no doubt evident; but the mere fact of their *not* having been even preserved by the Jews "shows beyond all reasonable doubt" that they were *not* "regarded as authoritative and sacred." Cf. *infra*, p. 68, the remarks of Josephus.

[2] The author of this book, to whose grandson we are indebted for the present Greek version, is said to have lived either 300 or 200 years before Christ. Cf. Hävernick's "Einleitung," 1er Th. 1er Abth., s. 29. That it was composed in Hebrew or Aramaic is clear from the Prologue, where the translator requests of his readers "to pardon us wherein we may seem to come short of some words which we have labored to interpret. For the same things uttered in Hebrew, and translated into another tongue, have not the same force in them."

The author, however, as I have observed, claims for himself full canonical authority. He writes: "I will yet make doctrine to shine as the morning, and will send forth her light afar off. I will yet pour out doctrine as prophecy, and leave it to all ages for ever. Behold that I have not labored for myself only, but for all them that seek wisdom."—ch. xxiv. 32–34. He assumes the prophetic tone: "Hear me, O ye great men of the people, and hearken with your ears, ye rulers of the congregation."—ch. xxxiii. 18. And he closes with the words:—"Blessed is he that shall be exercised in these things: and he that layeth them up in his heart shall become wise. For if he do them he shall be strong to all things: for the light of the Lord leadeth him."—ch. l. 28, 29.

[3] Pascal remarks: "Ils portent avec amour et fidélité le livre où Moise déclare qu' ils ont été ingrats envers Dieu toute leur vie, et qu' il sait qu' ils le seront encore plus après sa mort; mais qu' il appelle le ciel et la terre à témoin contre eux."—tom. ii. p. 188, ed. Faugère. To the same effect Mr. Davison remarks: "The words of the prophets are said to have beeen 'graven on a rock, and written with iron.' Had they not been so written and engraved, by an irresistible evidence of their inspiration, how could they have withstood the odium and adverse prejudice which they provoked? How could they have survived with the unqualified and public acknowledgment of their inspiration from the Jewish people, who hereby are witnesses in their own

The case of the New Testament is no less peculiar. It is plain that the primitive Christians did not consider Apostles as alone qualified to compose inspired documents; for, were such their belief, how can we acccount for the reception of the Gospels of S. Mark and S. Luke? Nor is the admission of these Gospels to be explained by saying, that no other memorials of the life of Christ existed than the four Evangelical narratives, and that the early Christians gladly collected every fragment of their Master's history:—for not only, as the best criticism explains, does the introduction of S. Luke's Gospel refer to "many who had taken in hand[1] to set forth" a narrative of the events of that period, but the earliest of the Fathers also (e. g. S. Irenæus, A. D. 167), describe the Apocryphal Gospels as being "countless in number."[2]

shame; and survive, too, with that admitted character, when every thing else of any high antiquity has been permitted to perish, or remains only as a comment confessing the inspiration of these prophetic writings? And the stress of the argument lies in this, that these writings were not merely preserved, but adopted into the public monuments of their Church and nation; strange archives of libel to be so exalted, if their authority could have been resisted. But the Jews slew their prophets, and then built their sepulchres and confessed their mission. There is but one reason why they did so, a constrained and extorted conviction."—*Discourses on Prophecy*, p. 51.

[1] Origen considers that this term conveys a latent reproof of those who undertook to write without the Divine commission. As the gift of "discerning of spirits," conferred upon the Jewish Church, enabled it to select the true Prophets, and to reject the false; so, he argues, in like manner did the Church of God choose four Gospels only, from the many writings which claimed that name. He says:

*Τάχα οὖν τὸ, ἐπεχείρησαν, λεληθυῖαν ἔχει κατηγορίαν τῶν προπετῶς καὶ χωρὶς χαρίσματος ἐλθόντων ἐπὶ τὴν ἀναγραφὴν τῶν εὐαγγελίων * * * τὰ δὲ τέτταρα μόνα προκρίνει ἡ Θεοῦ ἐκκλησία.*—*Hom. I. in Lucam.* tom. iii. p. 932. S. Ambrose, in his "Exposit Evang. sec. Lucam," adopts this passage, and gives an almost literal translation of it. Thus he renders nearly word for word the sentence omitted in the extract just given:

"Non conatus est Matthæus, non conatus est Marcus, non conatus est Johannes, non conatus est Lucas: sed Divino Spiritu ubertatem dictorum rerumque omnium ministrante, sine ullo molimine cœpta complerunt."—Lib. i. tom. I. p. 1265.

[2] *Ἀμύθητον πλῆθος ἀποκρύφων καὶ νόθων γραφῶν.*—*Cont. Hær.*, lib. I. xx. p. 91. So also S. Jerome, "Illud juxta Ægyptios, et Thomam, et Matthiam, et Bartholomæum, duodecim quoque Apostolorum, et Basilidis atque Apellis, ac reliquorum, *quos enumerare longissimum est.*"—*Procem in. Comm. super Matt.* tom. vii. p. 3. Cf. Gieseler, "Die Entst. der schriftl. Evang." s 8.

Incessant vigilance was required to guard the Canon of Scripture against such spurious additions. Thus Eusebius records that one Themison, a Montanist, in the second century, had "dared to imitate the Apostle (*ἐτόλμησε μιμούμενος τὸν Ἀπόστολον*) by composing a catholic epistle to instruct those who had a sounder faith than himself."—*Eccl. Hist.* v. xviii. p. 234.

Such attempts were severely punished. S. Jerome writes: "Igitur *περιόδους* Pauli et Theclæ, et totam baptizati Leonis fabulam, inter Apocryphas Scripturas computamus. Quale enim est, ut individuus comes Apostoli, inter cæteras ejus res hoc solum ignoraverit? Sed et Tertullianus, *vicinus eorum temporum*, refert Presbyterum quemdam in Asia *σπουδαστήν* Apostoli Pauli, convictum apud Joannem, quod esset auctor libri, et confessum se hoc Pauli amore fecisse, loco excidisse."—*De Viris Illust.*, t. II. c. vii. p. 827. The statement of Tertullian is as follows: "Quod si quæ Paulo perperam adscripta sunt, ad licentiam mulierum docendi tinguendique defend-

Nor, again, can we account for the admission into the New Testament of the writings of S. Mark and S. Luke, by alleging that, as companions and friends of Apostles, these Evangelists had opportunities of gaining such accurate information respecting the doctrines of the Christian faith as was not within the reach of others:—for, if this be so, why did the Church never recognise as canonical the Epistle of S. Clement of Rome—"my fellow-laborer," writes S. Paul, "whose name is in the book of life;"[1] or, what is still more remarkable, when we recollect the relation of S. Barnabas to S. Paul, how comes it to pass that the Epistle of S. Barnabas was rejected from the New Testament, while the Gospel of S. Mark, "his sister's son," was received?[2] It may

unt; sciant in Asia presbyterum, qui eam Scripturam construxit, quasi titulo Pauli de suo cumulans, convictum atque confessum id se amore Pauli fecisse, loco decessisse."—*De Baptismo*, c. xvii. p. 263.

The caution thus exercised by the Church was in obedience to express Apostolic commands. Thus S. Paul warns the Thessalonians not to be troubled "either by spirit, or by word, *or by letter as from us*."—2 Thess. ii. 2. So, again, S. John writes: "Beloved, believe not every spirit, but try the spirits whether they are of God."—1 S. John, iv. 1. When any book was offered to the Church's acceptance as being inspired, full proof of the fact, were its claims well founded, could and would be forthcoming in due time. On the other hand, if any uninspired book were once received as *Scripture*, it was *probable* that false doctrine would come in with it; and it was *certain* that the confidence of the people in the authority of the books which really were inspired would be rudely shaken. See Wordsworth "On the Canon," p. 260.

[1] Phil. iv. 3.

[2] Tholuck's account of the principle which guided the selection of the Books of the New Testament is not very clear. Having observed that S. Mark and S. Luke were not Apostles, and that it is at least a matter of doubt whether S. James and S. Jude (the authors of our Epistles) were so,—this writer goes on to say that the primitive Church was, nevertheless, led "by an unconscious but sure historico-religious tact" to receive their writings into the Canon of the New Testament. "This tact," continues Tholuck, "is vouched for especially by this, that none of the many impure, apocryphal Gospels—nay, not even the Ποιμήν of Hermas, so highly prized by individuals, but yet impure in spirit,—nor the Epistle of Barnabas, found admission into the Canon. On the other hand, the Epistle of Clemens, which was used in a wider circle, approaches most nearly the spirit of the Pauline Epistles; and can have been judged undeserving of reception into the New Testament Canon only on account of its want of originality."—*Comm. zum. Br. an die Hebr.*, Einleit, kap. vi. s. 84.

By the phrase "want of originality," Tholuck, I presume, means to repeat what he had just said of the approach of S. Clement "to the spirit of the Pauline Epistles." That the primitive Church did not consider such a fact any reason for refusing to receive a document as portion of Scripture, is demonstrated by the reception into the New Testament Canon of both the second Epistle of S. Peter, and the Epistle of S. Jude. Whichever of these two Epistles is of earlier date, the most careless reader cannot have failed to notice that one of them is not "original," and that its author has reiterated the inspired language of the other.

It has been doubted whether the "Shepherd of Hermas" was written by the individual named by S. Paul: "Salute Asyncritus, Phlegon, *Hermas*, &c."—Rom. xvi. 14. Origen, when commenting on these words (t. iv. p. 683) states his opinion that Hermas was the author, and expresses the highest respect for the work itself. Elsewhere (Hom. 35. in Luc. xii. 58, t. iii. p. 973) he implies that the authorship is doubtful. This doubt is confirmed by a passage in the celebrated Fragment preserved by Muratori, the date of which Credner ("Zur Geschichte des Kanons," s. 84.) places about

be said, it is true, that grave doubts exist as to whether the treatise which we now possess under the name of S. Barnabas was really written by the companion of S. Paul—although, if any weight be attached to external evidence, such doubts seem unintelligible;[1] but, admitting this, there can be no question that, so early as the days of Clement of Alexandria (A. D. 192) a work was well known in the Church which Clement constantly refers to as proceeding from S. Barnabas, whom he styles "the Apostle," "an Apostolic man," "one of the Seventy Disciples, and fellow-labourer of S. Paul."[2]

The several details connected with the general question here considered belong, however, to another department of theology:

the year 170. The writer of this Fragment, of which we possess only a Latin translation, having given a catalogue of the Books of the New Testament, proceeds to mention some other Christian compositions. I quote the following extract according to Dr. Routh's emendation of the very corrupt text: "Pastorem vero nuperrime temporibus nostris in urbe Roma Hermas conscripsit, sedente in cathedra urbis Romæ ecclesiæ Pio episcopo fratre ejus [i. e. A. D. 142–157]. Et ideo legi eum quidem oportet, sed publicari vero [ἀλλὰ δημοσιεύεσθαι δή] in ecclesia populo, neque inter Prophetas completos numero, [cf. S. Matt. xi. 13; S. Luke, xvi. 16.] neque inter Apostolos, in finem temporum potest."—*Reliq. Sacræ*, t. i. p. 396.

[1] On this question see Appendix E.

[2] The fact of Clement recognising this Epistle in such terms, has been met by the assertion that his acceptance of it arose from the correspondence of his own views with its general tone of doctrine. This allegation has been fully set aside by Gieseler: "The ancient testimony of Clement, that Barnabas was the author, cannot be ascribed to the partisan prejudice of an Alexandrian for the production of a kindred spirit: for neither could the Millenarian views (der Chiliasmus) of the Epistle (c. 15) please the Alexandrians; nor do all its interpretations suit Clement, who contradicts one of them (Pædag. ii. p. 221), and who prefers another interpretation of Ps. i. 1, to that given in our Epistle (Strom. ii. p. 464)."—*Kirchengeschichte*, 1er Band. s. 122. In the former of the two latter passages referred to by the learned historian, Clement observes: "Consider how Moses forbids to eat a hare or a hyena;" adding a reason which had been assigned for this prohibition, and which he quotes nearly verbatim from the Epistle of S. Barnabas, c. x. This quotation is introduced with the formula "they say" (*φασί*), and Clement goes on to refuse his assent to the allegorical interpretation annexed to it: *οὐ μέντοι τῇδε ἐξηγήσει τῶν συμβολικῶς εἰρημένων συγκατίθεμαι.*—*Pædag.* ii. p. 221; on which Potter observes: "Porro hoc loco Clemens Barnabæ contradicit, sed tanti viri reverentia ductus, nomen ejus reticet." In the last passage alluded to by Gieseler, Clement quotes this same chapter of the Epistle, where S. Barnabas refers Psalm i. 1, to the prohibition of Moses respecting meats: *Περὶ τῶν βρωμάτων μὲν οὖν* Μωσῆς *τρία δόγματα ἐν πνεύματι ἐλάλησεν * * * λαμβάνει δὲ τρίων δογμάτων γνῶσιν Δαβίδ.* To these words Clement refers with the single remark: *ταῦτα μὲν ὁ* Βαρνάβας. He then quotes another "wise man," who applies the three classes of "blessedness" in the Psalm in a different manner,—viz., to those who kept themselves apart from the Gentiles, the Jews, and the Heretics. But, adds Clement, "another explains the verse *with still greater propriety*," (*ἕτερος δὲ κυριώτερον ἔλεγεν*)—viz., understanding the words, in their literal sense, as conveying a moral lesson.

I have dwelt upon this point as it proves that the primitive Christians drew a broad line of distinction between inspired and non-inspired writings, even though the latter were composed by "Apostolic Men"—men, too, who possessed the same *natural* sources of information as the Apostles. For Clement's views on Inspiration, see Appendix G

I would merely add, and this even the most reluctant are forced to admit, that the reception of the different parts of the New Testament as Scripture took place without external concert,—from an inward impulse, as it were,—at the same time and in the most different places; and that, with scarcely an exception, each writing which it contains was all at once, and without a word of doubt, placed on a level with the Old Testament, which had hitherto been regarded as exclusively divine.[1] In short, the authority conceded to this new component of the Scriptures, seems to have grown up without any one being able to place his

[1] The importance of this circumstance, as bearing upon the inspiration of the New Testament, cannot be too highly estimated. Hug observes: "It was the distinguished and peculiar prerogative accorded to these writings, and for a long time the only mark of distinction which could be given them, that they were publicly read in the Christian assemblies. As in the religious meetings of the Jews, this honor was usually conferred only upon the Law and the Prophets, so among the Christians this eminent prerogative was granted only to the writings of the Apostles, together with the Old Testament which they retained from the Jews. Thus Peter reckons Paul's Epistles, while the author was still alive, among the γραφάς, Holy Scriptures (2 Pet. iii 15, 16)."—*Einleitung*, kap. iii. § 16. This fact is allowed even by De Wette: "Die heiligen Schriften des N. T. wurden in Einen Rang gestellt mit denen des A. T., welche ebenfalls vorgelesen wurden."—*Einleitung*, 6ste Ausg. 1er Th. § 25. s. 37. Cf. the extract from the Fragment of Muratori, already quoted, p. 57, note. See also Appendix D.

It will be observed that I have omitted to urge a fact on which modern writers on the New Testament seem to be unanimous, viz., that one Epistle *at least* of S. Paul has been lost. The absence, however, of all *external* evidence on this subject is, I cannot help thinking, sufficient to cause considerable doubt as to the fact. The *internal* evidence is contained in the words: "I wrote unto you in an Epistle (ἐν τῇ ἐπιστολῇ) not to company with fornicators."—1 Cor. v. 9. It may be well to remark that to the History of Moses of Chorene, published by W. and G. Whiston, in the year 1736, there is added (p. 371) an Appendix, "Quæ continet Epistolas duas, primam Corinthiorum ad Paulum Apostolum, alteram Pauli Apostoli ad Corinthios, nunc primum ex codice MS. Armeniaco integre pleneque editas, et Græce Latineque versas." The editor observes (p. 383, *note*.) that the Armenian Church did not receive the Scriptures before the end of Cent. IV.; and that these Epistles neither occur in their version of the Bible, nor are mentioned by any ancient Armenian writer. Cf. Thiersch, "Versuch zur Herstell. des hist. Standp." s. 104. But the list of "lost Epistles" does not stop here. Olshausen observes: "According to Bleek's conjecture, before the sending of our second Epistle [to the Corinthians], the Apostle wrote from Macedonia another Epistle to the Corinthians, couched in terms of strong reproof, which has not been preserved (so that Paul wrote to them in all *four* Epistles, of which two have been lost and two preserved), and I am much inclined to support this conjecture. For, unquestionably, the apprehension experienced by Paul in regard to the impression produced upon the Corinthians by his Epistle, and which the arrival of Titus first allayed (2 Cor. vii. 2–10.)—is not justified by the nature of the first Epistle."—*Die Br. an die Corinthier*, Einleit. s. 495. Olshausen further considers that "the Epistle from Laodicea" (Col. iv. 16.) was an Epistle from S. Paul to that Church, which is now "lost," and not the Epistle to the Ephesians. Prof. Moses Stuart thinks that 3 S. John, 9: "I wrote unto the Church, but Diotrephes * * * receiveth us not," also points to a "lost Epistle."—*On the Old Testament Canon*, p. 162.

Were these hypotheses correct, the conclusions stated above would be still more strongly confirmed.

finger upon the place or moment when adhesion to it was first yielded.

It may be urged, in explanation of such facts, that the very nature of the books themselves occasioned the preference given to them. It may be said that the difference, in point of style, and manner, and contents, as well of the books of the Old Testament from the Apocrypha, as of the New Testament from the writings of the Apostolical Fathers, is such as admits of no comparison; that the superiority of the books of Scripture is uncontested and incontestable; and that, as Hooker observes of the sacred writers, "a greater difference there seemeth not to be between the manner of their knowledge, than there is between the manner of their speech and others."[1] And, finally,—it may be further argued,—without any need of supposing special Divine guidance, the simple facts of the case account for the formation of the Canon, and enabled the early Christians, not only to judge certain writings to be unworthy of the name of Scripture, but also to select others as deserving such acknowledgment. Be it so. Such an explanation but serves to exalt the critical accuracy, the profound insight, the refined taste, of those who passed that judgment, and made that selection. The admission which such an explanation involves I claim wholly on the side of the present argument, and at once transfer it to the cause of Inspiration. That continued exercise of solid judgment which selected such writings, and such writings only; that critical sagacity which the most ingenious and subtle investigations of modern times have never been able to prove at fault; that unceasing caution and anxious vigilance, which never admitted into the Canon a single book for the rejection of which any valid reasons have ever been shown: such qualities, conceded to the Fathers of the first ages of the Church, only serve to enhance the value of their opinions upon every point connected with the Scriptures, and, above all, upon the subject of their Inspiration.

[1] Sermon on S. Jude, 17–21; vol. iii. p. 661, Keble's ed. To the same effect Neander observes: "In other cases, transitions are wont to form themselves by degrees; but in this instance we observe a sudden change to take place. There are here no gentle gradations, but, all at once, *a bound* (ein Sprung) from one style of language to another: which remark may lead us to an acknowledgment of the special activity, in the souls of the Apostles, of the Divine Spirit—the new, creative element of that first epoch."—*Allg. Gesch. der Kirche*, 1er Band. s. 1133.

In no nation was the universal belief of the ancient world[1] in an intercourse between earth and heaven, so deeply rooted as among the Jews. Their writings, composed subsequently to the completion of the Old Testament, afford the most decisive proof of their ascribing Inspiration to the authors of its several parts; and leave no doubt as to their conviction that the collection of Sacred Books was defined under the Divine guidance, and closed at the Divine command.[2] And I would here remark, that considerable misapprehension has arisen from not carefully distinguishing the opinions of the Jews who have lived since the coming of Christ, from the views of those who wrote before or at that period.[3] This feature of the case is peculiarly important, when we regard Inspiration, under its Christian aspect, as the characteristic function of the Holy Ghost. One of the principal doctrines of Christianity which Jews, of later times, have assailed with vehemence and vituperation, is that respecting the nature and operations of the Third Person of the Holy Trinity;[4] and to this fact we may, perhaps not unfairly, attribute the prevalence of a peculiar tenet, first advanced by Maimonides in the twelfth century: adopting whose theory, modern Jews ascribe to their sacred Books three degrees of Inspiration—the Mosaic, the Prophetical, and that of the Holy Spirit, which last they re-

[1] "*Vetus opinio est*, jam usque ab heroicis ducta temporibus, eaque et populi Romani et *omnium gentium* firmata consensu, versari quandam inter homines divinationem."—Cicero *de Divin* i. 1.

[2] "Let us only hear some of these testimonies which are just as decisive as they are unanimous; and every doubt must disappear as to the conviction that it was the *fact* of Inspiration which caused the reception of certain Books into the Canon, and the exclusion from it of others."—Hävernick, *Einleit.* 1er Th. 1te Abth. s. 51.

[3] This confusion is to be noted, for example, in Mr. Coleridge's "Confessions of an Inquiring Spirit."—Letter ii. p. 21.

[4] In proof of this assertion, I refer to J. A. Eisenmenger's "Entdecktes Judenthum." Königsberg, 1711, ch. vi. p. 264. For example: The Nizzachon, p. 12, observes on the words, "And lo, three men stood by him."—Gen. xviii. 2: "The heretics (המינים) [i. e. the Christians] say he saw three, and worshipped one; and these are the Father, the Son, and the impure spirit (הרוח הטומאה) whom they name the Holy Ghost; these three he saw in the form of one, and him he worshipped." At page 142 of this same work, occurs, according to Eisenmenger, the following passage:

"It stands, according to them, in the Gospel of Luke (בספר לוקש): Whoever sins against the Father, he finds forgiveness; whoever sins against the Son, he, too, finds forgiveness; but he who sins against the impure spirit (לרוח הטומאה) finds no forgiveness either in this, or that world. Now, when all three are one, why should he who sins against the impure spirit find no forgiveness?"

Eisenmenger adduces several passages to the same purpose, concluding "Ist dieses nicht eine erschreckliche Lästerung?"

gard as the lowest of all.[1] But to return to the early Jewish writers.

The writers of the Apocrypha invariably represent God as the real Author of the Law, which is styled "Holy," "made and given" by Him.[2] Moses is a "Holy Prophet:"[3] his words[4] are quoted with the form, "O Lord our God * * * as thou spakest by thy servant Moses in the day when thou didst command him to write thy Law."[5] That Law "which Moses commanded for an heritage unto the congregations of Jacob," is "the book of the covenant of the Most High God;" this covenant is "everlasting;" its "light is uncorrupt;" and its "decrees eternal."[6] "Faithfulness" and "truth," and the "showing secret things or ever they came," are the tokens of a Prophet.[7] On his predictions the most implicit reliance is placed. Thus it is said: "My son, depart out of Ninive, because that those things which the prophet Jonas spake shall surely come to pass;" and of Isaiah, "He saw by an excellent spirit what should come to pass at the last."[8] The study of the

[1] This theory has arisen from an attempt to explain the cause of the ancient division of the Old Testament writings—a division recognised by our Lord Himself (Luke, xxiv. 44.)—into the Law, the Prophets, and the Kethubim or Hagiographa:—the *ὁ νόμος καὶ οἱ προφῆται καὶ τὰ ἄλλα βιβλία*, of the Prologue to the Book of Ecclesiasticus:—the כתובים, נביאים, תורה of the Jews. The source of this distinction the Jewish Rabbins placed in the different degrees of Inspiration possessed by the writers of the respective parts of the Old Testament. The Mosaic degree of Inspiration, under which the Law was written, was the most exalted; in it no other man of God was thought to share, cf. Numb. xii 6–8: while Prophecy, properly so called (נבואה), was distinguished from that degree which was entitled "the Holy Spirit" (רוח הקדש). This view is developed at considerable length in the "Moreh Nebochim" of Maimonides. "Its leading idea amounts to this, that the degree of the Holy Spirit is lower than that of Prophecy. It consisted chiefly in a revelation by dreams, so that the authors of the Hagiographa knew only a part of the truth, while Prophecy, properly so called, is pure, i. e., unveils the truth completely. This theory has, perhaps, been borrowed from the Muhammedan philosophers, who make a similar distinction between the Koran and the Sunnah, or other alleged prophetical writings."—Hävernick, *Einleitung*, 1er Th. 1te Abth. s. 66. We have already seen (Lecture i. p. 34.) how this Jewish notion has been introduced into Christian Theology. For further remarks on the subject, see Appendix C.

[2] 2 Macc. vi. 23. *Τῆς ἁγίας καὶ θεοκτίστου νομοθεσίας.* Cf. Ecclus. xxviii. 7.

[3] Wisdom, xi. 1.

[4] "The Lord shall scatter you among the nations, and ye shall be left few in number among the heathen whither the Lord shall lead you."—Deut. iv. 27.

[5] Baruch, ii. 28.

[6] Ecclus. xxiv. 23; xvii. 12. Wisdom, xviii. 4. Tobit, i. 6.

[7] "By his faithfulness he [Samuel] was found a true Prophet, and by his word he was known to be faithful in vision."—Ecclus. xlvi. 15. So also of Isaiah: '*Ησαΐας ὁ προφήτης ὁ μέγας καὶ πιστὸς ἐν ὁράσει αὐτοῦ.* * * * *Ἕως τοῦ αἰῶνος ὑπέδειξε τὰ ἐσόμενα καὶ τὰ ἀπόκρυφα πρὶν ἢ παραγενέσθαι αὐτά.*—c. xlviii. 22, 25.

[8] Tobit, xiv. 8. Ecclus. xlviii. 24.

Law and Prophets is stated to be the source of wisdom.[1] Even life itself must be sacrificed by the Jew in their defence: "My sons," said their dying leader,[2] "be ye zealous for the Law, and give your lives for the covenant of your fathers." In fine, they represent these books as the shield and safeguard of their nation; and even when soliciting the alliance and friendship of the Gentiles,[3] they add, "Albeit we need none of these things, for that we have the holy books of Scripture in our hands to comfort us."

In addition to such writings, which, while they date events from the period of the cessation of prophecy,[4] direct the people to earnest prayer for its restoration,[5] we have the important remains of two contemporaries of the Apostles, Josephus and Philo, who may be regarded as representing respectively the Judaism of Palestine and of Alexandria.[6]

[1] Ecclus. xxiv. 18, &c,; xxxix. 1, &c. [2] Mattathias; 1 Macc. ii. 50.

[3] "This is the copy of the letters which Jonathan wrote to the Lacedemonians." —1 Macc. xii. 5. *Καὶ ἡμεῖς οὖν ἀπροσδεεῖς τούτων ὄντες, παράκλησιν ἔχοντες τὰ βιβλία τὰ ἅγια τὰ ἐν ταῖς χερσὶν ἡμῶν.*—ver. 9. This statement, observes Hävernick, "is a characteristic expression of the tone of thought which marks the Judaism of that period, which founded its high esteem for the Canonical Scriptures upon their holiness, their Divine origin, their Inspiration. * * * These opinions, [i. e. of the authors of the Apocrypha in general] far from betraying an uncritical spirit, rather denote the sharp line of distinction which they drew between canonical and uncanonical writings."—*Neue krit. Untersuch. über das B. Daniel*, s. 22. Hamburg, 1838. De Wette admits that, whatever may have been the reasons for admitting the several books into the Canon, the ancient Jews "regarded the authors as inspired (begeistert), and their writings as the product of holy Inspiration (als Früchte heiliger Begeisterung)."—*Einleitung*, s. 21: and to this effect he quotes R. Azaria Meor Enaim.: "Esras non admovit manus nisi ad libros, qui compositi sunt a Prophetis per Spiritum S. et in lingua sacra."

[4] "So there was a great affliction in Israel, the like whereof was not since the time that a prophet was not seen among them."—1 Macc. ix. 27. Cf. iv. 46; xiv. 41.

[5] "Give testimony unto those that thou hast possessed from the beginning, and raise up prophets that have been in thy name."—Ecclus. xxxvi. 15.

[6] Eusebius ("Præparat. Evang.") has preserved a few fragments of two Jewish writers of an earlier date, who represent in like manner the opinion of the Jews of Palestine and Alexandria—the high priest Eleazar, and Aristobulus. Eleazar, in his Epistle to Ptolemy Philadelphus (B. C. 285.) observes, that Moses had been instructed in all matters by God Himself: *ὑπὸ Θεοῦ κατεσκευασμένος εἰς ἐπίγνωσιν τῶν ἁπάντων*—*Præp. Ev.* viii. 9, t. ii. p. 282. ed. Gaisford. Aristobulus,—who endeavored to trace the philosophy of Aristotle in the Old Testament, as Philo aftewards sought in its pages for that of Plato,—is identified by Eusebius (*ibid.* p. 291.) with the individual mentioned 2 Macc. i. 10, where he is called "Aristobulus, King Ptolemeus' Master, who was of the stock of the anointed Priests." In his treatise *ἡ τῶν ἱερῶν νόμων ἑρμηνεία* (Euseb. *ibid.* vii. 13, p. 184.) addressed to Ptolemy Philometer (B. C. 180.), Aristobulus observes that competent judges marvel at the wisdom of Moses, and the Divine Spirit by whose inspiration he has been proclaimed a Prophet: *Οἷς μὲν οὖν πάρεστι τὸ καλῶς νοεῖν, θαυμάζουσι τὴν περὶ αὐτὸν σοφίαν, καὶ τὸ θεῖον πνεῦμα, καθ' ὃ καὶ προφήτης ἀνακεκήρυκται.*—*Ibid*, viii. 10, p. 292. In reply to H. Hody's denial (*Cont. Hist.* lxx. *Interp.* lib. I. c. ix. p. 49.) of the authenticity of this treatise, see

Philo[1] gives an elaborate theory of Inspiration, of which he distinguishes two species, 'Interpretation' and 'Prophecy.'[2] To the former he ascribes by far the higher dignity. To it are to be referred those divine oracles which are spoken in the person of God by the Prophet who is 'Interpreter;' who is thus united, as it were, in one person with the Deity, and thus becomes a living word of God, since he speaks in the person of the Divine Being. As the power of 'Interpretation,' thus understood, enters upon the profoundest mysteries of the Godhead, Philo declines to discuss its nature, as transcending the power of human understanding: and it is, perhaps, needless to conjecture how far this thought may have been suggested by some vague anticipation of the coming of the Divine Word Incarnate, the true source of all Revelation.[3] To 'Prophecy,' on the other hand, he frequently adverts. It includes as well those cases in which the Prophet inquires of God, and God answers and instructs him, as those in which God confers upon man the power of foreknowledge, by which he predicts future events. The distinction, however, be-

C. Valckenaer's *Diatribe de Aristobulo*, reprinted by Dr. Gaisford in his edition of the "Præparatio. Evang."—It is to be observed, that Eleazar and Josephus may be regarded as exponents of the views of the Essenes, while Aristobulus and Philo represent those of the Therapeutæ. The Therapeutæ, according to Philo, regarded the Law as a living organism (*ζῶον*) consisting of body and soul:

Ἅπασα γὰρ ἡ νομοθεσία δοκεῖ τοῖς ἀνδράσι τούτοις ἐοικέναι ζώῳ· καὶ σῶμα μὲν ἔχειν τὰς ῥητὰς διατάξεις, ψυχὴν δὲ τὸν ἐναποκείμενον ταῖς λέξεσιν ἀόρατον νοῦν.—De Vita Contempl. tom. ii. p. 483. Cf. Olshausen, "Ein Wort über tiefern Schriftsinn," s. 16, ff.

[1] See Gfrörer, "Philo und die alexandr. Theosophie." 1er Theil. s. 46. ff.; and also Eichhorn's "Einleitung in das A. T." 1er Band. s. 126. For a more extended examination of the opinions of Philo and Josephus, see Appendix F.

[2] *Ἑρμηνεία δὲ καὶ Προφητεία διαφέρουσι.—De Vita Mosis*, t. ii. p. 164.

[3] E. g. the following singular phrase is applied by Philo to the words of Moses, Deut. viii. 2: *ὁ π ρ ο φ ή τ η ς λ ό γ ο ς, ὄνομα Μωϋσῆς ἐρεῖ.—Lib. de Congr. quær. Erud. grat.* t. i. p. 543. "As if," observes Gfrörer, "Moses were the Prophet above all others, *προφήτης κατ' ἐξοχήν*."—*Philo*, s. 60. That Philo believed in the impersonation of the Logos is evident from numerous passages in his writings. Thus he applies the title of High Priest to the *λόγος*. The abode of the homicide in the city of refuge is not to terminate until the death of the High Priest (Numb. xxxv. 25). The inequality of punishment inevitable in this case affords Philo much perplexity. He solves the difficulty by allegorizing the command: *λέγομεν γὰρ, τὸν ἀρχιερέα οὐκ ἄνθρωπον, ἀλλὰ λ ό γ ο ν θ ε ῖ ο ν εἶναι, πάντων οὐχ ἑκουσίων μόνον, ἀλλὰ καὶ ἀκουσίων ἀδικημάτων ἀμέτοχον.—De Profugis*, t. i. p. 562. Cf. also "De Somniis," t. i. p. 683–692; "De Migrat. Abrah." t. i. p. 452. In like manner, the Logos is frequently called by Philo "the image of God" (*εἰκὼν Θεοῦ.* Cf. 2 Cor. iv. 4; Col. i. 15). Thus, speaking of Exod. xxiv. 10, "And they saw the God of Israel," Philo observes: "It is fit that they who are allied to knowledge should desire to behold Jehovah (*ἐφίεσθαι μὲν τοῦ τὸ Ὂν ἰδεῖν.* But if they cannot behold Him, at least, His image, the most sacred Word." (*Τὴν γοῦν εἰκόνα αὐτοῦ, τὸν ἱερώτατον λόγον*).—*De Ling Confus.* t. i. p. 419. Cf. Gfrörer, "Philo," 1er Th. s. 243, ff.

tween 'Interpretation' and 'Prophecy' is too subtle and too refined for Philo. He continually represents the 'Prophet' as an 'Interpreter;' what he utters as Prophet not being his own, but the sentiment of another. Hence we find the two ideas not unfrequently interchanged: for example, Philo says: "The prophets are 'Interpreters,' God making use of their organs to manifest His will." According to this theory, the state of the Prophet, under the influence of Inspiration, is one of total unconsciousness. He is, as it were, an instrument of music, moved invisibly by God's power; all his utterances proceed from the suggestions of another, the prophetic rapture having mastered his faculties, and "the power of reflection having retired from the citadel of his soul."[1] The Divine Spirit comes upon him, and dwells within him, and moves the entire organism of his voice, prompting to the announcement of all that he foretells.[2] To that aspect of this theory, which represents unconsciousness as the essential condition of the Prophet's inspiration, we shall advert again. I would only observe at present, that although in his definitions of the psychological basis of prophecy, Philo's statements are exaggerated, still his favorite explanation: "The Prophet is an 'Interpreter;' God within his soul suggesting what must be said,"[3] contains a main element of the truth.

The point of practical moment, however, to be noticed here, is the importance attached by Philo to the notion implied by the term *Prophet;* for we can thence understand the degree of estimation in which the authors of the Old Testament were held by him, when he applies to them, in general, that title:—thereby exhibiting, as it were unconsciously, the light in which he regarded their writings.[4] To Moses, Philo, after the manner of his

[1] The principle from which Philo draws this inference, powerfully illustrates how deeply he felt the reality of the Divine influence which actuated the Prophets: Τῷ *δὲ προφητικῷ γένει φιλεῖ τοῦτο συμβαίνειν· ἐξοικίζεται μὲν γὰρ ἐν ἡμῖν ὁ νοῦς, κατὰ τὴν τοῦ θείου πνεύματος ἄφιξιν, κατὰ δὲ τὴν μετανάστασιν αὐτοῦ, πάλιν εἰσοικίζεται.* Θέ*μις γὰρ ὀυκ ἔστι θνητὸν ἀθανάτῳ συνοικῆσαι.—Quis. Rer. Div. Hær.* t. i. p. 511.

[2] *Ἐνοικηκότος τοῦ θείου πνεύματος, καὶ πᾶσαν τῆς φωνῆς ὀργανοποιΐαν κρούοντος, και ἐνηχοῦντος εἰς ἐναργῆ δήλωσιν ὧν προθεσπίζει.—De Speciai. Leg.* t. ii. p. 343.

[3] *Ἑρμηνεὺς γάρ ἐστιν ὁ προφήτης, ἔνδοθεν ὑπηχοῦντος τὰ λεκτέα τοῦ* Θεοῦ.—*De Præm. et Pœn.* t. ii. p. 417.

Cf. Rudelbach's Essay, "Die Lehre von der Inspiration," 1840. 2es Kap. s. 17.

[4] Besides the title *προφήτης*, Philo employs various terms to denote the sacred writers: e. g. Μωϋσέως *ἑταῖρος*, or *θιασώτης. τις τῶν φοιτητῶν* Μωϋσέως, *ἱεροφάντης, μυσταγωγός*, &c. The greater portion of the Old Testament, moreover, is quoted so as

nation, ascribes the pre-eminence. He was "that purest mind, which received at once the gift of legislation and prophecy, with divinely inspired wisdom."[1] "He was breathed upon with heavenly love."[2] His words are "Oracles,"[3] and divinely true. To David, Philo expressly gives the title of Prophet;[4] to the Books of Kings he refers under the form, "As saith the sacred word."[5] He quotes Isaiah "as one of the Prophets of old who spake by divine Inspiration."[6] And he clearly intimates that such opinions were not peculiar to himself,[7] but were shared by his whole

to express the most undoubted belief in its inspiration; nor is there the least reason to suppose that Philo did not receive as canonical the Books which he does not refer to by name.

To give a few examples: Genesis is styled *ἱεραὶ γραφαί.*—*De Mund. Opp.*, t. i. p. 18.

Exodus, *ἱερὰ βίβλος.*—*De Migr. Abr.*, t. i. p. 438, where even Moses is styled *ὁ ἱεροφάντης.*

Leviticus, *ἱερὸς λόγος.*—*Alleg.* II. t. i. p. 85.

Numbers, *ἱερώτατον γράμμα.*—*Deus Immut.* t. i. p. 273.

Deuteronomy, *χρησμός.*—*De Migr. Abr.*, t. i. p. 454.

Joshua (ch. i. 5) is quoted as *λόγιον τοῦ ἵλεω θεοῦ.*—*De Ling. Confus.* t. i. p. 430.

The words of Ezra (ch. viii. 2) are called *τὰ ἐν βασιλικαῖς βίβλοις ἱεροφαντηθέντα.*—*Ibid.* t. i. p. 427.

Hosea (xiv. 8) is quoted as *παρά τινι τῶν προφητῶν χρησθέν.*—*De Plantat. Noe*, t. i. p. 350.

1 See "Liber de Cong. quær. Erudit. grat." t. i. p. 538.

2 On this phrase Gfrörer observes: "The complete perfection of Moses' nature (seines Wesens) is described in the third book, 'De Vita Mosis,' t. ii. p. 145, by the beautiful expression which includes in itself every other quality, *καταπνευσθεὶς ὑπ' ἔρωτος οὐρανίου.*"—*Philo*, i. s. 63.

3 The words of Moses, in general, are styled *λόγια* in the *locus classicus*, "De Vita Mosis," III. t. ii. p. 163. See Appendix F.

4 Quoting Ps. xxiii. 1: *οὐχ ὁ τυχών, ἀλλὰ προφήτης.*—*De Agricult.* t. i. p. 308. Ps. xxxviii. 4, is quoted with the form *ὁ τοῦ Μωϋσέως θιασώτης ἀνεφθέξατο.*—*De Plant. Noe*, t. i. p. 335. And of Ps. xciv. 9, Philo observes: *ὁ θεσπέσιος ἀνὴρ ἐν ὕμνοις λέγων ὧδε.*—*Ibid.* p. 334.

This mode of referring to the Psalms proves that Philo was unconscious of any distinction between the inspiration of the prophetical books, and that of the Hagiographa. See p. 62, note [1], *supra.*

5 The first Book of Samuel (ch. i. 11.) is quoted with the words: *ὡς ὁ ἱερὸς λόγος φησί.*—*De Ebrietat.* i. p. 379. This book was accounted by the Alexandrian Jews the "First Book of Kings."

6 *Τις τῶν πάλαι προφητῶν ἐπιθειάσας εἶπεν.*—*De Somniis*, t. i. p. 681. And Jeremiah is quoted with the words: *τοῦ προφητικοῦ θιασώτης χοροῦ, ὃς καταπνευσθεὶς ἐνθουσιῶν ἀνεφθέξατο.*—*De Ling. Confus.* t. i. p. 411.

7 It is to be observed, with reference to a common misapprehension, that although Philo often claims an exaggerated degree of insight into the sense of Scripture, he does not venture to compare himself with the sacred writers. Take, for example, the following passage, in which, while claiming the deepest insight into the divine mysteries, Philo represents himself as an humble disciple at the feet of the Prophet Jeremiah, who "announces his oracle filled with divine inspiration, and impersonating God:"—

Καὶ γὰρ ἐγὼ παρὰ Μωσεῖ τῷ θεοφιλεῖ μυηθεὶς τὰ μεγάλα μυστήρια, ὅμως αὖθις Ἱερεμίαν τὸν προφήτην ἰδών, καὶ γνοὺς ὅτι οὐ μόνον μύστης ἐστὶν, ἀλλὰ καὶ ἱεροφάντης ἱκανὸς, οὐκ ὤκνησα φοιτῆσαι πρὸς αὐτόν. Ὁ δὲ, ἅτε τὰ πολλὰ ἐνθου-

nation; for, describing how his countrymen had excited the anger of the Emperor Caligula by opposing his design of profaning the Temple, Philo adds, that the Jews would gladly embrace death, as immortality, sooner than overlook the abrogation of even the least of their country's laws.[1] Nor, while on this topic, should we omit to bear in mind Philo's entire system of allegorizing, exaggerated and forced though it was, but which, like that of Origen, was grounded upon the firm conviction that the most pregnant signification is couched beneath the literal meaning of each expression of Scripture.

The belief of Josephus in the authority of the Old Testament, and the nature of the Divine influence which actuated the Prophets, perfectly coincides with that of Philo. This agreement is particularly to be noticed with reference to the prophetic state, and to the manner in which both writers have employed the title 'Prophet.'[2] From this we can infer in what a profound sense Jo-

σιῶν, χρησμόν τινα ἐξεῖπεν ἐκ προσώπου τοῦ Θεοῦ λέγοντα πρὸς τὴν εἰρηνικωτάτην ἀρετὴν ταῦτα [*scil.* Jer. iii. 4].—*De Cherubim*, t. i. p. 147.

Gfrörer, having quoted a number of passages to prove that Philo occasionally claims supernatural aid *when interpreting* portions of the Old Testament, justly observes: "Doch muss man desswegen nicht glauben, dass unser Verfasser die Propheten des alten Bundes in eine Reihe mit den gewöhnlichen Menschen, oder mit dem lebenden Geschlechte, stellte."—*Philo*, i. s. 60.

[1] *Ἓν δὲ μόνον ἔθνος ἐξαίρετον τὸ τῶν Ἰουδαίων ὕποπτον ἦν ἀντιπράξειν, εἰωθὸς ἑκουσίους ἀναδέχεσθαι θανάτους, ὥσπερ ἀθανασίαν, ὑπὲρ τοῦ μηδὲν τῶν πατρίων περιϊδεῖν ἀναιρούμενον, εἰ καὶ βραχύτατον εἴη.*—*De Legat. ad Caium*, t. ii. p. 562.

M. Gaussen ("Theopneustia—The Plenary Inspiration of the Holy Scriptures," London, 1841.) observes, "The Jewish philosopher Philo in the narrative which he has left of his embassy to the Emperor Caligula, making use also of a term very similar to that of St. Paul [*θεόπνευστος*, 2 Tim. iii. 16.], calls the Scriptures '*oracles théocristes*,' that is to say, oracles given under an *unction from God*."—p. 24. But this writer has been led astray by not consulting the original authority. His note of reference is "*Θεόχριστα λόγια* P. 1022, Edit. Francof." Now, both in this edition of Philo's works, and in that of Mangey (t. ii. p. 577,), the words are, *Θ ε ό χ ρ η σ τ α γὰρ λόγια τοὺς νόμους εἶναι ὑπολαμβάνοντες* [*scil. οἱ Ἰουδαῖοι*]: and Philo uses them to prove how much more tenacious of their customs the Jews were than other nations. Since they believed, he argues, their laws to have "proceeded from Divine oracles," they would submit to every extremity rather than admit the erection of a statue in the Temple.

[2] Thus, Josephus represent Moses as a Prophet in so exalted a sense that his words are to be regarded as those of God: *προφήτης δὲ οἷος οὐκ ἄλλος, ὥς θ' ὅ τι ἂν φθέγξαιτο δοκεῖν αὐτοῦ λέγοντος, ἀκροᾶσθαι τοῦ Θεοῦ.*—*Ant.* IV. viii. 49, p. 258.

So sacred are the words of the Decalogue that Josephus dares not divulge them to the Gentiles except in the form of a brief summary: *οὓς* [*scil. λόγους*] *οὐ θεμιτόν ἐστιν ἡμῖν λέγειν φανερῶς πρὸς λέξιν, τὰς δὲ δυνάμεις αὐτῶν δηλώσομεν.*—*Ant.* III. v. 4, p. 129. Josephus gives another example of the reverence with which his countrymen regarded the Old Testament. He relates that when the Seventy Interpreters had completed their version, the King (Ptolemy Philadelphus) asked how it happened that no poet or historian had made any mention of so admirable a work. He was told, in reply, that the judgments of God had fallen upon all who had dared to treat of these Divine records: *ὁ δὲ Δημήτριος, μηδένα τολμῆσαι τῆς τῶν νόμων τούτων ἀνα-*

sephus calls Isaiah "a Prophet confessedly Divine;" and how much he intends to convey when he says that all the events of his nation had happened according to the predictions of the Twelve Minor Prophets.[1] But I must confine myself here to a few remarks on the celebrated passage in his work against Apion.[2] In this statement Josephus maintains that the records of no nation can compare with those of the Jews in point of historic truth. To establish this assertion he points out the care taken to preserve the Sacred Books, and also the strict rules which regulated their composition. The Sacred Books, he tells his opponent, were delivered to the charge of the High Priest, the purity of whose descent was guarded by the most stringent laws, and whose genealogy from father to son was set down in the public archives, and could be traced back for two thousand years. Such precautions, observes Josephus, to guard the purity of the sacerdotal race, are not only natural, but necessary. It is not in the power of every one to draw up such records, nor does any contradiction exist in them, because the privilege of writing them belongs to Prophets alone. They alone were acquainted with the facts of earliest date, which they have learned by direct inspiration from God. The history of their own times they have also written with unerring certainty, according as events occurred.[3] "With us," he continues, "there is no endless series of works, discordant and contradictory; two-and-twenty books contain the annals of all time, and are justly believed to be divine. * * * From the age

γραφῆς ἅψασθαι, διὰ τὸ θείαν αὐτὴν εἶναι καὶ σεμνὴν, ἔφασκε, καὶ ὅτι βλαβεῖεν ἤδη τινὲς, τούτοις ἐπιχειρήσαντες, ὑπὸ τοῦ Θεοῦ.—*Ant.* XII. ii. 13, p. 595.

And the case of the poet Theodectes (mentioned by Aristotle, "De Poet." xviii.) is adduced, who, desiring to dramatize some scriptural narrative, (*βουληθεὶς ἔν τινι δράματι τῶν ἐν τῇ ἱερᾷ βίβλῳ γεγραμμένων μνησθῆναι,*) was deprived, for a time, of sight.

[1] Alluding to the judgment pronounced by Isaiah against Hezekiah, 2 Kings, xx. 16: *ὢν δὲ οὗτος ὁ προφήτης ὁμολογουμένως θεῖος καὶ θαυμάσιος τὴν ἀλήθειαν, πεποιθὼς τῷ μηδὲν ὅλως ψευδὲς εἰπεῖν, ἅπανθ' ὅσα προεφήτευσεν ἐγγράψας βίβλοις κατέλιπεν, ἐκ τοῦ τέλους γνωρισθησόμενα τοῖς αὖθις ἀνθρώποις. Καὶ οὐχ οὗτος μόνος ὁ προφήτης, ἀλλὰ καὶ ἄλλοι δώδεκα τὸν ἀριθμὸν τὸ αὐτὸ ἐποίησαν· καὶ πᾶν εἴτε ἀγαθὸν εἴτε φαῦλον γίνεται παρ' ἡμῖν κατὰ τὴν ἐκείνων ἀποβαίνει προφητείαν.*—*Ant.* x. ii. 2, p. 515.

[2] Cont. Apion. i. 7, 8, t. ii. p. 441. This passage has been regarded from the earliest times as of the highest importance. Thus Eusebius quotes it, as giving *τὸν ἀριθμὸν τῆς λεγομένης παλαιᾶς τῶν ἐνδιαθήκων γραφῶν, τίνα παρ' Ἑβραίοις ἀναντίῤῥητα.*—*Eccl. Hist.* iii. 9, p. 103.

[3] *Εἰκότως οὖν, μᾶλλον δὲ ἀναγκαίως, ἅτε μήτε τοῦ ὑπογράφειν αὐτεξουσίου πᾶσιν ὄντος, μήτε τινὸς ἐν τοῖς γραφομένοις ἐνούσης διαφωνίας· ἀλλὰ μόνων τῶν προφητῶν τὰ μὲν ἀνωτάτω καὶ τὰ παλαιότατα, κατὰ τὴν ἐπίπνοιαν τὴν ἀπὸ τοῦ Θεοῦ μαθόντων, τὰ δὲ καθ' αὑτοὺς, ὡς ἐγένετο σαφῶς συγγραφόντων.*—*Cont. Apion.* i. 7.

of Artaxerxes, it is true, narratives of events extending to our day have been written, but they have not been counted of equal credit with books composed at an earlier period, because there has been no accurate succession of Prophets. Facts clearly prove how great trust we repose in our Sacred Books, for, although so many ages have passed away, no man has dared to add to, or take away from, or alter aught in them. Nay, it is implanted in every Jew, from the hour of his birth, to esteem as the ordinances of God, and to stand fast by these writings, and in defence of them, if need be, cheerfully to die."[1] This remarkable passage speaks for itself; and I would merely point out its illustration of a topic to which considerable weight was attached in the last Discourse, as forming the second "Condition" of the problem to be solved. The invariable rule that all writers of the Old Testament should be *Prophets*—the word being understood in the sense given to it by Josephus and Philo, and on which the former founds his proof of the unerring certainty of the Hebrew Scriptures—ensures that every portion of every book, whether relating to ancient events, or to facts which occurred in the lifetime of the writers, has been written under Divine *Inspiration*; while the direct communication from God of those matters the knowledge of which could not be naturally acquired by the Prophet, corresponds to the definition which I have assigned to *Revelation*.[2]

I cannot leave this branch of our subject without pausing to inquire whether, in that portion of the Bible which constitutes the New Testament, and which was written by the contemporaries of Philo and Josephus, we can find any traces of sentiments analogous to those which formed, as we have just seen, so important an element of the intense religious consciousness of the Jews. Such traces are to be found: and thus the stamp of Divine approval is given to the general features of the Jewish doctrine of Inspiration. A few instances will prove this. The phrase "oracles of God" is employed by Philo to denote not only the

[1] See Appendix F. Winer ("Real-Wörterbuch," art. "Sadducäer.") argues with great justice from these words of Josephus, that ancient and modern writers, from Tertullian ("Præscr. Hær." c. 45.) downwards, are in error when they assert that the Sadducees differed from the rest of the Jews in receiving as divine the Pentateuch alone. See also Hävernick, "Einleitung," t. i. s. 74.

[2] See Lecture i. p. 27.

Pentateuch, but also the Book of Joshua,[1] and therefore must be understood to apply to the entire of the Old Testament as a generic term. Now this is the very expression employed by S. Paul, in the text, to describe the inestimable value of the treasure committed to the Jews; and the word is of no unfrequent use in the New Testament in this same sense.[2] Josephus, as we have seen, has expressed the belief of his nation that the authors of the different Books of the Old Testament were all entitled to the appellation of Prophets. Adopting this principle as an undoubted truth, S. Peter, having quoted a prediction of Moses, goes on to enumerate the other sacred writers in the words: "Yea, and all the Prophets from Samuel and those that follow after." And Christ Himself, in the apologue of Lazarus and the rich man, represents Abraham as describing the Old Testament by the comprehensive phrase, "Moses and the Prophets."[3] Again; Philo observes, referring to the Prophet "like unto Moses"[4] who was at length to appear, that although he was to prophesy, and announce his oracles at the Divine instigation, yet his words *were not to be his own*, and that each utterance with which he had been inspired was to proceed from the suggestion of another.[5] It is impossible to avoid being struck by the general resemblance of this sentiment to an inspired statement of the New Testament in a much contested passage, on the meaning of which it casts considerable light: "No prophecy of the Scrip-

[1] *Λόγια*; see p. 66, note [3], *supra*. Compare too (p. 65, note [4]) Philo's expression for the book of Numbers—*ἱερώτατον γράμμα*—with the *τὰ ἱερὰ γράμματα* of S. Paul, 2 Tim. iii. 15.

[2] *Τὰ λόγια τοῦ θεοῦ.*—Rom. iii. 2. S. Stephen (Acts, vii. 38.) reminds the Jewish Council how Moses "received the lively *oracles* (*λόγια ζῶντα*) to give unto us." So, again, 1 Peter, iv. 11, *εἴ τις λαλεῖ, ὡς λόγια θεοῦ*; and Heb. v. 12, *τῆς ἀρχῆς τῶν λογίων τοῦ θεοῦ*. As a further instance of such analogies, cf. Gal. iv. 22, &c., which contains the allegorical exposition of the history of the two sons of Abraham. The Apostle's inference is prefaced by the words, "which things are an allegory," *ἅτινά ἐστιν ἀλληγορούμενα*, ver. 24.—language intimating a view of the Old Testament altogether analogous to that which characterizes the writings of Philo. For example:—Philo's sentiments as to the relation of the *letter* of Scripture, to its spiritual or allegorical sense, may be illustrated by his remark on the migrations of Abraham: *αἱ δηλωθεῖσαι ἀποικίαι, τῷ μὲν ῥήματι τῆς γραφῆς, ὑπ' ἀνδρὸς σοφοῦ γεγόνασι, κατὰ δὲ τοὺς ἀλληγορίας νόμους, ὑπὸ φιλαρέτου ψυχῆς, τὸν ἀληθῆ ζητούσης θεόν.*—*De Vita Abrah.* t. ii. p. 11. But see *infra*, Lecture vii.

[3] Acts, iii. 22–24. S. Luke, xvi. 29, 31.

[4] Deut. xviii. 18.

[5] * * * *τις ἐπιφανεὶς ἐξαπιναίως προφήτης θεοφόρητος θεσπιεῖ καὶ προφητεύσει, λέγων μὲν οἰκεῖον οὐδέν* * * * *ὅσα δ' ἐνηχεῖται, διελεύσεται καθάπερ ὑποβάλλοντος ἑτέρου.*—*De Monarch.* I. t. ii. p. 222. And again, *προφήτης γὰρ ἴδιον μὲν οὐδὲν ἀποφθέγγεται, ἀλλότρια δὲ πάντα ὑπηχοῦντος ἑτέρου.*—*Quis Rer. Div. Hæres*, t. i. p. 510.

tures," writes S. Peter, "is of any *private interpretation;*[1] for the prophecy came not in old time by the will of man; but holy men of God spake as they were moved by the Holy Ghost." But a higher instance still remains. "Moses alone," writes Philo, "has fully realized the qualities of a legislator. All know this who are versed in the sacred books, which none could have written without the guidance of God,—those most glorious of possessions, the image and copy of models stamped upon his soul. That these laws are truly Divine, and omit nothing needful, is our surest trust. The words of Moses alone, steadfast and unshaken, stamped, as it were, with the seal of nature itself, remain fixed since the day they were written until now; and our hope is that for all future time they will abide immortal as long as sun and moon, and the universal heaven, and the world itself endure."[2] It is almost unnecessary to point out the striking resemblance of these words to the language of our Lord Himself when speaking of the Law: "Verily I say unto you, till heaven and earth pass, one jot or one tittle shall in no wise pass from the Law, till all be fulfilled;" or, again: "It is easier for heaven and earth to pass, than one tittle of the Law to fail."[3]

But it may be said that Christ and His Apostles, by adopting this language, merely 'accommodated' themselves to the prejudices of the Jewish people; and that by this principle of 'accommodation' are to be explained all the strong expressions

[1] *Ἰδίας ἐπιλύσεως*.—2 Peter, i. 20, of which passage several commentators give the following interpretation: "The writings of the Prophets are not of *their* (the Prophets') *own* revelation, disclosure, *propriæ patefactionis;* they did not communicate their own thoughts, but the counsels of God." Mangey observes on the sentiment of Philo here referred to: "Non multum a Philone discrepat D. Petrus, 2 Ep. i. 20, ubi *ἐπιλύσεως* non *de interpretatione*, ut vulgo, sed de *motu*, et suggestione est exponendum ob sequentia."—t. i. p. 510. Whether Mangey's exposition of this obscure passage be correct or not, the principle conveyed by it is quite consistent with that which will be laid down in Lecture v., *infra*.

[2] Τὰ *δὲ τούτου μόνου βέβαια, ἀσάλευτα, ἀκράδαντα, καθάπερ σφραγῖσι φύσεως αὐτῆς σεσημασμενα, μένει παγίως ἀφ' ἧς ἡμέρας ἐγράφη μέχρι νῦν, καὶ πρὸς τὸν ἔπειτα πάντα διαμενεῖν ἐλπὶς αὐτὰ αἰῶνα ὥσπερ ἀθάνατα, ἕως ἂν ἥλιος καὶ σελήνη καὶ ὁ σύμπας οὐρανός τε καὶ κόσμος ᾖ.*—*De Vita Mosis*, t. ii. p. 136.

[3] S. Matt. v. 18; S. Luke, xvi. 17. Mangey's note on the passage just quoted from Philo is as follows:—"Legem Mosis, quoad morum saltem præcepta, esse perpetuam, non Philo solus docuit, id enim sibi spondebant Judæi omnibus fere seculis. Siracid. xxxvii. 25, *καὶ αἱ ἡμέραι τοῦ Ἰσραὴλ ἀναρίθμητοι.* * * * Joseph. Ant. lib. iii. c. 8, circa finem. *νόμων οὓς, κρείττονας ἢ κατὰ σύνεσιν ἀνθρωπίνην ὄντας, εἰς τὸν ἅπαντα βεβαίως αἰῶνα συνέβη φυλαχθῆναι, δωρεὰν εἶναι δόξαντας τοῦ Θεοῦ*, &c.

Compare also with Christ's language as to the Law, the language of the book of Baruch, c. iv. 1: "This is the book of the commandments of God, and the Law that endureth for ever."

employed in the New Testament respecting the authority and inspiration of the Old. This objection will meet us again in the course of our investigation, and it may be well to discuss it here, once for all.

It is plain, that in any communication from an infinite Being to creatures of finite capacities, one of two things must happen. Either the former must raise the latter almost to His own level; or else He must suit the form of His communication to their powers of apprehension. In a word, unless God's Revelation be meant to extend to the removal of every error, and to afford man an unclouded view of the Divine councils and nature,—and we have no reason to suppose that either our senses could perfectly take in, or the capabilities of language correctly convey, such knowledge,—unless, I repeat, this be insisted upon, we must believe that Revelation *has* been 'accommodated' to the understanding and opinions of mankind; in all points in which it was not God's will further to enlighten the understanding, or specially to correct such opinions.[1] Indeed, by insisting upon the former part of this alternative, a late writer attempts to defend his denial of the possibility of a Revelation;—"Even the Omnipotence of God," he observes, "cannot infuse infinite conceptions into finite minds."[2] If we turn to Scripture, however, we shall see how this matter is decided. In God's dealings with men we find "wrath," "jealousy," "repentance," and other affections, ascribed to the Divine

[1] Cf. Arnold,—"On the Right Interpretation of the Scriptures," Sermons, 4th Ed. vol. ii. p. 385; who also observes: "When God chooses a being of finite knowledge to be the medium of His revelations, it is at once understood that the faculties of this being are left in their natural state, except so far as regards the especial message with which he is intrusted. But, perhaps, we do not enough consider how in the very message itself there must be a mixture of accommodation to our ignorance;—for complete knowledge on any one point could not be given without extending itself to other points;—nay, the very means by which we receive all our knowledge, that is, language, and the observation of our senses, are themselves so imperfect, that they could not probably convey to the mind other than imperfect notions of truth."

[2] "The Creed of Christendom;" by William Rathbone Greg. London, 1851. "Being finite, we *can* form no correct or adequate idea of the Infinite: being material, we *can* form no clear conception of the Spiritual. The question of a Revelation can in no way affect this conclusion; since even the Omnipotence of God cannot infuse infinite conceptions into finite minds,—cannot, without an entire change of the conditions of our being, pour a just and full knowledge of His nature into the bounded capacity of a mortal's soul. Human intelligence could not grasp it; human language could not express it."—*Preface*, p. x. Even Mr. Coleridge has so completely overlooked the fact which we are now considering, as to observe: "How can absolute infallibility be blended with fallibility? How can infallible truth be infallibly conveyed in defective and fallible expressions?"—*Confessions of an Inquiring Spirit*, Letter II. p. 21. What! not even in the words of Christ?

See also Mr. Coleridge's remarks on 'accommodation,' *supra*, p. 53, note.

Being. He is described "as sitting on a throne;" His eyes are said "to behold the children of men;" not to mention other instances, which must suggest themselves to every one, in which God condescends to convey to us, not the very reality indeed, but something as near the reality as He sees it expedient for us to know. Without this species of 'accommodation' there could be no such thing as instruction.[1] Every instructor must begin upon ground common to his pupils, with principles presupposed as known to them, in order to extend the sphere of their knowledge to other truths. The missionary, for example, must adopt some such process when he speaks of "God" to a heathen; he adopts the term of the heathen dialect, but he refines and exalts its meaning.[2] In fact, the principle of all such adaptations is expressed in the explanation of S. Paul to the Athenians: "Whom ye ignorantly worship, Him declare I unto you."[3]

[1] Thus, Dante writes:

"Così parlar conviensi al vostro ingegno,
Perocchè solo da sensato apprende
Ciò che fa poscia d' intelletto degno.
Per questo la Scrittura condiscende
A vostra facultate; e piedi e mano
Attribuisce a Dio, ed altro intendre."

Paradiso, Canto IV.

[2] In this task the missionary is beset with no small difficulties; a consideration of which will illustrate the necessity of Divine guidance in order thus to refine the sense of human language, and to overcome its imperfections. See, for example, "An Inquiry into the proper mode of rendering the word 'God,' in translating the Scriptures into the Chinese language;" by Sir G. S. Staunton, 1849, who writes: "Drs. Morrison, Milne, and Marsham, used SHIN to render *Elohim* and *Theos* in all cases. Dr. Medhurst and Mr. Gutzlaff used SHANG-TEE to render these words, when the true God was referred to, and SHIN when the reference was to a false God." The early Christian missionaries "accepted without scruple TIEN and SHANG-TEE, which they found in popular use, to convey the Scriptural ideas of heaven and the true God." "In 1715 the Dominicans obtained from the Pope an apostolic precept, ordaining among other things that the term SHANG-TEE should be no longer used in the Christian Ritual of the Chinese, and that the term TIEN-CHU, signifying literally, 'Lord of heaven,' and already occasionally used, should be substituted in its place." * * * "It has been shown that SHANG-TEE, or *Tien*, may be said to be the immediate object of the Emperor's public worship on certain State occasions. Yet it must be confessed that neither *Tien* nor SHANG-TEE, practically speaking, is viewed by the people of China generally, as an object of direct worship at all! The religious worship of the Chinese people, such as it is, is practically transferred to the multitude of SHIN ('gods,' according to some translators, and 'spirits,' according to others), whose images are honored under various names."—pp. 2–18. The Protestant missionaries propose to introduce the word SHIN.—p. 27.

[3] Acts, xvii. 23. I have not alluded to the use of the term Λόγος by S. John, which is commonly adduced as an illustration. Thus, Olshausen, on S. John, i. 1, observes: "If it be assumed (and this, if it cannot be demonstrated, cannot be proved untrue), that John was acquainted with the writings of Philo, * * * we have then an external reason for the use of this term; only we are not to assume that John

The importance of this subject has called attention to it from the earliest period of Christianity: and while the Fathers recognise and state with accuracy the nature of this 'economy' (*οἰκονομία*), or 'condescension' (*συγκατάβασις*), or 'accommodation' (*συμπεριφορά*), as it is exhibited in God's revelations, or in the inspired teaching of the Apostles, they are careful to point out the distinction between this characteristic of the language of Scripture, and the 'hypocrisy' (*ὑπόκρισις*), which through cowardice conceals a truth, or the 'dissimulation' (*dissimulatio*), which to attain its ends stoops to tolerate error.[1] In modern times much attention has been directed to the principle of 'ac-

gained the *idea itself* through any historical medium whatever. Even if he did receive some external notice of it, he obtained it first in reality through the illumination of the Spirit." See also some interesting remarks on this subject in a Lecture "On the Platonic Philosophy," by the late Professor W. A. Butler, published in the Irish Eccl. Journal for October, 1849, p. 342.

[1] A few illustrations will suffice to prove this statement: S. Cyril of Alexandria writes of the Holy Ghost:—*Ὅτι τέλειον τὸ Πνεῦμα τὸ Ἅγιον καὶ οὐδὲν ἀτελὲς ἐν αὐτῷ· κἂν γὰρ φέρηταί τινα περὶ αὐτοῦ παρὰ ταῖς θείαις γραφαῖς, ὑπεμφαίνοντά τι τοιοῦτον, τῆς οἰκονομίας ἕνεκα τῆς δι' ἡμᾶς εἰρῆσθαι δώσομεν.*—*Thesaur. Assert.* xxxiv. t. v. p. 343. The recognised use of *οἰκονομία* to signify the mystery of the Incarnation comes under this head: *Τὴν ἐνανθρώπησιν τοῦ Θεοῦ Λόγου καλοῦμεν οἰκονομίαν.*—Theodoret. *Dial.* II. t. iv. p. 62.

S. Paul circumcised Timothy "because of the Jews."—Acts, xvi. 3. On this, Clement of Alex. justly refers to the words 1 Cor. ix. 19–22, ending: "I am made all things to all men, that I might by all means save some;" adding the remark (according to Potter's emendation of the text): *Ὁ τοίνυν μέχρι τῆς συμπεριφορᾶς συγκαταβαίνων ψιλῆς, διὰ τὴν τῶν δι' οὓς συμπεριφέρεται σωτηρίαν, οὐδεμίας ὑποκρίσεως διὰ τὸν ἐπηρτημένον τοῖς δικαίοις ἀπὸ τῶν ζηλούντων κίνδυνον μετέχων, οὗτος οὐδαμῶς ἀναχάζεται.*—*Strom.* VII. ix. p. 863.

Similarly, S. Chrysostom,—speaking of S. Paul's conduct, Acts, xxi. 20–26:—*ὁρᾷς ὅτι ἡνίκα μὲν καιρὸς συγκαταβάσεως ἦν, καὶ Παῦλος ἰουδάϊζεν.*—*Hom. in Gal.* ii. 11, t. iii. p. 372.

While the fact of such 'accommodation' is thus distinctly admitted, all notion of 'dissimulation' is as rigidly excluded. Thus: Tertullian, referring to S Mark, x. 46–52, where the multitude charge the blind Bartimæus that he should hold his peace, rejects a cavil of Marcion:—"Aut doce increpantes illos scisse quod Jesus non esset filius David; ut idcirco silentium cæco indixisse credantur. Sed et si doceres, facilius illos ignorasse præsumeretur, *quam Dominum falsam in se prædicationem sustinere potuisse.* Sed patiens Dominus: non tamen confirmator erroris, immo etiam detector Creatoris; ut non prius hanc cæcitatem hominis illius enubillasset, ne ultra Jesum filium David existimaret. Atquin, ne patientiam Ejus infamaretis, nec ullam rationem *dissimulationis* Illi affingeretis, nec filium David negaretis, manifestissime confirmavit cæci prædicationem, et ipsa remuneratione medicinæ et testimonio fidei. Fides, inquit, tua te salvum fecit."—*Advers. Marc.* iv. 36, p. 564.

Bretschneider ("Handbuch der Dogmatik," 1er Band. s. 422) justly observes that Origen rejects all false 'accommodation' when he explains, as follows, the calumny of the Jews: "Say we not well that thou art a Samaritan" (S. John, viii. 48): *εἰκὸς δὲ καὶ ὅτι τινὲς ᾤοντο αὐτὸν* [*scil.* Christ] *μὴ ἀπὸ διαθέσεως τὰ περὶ μέλλοντος αἰῶνος, καὶ τὰ περὶ κρίσεως, καὶ ἀναστάσεως διδάσκειν, διακείμενον μὲν Σαμαρειτικῶς, ὡς μηδενὸς μετὰ τὸν βίον ἀποκειμένου τοῖς ἀνθρώποις, προσποιήσεως δὲ ἕνεκεν, κατὰ τὸ ἔνδοξον καὶ ἀρέσκον τοῖς Ἰουδαίοις, τὰ περὶ ἀναστάσεως καὶ τῆς αἰωνίου ζωῆς προφερόμενον.*—*Comm. in Joann.* t. iv. p. 353.

For further instances, cf. Suicer, "Thesaurus," *sub voc. οἰκονομία.*

commodation,' in consequence of the uses to which it has been perverted by Rationalists of every school.[1] It has been distinguished into 'accommodation in the *form*,' and 'accommodation in the *matter*,' of the information communicated.[2] To the former belong the style and popular mode of instruction employed by Christ and His Apostles, as well as their practice of clothing the truths of religion in parables, or allegories, or similitudes borrowed from the range of ordinary experience. Take, for example, the figurative analogies which Christ applies in the twelfth chapter of S. Matthew's Gospel, like a parable, in order to exhibit an idea vividly to His hearers—the connexion being such that He could not possibly be misunderstood.[3] 'Accommodation in the *matter*' of the information communicated is laid down as being twofold: *negative* and *positive*. Negative accommodation is that in which either a command is not enforced in its full rigor, or in which the whole truth is not at once disclosed, but is imparted gradually. As an instance of not insisting upon the strict letter of a Divine injunction, we may cite the relaxation of the law of marriage, by which a system of divorce was permitted to the Jews "because of the hardness of their hearts;"[4] but even here the moral obligation of the command was never allowed to be forgotten, as is plainly intimated by the Prophet Malachi.[5] As cases in which the truth is unfolded gradually, we

[1] Spinoza, in this, as in other kindred topics, seems to have led the way: "Nec aliter de Christi rationibus, quibus Pharisæos contumaciæ et ignorantiæ convincit discipulosque ad veram vitam hortatur, statuendum; quod nempe suas rationes opinionibus et principiis uniuscujusque *accomodavit*. Ex. gr. Cum Pharisæis dixit, vide Matt. xi. 26, 'et si Satanas Satanam ejicit, adversus seipsum divisus est,' &c., nihil nisi Pharisæos ex suis principiis convincere voluit, non autem docere, dari Dæmones, aut aliquod Dæmonum regnum." Spinoza adds: "Si mihi enumeranda essent omnia Scripturæ loca, quæ tantum *ad hominem, sive ad captum alicujus scripta sunt*, et quæ non sine magno Philosophiæ præjudicio tanquam divina doctrina defenduntur, a brevitate cui studeo longe discederem."—*Tractatus Theol. Polit.* cap. ii. *circ. fin.*

[2] Cf. Bretschneider, "Handb. der Dogm." § 42, ss. 418–430; whose rationalistic views here, as elsewhere, disfigure the accuracy of his distinctions.

[3] S. Matt. xii. 43–45. "When the unclean spirit is gone out of a man, he walketh through dry places, seeking rest, and findeth none," &c.

[4] S. Matt. xix. 8.

[5] "The Lord hath been witness between thee and the wife of thy youth, against whom thou hast dealt treacherously: yet is she thy companion, and the wife of thy covenant. And did not He make one? * * * Therefore take heed to your spirit, and let none deal treacherously against the wife of his youth."—Mal. ii. 14, 15. Cf. too, Christ's appeal to the original law of marriage, S. Matt. xix. 4: "Have ye not read," &c. Mr. Greg asserts that our Lord "contradicted Moses, and abrogated his ordinances in an authoritative and peremptory manner, which precludes the idea that he supposed himself dealing with the direct commands of God. This is done in many points specified in Matt. v. 34–44;—in the case of divorce in the most positive and

may adduce the passages in which S. Paul tells the Corinthians that he had "fed them with milk, and not with meat;"[1] and in which Christ Himself told His disciples:—"I have yet many things to say unto you, but ye cannot cannot bear them now."[2]

Positive accommodation, however,—which brings us to the objection from which we started,—is that in which the teacher adopts as true, principles which he knows to be erroneous, and uses them so as to confirm his pupils in their errors. Of this a remarkable instance occurs in the New Testament, in the case of S. Peter's "dissimulation" at Antioch; and there it is treated with severe and marked reprobation. "I withstood him to the face," writes S. Paul, "because he was to be blamed."[3]

It will be easily seen how the other examples of just and necessary 'accommodation' to human imperfection, have supplied to over-ingenious and perverse minds that coloring of truth which has served to lend even a semblance of plausibility to their statement, when they ascribe positive or false 'accommodation' to our Lord and His disciples. In the particular case before us, in which, as I have shown, Christ has given His sanction to the sentiments of the Jews respecting the permanence of the Law, and the authority of the Old Testament, His discourses were, it is true, delivered to the multitude on the Mount, and to the Pharisees: but we find Him still urging these same principles when alone with His most trusted friends both before and after His Resurrection;—His chief argument, in all cases, being an appeal to the Prophecies respecting Himself.[4] S. Paul, too, when writing to his confi-

naked manner."—*Creed of Christendom*, p. 11. On this subject Mr. Davison, with his usual accuracy, observes: "The Law forbore, in some few points, a perfection of its discipline. It practised an unwilling condescension, in yielding to the 'hardness of heart,' the gross and refractory temper of the people to whom it was given. This was seen in its non-prohibition of a plurality of wives, and in its permission of divorce. But the Holy Jesus, who came to restore the Divine Law to its first integrity, as well as to make atonement for the transgression of it, He, in His Institutes, reformed these temporary concessions. Meanwhile, one of the Prophets [Malachi] had given a clear intimation that God approved not the permission so allowed, but would draw the domestic charities into stricter bonds of union and severity."—*Discourses on Prophecy*, p. 44.

[1] 1 Cor. iii. 2. [2] S. John, xvi. 12.

[3] Gal. ii. 11–18. "The other Jews *dissembled* likewise with him (συνυπεκρίθησαν); insomuch that Barnabas also was carried away with their *dissimulation* (ὑποκρίσει)."—ver. 13. Cf. the words of Clement of Alex. already quoted, p. 74, note. On the question of S. Peter's conduct at Antioch, see Lecture v.

[4] E. g. S. Matt. xxvi. 24, 54; S. Luke, xxiv. 44–47. Even in prayer to His Father, our Lord appeals to the Old Testament: "While I was with them in the world, I kept them in Thy name: those that Thou gavest Me I have kept, and none of them

dential disciple Timothy, and to those most opposed to Judaism at Corinth[1]—for the Judaizing Christians were surely not those who boasted that they were "of Paul," or "of Apollos,"—S. Paul, I say, maintains the Divine inspiration of the Old Testament as strictly as the most rigid Israelite of the school of Philo. But our denial of the use of false 'accommodation' is not to be limited to this one point. It may be confidently affirmed, that the teaching of the New Testament affords no single instance of such deception. Christ neither denies the existence of Spirits in order to conciliate the Sadducees, nor does He instruct the woman of Samaria in doctrines which He opposed before the Jews. S. Paul proclaims the same Divine truths before kings and rulers, before Jews and Greeks ; and he tells us that the doctrine of a crucified Redeemer was alike offensive to both. In a word, we find Christ quoting Moses and the Prophets to friend and to foe ; to Pharisee and to Sadducee ; to the people and to His disciples ; in the desert[2] and in the Temple ; at the commencement of His ministry and at its close ; in exposition by acts and exposition by doctrine,—combining it, in all matters, with the new revelation as being conveyed by the same Spirit.

From all this, therefore, it may be concluded, that the sentiments of Philo and Josephus and the early Jews, were not the mere private assertions of good and pious men, or the exaggerated expression of Hebrew nationality : those sentiments rather exhibit authentic information respecting the real character of the Old Testament ; information stamped with the seal of Christ Himself,—the source of all Revelation—who would have counteracted His own sole purpose had he ascribed to the ancient Scriptures authority to which they could lay no claim.

I now turn to the evidence afforded by the Christian Church ;[3] and in doing so it may be well to notice, in the first instance, any traces that exist of exceptions to the singular uniformity which

is lost, but the son of perdition, *that the Scripture might be fulfilled.*"—S. John, xvii. 12. Cf. xiii. 18.

[1] 2 Tim. iii. 16 ; 1 Cor. iii. 4. The great majority of S. Paul's Epistles, and, to a great degree, the Gospels, were intended for those who were *not* Jews, and who, therefore, could not have been *prejudiced* in favor of the Old Testament.

[2] See especially the accounts of His Temptation,—S. Matt. iv. ; S. Luke, iv.

[3] For a more extended discussion of the opinions of the Fathers, see Appendix G. So unexceptionable a witness as De Wette introduces his list of authorities from the early Christian writers, from S. Irenæus downwards, with the remark : "Man erkannte diese Bücher als heilig und göttlich."—*Einleit.* § 22, s. 30.

has prevailed upon the question of Inspiration in every age. It has become the fashion, indeed, among modern writers, following, I apprehend, in the footsteps of Neander,[1] to point to the celebrated Theodore of Mopsuestia, who lived at the opening of the fifth century, as having led the way in questioning the inspiration of the Scriptures.[2] I believe this charge to be altogether without

[1] Neander observes, in the first edition of his history (A. D. 1829): "The germs of this tendency [viz. to a "grammatico-logical" method of interpreting the Bible] were still further developed by distinguished men in the fourth century and in the commencement of the fifth * * * above all by the acute and original Theodore of Mopsuestia. * * * We find, in fact, traces of a more free mode of apprehending the idea of Inspiration in this period, only in those cases where a more unprejudiced grammatico-logical interpretation of the Bible conduced to that result, as in the case of a Jerome, a Theodore of Mopsuestia, and a Chrysostom."—*Allg. Gesch. der Kirche*, 2er Band. s. 503. Neander has considerably modified his opinion as to the views respecting Inspiration maintained by the three writers named in this extract. In the second edition of his history, published in 1846, the entire of the section, from which I have just quoted, has been re-written to the extent of several pages; the author contenting himself with adducing a series of quotations from Theodore, S. Chrysostom, and S. Jerome, to illustrate the proposition, that in consequence of the principles according to which those writers expounded the Bible, they have advanced certain ideas, "*at the foundation of which* lies a peculiar modification of the notion of Inspiration."—2te Aufl. 2er Band, s. 661, ff.

For an examination of Theodore's estimation of Scripture, see Appendix G. The reader may form a judgment with respect to S. Jerome's views from the following comment on Eph. iii. 6:—"Scio appositionem conjunctionis ejus, per quam dicitur, 'cohæredes, et concorporales, et comparticipes,' indecoram facere in Latino sermone sententiam. Sed *quia ita habetur in Græco, et singuli sermones, syllabæ, apices, puncta, in divinis Scripturis plena sunt sensibus*, propterea magis volumus in compositione structuraque verborum, quam intelligentia periclitari."—T. vii., p. 591. For S. Chrysostom's theory of Inspiration, see, for the present, p. 88, note [6], *infra.*

[2] Thus, for example, M. Gaussen writes: "With the exception, we say, of Theodore de Mopsueste, the long period of the first eight centuries of Christianity did not produce a single theologian who disavowed the plenary inspiration of the Scriptures, save only among the most violent of the heretical sects which have troubled the Christian Church; I mean the Gnostics, the Manichæans, the Anomœans, and the Mahometans."—*Theopneustia*, p. 353.

One feels more surprise, however, at so well-informed a writer as Rudelbach making the same assertion; especially since he adduces as his sole grounds the fact of Theodore having denied the Canonical authority of the Book of Job, of Proverbs, and of Ecclesiastes. See his "Zeitschrift" for 1840: "Die Lehre von der Inspir.," 2es Kap., s. 46. I have already observed (p. 46), when referring to the similar error of Luther as to certain Books of the New Testament, that it is an obvious mistake to represent the denial of the Canonicity of a particular Book as being equivalent to a denial of the inspiration of Scripture in general. In Theodore's, as in Luther's case, the low estimate in which particular Books were regarded, arose from the exalted sense in which the Divine character of Scripture was felt and recognised:—their common error consisting in the belief, that such and such portions of the Bible did not satisfy the tests of Inspiration which they ventured to define. This distinction, Rudelbach insists upon when speaking of Luther, while he forgets to acknowledge its existence in the parallel case of Theodore of Mopsuestia. He remarks: "Passages lie before us from Luther's writings, writings, too, composed at very different periods of his life, (even at the date of his rude decision as to the Epistle of James,) which satisfactorily prove that he never ceased to assert the verbal inspiration of the Holy Scriptures, and that we, consequently, do violenee to his words if we impute to him any other principle."—*Ibid.* 4es Kap. s. 8. See Appendix C.

foundation. Suffice it here to observe, that when the doctrinal views of Theodore were condemned at the Fifth General Council, nearly one hundred and thirty years after his death; and when every imputation which controversial animosity could suggest, was cast in after-times upon his memory by individual opponents[1]—no allusion whatever was made to his having deviated, on this cardinal point, from the universal belief of Christendom. This harmony of opinion, indeed, will appear the more striking when the nature of the exceptions which do exist is duly considered.

It is a common and a just remark of Christian writers from the earliest times, that amid the various contests in which the Church has had to engage with the different forms of heresy, both sides have appealed to the Divine authority of the Bible.[2] The single exception to this uniformity of sentiment which the records of antiquity appear to afford occurs in the case of such a controversy. This contradiction of the unanimous voice of the Church proceeded from the Anomœans—that extreme section of the Arians, in the fourth century, whose heretical tenet of the complete dissimilarity between the Father and the Son gave rise to their name. Of this party S. Epiphanius tells us, and he mentions it as an offence unheard of in any previous controversy, that when pressed by arguments from Scripture, its defenders replied,

[1] E. g. Leontius of Byzantium (A. D. 590), in his work "Contra Nestorianos et Eutychianos," of which merely a Latin version had been published by Canisius, in his "Lectiones Antiquæ," (ed. Basnage. Ant. 1725. t. i. p. 525.) the original Greek text not having been accessible before the year 1844, when it was given by Cardinal Mai in his "Spicilegium Romanum," t. x. pars ii. p. 1, &c. While defending Theodore from the charge of having called in question the inspiration of Scripture, I must altogether disclaim any desire to defend his orthodoxy on other points: "Est enim manifestum, Theodorum Nestorii magistrum, utpote Nestoriani erroris auctorem, a veteribus vocari."—O. F. Fritsche, *De. Theodori Vita*, p. 15. His merit, however, as an expositor of Scripture has never been called in question. Cardinal Mai, in the Préface to his edition of Theodore's Commentary on the Twelve Minor Prophets, ("Scriptorum Veterum Collectio," Romæ, A. D. 1832. tom. vi.) expresses the estimation in which he was held: "Ab Orientalibus 'Sapientiæ mare,' et Scripturarum 'Interpres *κατ' ἐξοχὴν*' dictus, universæ Ecclesiæ Doctor interdum appellatus, et Magni denique, cognomento donatus."—p. v. Cardinal Mai, having pointed out the faults usually noted in Theodore's Commentaries, goes on to speak in the highest terms of his exposition of the Minor Prophets; observing, that notwithstanding the obscurity of the subject, Theodore "non verba legere, sed in Prophetæ cujusque mentem oculorum aciem intendere videatur. Quamobrem, non sine causa, a multis arcem Interpretum tenere dictus est."—p. xv.

[2] Thus S. Irenæus writes: "Tanta est autem circa Evangelia hæc firmitas, ut et ipsi hæretici testimonium reddant eis, et ex ipsis egrediens unusquisque eorum conetur suam confirmare doctrinam."—*Cont. Hær.* lib. iii. 11. p. 189. So also Theodoret, in his Dialogues, makes the representative of heresy observe: Μ*ή μοι λογισμοὺς ἀνθρωπίνους προσενέγκῃς. ἐγὼ γὰρ μόνῃ πείθομαι τῇ θείᾳ γραφῇ.* *Eranistes*, Dial. I. t. iv. p. 13.

either—"The Apostle makes that statement merely as a man;" or,—"Why do you quote the Old Testament against me?"[1] It is generally believed, too, that the objections noticed by S. Jerome in his Preface to the Epistle to Philemon proceeded in like manner from the Anomœans.[2] The only other instance which I have been able to discover of the subsequent revival, in any part of the Church, of erroneous views upon the subject of Inspiration, is in the case of a monk of Constantinople, of the twelfth century.[3]

The positive testimonies to which I now proceed may with some propriety be arranged under three heads: the First, relating to the Divine influence exerted in the composition of the Bible; the Second, to the human agents selected to write the different books; the Third, to the nature of the writings thus produced. I shall not attempt here[4] to give more than a rapid sketch of the nature and weight of the proofs which may be adduced; and I would merely observe, before entering upon this branch of the subject, that we must not expect to find in the annals of the early Church any such elaborate theory, or series of systematized propositions on the subject of Inspiration, as we meet with in the case of other doctrines. The absence, indeed, of dogmatic teaching on this question during the first fifteen centuries of the Church affords a clear illustration of the harmony of opinion which prevailed respecting it; while the unhappy distractions of modern

[1] *῞Οταν ἐλεγχόμενοι ὑπὸ τινων ὑπωπιάζωνται, εὐθὺς ἀποτρέχοντες καὶ ἀποπηδῶντες, καὶ λέγοντες, τοῦτο ὁ Ἀπόστολος ὡς ἄνθρωπος ἔφη. ἄλλοτε δὲ, τί μοι φέρεις τὰ τῆς παλαιᾶς διαθήκης;* "Nor is this strange," proceeds S. Epiphanius, "for 'if they have called the master of the house Beelzebub, how much more shall they call them of His household?' viz. His Prophets and Apostles."—*Adv. Hær.* lib. iii. Hæresis 76. t. i. p. 992. Cf. Rudelbach, *loc. cit.* 2es Kap. s. 45.

[2] This seems to be the earliest allusion to the vulgar objection against Inspiration, founded upon the Apostle's words—"The cloke which I left at Troas," &c.—2 Tim. iv. 13. On such passages the heretics founded the conclusion: "Non semper Apostolum, nec omnia, Christo in se loquente dixisse."—S. Jerome, *Pref. in Ep. ad Philem.* t. vii. p. 742.

[3] Euthymius Zigabenus, A. D. 1116. S. Mark (ii. 27) adds to the words of our Lord recorded by S. Matthew (xii. 8), the saying: "The Sabbath was made for man, and not man for the Sabbath." On this Euthymius observes, that we need not wonder at such variations, for the Evangelists wrote many years after these words were spoken; and since *they were but men*, it is natural they should occasionly *forget* what had been said: *οὐ χρὴ δὲ θαυμάζειν εἰ τὰ μὲν οὗτος ὁ εὐαγγελιστὴς προστίθησι, τὰ δὲ ἐκεῖνος παραλιμπάνει. καὶ γὰρ οὐχ ἅμα τῷ λέγειν τὸν Χριστὸν ἔγραφον τὰ εὐαγγέλια ἵνα καὶ πάντων ὁμοῦ τῶν αὐτοῦ λόγων ἀπομνημονεύειν ἔχοιεν· ἀλλὰ μετὰ πολλοὺς ὕστερον ἐνιαυτούς. καὶ εἰκὸς, ἀνθρώπους ὄντας αὐτοὺς ἐπιλαθέσθαι τινῶν.*—*Comm. in S. Matt.* xii. 8. t. i. p. 465. Ed. Matthæi. Leipzig, 1792.

[4] See Appendix G.

times, sufficiently account for the want of any authoritative decision since the sacred precincts have been invaded. This absence, however, of recognised theory or system serves but to exhibit in bolder relief how profoundly incorporated with the Christian consciousness of those times was the belief in the inspiration of Scripture; and undesignedly represents its depth, its fervor, and its source.

I. The evidence as to the belief of the Church in the Divine influence exerted in the composition of the Bible, naturally starts from that Article of the Creed in which Christians to the present day profess:—"We believe in the Holy Ghost, the Lord, the Life-giver * * * who spake by the Prophets."[1] This Confession not only defines the inspiration of the sacred writers to be the act of the Holy Ghost; but it also lays down as a fundamental doctrine of Christianity, that Old and New Testament have proceeded from the same source, and are alike Divine. That to this latter truth the Article of the Creed chiefly refers, admits of no doubt. In fact, it merely embodies a tenet maintained from the very first in opposition to the various phases of Gnosticism; for in the earliest writings composed in defence of Christianity, the epithet 'Prophetic' (προφητικόν) is the title usually assigned to the Holy Ghost.[2] We observe this co-ordination of Old and New Testament so early as the days of S. Polycarp, who, when referring to "the Scriptures," combines in one quotation a passage from the Psalms, and a text from the Epistle to the Ephesians.[3] So also S. Justin Martyr having quoted to the Jew Trypho the words of the Prophet Malachi,[4] breaks forth into praise of God's goodness, adding: "These words have not been devised by me,

[1] Πιστεύομεν * * * εἰς τὸ Πνεῦμα τὸ ἅγιον, τὸ κύριον, τὸ ζωοποιόν * * * τὸ λαλῆσαν διὰ τῶν προφητῶν.—*Symb. Constant.* Mansi. t. iii. p. 565.

[2] E. g. by S. Justin Mart.: 'Εκεῖνον τὲ, καὶ τὸν παρ' Αὐτοῦ 'Υιὸν ἔλθοντα * * * Πνεῦμα τὲ τὸ προφητικὸν σεβόμεθα, καὶ προσκυνοῦμεν.—*Apol.* i. § 6. p. 47. And, again, quoting Gen. xlix. 10: ὡς προεῤῥέθη ὑπὸ τοῦ θείου ἁγίου προφητικου Πνεύματος διὰ τοῦ Μωϋσέως, μὴ ἐκλείψειν ἄρχοντα κ. τ. λ.—*Ibid.* § 32. p. 63.

[3] This passage, which is extant only in the old Latin version, is quite obscure according to the ordinary punctuation. I quote it after Dr. Jacobson's judicious suggestion ("Patres Apostolici," ed. 3tia, t. ii. p. 527.): "Confido enim vos bene exercitatos esse in sacris literis, et nihil vos latet; mihi autem non est concessum [*post* "concessum," vos ædificare, *ex verbis ad fin.* § 11, *subaud.*] Modo ut HIS SCRIPTURIS dictum est; *Irascimini, et nolite peccare* [Ps. iv. 4, LXX.]; et, *Sol non occidat super iracundiam vestram* [Eph. iv. 26]."—S. Polycarpi, *Ep. ad Philipp.* § 12.

[4] "I have no pleasure in you, saith the Lord of Hosts, neither will I accept an offering at your hand. For from the rising of the sun even unto the going down of the same, My Name shall be great among the Gentiles," &c.—Mal. i. 10, 11.

6

nor have they been embellished by any human skill. Such were the songs of David; so Isaiah proclaimed glad tidings, and Zechariah preached, and Moses composed his record. Dost thou recognise them, Trypho? They are preserved in the writings of your people—nay, I should rather say, in ours; for we obey them, but you, though reading them, do not discern their sense."[1] And the belief that both Testaments enforce the same lesson is implied in the striking parallel of Origen: "When the people murmured against Moses in the wilderness, he led them to the rock to drink; and even now he leadeth them to Christ."[2]

The ordinary style in quoting Scripture was, either to omit the writer's name—"Thus spake the Holy Ghost;" or to supply it thus—"So spake the Spirit by Solomon," or "by Isaiah," or "by Paul."[3] "It is needless to seek," said S. Gregory the Great, "who wrote the Book of Job, since we may faithfully believe that the Holy Ghost was its author."[4] "What avails it," said Theodoret, "to know whether all the Psalms were written by David, it being plain that all were composed under the influence of the Divine Spirit?"[5] Hence the numerous epithets applied to every part of Scripture:—"The Scriptures of the Lord;" "the Divine Scriptures;" "Heavenly Letters." The phrase, however, most usually employed is that of S. Paul: "Scriptures given by inspiration of God." In a word, the evidence under this head may be summed up in the language of S. Clement of Rome:

[1] *Οὐ γὰρ ὑπ' ἐμοῦ συνεσκευασμένοι εἰσὶν οἱ λόγοι, οὐδὲ τέχνῃ ἀνθρωπίνῃ κεκαλλωπισμένοι, ἀλλὰ τούτους Δαβὶδ μὲν ἔψαλλεν, Ἠσαΐας δὲ εὐηγγελίζετο, Ζαχαρίας δὲ ἐκήρυξε, Μωϋσῆς δὲ ἀνέγραψεν. Ἐπιγινώσκεις αὐτοὺς, Τρύφων; Ἐν τοῖς ὑμετέροις ἀπόκεινται γράμμασι, μᾶλλον δὲ οὐχ' ὑμετέροις, ἀλλ' ἡμέτεροις· ἡμεῖς γὰρ αὐτοῖς πειθόμεθα· ὑμεῖς δὲ, ἀναγινώσκοντες, οὐ νοεῖτε τὸν ἐν αὐτοῖς νοῦν.*—*Dial. cum Tryph.* c. 29. p.127.

[2] "Murmuraverunt adversus Moysen, et propterea jubet Dominus ut ostendat eis petram, ex qua bibant. Si quis est, qui legens Moysen murmurat adversus eum, et displicet ei lux, quæ secundum literam scripta est * * * ostendit ei Moyses petram, quæ est Christus, et adducit eum ad ipsam ut inde bibat, et reficiat sitim suam."—*Hom. in Exod.* xi. 2, t. ii. p. 169.

[3] For example, S. Cyprian: "Loquitur per Salomonem Spiritus S."—*De Opere et Eleemos.* p. 240. Tertullian:—"Spiritus Sanctus hanc Scripturæ suæ rationem constituit, ut cum quid ex aliquo fit, et quod fit, et unde fit, referat. 'Fruticet,' inquit, 'terra herbam fœni, seminantem semen,'" &c. &c.—*Adv. Hermogen.* cap. xxii. p. 276. To the same effect Clemens Alex.:

*ἔχεις τὸν χορὸν πάντα τὸν προφητικὸν, τοὺς συνθιασώτας τοῦ Μωϋσέως. τί φησὶν αὐτοῖς τὸ Πνεῦμα τὸ Ἅγιον διὰ Ὠσηὲ, ὀυκ ὀκνήσω λέγειν * * * ἔτι δὲ καὶ διὰ Ἡσαΐου κ. τ. λ.*—*Cohortat. ad Gentes*, c. viii. p. 67.

[4] "Sed quis hæc scripserit, valde supervacue quæritur, cum tamen auctor libri Spiritus Sanctus fideliter credatur."—*Præf. in Moralia in Lib. Job.* t. i. p. 7.

[5] *Ἐγὼ δὲ περὶ τούτων μὲν οὐδὲν ἰσχυρίζομαι. ποίαν γάρ μοι προστίθησιν ὠφέλειαν, εἴτε τούτου πάντες, εἴτ' ἐκείνων εἰέν τινες· δήλου γέ ὄντος, ὡς ἐκ τῆς τοῦ θείου Πνεύματος ἐνεργείας συνεγράφησαν ἅπαντες;*—*Protheoria in Psalmos*, t. i. p. 395.

"Give diligent heed to the Scriptures, the true sayings of the Holy Ghost."[1]

From such principles the Church inferred the sufficiency, the infallible certainty, and the perfection of Scripture. On this foundation S. Athanasius argues against the Gentiles: "The holy and divinely inspired Scriptures are sufficient to express the truth."[2] So, again, the critical and unimpassioned Eusebius, alluding to an assertion that in the superscription of the thirty-fourth Psalm, the name Abimelech had been, by an oversight, substituted for Achish, rejects the idea with indignation: "I hold it," he observes, "to be alike rashness and presumption to venture to prove that the Divine Scriptures have erred."[3]

I may also observe that the joint participation of the Eternal Word and of the Holy Spirit in bringing the Scriptures into being, to which I have already drawn attention, was a truth fully appreciated by the Fathers. The sacred writers are said to "have been moved by the Spirit," as well as "moved by Christ."[4] "They who prophesy," said S. Justin M., "are actuated by no other than the Divine Logos."[5] On other occasions this same writer ascribes the prediction to "the Prophetic Spirit."[6] And in one place he combines the two ideas: "Think not that the words which you hear the Prophet speaking in his own person were uttered by himself, when filled with the Spirit, but by the Divine Word who moved him."[7]

[1] Ἐν [κύπτετε] εἰς τὰς γραφάς, τὰς ἀληθεῖς [ῥήσεις] Πνεύματος τοῦ Ἁγίου.—*Ad Corinth.* c. 45. t. i. p. 162. ed. Jacobson.

[2] Αὐτάρκεις μὲν γάρ εἰσιν αἱ ἅγιαι καὶ θεόπνευστοι γραφαὶ πρὸς τὴν τῆς ἀληθείας ἀπαγγελίαν.—*Or. cont. Gentes*, t. i. p. i. Still more strongly, on another occasion, this great Father writes:

Μάτην γοῦν περιτρέχοντες προφασίζονται, διὰ πίστιν ἠξιωκέναι, γενέσθαι τὰς συνόδους. ἔστι μὲν γὰρ ἱκανωτέρα πάντων ἡ θεία γραφή.—*Epist. de Synodis Arim. et Seleuc.* t. i. p. 720.

[3] Ὁ μὲν οὖν τις ἐρεῖ, ἐπεὶ μὴ ἐμφέρεται ἐν τῇ ἱστορίᾳ τῇ κατὰ τὸν Ἀχιμέλεχ· ἀλλοιώσας τὸ πρόσωπον αὐτοῦ ὁ Δαυὶδ, κατὰ σφάλμα κεῖσθαι τὸ ὄνομα τοῦ Ἀβιμέλεχ ἀντὶ τοῦ ὀνόματος Ἀγχούς. σαφῶς γὰρ ἐπὶ τοῦ Ἀγχοὺς εἴρηται· ἀλλοιώσας τὸ πρόσωπον κ. τ. λ. [1 Sam. xxi. 13] * * * ἔργον δὲ θρασὺ καὶ προπετὲς εἶναι ἡγοῦμαι τὸ ἀποφήνασθαι τολμᾷν τὴν θείαν γραφὴν ἡμαρτῆσθαι. —*Comment. in Psal.* ed. Montf.—*Coll. nov. Patr.* t. i. p. 129.

[4] Πνευματοφόροι.—Theophilus, *ad Autolyc.* lib. ii. 9, p. 354.

Χριστοφόροι.—S. Athanasius, *Cont. Gentes*, 5. t. i. 5.—*De Incarnatione*, 10. t. i. p. 56.

[5] Ὅτι δὲ οὐδενὶ ἄλλῳ θεοφοροῦνται οἱ προφητεύοντες εἰ μὴ Λόγῳ θείῳ, καὶ ὑμεῖς ὡς ὑπολαμβάνω φήσετε.—*Apol.* I. § 33. p. 64.

[6] Ὁ αὐτὸς προφήτης Ἡσαΐας θεοφορούμενος τῷ Πνεύματι τῷ προφητικῷ ἔφη.—*Ibid* § 35. p. 65.

[7] Ὅταν δὲ τὰς λέξεις τῶν προφητῶν λεγομένας ὡς ἀπὸ προσώπου ἀκούητε, μὴ ἀπ' αὐτῶν τῶν ἐμπεπνευσμένων λέγεσθαι νομίσητε, ἀλλ' ἀπὸ τοῦ κινοῦντος αὐτοὺς

II. Under the second head may be comprised all allusions to the effect of the Divine influence upon the intellectual faculties of the Prophets. The Fathers of the Church at a very early period expressed their opinions on the subject; and this fact is the more important, inasmuch as by their contact with heathenism on the one side, and the impure element of Montanism on the other, they stood sufficiently near the phenomena presented by those false systems to be conscious of their tendency, and to feel the necessity of guarding against either extreme. We know from the writings of Plato that the Seers or Diviners (*μάντεις*) of the heathen were so called from the state of phrensy in which they uttered their oracles; the Prophet (*προφήτης*) being merely the interpreter of the unconscious Diviner (*μάντις*.)[1] The early Church clearly perceived that the difference between this natural divination—the *Mantike* of the old world—and true prophecy, is essential and specific. Origen argues, at some length, that the ecstatic and phrensied condition of the Pythian prophetess, whose hallucinations Celsus had adduced in opposition to the Prophets of the Old Testament, could not be the product of the Spirit of God. The Jewish Prophets, he urges, "were illuminated by the Divine Spirit; their understanding becoming more perspicacious, and their souls more lucid by the touch, as it were, of the Holy Ghost. But if the Pythia, while delivering her oracle, is in ecstacy, and no longer self-possessed, what sort of spirit must we deem that to be which darkens her understanding, and clouds the faculties of her mind?"[2]

θείου Λόγου.—*Ibid.* § 36. p. 65. The principle expressed by this language, and which I have already stated, Lecture i. p. 25, note [1], is clearly laid down by S. Athanasius: *οὐ γὰρ ἐκτός ἐστι τοῦ Λόγου τὸ Πνεῦμα, ἀλλὰ ἐν τῷ Λόγῳ ὄν, ἐν τῷ Θεῷ δι' αὐτοῦ ἐστιν· ὥστε τὰ χαρίσματα ἐν τῇ Τριάδι δίδοσθαι*.—*Epist.* iii. *ad Serap.* 5. t. i. p. 694.

[1] See above, p. 65, the opinion of Philo. Baumgarten Crusius observes that the word *προφήτης* is employed by the Alexandrian writers in a sense different from its classical usage. With the Alexandrians it denotes merely 'one who foretells;' with the Greeks, 'one who announces' (*ἑρμηνεύς, ἐξηγητής*, cf. Ruhnken on Timæus), what the *μάντις* had uttered.—*Grundzüge der bibl. Theologie*, s. 40.

"The derivation [of *μάντις*] from *μαίνομαι* is found as early as Plato (Tim. 72 b.) where he distinguishes *μάντεις* from *προφῆται*, the former being *persons who uttered oracles in a state of divine frenzy*, the latter the *interpreters of those oracles*."—*Liddell and Scott*. I shall have occasion to return to the point here adverted to.

[2] *Ἀλλὰ καὶ τὸ εἰς ἔκστασιν καὶ μανικὴν ἄγειν κατάστασιν τὴν δῆθεν προφητεύουσαν, ὡς μηδαμῶς αὐτὴν ἑαυτῇ παρακολουθεῖν, οὐ θείου Πνεύματος ἔργόν ἐστιν* * * * *ὅθεν ἡμεῖς ἀποδείκνυμεν, συνάγοντες ἀπὸ τῶν ἱερῶν γραμμάτων, ὅτι οἱ ἐν Ἰουδαίοις προφῆται, ἐλλαμπόμενοι ὑπὸ τοῦ θείου Πνεύματος τοσοῦτον, ὅσον ἦν καὶ αὐτοῖς τοῖς προφητεύουσι χρήσιμον, προαπέλαυον τῆς τοῦ κρείττονος εἰς αὐτοὺς ἐπιδημίας· καὶ διὰ*

The principles of Montanism,[1] on the other hand, grew out of the desire to see perpetuated, through all future ages of the Church, that extraordinary effusion of spiritual gifts poured out in the days of the Apostles. It was held by the sect which acknowledged Montanus as its leader, that the office of Prophet was to be permanent; and that by the existence of this order of ministers was to be fulfilled Christ's promise of the Paraclete, whose continued revelations were to possess equal or even superior authority to the voice of Scripture.[2] According to this system, the influence of the Spirit, when exerted, produced a state of ecstacy in which the consciousness of the Prophet is altogether suppressed; and God alone speaks, as if in His own name, from the soul of which He takes possession.[3] With reasoning similar to that adopted in rejecting the heathen divination, the Church rose in opposition to this fanaticism"; and here also it was argued, that the existence of a state of unconsciousness proved that Montanism was in no sort allied to the true prophetic Spirit. Thus, S. Epiphanius urges against Montanus, "that whatsoever the Prophets have said, they spake with understanding;" he refers to their "settled mind," "their self-possession," and their not

*τῆς πρὸς τὴν ψυχὴν αὐτῶν, ἵν' οὕτως ὀνομάσω, ἁφῆς τοῦ καλουμένου Ἁγίου Πνεύματος, διορατικώτεροί τε τὸν νοῦν ἐγίνοντο, καὶ τὴν ψυχὴν λαμπρότεροι * * * εἰ δ' ἐξίσταται, καὶ οὐκ ἐν ἑαυτῇ ἐστιν ἡ Πυθία, ὅτε μαντεύεται· ποδαπὸν νομιστέον πνεῦμα, τὸ σκότον κατεχεύαν τοῦ νοῦ καὶ τῶν λογισμῶν, ἢ τοιοῦτον ὁποῖόν ἐστι καὶ τὸ τῶν δαιμόνων γένος.—Cont. Cels.* vii. 4. t. i. p. 696.

[1] Cf. Bishop Kaye's "Account of the Writings of Tertullian," ch. i.: and especially Neander's "Allgemeine Geschichte der Kirche," 1er Band, 2te Aufl. s. 877 ff; as well as the comparison of Gnosticism and Montanism in the Introduction to this latter writer's "Antignosticus."

[2] The revelations of the Paraclete were to render perfect, and even supersede, all previous divine commands. Thus Tertullian writes: Si enim Christus abstulit quod Moyses præcepit, quia ab initio non fuit sic [S. Matt. xix. 8] * * * cur non et Paracletus abstulerit, quod Paulus indulsit."—*De Monogamia*, c. 14, p. 686. Tertullian elsewhere insists upon a similar gradation in the divine communications. e. g. "Etenim est *prophetica vox veteris Testamenti*, 'Sancti eritis,' &c. * * * Debemus enim ita ingredi *in disciplina Domini* * * * *Ita enim et Apostolus dicit* 'quod sapere secundum carnem,' &c. * * * *Item per sanctam prophetidem Priscam* ita evangelizatur," &c.—*De Exhort. Castit.* c. 10. p. 670. See also t. i. p. 752, ed Oehler, Lipsiæ. 1853; for I should add, that this reference to Prisca is not received by Rigaltius in his edition. It occurs only in the "Codex Agobardinus."

[3] Take, for example, one of the passages from Tertullian to which Bishop Kaye (p. 52) has referred, as containing "positive allusions" to the system of Montanus: "In spiritu enim homo constitutus, præsertim quum gloriam Dei conspicit, vel *quum per ipsum Deus loquitur*, necesse est excidat sensu obumbratus scilicet virtute divina."—*Adver. Marc.* iv. c. 22. p. 537. Again: Adam, observes Tertullian, prophetically announced the mysterious union of Christ and the Church, when he spoke of the marriage tie—Gen. ii. 24; cf. Eph. v. 31. On that occasion "in illum Deus *amentiam* immisit, spiritalem vim *qua constat prophetia*."—*De Anima*, c. 21. p. 324.

being "carried away as if in ecstacy."[1] So also S. Cyril of Jerusalem, alluding to this question, says of the true Spirit: "His coming is gentle; most light is His burden; beams of light and knowledge gleam forth before His coming."[2]

With such extremes, however, on either side, which it alike opposed and rejected, the primitive Church did not shrink from expressing a decided opinion as to the effect produced upon the sacred penmen while actuated by the Spirit's influence;—an opinion clearly indicated by the series of similitudes which the different writers employed who approached the subject of Inspiration, and which were admirably calculated, had there been occasion to develop them, to illustrate that mutual co-operation of the Divine and Human agencies, which, as we have seen, forms the first Condition of our problem.[3] The language made use of plainly denotes that the human element was not thought to have been suppressed or suspended, but to have been filled and exalted by the divine illumination; and to this notion belongs that entire system of illustration so familiar to the Fathers from the earliest times.

They compared the soul of the man of God, when subjected to the Divine influence, to an instrument of music into which the Holy Spirit breathes, or the strings of which He sways,[4]

[1] See Hær. XLVIII. lib. ii. t. i., *passim*. E. g. *ὁ προφήτης μετὰ καταστάσεως λογισμῶν, καὶ παρακολουθήσεως ἐλάλει καὶ ἐφθέγγετο ἐκ Πνεύματος Ἁγίου, τὰ πάντα ἐρρωμένως λέγων.*—*Ibid.* p. 404. It may be well to observe here, that what the Fathers denounce as false in this system is *not* the allegation that prophets received Divine Revelations while in a state of ecstacy, but,—and this they almost unanimously point out, as a proof of the falsehood of the claims of Montanus,—that his Prophetesses *gave utterance* to their asserted revelations *during* their state of unconsciousness. This fact seems to have been wholly overlooked by late writers. But on this subject see Lecture v., and Appendix G.

[2] *Ἥμερος ἡ παρουσία· εὐώδης ἡ ἀντίληψις· κουφότατον τὸ φορτίον· προαπαστράπτουσιν ἀκτῖνες φωτὸς καὶ γνώσεως, πρὸ τῆς παρουσίας.*—*Catech.* xvi. 16. p. 252. Cf. the remarks of the Benedictine Editor on the word *ἀντίληψις*.

[3] See Lecture i. pp. 35–39.

[4] Thus Athenagoras writes: *συγχρησαμένου τοῦ Πνεύματος, ὡσεὶ καὶ αὐλητὴς αὐλὸν ἐμπνεῦσαι.*—*Legat. pro Christ*, ix. p. 286. For a catena of such illustrations see Appendix G.

I must here express my dissent from a remark of Mr. Westcott, in his valuable "Catena on Inspiration," to the effect that "the language of Athenagoras * * * has been regarded, with good reason, as expressing the doctrine of Montanism."—*Elem. of Gosp. Harm.* p. 166. It is true that Athenagoras considers the Prophets of the Old Testament to have *uttered* their predictions while in a state of ecstacy—thus adopting the sentiments of Philo; but that he held, on any point, the extravagant opinions of Montanus, cannot, I apprehend, be alleged with any justice. Thus Neander observes: "Neither the remarks of Athenagoras concerning the second marriage, nor what he *says of the ecstacy of the Prophets*, when acting as blind organs of the operation of the Divine Spirit, can prove that he was a Montanist; for, as we remarked above, the Montanists said nothing on these points that was altogether new: they

like the plectrum of a harp or lyre, in order to evoke its vital tones. Such illustrations were obviously suggested by the very etymology of the word Inspiration—or, as S. Paul terms it, *Theopneustia*;[1] and when they are applied to men, as the agents of the Holy Spirit, we should remember that the tone and quality of the note depend as much upon the instrument itself, as upon the hand which sweeps over its strings.[2] And carrying out the analogy, we can easily see, when we reflect upon the full and deep harmonies of Scripture, how much of their power and beauty lies in the Divine union of the different human instruments through which we listen to the breathings of the Spirit. Thus, Origen, speaking of the consistency of the various parts of Scripture, finely observed: "Scripture, as a whole, is God's one, perfect, and complete instrument; giving forth to those who wish to learn its one saving music from many notes combined; stilling and restraining all strivings of the evil one, as David's music calmed the madness of Saul."[3] All such illustrations, no doubt, clearly recognise a relatively passive state in the sacred penmen; but they by no means imply that such a state involved inaction or unconsciousness. On the contrary, the decided manner in which the very writers, who have made use of the similitudes in question, opposed the erroneous views as to Prophecy with which they had to contend, proves how sensibly they felt the distinction which subsists between the vibration of the strings of an instrument of music, and the pulsations of a human heart touched and animated by the Spirit of God.[4] Add to this, the marked omis-

merely pushed to the extreme a way of thinking on religious and moral subjects which was already existing."—*Allg. Gesch. der Kirche*, 1er Band, s. 1162.

[1] 2 Tim. iii. 16. *Πᾶσα γραφὴ θεόπνευστος.*

[2] I avail myself here of some exeellent remarks of Mr. Westcott (p. 164), whose language also I make use of, with a few alterations.

[3] *Ἓν γὰρ τὸ τέλειον οἶδε καὶ ἡρμοσμένον ὄργανον τοῦ Θεοῦ εἶναι πᾶσαν τὴν γραφὴν, μίαν ἀποτελοῦν ἐκ διαφόρων φθόγγων σωτήριον τοῖς μανθάνειν ἐθέλουσι φωνὴν, καταπαύουσαν καὶ κωλύουσαν ἐνέργειαν πᾶσαν πονηροῦ πνεύματος, ὡς κατέπαυσεν ἡ Δαβὶδ μουσικὴ τὸ ἐν τῷ Σαοὺλ πονηρὸν πνεῦμα.*—*Comm. in Matt.* v. 9, t. iii. p. 441.

[4] This idea is beautifully expressed by Hooker, at the close of a passage already quoted, Lecture i. p. 35, note [4]; where he refers to Ezek. iii. 3, on which text that passage is a comment: "'*I ate it, and it was sweet in my mouth as honey*,' saith the Prophet. Yea, sweeter, I am persuaded than either honey or the honeycomb. For herein they were not like harps or lutes, but they felt, they felt the power and strength of their own words. When they spake of our peace, every corner of their hearts was filled with joy. When they prophesied of mourning, lamentations, and woes, to fall upon us, they wept in bitterness and indignation of spirit, the arm of the Lord being mighty and strong upon them."—*Sermon* v. *on S. Jude*, 17–21. Vol. iii., p. 663. Keble's ed. Cf. also Rudelbach, *loc. cit.* 2es Kap. s. 27.

sion by the Fathers,[1] while adopting the language and analogies employed by Philo, of any allusion to that suppression of intellectual energy and of the exercise of reason, which, as we have seen, was so much insisted upon by the Jewish philosopher.

Neander, indeed, alleges that the opposition of the Church to Montanism introduced a considerable modification into its sentiments respecting Inspiration ; and that the mode of regarding the operation of the Divine influence, which has just been considered, gradually disappeared.[2] I believe this opinion of the learned historian to be opposed to facts. The theory of Inspiration, which is founded upon the illustration of the lyre, began with S. Justin Martyr,[3] about the year 140, and prior to the rise of Montanism :[4] and although the opinions of Montanus were still maintained in the sixth century,[5] we can trace a series of writers by whom the same similitude was employed, down to S. Chrysostom, who on more than one occasion falls into the same train of thought. For example, he describes S. Paul as "the chosen vessel, the temple of God, the mouth of Christ, the lyre of the Spirit."[6]

III. To the third division of our subject belong those testimonies of the Fathers which relate to the nature of the Bible as a written document, the joint product of the Holy Spirit and the men of God. The evidence on this point is varied and extensive ; a few quotations, however, must, for the present, suffice.

There is nothing superfluous in the Bible. In S. Mark's account of our Lord's miracle at Jericho, the blind Bartimæus, "casting away his garment, rose, and came to Jesus."[7] Origen asks upon this : "Shall we venture to say that these words have

[1] With the exception, of course, of Athenagoras. See p. 86, note [4], *supra*.

[2] "That mode of regarding Inspiration, which had passed over from the Jews, had up to this time [viz. of Tertullian] prevailed even among the teachers of the Church; but now, in consequence of the opposition to Montanism, this view was gradually suppressed."—*Allg. Gesch. der Kirche*, B 1, s. 895.

[3] *Οἷς οὐ λόγων ἐδέησε τέχνης * * * ἀλλὰ καθαροὺς ἑαυτοὺς τῇ τοῦ θείου Πνεύματος παρασχεῖν ἐνεργείᾳ, ἵν' αὐτὸ τὸ θεῖον ἐξ οὐρανοῦ κατιὸν πλῆκτρον, ὥσπερ ὀργάνῳ κιθάρας τινὸς ἢ λύρας, τοῖς δικαίοις ἀνδράσι χρώμενον, τὴν τῶν θείων ἡμῖν καὶ οὐρανίων ἀποκαλύψῃ γνῶσιν.*—*Cohort. ad Græc.* 8, p. 13.

[4] Eusebius (Eccl. Hist. iv. 27), mentions that Apollinaris of Hierapolis (*circ.* A. D. 170,) wrote against a sect of the Montanists. S. Epiphanius places the rise of Montanism in the year 157. See Kaye's "Tertullian," p. 13.

[5] See Gieseler, "Lehrbuch der Kirchengeschichte," 1te Periode, § 47, s. 168; who observes, that the last edicts against Montanism occur in the Code of Justinian, A. D. 530–532.

[6] *Παῦλος ὁ ἀπόστολος, τὸ σκεῦος τῆς ἐκλογῆς, ὁ ναὸς τοῦ Θεοῦ, τὸ στόμα τοῦ Χριστοῦ, ἡ λύρα τοῦ Πνεύματος.*—*De Lazaro*, Concio VI. t. i. p. 786.

[7] S. Mark, x. 50.

been inserted in the Gospel without a purpose? I do not believe that one jot or one tittle of the Divine instruction is in vain."[1] Again: that Scripture can contain no contradictions is the uniform language of every writer. Julius Africanus, having proposed one of the most ingenious modes of harmonizing the genealogies of Christ which has ever been suggested,[2] concludes his remarks by observing: "Whether this explanation be correct or not, the Gospels in all points state the truth."[3] His Jewish adversary had attempted to force S. Justin Martyr to admit that, according to the Christian exposition of the Old Testament, he must allow the existence of contradictions. S. Justin replies: "I dare not either imagine or assert, that the Scriptures contradict each other; but were any passage to be adduced which has even the semblance of being opposed to another, being altogether persuaded that no such opposition really exists, I will rather confess that I myself do not understand what is said."[4] No less

[1] *Καὶ τολμήσομεν φῆσαι μάτην ταῦτα προσερρίφθαι τῷ εὐαγγελίῳ; ἐγὼ μὲν οὖν ἰῶτα ἓν ἢ μίαν κεραίαν οὐ πιστεύω κενὴν εἶναι θείων μαθημάτων.—Comm. in* Matt. xvi. 12. t. iii. p. 734.

[2] The apparent discrepancy in the accounts of the Genealogies has attracted attention from the earliest times. Olshausen on S. Matt. i. 1, observes: "Julius Africanus especially (Euseb. H. E. i. 7.) had his attention engaged in it. Three hypotheses were formed with unusual acuteness for the solution of this difficulty." That of Julius Africanus is as follows:—he supposes Heli (S. Luke, iii. 23) and Jacob (S. Matt. i. 15) to have been half-brothers *by the same mother*; the *same father* would, clearly, have rendered the genealogies identical: and he also supposes Heli to have died without issue, on which, by the law of the Levirate marriage (Deut. xxv. 5, 6)—so called from *Levir*, a husband's brother—Jacob married the widow. From this union was born "Joseph the husband of Mary, of whom was born Jesus, who is called Christ." —S. Matt. i. 16. This hypothesis of Julius Africanus is thus stated in his Epistle to Aristides: *ἐκ διαφόρων δύο γενῶν εὑρήσομεν τόν τε Ἰακὼβ καὶ τὸν Ἡλὶ ὁμομητρίους ἀδελφούς. ὧν ὁ ἕτερος Ἰακὼβ ἀτέκνου τοῦ ἀδελφοῦ τελευτήσαντος Ἡλὶ, τὴν γυναῖκα παραλαβὼν, ἐγέννησεν ἐξ αὐτῆς τρίτον τὸν Ἰωσήφ.*—Routh, *Reliq. Sacræ*, t. ii. p. 234.

[3] *Εἴτ' οὖν οὕτως, εἴτ' ἄλλως ἔχοι, * * * τὸ μέντοι εὐαγγέλιον πάντως ἀληθεύει.—Ibid.* p. 237.

[4] Trypho, pressed by quotations from the prophetical writings, had appealed to Isai. xlii. 8, in proof that God would not communicate His glory to another. S. Justin proceeds to reply:

Κἀγώ· εἰ μὲν ἁπλῶς καὶ μὴ μετὰ κακίας τούτους τοὺς λόγους εἰπὼν, ἐσίγησας, ὦ Τρύφων, μήτε τοὺς πρὸ αὐτῶν προειπὼν, μήτε τοὺς ἐπακολοθοῦντας συνάψας, συγγνωστὸς εἶ. εἰ δὲ χάριν τοῦ νομίζειν δύνασθαι εἰς ἀπορίαν ἐμβάλλειν τὸν λόγον, ἵν' εἴπω ἐναντίας εἶναι τὰς γραφὰς ἀλλήλαις, πεπλάνησαι. οὐ γὰρ τολμήσω τοῦτό ποτε ἢ ἐνθυμηθῆναι, ἢ εἰπεῖν· ἀλλ' ἐὰν τοιαύτη τὶς δοκοῦσα εἶναι γραφὴ προβληθῇ, καὶ πρόφασιν ἔχῃ ὡς ἐναντία οὖσα, ἐκ παντὸς πεπεισμένος ὅτι οὐδεμία γραφὴ τῇ ἑτέρᾳ ἐναντία ἐστὶν, αὐτὸς μὴ νοεῖν μᾶλλον ὁμολογήσω τὰ εἰρημένα.—Dial. cum Tryph. c. 65, p. 162.

To the same effect, S. Dionysius of Alexandria—(*obiit* A. D. 264; and of whom Mosheim says, "the ancients used no flattery when they styled him Dionysius the Great,"—Cent. III. part ii. ch. 2.)—referring to one of the difficulties connected with the harmony of the Resurrection, observes: "Let us not suppose that the Evangelists differ, or that they are at variance with each other; but even though there shall seem to be some trifling question as to the matter in hand * * * still let us be

marked, from the very first, was the importance ascribed to each phrase which the sacred penmen employ. S. Irenæus observes, that "S. Matthew might, no doubt, have said: 'The generation of *Jesus* was on this wise;' but the Holy Ghost, foreseeing that men would deprave the truth, and fortifying us against their deceptions, says, by Matthew, 'the generation of *Christ* was on this wise.'"[1] One instance more may be added, which places in the clearest light the belief, both of the members of the Church at large, and of the greatest of the Fathers, in the Divine source of the language of Scripture. I allude to a passage in the correspondence between S. Augustine and S. Jerome, with reference to the labors of the latter in expounding and translating the Bible; and this instance is the more significant for our purpose when we consider the question discussed, as well as the solemn manner in which S. Augustine solicits a reply. The Bishop of a certain city, which is not named, had desired to introduce S. Jerome's new version of the Old Testament. On the first occasion of its being used in public worship, the portion of Scripture read was the fourth chapter of the Book of Jonah, where it is said, at the sixth verse, that "the Lord God prepared a gourd, and made it to come up over Jonah." In this passage the word rendered in the old Italic version—"*gourd*" (*cucurbita*), had been taken by S. Jerome to signify "*ivy*" (*hedera*). The change was at once discovered, and a violent tumult was excited among the people, especially among such of them as were Greeks, who accused the Bishop of corrupting the text of the Bible. The result, S. Augustine tells us, was, that the Bishop was compelled to restore the old translation, "not wishing, after the great danger he had encountered, to continue without a flock."[2]

zealous honestly and faithfully to harmonize what has been said." (Μηδὲ *διαφωνεῖν, μηδὲ ἐναντιοῦσθαι τοὺς εὐαγγελιστὰς πρὸς ἀλλήλους ὑπολάβωμεν· κ. τ. λ.*)—*Epist. Canon.* ap. Routh, *Rel. Sacræ*, t. iii. p. 225.

[1] "Potuerat dicere Matthæus: 'Jesu verò generatio sic erat;' sed prævidens Spiritus S. depravatores, et præmuniens contra fraudulentiam eorum, per Matthæum ait: 'Christi autem generatio sic erat.'"—*Cont. Hær.* lib. III. xvi. 2, p. 204. It is clear that had the copy of the Gospels used by S. Irenæus given the correct reading of S. Matth. i. 1, viz., "Jesus Christ," his argument would have been considerably strengthened. See D. Massuet's note *in loc.*

[2] "Quidam frater noster Episcopus, cum lectitari instituisset in ecclesia cui præest, interpretationem tuam, movit quiddam longe aliter abs te positum apud Jonam Prophetam, quam erat omnium sensibus memoriæque inveteratum, et tot ætatum successionibus decantatum. Factus est tantus tumultus in plebe, maxime Græcis arguentibus et inclamantibus calumniam falsitatis, ut cogeretur Episcopus (ea quippe

I have thus attempted to give some idea of the sentiments cherished in every age by both Jews and Christians, as to the nature and value of the sacred documents committed to their charge.[1] This belief was no merely speculative tenet; nor did it rest upon some general feeling that the writings which taught the doctrines of revealed religion were deserving of reverence. Their conviction of the Divine source of that faith which the Bible unfolds, was not more firm than their conviction that the origin of the records which contain its history was, in like manner, Divine. Proofs, equally incontrovertible, were given of both. The soldier of the Cross, in our day, goes forth to heathen lands, supported, it is true, by the sense of duty, and animated by his glorious message: but he is also cheered on his path, and stimulated in his toil,—for he is but man,—by the consciousness of universal sympathy, and the tokens of public applause. Once this was not so. There were days when the Christian missionary, although in the land of his fathers, and surrounded by the civilization of the world, was encountered on every side, did he suffer his thoughts to dwell upon aught but the task before him, by the certainty of persecution, and contumely, and wrong. "If the Tiber," said Tertullian, "floods to the walls, if the Nile does not irrigate the fields, if the heavens are shut, if the earth

civitas erat,) Judæorum testimonium flagitare. Utrum autem illi imperitia an malitia, hoc esse in Hebræis codicibus responderunt, quod et Græci et Latini habebant atque dicebant. Quid plura? Coactus est homo velut mendositatem corrigere, volens, post magnum periculum, non remanere sine plebe."—*August. ad Hieron.* Epist. lxxi. t. ii. p. 161; S. Augustine concluding with the words: "Sed obsecro te per Dominum, ne te pigeat ad omnia respondere."

S. Jerome in his reply explains the cause of the commotion: "Dicis me in Jonam Prophetam male quiddam interpretatum, et seditione populi conclamante, propter unius verbi dissonantiam Episcopum pæne Sacerdotium perdidisse; et quid sit illud * * * subtrahis * * * nisi fortè, ut ante annos plurimos, cucurbita venit in medium, asserente illius temporis Cornelio et Asinio Pollione, me *hederam* pro *cucurbita* transtulisse. Super qua re in commentario Jonæ Prophetæ plenius respondimus."—*Hieron. ad August.* Ep. cxii. t. i. p. 748.

[1] The kind of *effect* which the argument built upon this universal consent, is calculated to produce, has been beautifully expressed by Mr. Coleridge: "In every generation, and wherever the light of Revelation has shone, men of all ranks, conditions, and states of mind, have found in this Volume a correspondent for every movement toward the Better felt in their own hearts * * * As if on some dark night a pilgrim, suddenly beholding a bright star moving before him, should stop in fear and perplexity. But lo! traveller after traveller passes by him, and each, being questioned whither he is going, makes answer, 'I am following yon guiding Star!' The pilgrim quickens his own steps, and presses onward in confidence. More confident still will he be, if by the wayside he should find, here and there, ancient monuments, each with its votive lamp, and on each the name of some former pilgrim, and a record that there he had first seen or begun to follow the benignant Star!"—*Confess. of an Inquiring Spirit,* Letter vi. p. 73.

quakes, if there is a famine or a pestilence,—at once the cry is raised, CHRISTIANOS AD LEONEM."[1] In attestation of the truth and origin of the facts on which Christianity relies, no more convincing proof can be alleged than the endurance of such trials, and the triumphs thus achieved. The proof, too, is one of which Christian Apologists in every age have not been slow to avail themselves.[2] But the argument should not pause here. It exhibits the Church's belief in the Divine character and inspiration of the Bible, no less than in the truth and heavenly origin of its contents. Jew and Christian alike were eager to sacrifice life itself, not merely in defence of the doctrines of revealed religion, but of the very documents in which those doctrines were contained. Within so short a space of time as ten years before the public recognition of Christianity, the persecution of Diocletian carried torture and death to every section of the Church. The trial of the martyr's faith was not now to sacrifice to the gods, or to adore the Emperor;—the edict went forth, 'Give up your sacred writings, or die.'[3] There was no longer that actual

[1] "Si Tiberis ascendit ad mœnia, si Nilus non ascendit in arva, si cœlum stetit, si terra movit, si fames, si lues, statim, CHRISTIANOS AD LEONEM."—*Apolog.* c. 40, p. 36.

[2] Thus S. Justin Mart. writes:

Οὐδένα οὐδέποτε ἰδεῖν ἐστὶν ὑπομείναντα διὰ τὴν πρὸς τὸν ἥλιον πίστιν ἀποθανεῖν· διὰ δὲ τὸ ὄνομα τοῦ Ἰησοῦ, ἐκ παντὸς γένους ἀνθρώπων καὶ ὑπομείναντας καὶ ὑπομένοντας παντα πάσχειν ὑπὲρ τοῦ μὴ ἀρνήσασθαι Αὐτὸν, *ἰδεῖν ἐστί.*—*Dial. cum Tryph.* c. 121. p. 214. Cf. Apol. ii. 12, p. 96.

[3] Credner, in his treatise "Zur Geschichte des Kanons." p. 65, quotes "two documents which are the most ancient which we possess on this subject." In the Donatist controversy, Felix, Bishop of Aptungis, was accused of having been a "Traditor," or one who had given up his sacred books, in the persecution of Diocletian. Felix was tried on this charge in the year 320, on which occasion were adduced the official documents, which had been received in his house in the year 303. The former of these documents runs as follows: "Diocletiano VIII. et Maximiano VII. Coss.; XIV. Kal. Jun., ex actis Munatii Felicis, flaminis perpetui, Curatoris coloniæ Cirtensium. Cum ventum esset ad domum in qua Christiani conveniebant, Felix flamen perpetuus Curator Paulo Episcopo dixit, '*Proferte scripturas legis*, et si quid aliud hic habetis, ut præcepto et jussioni parere possitis, &c.'" This document is taken from the "Monumenta vetera ad Donat. hist. pertinentia," published by Dupin in his edition of the treatise of S. Optatus, "De Schism. Donatistarum," Ant. 1702, p. 168.

In the second document which Credner quotes, and which also is of the year 303, occurs a letter from Felix to Cæcilianus, to the effect that inquiry had been made "an aliquæ *scripturæ legis vestræ* secundum sacram legem *adustæ sint*, &c."—*Ibid.* p. 164.

Ruinart refers to this same Edict, with the addition: "et propositum est per colonias et civitates Principibus et Magistratibus, suo cuique loco, ut LIBROS DEIFICOS peterent de manu Episcoporum et Presbyterorum."—*Acta Primorum Martyr.* p. 355.

In pursuance of this Edict "the divinely inspired Scriptures"—Eusebius records as an eye-witness—were publicly committed to the flames: *τὰς δὲ ἐνθέους καὶ ἱερὰς γραφὰς κατὰ μέσας ἀγορὰς πυρὶ παραδιδομένας αὐτοῖς ἐπείδομεν ὀφθαλμοῖς.*—*Ecc. Hist.* lib. viii. 2 p. 377. Lactantius fixes the day on which this persecution commenced, as the Terminalia "a. d. vii. Kal. Martias" (A. D. 303) "Qui dies cum illux-

knowledge of the facts of Christ's life, or of the teaching of His Apostles, which had cheered the martyr Stephen, and supported the dying Polycarp. The personal recollection of such matters had now ceased; the belief in the facts had become, as with us, but historical: and yet such was the firm conviction of the Divine inspiration and heavenly origin of the Scriptures of Truth, that death with all its horrors was embraced rather than resign them to the heathen.[1] To use the profound observation of Pascal:[2] "This is a sincerity which has no example in the world, nor its root in nature."

isset * * * repente, adhuc dubia luce, ad ecclesiam profectus * * * revulsis foribus, simulacrum Dei quæritur: *Scripturæ repertæ incendundur*," &c.—*De Mort. Persecut.* c. xii.

[1] Take the case of the martyrdom of the Bishop of Tibiura, in Africa:

* * "Postera autem die Felix Episcopus venit Carthagine Tibiuram * * * cui Magnilianus Curator dixit, 'Felix Episcope, da libros, vel membranas quascunque habes.' Felix Episcopus dixit, 'Habeo, sed non do.' Magnilianus Curator dixit, 'Prius est quod Imperatores jusserunt, quam quod tu loqueris. Da libros, ut possint igni aduri.' Felix Episcopus dixit, 'Melius est me igne aduri, quam Scripturas Deificas: quia bonum est obedire Deo magis quam hominibus' * * * Magnilianus C. dixit, 'Ibis ergo ad Proconsulem' * * * Tunc profectus est Felix a Tibiura * * * cui dixit Proconsul, 'Quare scripturas supervacuas non reddis?' Felix Episcopus dixit, 'Habeo sed non dabo.' * * * Tunc præfectus jussit Felicem de vinculis eripi; et dixit, 'Felix, quare *Scripturas Dominicas* non das? aut forsitan non habes?' Cui respondit, 'Habeo quidem, sed non do.' Præfectus dixit, 'Felicem gladio interficite.' Felix Episcopus, dixit voce clara, 'Gratias tibi Domine, qui me dignatus es liberare.'"—*Acta S. Felicis, Episc. et Mart.*, ap. Ruinart, p. 356.

Again: in the year 304 several ladies of Thessalonica, named Agape, Chionia, Irene, &c., were burned alive under circumstances of revolting atrocity. The Prefect, we are told, addressed Irene as follows:

"Dulcetius vero: 'Quisnam tibi auctor fuit ut membranas istas atque scripturas ad hodiernum usque diem custodires?' 'Ille,' inquit Irene, 'Deus Omnipotens, qui jussit nobis ad mortem usque Ipsum diligere. Qua de causa non ausæ sumus Eum prodere, sed maluimus aut viventes comburi, aut quæcumque alia nobis acciderint perpeti, quam talia scripta prodere.'"—*Ibid.* p. 394.

[2] Pascal is speaking of the Jews:—"Cependant ce livre qui les déshonore en tant de façons, il le conservent aux dépens de leur vie. C'est une sincérité qui n'a point d'exemple dans le monde, ni sa racine dans la nature."—ed Faugère, t. ii. p. 189.

In proof of this assertion, we may adduce the language of Philo:

Καὶ πλειόνων ἐτῶν διεληλυθότων, τὸ μὲν ἀκριβὲς οὐκ ἔχω λέγειν ὁπόσα, πλέω δ' οὖν ἢ δυσχίλια ἔτη, μὴ ῥῆμά γε αὐτοὺς μόνον τῶν ὑπ' αὐτοῦ [*scil.* Moses] *γεγραμμένων κινῆσαι, ἀλλὰ κἂν μυριάκις αὐτοὺς ἀποθανεῖν ὑπομεῖναι θᾶττον, ἢ τοῖς ἐκείνου νόμοις καὶ ἔθεσιν ἐναντία πεισθῆναι.*—*De Judæor. ex Egypto Profect.* t. ii. p. 628. As to the sense of *ἔθος*, in this passage, compare the following:

Οὓς ὁ ἱερὸς λόγος διδάσκει χρηστῆς ὑπολήψεως πεφροντικέναι, καὶ μηδὲν τῶν ἐν τοῖς ἔθεσι λύειν, ἃ θεσπέσιοι καὶ μείζους ἄνδρες ἢ καθ' ἡμᾶς ὥρισαν.—*De Migr. Abr.* t. i. p. 450. In both these places *ἔθος* clearly denotes not merely *customs, rites;* but the *Law* itself. Cf. Acts, vi. 14; xv. 1; xxi. 21.

LECTURE III.

THE OLD TESTAMENT AND THE NEW—THE LOGOS THE REVEALER.

Προκείσθω τοίνυν * * * *τῆς ἡμετέρας πίστεως ὁ λόγος, καὶ Εὐαγγελίου ὁ ὅρος, καὶ τῶν Ἀποστόλων τὸ κήρυγμα, καὶ τῶν Προφητῶν ἡ μαρτυρία.*

S. ATHANASIUS, *Cont. Apollinar.* ii. 4.

"Scriptura omnis in duo Testamenta divisa est * * * Judæi Veteri utuntur, nos Novo: sed tamen diversa non sunt, quia Novum Veteris adimpletio est, et in utroque idem Testator est Christus."

LACTANTIUS, *Divin. Instit.* iv. 20.

"Prophetæ, ab Ipso habentes donum, in Illum prophetaverunt."

S. BARNABAS, *Epist.* § v.

Πάντα δι' Αὐτοῦ, καὶ εἰς Αὐτὸν ἔκτισται. οὕτω δὲ, ὡς ἀληθῶς ὄντος καὶ ἐνεργοῦντος, ὡς Λόγου ἅμα καὶ Θεοῦ· δι' οὗ ὁ Πατὴρ πάντα πεποίηκεν, οὐχ ὡς δι' ὀργάνου, οὐδ' ὡς δι' ἐπιστήμης ἀνυποστάτου * * * *τοῦτον εἶναι, ὃς ἐκπληρῶν τὴν πατρικὴν βουλὴν τοῖς πατριάρχαις φαίνεται* * * * *ποτὲ μὲν ὡς Ἄγγελος, ποτὲ δὲ ὡς Κύριος, ποτὲ δὲ Θεὸς μαρτυρούμενος.*

SYN. ANTIOCH. *Adv. Paulum Samosat.*

Ἀκόλουθα εὑρίσκεται καὶ τὰ τῶν Προφητῶν καὶ τὰ τῶν Εὐαγγελίων ἔχειν, διὰ τὸ τοὺς πάντας πνευματοφόρους ἑνὶ Πνεύματι Θεοῦ λελαληκέναι.

THEOPHILUS, *Ad Autolycum*, iii. 12.

LECTURE III.

THE OLD TESTAMENT AND THE NEW: THE LOGOS THE REVEALER.

NO MAN KNOWETH WHO THE SON IS, BUT THE FATHER; AND WHO THE FATHER IS, BUT THE SON, AND HE TO WHOM THE SON WILL REVEAL HIM."—*S. Luke*, x. 22.

THE course of our inquiry respecting the inspiration of Holy Scripture has brought us to the examination of the Scriptures themselves. We have now to seek for the intimations given by the sacred writers as to the nature of the influence by which they were actuated; and also to collect whatever inferences, relating to the manner of the Divine co-operation, can be drawn from the internal structure of the Bible in confirmation of the claim to infallible authority which it asserts for itself, and which, as we have seen, has been in all ages ascribed to it by the Church of God.

This line of argument is by no means fairly open to an objection often urged against it. You require us, it is said, to receive the Bible as true because it is inspired, and you then undertake to prove its inspiration from its own pages. This is not so. It will be remembered that, from the outset, the present investigation has taken for granted the entire array of Christian evidence—embracing, together with the proofs of supernatural agency, the vast extent of antiquarian and grammatical criticism, the profound argument from the analogy of nature,[1] as well as a

[1] Bishop Butler observes, in a well-known passage: "Hence, namely from analogical reasoning, Origen has with singular sagacity observed, that 'he who believes the Scripture to have proceeded from Him, who is the Author of Nature, may well expect to find the same sort of difficulties in it as are found in the constitution of Nature.' And in a like way of reflection, it may be added, that he who denies the Scripture to have been from God, upon account of these difficulties, may, for the very same reason, deny the world to have been formed by Him."—*Analogy*, Introd.

The passage which Butler has here quoted continues as follows: ἔστι δέ γε καὶ ἐν τῇ

comparison of our sacred records with the whole range of profane history, and with the present aspect of the world. On such evidence we are entitled to assume the genuineness, the authenticity, and the perfect truthfulness of the several books to which the name of Holy Scripture has been assigned. To examine, therefore, the nature of the influence under which those books have been drawn up, by the light which they themselves afford, can never be justly charged with logical fallacy. As well might we reject the personal statements of an ambassador, with respect to the nature of his powers and the source of his instructions, after we had verified his credentials, and satisfied ourselves as to his veracity. And thus the adducing arguments from Scripture itself, in proof of its own inspiration, is no *petitio principii.* It would only become so, were we to assume the fact of its inspiration in order to infer therefrom the *credibility* of its contents. This credibility we establish by independent proofs. We regard the sacred books, in the first instance, as historical documents drawn up by men whose honesty and truthfulness rest upon the ordinary grounds of human belief, and whose qualifications are further attested by that Society, to whose charge the writings which they composed have confessedly been committed. Having thus convinced ourselves of the authority of the Bible, that its doctrines are revealed, and that its facts are true, we can feel no scruple in admitting as accurate the character which its own writers ascribe to it.

Still less can any objection be made to our drawing inferences as to the nature of the influence under which the Bible was composed, from the phenomena which its pages present to view, or its contents record. Such a process of reasoning is as sound as it is philosophical. The argument from Final Causes is admitted by all to afford the plainest evidence that the Creator of the world is God. The traces of design which are engraved upon the face of Nature, are universally received as the clearest proof that its Author is Divine. On the whole, then, the Bible, as history, testifies of Christ: Christ, moreover, as the Lord who animates His Church with His Spirit, testifies that Scripture is "Holy

*κτίσει τινὰ ἀνθρωπίνῃ φύσει δυσεύρετα ἢ καὶ ἀνεύρετα. καὶ οὐ διὰ τοῦτο κατηγορητέον τοῦ ποιητοῦ τῶν ὅλων. φέρε εἰπεῖν, ἐπεὶ οὐχ εὑρίσκομεν αἰτίαν βασιλίσκων κτίσεως, καὶ τῶν ἄλλων ἰοβόλων θηρίων * * * οὕτω τοίνυν καὶ ἐν ταῖς θείαις γραφαῖς χρὴ ὁρᾷν, ὅτι πολλὰ ἀπόκειται ἐν αὐταῖς δυσαπόδοτα ἡμῖν.*—*Selecta in Psalmos*, t. ii. p. 528.

Scripture :"[1] and hence we do not, at starting, believe what is contained in the Bible, because it is inspired ;—but, having previously established its claims to our belief, we are fully entitled to draw our main argument for its inspiration from its own pages.[2]

The present stage of our inquiry brings before us a fact to which attention has been already drawn :—I mean the indissoluble connection, and coequal authority, of the two great divisions of the inspired record. These two collections of ancient documents we receive on the testimony of the bodies of men to whose trust they were respectively committed. The Jewish Church, in its day, has borne witness to the Old Testament : the Christian Church, in like manner, bears witness to the New.[3] The Christian Church, moreover, has an additional testimony to offer ;—testimony, I mean, to the continuity of both Old and New Testament, to their mutual relation, and to the identity of their Divine Author.[4] From the very dawn of Christianity, it is true,

[1] "Die Schrift, als Geschichte, beweiset für Christus; Christus, als der seine Gemeine mit seinem Geiste belebende Herr, beweiset für die Schrift als heilige Schrift. Hiedurch entgehen wir gründlich dem mit Recht gerügten Zirkel, dem in der Schrift Enthaltenen zu glauben, *weil* sie inspirirt ist, aber *dass* sie inspirirt sei, wiederum aus den Aussagen der Schrift zu beweisen."—Sack, *Apologetik*, s. 429.

[2] Modern writers have drawn a distinction between the *fides humana* and the *fides divina* of Scripture. The *fides humana* of the Bible is founded upon its authenticity, its credibility, and its integrity. By the *authenticity* (*αὐθεντία*) of a writing is meant, that it has been composed by the author to whom it is ascribed; or, if the author has not named himself, that it has been composed at the time, among the people, and under the circumstances assigned in its contents. The *credibility* (*ἀξιοπιστία*) of a writing, which depends on the credibility of its author, and on its contents, consists in those particulars which gain for it public belief. The *integrity* of a writing appears from the proofs given that we possess it in the form in which it was originally composed, and that it has undergone no such falsifications as render its use uncertain, or its author's meaning undiscoverable. The *fides divina* of Scripture presupposes the *fides humana*. Cf. Bretschneider, "Handb. der Dogm." i. s. 338.

[3] In his review of Twesten's "Vorlesungen," Nitzsch well describes the function of the Church : "Die Kirche ist veranlassende, vermittlende, vorbereitende Ursache unserer Ueberzeugung von der Göttlichkeit einer Schrift."—*Studien u. Kritiken*, 1828. s. 240.

[4] On such testimony rests "The Canon of Scripture." According to Christian usage, the word *κανών* does not differ in signification from what, in heathen philosophy, was termed *decretum* or *δόγμα*,—namely, the leading principles of a philosophical system. Thus Seneca writes: "Nulla ars contemplativa sine decretis suis est, quæ Græci vocant *δόγματα*. * * * Aliqua vel casu vel exercitatione, exibunt recta: sed non erit in manu *regula*, ad quam exigantur, cui credat recta esse quæ fecit."—*Epist.* 95. Hence the phrases *κανὼν ἐκκλησιαστικός*, and *regula fidei*, were used as synonymous, and as denoting both Old and New Testaments. Clemens Alex. defines the *κανὼν ἐκκλησιαστικός* to be "the harmony of the Law and the Prophets with the New Testament." It is—*ἡ συνῳδία καὶ ἡ συμφωνία νόμου τε καὶ προφητῶν, τῇ κατὰ τὴν τοῦ Κυρίου παρουσίαν παραδιδομένῃ διαθήκῃ*.—*Strom.* vi. 15. p. 803. Thus, too, Tertullian says of the Church of Rome in his day: "Legem et Prophetas cum Evangelicis et Apostolicis literis miscet, et inde potat fidem."—*De Præscr. Hær.* c xxxvi. p 245. See Credner, "Zur Geschichte des Kanons," s. 20–22. The firm

some have been found to question that identity, and even to assert that the two portions of the Bible are heterogeneous and opposed. Of such importance, however, has the exposure of this error been always deemed, that, as I have already pointed out, the Church declares by an express article of the Creed, that it was the Holy Ghost "who spake through the Prophets."[1]

The revival, in our own day, of opinions whose tendency at least is not dissimilar,[2] may, to a certain extent, be inferred from the absence of any reference to the Old Testament, in the great majority of modern treatises which allude to the subject of Inspiration; an omission so remarkable, that a reader, unfamiliar with the Bible, might imagine that no Church of old had ever received "the oracles of God;" that no prophet had ever foretold the Advent of the Messiah; that no elaborate ceremonial had ever typified the mysteries of the Kingdom of Christ. The revival of such views with respect to the Old Testament is not, however, a matter of mere inference. The opinion has been openly avowed, and eagerly defended, that the Old Testament is either totally unconnected with the New—except indeed by chance; or that its importance has passed away, and that the Gospel dispensation can tolerate no remnant of the covenant under which the Jewish nation was chosen.[3] It is needless to inquire to what

belief of the Church in the continuity of both Old and New Testament is well described in the following verses of S. Gregory of Nazianzum:

Χάρισμα δ' οἶδα Πνεύματος θείαν δόσιν.
Κήρυγμ' ἀδήλων, τὴν προφητείαν λέγω·
Εὐαγγέλιον δὲ, τῆς νέας σωτηρίας·
'Αποστολὴν δὲ, συμμαχίαν κηρύγματος·
Λόγου δὲ γνῶσιν, τὴν κατήχησιν, νέοις·

Carmen xxxiv. t. ii. p. 622.

[1] See Lecture ii. p. 81.

[2] Thus Mr. Morell writes:—"If the Jewish dispensation was Divine, if God communed in secret with the nation, if His Spirit was in the Church, then the writings which embody this religious state *are inspired*,—inspired, however, not as being penned under any specific commission from heaven, but as being the productions of those who were enlightened by special influences, and as being universally received by the Jews as the purest representations both of their national and their individual religious vitality. In such representations of course we could not expect to see described a *higher religion* or a more perfect morality than *actually existed* in those times; hence accordingly the imperfections both in moral and religious ideas which are mixed up with all their sacred writings."—*Philosophy of Religion*, p. 169.

[3] Bretschneider argues, that since "doctrines relating to God and morality are far more perfectly stated in the New Testament by Jesus and the Apostles, and have been sufficiently attested by the latter as Divine; and since this system of teaching requires no attestation by means of the Old Testament, it is clear that there is no need of a theory of Revelation for the Old Testament, which cannot be 'judex et norma fidei et vitæ' for Christians in the same sense as the New Testament."—*Handb*

extent we are to look upon such conclusions as the result of a false conception of spiritual religion, or how far they may be traced to certain dogmatic views on points of Christian doctrine; it is more to our purpose to examine whether such sentiments have any foundation, and, if not, to expose their falsehood. Let us then examine, in the first place, under what aspect the Old Testament is presented to us in the New;[1] and inquire, secondly, whether a comparison of the two great divisions of the Bible offers such analogies, as may justify our maintaining that their authors equally shared in the same guiding influence of the Spirit of God.

der Dogm. I. s. 159. See, too, the remarks of Twesten, quoted Lecture i. p. 27, note[3]; where also the opinions of Schleiermacher have been referred to, and where we have seen (note[2]) how this latter writer has gone so far as to consider "the expressions of the nobler and purer heathenism" of equal value for Christians as the sentiments of the Old Testament. To which I may add that in his chapter, "Von der Methode der Dogmatik," Schleiermacher refuses to quote the Old Testament in support of his views, alleging it to be, as an authority, "superfluous:"—Mithin erscheint das alte Testament doch für die Dogmatik nur als eine überflüssige Autorität."—*Der christl. Glaube*, I. s. 147. It may be well to observe, as bearing upon a topic to be discussed in the present Lecture, that Schleiermacher's views on this subject appear to have arisen, from his having perceived but partially the connexion of Revelation with the Person of Christ. The leading feature of his system is, that *the Person* of the Redeemer, and *it alone*, is the Revelation to man: and that a belief in the reality of *this Person* forms the essence of (what Schleiermacher terms) "the Christian consciousness." Thus he concludes, "that if belief in the Revelation of God in Christ, and in the Redemption through Him, has not already sprung up spontaneously and originally (auf dem ursprünglichen Wege), by means of experience as the demonstration of the Spirit and of power, neither miracles nor prophecies can produce it; nay more, that this belief would be just as immoveable, even if Christianity could point to neither prophecies nor miracles."—*Ibid.* s. 97. According to this theory, therefore, all Revelation is excluded, except the fact of Christ's Personal appearance, and the Redemption which He effected:—in other words, because Christ is Himself (in the highest sense) *the* Revelation of God, Schleiermacher infers that He cannot have communicated Divine knowledge by the intervention of human agents. Hence his denial of any revelation in the Old Testament, and his undervaluing Inspiration in general. See Lecture i. pp. 34, 35, *supra*.

Sack, commenting on the various modes of stating this principle in the successive editions of the "Christliche Glaube," truly remarks that all those statements have this in common, "dass eigentliche Offenbarung nur in der Person Christi sei, ausser derselben nur in dem allgemeineren Sinne, wie man es auch von Entstehung eines neuen Kunstlebens sagen könne.—*Apologetik.* s. 123. And Nitzsch justly sums up this theory of Schleiermacher by saying: "This theologian has taken his idea of Revelation, not from the Holy Scriptures, but from the philosophy of the general usage of language; and indeed this is the reason why he considers this idea as too *slight* to express the peculiarity of Christianity. That which is wholly direct in the Revelation would appear to him to be perfectly applicable only to Christ, as an intelligent recipient; but it is deserving of remark that, according to Scriptural guidance, this view is here inapplicable; for * * * an ἀποκάλυψις, or revelation in the above sense, has not been given to Christ. That He taught what He heard is something quite different, for that even does the Holy Spirit."—*System der Christl. Lehre*, § 24.

[1] As to the *principle* on which the writers of the New Testament have appealed to the Old, see *infra*, Lecture vii.

Now when we seek for the judgment passed by Him, who is the central point to which all the rays of Revelation converge, we are at once met by a statement, which might seem to set this question at rest for ever. Christ has said, "Search the Scriptures"—that is, of the Old Testament—"they are they which testify of Me."[1] In the vision of the Prophet Evangelist, the same truth has been repeated by a messenger from heaven: "The testimony of Jesus is the spirit of prophecy."[2] The Old Testament, then, "testifies" of Christ—and this by no isolated predictions; for the entire history of God's Revelation, under the former dispensation, is one great reference to the future Messiah: and upon that revelation by *facts*, and prediction by *facts*, is grounded that series of predictions by *words*, which God has been pleased to communicate, in a supernatural manner, by His special agents.

[1] S. John, v. 39. The constant use which our Lord Himself makes of the Old Testament may, indeed, be considered to decide this question:—especially His manner of quoting it on the occasion of His Temptation (S. Matt. iv. 4, 7, 10). Parallel to this instance is that in which the angel, when announcing the birth of John the Baptist (S. Luke, i. 17), makes use of the prediction of Malachi: "Behold I will send you Elijah the prophet, before the great and dreadful day of the Lord. And he shall turn the heart of the fathers to the children," &c.—Mal. iv. 5, 6: on which Olshausen profoundly observes:—"Such cases are clearly not to be understood as if angels quote *from* Scripture, but the words occur *in* Scripture, because it has been so resolved in the heavenly world to which the spiritual beings who speak belong. The supporting a thought by the words of Scripture is to be regarded only as the clothing it in the form accessible to man, and which he can comprehend. Angels, therefore, do not quote the language of Scripture, *because* they desire to take a proof from the Bible, or a reference for their words; but the thoughts applied are to be found in the Bible, because they contain a truth which holds good as well in heaven as upon earth."—*Comm. üb. Luc.* i. 17, B. i. s. 93.

[2] Rev. xix. 10, "I am thy fellow servant" said the Angel to S. John, "and of thy brethren that have *the testimony* (*τὴν μαρτυρίαν*) of Jesus: * * * for the testimony (*ἡ μαρτυρία*) of Jesus is the spirit of prophecy:" i. e. (as Bishop Hurd remarks)—"the testimony of, or concerning Jesus. * * * I affirm its sense to be 'That the scope and end of Prophecy was the testimony of Jesus.'" *On Prophecy*, Sermon ii. Compare with this our Lord's own words just quoted: *ἐρευνᾶτε τὰς γραφάς* * * * *καὶ ἐκεῖναί εἰσιν αἱ μαρτυροῦσαι περὶ ἐμοῦ.*—S. John, v. 39.

The view adopted by Hengstenberg is but slightly different: "The testimony of Jesus is the testimony which Jesus delivers. According to the point of view taken in the Apocalypse, the testifier is always properly Christ—cf. at ch. i. 2; vi. 9. * * * All doubt is removed by the explanation given in this passage itself. According to it, 'those who have the testimony of Jesus' is equivalent to those who have the Spirit of Prophecy. * * * The *for* introduces the reason, on account of which the angel had spoken of a *testimony* of Jesus. It stands in this, that the testimony of Jesus, which alone could here be made account of, is all one with the Spirit of Prophecy. That the testimony *concerning* Christ, is, at the same time, the testimony *of* Christ; and,—*prophecy* has its source in the *spirit* of prophecy,—these correspond to each other. Christ testifies in the prophets through His Spirit (1 Pet. i. 11)."—*The Revelation of S. John expouuded.* (Clarke's For. Theol. Lib. vol. ii. p. 256.) It will be seen, as we proceed, how this view of the passage falls in with the main object of this Lecture.

Those parts of the New Testament in which the Holy Ghost has brought to full maturity the spirit of the Old Testament revelations are, the Gospel of S. Matthew, the Epistle to the Hebrews, and the discourse of S. Stephen in the seventh chapter of the Acts of the Apostles.[1] S. Stephen, when defending himself from the charge of "blaspheming the holy place and the Law,"[2] takes occasion to prove, *negatively*, that the Law and the Temple, though Divine, were not the highest and last form of God's Revelation.[3] S. Matthew takes the *positive* line of argument, that Jesus is the promised seed of Abraham, "the Son of David:"—an argument which opens by exhibiting the three great periods of the Genealogy,[4] and which unfolds itself on the

[1] Cf. "Der Brief an die Hebräer erklärt," von Dr. J. H. A. Ebrard, Königsberg, 1850. Einleit., s. 5. There is no portion of the New Testament on which so little attention has been bestowed by commentators, or which has suffered so much from misconception, as that passage in the Acts of the Apostles which relates to S. Stephen. Some remarks on the subject of his address, and, especially, of the "demonstrable historical mistakes" charged against him (see Alford's Greek Testament, *Proleg*, vol. i. § 6.), will be found in Appendix H. Meanwhile I would draw attention to the impressive manner in which S. Luke dwells upon the character of the First Martyr. He alone of the Deacons is described as "a man full of faith and of the Holy Ghost."—Acts, vi. 5. "Stephen," it is added, "full of faith and power, did great wonders and miracles among the people" (ver. 8); the learning of the Jewish synagogue was unable "to resist the wisdom and the Spirit by which he spake" (ver. 10); and at ch. vii. 55, it is said of him again, ὑπάρχων δὲ πλήρης Πνεύματος Ἁγίου, ἀτενίσας εἰς τ. οὐρ.—that he *was* a person "full of the Holy Ghost," not one who *became so* (γενόμενος) at that moment;—as appears from the junction of the aorist ἀτενίσας, with ὑπάρχων. Cf. Luger, "Die Rede des Stephanus," s. 9.

[2] "Then there arose certain of the synagogue * * * disputing with Stephen * * * and set up false witnesses which said, This man ceaseth not to speak blasphemous words against this holy place and the Law."—Acts, vi. 9, 13.

[3] S. Stephen, reviewing the course of Jewish history, argues: (1.) That the Law is not to be regarded as an isolated revelation, but as that in which the promise already given to Abraham (Acts, vii. 5) received its fulfilment; nay, more, that it carried in itself the pledge of another revelation still future, and connected with the accomplishment of the former promise:—"A Prophet shall the Lord your God raise up unto you," &c. (ver. 37). The Law was added, writes S. Paul, "till the Seed should come to whom the promise was made."—Gal. iii. 19. (2.) That the temple built by Solomon could not have been the full realization of the Divine purpose: "The Most High dwelleth not in temples made with hands," &c. (ver. 46–50). (3.) To the Jews it was particularly offensive that Jesus, whom they had crucified, should be represented as the great Prophet of the new dispensation. S. Stephen argues, therefore, that such a fact could form no objection whatsoever against Jesus, for this same rejection of God's messengers had accompanied every former phase of Revelation: "Which of the Prophets have not your fathers persecuted?" (ver. 52). See Ebrard, "Kritik der Evang. Geschichte," s. 689; and Luger, "Die Rede des Stephanus," s. 27.

[4] I. The period ascending to David. II. That descending to Jechonias. III. That, in which the house of David is found in poverty, extending to the Blessed Virgin. Cf. Ebrard, "Der Br. an die Hebr." s. 5. Or, as Townson expresses it: "He begins with entitling Jesus Christ 'the son of Abraham,' and the 'son of David:' and divides his genealogy into three parts, answering to so many remarkable periods in their history; every one of which was early distinguished by predictions concerning the Messiah, peculiarly interesting to them: the first by the promise to Abraham,

field of the New Testament narrative.[1] The Epistle to the Hebrews, on the other hand, sets out from the Old Testament, the leading features of which it formally develops in a systematic treatise; and points out how the former Scriptures, in all their details, ever refer to Jesus. It proves that the Revelation and Redemption by the Messiah, promised in the Old Testament, have already become absolute and complete; and that, while by His coming, the types of the Law, if understood literally, have received their full accomplishment, their spiritual signification, nevertheless, and allusive power, abide for ever as exponents of the Person and Office of Christ.[2] But to proceed with somewhat more particularly.

We observe that our Lord, throughout the entire duration of His ministry, represents Himself as fulfilling, in Person, the scheme of the former covenant: we know, too, that He has made the Old Testament the basis of His teaching, continually employing it, as it was received in His time by the Jews, without letting fall the slightest hint that any portion of it was done away. So far from stating anything to that effect, He has expressed Himself in a manner which proves the very reverse, employing language by which He has not only defined the permanent authority of the Old Testament, but also indicated its true place in the new dispensation. The words are recorded by S. Matthew, whose Gospel, we also know, was designed to illustrate the connection of the two Covenants:—"Think not," said Christ,

that 'in his seed all the nations of the earth should be blessed,' (Gen. xxii. 18) * * * the second, by assurances to David, that the promised seed should spring from his loins (2 Sam. vii. 16) * * * the third, by marking an era of seventy weeks, or 490 years, before the end of which the Messiah should come (Dan. ix. 24–27)."—*Discourses on the Four Gospels*, iv. § 5, p. 116, Elrington's ed.

[1] For references to the title "Son of David," cf. S. Matt. ix. 27; xii. 23; xv. 22; xx. 30, 31; xxi. 9; xxii. 42, 45.

[2] "The history of the people, as well as its sacred rites, are all applied to Christian relations. In the fourth chapter, the march of Israel from Egypt to the land of Canaan, is used as a type of the march of the people of God, in spirit, to the land of eternal repose. With the High Priest of the Old Testament is Christ—the Eternal High Priest—compared; and in the seventh chapter, He is found again in Melchizedek, the king of Righteousness and of Peace. In the ninth chapter, follows a widely-drawn parallel of the spiritual blessings of the New Testament, its ordinances and privileges, with the institutions of the old Levitical Priesthood; of the Tabernacle of Testimony, with the perfect Tabernacle of God not made with hands; of the sacrifice, with the eternal, atoning Sacrifice of the Son of God. Even the parts of the Tabernacle of Testimony are again referred to in a spiritual sense: the flesh of the Son of God, it is said, is the veil; through the blood of Jesus we have boldness to enter into the Holy Place,—He has prepared it for us as a new and living way."—Olshausen, *Ein Wort uber tiefern Schriftsinn*, s. 59.

"that I am come to destroy the Law or the Prophets: I am not come to destroy, but to fulfill."[1] Christ here points out that, of what might appear *new* in His office or His teaching, there was nothing which could be separated from its historical foundation. In this passage He exhibits the internal connection of Old and New Testament. His words denote, in the first place, the unquestionable authority of the former Scriptures; secondly, that the New Testament can be regarded only as their fulfilment; thirdly, that the Law, consummated in this sense, is Divine and Everlasting. In the former part of this statement our Lord declares that the Old Testament was not abrogated—an opinion then held, perhaps, by His followers;[2] in the latter, He announces that such was not the object of His ministry. And it is to be well noted that the language employed by Him, in the verses which follow, to express the permanence of the Old Testament,[3] He has elsewhere made use of, in order to assert the same of His own revelations: "Heaven and earth shall pass away, but My words

[1] S. Matt. v. 17. This passage has been felt, from the earliest times, to be the authoritative announcement of the connexion of Old and New Testament. It was, accordingly, the chief difficulty of Marcion; and, in general, of the Gnostic school. Thus Tertullian writes: "Venisse Se [scil. Christum] non ut Legem et Prophetas dissolveret, sed ut potius adimpleret. Hoc enim Marcion, ut additum, erasit."—*Adv. Marcion*, iv. 7, p. 507. The manner in which the Marcionites attempted to evade the force of this text by a different reading, is stated in the Dialogue "De recta fide adv. Marcionitas:" A. *φανερῶς γοῦν τοῦ Σωτῆρος πληρῶσαι ἐλθόντος τὸν νόμον, οὗτοι καταλύειν φάσκουσι.* MA. Τοῦτο *οἱ* Ἰουδαϊσταὶ *ἔγραψαν, τὸ· οὐκ ἦλθον καταλῦσαι τὸν νόμον, ἀλλὰ πληρῶσαι· οὐχ οὕτως δὲ εἶπεν ὁ* Χριστός· *λέγει γὰρ, οὐκ ἦλθον πληρῶσαι τὸν νόμον, ἀλλὰ καταλῦσαι.—Ap. Origenis Opp.*, t. i. p. 830.

The opposition to the force of this text was further encountered by S. Augustin. (cont. Faust. xix. 6, t. viii. p. 316), S. Isidor. Pelus. (lib. I. Epist. 371, ad Pansoph. p. 97), Theodoret. (Hæret. Fab. lib. v. § 17, t. iv. p. 291). Cf. Tholuck, "Auslegung der Bergpredigt," s. 131.

[2] The intention of Christ's words, "Think not (*μὴ νομίσητε*), &c."—was, it may be, to set aside a misconception of the passage: "Behold the days come, saith the Lord, that I will make *a new covenant* with the house of Israel, and with the house of Judah: *not according to the covenant that I made with their fathers,*" &c.—Jer. xxxi. 31, 32.

[3] "Verily I say unto you, till heaven and earth pass (*ἕως ἂν παρέλθῃ*), one jot, or one tittle shall in no wise pass from the Law till all be fulfilled."—ver 18. Cf. too, ver 19, as further illustrating the importance to be attached to the Law: "Whosoever, therefore, shall break one of these least commandments (*τῶν ἐντολῶν τούτων τῶν ἐλαχίστων*), &c." It is to be remarked also, that the words of Christ, fixing, as it were, a certain period when the Law *shall* pass away—*ἕως ἂν πάντα γένηται*—point to a certain epoch of which Prophets and Apostles have spoken. Cf. for example, the references to the "new heavens and the new earth" by Isaiah (ch. lxv. 17; lxvi. 22), and by S. John (Rev. xxi. 1.): see also 1 Cor. xv. 24. Our Lord, therefore, here expresses something more than a mere proverbial description of the permanence of the Law, such as He has given elsewhere—"It is easier for heaven and earth to pass, than one tittle of the law to fail."—S. Luke, xvi. 17. See Ritschl, "Die Entsteh. der altkath Kirche," s. 28.

shall not pass away,"[1]—that is, the Old Testament and the sayings of Christ are alike imperishable, because both are the Word of God. Nor does our Lord confine this solemn ratification to any particular portion of the former Scriptures. Here, it is true, he speaks but of "the Law and the Prophets," and in another place[2] He refers merely to "the Prophets;" but we know that in S. John's Gospel[3] He frequently cites certain words from the Psalms, which, He observes, were "written in the Law;" and in S. Luke's He adopts the Old Testament in full, according to the received division of the Jews, when He says that "all things must be fulfilled which were written in the Law of Moses, and in the Prophets, and in the Psalms concerning Me."[4]

But further:—in this passage from the fifth chapter of S. Matthew, the expressions "to destroy," and "to fulfill," do not of themselves present an immediate contrast.[5] Opposed to the

[1] S. Matt. xxiv. 35. The fact that S. Matthew, alone of the Evangelists, has preserved both these expressions of our Lord, is not to be overlooked. There can be no doubt the design was, that one passage should illustrate the other.

[2] S. Luke, xviii. 31.

[3] S. John, x. 34; xii. 34; xv. 25. Cf. also S. Matt. xiii. 35, where words from the Psalms are quoted as "spoken by the Prophet."

[4] S. Luke, xxiv. 44. Rudelbach observes:—"The threefold division here,—where, for the last time, an allusion to the Old Testament falls from the lips of Jesus,—combined with the earlier mode of citation, 'the Law and the Prophets,' is not without deep significance. The Lord has hereby sanctioned *all* the divisions which were current in the Jewish Church, and attested in the most perfect manner the integrity of the whole of the Old Testament."—*Die Lehre von der Inspir.*, 1841, H. iv. s. 38. S. Paul (1 Cor. xiv. 21) quotes Isai. xxviii. 11, with the words, "In the Law it is written;" and in Rom. iii. 19, he describes his previous citations from both Isaiah and the Psalms as "what the Law saith." Cf. too, the words recorded by Josephus: *ὃς ἐδίδασκεν ἡμᾶς, ἔτι ὢν σὺν ἡμῖν, τὸν νόμον καὶ τοὺς προφήτας.*—*De Maccabæis*, 18, t. ii. p. 519; under which description the speaker expressly includes Daniel, the Psalms, and the Proverbs;—each of these instances clearly proving how completely unsupported, by ancient Jewish usage, is that theory of the modern Rabbins as to the different *degrees* of Inspiration under which the Old Testament was written (see Lecture ii. p. 62, note [1]). The quotations here adduced show, beyond any doubt, that in the days of Christ the Jews included the whole body of the Old Testament writings under the name of the Law, which portion of the Bible their modern representatives would exalt so highly above all the other books.

[5] *Καταλῦσαι, πληρῶσαι.* The phrase *καταλύειν νόμον*, in Hellenistic as in classic Greek, is equivalent to *ἀκυροῦν*: see S. Matt. xv. 6 ("Ye *have made* the commandment of God *of none effect*;" or rather, "Ye have cancelled, abrogated the word of God"); or Gal. iii. 17 ("The law cannot *disannul*" the covenant.) In this latter instance follows S. Paul's customary phrase *καταργῆσαι*, expressing the result which must have attended the *ἀκύρωσις νόμου*;—the "disannulling of the covenant" must, of itself, "make of none effect," "leave idle, or useless," "the promises." (Cf. S. Luke, xiii. 7, the barren fig-tree "cumbereth," "*makes* barren," *καταργεῖ*, "the ground.") On the other hand, *πληροῦν νόμον* signifies, in Hellenistic as in classic Greek, *explere legem, peragere quæ sunt officii.* (Cf. S. Matt. iii. 15, "Thus it becometh us to fulfil—*πληρῶσαι*—all righteousness." Acts, xiv. 26, "The work which they fulfilled"—*ὃ ἐπλήρωσαν*). Its use is sometimes founded on the trope of *filling a measure*: "Fill ye up then (*πληρώσατε*) the measure of your fathers." S. Matt. xxiii. 32.

abrogation of a Law we should rather look for its confirmation, or its re-institution; and S. Paul, in his Epistle to the Galatians, supplies the complete idea, when he places in opposition, the phrases "to destroy," and "to build again."[1] It was not, however, the Divine will to perpetuate the former scheme, but to extend and to develop it;[2] and hence the absence of complete antithesis in the expressions which we are considering. By them our Lord would seem to suggest the significant figure of a building, to the foundations of which additional strength has been given, and which has been in part remodelled, but which, at the same time, has been renovated and brought to completion on its former foundations;—the Architect now bringing to light certain features of His original design which had previously been concealed from view, hereby exhibiting their relation to the stability of the entire structure.[3] Hence the Old Testament is the basis, on which the New was to be erected. It presents the outlines of the picture, which were afterwards to be filled up. It affords the shadow of good things, while the body was of Christ.[4] No stronger confirmation, indeed, can be given of the fact that Christ was, in His own Person, the fulfilment of the Old Testament, than His statement that He could not withdraw Himself

For its signification, "to fulfil" a prophecy, see Lecture iv. Cf. Tholuck, "Die Bergpredigt," s. 133.

1 "If I *build again* the things which I *destroyed*"—Εἰ γὰρ ἃ κατέλυσα, ταῦτα πάλιν οἰκοδομῶ.—Gal. ii. 18. See Olshausen on S. Matt. v. 17. B. i. s. 212.

2 It has been already pointed out (Lecture i. p. 28), that this principle of development has been, from the first, the characteristic of Revelation.

3 Twesten forcibly observes of the words of Christ and His Apostles, which refer to the Old Testament, that "λῦσαι is ever a πληρῶσαι; that καταργῆσαι is, at the same time, a στῆσαι." Thus S. Paul writes, "Do we then make void (καταργοῦμεν) the Law through faith? God forbid: yea, we establish (ἱστάνομεν) the Law." (Rom. iii. 31.)—*Vorles. über die Dogm.* 1er Band, s. 333. Compare, too, the Apostle's language at the close of this Epistle (ch. xiii. 8–10), "Love is the fulfilling (πλήρωμα) of the Law."

4 Col. ii. 17. Olshausen has remarked in his second Tract on "The deeper sense of Scripture" that—"The Law, with all its ordinances, is like a grain of seed which includes in itself the whole law of formation of the plant. Should the plant spring up, the grain of seed must die; a power, which would cause it to continue in its isolated subsistence, would be just as destructive as the Judaizing teachers, with whom Paul was forced to contend. But notwithstanding such a fact, the law of the germ which lives no longer, invisibly penetrates the entire plant; so that in the plant's concentrated formations, the law, renewing its youth, repeatedly presents itself again in the fruit. Thus the Law was apparently dissolved by Christ, but only in order to be fulfilled, in its spirit, in every iota."—*Noch ein Wort, &c.*, s. 23. Jehovah, Himself, announced this same truth by the last of the Prophets: "From the rising of the sun, even unto the going down of the same, My name shall be great among the Gentiles; and in every place incense shall be offered unto My name, and a pure offering."—Mal. i. 11.

from that death, the mere prospect of which overpowered His soul, because He would thereby contravene the language of Prophecy,—"How then shall the Scriptures be fulfilled that it must be?"[1]

It has been attempted by some writers to take a sort of middle course in this question, and to make a distinction between the contents of the Old Testament. Divine authority they allow to those parts only which bear directly upon the office of Christ; while they deny Inspiration to those other portions which, they conceive, must be opposed to the Christian scheme: and in this latter class, the writers in question place the Law, as being that one of "the two covenants" contrasted by S. Paul,[2] "which gendereth to bondage," and the ministration of which he elsewhere terms that "of the letter."[3] Such writers are, however, forced of themselves to admit, that the exact line of distinction cannot be drawn; that the Law, too, has its prophetical side; and that we have it upon the authority of Christ himself, that Moses "wrote" of Him.[4] In truth, this notion, which would represent the doctrines of Scripture as distinct from its history, and which assumes that portions of the Old Testament, which it regards merely as the annals of a particular nation,[5] do not treat of Christ,

[1] S. Matt. xxvi. 54. Compare, also, the striking passage: "After this Jesus,—knowing that all things were now accomplished,—*that the Scripture might be fulfilled, saith,* I thirst."—S. John, xix. 28. A short time previously he had rejected the proffered "wine mingled with myrrh" (S. Mark, xv. 23); but at this moment, in the extremity of bodily exhaustion (Ps. xxii. 15), he accepts the "vinegar to drink" (Ps. lxix. 21);—the Evangelist expressly pointing out the fulfilment of the prediction: Jesus said "It is finished (τετέλεσται); and He bowed His head, and gave up the ghost."—S. John, xix. 30. See the excellent remarks of Rudelbach, "Die Lehre von der Inspir." 1841, H. iv. s. 35.

[2] Gal. iv. 24.

[3] 2 Cor. iii. 6.

[4] S. John, v. 46. Thus Twesten writes:—"We have distinguished in the Old Testament elements of two kinds, those whereby it is related to the New, and those whereby it is opposed to it. It lies in the nature of the case, that the former only, not the latter, can be referred to the Spirit of Christ: not the Law, but the Promises. Moreover, all those passages which prove an inspiration of the Old Testament, relate, in point of fact, to prophetic writings, including the Psalms (for David also was a prophet, Acts, ii. 30). Hence Paul contrasts the two Testaments, as the son of the bondmaid born after the flesh, and the son of the freewoman born after the Spirit (Gal. iv. 24, 29): their service, too, he opposes as that of the letter and of the spirit (2 Cor. iii. 6, &c). Since, however, even Moses has written of Christ (John, v. 46), since even the Law has a typical and also a prophetical side,—one dare not separate mechanically what is inspired in the Old Testament from what is not."—*Vorles. über die Dogm.*, 1er Band, s. 412. Cf. Lecture i. p. 27, note [3].

[5] The true conception of the historical parts of Scripture, has been laid down by the Schoolmen with their customary acuteness. Thus Alexander Alensis—the "Irrefragable Doctor"—discussing the question, 'An Theologia sit scientia'? points out the essential distinction between sacred and profane history:—"Aliter est historia in

—is of itself untenable. It is forgotten that the Jewish people themselves, their history, their ritual, their government, all present one grand prophecy of the future Redeemer;[1] that in the New Testament, fully to the same extent as in the Old, doctrines are based upon history; and that the Old Testament is as entirely occupied with the Messiah still future, as the New with the Christ who has already come. Thus the Apostles see the Christian element in the narrative of Hagar and Ishmael;[2] of the miracle of the water which flowed from the rock at the word of Moses;[3] of the vision of the Lord of Hosts by Isaiah.[4] Does not the New Testament explain the saying of the prophet—"Behold I, and the children which God hath given me,"[5] to have been fulfilled in Christ as perfectly as the words of any Messianic Psalm; and in the same degree as what is specially honored,

sacra Scriptura; aliter in aliis. In aliis enim historia significatione sermonum exprimit singularia gesta hominum; *nec est intentio significationis interioris.* * * * In sacra vero Scriptura ponitur historia non ea ratione seu fine, ut significentur singulares actus hominum significatione sermonum; sed ut significentur universales actus: et conditiones pertinentes ad informationem hominum, et contemplationis divinorum mysteriorum significatione rerum. * * * Introducitur ergo in historia sacræ Scripturæ factum singulare ad significandum universale: et inde est, quod ejus est intellectus et scientia. * * * In litterali historia Abrahæ, et Job, singulare est, quod narratur: sed ad hoc in Scriptura narratur, ut exemplar sit vitæ et conversationis bonorum: unde Rom. xv. 'Quæcunque scripta sunt, ad nostram doctrinam scripta sunt.' Et Jacob. ult. 'Exemplum accipite patientiæ et longanimitatis prophetas.'"—*Summæ Theolog.* Pars. 1ma, qu. i. Albertus Magnus, "Summæ Theol. Tract. i.," argues precisely in the same manner.

[1] "Tota divina οἰκονομία priorum temporum hunc ipsum Christum ejusque res gestas, ut pulcherrimam ac perfectissimam speciem, perpetuo velut ante oculos habens, cætera omnia ad illud instar effinxit."—*Grotius* ad Matt. i. 22; Opp. Theol. t. ii. p. 11 (quoted by Rudelbach, 1842, H. ii. s. 39). Take as a single illustration, the parallel between Israel and Christ: "Thou shalt say unto Pharaoh, Thus saith the Lord, Israel is My son, even My first born: and I say unto thee, Let My son go," &c.—Exod. iv. 22. The Prophet applies the words: "When Israel was a child, then I loved him, and called My son out of Egypt."—Hosea, xi. 1. The Evangelist, in fine, fills up the outlines of the history: Joseph "took the young child and His mother, and departed into Egypt * * * *that it might be fulfilled* (ἵνα πληρωθῇ) which was spoken of the Lord by the Prophet, saying, Out of Egypt have I called My Son."—S. Matt. ii. 14, 15.

[2] Gal. iv. 24–26. The argument of S. Paul in this passage affords a striking illustration of that characteristic of Revelation, according to which it is fully developed by means of a *succession* of repeated acts on God's part. The Law, so far from disannulling the promise to Abraham, and the covenant of circumcision made with him, was, in its day, the fulfilment of that promise, and the ratification of that covenant. In its turn the Law, in like manner, received its further completion in the Christian scheme:—the son of "the freewoman" has now become the son of "the bondmaid," through the coming of the "Jerusalem which is above." "Agar is Mount Sinai in Arabia, and *is in the same rank with* (as the margin of our version renders the original —συστοιχεῖ δέ) Jerusalem *which now is*, and is in bondage with her children; *but Jerusalem which is above is free, which is the mother of us all.*" Cf. Luger, "Die Rede des Stephanus, s. 28.

[3] 1 Cor. x. 4. [4] S. John, xii. 41. [5] Heb. ii. 13; Isai. viii. 18.

as the Christian element of the Old Testament? Nay, S. Paul teaches Timothy,[1] that by "the holy Scriptures"—that is, of the Old Testament taken in its entire extent—"is the man of God" "made wise unto Salvation through faith which is in Christ:" in other words, because Christ is their object.

The manner in which S. Paul relies upon the Old Testament is peculiarly striking. Men are almost invariably tempted, after a change of opinion, to make little of the system which they have left; nay, even to reject what truth may be in it, rather than transfer any of their former views to their new line of thought. Had S. Paul acted as men are wont to do, he must, unquestionably, have rather avoided attaching importance to, or upholding the authority of the Old Testament;—especially as his chief task was, that of opposing the introduction of Jewish practices into Christianity. We know, for example, how Marcion and his followers, from their hostility to Jewish opinions, rejected the Old Testament altogether.[2] Now, S. Paul adopts a course the very reverse of this.[3] He recognises the Old Testament as an essential component of the Faith, profitable for all times; and as containing in its doctrines, in its types, in its history, the germs of all the leading truths of Christianity. For example: Moses and the Prophets had laid down in express terms, that the true end and design of the Law was the circumcision of the heart.[4] Need one point out how forcibly S. Paul insists that "that is not circumcision, which is outward in the flesh;" and that the true circumcision is that of the heart?[5] The very sense, indeed, in which he teaches that the Law is annulled, assumes not only a continual connexion of it with the New Testament, but also the union of

[1] 2 Tim. iii. 15.

[2] "Cerdo preceded him in this, as in his tenets generally; having at an earlier period asserted this contrariety between the two Testaments. * * * It would appear that Marcion went beyond his master in this matter, since he not only maintained a contrariety between the two Testaments, but even assumed a contrariety between the Apostles in the New * * * Relying upon this contrariety, he charged a Jewish bias upon the writings of all the Apostles, with the exception of Paul, who has declared the abolition of Judaism without indulgence." Hug, *Enleitung*, 1er Th. Kap. 1, § 8. (Fosdick's transl. p. 44.)

[3] It is interesting to observe that the Apostle designates the gross immorality of Heathenism, when contrasting it with Judaism, by the term ἀνομία.—2 Cor. vi. 14; Rom. vi. 19.

[4] "Circumcise, therefore, the foreskin of your heart, and be no more stiffnecked." —Deut. x. 16. Cf. xxx. 6. Again: "Circumcise yourselves to the Lord, and take away the foreskin of your hearts, ye men of Judah, and the inhabitants of Jerusalem."—Jer. iv. 4.

[5] Rom. ii. 28, 29. Cf. Col. ii. 11; Phil. iii. 3.

both in one Divine plan. Look to the fourth chapter of the Epistle to the Romans, and the entire treatment of the subject of Faith. The Apostle shows that the object of the Divine Author of the Pentateuch was neither temporary, nor restricted to the immediate subject of its history. It was not written for Abraham's sake only that his faith was imputed to him for righteousness, but for us also.[1] When addressing the Gentile church at Corinth—a church for which the Jewish law, *as such*, could possess neither interest nor importance,—the Apostle enforces the practical lesson which he was inculcating, by assuming the Divine nature and standing authority of that Law, as opposed to anything human: "Say I these things as a man? or saith not the Law the same also?"[2] In proof of this position, he goes on to quote—as being "written in the Law of Moses"—the apparently trivial command, "Thou shalt not muzzle the mouth of the ox, that treadeth out the corn;" observing, in explanation, "for our sakes no doubt this is written:" and in the tenth chapter of the same Epistle he adds, that the history of Israel is our "example."[3] Again, in the second chapter of the Acts of the Apostles, S. Peter, and, in the thirteenth chapter, S. Paul, demonstrate to the Jews, from the pages of the Old Testament, that the "same Jesus whom they had crucified was both Lord and Christ:"[4] the former Apostle further teaching that the Spirit of Christ which was in the Prophets "testified beforehand the sufferings of Christ, and the glory that should follow;"[5] and the

[1] Rom iv. 23, 24. Cf *supra*, p. 108, n. 5.

[2] 1 Cor. ix. 8; and the Apostle proceeds: "For it is written in the Law of Moses (ἐν γὰρ τῷ Μωϋσέως νόμῳ γέγραπται), Thou shalt not muzzle the mouth of the ox that treadeth out the corn. *Doth God take care for oxen?* Or saith He it *altogether* for our sakes? For our sakes no doubt this is written."—ver 9, 10; S. Paul clearly intimating by the question, "Doth God take care for oxen?" that the Holy Spirit had from the first intended that the expression should apply to human laborers. It is worth noticing, too, in how unconnected a manner, if we take them in their bare literal sense, the original words occur in Deut. xxv. 4. This same quotation is made for a kindred purpose in 1 Tim. v. 18; where in the next verse the Apostle goes on to apply the ordinance of the Law (Deut. xvii. 6; xix. 15): "At the mouth of two witnesses, or at the mouth of three witnesses shall the matter be established;—an ordinance to which he had already referred,—2 Cor. xiii. 1; and to which our Lord Himself had on two occasions appealed,—S. Matt. xviii. 16; S. John, viii. 17.

[3] "With many of them [viz., "our fathers"] God was not well pleased: for they were overthrown in the wilderness. Now these things were our examples (τύποι)."—1 Cor. x. 5, 6.

[4] "Therefore let all the house of Israel know assuredly, that God hath made that same Jesus, whom ve have crucified, both Lord and Christ."—Acts, ii. 36.

[5] 1 Peter, i. 11

latter reminding the church of Corinth how, from the first, he had taught them that Christ had died, was buried, and rose again "the third day, according to the Scriptures."[1] And this same doctrine, expressing as it does the complete harmony of the two great divisions of the Bible, S. Paul again proclaims, if possible, more clearly, before King Agrippa: "I continue unto this day, witnessing both to small and great; saying none other things than those which the Prophets and Moses did say should come."[2]

In short, the words and the Spirit of Christ alike guided the Apostles to combine their teaching and their acts, their faith and their hopes, with the substance and language of the Old Testament. Hence it is that, in presence of the Christian Church, they insist not only upon the preparatory relation of the former Scriptures to Christ, but also upon their permanent authority as a Divine source of life.[3] Their type of Truth is declared to preform in itself the image of the future destinies of the world to the final consummation:—"The heaven," said S. Peter, "must receive Jesus Christ until the times of restitution of all things which God hath spoken by the mouth of all His holy prophets since the world began."[4] The centuries, therefore, which are still future, and the hidden germs of whose development the Old Testament bears within it, will successively unfold its exposition and fulfilment, just as the Old Testament itself, during the centuries which are now past, had beforehand indicated and prepared for the arrival of the Lord. In a word, we find Christ Himself addressing His disciples in the language of the Theocracy, even when He refers to the consummation of the Christian scheme. Then, he tells them, they also "shall sit upon twelve thrones, judging the twelve tribes of Israel."[5] He employs the phraseology of the Old Testament when He speaks of His own return and its signs.[6] He applies the predictions of Joel and of Daniel, and adds nothing to what those prophets had announced

[1] 1 Cor. xv. 3, 4.

[2] Acts, xxvi. 22. Cf. xxviii. 23.

[3] To the *μόρφωσις τῆς γνώσεως καὶ τῆς ἀληθείας* in the Old Testament (Rom. ii. 20) corresponds in Christianity the *πλήρωσις*. While the *νόμος τῶν ἐντολῶν*, so far as it was contained *ἐν δόγμασιν* was abolished by Christ (Eph. ii. 15; cf. Col. ii. 14) the substance of the Law, its *δικαίωμα*—as the *ἐντολαί* prove it to be—remains and receives its full accomplishment. See Rom. iii. 31; viii. 4. Cf. Beck, "Propäd. Entwickl.," s. 247.

[4] Acts, iii. 21.

[5] S. Matt. xix. 28.

[6] S. Matt. xxiv.; S. Mark, xiii.; S. Luke, xxi.

beyond what was disclosed by His personal humiliation.[1] The Apostles, too, when they describe the features of their Master's life, simply present them as the accomplishment of what had "been written aforetime :" so that the whole record of Prophecy revives, as it were, in their testimony, standing there in its full brilliancy, as Moses and Elias near Christ upon the Mount of Transfiguration.[2] Even S. John, in after times, when he beheld the felicity of the Saints in Glory, and was permitted to hear the voice of praise and thanksgiving with which the courts of heaven resound, records how both Old and New Testament furnish, even there, the language of adoration. He tells us how those "who have gotten the victory, and who have the harps of God," still sing "the song of Moses the servant of God, and the song of the Lamb."[3] In fine, in the historical, the didactic, the prophetical portions of the New Testament alike, we discern the Old Testament, "the old Law, living again," as it has been finely remarked, "in a new and spiritual life ; not embalmed and laid with reverential care aside in the grave, but arisen from the dead and alive for evermore, like its own Divine Founder."[4]

The passages of Scripture, which have been reviewed in the remarks just made, not only enable us to refute those systems which reject or disparage one portion of the inspired writings, but also supply an argument bearing with great force upon our more immediate subject. The summary, which has been given, pre-

[1] See Hofmann, "Weissagung und Erfüllung," s. 59.

[2] "Inde apparent Moyses et Elias, hoc est, Lex et Prophetia cum Verbo; neque enim Lex potest esse sine Verbo: neque propheta, nisi qui de Dei Filio prophetarit. Et illi quidem filii tonitrui corporali gloria Moysen quoque et Eliam speculati sunt: sed etiam nos quotidie videmus Moysen cum Dei Filio; videmus enim Legem in Evangelio cum legimus: 'Diliges Dominum Deum tuum.' Videmus Eliam cum Dei Verbo, cum legimus: 'Ecce Virgo, in utero accipiet.' "—S. Ambros., *Exposit. Evang. sec. Luc.* lib. VII. t. i. p. 1413.

[3] Rev. xv. 3. Compare this verse with the allusion in Isai. xii. 1, 2, to Exod. xv. 1, &c. Olshausen, having observed that Heb. iv. shows how the Jews must have understood the spiritual import of the departure from Egypt, and the entrance under Joshua into the promised land, proceeds to say :—"In accordance with this conception, the miraculous passage through the Red Sea, was the miraculous aid whereby the Lord perfects the deliverance from the power of the evil one; and the song of Moses which was based upon that event becomes the triumphal song of the Elect. * * * If the Law has led on the way to the land of rest, as far as Jordan, so the heavenly Joshua has guided with strong hand, through its waves, into the fatherland. Not otherwise are all of mankind, who have been ordained to life, guided, like Israel, through the wilderness, after they have been drawn out of darkness, in order to enter once for all into the eternal land of peace, and to sing the song of Moses and of the Lamb, when the land of darkness lies behind."—*Ein Wort.*, &c., s. 52, *u.* s. 95.

[4] Williams on the Apocalypse, Preface, p. vi. For some further remarks on the use of the Old Testament in the New, see *infra*, Lecture vii.

sents in a tangible shape, one of the strongest proofs of the continuous exercise of the Divine influence, throughout every page of the Bible. It exhibits, as a matter of fact, the unity of design which pervades writings of such various forms, and such diversified contents : writings, too, which were not the product of a single age, or of one particular stage of human civilization, but whose authors are scattered over more than twenty centuries. So intimate, indeed, is the connexion which subsists between the Old and New Testament, in language, in thought, and in the mutual relation of means and end, that we can regard their several books no otherwise than as the different members of one organized whole ; each member fulfilling its own proper function, and, by its perfect adaptation to the great purpose, which all the parts alike subserve, pointing to One Divine Author.

This same conclusion presents itself no less forcibly if we turn our view to the supernatural means employed under both dispensations. The analogy, which has subsisted from the first between the different phases of the Divine operations, is as striking as it is perfect. "The divers manners" in which God had of old time spoken by the prophets, are repeated, in strictly identical forms, in the case of those servants of God, of whose acts the New Testament gives the history. In both narratives the Divine suggestions are represented as having been conveyed by the same channels :—Angelic appearances, Dreams, Visions, Ecstacy, Voices from heaven,[1] Symbolic acts. The angel Gabriel informs Daniel when "Messiah the Prince" should come ; the same celestial messenger announces to the blessed Virgin the Incarnation of Christ.[2] The dreams by which warnings were conveyed, and commands issued to Joseph, as related in the opening chapters of S. Matthew's Gospel, in no respect differ from the dreams of

[1] E. g. we read that, at S. Paul's conversion, "there shined round about him a light from heaven: and he fell to the earth, *and heard a voice* saying unto him, Saul, Saul, why persecutest thou Me?"—Acts, ix. 3, 4; just as we read that when the Prophet of God had heard the "still small voice," "he wrapped his face in his mantle, and went out, and stood in the entering in of the cave. And behold *there came a voice* unto him and said, What doest thou here, Elijah?"—1 Kings, xix. 12, 13. As a further example of these analogies between the Old and New Testaments, we may add the election of Matthias by lot (Acts, i), as being parallel to the singling out of Achan (Josh. vii.); of Jonathan (1 Sam. xiv. 41); of Jonah (ch. i. 7): the principle of such acts being stated in the words: "The lot is cast into the lap, but the whole disposing thereof is of the Lord."—Prov. xvi. 33.

[2] Dan. ix. 21–25; S. Luke, i. 26.

the Patriarchs.[1] The visions recorded by S. Luke in the Acts of the Apostles, are but a repetition of those seen by men of God in other days.[2] The trance of S. Peter, mentioned in the tenth chapter of the Acts, and that of S. Paul, of which he speaks in the twelfth chapter of the Second Epistle to the Corinthians, resemble in every particular the states of prophetic rapture. We read, moreover, that revelations were constantly conveyed to men, under the Old Testament, by means of symbolical actions;—the writings of Jeremiah or Ezekiel will supply abundant illustrations.[3] This fact presents itself no less prominently in the New Testament. Agabus[4] makes use of a symbolical act, when predicting S. Paul's approaching captivity: and Christ Himself adopted symbolical language when alluding to the manner of S. Peter's death;[5]—this latter instance being, in strict conformity with similar prophetic intimations, both brief and obscure.

[1] Neander, alluding to this portion of the evangelical history, makes the strange remark: "We need be the less afraid of a free, unliteral interpretation, when we find a difference *in the subjective conception* of these events by even the Evangelists themselves, Matthew speaking *only* of dreams and visions, and Luke of objective phenomena, viz. the appearance of angels."—*The Life of Jesus Christ*, § 14. (Bohn's Transl., p. 21.) Mr. Westcott, in reply to this attempt to exhibit the statements of the Gospels as a result of the "subjective" influence of each writer's mind, observes:—"But surely those are right who see in this difference an adaptation to the peculiar state of the recipient,"—(*Elements of the Gospel Harmony*, p. 77),—meaning, I presume, that an announcement by a dream was the form of Revelation best suited to the apprehension of Joseph; while the appearance of an angel was adapted to the more spiritual mind of Mary. This may be so,—if we merely regard the *manner* of the Divine communication. But the natural remark, that each Evangelist wrote as he has written, simply because he was narrating *facts*, affords the direct answer: and Mr. Westcott completely overturns the notion that S. Matthew, in consequence of his "subjective" views, refrains from allusion to angelic appearances—by referring to this Evangelist's description of the angel of the Lord, who appeared at the Sepulchre (S. Matt. xxviii. 2–7); while the visions recorded in the Acts of the Apostles prove that no "subjective" prejudice in favor of "objective phenomena" induced S. Luke to write only of angels. See Acts, xvi. 9; xviii. 9, 10. Cf. ch. xxvii. 23.

[2] See last note. Compare for example, the statement: "Then spake the Lord to Paul in the night by a vision," &c. (Acts, xviii. 9);—with the language of the Old Testament: "It came to pass that night that the word of the Lord came unto Nathan * * * and according to all this vision so did Nathan speak unto David."—2 Sam. vii. 4, 17.

[3] E. g. "Thus saith the Lord unto me, Make thee bonds and yokes, and put them upon thy neck."—Jer. xxvii. 2. Again: "Thou also, son of man, take thee a tile, and lay it before thee, and pourtray upon it the city, even Jerusalem."—Ezek. iv. 1.

[4] "And when he was come unto us, he took Paul's girdle, and bound his own hands and feet, and said, Thus saith the Holy Ghost, So shall the Jews at Jerusalem bind the man," &c.—Acts, xxi. 11.

[5] "Verily, verily, I say unto thee, when thou wast young, thou girdedst thyself, and walkedst whither thou wouldest: but when thou shalt be old thou shalt stretch forth thy hands and another shall gird thee," &c.—S. John, xxi. 18. Cf. Olshausen *in loc.*, who quotes: "Tunc Petrus ab altero cingitur, quum cruci adstringitur."—Tertullian. *Scorpiace*, § 15, p. 633. "It is worthy of notice that Jesus is represented as veiling the great mystery of His death under symbolic language, both in S. John and

In the structure, too, of both divisions of the Bible, we notice the same resemblance. The history of events occupies a considerable portion of each. Without such details, their other portions would be unintelligible; and accordingly, both Testaments combine the history and the doctrines of religion. As a single instance of didactic teaching in the New Testament, we may adduce the Epistle of S. James; who, after the manner of the ancient Prophets, raises his voice against the rich, and whose words, in their Hebrew form, bear all the stamp of Old Testament Prophecy.[1] Again, the hymns of Mary and Zacharias, in the opening of S. Luke's Gospel, present a perfect sample of the Hebrew type of the Psalms.[2] Many other analogies, similar to those just pointed out, will meet us in the course of this inquiry: it must suffice, for the present, to allude to one other of much interest;—I mean the echo of the last tones of Old Testament prophecy in the Revela-

in the Synoptists. Cf. John, iii. 14; Matt. xii. 40; John, ii. 22; Luke, xiii. 32. For a still earlier revelation of the same truth, cf. John, i. 29; Luke, ii. 35."—Westcott, *Elem. of Gosp. Harm.*, p. 60.

[1] "The Christian Jeremiah."—Wordsworth, *On the Canon*, p. 257.

[2] "The hymns of Mary and Zacharias perfectly represent the Old Hebrew type of the Psalms, and may be restored word for word, into pure Hebrew."—Thiersch *Versuch zur Herstell. für die Krit. der N. T. Schriften*, s. 48. The hymn of the Blessed Virgin (S. Luke, i. 46, &c.) may be regarded as the closing Psalm of the Old Testament—"Dieser Lobgesang ist ja eigentlich der Schlusspsalm des alten Testamentes." —Ebrard, *Kritik der Evang. Gesch.*, s. 221. It may not be amiss to observe, that the nature of these hymns affords a powerful argument against the mythic theory of Strauss. The hope of the *coming* Messiah is here depicted, colored with all the hues of Hebrew nationality. The strain of sentiment is purely Israelitic throughout: e. g. the raising up "the horn of salvation" in the house of David; the fulfilment of the promise to Abraham, &c.—S. Luke, i. 68–79: while the blessing of salvation through the remission of sins—"which the song of Simeon expands further to a light to lighten the Gentiles, as well as the peculiar glory of God's ancient people, is spoken of as one yet to be revealed." These hymns, in short, "differ in no other respect from the ordinary tenor of the Psalms, and other ancient predictions of the same mercies, than in the announcement of their *time* as now at length close at hand; and the designation of the *instruments* of their approaching but yet unreached fulfilment, as now actually present. Could this have been the case, if they were written in the times of Christianity? * * * They who saw in the Incarnate Godhead, vanquishing death by death * * * a reign more glorious and more secure than any earthly image whatever could adequately reach,—could they have failed to exhibit some *explicit* statement of this, bursting through the more sensible imagery with which it is encompassed, *as we see continually in the visions of the Apocalypse* [e. g. ch. v. 5–14] * * * Such a vision of coming power, and light, and majesty, as these hymns indicate, * * * could belong only to the particular position assigned to it in the boundary of the old and new covenants. The projection of a vision like this from the point of view under the New Testament, is what cannot in sound reason or just criticism be maintained: with the possession of such explicit knowledge as even Christ's earthly life supplied,—but still more His death, and the events that followed,—such reserve, united to such imagined anticipation, were to an earnest mind, unnatural, to a deceitful mind, impossible."—W. H. Mill, *The Christian Advocate's Publication for* 1841, p. 44–51.

tion of S. John. It does not arise from accidental coincidence, or mere subjective peculiarities, that S. John follows so nearly the closing prophets of the Old Testament,—Ezekiel, Daniel, Zechariah;[1] it rather springs from the serial character of Scripture in general, and of the prophets in particular. As the Bible is no fortuitous assemblage of writings, but one organic whole, S. John had the double end in view of connecting what he wrote with the preceding books of the New Testament, and with the last predictions of the Old, whose authors he, in a certain sense, immediately follows, as the writer of the only prophetical *book* of the New Testament.[2] One feature of this analogy may be mentioned. The Apocalypse opens with the words: "The revelation of Jesus Christ, which God gave Him, and He signified it by His angel to His servant John;" and again, in its closing chapter,[3] Christ reveals the knowledge of the future by the mediation of His angel. Here then we find that, together with the Divine Revealer—the Eternal Word—an angel is placed in a subordinate relation to Him, as His ministering attendant. So also, in those prophetical books with which the Apocalypse has the closest affinity, a particular angel is brought into notice, who in like manner stands beside the Eternal Son as the mediating agent of His revelations.[4] Thus Daniel writes:—"And I heard a man's voice between the banks of Ulai, which called and said, Gabriel, make this man to understand the vision."[5]

[1] To take a few out of many examples: "Behold He cometh with clouds; and every eye shall see Him, and they also which pierced Him, and all kindreds of the earth shall wail because of Him."—Rev. i. 7. This passage, while it is a reflexion of Christ's words, S. Matt. xxiv. 30, literally repeats the language of the prophets:—of Daniel, who speaks of the Son of Man coming in the clouds of heaven (ch. vii. 13); and of Zechariah, who writes: "They shall look upon Me whom they have pierced, and they shall mourn for Him."—xii. 10. Again, S. John, in his Gospel, had merely pointed to his own name by implication, but here he states it: at ver. 9, we read "I John;"—a phrase which follows the style of Daniel, who alone of the prophets says "I Daniel" (vii. 28; viii. 1; ix. 2; x. 2): "We find the same difference in the Old Testament also, between the historical and the prophetical writings of the prophets. The *history* had its security in the joint knowledge of contemporaries; but in *Prophecy* personality is of the greatest moment, and the anonymous is excluded. Nameless prophecies have no place in Old Testament Scripture."—Henstenberg, *The Revelation of S. John*, (Clarke's For. Theol. Lib., i. p. 52.) The doubts which have been insinuated against this portion of the New Testament add great importance to this remark. Compare, also, Zech. iv. 2, with Rev. i. 12; and Ezek. ii. 9; iii. 1–3, with the language of Rev. x.

[2] Hengstenberg on Rev. i. 9, *ibid.* p. 85.

[3] "The angel which showed me these things."—Rev. xxii. 8.

[4] Cf. Hengstenberg, *ibid.* p. 50.

[5] Dan. viii. 16. Again: "The man Gabriel whom I had seen in the vision at the beginning, being caused to fly swiftly, touched me * * * and said, O Daniel, I

This latter remark leads directly to the chief bond of union between the two parts of the inspired record. It has been shown in the first of these Discourses, that one of the two conditions which must be satisfied by any solution of the problem now under consideration, is imposed by the essential distinction which subsists between Revelation and Inspiration.[1] According to that distinction, while Scripture is, throughout all its parts, *inspired*, it cannot be said that all its contents are *revelations*. This principle, which is suggested by the mere inspection of the contents of the sacred volume, is connected with a fact already adverted to, and of which some proof must now be given; namely, that while Inspiration (as the signification of the term denotes) is the peculiar function of the Holy Ghost,—so, in like manner, to reveal is the office appropriated to the Eternal Word.[2] In the New Testament this fact is obvious. In its pages we see the Divine Logos,—the Eternal Word Himself Incarnate—no longer by His mediating angel, but in His own Person leading to their completion, the disclosures of the Divine will which had been given through "all His holy prophets since the world began." In the Gospel history, we see the Son of God combining in His own Person the two great phases of all *immediate* Revelation; unfolding, that is, the mystery of the Divine counsels by His words; displaying the wonders of Divine power by His acts.[3] In days of old the Creator of the physical world—for God has "created all things by Jesus Christ,"[4]—He is here manifested as the restorer of the moral world, as the author of "a New Creation."[5] The scheme of Revelation was not, indeed, completed by Himself while on earth. "I have yet many things to say unto you,"[6] was His statement to His disciples on the eve of His

am now come forth to give thee skill and understanding."—ix. 21, 22. So also Zechariah writes: "And the Lord answered the angel that talked with me with good words. * * * So the angel that communed with me said unto me, Cry thou saying, Thus saith the Lord of Hosts, I am jealous," &c.—Zech. i. 13, 14.

[1] Lecture i. p. 40.

[2] "Non enim aliter nos discere poteramus quæ sunt Dei, nisi Magister noster, Verbum existens, homo factus fuisset. Neque enim alius poterat enarrare nobis quæ sunt Patris, nisi proprium ipsius Verbum. *Quis enim* alius *cognovit sensum Domini? aut quis* alius *ejus consiliarius factus est?*"—S. Irenæus, *Cont. Hær.*, lib. v. i. 1, p. 292.

[3] See Lecture i. p. 24.

[4] Eph. iii. 9.

[5] Ὥστε εἴ τις ἐν Χριστῷ, καινὴ κτίσις.—2 Cor. v. 17. "For in Christ Jesus neither circumcision availeth anything, nor uncircumcision, but *a new creation* (καινὴ κτίσις).—Gal. vi. 15. Cf. the remarkable words—"And He that sat upon the throne said—Behold, I make *all things new* (καινὰ ποιῶ πάντα)."—Rev. xxi. 5.

[6] S. John, xvi. 12.

departure from them; and although He may have disclosed many of such things during the "forty days" of His appearance "after His Passion," when He spake to them "of the things pertaining to the kingdom of God,"[1] yet we know that, even after Pentecost, new revelations were needed by them, and that new revelations were given.

But whence did these proceed, and by what channels were they conveyed? He Himself has told us how this was to be. "When He, the Spirit of truth is come, He will guide you into all truth: for He shall not speak of Himself; but whatsoever He shall hear, that shall He speak; and He will show you things to come. He shall glorify Me; for *He shall receive of Mine*, and shall show it unto you."[2] These words place it beyond question, that the entire scheme of the new dispensation (not only that portion of it unfolded by Himself while on earth, but also what was revealed to the Apostles after His Ascension), proceeded *directly* from the Eternal Son; while the Divine Being under whose influence the Apostles were enabled to apprehend such mysteries, and who shielded them from all error,—who taught them "all things," and who brought "all things to their remembrance,"—who gave them, in fine, "a mouth and wisdom which all their adversaries could neither gainsay nor resist"[3]—was the Spirit of Truth, the Holy Ghost, the source of Inspiration. This very principle, indeed, that from the revelations of the Eternal Son alone, can man attain to any knowledge of God, His nature, or His counsels, is expressly defined in the passage which I have chosen as the text of this Discourse: "No man knoweth who the Son is, but the Father; and who the Father is, but the Son, and he to whom the Son wills to reveal Him."[4] Thus it is, that S. Paul, when referring to the source of his knowledge of Christian truth, writes so explicitly—"I neither received it of man,

[1] Acts, i. 3.
[2] S. John, xvi. 13, 14.
[3] S. John, xiv. 26. S. Luke, xxi. 15.
[4] *ᾧ ἂν βούληται ὁ Υἱὸς ἀποκαλύψαι.* Baumgarten Crusius attempts to maintain, without adducing a particle of proof, that in the preceding verse, and in the parallel passage, S. Matt. xi. 25, the word *ἀπεκάλυψας*, in the sentence, "Thou hast hid these things from the wise and prudent, and *hast revealed* them unto babes (*νηπίοις*)," merely signifies, "hast made it possible for them to understand;"—thus losing the entire force of the idea "to reveal." In a note, however, this writer qualifies his assertion, and considers that the sense which he assigns to *ἀπεκάλυψας* may lie in the word *νηπίοις* ("ad intelligentiam eorum"), and *ἀποκαλύπτειν* still retain its proper signification: "Cause it to be known through Me," i. e. Christ.—*Grundzüge der Bibl. Theologie*, s. 223.

neither was I taught it, but by the revelation of Jesus Christ;"[1] while he further informs us of the channel of conveyance,—" God hath revealed them unto us by His Spirit."[2] In fine, the first words of the Apocalypse announce that the Book is " the *revelation* of Jesus Christ:" and S. Peter teaches, generally, respecting the Prophets of the Old Testament, that it was " the Spirit of Christ, which was in them."[3]

But do the statements of the Old Testament itself correspond to these intimations of the New? While proceeding to seek for the evidence which is there supplied, let us reflect for a moment on the idea of the Divine Word, as Creator of all things. The original *act* of Creation is the foundation of all exhibitions of supernatural power, whether by *word* or by *act*:—whether they be, in short, Revelations, properly so called, or Miracles.[4] Could we conceive this world of ours to have existed from eternity, the subject of fixed determinate laws, then, indeed, the introduction among the phenomena which surround us, of any power which does not follow the course of nature, must positively disturb and disorganize the adjustments of the universe. But seeing that all

[1] *Δι' ἀποκαλύψεως Ἰησοῦ Χριστοῦ.*—Gal. i. 12.

[2] *Ἡμῖν δὲ ἀπεκάλυψεν ὁ Θεὸς δ ι ὰ τ ο ῦ Π ν ε ύ μ α τ ο ς.*—1 Cor. ii. 10.

[3] "Of which salvation the prophets have inquired * * * who prophesied of the grace that should come unto you: searching what or what manner of time the Spirit of Christ which was in them (*τὸ ἐν αὐτοῖς Πνεῦμα Χριστοῦ*) did signify, when it testified beforehand," &c.—1 Pet. i. 10, 11. These intimations of Scripture have been accurately interpreted by the Fathers. See the passages quoted, Lecture ii. p. 83. To which may be added the express language of two disciples of the Apostles,—S. Clement of Rome, and S. Ignatius. S. Clement, referring to Psalm xxxiv. 11–17, writes as follows: *ταῦτα δὲ πάντα βεβαιοῖ ἡ ἐν Χριστῷ πίστις· κ α ὶ γ ὰ ρ Α ὐ τ ὸ ς διὰ τοῦ Πνεύματος τοῦ Ἁγίου οὕτως προσκαλεῖται ἡμᾶς· Δεῦτε, τέκνα, κ. τ. λ.*—*Ad Corinth.* xxii. And S. Ignatius observes: *πῶς ἡμεῖς δυνησόμεθα ζῆσαι χωρὶς Αὐτοῦ* [*scil.* *Ἰησοῦ Χριστοῦ*], *οὗ καὶ οἱ προφῆται μαθηταὶ ὄντες τῷ Πνεύματι ὡς διδάσκαλον Αὐτὸν προσεδόκουν.*—*Ad Magnes.* ix.

[4] In the case of the physical world, as Twesten justly observes, there have been certain epochs in which plants, and animals, and man, have for the first time appeared; and it is capable of demonstration that, up to a certain point of time, none of these existences had as yet made their appearance. If we cannot avoid acknowledging here, that certain forces were exercised at such epochs, why not acknowledge the same in the realm of history? Jean Paul writes: "Wenigstens zwei Wunder oder Offenbarungen bleiben euch unbestritten, nämlich die Geburt der Endlichkeit, und die Geburt des Lebens, mitten ins dürre Holz der Materie hinein."—*Levana*, Th. 1, s. 126. Religion, continues Twesten, "represents itself to our inward experience as a *power* to make happy, as a *principle* of new operations,—nay, of a transformation of the whole thought and will; as a new *power of life*, elevated above that to which we formerly belonged, as high as human life is raised above the animal, or the physical power of life above the merely mechanical and chemical processes of inanimate nature. Therefore we can regard the origin of Christianity [qu. Revelation] in no other light than the origin of vegetable or animal life,—of the instincts of brutes, or the consciousness of man; in short, as a New Creation."—*Vorlesungen*, 1er Band, s. 352, ff.

around us has been called into being at the fiat of Omnipotence, each manifestation of supernatural agency, is but a re-appearance of the original Creative Power[1] penetrating the veil of nature, determining anew, and giving a new direction to the course of this world's history. The immediate intervention of God in such cases, is not to be referred merely to His general activity in Nature, but must rather be regarded as a concentration, as it were, of that activity in certain definite *acts*, or in certain definite *organs* which represent the spirit and power of the universal Revelation. This concentration, again, can come to pass only through the creative and revealing Presence of that Divine Being, who, having ordained the laws of Nature, and provided for their permanence by His unceasing energy, nevertheless at times further unveils His character and His will in new and special revelations.[2] The Old Testament, in remarkable language, intimates that the special miracles of Revelation have ever proceeded from such renewed activity of the Creative[3] Power; while it describes those miracles as being themselves *new centres*, as it were, of Creation, from which new epochs date, and which manifest, once more, as on the first day, the glory of Jehovah.[4] The sacred

[1] "When mankind," writes Bishop Butler, "was first placed in this state, there was *a power exerted*, totally different from the present course of nature. Now whether *this power* stopped immediately after it had made man, or *went on and exerted itself farther in giving him a revelation*, is a question," &c., &c.—*Analogy*, part ii. ch. 2.

[2] "Miracles and Prophecy are, properly speaking, nothing more than particularly energetic displays of the 'demonstration of the Spirit and of power' (*ἀποδείξεως πνεύματος καὶ δυνάμεως* 1 Cor. ii. 4); and accordingly only different modes of operation of one and the same Cause. What the Miracle is in the department of action, Prophecy is in the department of knowledge (*miraculum potentiæ. scientiæ*)"—Beck, *Propäd. Entwicklung*, s. 178. Hence the scriptural titles of such exhibitions of the Divine energy, *δυνάμεις, τέρατα, σημεῖα*. Cf. Acts, ii. 22; 2 Cor. xii. 12. "*Δύναμις* expresses rather the objective idea of miracle; *τέρας*, the subjective; *σημεῖον* the visible sign of the spiritual fact of God's kingdom."—Nitzsch, *Syst. der Christl. Lehre*, § 34. (Montgomery's transl., p. 84.) Sack truly observes: "Die Offenbarung ist nicht Natur im empirisch-kosmischen Sinne, sie tritt zwar in die Natur hinein, aber sie ist wesentlich über der Natur, oder übernatürlich, da sie die Selbstdarstellung des Schöpfers und Herrn der Natur ist."—*Apologetik*, s. 121. And he quotes the apposite remark of Dr. Julius Müller: "Ut miraculum non possit non obscurum esse a parte legis naturalis, tamen apertum est a parte superioris ordinis."—*Ibid.* s. 138.

[3] Mr. Rogers, in his Essay, "Reason and Faith," observes that the time "is coming when even those who shall object to the *evidence* which sustains the Christian miracles will acknowledge that philosophy *requires* them to admit that men have no ground whatever to dogmatise on the antecedent impossibility of miracles in general * * * not only because the geologist will have familiarized the world with the idea of successive interventions, and, *in fact, distinct creative acts, having all the nature of miracles*," &c.—p. 43.

[4] For example: "Because all those men which have seen My glory, and My miracles which I did in Egypt and in the wilderness," &c.—Numb. xiv. 22. Again.

writers represent God as concentrating His "great and unsearchable" doings,[1] in single, visible acts of *Creation*, whereby elements absolutely new are introduced into the usual series of events. For example, Moses thus announces the Divine punishment inflicted for the rebellion of Korah: "But if the Lord *make a new thing* (the margin of our version renders the original literally, "create a creature,")[2] and the earth open her mouth, and they go down quick (or still living) into the pit, then ye shall understand that these men have provoked the Lord." In the same manner Jeremiah announces the grand miracle of the Incarnation: "The Lord hath *created a new thing*[3] in the earth." And—to quote a passage which expands the idea implied by the texts just adduced—the Lord of Hosts is described by Isaiah as upbraiding the house of Jacob for its "obstinacy:" "I have even from the beginning declared it to thee, before it came to pass I showed it thee. * * * I have showed thee *new things* from this time, even hidden things, and thou didst not know them. They are *created* now, and not from the beginning * * * lest thou shouldest say, Behold I knew them."[4]

But the Old Testament does not confine itself to this representation of the fact, that the revelations which it contains are but new instances of Creative Power, thereby leading us back to

"This beginning of miracles did Jesus in Cana of Galilee, and manifested forth His glory."—S. John, ii. 11. Cf. ix. 3–5; xi. 40.

[1] "Which doeth great things, and unsearchable; marvellous things without number."—Job, v. 9. For this conception of the question I am largely indebted to the profound remarks of Beck, *loc cit.* s. 186 ff.

[2] בריאה יברא.—Numb. xvi. 30. To take another example from the Pentateuch:—"Behold I make a covenant: before all thy people will I do marvels, such as *have not been done* [i. e. *created*, אשר לא־נבראו] in all the earth."—Exod. xxxiv. 10. Gesenius thus explains the term rendered "marvels," נפלאות: "*Mirabiliter facta, miracula* Dei, tum in mundo creando et sustentando (Ps. ix. 2; xxvi. 7; xl. 6), tum in populo suo juvando patrata (Ex. xxxiv. 10; Jos. iii. 5)."

[3] ברא יהוה חדשה.—Jer. xxxi. 22.

[4] Isai. xlviii. 5–7. "New things," חדשות; "they are created," נבראו.

Cf. also the following texts: "Behold the former things are come to pass, and *new things* (חדשות) do I declare," Isai. xlii. 9); "Remember ye not the former things, neither consider the things of old. Behold I will do *a new thing* * * * I will even make a way in the wilderness, and rivers in the desert" (xliii. 18, 19). Cf. Isai. iv. 5; xli. 20; xlv. 8. That the ideas expressed by the terms ברא and חדש are considered by the sacred writers strictly cognate, will appear from the following passages: "So is this great and wide sea wherein are things creeping innumerable, both small and great beasts. * * * Thou sendest forth Thy Spirit, they are *created* (יבראון): and thou *renewest* (ותחדש) the face of the earth."—Ps. civ. 30. "*Create* (ברא) in me a clean heart, O God; and *renew* (חדש) a right spirit within me."—Ps. li. 10. "Behold I *create new* heavens (בורא שמים חדשים], and a new earth."—Isai. lxv. 17; cf. lxvi. 22.

the Author of all creation—the Eternal Son ;[1] it presents Him directly to our view, as unfolding in Person the Divine counsels, under the mysterious character of the ANGEL OF JEHOVAH. To this title,—employed for the first time to describe His appearance in the age of Abraham, laying the foundation, as it were, of all future revelations to the chosen race,—some attention must be devoted.

The passages of the Old Testament which refer to this aspect of Revelation may be reduced to three heads.[2] In the first place, the Angel of Jehovah, by the use of the first person singular, identifies Himself with the Divine Nature. Thus, "The Angel of the Lord[3] said unto Hagar, I will multiply thy seed exceedingly ;" and in a subsequent verse we read, that "She called the name of JEHOVAH that spake unto her, Thou God seest me." Secondly, reference is made to the Angel, so as to prevent our understanding any other than a Being essentially Divine. For example, Jacob says, "God, before whom my fathers Abraham and Isaac did walk, the God which fed me all my life long unto this day, the ANGEL which redeemed me from

[1] Bishop Bull writes : "Esto igitur, inquies, fuerit Deus, qui in veteri Testamento, sive per Angelum, sive sub Angelica repræsentatione sanctis viris apparuit, et locutus est ; at qua demum ratione adducti crediderunt Doctores, fuisse Dei Filium ? Respondeo : Ratione, ni fallor, optima, quam ex traditione Apostolica edidicerant. Scilicet Deus Pater, quemadmodum per Filium Suum mundum primitus condidit creavitque ; ita per eundem Filium Se deinceps mundo patefecit."—*Defensio Fid. Nicenæ*, sect. I. ch. i. § 12, p. 11. ed. 1721.

[2] This classification of the passages in question, I borrow from Sack, "Apologetik," s. 170 ff.

[3] מלאך יהוה.—Gen. xvi. 9–11. Again we read: "And the Angel of the Lord (מלאך י״י) called unto him out of heaven and said, Abraham, Abraham ; and he said, Here am I. And He said, Lay not thine hand upon the lad * * * for now I know that thou fearest God (אלהים), seeing thou hast not withheld thy son, thine only son from ME" (לא חשכת ממני).—Gen. xxii. 11, 12. So also Exod. iii. 2 : "The Angel of the Lord (מלאך י״י) appeared unto" Moses "in a flame of fire out of the midst of a bush ;" * * * "And when the Lord (יהוה) saw that he turned aside to see, God (אלהים) called unto him out of the midst of the bush" (ver. 4) * * * "Moreover He said, I am the God of thy father, the God of Abraham, the God of Isaac, and the God of Jacob. And Moses hid his face ; for he was afraid to look upon God (האלהים־אל). And the Lord (יהוה) said" &c. (ver. 6, 7). Bishop Bull observes : "Cum Patres *communiter asserunt*, Angelum, qui Abrahamo et Mosi apparuit, cuique nomen Jehovæ, et divini honores tribuuntur, fuisse Dei Filium, duplicem id sensum admittit : nempe, vel fuisse Deum, i. e. Filium Dei, nomine Angeli significatum, quia Ipse corpus assumserit, sive speciem visibilem, qualem Angeli usurpare solent ; vel Filium Dei fuisse in Angelo, hoc est, Angelum fuisse, qui corpus assumsit, et Filium Dei fuisse in Angelo, per assistentiam nempe et præsentiam singularem."—*Def. Fid. Nic.*, Sect. I. ch. i. § 11, p. 10. Bishop Bull considers the latter of these senses to be that which the Ancients approved. E. g. he quotes the words of S. Athanasius on Exod. iii. 2–6 (Cont Arian. Orat. iii. § 14, t. i. p. 563) : "What was seen was an Angel ; but God spoke in him ;" and he refers, in confirmation of this view, to Exod. xxiii. 20, "My NAME is in Him,"—words which will be considered under the third head.

all evil, bless the lads;'[1]—where the identification of the Angel with Him from whom alone all blessing flows, and who redeems from evil, cannot be doubted. Thirdly, a certain distinction is made between the Angel of Jehovah and Jehovah Himself; but in such a manner as to represent that the essence of Deity had become *manifest* and *operative* in the former. Thus Jehovah says: "Behold I send an ANGEL before thee to keep thee in the way. * * * Beware of Him, and obey His voice; provoke Him not; for He will not pardon your transgressions: for My NAME is in Him;"[2]—where, even without dwelling upon the signification of the phrase "the Name of Jehovah," we can only understand such words as describing a distinct, Divine Personality.[3]

An expression in the Epistle to the Hebrews, casts further light on the class of texts which have been just considered. The sacred writer observes: "Wherefore, holy brethren, partakers of

[1] Gen. xlviii. 15, 16. S. Athanasius writes: "None of created and natural angels did he join to God their Creator, nor rejecting God that fed him did he from angel ask the blessing on his grandsons; but in saying 'Who delivered me from all evil' [המלאך הגאל מכל־רע] he showed that it was no created angel, but the WORD OF GOD, whom he joined to the Father in his prayer, through Whom, whomsoever He will, God doth deliver. For knowing that He is also called the Father's 'Angel of great counsel' [Isai. ix. 6, *μεγάλης βουλῆς* Ἄγγελος, LXX.], he said that none other than He was the Giver of blessing, and Deliverer from evil. Nor was it that he desired a blessing for himself from God, but for his grandchildren from the Angel, but Whom he himself had besought saying, 'I will not let Thee go except Thou bless me,' (for that was God, as he says himself, 'I have seen God face to face,' [Gen. xxxii. 26, 30])—Him he prayed to bless also the sons of Joseph."—*Cont. Arian.* Orat. iii. § 12. t. i. p. 561. (Oxf. Transl. p. 418.)

[2] Exod. xxiii. 20, 21. Hence Sack concludes "that מלאך י״י is to be translated not "an Angel of Jehovah," but "the Angel of Jehovah,"—or the *appearing*, the *revelation* of Jehovah; the idea being 'Jehovah in His visibility.'"—*Apologetik*, s. 171. Cf. the promise vouchsafed on the withdrawal (see *infra*, p. 127, note [1]) of the Uncreated Angel ("My Presence (פני) shall go with thee, and I will give thee rest"—Ex. xxxiii. 14), with the statement: "In all their afflictions he was afflicted, and the Angel of His Presence (מלאך פניו) saved them."—Isai. lxiii. 9. On the phraso here employed Olshausen observes: "In Exod. xxxiii. 20, 23, פנים is used for the mysterious, invisible God; while His becoming revealed, and therefore the Son [das Offenbarwerdende (also der Sohn,)] is called 'His back' אחריו. In Isaiah, lxiii. 9, however, the Revealer of God Himself is called מלאך פנים."—*Comm. über Johann*, i. 1, B. ii. s. 34.

[3] The manner in which Jewish writers have understood the texts just quoted will be seen from the following extracts:—Philo writes: *Ἕως μὲν γὰρ οὐ τελείωται, ἡγεμόνι τῆς ὁδοῦ χρῆται λόγῳ θείῳ· χρησμὸς γὰρ ἐστιν, Ἰδοὺ ἀποστέλλω τὸν ἄγγελόν μου πρὸ προσώπου σου κ. τ. λ.* [Exod. xxiii. 20].—*De Migr. Abr.* t. i. p. 463. In the remarkable personification of the Divine Wisdom to be found in the Apocrypha, we find this same truth developed. We are told that wisdom guided them in a marvelous way, and was unto them for a cover by day and a light of stars in the night season; brought them through the Red Sea * * * drowned their enemies," &c.—Wisdom, x. 17–19. Compare the words of S. Paul,—"Neither let us tempt Christ as some of them also tempted, and were destroyed of serpents."—1 Cor. x. 9.

the heavenly calling, consider the Apostle and High Priest of our profession, Christ Jesus."[1] The true force of these words will at once appear, if we compare the etymology of the expression "Apostle," with that of the title applied in the Old Testament, as we have seen, to the Person of the Eternal Word, in His character of Revealer. Christ is here called "Apostle," or "Messenger," with plain reference to His office, under the former dispensation, as "Angel of Jehovah." The *term* "Angel," indeed, could not have been employed without confusing the meaning; for, in the two preceding chapters, it had been used to denote the *species* of Angels as distinguished from the human race; and hence, it could not fitly describe, in the passage before us, the peculiar office of Christ as "*the* Angel." The inspired writer, accordingly, selects for this purpose the term "Apostle;" which equally denotes the same idea, and which is borrowed from a verb continually employed by S. John, in a strictly technical sense, to signify the 'mission' of the Eternal Son into the world, —this Evangelist repeatedly describing Christ as "the Apostle," or as He "whom God *hath sent*."[2] S. Paul, therefore, in the

[1] Heb. iii. 1. It is to be observed that in the previous portion of this Epistle (ch. i. 4; ii. 9), a contrast is drawn between Christ and *angels* (*ἄγγελοι* in the plural). At first sight it might appear that this contrast would have been heightened, had the opposition been drawn between the Son of God and "The Angel of Jehovah" (מלאך י״י), so often referred to in the Old Testament. The remarks already made explain why this has not been done:—"the Angel of Jehovah" was no definite angelic being. The מלאך י״י was not a person in subordination to God,—was no individual of the number of created angels, of whose instrumentality God might have availed Himself,—but He was Himself God, as he appeared in the form of an Angel. See Ebrard, "Der Brief an die Hebräer," s. 33.

[2] *Ὃν γὰρ ἀπέστειλεν ὁ Θεός.*—S. John, iii. 34. *ὁ Πατήρ με ἀπέσταλκεν.*—v. 36. Cf. vi. 29; x. 36; and in fine: "As my Father hath sent (*ἀπέσταλκεν*) Me, even so send (*πέμπω*) I you"—xx. 21, where the difference of the two verbs, clearly denotes the technical application of the former. This same technical signification of the verb, by which S. John denotes the 'mission' of the Son into the world, we find elsewhere in the language of S. Paul: "When the fulness of time was come, God sent forth (*ἐξαπέστειλεν*) His Son."—Gal. iv. 4. See Ebrard, *ibid.* s. 126.

C. A. Keil ("Opuscula Academica" Lipsiæ, 1821.) gives some important references, which illustrate that view of the text in the Epistle to the Hebrews which I have taken from Ebrard, and also the general notion of the Logos as the Revealer. E. g. *Θεὸς οὖν ὢν ὁ Λόγος, καὶ ἐκ Θεοῦ πεφυκώς, ὁπότ' ἂν βούληται ὁ Πατὴρ τῶν ὅλων, πέμπει αὐτὸν εἴς τινα τόπον, ὃς παραγινόμενος καὶ ἀκούεται καὶ ὁρᾶται.*—Theophilus, *Ad Autolyc.* ii. § 22. p. 365. "Atque hac ipsa de causa [observes Keil] *Θεοῦ* etiam *ἄγγελος* et *ἀπόστολος* iis [*scil.* Patribus] dicitur, quod diserte docent Justini Mart. et Originis loca, quorum ille quidem ita habet: *καὶ ἄγγελος δὲ καλεῖται, καὶ ἀπόστολος. αὐτὸς γὰρ ἀπαγγέλλει ὅσα δεῖ γνωσθῆναι, καὶ ἀποστέλλεται μηνύσων ὅσα ἀγγέλλεται.*—*Apol.* i. § 63, p. 81; hic autem sic: *δύναται δὲ καὶ ὁ Λόγος Υἱὸς εἶναι παρὰ τῷ ἀπαγγέλλειν τὰ κρύφια τοῦ Πατρὸς ἐκείνου* * * * *καὶ καθὸ Λόγος ἐστὶ μεγάλης τυγχάνει βουλῆς Ἄγγελος ὤν. κ. τ. λ.*—*Tom.* i. *in Joan.* t. iv. p. 45 [cf. the use of this quotation from the LXX. of Isaiah, ix. 6, by S. Athanasius, *supra*, p.

Epistle to the Hebrews alludes to the Angel of Jehovah, who, under the Law, had revealed God to the people; referring at the same time to the High Priest who was the representative of the people before God.[1] With these features of the Theocratic dispensation he compares the Christian scheme. "Consider," he writes, "the Apostle and High Priest of *our* (i. e. the Christian) profession;" and he then goes on to develop at some length the comparison thus instituted.

These statements of Scripture having been premised, let us look to the circumstances under which the immediate intervention of the Uncreated Angel was withdrawn.[2] As in after times the Jewish people "denied the Holy One and the Just," so in the days of Moses they rebelled against their Divine Guide: they despised the stern warning of Jehovah, and worshipped the calf in Horeb. On that occasion the solemn promise, that the Uncreated Angel should continue to precede the armies of Israel, was as solemnly revoked, and a created angel assigned as their leader. "I will send an angel before thee," said the Lord, " * * * for I will not go up in the midst of thee, for thou art a stiff-necked people: lest I consume thee in the way."[3]

124, note [1]]. "Hinc vero jam illud etiam repetendum est, quod hunc *Λόγον* Vet. quidem Test. temporibus non modo sub variis formis hominibus docuerunt adparuisse, sed prophetis etiam, quæ tradi ab iis vellet, suppeditasse. Nov. autem Test. temporibus in Mariam eum dicebat se demisisse, hominemque factum esse."—p. 503. To which I may add the words of Clemens Alex.: *τὸ μὲν οὖν πρότερον τῷ πρεσβυτέρῳ λαῷ, πρεσβυτέρα διαθήκη ἦν, καὶ νόμος ἐπαιδαγώγει τὸν λαὸν μετὰ φόβου, καὶ Λόγος ἄγγελος ἦν· καινῷ δὲ καὶ νέῳ λαῷ, καινὴ καὶ νέα διαθήκη δεδώρηται, καὶ ὁ Λόγος γεγένηται * * * καὶ ὁ μυστικὸς ἐκεῖνος* Ἄγγελος Ἰησοῦς *τίκτεται.*—*Pædagogus.* lib. i. c 7. p. 133.

[1] Ebrard writes as follows: "Betrachten wir nun das Attribut *τὸν ἀπόστολον καὶ ἀρχιερέα τῆς ὁμολογίας ἡμῶν* näher. Ἀπόστολος heisst Jesus nach seiner Analogie mit dem מלאך י״י, als Bote Gottes an die Menschen, *ἀρχιερεύς* nach seiner Analogie mit dem כהן הגדול als Vertreter der Menschen vor Gott."—*Ibid.* s. 125.

[2] The view which I take of this question is, I am aware, attended with some difficulty. So profound a theologian as Bishop Bull has observed: "Ad *ἐπιφανείας* sub Veteri Testamento quod attinet, hactenus cum Augustino consentimus, non semper in Angelo præsentia singulari adfuisse Deum; sed multa per solos angelos administrasse: quin et modum excessisse in hac questione Veteres nonnullos, haud negamus. Præterea quando merus angelus, quando autem Deus in Angelo apparuerit, sæpe difficilem esse conjecturam, ultro fatemur."—*Def. Fid. Nic.* Sect. iv. cap. iii. § 15, p. 245. The difficulty has been also noticed by S. Athanasius: "Nor on seeing an angel would a man say he had seen the Father; for angels, as it is written, are 'ministering spirits sent forth to minister' [Heb. i. 14], and are heralds of gifts given by Him through the Word to those who receive them. * * * And he who beholds a vision of angels knows that he has seen the angel, and not God. For Zacharias saw an angel: and Esaias saw the Lord. Manoe, the father of Samson, saw an angel; but Moses beheld God. Gideon saw an angel, but to Abraham appeared God."—*Cont. Arian.* Orat. iii. § 14. t. i. p. 563 (Oxf. Transl. p. 420.)

[3] Exod. xxxiii. 2, 3.

Here, then, as in the age of the Incarnation, the Personal Presence of the Eternal Son is withdrawn; and here, too, although in a veiled and mysterious manner, that Presence was supplied. God promises the people that they should not be forsaken: "My Presence shall go with thee, and I will give thee rest."[1] Henceforward, as in the Gospel times,[2] God's dispensation was no longer administered by the Personal Presence of the Eternal Son; but in both cases certain glimpses of His appearance were, from time to time, vouchsafed. Not to dwell upon other instances, Daniel[3] saw "one like the Son of Man, who came to the Ancient of Days;" just as S. Stephen[4] beheld "the Son of Man, standing on the right hand of God." So, too, the object of Zechariah's vision seems to have been identical with the Divine

[1] *Ibid.* ver. 14. Dr. Mill writes as follows:—"That the Angel of the Lord who preceded the children of Israel from Egypt in the cloud and in the fire was (agreeably to Exod. xiii. 20, 21; coll. xiv. 19, 20; Numb. xx. 6, &c.), the Lord Himself, possessor of the incommunicable name יהוה; and that this Angel of the Covenant, as he is termed in Mal. iii. 1 coll. Gen. xlviii. 15, 16, &c., is the Uncreated Word, who appeared in visible form to Jacob and Moses, and who was in the fulness of time incarnate in the Person of Jesus Christ, is the known undoubted faith of the Church of God, and needs not to be enlarged on here. This same Uncreated Angel, in whom was the Name of the Lord, is promised by the mouth of Moses in Exod. xxiii. 20–23, to continue to precede the armies of Israel, and cut off the Canaanites before them: but with an awful caution annexed, that they should be careful not to provoke that august Presence, intolerant of any contact with sin. But after the transgression of the calf in Horeb, it is as solemnly propounded in Exod. xxxiii. 2, 3, that another angel, expressly distinguished from the Divinity, and therefore a created being, should execute that part of the former's province which consisted in preceding their host and exterminating their enemies; the Divine Presence which would otherwise consume them being withdrawn. And though the worst part of this sentence was removed, as we find in the subsequent part of the chapter, by the intercession of Moses,—and the cloudy pillar that indicated the Divine Shekinah or inhabitation was restored to the tabernacle, and continued there,—there is no proof that the function assigned in ver. 2 to the created angel should be superseded; while in the later Prophets, and in the testimony of the New Testament respecting the elder Sinaitic dispensation as subjected to created angels (Acts, vii. 53; Gal. iii. 19; Heb. i.; ii. 2–5), we have a strong argument for its continuance."—*The Christian Advocate's Publication for* 1841, Note A, p. 92.

Dr. Mill then proceeds to consider the passage, where one who describes himself as *Captain* or *Prince of the host of the Lord* (שר־צבא־יהוה), appears to Joshua.—Josh. v. 13–15. "In expressing the belief that this leader of the heavenly host, who conducted the people of Israel into Canaan, and vanquished their enemies before them, was a created angel, i. e. the Michael of Daniel, to whom the same functions with respect to Israel are ascribed,—and not, as many have supposed, the Divine Word or Angel of the Presence, who appeared in various manners to Jacob in Peniel, to Moses in the flaming bush, and elsewhere, I follow the general consent of ancient interpreters, and what appears to me the obvious sense of the Scripture."—*Ibid.* p. 54. For Dr. Mill's remarks on this question see Appendix I.

[2] "When the Comforter is come, whom I will send unto you from the Father, * * * He shall testify of me."—S. John, xv. 26. "It is expedient for you that I go away."—xvi. 7.

[3] Dan. vii. 13.

[4] Acts, vii. 56.

Being whom S. John describes: "And I saw heaven opened, and behold a white horse; and He that sat upon him was called Faithful and True: * * * and He was clothed with a vesture dipped in blood, and His name is called THE WORD OF GOD."[1] At all events, we know that, subsequently to the age of Moses, the *immediate* communications of Jehovah, as a general rule, ceased; and that certain means were made use of for conveying His revelations: "There arose not"—such is the definite information given in the last words of the Pentateuch—"There arose not a prophet since in Israel like unto Moses, whom Jehovah knew face to face." For the Prophets who followed, God appointed certain channels, through which His revelations were to flow. "If there be a prophet among you, I the Lord will make myself known unto him in a vision, and will speak unto him in a dream."[2]

But although the Personal Presence of the Logos was thus withdrawn, the language in which the sacred writers who followed Moses speak of the Divine influence under which they acted, while it distinctly points to an intermediate agency, intimates, at the same time, the indissoluble connexion with, and relation to the Eternal Word, of the means by which His Presence was supplied, and His revelations were communicated. Let us briefly consider how the agency now introduced is spoken of. It is described, generically, as "the Spirit of God." Thus "the Spirit of God" comes equally upon Balaam and Saul, as upon the prophets Azariah and Ezekiel.[3] The exercise of the Divine influ-

[1] Rev. xix. 11–13. Cf. "I saw by night, and behold a man riding upon a red horse, and he stood among the myrtle trees that were in the bottom; and behind him were there red horses speckled and white," &c.—Zech. i. 8.

[2] Numb. xii. 6. Besides those passages in which mention is made of the Personal appearance of the Divine Being, the Old Testament refers to a twofold manifestation of God in the world: (1.) He dwells in the midst of Israel:—"Let them make me a sanctuary that I *may dwell* (ושכנתי) among them"—Ex. xxv. 8; cf. Deut. xxxiii. 12, 16. (2.) The Lord continually *speaks* with Patriarchs and Prophets. "For both exhibitions of the divine agency, the Jewish Mystics have formed peculiar expressions—the Shekinah and the Memra (מימרא and שכינה). * * * The term Shekinah is found as well in the purely Pharisaical books (e. g. the Talmud) as in the Mystical. The Memra, on the other hand, belongs merely to the Targums." * * * "In fact, the Memra is a Hebrew coloring of the Alexandrine Logos."—Gfrörer, *Das Jahrhundert des Heils*, i. s. 300 ff. The term ἐπισκηνώσῃ in the New Testament ("that the power of Christ *might rest upon me*," 2 Cor. xii. 9), has been thought to contain an allusion to the Shekinah.

[3] In such cases we find the "Spirit of Jehovah," and the "Spirit of Elohim" used indifferently. Thus, "The Spirit of God (רוח אלהים) came upon" Balaam—Numb. xxiv. 2; Samuel tells Saul that "the Spirit of the Lord (רוח יהוה) will come upon" him.—1 Sam. x. 6; and at ver. 10 we read that "the Spirit of God (רוח אלהים) came

ence, however, is more frequently represented by certain metaphorical expressions. Of Ezekiel, for example, we read: "The Spirit of the Lord *fell upon me*, and said unto me,"[1]—words which are immediately preceded by the statement: "The Spirit lifted me up, and brought me unto the east gate of the Lord's house;" which passages, taken together, denote that by the power of the Spirit he was raised to the state of prophetic ecstacy, analogous to that described in the New Testament, where it is said of S. Peter, that "a trance or ecstacy *fell upon*" him.[2] Again, it is said of Zechariah the son of Jehoiada, of Amasai, and of Gideon, that they were "clothed" (as the margin of our version correctly renders the Hebrew term) with the Spirit;[3] a phrase identical with that employed by our Lord Himself: "Tarry ye in the city of Jerusalem, until ye *be endued* with power from on high."[4]

The Divine influence is also frequently denoted by the expression, "the hand of the Lord." Thus we read that "the hand of the Lord was on Elijah."[5] Ezekiel writes: "The hand of the Lord God fell there upon me"[6]—meaning that he there became conscious of the mental excitement produced by the Spirit. And to the same effect, Jeremiah says: "I sat alone, because of Thy hand;" or, in the language of Isaiah, "The Lord spake thus to me with a strong hand." This latter phrase is repeated by Ezekiel,—"The hand of the Lord was strong upon me," and denotes: "I was impelled by Divine Spirit:" or, as the Chaldee paraphrase renders, "I was under the influence of prophecy."[7]

upon him." Again, "The Spirit of God (רוח אלהים) came upon Azariah the son of Oded,"—2 Chron. xv. 1; while Ezekiel writes: "The Spirit of the Lord (רוח יהוה) fell upon me."—xi. 5. In Isaiah we meet with a slight variation of the phrase, "The Spirit of the Lord God (רוח אדני יהוה) is upon me."—lxi. 1. Hence the New Testament phrase to denote the state in which revelations were received, ἐν πνεύματι = ברוח. E. g. our Lord says: "How then doth David in spirit (ἐν Πνεύματι) call Him Lord?"—S. Matt. xxii. 43; and S. John,—"I was in the Spirit (ἐν Πνεύματι) on the Lord's day."—Rev. i. 10; iv. 2; xvii. 3: cf. ἐν ἐκστάσει.—Acts, xi. 5.

[1] Ezek. xi. 5. ותפל עלי רוח י״י. At ver. 1, we read simply רוח.

[2] Acts, x. 10, Griesbach reads, ἐπέπεσεν; Lachmann and Tischendorf, ἐγένετο. In either case, however, the parallel holds; for while we find נפל in the case before us, we read היה in several others, e. g. Numb. xxiv. 2; 2 Chron. xv. 1, &c. &c. In support of ἐπέπεσεν, cf. Gen. xv. 12 (LXX.) ἔκστασις ἐπέπεσε (נפלה) τῷ Ἄβραμ.

[3] Of Zechariah (2 Chron. xxiv. 20), it is said, רוח אלהים לבשה. Of Amasai (1 Chron. xii. 18), simply רוח לבשה. Of Gideon (Judges, vi. 34), רוח יהוה לבשה.

[4] S. Luke, xxiv. 49. ἐνδύσησθε.

[5] 1 Kings, xviii. 46. יד י״י היתה.

[6] Ezek. viii. 1. ותפל עלי שם יד אדני יהוה.

[7] Jer. xv. 17; Isai. viii. 11; Ezek. iii. 14. Gesenius translates the original of Isai. viii. 11, by the words: "Denn also sprach Jehovah zu mir in der Entzückung;" on which he observes:—"Of the spiritual influence (Begeisterung) which comes

That this is the true signification of the metaphor, "the hand of the Lord," will appear more distinctly from a statement of Ezekiel: "The hand of the Lord was upon me, and carried me out in the Spirit of the Lord,"—a condition analogous to that described more concisely by S. John in the Apocalypse, as being "in the Spirit."[1] With reference to this subject the New Testament, indeed, but repeats the language of the Old. For example: S. Luke writes of S. John the Baptist: "The hand of the Lord was with him;"[2] and the same Evangelist records the expression of Christ: "If I by the finger of God"—that is, as S. Matthew in the parallel passage explains the words, "If I by the Spirit of God"—"cast out devils."[3] This phrase, "the hand of the

upon the Prophet, when the Deity appears to him, and urges him to speak, to act, and to work in Its name, the Hebrew says not merely: 'the Spirit of God came upon him' (Ezek. xi. 5), but still more frequently: יד י״י היתה על—'the hand of Jehovah came upon' (Ezek. i. 3; iii. 14, 22; xxxiii. 22; xxxvii. 1, and with נפל 'fell upon me,' viii. 1), and once: 'the hand of the Lord was strong upon me,' עלי חזקה יד י״י—Ezek. iii. 14 [Gesenius translates "die Hand Jehova's trieb mich an"], cf. on חזק Exod. xii 33. ["The Egyptians were urgent"]. Hence יד־יהוה directly implies the spiritual influences which constitute a Prophet, and the revelations which he received. Thus Jer. xv. 17: 'I sat not in the assembly of the mockers, nor rejoiced; I sat alone because of Thy hand:'—מפני ידך בדד ישבתי ("wegen deiner Offenbarungen sass ich einsam"). To the latter passages, and especially Ezek. iii. 14 (a comparison which Jarchi has already with great aptness pointed out), the passage before us (Isai. viii. 11) is to be joined: בחזקת היד, properly 'in the impulse of the hand of God' (im Antrieb der Hand Gottes), i. e. when I was urged by the Divine Spirit, when God revealed Himself to me. Excellently the Chaldee: במתקף נבואתא, *in impetu propheticæ.* * * * The Syriac, Luther, Lowth, &c. explained, from an unacquaintance with this usage of language, 'while,' or 'as if He caught me by the hand' (indem, od. als ob er mich bey der Hand fasste); cf. החזיק ביד *to catch by the hand.*"—*Der Prophet Jesaia*, i. s. 338.

[1] Ezek. xxxvii. 1; Rev. i. 10. This conclusion is fully confirmed by the following striking passage: "All this, said David, the Lord made me understand in writing by his hand upon me," (הכל בכתב מיד י״י עלי השכיל), 1 Chron. xxviii. 19; as well as by the statement of the New Testament, that the men of God spake *ὑπὸ Πνεύματος Ἁγίου φερόμενοι.*—2 S. Pet. i. 21.

[2] S. Luke, i. 66 *χεὶρ Κυρίου*=יד יהוה. This sense of יד denoting *power*, *influence*, is quite in accordance with Hebrew usage. E. g. "Their inhabitants *were of small power.*" 2 Kings, xix. 26; where the marginal reading "short of hand" gives a literal rendering of the original, קצרי־יד. We may also compare the use, by the New Testament writers, of *δύναμις* and *δύναμις ὑψίστου*, parallel with a reference to the Holy Ghost—S. Luke, i. 35; Acts, x. 38; 1 Thess. i. 5.

[3] S. Luke, xi. 20, *εἰ δὲ ἐν δακτύλῳ Θεοῦ ἐκβάλλω.* S. Matt. xii. 28, *εἰ δὲ ἐν Πνεύματι Θεοῦ ἐγὼ ἐκβάλλω.* Cf. Exod. viii. 19 [15], "This is the finger of God," אצבע הוא אלהים:—LXX. *Δάκτυλος Θεοῦ ἐστὶ τοῦτο.* This parallelism has been noticed from a very early period. Thus Didymus of Alexandria (flor. A. D. 370, "Magna, apud omnes, admiratione habitus."—Cave, *Hist. Lit.*) writes:—"Salvator ait: 'Si autem ego in digito Dei ejicio dæmonia, ergo supervenit in vos regnum Dei.' Hunc eundem locum alius Evangelista describens, loquentem intulit Filium: 'Si autem ego in Spiritu Dei ejicie dæmonia.' Ex quibus ostenditur, digitum Dei esse Spiritum Sanctum. Si ergo conjunctus est digitus manui, et manus ei cujus manus est: et digitus sine dubio ad ejus substantiam refertur cujus digitus est."—*De Spiritu Sancto*, c. xx. (ap. Galland. t. vi. p. 271.)

Lord," we meet in combination with another as frequently employed, and no less important: "The word of the Lord came expressly unto Ezekiel, * * * and the hand of the Lord was there upon him."[1] It is needless to adduce examples of the recurrence of the expression—"The word of the Lord" came to such or such a prophet: Moses thus denotes revelations in the time of Abraham; it is used by David,[2] as well as by those who were officially prophets. In the Gospels, too, the phrase is applied to S. John the Baptist in the very language and tone of the Old Testament: "The word of God came unto John the son of Zacharias in the wilderness;"[3]—the identity of expression in-

[1] Ezek. i. 3. While considering such phrases, the following unique form of quotation cannot be passed over. Our Lord Himself says: "Therefore also said the Wisdom of God (διὰ τοῦτο καὶ ἡ Σοφία τοῦ Θεοῦ εἶπεν), I will send them prophets," &c.—S. Luke, xi. 49. The parallel passage in S. Matthew (xxiii. 34) simply gives—"Wherefore behold *I send unto you* prophets," &c.—without any indication of the words being a quotation. One can hardly doubt, however, that our Lord expressly refers to 2 Chron. xxiv. 19: "Yet He sent prophets to them, to bring them again unto the Lord; and they testified against them: but they would not give ear;"—especially as this statement of the sacred writer is at once followed by the account of the putting Zechariah to death, to which event Christ has alluded, in immediate connexion with the words just adduced from S. Luke and S. Matthew. The difficulty arising from the want of exact agreement of this quotation with any passage of the Old Testament is somewhat exaggerated by Olshausen; nevertheless, assuming that there is a reference, he acutely observes: "If this be so, then the Redeemer in Matthew speaks not merely as a Person bounded by the limits of a temporal life, but as the Son of God, as the essential Wisdom (Prov. viii.; Ecclus. xxiv.), which S. Luke introduces as speaking, and by whose intervention from the beginning all prophets and holy men of God have entered on their office (Wisd. vii. 27). ["In all ages entering into holy souls, she (Wisdom) maketh them friends of God, and prophets"]. In this case there would be no essential difference between Matthew and Luke." Olshausen adds, "if Jesus calls Himself, in John, the Truth, the Resurrection, and the Life, why shall He not also describe Himself as Wisdom?"—*Comment.* B. i. s. 850. That an absence of literal agreement is no proof that the Old Testament has not been directly referred to, will be shown in Lecture vii. *infra*.

[2] "The word of the Lord came unto Abram."—Gen. xv. 1. "And David said to Solomon * * * the word of the Lord came to me."—1 Chron. xxii. 8. In both cases we read דבר־יהוה: the LXX., however, have translated the original in the former of these passages by ῥῆμα Κυρίου, in the latter by λόγος Κυρίου,—employing ῥῆμα and λόγος indifferently. See *infra*, p. 132, &c. With such phrases we may compare the words of Simeon (S. Luke, ii. 29): "according to Thy word"—κατὰ τὸ ῥῆμά Σου (*scil.* πρὸς ἐμὲ ἐρχόμενον); in which expression he, of course, refers to the fact stated by the Evangelist: καὶ ἦν αὐτῷ κεχρηματισμένον ὑπὸ τοῦ Πνεύματος τοῦ Ἁγίου (ver. 26), on the *form* of which χρηματισμός S. Luke is silent. As to the term by which the Divine communication is here expressed, it is to be noted that "χρηματίζειν, in profane Greek, denotes 'to transact public business,' 'to communicate answers and decrees;'—εσθαι, 'to receive such decrees, &c.' In Hellenistic Greek, the expression appears in the same sense, with a reference, however, to the province of Divine things: χρηματίζειν, 'to give Divine commands' (cf. Heb. xii. 25);—εσθαι, 'to receive the same.' [So Jer. xxvi. 2; xxix. 23.] Cf. S. Matth. ii. 12, 22. For the signification, 'to take and bear a title or name,' quite usual among profane writers, see Acts, xi. 26; Rom. vii. 3."—Olshausen, *Comment.*, i. s. 69.

[3] S. Luke, iii. 2. On this passage Olshausen observes:—"Peculiar to Luke, iii. 2, is the addition, ἐγένετο ῥῆμα Θεοῦ ἐπὶ Ἰωάννην, which corresponds to the phrase so

dicating, doubtless, the continuity of the Baptist's position with that of the servants of God, under the old dispensation whose ranks he closed: "For the Law and the Prophets were until John."

The New Testament usage of the expression, "The word of God" (ῥῆμα Θεοῦ, in the singular, as employed by S. Luke in the passage just quoted,) may help to discover its true force. It results from an examination of the texts in which the phrase occurs, that it invariably implies the Divine spiritual influence.[1] To

usual among the prophets, היה דבר י״י על. This remark represents, in the first place, the public appearance of John as an act not proceeding from his own reflexion, but as conditioned by a higher impulse. Secondly, the mode of operation of the higher world upon the mind of John appears hence not to differ from that which took place in the prophets of the Old Testament."—B. i. s. 157. Olshausen subsequently resumes the subject when commenting on S. John, i. 1:—" The writers of the Old Testament are, no doubt, acquainted with the idea of the Divine Utterance (des göttlichen Sprechens), and in like manner with the plurality of Persons in God; but the WORD Itself nowhere appears as a Personality, but only as an Activity of God. Even in the remarkable passage, Ps. xxxiii. 6, where the Word is placed in conjunction with the Spirit, we can, no doubt, looking backwards from the stand-point of the New Testament, recognise the Eternal Word; but the idea of Personality is not as yet distinctly expressed, even in this passage. * * * Nay, even in the New Testament, the Divine Utterance (ῥῆμα τοῦ Θεοῦ) appears still to predominate merely as Divine Activity,—whether it be a *single* operation which is to be described by the phrase, or the *collective* Activity of the Divine Nature (cf. Heb. iv. 12; xi. 3). Only in the language of John is the idea of the Personality of the Word distinctly expressed (cf. 1 John, i. 1; Rev. xix. 13). The other writers use for this exalted Personality a different name. It is called ὁ Υἱὸς τοῦ Θεοῦ, as born from God's Nature; ὁ Υἱὸς τοῦ ἀνθρώπου = בר אנש (Dan. vii. 13) as the original type of Humanity [cf. Gen. i. 26, 27]. Only in the profound language of the Book of Proverbs (viii. 22, ff.; cf. with xxx. 4), does the idea of the Logos appear, which is there introduced under the name of Wisdom, as if in the transition, from the more universal impersonal conception, to the personal. However, the name 'Word of God' is wanting for the idea, in Prov. xxx. 4; it appears, on the contrary, in the New Testament name 'Son of God.'"—*Comm.* B. ii. s. 33.

[1] Viz., (1) S. Luke, iii. 2; (2) Rom. x. 17, "Faith cometh by hearing, and hearing by the word of God." (Lachmann reads ῥήματος Χριστοῦ.) (3) Eph. vi. 17 (see next note). (4) Heb. vi. 5, "Were made partakers of the Holy Ghost, and have tasted the good word of God." (Καλὸν should, perhaps, be rather taken as the predicate.) (5) Heb. xi. 3, "Through faith we understand that the worlds were framed by the word of God." (Cf. Heb. i. 3—τῷ ῥήματι τῆς δυνάμεως Αὐτοῦ.) The texts, S. Luke iv. 4, and 1 S. Pet. i. 25, are quotations. On Rom. x. 17, Olshausen observes:—"ῥῆμα Θεοῦ is, no doubt, to be referred to the *doctrine* of the revelation which forms the foundation of preaching, but yet so that this doctrine is conceived as being wholly animated (beseelte und belebte) by the Spirit of God, so that it might even have been written: ἡ δὲ ἀκοὴ διὰ Πνεύματος Θεοῦ."—B. iii. s. 388.

To these texts may be added Eph. v. 26, "That he might sanctify and cleanse it with the washing of water *by the word*, that He might," &c. "There is some uncertainty as to the explanation of ἐν ῥήματι. Most interpretations are seen, at the first glance, to be false, as, e. g., that of Koppe, according to which ἐν ῥήματι ἵνα forms one phrase, which stands, as he believed, for the Hebrew על דבר אשר, words which the LXX. never translate in this manner. Against the connexion with ἁγιάσῃ there is the position of the words; otherwise the junction of the expressions would not be unsuitable, according to the analogy of the ἁγιάζειν ἐν ἀληθείᾳ of John, xvii. 17 and 19. The words can only be united with λουτρὸν τοῦ ὕδατος. In this connexion take a single instance, S. Paul writes: "The sword of the Spirit, which [Spirit] is the word of God."[1] In fact, when the term ῥῆμα is employed in the New Testament *in the singular number*, and as distinct from that which usually implies the same idea (λόγος), it points to some Divine agency which always accompanies, or proceeds from, the Eternal Word;—an operation which He produces, but not the Divine Logos Himself. It is only in the language of S. John that the idea of the *Personality* of the WORD is expressed; and it is deserving of remark that this term (ῥῆμα) which denotes the Divine utterance does not occur *in the singular* in his Gospel.[2] In the Old Testament, with the exceptions already noted, Christ appears to act rather through the medium of this operative power, than after the manner of a Person; and thus, in the passage, "Through faith we understand that the worlds were framed by *the word of God*,"[3] not the Personal Word (Λόγος), but this Divine operative energy (ῥῆμα Θεοῦ) is represented as the immediate source of all created things. In conformity with this

writers usually recur either to the ordinance of Christ in the institution of Baptism, whereby 'the washing of water' (das Wasserbad) receives its purifying power; or to the word of reconciliation and forgiveness of sins. But in neither allusion do we see how the article before ῥήματι could be omitted; for in either case the Apostle would have had a definite word in view. Here ἐν ῥήματι rather stands as equivalent in signification to ἐν πνεύματι (Eph. ii. 22): and this with the design of pointing out that Baptism is no mere 'washing of water,' but a 'washing of water *in the word*;' i. e. by means of which man is born again of water, and of the Spirit (John, iii. 5). * * * Ῥῆμα is therefore, here, as in Heb. i. 3, xi. 3, a description of the Divine power and agency in general, which according to their nature must be a spiritual influence."—Olshausen, *in loc.* B. iv. s. 279.

[1] Eph. vi. 17. (τὴν μάχ. τοῦ Πνεύματος, ὅ ἐστιν ῥῆμα Θεοῦ.) "How Paul can add as an explanation of the Spirit, ὅ ἐστιν ῥῆμα Θεοῦ, presents some obscurity. That this expression describes some one particular of the word of God,—His threats against the wicked, or the commands of Christianity,—is, considering the universality of the phrase, highly improbable. * * * But how can this 'word of God' be described as the Spirit Himself? The Holy Spirit, it appears, exerts an influence which accompanies the word of God,—an agency which the word of God calls forth, but which is distinct from the word of God itself. * * * Whether it be conceived as word of God the Father, or as word of Christ (Col. iii. 16), or as influence of the Holy Spirit, depends solely on the manner in which the writer regards it: as Revelation of the Triune God, it also reconciles the different relations to the Trinity."—Olshausen, *Comm.* B. iv. s. 298.

[2] Mr. Westcott, although his attention has been directed to this subject, has not noticed the distinct signification of these phrases. He merely observes: "It is important to notice the difference between τὸ ῥῆμα τοῦ Θεοῦ and ὁ λόγος τοῦ Θεοῦ, which are both translated in E. V. 'the word of God.'"—*Elem. of Gosp. Harm.*, p. 12. He then contents himself with referring to the passages in which these expressions occur; and among others to S. John, iii. 34; viii. 47, in which texts we find *the plural form*—τὰ ῥήματα τοῦ Θεοῦ.

[3] Heb. xi. 3.

idea S. Peter tells us that it was "the Spirit of Christ" which spake in the prophets.[1]

In bringing to a close this branch of our inquiry, I would briefly draw attention to the powerful evidence for the essential Divinity of Christ, which is afforded by a comparison of the language employed when referring to His inspired servants, with that in which Scripture alludes to Himself. The words "to reveal," "to manifest," or kindred expressions, are never applied *to* Christ, although often used *of* Him.[2] S. Paul writes: "It pleased God to *reveal* His Son in me;"[3] and S. John: "The Son of God was *manifested* that He might destroy the works of the Devil."[4] Christ was the Revealer, but received no revelation: He was the source of all Divine communications, not the channel merely through which they were to be derived. To Him belongs the necessary and essential possession of knowledge; the highest perfection of mere human nature consists in its acquisition. The knowledge of Him is as essential to the life of the soul as that of the Father—"This is life eternal, that they might know Thee, the only true God, and Jesus Christ whom thou hast

[1] 1 S. Pet. i. 11. This discussion will suitably terminate with the following quotations. S. Athanasius writes: *ἀμέλει οὕτως ἐστὶ τὸ Πνεῦμα ἀδιαίρετον πρὸς τὸν Υἱὸν, ὡς μὴ ἀμφιβάλλειν ἐκ τοῦ λεγομένου. ὅτε γὰρ ὁ Λόγος ἐγίγνετο πρὸς τὸν προφήτην, τὰ παρὰ τοῦ Λόγου ἐν τῷ Πνεύματι ἐλάλει ὁ προφήτης.*—*Ad Serapion.* Ep. iii. 5. t. i. p. 694. This great writer goes on to quote S. Peter's saying, that "the Holy Ghost spake by the mouth of David" (Acts, i. 16); and the words of S. Paul: "Since ye seek a proof of Christ speaking in me" (2 Cor. xiii. 3); which he compares with the Apostle's remark, "The Holy Ghost witnesseth in every city," &c.—Acts, xx. 23. Cf. also the reference to S. Athanasius, Lecture ii. p. 84, note.

Didymus of Alexandria observes:—"Porro jam frequenter ostendimus ejusdem operationis esse Spiritum Sanctum, cujus est Pater et Filius, et in eadem operatione unam esse substantiam; et reciproce eorum quæ *ὁμοούσια* sunt, operationem quoque non esse diversam."—*De Spiritu Sancto*, c. xxxii, (ap. Galland. t. vi. p. 275.)

[2] "Ubi scientiæ religionis, quæ in Jesu fuerit, divina origo describitur, non usurpari solent verba *ἀποκαλύπτεσθαι* aut *φανεροῦσθαι*; id quod nos jam admonere potest, Eum revelationis, quæ vulgo laudetur, non fuisse participem. In unico tantum loco Apoc. i. 1, vox *ἀποκάλυψις* ita adhibetur * * * ad indicandam Ejus veritatem et divinam auctoritatem verba addebantur: *ἣν ἔδωκεν Αὐτῷ ὁ Πατήρ.* Atque hæc verba etiam verti possunt: quam demandavit Ei Pater. Hic igitur locus ne continere quidem videtur exemplum contrarium. * * * Spiritum illum, qui Apostolos edocturus et adjuturus erat, non minus sibi ipsi vindicat Jesus, quam Patri. 'De Meo Ille sumet,' inquit, (Joan. xvi. 14) 'quæ vos edoceat;' causam interserens Se omnia cum Patre communia habere. * * * Dicitur Ipse de cœlo venisse, et in cœlo versari (Joan. iii. 13); dicitur Patri proximus assidere (i. 18), cernere quæ Pater agat (v. 19 sq.), solus vidisse Patrem (vi. 46), solus, qualis sit Pater, scire, aliisque pro benignitate Sua patefacere (Luc. x. 22). Sic describitur non tam acquisitio quam necessaria possessio scientiæ."—C. L Nitzsch, *De Revel. externa eademque publica*, pp. 10–12.

[3] Gal. i. 15, 16—*ἀποκαλύψαι.*

[4] 1 S. John, iii. 8—*ἐφανερώθη.*

sent."[1] And that it is the office of the Eternal Son alone to convey such knowledge to mankind, and that at His good pleasure alone it can be imparted, we learn from the words of our text: "No man knoweth who the Son is, but the Father; and who the Father is, but the Son, and he to whom the Son wills to reveal Him."

[1] S. John, xvii. 3.

The argument for the Divinity of Christ, to which I have here drawn attention, has not been unnoticed by the Fathers. S. Gregory Naz., describing the nature of Inspiration as possessed by the sacred writers of both Testaments, observes to this effect: Τοῦτο [*scil.* τὸ Πνεῦμα] *ἐνήργει * * * ἐν τοῖς πατράσι, καὶ ἐν τοῖς Προφήταις, ὧν οἱ μὲν ἐφαντάσθησαν Θεὸν, ἢ ἔγνωσαν, οἱ δὲ καὶ τὸ μέλλον προέγνωσαν τυπούμενοι τῷ Πνεύματι τὸ ἡγεμονικὸν, καὶ ὡς παροῦσι συνόντες τοῖς ἐσομένοις. τοιαύτη γὰρ ἡ τοῦ Πνεύματος δύναμις. ἔπειτα ἐν τοῖς Χριστοῦ μαθηταῖς· ἐῶ γὰρ Χριστὸν εἰπεῖν, ᾧ παρῆν, οὐχ ὡς ἐνεργοῦν, ἀλλ' ὡς ὁμοτίμῳ συμπαρομαρτοῦν· καὶ τούτοις τρισσῶς, καθ' ὅσον οἷοί τε ἦσαν χωρεῖν, καὶ κατὰ καιροὺς τρεῖς.* —*Orat.* xli. c. 11. t. i. p. 739.

These three stages are to be dated, as S. Gregory explains,—(1) from before Christ's glorification by His Passion; (2) from His Resurrection; (3) from His Ascension.

LECTURE IV.

REVELATION AND INSPIRATION.

"Ecce apertis eisdem oculis fidei, David, Amos, Danielem, Petrum, Paulum, Matthæum intueor, et Sanctus iste Spiritus qualis sit Artifex, considerare volo, sed in ipsa mea consideratione deficio. Implet namque citharœdum puerum, et Psalmistam facit. Implet pastorem armentarium sycomoros vellicantem, et Prophetam facit. * * * Implet piscatorem, et Prædicatorem facit. Implet persecutorem, et Doctorem gentium facit. * * * O qualis est Artifex iste Spiritus! Nullâ ad discendum morâ, agitur in omne quod voluerit. Mox ut tetigerit mentem docet; solumque tetigisse docuisse est."

S. GREGOR. M., *Homil.* XXX. c. 8.

*Σαφῶς ἔδειξε τοῦ Δεσπότου Χριστοῦ καὶ τῶν Προφητῶν τὸ διάφορον * * * τὸ μέντοι πολυμερῶς, τὰς παντοδαπὰς οἰκονομίας σημαίνει· τὸ δὲ πολυτρόπως, τῶν θείων ὀπτασιῶν τὸ διάφορον. ἄλλως γὰρ ὤφθη τῷ Ἀβραὰμ, καὶ ἄλλως τῷ Μωυσῇ * * * καὶ Ἡσαΐας δὲ, καὶ Δανιὴλ, καὶ Ἰεσεκιὴλ διάφορα ἐθεάσαντο σχήματα. τοῦτο διδάσκων ὁ τῶν ὅλων ἔφη Θεός· Ἐγὼ ὁράσεις ἐπλήθυνα, καὶ ἐν χερσὶ Προφητῶν ὡμοιώθην. οὐ γὰρ πολύμορφος ἡ Θεία φύσις, ἀλλὰ ἀναείδεός τε καὶ ἀσχημάτιστος * * * οὐκ αὐτὴν τοίνυν ἑώρων τὴν ἀνέφικτον φύσιν, ἀλλὰ τινὰ σχήματα, ἃ πρὸς τὴν χρείαν ὁ ἀόρατος ἐδείκνυε Θεός.*

THEODORETUS, *In Epist. ad Heb.* i. 1.

"Qui a nobis Prophetæ, in Vetere Testamento Videntes appellabantur: quia videbant ea quæ cæteri non videbant, et prospiciebant ea, quæ in mysteriis abscondita erant."

S. ISIDORUS, Hispal. *Etymolog.* lib. vii. 8.

LECTURE IV.

REVELATION AND INSPIRATION.

I HAVE ALSO SPOKEN BY THE PROPHETS, AND I HAVE MULTIPLIED VISIONS, AND USED SIMILITUDES BY THE MINISTRY OF THE PROPHETS.—*Hosea*, xii. 10.

WHEN entering in the last Discourse upon an examination of the Scriptures themselves, it was necessary, in the first instance, to define the field over which that examination must extend. It was accordingly shown, from a comparison of both portions of the inspired record, and from a consideration of the specific analogies which present themselves at every step of our progress, that the same organic relation subsists between the Old and the New Testament, as between the germ and the flower;[1] and that no just or satisfactory theory of Inspiration can be proposed, which does not exhibit the inseparable connexion of the different books which the Bible combines; or which does not recognise the claim of their respective authors to an equal share in the controlling influence and active co-operation of the Holy Ghost.

The facts by which we must be guided, when attempting to form any definite idea of Inspiration, may be reduced to two classes. Of these classes, one consists of those indications, which enable us to infer, with absolute certainty, that the subject matter of many portions of Scripture must have been supernaturally revealed, while they, with equal clearness, denote that other de-

[1] This relation is very clearly illustrated by a remark of Dr. Mill in "The Christian Advocate's Publication" for 1844, p. 413, note: "The Catholic interpretation of the citation of Hosea [xi. 1.] by S. Matthew [ii. 15] makes Israel and the promised Seed to stand in the place of type and antitype, the latter the full development of what the other was in germ; *ῥητῶς*—as Eusebius says, when Joseph in this instance brought the infant Jesus from literal Egypt,—*κατὰ διάνοιαν δὲ, ὁπηνίκα ἐκ τῆς νοητῆς Αἰγύπτου καὶ τῶν τῇδε τόπων ἐπὶ τοὺς οὐρανοὺς ἅμα λαμβάνων αὐτὸν ὁ Πατὴρ ὡδήγησεν.*—*Eclog. Prophet.* p. 48, ed. Gaisford." Cf. Lect. iii. p. 109, note [1], and *infra*, p. 153, note [1].

tails of the sacred history have been derived from natural sources. Such indications are presented by the *contents* of both the Old and the New Testament. The other class of facts—presented by its whole manner, and language, and style—comprises, not only the direct evidence which the Bible itself bears to the constant presence of the Divine element involved in its composition, but also certain phenomena which no less plainly attest the coexistence of a human element. To show how these elements, apparently so heterogeneous, may be combined ; to exhibit them as not merely concurrent, but as absolutely amalgamated in one distinct energy ;—to prove, moreover, that under the controlling influence of the Divine principle, there has hence resulted the perfect inspiration of all the parts of Scripture, whatever be their subject matter,—such is the task to which I must now address myself.

In adopting this course, the *direct* evidence which the Bible supplies is necessarily postponed. That evidence is made up of those statements in which the sacred penmen tell us that promises of spiritual guidance were given them ;—of the intimations which they convey that such promises were fulfilled ;—and of the claims to infallible authority which they consequently advance on behalf of their own writings, or which they ascribe to the writings of their fellows. This portion of the subject will be considered on a future occasion.[1] Our attention must, for the present, be restricted to the facts which attest the coexistence of the Divine and human elements in the composition of the Scriptures, and which supply us with one of the conditions to be satisfied by any theory of Inspiration that can claim respect, or challenge impartial consideration.

Two such conditions I have already pointed out,[2] as being necessary and sufficient for the satisfactory solution of the problem before us. In the first place, we know, as a matter of fact, that the authorship of the different books of both the Old and the New Testament must be referred to certain human agents ; and we further perceive, on every page of those books, traces of the distinct individuality and personal characteristics of their respective authors.[3] This co-existence of human agency with the im-

[1] See *infra*, Lecture vi.

[2] Lecture i. pp. 35–40.

[3] Bishop Lowth, referring to the qualities called by Longinius *Grandeur of Con-*

pelling influence of the Holy Spirit, constitutes the first Condition to be satisfied by our theory. The facts which impose this Condition are not to be questioned. The language, the imagery, the forms of expression made use of by the writers of Scripture, all correspond, in their most minute details, with what we might of ourselves expect from men whose education, and social position, and native temperament, were such as theirs are known to have been. This feature of the inspired record will appear more clearly as we proceed. The style, too, in which the different books are written is adapted with the strictest propriety to their subject. The grave and unimaginative language which befits historical narrative; the solemn tone appropriate to didactic composition; the poetic coloring naturally suited, as we shall see, to Prophecy—all such characteristics meet our view in the several divisions of the Bible. In a word, the agents upon whom the Divine influence was exerted, were men whose whole lives exemplified, and whose writings, now before us, exhibit, all the peculiarities of genius, character, thought, and feeling, belonging to their nature as human beings, and resulting from the several social positions which they respectively occupied, as represented in the sacred history.

In the combination of the two elements thus co-operating, —namely, the actuation by the Spirit of God, and the distinct, but subordinate, agency of man,—consists what has been usually termed the 'dynamical' theory of Inspiration. According to this theory the Holy Ghost employs man's faculties in conformity with their natural laws;[1] at the same time, animating, guiding, moulding them so as to accomplish the Divine purpose:[2] just as

ception, and *Vehemence* or *Enthusiasm of Passion*, observes:—"To each of these we must have recourse in the present disquisition, and in applying them to the sacred Poets, I shall endeavor to detract nothing from the dignity of that Inspiration which proceeds from higher causes, while I allow to the genius of each writer his own peculiar excellence and accomplishments. I am indeed of opinion, that the Divine Spirit by no means takes such an entire possession of the mind of the Prophet as to subdue or extinguish the character and genius of the man: the natural powers of the mind are in general elevated and refined, they are neither eradicated nor totally obscured; and though the writings of Moses, of David, and of Isaiah, always bear the marks of a Divine and celestial impulse, we may nevertheless plainly discover in them the particular characters of their respective authors."—*On the Sacred Poetry of the Hebrews*, Lect. xvi. (Gregory's transl., vol i. p. 346).

[1] See Westcott's "Elements of the Gospel Harmony," p. 8, note [1].

[2] For some remarks respecting the design and structure of the Bible, see Lecture i. p. 28, &c. How admirably even the structure of the inspired writings has been adapted to the wants and imperfections of mankind, has been noticed in very striking

in nature, the principle of life, when annexed to certain portions of matter, exhibits its vital energy in accordance with conditions which that matter imposes ; while it governs and directs, at the same time, the organism with which it is combined.[1] We must, therefore, look upon Inspiration as a Divine power acting not only *on*, but *through*, man. We must not regard the sacred penmen, on the one hand, as passive machines, yielding to an external mechanical force[2]—such a view takes in merely the

language by S. Basil when explaining the nature of the Psalms (Homil. in Ps. i., Opp. t. i. p. 90). This passage is quoted by Hooker, where he observes that the Church's use of psalmody is (as Rabanus Maurus had expressed it) "to the end that unto grosser and heavier minds, whom bare words do not easily move, the sweetness of melody might make some entrance for good things." "S. Basil," continues Hooker, "himself acknowledging as much, did not think that from such inventions the least jot of estimation and credit thereby should be derogated,—'For' (saith he) 'whereas the Holy Spirit saw that mankind is unto virtue hardly drawn, and that righteousness is the less accounted of by reason of the proneness of our affections to that which delighteth ; it pleased the wisdom of the same Spirit to borrow from melody that pleasure, which mingleth with heavenly mysteries, causeth the smoothness and softness of that which toucheth the ear, to convey as it were by stealth the treasure of good things unto man's mind. To this purpose were those harmonius tunes of psalms devised for us, that they which are either in years but young, or touching perfection of virtue as not yet grown to ripeness, might, when they think they sing, learn. O the wise conceit of that Heavenly Teacher, which hath by His skill found out a way, that doing those things wherein we delight, we may also learn that whereby we profit!' "—*Eccl. Pol.* B. v. 38. Keble's ed. vol. ii. p. 162.

[1] I have already (Lect. i. p. 39) adduced this illustration, as well as that supplied by the received doctrine of the Church, respecting the co-operation of Divine Grace. That in the *ordinary* exercise of the Holy Spirit's influence, man's distinct working must ever be combined with God's continual aiding, is expressly taught by S. Paul: "Work out your own salvation with fear and trembling, FOR it is God which worketh in you both to will and to do." (*Τὴν ἑαυτῶν σωτηρίαν κατεργάζεσθε· Θεὸς γάρ ἐστιν ὁ ἐνεργῶν ἐν ὑμῖν.*)—Phil. ii. 12, 13. On this statement of Scripture is founded S. Augustine's great proposition, incorporated by the Anglican Church in her Tenth Article: "Sine Illo vel operante ut velimus, vel co-operante cum volumus, ad bona pietatis opera nihil valemus."—*De Gra. et Lib. Arbit.* § 33. t. x. p. 735. See also *supra*, p. 44. It must be borne in mind, however, that no more than an *analogy* exists, between this *ordinary* influence of the Holy Ghost upon Christians in general, and that Inspiration which prompted and guided the sacred writers. These two agencies of the same Spirit, although *analogous*, are *specifically distinct*. This question will be discussed in Lecture v.

[2] The objections, to which such a view of Inspiration is obnoxious, have been briefly noticed in Lecture i. p. 36 ; to which remarks I may here add the observations of a celebrated writer to the same effect. Bishop Warburton, arguing against what he calls the "idea of organic [or as it is now usually termed 'mechanical'] Inspiration," objects, among other matters: "(1.) It would be putting the Holy Spirit on an unnecessary employment; for much of these sacred volumes being historical, and of facts and discourses which had fallen under the observations of the writers, they did not need His immediate assistance to do this part of their business for them. (2.) Had the Scriptures been written under this organic Inspiration, there must have been the most perfect agreement amongst the four Evangelists, in every circumstance of the smallest fact. But we see there is not this perfect agreement. * * * (3.) Were this the true idea of Scripture-inspiration, that each writer was but the mere organ of the Spirit, the phraseology or turn of expression had been one and the same throughout all the sacred books written in the same language."—*A Discourse on the Office of the Holy Spirit*, ed. 1788, vol. iv. p. 566. In avoiding one extreme, however,

objective side of Inspiration: on the other hand, if we dwell solely upon the *subjective* phase of this influence, we lose sight of the living connexion of the writer with God. Were this latter conception correct, the authors of Scripture, following the impulse of their own genius, and in accordance with their own judgment, proceeded, in the natural course of things, to develop new inferences from the germ of Truth implanted within them;[1] and hence, as some have argued, we cannot accept all the conclusions at which they have arrived as either infallible or authoritative. The true theory, as it recoils from any such negation of the Divine majesty of the Bible, so it equally ignores the defective estimate of the opposite extreme.[2] The human element,

Bishop Warburton has fallen into another. His definition of Inspiration opens with the statement: "That the Holy Spirit so directed the pens of these writers that *no considerable error* should fall from them * * * by preserving them by the more ordinary means of Providence, from any *mistakes of consequence*," &c.—p. 568: to which remarks he appends the curious conclusion: "This seems to be the true idea of the Inspiration in question. This only doth agree with all appearances; and will fully answer the purpose of an inspired writing, which is to afford an INFALLIBLE RULE [the emphasis is the Bishop's own] for the direction of the Catholic Church."

1 "A gift," observes Mr. Morell, speaking of the Pentateuch, which its author "was left to make use of as necessity or propriety might suggest." See the passage already quoted, p. 27, note [4]. "I *know*," continues Mr. Morell, "that I am speaking the conviction of many learned men and devout Christians, when I say, that the blind determination to represent every portion of the Old Testament as being alike written entirely under the guidance of God, and by the special direction of the Spirit, has been one of the most fearful hinderances which ever stood in the way of an honest, firm, and rational belief in the reality of a Divine Inspiration at all."—*Philosophy of Religion*, p. 178.

2 "The earliest apologists of modern times confined themselves to the literal assertion of a mechanical power. They regarded the Divine agency as operating externally and not internally;—as acting *on* man and not *through* man; they lost the idea of an active energy in that of a passive state. At present the case seems reversed, and the reason is evident. Our predecessors had to assert the reality of Inspiration against those who ridiculed its very name, and denied the possibility of a revelation; while we have to show that it is a peculiar influence, against those who see in the Apostles only the ordinary working of God. They had to contend with those who denied the spirit through the outward form; while we have to resist those who deny the outward form to secure the spirit,—who claim as the primal attributes of man what we hold to be the after-gifts of heaven."—Westcott, *Elements of the Gospel Harmony*, p. 5. Mr. Morell again supplies us with an illustration which will exhibit the justice of Mr. Westcott's remark: "If it be said that the Providence of God *must* have watched over the composition and construction of a canonical book, which was to have so vast an influence on the destiny of the world,—we are quite ready to admit, and even ourselves to assert it. But in the same sense Providence watches over every other event which bears upon the welfare of man, although the execution of it be left to the *freedom* of human endeavor. And what, after all, *need* we in the Scriptures more than this? Why should we be perpetually craving after a stiff, literal, verbal infallibility? Christianity consists not in propositions—it is a life in the soul; its laws and precepts are not engraven on stone; they can only be engraven on the fleshy tables of the heart."—*Ibid.* p. 183. Few, indeed, will be found to deny that "Christianity consists not *in* propositions:"—as few, perhaps, as would allege that an electric current consists *in* the formulæ by which Gauss or Faraday

instead of being suppressed, becomes an integral part of the agency employed;—moulded, it is true, and guided, and brought into action by the co-operation of the Spirit, but not the less really, on that account, participating in the result produced. Nay more, the peculiar type of each writer's nature was even essential to the due reception of that particular phase of truth presented by his statements: his share in the great work was apportioned to the order of his intellect and the class of his emotions; while his characteristic form of expression was absolutely requisite, for the adequate and complete conveyance of his Divine message. Without the moving power, man could not have grasped the Divine communications; without the living instrument those communications could not have received fitting expression. The Bible, it has been well observed, "is authoritative, for it is the voice of God; it is intelligible, for it is in the language of men."[1]

It appears to me, however, that the 'dynamical' theory, taken alone, is not sufficient to account for all the phenomena which the Bible presents to our view. By it, the first Condition, only, of our problem is satisfied. We must, therefore, seek for a further principle, according to which the remaining Condition, which the nature of the case equally imposes, may be complied with. This Condition arises from that class of facts which indicate, as I have observed above, that a considerable portion of what the Bible contains consists of matters already known to the sacred writers, or the knowledge of which might be—nay, which we actually know often was—derived from the ordinary sources of information that were at their command.[2] Other portions, again, are such as they could not have become acquainted with, except by an immediate communication from heaven.[3] The

have expressed its laws. The *knowledge*, however, of what Christianity is, as well as of the laws of electricity, *must* be communicated *by* propositions; and it is not more unnatural that the Christian should "crave" for an assurance that God's Revelation has came to him unclouded by human error, than that the student in the exact sciences should "crave" for perfect accuracy in the structure of the formulæ, by which the philosopher from whom he derives his information, has expressed the secrets of Nature. For some remarks on the meaning of the phrase 'Christian knowledge,' see *infra*, Lecture vi.

[1] Westcott.—*Ibid.* p. 8.

[2] See, for example, the statement of S. Luke in the introduction to his Gospel,—the opening of S. John's First Epistle, &c. Compare also the remarks on this subject in Lecture i. pp. 39, 40, &c.

[3] E. g. The announcements of the future; the account of the Creation, &c. I

principle which satisfies this Condition is that of the distinction between Revelation and Inspiration. I have shown, on a former occasion,[1] that this distinction is specific, and not merely one of degree ; and we perceived, in the last Discourse, that the sources, too, from which Revelation and Inspiration respectively proceed, are also different :—the former having as its author the Second, the latter the Third, Person, in the Holy Trinity.

It may be well, moreover, again to observe, that the gift of Inspiration was equally required by those among the authors of Scripture who had received revelations, as by those to whom Divine knowledge was never thus imparted. In the former case Inspiration was necessary, not only in order to enable the sacred writer correctly to apprehend, and faithfully to express, the substance of the Divine communication ;[2] but also for a further reason. It is to be remembered, that when a revelation had been once conveyed to any individual and publicly announced by him, it became as much a matter of history as any natural event of which the Bible takes notice. We have reason to believe that, in the great majority of cases, the Divine communications were not committed to writing, for some time after they were received :[3] there are even instances of several years having elapsed before they were thus placed on record.[4] Now, in all such cases the co-

do not, of course, mean to deny that some of the sacred writers received immediate revelations even of matters of fact which they might have learned from human testimony. I have already adduced one instance of this kind, recorded in the passage quoted (p. 40, note [2]) from 1 Kings, xiv. 5. The case of S. Paul is still more to the point. He tells us of "the Gospel which was preached of him," that he "neither received it of man, neither was he taught it, but by the revelation of Jesus Christ"—Gal. i. 11, 12 ; and we know from 1 Cor. xi. 23 ; xv. 3, that such revelations conveyed the knowledge of matters of fact which he might have learned from the other Apostles, as well as of matters of doctrine. It is plain, however, that such cases were exceptions to the usual course of the Divine Economy—see e. g. the last note.

[1] Lecture i. p. 42, &c.

[2] See Lecture i. p. 43, and *infra*, p. 175, note [2].

[3] This obviously took place whenever God's will was unfolded by means of *dreams;* whether we regard the dreams of men who were never inspired,—as Pharaoh, Nebuchadnezzar, &c.,—or those of prophets, who were also to the fullest extent guided by Inspiration. Thus Daniel writes: "In the first year of Belshazzar king of Babylon, Daniel had a dream and vision of his head upon his bed: then he wrote the dream, and told the sum of the matters. Daniel spake and said, I saw in my vision by night," &c.—vii. 1, 2. The same is to be said of the communications from heaven which the Patriarchs received, and which Moses has recorded in the Book of Genesis. We cannot doubt that the promises to Abraham, for example, were handed down and preserved by his descendants; and that Moses was familiar, from his childhood, with those revelations which unfolded the future glories of his nation. Thus, too, in the New Testament, S. Luke has given an account of the Annunciation (ch. i. 26-38), of the communication of the Angel to Cornelius (Acts, x.), &c. &c.

[4] Thus we read: "And it came to pass in the fourth year of Jehoiakim, the son of

operation of the Holy Spirit was indispensable, in order both to bring the original revelation before the mind of the sacred writer, in its primitive perfection, and to enable him to record it with infallible accuracy.[1]

By attending to these principles, which satisfy the second Condition of our problem, we are able at once to perceive the weakness of the great mass of those arguments, which are commonly brought forward in order to prove the existence of error or imperfection in the Bible.[2] In such objections it is tacitly assumed that the matters, to which exception is taken, are recorded as being actually *revelations* from God; while in truth they are often nothing more than historical details, which have been inserted, as simple matters of fact, in the Scripture narrative, under the guidance of its Divine Author.[3]

Josiah king of Judah, that this word came unto Jeremiah from the Lord, saying, Take thee a roll of a book, and write therein all the words that I have spoken unto thee against Israel, and against Judah, and against all the nations, from the day I spake unto thee, from the days of Josiah, even unto this day."—Jer. xxxvi. 1, 2. But we also know that such revelations were given during a period of twenty-three years: "The word that came to Jeremiah concerning all the people of Judah in the fourth year of Jehoiakim * * * saying, from the thirteenth year of Josiah * * * even unto this day, that is, *the three and twentieth year*, the word of the Lord hath come unto me, and I have spoken unto you rising early and speaking."—Jer. xxv. 1–3.

[1] E. g. in the case to which the last note refers, "after that the king had burned the roll" on which the prophet had written all that God had commanded him—"the word of the Lord came to Jeremiah * * * saying, Take thee again another roll and write in it *all the former words* that were in the first roll."—Jer. xxxvi. 27, 28. Indeed, if a record of Prophecy was to be preserved at all, this Divine guidance was obviously indispensable. Eichhorn observes that Greek antiquity seems to have attached no importance to such preservation of the words of an oracular announcement. Hence, when one writer has not copied another, such oracles have been handed down in different forms, which often convey meanings altogether dissimilar. E. g.—When the Thasians, in obedience to the laws of Draco, cast into the sea the statue of the athlete Theagenes (by the fall of which a man had been accidentally killed), the Pythia, consulted on the subject of a famine which occurred shortly afterwards, replied: Θεαγένην δ' ἄμνηστον ἀφήκατε τὸν μέγαν ὑμέων—according to the version given by Pausanias (Lib. vi. 11); while the form in which it is reported by Eusebius ("Præpar. Evang." v. 34), is altogether different: Εἰς πάτρην φυγάδας κατάγων Δήμητραν ἀμήσεις. See his "Einleitung in das A. T." B. iv. s. xxiii.

[2] As exemplifying the neglect of the distinction here insisted upon, and its results, I may adduce the words of M. Athanase Coquerel: "God's share in Revelation is called Inspiration. Inspiration is a transmission of ideas from God to man."—*Christianity*, p. 202. "Religious and moral truth exist in Revelation in a relative degree only; scientific truth, therefore, could not be found there in an absolute degree. These considerations end in leading to the discovery that Revelation *must* contain errors in what regards scientific truth. This was a condition *strictly necessary* to the gift of Revelation."—*Ibid.* p. 211.

[3] See, for example, the quotation from Mr. Coleridge, *supra*, Lecture i. p. 41, note [1]. Or, still more to the point, take the class of objections founded, as in the case of M Coquerel, upon the (alleged) mistakes committed by the writers of Scripture, when touching upon matters of science. As illustrating the bearing of the distinction between Revelation and Inspiration in answering such objections, I would refer the

Having made these preliminary remarks, I now proceed to state the arguments by which the 'dynamical' theory of Inspiration may be supported. Inspiration, I must again repeat, is to be understood as denoting that Divine influence, under which *all* the parts of the Bible have been committed to writing—whether they contain an account of ordinary historical facts, or the narrative of supernatural revelations. In the reception and utterance of such revelations, it is admitted by all who allow that any communication has taken place between earth and heaven, that the human agent can be regarded in no other light than as an instrument in the hand of God, by whose intervention His counsels have been made known to man. If in any case here assuredly, the strict 'mechanical' theory of Inspiration (if true) must hold good;—a theory according to which each phrase and expression in the Bible has been set down by the sacred penmen at the dictation of the Holy Ghost. But if the facts which we are about to consider warrant our asserting that, even in the reception of what are, in the most literal sense, revelations, human agency has had its full scope; and that each prophetic announcement, as recorded in the pages of Scripture, bears the undoubted stamp of the genius, and mental culture, and circumstances of the prophet who has given it utterance;—we are surely justified in concluding that, when relating matters of history or drawing inferences from previous revelations, the same scope, at least, was allowed to the individual characteristics of the inspired writers.

The general method according to which the Divine Scheme has been developed, might, indeed, of itself, justify such a conclusion. We are expressly taught by the whole tenor of Scripture, that the course which God has pursued in conveying His revelations to man has been always singularly marked by the employment of *natural* means: and further, that at each step in the progress of His providential dispensations, and in the accomplishment of prophetic announcements, the expenditure (if one may reverentially use the term) of miraculous agency has

reader to the remarks on "Joshua's Miracle," Lecture viii. *infra*, where other topics of this nature will be considered. With great truth Jahn observes: Diese Bestimmung des Begriffs der Inspiration, und der Unterschied von Offenbarung muss sorgfältig beobachtet werden, indem beyde sehr häufig verwechselt werden, woraus dann grosse Schwierigkeiten erwachsen."—*Einleit.* 1er Th. s. 92.

ever been strikingly sparing. This principle may be briefly illustrated. Take, for example, a fact pointed out by a distinguished writer on Prophecy. David was anointed, and therefore predicted, as king long before he ascended the throne. "By a series of events, following in the ordinary course of Providence, without any miracle interposed, this prediction was brought to pass. * * * No other single narrative of Scripture is so prolix and circuitous as that which describes the accomplishment of this particular prediction. The sequel of things described is protracted, often retrograde in the expectation, and apparently receding from the event; and it fills many chapters[1] before it is brought to a close. Upon which I would observe," continues Mr. Davison, "that it offers, and seems to be designed to offer, an example, in the actual development, of the progress of Prophecy to its completion, whatever may be the mazes and flexures through which it has to work its way; and suggests to us, in other cases not so particularly narrated, how the Divine prescience penetrates through the perplexity of human affairs, and its predictions, *without a sensible miracle*, pass to their near or their remote fulfilment."[2] To this acute observation another illustration may be added. In considering the single predictions of Scripture apart from the complete structure of Prophecy, we may observe, that a certain method has been almost uniformly pursued, which constitutes, as it were, the *Law* according to which the different portions of God's Revelation have been communicated:[3]—namely,

[1] From 1 Sam. xvi. to 2 Sam. v.

[2] "Discourses on Prophecy," pp. 183, 4.

[3] I am anxious to speak here with the utmost caution; as my object is merely to illustrate the ordinary course of Revelation, not to take any part in the controversy which has arisen on a subject with which the present work is concerned but indirectly. Some valuable remarks on this controversy are to be found in the opening chapter of Hofmann's treatise—"Weissagung und Erfüllung." Many writers of recent times, it is there pointed out, have laid down such 'Laws' of the relation of Prophecy to its fulfilment, as only embrace certain cases; and consequently they exclude from the rank of Prophecy all those parts of Scripture to which their arbitrary 'Law' does not apply. Others, again, fearing the excesses to which such views have led, have gone into the opposite extreme; and by looking merely to the single phenomena, have given up, from the first, all idea of the existence of any relation or order in the scheme of Prophecy:—of this latter class Hengstenberg may be adduced as an example (see *infra*, p. 150, note [1]). Among writers of the former class may be reckoned Dr. Arnold. "Prophecy," he observes, "fixes our attention on principles, on good and evil, on truth and falsehood, on God and on His enemy. * * * Prophecy then is God's voice, speaking to us respecting the issue, in all time, of that great struggle which is the real interest of human life, the struggle between good and evil. * * * The Seed of the woman shall bruise the serpent's head, but the serpent notwithstanding shall first bruise His heel. So completely is the earliest

that each prediction, with scarcely an exception, proceeds from and attaches itself to some definite fact in the historical present.[1] In other words, when the future is to be foreshadowed, certain events of the time, historical or incidental, are selected as occasions on which may be founded the several disclosures of the Divine will.[2] The Almighty—who can question

prophecy recorded in Scripture, the sum and substance, so to speak, of the whole language of Prophecy, how diversified soever in its particular forms."—*Sermons*, 5th ed. vol. i. p. 377. And again: "Other events, lesser mercies, earthly deliverances, are in part the subject of Prophecy, and in part its fulfilment. But its language, the language of hope in God, naturally goes beyond these. * * * And therefore it seeks elsewhere its real fulfilments; it tarries not on those lower heights which would receive it on its first ascent from the valley, but ascends and mounts continually to the mountain of God."—*Ibid.* p. 400, note. Almost to the same effect Olshausen remarks, that the Bible represents the contest between Good and Evil as foreshadowed by the relation between Israel and other nations. "Israel has continually its opponents among the other nations, who contravene its efforts towards Good, but who serve, at the same time, in the season of its disobedience, as a scourge in the hand of God. First, the Egyptians with their Pharaoh; then, the Canaanites with their kings; again, Babylon with its despots; Rome, in fine,—the eagles who devour the carcass. These references, the Bible again understands in a higher sense of humanity, of the spiritual Israel, which struggles towards its lofty aim: it, too, has its Egyptians, its Babylon, as well as 'Israel after the flesh' (Rev. xi. 8; xiv. 8)."—*Ein Wort üb. tief. Schriftsinn*, s. 96.

This mode of regarding Prophecy involves much that is just as well as profound; and the principle of the pregnant signification of Scripture which it implies will be adverted to in Lecture vii. The objection, however, to which Dr. Arnold's view is obnoxious, refers to the *exclusive* manner in which he has applied this principle, and to the consequences which he has inferred from it. In the year 1825 he wrote as follows:—"I think that, with the exception of those prophecies which relate to our Lord, the object of Prophecy is rather to delineate principles and states of opinion which shall come, than external events. I grant that Daniel seems to furnish an exception."—*Life and Correspondence*, 6th ed. p. 59. In 1840, however, the full result is stated: "I am very glad, indeed, that you like my Prophecy Sermons: the points in particular on which I did not wish to enter, if I could help it, but which very likely I shall be forced to touch on, relate to the latter chapters of Daniel, which, if genuine, *would be a clear exception to my canon* of interpretation, as there can be no reasonable spiritual meaning made out of the Kings of the North and South. But I have long thought that the greater part of the book of Daniel is most certainly a very late work, of the time of the Maccabees; and the pretended prophecy, about the kings of Grecia and Persia, and of the North and South, is mere history, like the poetical prophecies in Virgil and elsewhere * * * that there may be genuine fragments in it, is very likely."—*Ibid.* p. 505.

[1] "Die ächte Prophetie wurzelt zunächst auf dem historischen Grunde der Gegenwart."—Hävernick, *Einlet.* Th. II. Abth. ii. s. 52. S. Augustine clearly recognises this principle, when, speaking of the prediction of Nathan, 2 Sam. vii. 12–14 (see *infra*, p. 152, note [1]); he observes:—"Facta est quidem nonnulla imago rei futuræ etiam in Salomone, in eo quod Templum ædificavit, et pacem habuit secundum nomen suum * * * sed eâdem suâ personâ per umbram futuri prænunciabat etiam ipse Christum Dominum nostrum, non exhibebat. Unde quædam de illo ita scripta sunt, quasi de ipso ista prædicta sint, dum Scriptura Sancta etiam rebus gestis prophetans, quodam modo in eo figuram delineat futurorum."—*De Civ. Dei*, xvii. 8, t. vii. p. 471.

[2] Otto Strauss, in his "Exposition of the Prophecy of Nahum, illustrated from the Monuments of Assyria" (Berlin, 1853) has pointed out the important bearing of this principle upon the interpretation of Prophecy: "Sacros Israelitarum prophetas constat non temere nec nulla provocatos occasione et necessitate fuisse vaticinatos. * * * Cujusvis igitur vaticinii causa et ratio e temporis sui conditione eruenda

it ?[1]—could in all cases have unveiled His purpose, without observing any such method, or acting in accordance with any such Law: but, He has not only thought fit to disclose His will *gradually*—as the Scripture narrative clearly implies,—

est."—c. II. p. xix. As an example of this, we may adduce the connexion of the sins of Manasseh with the predictions respecting the Exile in Babylon (cf. 2 Kings, xxiv. 3; Jer. xv. 4). Observe, too, that the duration of that exile exactly corresponded with the space of time which elapsed between the first year of the reign of Manasseh, and the carrying out of the reformation by Josiah. Manasseh reigned fifty-five years (2 Chron. xxxiii. 1); Amon, two years (ver. 21); and in the twelfth year of his reign Josiah "*began* to purge Judah and Jerusalem from the high places" (2 Chron. xxxiv. 3), Now 55 + 2 + 13 = 70. See O. Strauss, *ibid.* p. xxx.

[1] This the objection of Dr. Hengstenberg, who is quoted by Hofmann (*loc. cit.* s. 3) as a type of the second class of writers to whom I have referred, p. 149, note; and who contend that prediction is to be prized the more, the more isolated it appears, —its superhuman origin being thus rendered, it is thought, of easier proof. Hengstenberg's words are: "Wer will Gott die Regel vorschreiben, welche er bei seinen Offenbarungen befolgen soll? Wer will sagen, dass er das was er in der Regel nicht thut, nie thun dürfe?"—*Christologie des A. T.*, I. ii. s. 193. And he elsewhere alleges, as a reason for his rejection of the 'Law' of Prophecy now before us, that what is thus connected with an actual event might easily be regarded, not as a Divine revelation, but as a mere subjective foreboding—"blosse subjective Vorahnung."—*Beiträge zur Einleit. ins A. T.*, i. s. 188. This latter remark, I should observe, is directed immedietely, and with justice, against the theory of Nitzsch, that Prophecy is "the represented future of the kingdom of God, grounded on an internal perception of the Divine decree, which, ever proceeding from a definite point of the historical present, points out with more or less dictinctness of detail the completion of the Divine economy; and whilst it is conversant with the Divine in history, *but not with the outward matter*, characterizes *reality* only in those leading points wherein it especially accords with truth."—*System der christl. Lehre*, s. 67. (Montgomery's transl. § 35, p. 88.) On such a theory (as Hengstenberg truly observes), all that is Divine in Prophecy would disappear, and "the prophecy of Redemption in general could be derived from man's need of Redemption, combined with the knowledge of Divine love."—*Beiträge, l. c.*

But still the perversion of a principle must not induce us to overlook its truth, or tempt us to pass over the facts which Scripture offers to our view. No doubt the Lord Almighty can convey the knowledge of His will when and how He pleases; and they who venture to argue, *à priori*, that such or such a 'Law' expresses the relation of *all* Prophecy to its fulfilment, enter upon depths which human reason cannot pretend to fathom: but we may reverentially approach this inquiry, following the course allowed to be just and reasonable in all sound philosophy. In other words, we may investigate *the occasions* on which, as the Bible tells us, God's revelations have been given; and we may inquire,—not assuredly what has *determined* the course of the Divine conduct,—but what, in point of fact, has *constituted* it. In short, we may seek in the pages of Scripture whether the revelations of God have come to man without order, or connexion, or method;—or whether they have been communicated (to borrow the language of philosophy) according to some 'Law.' Now the Bible, by no means obscurely, points out the existence of a remarkable relation between the Divine announcements and certain historical events; nay more (in opposition to the doctrine laid down by Nitzsch), we can continually point out the mutual connexion which subsists between the Divine element in history, and *its external matter*. Thus Israel, in all its institutions, as well as in its external history, is one grand prophecy of the future. Take, e. g. the 78th Psalm, in which the entire history of the chosen people is specially particularized, and expounded in a spiritual manner. The New Testament (1 Cor. x.) informs us how S. Paul understood this Psalm, and applied it to Christ: nay more, an Evangelist places its Messianic reference beyond any doubt, by his adoption of its opening words to describe the Saviour's mode of instruction: "Without a parable spake He not unto them: *that it might be fulfilled which was*

He has also, as a general rule, availed Himself (if we may use the phrase) of certain occasions which were presented from time to time, and which formed a species of natural channel for the conveyance of His revelations.[1] Instances of

spoken by the prophet, saying, I will open my mouth in parables; I will utter things which have been kept secret from the foundation of the world."—S. Matt. xiii. 35.

In opposition to the view here stated, Hengstenberg considers it a needless task to seek for the relation of Prophecy to the time and occasion of its delivery. His error will be seen at once, if we bear in mind his mode of treating the Psalms, in which it is especially important to trace those *occasions* in David's history, which were selected as points to which predictions respecting Christ might be, as it were, attached. Neglecting this principle, Hengstenberg regards the fulfilment in our Lord's history of some of the Psalms to be merely casual; and excludes from his "Christology" others which the New Testament unquestionably represents as Messianic. In that work (B. I. i. s. 94, *u.* s. 154), he divides those Psalms which alone he allows to be Messianic, into two classes: (1) those which describe the Messiah in Glory; viz., Psalms ii., xlv., lxxii., cx.; (2) those in which a suffering Messiah is depicted; viz., Psalms xvi., xxii., xl. Hofmann with reason observes: "Why is the 45th Psalm to be preferred to the 8th, when both are referred in the same manner to Jesus in the Epistle to the Hebrews, and nowhere else? Jesus Himself quotes a passage from Ps. xli. with the words, "that the Scripture may be fulfilled," and refers it to Himself [viz. Ps. xli. 9, "He that eateth bread with Me hath lifted up his heel against Me"—S. John, xiii. 18]; is this Psalm to be regarded as less Messianic than the 22nd? We clearly see why Hengstenberg has omitted the 8th and 41st Psalms; he found it impossible to refer them throughout to Jesus."—*loc. cit.* s. 4.

[1] We can trace this 'Law' of Prophecy even in cases which may appear to present an exception: I mean the announcement by name, so many years before their appearance, of Josiah (1 Kings, xiii. 2), and Cyrus (Isai. xliv. 28; xlv. 1),—the solitary instances of this kind of prediction to be found in the Old Testament. In each of these cases there is the closest connexion with the immediate occasion of the prophetic communication. In 1 Kings, xiii. 2, the name Josiah (יאשיהו) expresses the fundamental thought of the prediction of which it is a part. The prediction directly refers to the signification of this name [Gesenius explains it to mean: "quem Jehovah sanat: a rad. אשה *sanavit*, et יהו"], which is as expressive here, as is that of Immanuel, when employed by Isaiah (ch. vii. 14). The announcement of "the man of God" that "Jehovah founds, or supports"—which is implied by the name Josiah —is obviously opposed to the erection of that altar by Jeroboam, the destruction of which it was the prophet's immediate design to proclaim: "O altar, altar, thus saith the Lord; Behold a child shall be born unto the house of David, Josiah by name. * * * And he gave a sign the same day, saying * * * Behold the altar shall be rent," &c.,—in other words, Jehovah, not Jeroboam, is the true founder of the altar. In the next place, as to Isaiah's prediction of Cyrus:—(1.) We are to notice how completely ideal is the prophet's description of this king. By him, for the first time among the rulers of the heathen, will homage be paid to the God of Israel. He is to be the counterpart to Egyptian Pharaoh: "He shall build My city, and he shall let go My captives, not for price nor reward, saith the Lord of Hosts."—Isai. xlv. 13. He is God's "shepherd," His "anointed." Jehovah declares of him: "I have raised up one from the north, and he shall come: *from the rising of the sun* (ממזרח-שמש) shall he call upon My Name."—xli. 25. (2.) The passage just quoted, combined with the statements that "the righteous man" (xli. 2), and "a ravenous bird" (xlvi. 11) were to come "from the east," supplies *the occasion* on which is founded the prophet's allusion to the primary signification of the name Coresch (כורש), or Cyrus, which corresponds to the old Persian—"huarĕ ksaêta," i. e. *Sol rex* (the final ש belonging to the nominative). The name, therefore, is to be regarded as a regal appellative; as a 'nomen dignitatis.' It is, moreover, certain, that Cyrus before he ascended the throne was called Agradates, the title Cyrus being a species of apotheosis. Bournouf observes: "Le titre de *soleil* s'est naturellement attaché au nom du monarque, surtout dans un pays comme la Perse, où cet astre recevait sous son propre

this mode of acting will present themselves to every mind. Suffice it here to mention the memorable example afforded by the narrative contained in the seventh chapter of the second Book of Samuel, where God employs the occasion of correcting the error into which Nathan's precipitancy had led him, for the purpose of conveying the fundamental prediction, which represents Christ as the Son of David, and on which are founded all the Messianic Psalms.[1] By this fact of the connexion of single

nom de 'huarĕ' les adorations des hommes." The employment by Isaiah of the foreign word Coresch, is not more strange than the use by Nahum (ch. iii. 17) of the Persian טפסר, which our version renders "captains," and Gesenius "Satraps." There is, besides, a strong resemblance in sound between כורש, and the Hebrew חרס which occurs in Isaiah, xix. 18, and where it is rendered in the margin of our Bibles, "Heres or the Sun." That Isaiah himself employs Coresch merely as a "nomen dignitatis," and that he is unconscious (see *infra*, Lecture v.) of its personal application, is further confirmed by the absence, in his use of the word, of the predicate "King of Persia," by which Cyrus is invariably designated when named elsewhere in the Old Testament,—in Chronicles, in Ezra, and in Daniel. See Hävernick's "Einleitung," Th. II. Abth. ii. s. 163 ff. Gesenius' remark on כורש is "Græci hoc nomen Persis *solem* notasse observant (v. Ctesias ap. Plut. Artax. Opp., t. i. p. 1012. Etym. M. Κῦρος κοῦρος ἥλιος), et recte quidem."

[1] "And when thy days be fulfilled, and thou shalt sleep with thy fathers, I will set up thy seed after thee * * * and I will establish his kingdom. He shall build an house for My Name, and I will establish the throne of his kingdom for ever. I will be his Father, and he shall be My son."—vers. 12–14. "Almost all the more ancient Christian expositors, and several of the Jewish, refer this prediction to Christ: * * * the majority of the earlier Christian writers discern in it a 'double sense,' either by referring part of it to Solomon, and part to Christ; or by regarding Solomon as its proper object, and representing him and his kingdom as types of the Kingdom of Christ."—Sack, *Apologetik*, s. 274.

Ebrard, in his comment on Heb. i. 5, points out how the inspired writer exhibits, in that passage, the connexion of the Messianic Psalms with this grand announcement of Nathan, by combining it with the unquestionable prediction of the Second Psalm: "For," argues the Apostle, "unto which of the angels said He at any time, Thou art My Son, this day have I begotten Thee? And again, I will be to Him a Father, and He shall be to Me a Son." The language of Gen. iii. 15, and Deut. xviii. 15, denoted, it is true, the Messiah in general terms: in the words of Nathan, however, was it for the first time revealed, that He should spring from the line of David; and also that His Sonship should be such as could not properly be derived from David, but only from God. S. Augustine has acutely remarked, that the fact of Solomon having been anointed king, during David's lifetime (1 Kings, i. 32–53), of itself proves that this prediction of Nathan could not have been fulfilled literally in his person: "Nec ob aliud, vivente adhuc patre suo David, regnare Salomon cœpit, quod nulli illorum regum contigit, nisi ut hinc quoque satis eluceat, non esse ipsum, quem prophetia ista præsignat, quæ ad ejus patrem loquitur, dicens 'Et erit cum repleti fuerint dies tui,'" &c.—*De Civ. Dei*, xvii. 8. t. vii. p. 471. Indeed, Solomon himself implies as much, 1 Kings, viii. 27. "Not less clearly," writes Ebrard, "was David conscious of the fact that Nathan's words were to find their full accomplishment, for the first time, 'in the distant future (למרחוק) in a Man, who is Himself the Lord Jehovah.'—2 Sam. vii. 19 ["Thou hast spoken also of Thy servant's house for a great while to come. And is this the manner of man, O Lord God?" E.V.:—the latter words meaning, according to Ebrard: "And this is the manner of the Man, The Lord Jehovah"]; or as it is explained 1 Chron. xvii. 17, 'in a Man who is exalted to the rank of Jehovah.' [The English version reads here: "Thou hast regarded me according to the estate of a man of high degree, O Lord God."] On this promise, so well understood, David builds the hope which he expresses in the Second Psalm."—s. 42. (Cf. Acts, ii.

predictions with the historical present, may be explained, I conceive, that characteristic of Prophecy which consists in its 'double sense;'[1] according to which the *particular* is brought forward as a pledge of what lies far beyond, without representing the former as the true or highest end. Thus the prediction which foreshadowed the restoration of Judah from captivity in Babylon,[2] had a further end. "It is a subject," observes Mr. Davison, "akin to the Evangelical Restoration. Every Christian understands the resemblance."[3]

30, 31). Of the manner in which the English Version renders these passages Ebrard remarks: "If אדני י״י were not in apposition to תורת־אדם, but a vocative, the latter words would be altogether without meaning."—*Ibid.* For an analogous, but different, interpretation, see Kennicott's "Remarks on select passages in the Old Testament," p. 115.

[1] "This age of Prophecy [viz. that of David and Solomon], in particular, brings the doctrine of the 'double sense,' as it has been called, before us. For Scripture Prophecy is so framed in some of its predictions, as to bear a sense directed to two objects, of which structure the predictions concerning the kingdom of David furnish a conspicuous example; and I should say, an unquestionable one, if the whole principle of that kind of interpretation had not been by some disputed and denied. * * * The double sense of Prophecy, however is of all things the most remote from fraud or equivocation, and has its ground of reason perfectly clear. For what is it? Not the convenient latitude of two unconnected senses, wide of each other, and giving room to a fallacious ambiguity; but the combination of two related, analogous, and harmonizing, though disparate subjects, each clear and definite in itself; implying a two-fold truth in the prescience, and creating an aggravated *difficulty*, and thereby an accumulated proof in the completion."—Davison, *Discourses on Prophecy*, p. 195. In his application of this important principle, Mr. Davison appears to me to exhibit too great caution when he observes: "I would understand the double sense to obtain only in some of the more distinguished monuments of Prophecy."—p. 198. Olshausen seems to have had a more just apprehension of its applicability. Equally cautious with Mr. Davison, he guards against the abuse of this principle of the 'double sense,' by refusing to accept any interpretation of Scripture which *the words of Scripture* do not justify:—"This is to be laid down, in the first instance, as the rule of every system of exposition, that Scripture has no other meaning in addition to the simple meaning of its own words; but yet *under* this it again has the same, only lying somewhat more deeply. * * * A firm, necessary connexion must always be maintained between the literal sense of the words, and the more profound import of this verbal sense."—*Ein Wort*, &c. s. 90. This pregnant sense of the language of Prophecy has been clearly pointed out by Bacon: "Secunda pars [Historiæ Ecclesiasticæ] quæ est historia ad prophetias, ex duobis relativis constat; prophetia ipsa, et ejus adimpletione * * * atque licet plenitudo et fastigium complementi eorum [vaticiniorum] plerumque alicui certæ ætati vel etiam certo momento destinetur; attamen habent interim gradus nonnullos et scalas complementi, per diversas mundi ætates."—*De Augm. Scient.* lib. II. c. xi. The importance of giving due weight to the comprehensive signification of the language of Scripture will be shown more fully in Lecture vii. Meanwhile I may refer to a remarkable illustration already given, Lecture iii. p. 109, note [1].

[2] Isai. lii.; Jer. xxxi. "In like manner the prophecy of the judicial destruction of Jerusalem with the dissolution of the Jewish Economy, symbolizes with that which relates to the final judgment, which will shut up the whole temporal Economy of God at the end of the world. In the New Testament they are united."—Davison, *Discourses*, p. 199.

[3] *Ibid.* p. 198. It may be well to observe here, that the whole system of Types to which the Bible attaches so much importance, affords an obvious illustration of the 'double sense' of prophecy. See on this subject Lecture v. *infra*.

What we know respecting the *occasional* composition of the several books of the New Testament, supplies a striking analogy to that 'Law' of Prophecy to which I have now drawn attention. The external *occasions* which have called forth the successive components of the New Testament, are precisely parallel to the historical events to which particular predictions have been annexed; and may, in this light, be regarded as the providential element, by which the free agency of the sacred writers was brought under the guidance of Inspiration. The Epistles of S. Paul to the Corinthians, for example, were called forth by certain events in one of the churches which he had planted. This was confessedly their primary intent. And yet such was the occasion made use of by the Holy Ghost for the purpose of conveying Divine instruction to the remotest futurity.[1]

Before entering upon an examination of the particular facts by which, as I have said, the 'dynamical' theory of Inspiration may be proved, it is necessary to consider the nature of the Prophetic Office.

The great doctrine of Monotheism formed the essence of the Patriarchal Creed; and presented, as taught by Moses, the leading idea of the Jewish nation. On Sinai was announced from heaven the complete polity of Israel, according to which the people were to acknowledge Jehovah as their invisible Lord and King. The duty of the Hebrew as a citizen thus became equivalent to his religious duty;—each particular of his life being referred to his duty to God. In the words of the Prophet—"Jehoveh was

[1] We learn from a passage in Tertullian's controversy with Marcion, that the Church has, from the first, recognised the principle that the *external occasion* of each inspired document is altogether subordinate to its destination for the future: "Ecclesiæ quidem veritate epistolam istam ad Ephesios habemus emissam, non ad Laodicenos; sed Marcion ei titulum aliquando interpolare gestiit, quasi et in isto diligentissimus explorator. Nihil autem de titulis interest, *cum ad omnes Apostolus scripserit, dum ad quosdam.*"—*Adv. Marcion*, v. 17, p. 607. So also in the Fragment preserved by Muratori (*see supra*, Lecture ii. p. 57, note [2]), we read: "Cum ipse beatus Apostolus Paulus sequens prædecessoris sui Johannis ordinem, nonnisi nominatim septem Ecclesiis scribat. * * * Et Johannes enim in Apocalypsi licet septem Ecclesiis scribat, TAMEN OMNIBUS DICIT."—ap. Routh, *Reliq Sacræ.* t. i. p. 395. Of this passage Credner, having remarked that S. John is called the "prædecessor" of S. Paul with reference to Gal. i. 17 (*οἱ πρὸ ἐμοῦ 'Απόστολοι*)—gives the following paraphrase: "Although Paul has directed Epistles to seven churches defined by name, still these writings possess a value not merely local, but rather universal; just as the Revelation of John addressed, in the first instance, to seven churches has a universal value. This comparison is rendered a demonstration by the fact that in the Revelation itself (ch. ii. 23), what is said to the Seven Churches is extended to all, by the words: *καὶ γνώσονται πᾶσαι αἱ ἐκκλεσίαι.*"—*Zur Geschichte des Canons*, s. 86.

their Judge, Jehovah was their Lawgiver, Jehovah was their King."[1] This conception received from Josephus the appropriate appellation of the "Theocracy."[2] In it consisted the germ of that future Kingdom of God, the erection of which was the great end of the former Covenant. In the different features of the Theocracy can be traced the outline of that agency which has been ordained by the Divine decree for the Redemption of mankind. Here were displayed the preparations for, and the types of, that Church of Christ to be founded in "the latter days," and unto which all nations are yet to flow;—"which stretches out her boughs unto the sea, and her branches unto the river;"—of which "kings shall be the nursing fathers, and queens the nursing mothers;"—"She that looketh forth as the morning, fair as the moon, clear as the son, terrible as an army with banners!"[3]

The Theocracy presents two great periods: the one starting from Moses, the other taking its rise from Samuel. During the former, its chief ministers were the Priests, who, to the end, represented one of the most essential elements of the Law. To them was intrusted the sacred symbolism of Divine worship, to which even the oral teaching of the Law yielded in importance;[4] the sacerdotal instruction, throughout the entire course of the Theocracy, being a system of teaching by acts. Together with the institution of the Sacerdotal Order, the germ of a new ministry—that of the Prophets—was placed by Moses in the Law,[5]

1 Isai. xxxiii. 22. Cf. 1 Sam. viii. 7; Micah, iv. 7. Cf. on this subject the remarks of Baumgarten Crusius, "Grundzüge der bibl. Theol.," s. 35.

2 Alluding to the various forms of earthly governments, Josephus observes: *ὁ δ' ἡμέτερος νομοθέτης εἰς μὲν τούτων οὐδοτιοῦν ἀπεῖδεν· ὡς δ' ἄν τις εἴποι βιασάμενος τὸν λόγον, Θεοκρατίαν ἀπέδειξε τὸ πολίτευμα, Θεῷ τὴν ἀρχὴν καὶ τὸ κράτος ἀναθεὶς, καὶ πείσας εἰς ἐκεῖνον ἅπαντας ἀφορᾷν ὡς αἴτιον μὲν ἁπάντων ὄντα τῶν ἀγαθῶν.*—*Cont Apion*, II. xvi. t. ii. p. 482.

3 Ps. lxxx. 11; Isai. xlix. 23; Cant. vi. 10.

4 Hävernick justly rejects the opinion that the Priests represent merely the formal and external side of the Theocracy, while the Prophets exhibit its spiritual tendency and internal character. The symbolical ordinances and the oral teaching of the Law are placed side by side, in the following command of the Lord to Aaron: "It shall be a statute for ever throughout your generations: and that ye may put difference between holy and unholy, and between unclean and clean; and that ye may teach the children of Israel all the statutes which the Lord hath spoken unto them by the hand of Moses."—Lev. x. 9–11. "Einleit." Th. II. Abth. ii. s. 4.

5 "Prophecy belongs rather to the promissory side of the Law, than to its commands. The Prophets are a free gift of Divine Grace, designed to bless the Theocracy as instruments of Jehovah, and in whom His love for His people finds expression."—Hävernick, *loc. cit.* s. 5. This writer further points out how fully the *freedom* of the Spirit's influence was exhibited, even under the Old Covenant, by the fact,—so remarkable when Oriental manners are taken into account,—that the exercise of the

although its full development was reserved for a later period. That the Spirit of Prophecy was poured out in his days, appears not only from the account of the seventy Elders who "prophesied" (as we read in the eleventh chapter of the book of Numbers),[1] but also from the tests which the Law had already defined for distinguishing between true and false prophets.[2] The age of the Judges, towards its close, presents an instance in which the gift of Prophecy was conferred even to the fullest extent, in the case of the "man of God" who came "unto Eli, and said unto him, Thus saith the Lord ;"[3] and whose announcements are conceived in a form, and expressed in a manner, identical with those of subsequent prophets. As time went on, together with the total degeneracy of the Priesthood, this dawning light of Prophecy was almost quenched in Israel.[4] Under such circumstances, Somuel was called by God, not only to reform the Sacerdotal Order, but also to restore Prophecy to its true legal basis, by

prophetic agency was independent of sex. This is proved by the examples of Miriam (Exod. xv. 20), Deborah (Judg. iv. 4)—whose genuinely prophetical song is a sublime echo of the age of Moses,—and Huldah (2 Kings, xxii. 14); to each of whom the *official* title (see *infra*, p. 158, note [1]), of Prophetess—נביאה, is applied. Mention is also made of the existence of Prophetesses in the age of the New Testament: e. g. Anna (S. Luke, ii. 36), and the daughters of Philip the Evangelist (Acts, xxi. 9).

[1] Moses, filled with a growing sense of his powerlessness to keep the people true to their allegiance to God, had said unto the Lord: "I am not able to bear all this people alone, because it is too heavy for me. * * * And the Lord came down in a cloud, and spake unto him, and took of the Spirit that was upon him, and gave it unto the seventy Elders: and it came to pass that when the Spirit rested upon them they prophesied (ויתנבאו), and did not cease. * * * And there ran a young man, and told Moses and said, Eldad and Medad do prophesy in the camp. * * * And Moses said unto [Joshua], Enviest thou for my sake? would God that all the Lord's people were prophets (נביאים), and that the Lord would put his Spirit upon them!"—vss. 14, 25, 27, 29; which latter words, observes Hävernick, "express as well an earnest longing for the perfection of the Theocracy, as a profound insight into the essence of the Kingdom of God,—nay more, which contain a prophetic announcement of Its glorious future."—*loc. cit.* s. 17.

[2] "If there arise among you a prophet (נביא) * * * and the sign or the wonder come to pass whereof he spake unto thee, saying, Let us go after other gods * * * thou shalt not hearken unto the words of that prophet."—Deut. xiii. 1–3. "The prophet (הנביא), which shall presume to speak a word in My Name, which I have not commanded him to speak, or that shall speak in the name of other gods, even that prophet shall die."—Deut. xviii. 20. These preparatory ordinances pointing to the institution of a Prophetic Order, although the office itself was not as yet fully developed, are perfectly analogous to the directions which related to the future introduction of kingly rule: e. g. "And it shall be, when he sitteth upon the throne of his kingdom, that he shall write him a copy of this Law in a book," &c.—Deut. xvii. 18.

[3] Sam. ii. 27–36.

[4] The influence of the Spirit of God was, however, still exerted, although in a lower and far different manner, in the persons of the Judges, by whom, during this interval, the Theocracy was administered. E. g. "The Spirit of the Lord came upon Gideon."—Judges, vi. 34; "upon Jephthah,"—xi. 29; upon Samson, xv. 14, &c. &c.

proving that the guidance of the people must rest upon an inward religious life. His function was not, as has been erroneously maintained, to create anew, but simply to re-organize ;[1] and the sacred history informs us of his success. The child Samuel saw a time "when the word of the Lord was precious," when there was "no open vision :"[2]—the man Samuel beheld around him a host of prophets, who, together with him, served Jehovah, sang His praises, received His revelations, and proclaimed His Name.[3] In the interval between Moses and Samuel, the *official* title of the Prophetic Order, (Nabi),[4] together with the office itself, had

[1] "As the whole tendency of Samuel's labors," observes Hävernick, "can only be understood by looking constantly to the Law,—as he is to be accounted merely the Theocratic Reformer, not the founder of Theocracy,—such is also his relation to Prophecy."—*loc. cit.* s. 18. Indeed Samuel's entire life was, as it were, a reflection of that of Moses ; and hence he is referred to in Scripture as a second Law-giver: "Then said the Lord unto me, Though Moses and Samuel stood before Me."—Jer. xv. 1. And again: "Moses and Aaron among His Priests, and Samuel among them that call upon His name."—Ps. xcix. 6. Although no information on the subject is given in 1 Sam. i., we learn from 1 Chron. vi. 22–28, that Samuel was of the tribe of Levi, and the family of Kohath; while we can infer that he performed the functions of a Priest from 1 Sam. vii. 9. (See Winer, "Real Wörterb." *Art.* 'Samuel.') He was not High Priest, Eli having been the last individual who filled at once the highest ecclesiastical and civil offices.

[2] 1 Sam. iii. 1.

[3] The system of Revelation is most plainly exhibited by a review of the periods which start from Moses and Samuel respectively. I have already alluded (Lecture i. pp. 23, 24.) to the distinction which exists between God's revelations by Act, and by Word; i. e. between the manifestation of His power over the material universe, and the proofs of His omniscience by the mouth of His prophets. The former is chiefly attested in that series of sublime acts of Omnipotence, displayed during the space of time which elapsed from the Exodus to the conquest of Canaan:—for, although in the Patriarchal age also, there were exhibited proofs of miraculous power, they were comparatively few and far between. "This relative withdrawal of miracles in the history of the Patriarchs," observes Sack, "is an incomparable proof of the historic truth and the Divine nature of the Patriarchal Revelation. What opportunities has a mythico-poetical narrative here let slip!"—*Apologetik*, s. 174. After the possession of Canaan was secured, displays of miraculous power appear to have been gradually withdrawn; and the course of Revelation was now marked by the series of prophetic announcements which signalized the period from Samuel to Malachi. We must, however, bear in mind that, as in the Divine economy in general there are no abrupt transitions, so here, too, each of these phases of Revelation fades away into the other. In the age of Moses there were displays of omniscience; in the Prophetic period there were exhibitions of miraculous power. After Malachi there was indeed, for a considerable time, a cessation from such supernatural revelations; but this was merely the prelude to the advent of the Divine Revealer Himself, in whom both phases were united. Cf. Köppen, "Die Bibel ein Werk der göttl. Weisheit." B. ii. s. 100.

[4] The earliest occasion on which the word Nabi is used in Scripture, is when God commands Abimelech to restore Sarah to Abraham, adding: "He is a Prophet (כי־נביא הוא) and he shall pray for thee, and thou shalt live."—Gen. xx. 7. "Here Abraham is so called, for the Patriarch combined in his person the kingly, the sacerdotal, and the prophetical office."—Hävernick, *Einleit.* Th. I. Abth. i. s. 54. Cf. Ps. cv. 15. During the age of Moses mention is made, as we have seen (p. 156, notes [1] and [2]), of both Prophets and Prophetesses: e. g. "If there be a Prophet (נביא) among you, I the Lord will make Myself known unto him in a vision," &c.—Num. xii. 6. It is to be observed that Moses himself is styled Nabi in Hos. xii. 13 [14].

fallen into oblivion; and hence it was said in the days of Samuel: "He that is now called a Prophet (Nabi) was beforetime called a Seer (Roeh)."[1] A regular line of prophets having been formed by Samuel, the title, defined by the Law, was restored; and the appellation "Prophet" (Nabi) henceforward denotes the *official* character of chosen ministers of the Theocracy, who are distinguished by this title from those other men of God, who possessed, indeed, the prophetic *gift*, but not the prophetic *office*. The signification of the term *Nabi* may be inferred, not only from its admitted etymology,—according to which it implies "a speaker," "one who announces the sayings and revelations of God,"[2]—but also from the explanation given by Jehovah Himself: "The Lord said unto Moses, See, I have made thee a god (Elohim) to

[1] 1 Sam. ix. 9. There are three distinct Hebrew terms, for which our English version gives but these two equivalents: viz. נביא (Nabi, i. e. the official title of the chief agent of the Theocracy)—which is translated *a Prophet;* ראה (Roeh), and חוה (Chozeh), which are rendered by the single term *a Seer.* The question whether any or what distinction exists between these three terms has been much discussed. It seems plain, however, notwithstanding some apparent exceptions, that they are not employed indiscriminately by the sacred writers. E. g. in 1 Chron. xxix. 29, Samuel is styled "Roeh;" Nathan, "Nabi;" and Gad, "Chozeh;"—the English version, here as elsewhere, making no distinction between Roeh and Chozeh. The conclusion at which I have arrived, and which in some respects differs, so far as I am aware, from any which has been hitherto suggested, is that Nabi and Roeh are equivalent in their meaning—as, indeed, the text 1 Sam. ix. 9, of itself intimates; each denoting the *official* minister of the Theocracy, and Roeh being merely the archaic form of expression. Chozeh, on the other hand, is the general title applied to any agent of God to whom revelations were *occasionally* made; and to whom, on certain exigencies, Divine communications were vouchsafed. According to this view every "Nabi" could receive the title "Chozeh," but not conversely. But on this question see Appendix J.

I may add, that the LXX. invariably render נביא by *προφήτης* (or *ψευδοπροφήτης*, e. g. Jer. vi. 13); and that they make no distinction between ראה and חוה (see 1 Chron. xxix. 29, where both terms are rendered *βλέπων*), translating in numerous places by *ὁρῶν*, *βλέπων*, and *προφήτης* indifferently: see 2 Sam. xxiv. 11; 1 Chron. xxvi. 28. This general use of *προφήτης* to denote all classes of God's messengers, is further exhibited by the writings of Philo and Josephus. See Lecture ii. p. 65, &c. The term *προφήτης*, Eusebius observes, is derived *παρὰ τὸ προφαίνειν καὶ προφωτίζειν ἐν αὐτοῖς τὸ Θεῖον Πνεῦμα, μὴ μόνον τὰ παρόντα, ἀλλὰ καὶ τῶν μελλόντων ἀληθῆ καὶ ἀκριβῆ γνῶσιν.*—*Demons. Evang.*, lib. v. p. 209, ed. Paris. On the other hand, S. Isidore of Seville observes: "Quos gentilitas *vates* appellat, hos nostri *prophetas* vocant, quasi præfantores, quia porro fantur, et de futuris vera prædicunt."—*Etymolog.*, lib. VII. c. viii. p. 60.

[2] Both Knobel ("Der Prophetismus der Hebräer," Th. i. s. 137) and Hävernick explain נבא (which is found only in Niphal and Hithp.) to mean "to stream forth," "to gush forth from a source," after the analogy of נבע, *scaturivit.* Cf. נחל נבע, "a stream *gushing out*," or "*flowing* brook."—Prov. xviii. 4. Hence, by a transition not unusual, it is transferred to the flow of words; see Ps. lxxviii. 2. Compare the manner in which הטיף (which literally signifies *stillavit*), is used to express the idea of *prophesying;*—see Micah, ii. 6, and cf. Ezek. xxi. 2. The trope cannot be better expressed than by the words: "My doctrine shall drop as the rain, My speech shall distil as the dew."—Deut. xxxii. 2.

Pharaoh: and Aaron thy brother shall be thy prophet (Nabi;)" the Lord having previously announced to Moses,—Aaron "shall be thy spokesman to the people: and he shall be to thee instead of a mouth: and thou shalt be to him instead of God."[1] And thus the official Prophet was, above all others, God's spokesman to the people; the mouth, as it were, by which Jehovah uttered His commands.

Closely connected with the organization of the Prophetic Order, was the institution of those Societies or Schools established by Samuel at Ramah, Bethel, Gibea, Jericho, and Gilgal; the members of which were called "prophets," or "sons of the prophets," indifferently.[2] Over these Societies the leading prophets of

[1] Exod. vii. 1; Exod. iv. 16 ("and he shall be thy spokesman"—ודבר־הוא לך). Knobel observes that Onkelos has rendered נביא ("*prophet*") in the former of these passages, as well as פה ("*mouth*") in the latter, by the word מתורגמן *interpres.—Ibid.* Th. i. s. 104. In this sense Jehovah promises Jeremiah: "If thou take forth the precious from the vile, thou shalt be as *My mouth*"—Jer. xv. 19; and also declares respecting "the Prophet like unto Moses"—"I will put My words in *his mouth.*"—Deut. xviii. 18.

[2] 1 Sam. x. 5, 10; xix. 20; 2 Kings, ii. 3, 5; iv. 38. Cf. too, 2 Kings, xxii. 14, and 2 Chron. xxxiv. 22, where it is said of "Huldah the Prophetess" that "she dwelt in Jerusalem, in the *College*," (משנה, which the Chaldee paraphrast renders *domus doctrinæ*, and Kimchi *a school*—see "Select Discourses" by John Smith, of Cambridge, "On Prophecy," ch. ix.) Hävernick thinks that Samuel did not appoint any fixed constitution of these assemblies, merely because we do not meet the phrase "Sons of the Prophets" until after his death: during his lifetime they were called "the company (חבל, להקה) of the Prophets." That their number was considerable, may be inferred from the fact that Ahab on one occasion "gathered the prophets together about four hundred men"—1 Kings, xxii. 6; and that in Jezebel's persecution "Obadiah took an hundred prophets and hid them by fifty in a cave."—1 Kings, xviii. 4. See Knobel, "Der Proph. der Hebräer," Th. ii. s. 39 ff. Over these Schools, as I have said, one of the leading prophets of the age usually presided. Thus Saul's messengers "saw the company of the prophets prophesying, and Samuel standing as appointed over them"—1 Sam. xix. 20: so also, when Elisha came again to Gilgal * * * the sons of the prophets were sitting before him"—2 Kings, iv. 38. Hence the title "Sons or pupils of the Prophets." That such was the origin of the phrase is evident from the question asked, on one occasion, respecting them: "But who is their father?"—1 Sam. x. 12. In this sense, too, Elisha addressed Elijah when taken from him to heaven: "My father, my father, the chariot of Israel, and the horsemen thereof."—2 Kings, ii. 12. See J. Smith, *loc. cit.* They were also sometimes called simply prophets:—as we learn from 1 Kings, xx., where the person who, at ver. 35, is described as "a certain man of the sons of the prophets," is named at ver. 38 "the prophet;" see also 2 Kings, ix. 1, 4:—in both of which cases we observe that the individual named executed a Divine commission. Indeed we can infer that Divine revelations were at times made to these assemblies collectively: e. g. "The sons of the prophets that were at Bethel came forth to Elisha and said unto him, Knowest thou that the Lord will take away thy master from thy head to-day?"—2 Kings, ii. 3, 5. That "the Master" or chief Prophet was always regularly instituted in his functions, we may, perhaps, conclude from the command of God to Elijah: "Elisha, the son of Shaphat of Abelmeholah, shalt thou anoint to be Prophet in thy room."—1 Kings, xix. 16. From these Societies the selection of the leading prophets was ordinarily made. "Elisha himself was trained up by Elijah as his disciple [see e. g. 1 Kings, xix. 21, 'Then Elisha arose, and went after Elijah. and ministered unto him;' and also 2 Kings, ix. 1] and therefore in 2 Kings, iii. 11, it was thought a reason

the age presided; and the course of instruction imparted in them appears to have embraced the following subjects: music,[1]—which so far back as the time of Moses formed an important feature of Divine worship; the composition of lyrical poetry,—the connexion of which with Prophecy is shown by the predictions of Balaam, and the songs interwoven in the writings of Isaiah (both instances exhibiting how closely Prophecy bordered upon sacred lyrics;)[2] and above all, as we may safely conclude from the char-

good enough to prove that he was a prophet, for that he had been Elijah's disciple, and 'poured water upon his hands,' as all the Jewish scholastics observe. * * * And hence it was that Amos urgeth the extraordinariness of his commission from God: 'I was no prophet, nor was I a prophet's son' (Amos, vii. 14)—'He was not prepared for Prophecy, or trained up so as to be fitted for a prophetical function by his discipleship,' as Abarbanel glosseth upon the place. And therefore Divine Inspiration found him out of the ordinary road of Prophets, among his herds of cattle." —J. Smith, *loc. cit.*

[1] Carpzovius observes:—"Notamus eam [musicam] partim ad prophetarum exercitia, et munia, partim ad dispositiones pertinere eorum qui huic se muneri destinabant."—*Introd.*, § ix. p. 21. The most obvious proof of the latter fact here adverted to, is afforded by the case of Elisha when solicited to declare the Lord's will to King Jehoram: "And Elisha said, As the Lord of Hosts liveth * * * surely were it not that I regard the presence of Jehoshaphat the King of Judah, I would not look toward thee, nor see thee. But now bring me a minstrel. And it came to pass, when the minstrel played, that the hand of the Lord came upon him. And he said, Thus saith the Lord" &c.—2 Kings, iii. 14–16. The relation of music to the functions of a prophet, may be noticed so early as the age of Moses:—"Then sang Moses and the children of Israel this song unto the Lord. * * * And Miriam the prophetess * * * took a timbrel in her hand," &c.—Exod. xv. 1, 20. Cf. Judges, iv. 4; v. 1. The intimate connexion of music with the prophetical office, and of both with the service of the Temple, we learn from 1 Chron. xxv. 1, where David "separated to the service of the sons of Asaph, &c. who should prophesy (הנבאים) with harps, with psalteries, and with cymbals." The word למנצח, too,—which must be rendered "to the chief musician," and which stands at the head of fifty-three Psalms, affords a proof that the Psalms, in the superscription of which it occurs, were intended for public use in the Temple. Compare Hab. iii. 19, where the prophet manifestly imitates the superscription of the Psalms: "the words (למנצח בנגינותי), with which the song of the Church is there closed, can be no otherwise explained than as meaning, 'to the chief musician upon my (Israel's, for it is the Church that speaks through the whole chapter) stringed instrument,' assigned to the chief musician, that he might publicly sing it with the accompaniment of sacred music in the Temple."—Hengstenberg, *Comm. on* Ps. iv. (Clarke's For. Theol. Lib., i. p. 57.) While considering the Divine institution of the musical element of the Temple worship, we must not forget the *external* qualifications which Moses possessed, in consequence of his Egyptian education. C. F. Keil, in his continuation of Hävernick's "Einleitung," (s. 6) calls attention to the words of Philo, in which he enumerates the human acquirements of Moses: * * * *τήν τε ῥυθμικὴν καὶ ἁρμονικὴν καὶ μετρικὴν θεωρίαν, καὶ μουσικὴν τὴν σύμπασαν, διά τε χρήσεως ὀργάνων* * * * *Αἰγυπτίων οἱ λόγιοι παρέδοσαν*—*De Vita Mosis*, I. t. ii. p. 84,—a statement which is quoted by Clemens Alex., Strom. i. p. 413. It is to be observed, moreover, that not the sacred music alone, but everything relating to the worship of Jehovah, was the result of Divine command: "And the Lord spake unto Moses saying, See I have called by name Bezaleel * * * and I have filled him with the Spirit of God * * * to devise cunning works, to work in gold," &c.—Exod. xxxi. 1–4.

[2] By sacred lyrical poetry is meant songs of praise and thanksgiving to Jehovah, as distinguished from those poetical compositions which are stamped with the strictly prophetical character. The song of the children of Israel, after the passage of the

acter of the founder, Samuel,—the Divine ordinances of the Law, and the spirit of the Theocracy. This necessity of systematic education, in order to qualify men to become spokesmen of God, is in every respect analogous to that course of instruction and experience, and personal companionship with their Master, which was required under the New Testament by the Apostles, before

Red Sea (Ex. xv.), is an example of the former; the Messianic Psalms, of the latter. That the lyrical poetry of Israel, like all the other features of the Theocracy, must be traced to a Divine source, is proved by Keil in the work referred to in the last note. The attempt to trace its origin in the warlike spirit of the people, is utterly without support. Of such songs as must, if this theory were correct, have been produced in the earlier times, we know absolutely nothing. Neither the "Book of the wars of Jehovah" (Numb. xxi. 14), nor the war song of Deborah (Judges, v.) form exceptions,—for the genuine Theocratic character is stamped upon both. In the history of the Hebrews there occurs no such "Heroic Age," to which the origin of the poetic art can be ascribed. The poetry of Israel was most copious in those times when religion had the greatest power over the popular mind; not in those periods when war was the leading tendency, as during the rule of the Judges. In short, there is no historical foundation for such an opinion: it rests upon a perfectly defective view of the true characteristics of Hebrew poetry. "If, with the Hebrews, Religion is related to Poetry as cause to effect, it is clear that even the historical formation of their poetry must be connected, in the most intimate manner, with the entire course of development of the Theocracy. The sacred lyrics, consequently, received their condition wholly from the revelations of God in word and act, so that they are to be regarded as the corresponding echo of the faithful community."—Keil, *loc. cit.* s. 5. The song of Moses (Exod. xv.) is a poetic piece in a highly cultivated form, and Ps. xc. is also ascribed to him in its superscription. That in his age the arrangements of public worship required a liturgical use of such songs, is placed beyond any doubt by Numb. x. 35, 36 (cf. Ps. lxviii. 1;) nor was this species of inspired poetry ever discontinued (see Judges, v; 1 Sam. ii. 1–10, which pieces have the greatest community with Ex. xv.) We have also to notice another species of versification of a less formal nature, and more akin to the original character of poetry. It is characterized by the name of the poets—המשלים, "they that speak in proverbs" —Numb. xxi. 27, of which class of sayings that chapter affords a remarkable example (ver. 27–30:) such are also the adages or "parables" of Balaam (Numb. xxiv. 3). (In proof of Balaam's inspiration see Lecture v.)

We must remember, however, that all Hebrew poetry was not inspired. Although it is said of Solomon that "his songs were a thousand and five" (1 Kings, iv. 32), yet only two of his poetical compositions stand in the Canon (Ps. lxxii. and cxxvii.) From the age of Solomon, to the opening of the Chaldean catastrophe, we possess (in addition to some Psalms of Asaph and the sons of Korah, from the times of Jehoshaphat and the Assyrian invasion,)—the song of Jonah (ch. ii.), of Hezekiah (Isai. xxxviii. 10, &c.), and some hymns interwoven in the prophecies of Isaiah (ch. xii. and xxvi.) To these prophetical songs belongs the hymn of Habakkuk (ch. iii.), which in part relates to Ps. lxxvii.; and which repeats in lyrical form the impression produced by the revelation which the prophet had received. Bishop Lowth observes:—"It is sufficiently evident that the Prophetic Office had a most strict connexion with the poetic art. They had one common name, one common origin, one common author,—the Holy Spirit. Those, in particular, were called to the exercise of the Prophetic Office who were previously conversant with the sacred poetry. It was equally a part of their duty to compose verses for the service of the Church, and to declare the oracles of God: it cannot, therefore, be doubted that a great portion of the sacred hymns may properly be termed prophecies, or that many of the prophecies are in reality hymns. * * * Of this we have an illustrious proof in that prophetic ode of Moses (Deut. xxxii.) which he composed by the especial command of God, to be learned by the Israelites."—*The Sacred Poetry of the Hebrews* Lect. xviii. (Gregory's transl., vol. ii. p. 18).

they could enter upon their peculiar functions. That such preparatory discipline was necessary, is proved by the statement of S. Peter, that the successor to the Apostleship of Judas should be one "who had companied" with the disciples, "beginning from the baptism of John:" for to those who were qualified by knowledge thus acquired S. Peter restricts the choice; declaring that from such persons only "must one be ordained to be a *witness*" of Christ's Resurrection.[1] The case of S. Paul, it is true, proves, that while this was the ordinary rule of God's selection, certain other agents of the Divine will could be raised up, who were not thus qualified by personal experience;—just as the preparatory training of a Prophet under the Old Testament might be dispensed with. Amos, for example, replied to the cavils of Amaziah—"I was no prophet, neither was I a prophet's son; but I was an herdman, and a gatherer of sycamore fruit: and the Lord took me as I followed the flock, and the Lord said unto me, Go, prophesy unto My people Israel."[2] Such cases, however, were exceptions: and the ordinary method by which the scheme of Revelation was carried on, was the employment of men whose education, experience, and natural capacity qualified them to become ministers of God's will.

This remark brings immediately before us the facts to which I have adverted above; or, in other words, the process by which the revelations of God have been introduced into the sphere of human knowledge. And here, at the outset, I would observe,—although after what has been said the caution may appear unnecessary,—that we must ever keep in mind, that the internal suggestion which prompts his utterance neither proceeds from, nor is produced by, the prophet's natural powers or personal condition:[3] it is a *new* principle which is infused into his soul, with

[1] Acts, i. 21, 22. See on this point Lecture vi.

[2] Amos, vii. 14. Cf. ver. 12, where Amaziah calls him "seer" (חזה); see *supra*, p. 159, note [2]. Hävernick, (Th. II. Abth. ii. s. 303 ff.) observes that, in consequence of the circumstances which thus marked the call of Amos, we have more minute information concerning his history than is usual in the case of the minor prophets. He was "among the herdmen of Tekoa * * * in the days of Uzziah King of Judah, and in the days of Jeroboam, the son of Joash, King of Israel, two years before the earthquake."—Amos, i. 1.

[3] "God reveals Himself externally in the history of the people; internally in the spirit of man by His Spirit: while neither the world nor humanity are brought into any false identity with the Divine Being. Thus Hebrew Prophecy, according to its *subjective* starting-point, stands in contrast to all heathen notions, according to which the Divine life comes forth in the multiplicity of the powers of Nature. Prophecy is not, like the heathen *Mantik*, tied to the concealed, mysterious, gloomy energies and

an energy transcending all that is human. This fact is completely established by the uniformity with which the prophets themselves point out one characteristic of every species of Divine revelation. They invariably represent their knowledge as proceeding from *an immediate intuition.*[1] Such is the obvious sense of the constant expressions, "Seer," "Vision."[2] All revelations were "seen," or "gazed upon;" and were, therefore, apprehended by the inward intelligence instantaneously, and in a manner analogous to the reception of impressions by the outward senses. Thus the revelations which the prophets received, could be neither the mere result of their own power of reflection, nor fictions suggested

powers of Nature. Hence there is found in genuine Hebraism no divination of many different kinds; no uncertain, fluctuating struggle and effort to place one's self in community with the Deity. * * * The essence and subjective peculiarity of prophetic inspiration lies in this, that it finds its origin, not in the natural consciousness of man, nor yet in any eminent natural parts and abilities, but proves itself to be the higher supernatural operation of the Spirit of God."—Hävernick, *Einleitung, loc. cit.* s. 29 ff. The Bible notion of Revelation, says Baumgarten Crusius, proceeds from the idea of the guardian God of Israel, and of the union with the people of Him who is also Deity of the Universe. With the Greeks and Romans the notion was connected with that of Deity *in* the Universe (in a Pantheistic or Polytheistic sense); or it was related (as in the case of Socrates), to a mystic conception of a union with God; or, in fine, as denoting something exalted and excellent.—*Grundzüge der bibl. Theol.*, s. 215.

[1] "The perception of the 'word' which God communicated to the prophets, was made by means of the spiritual sense, the apprehension of which is named, in reference to the noblest of the natural senses, a *seeing.* * * * As the Divine idea presents itself not mediately through the natural sense, but directly to the spirit of the prophet, the notion of *seeing* is in its proper place."—Delitzsch, *Der Proph. Habak.* s. 3. (Fairbairn's "Ezekiel," p. 96.) Hence the comprehensive, and significantly descriptive terms חזה, חזון, ראה, מראה, &c. Thus Isaiah "*saw* the vision concerning Judah."—i. 1. Ezekiel "*beheld*" the vision of "dry bones."—xxxvii. 8. Micah "*saw* the word of the Lord concerning Samaria,"—i. 1; and, in like manner, we read of "the burden which Habakuk the Prophet did *see.*"—i. 1. On the word משא, translated "burden" in the passage last quoted, S. Jerome observes: "MASSA nunquam præfertur in titulo, nisi quum grave, et ponderis laborisque plenum est quod videtur."—*Comment in Abac.* Prol. t. vi. p. 587. And to the same effect, in his Prologue to Nahum: "*Assumptio*, quam LXX. interpretantur *λῆμμα* [they also render by *ὅραμα, ὅρασις, ῥῆμα*,] et Aquila *ἆρμα* interpretatus est, apud Hebræos MASSA ponitur, id est, *grave onus:* eo quod eam adversus quam videtur premat, nec sinat elevare cervicem."—*Ibid.* p. 535. On Isai. xiii. 1, see t. iv. p. 169. Hengstenberg ably defends this interpretation against those moderns (viz., Vitringa, Michaelis, Gesenius, &c.) who have revived the notion of the LXX. See his "Christologie," ii. s. 102; and s. 272, where he proves that the only passage urged in opposition to S. Jerome's view (viz. Zech. xii. 1) does not really militate against it.

[2] When S. John says that he "bare record of the word of God, and of the testimony of Jesus Christ, and of *all things that he saw.*"—Rev. i. 2,—the latter words clearly signify the Apostle's prophetic visions. On the passage, "The *book of the vision* (ספר חזון) of Nahum the Elkoshite," &c., Nah. i. 1, Otto Strauss observes: "Adjectus genitivus חזון *omnino propheticum esse librum* ostendit; monemur, describendum hostium interitum nec conspectum oculis esse, nec post eventum enarratum, neque ratione antea et conjectura nuntiatum, sed animo extrinsecus rapto oblatum per speciem et visionem, et sic perceptum literis exinde exaratum."—*Nahumi de Nino Vaticin.*, p. 7. The words, "the book of the vision," point to the Divine Author; while the addition of the prophet's name directs attention to the human agent.

by their own imagination.[1] Of this there can be no clearer proof, than the plain and unaffected manner in which they intimate, that their gift of prophesying was neither permanent, nor the result of their own volition, but depending wholly on the Divine pleasure. For example, when the Shunamite fell at the feet of Elisha, and his servant "came near to thrust her away, the man of God said, Let her alone; for her soul is vexed in her, and the Lord hath hid it from me, and hath not told me." In like manner S. Paul does not scruple to declare—"I go bound in spirit unto Jerusalem, not knowing the things that shall befall me there."[2] In short, the men of God were as fully assured of the objective reality of the Divine communications, conveyed thus immediately to their souls, as we are of the objective reality of the world which surrounds us.[3]

The revelations conveyed to God's servants may, speaking generally, be reduced to two classes.[4] They were either com-

[1] "The prophets feel themselves elevated to a new and higher sphere,—a world living beyond common reality; in the midst of which they hear the Truth—the voice of God. God is Himself the author of such a state: He qualifies the soul of the prophet for those intuitions, causes him to 'see visions,' 'opens his ear,' &c.; and also endows the inward organs of his spirit, so that they are capable of attaining to those intuitions (Anschauungen). By means of this Divine starting-point, as the principle operating in the prophets, the prophetic intuitions do not fall into the category of mere subjectivity; but lay just claim to be entitled actual states which have an objective reality."—Hävernick, *loc. cit.*, s. 34.

[2] 2 Kings, iv. 27; Acts, xx. 22. Cf. also what we read of Jeremiah having addressed prayers to God, at the request of his countrymen; promising them that "whatsoever thing the Lord shall answer you, I will declare it unto you."—xlii. 4. Although his prayer was offered at a season of urgent emergency (cf. ch. xli. 17, with xlii. 15–19), several days elapse before the prophet receives his answer. "And it came to pass after ten days, that the word of the Lord came unto Jeremiah."—ver. 7.

[3] For some further remarks on this question, see Lecture v.

[4] I have not attempted any formal classification of the various means by which revelations have been conveyed to man. Attempts of this nature must to a great extent be arbitrary, and inexact; nor is such a classification at all essential to the present subject. I may, however, adduce that which has been given by S. Isidore of Seville (*circ.* A.D. 595)—"Prophetiæ autem genera sunt septem. Primum genus, *Ecstasis*, quod est mentis excessus: sicut vidit Petrus vas illud submissum de cœlo, in stupore mentis, cum variis animalibus. Secundum genus, *Visio:* sicut apud Esaiam dicentem, 'Vidi Dominum sedentem,' &c. (cap. vi.). Tertium genus, *Somnium:* sicut Jacob subnixam in cœlum scalam dormiens vidit. Quartum genus, *per Nubem:* sicut ad Moysem et ad Job post plagam loquitur Deus. Quintum genus, *Vox de cœlo:* sicut ad Abraham sonuit dicens: 'Ne injicias manum tuam super puerum;' et ad Saulum in via: 'Saule, Saule, quid Me persequeris?' Sextum genus, *Accepta parabola:* sicut apud Salomonem in Proverbiis, et apud Balaam cum evocaretur a Balac. Septimus genus, *Repletio Sancti Spiritus:* sicut pæne omnes Prophetas."—*Etymolog.* lib. VIII. c. viii. p. 61. S. Isidore adds: "Alii tria genera visionum esse dixerunt." I. "Secundum oculos corporis,"—(as Abraham saw the three men under the oak at Mamre). II. "Secundum spiritum, quo imaginamur ea, quæ per corpus sentimus,"—(as S. Peter's vision, Acts, x.) III. "Quod neque corporeis sensibus, neque ulla parte ani-

munications made when the action of the external senses was suspended, and there was no consciousness of passing events; or they were communications made in the natural waking state, when the prophet was conscious of all that took place around him.[1] This division, to some extent, corresponds with that intimated in the words of S. Paul—"I will come to visions and revelations of the Lord:"[2] where the term Visions implies that certain ideas had been imparted by means of an image, while by Revelations is denoted an unfigurative communication from the Divine to the human spirit.[3] Of these classes both may be, and often are, united, but always so that one or other predominates: here, however, we are chiefly concerned with the former, in which the action of the outward senses was suspended, and in which state the human soul, like a pure mirror undimmed by any cloud of earth, received and reflected the beams of Divine Truth which were presented to it.[4] This class comprises but two species of revelations,—revelations by Dreams, and revelations by Ecstatic Visions; which channels of the Divine communications seem to differ principally in this, that in Ecstasy the activity of the men-

mæ qua corporalium rerum imagines capiuntur: sed per intuitum mentis, quo intellecta conspicitur veritas: sicut Daniel, hoc præditus, mente vidit, quod Balthasar viderat corpore." For the distinctions of the mediæval Jews, see Appendix C.

[1] S. Thomas Aquinas discusses this subject with his usual acuteness. Considering the question "De modo propheticæ cognitionis,"—he observes: "Prophetica Revelatio fit secundum quatuor, scil. secundum influxum intelligibilis luminis; secundum immissionem intelligibilium specierum; secundum impressionem, vel ordinationem imaginabilium formarum; et secundum expressionem formarum sensibilium. Manifestum est autem quod non fit abstractio a sensibus, quando aliquid repræsentatur menti prophetæ per species sensibiles, sive ad hoc specialiter formatas divinitus, sicut rubus ostensus Moysi (Ex. iii.) * * * Similiter etiam non est necesse ut fiat alienatio a sensibus exterioribus per hoc quod mens Prophetæ illustratur intelligibili lumine, aut formatur intelligibilibus speciebus. * * * Sed quando fit revelatio prophetica secundum formas imaginarias, necesse est fieri abstractionem a sensibus, ut talis apparitio phantasmatum non referatur ad ea quæ exterius sentiuntur."—*Summ. Theol.* 2da 2dæ, qu. clxxiii. art. 3. t. xxiii. p. 307.

[2] 2 Cor. xii. 1, *ἐλεύσομαι γὰρ εἰς ὀπτασίας καὶ ἀποκαλύψεις* Κυρίου. The verb *ἁρπάζεσθαι* ("caught up," ver. 2) points out the ecstatic condition, in which the vision was accompanied by impressions upon the sense of hearing—*ἤκουσεν ἄῤῥητα ῥήματα* (ver. 4).

[3] Thus Hävernick distinguishes between 'Prophecy,' and 'Vision' understood in the strict sense of the word. In the former, Divine truth is represented to the Prophet's mind in a more simple, spiritual, and unveiled manner; in the latter, in a more concrete manner, under the veil of symbols. Modern writers, overlooking the fact, already adverted to (p. 164, note [1]),—viz. that the notion of *Intuition* (Anschauung) is essential to *all* kinds of Prophecy, have applied it solely to *Visions*, which are but a particular species of Intuition. See his "Einleitung," Th. II. Abth. ii. s. 39.

[4] *Πῶς προεφήτευον αἱ καθαραὶ καὶ διαυγεῖς ψυχάι; οἱονεὶ κάτοπτρα γινόμενα τῆς θείας ἐνεργείας, τὴν ἔμφασιν ῥανὴν καὶ ἀσύγχυτον, καὶ οὐδὲν ἐπιθολουμένην ἐκ τῶν παθῶν τῆς σαρκὸς ἐπεδείκνυντο. πᾶσι μὲν γὰο πάρεστι τὸ* Ἅγιον Πνεῦμα.—S. Basil *Comm. in Esai.* Proœm. § 3, t. i. p. 379.

tal faculties was called into exercise. We meet with Dreams in the case of Jacob, Solomon, Daniel, and others in the Old Testament; in the case of Joseph in the New.[1] In all such instances we see how one of the most ordinary of natural facts was made use of, as the means of conveying a revelation; and how the action of the senses was suspended by purely natural causes. In the state of Ecstasy,—itself also to be met with, although more rarely, in the department of natural facts,—the suspension of certain faculties was produced, either by the sublime and overpowering character of the conceptions infused into the mind, or by the direct operation of the Divine energy, or by both causes conjoined.[2] A striking example of the ecstatic condition is supplied by the trance of S. Peter, recorded in the Acts of the Apostles; which at the same time affords a complete proof of how the natural condition and circumstances of the person who

[1] Gen. xxviii.; 1 Kings, iii. 5; Dan. vii. 1; S. Matt. i. 20; ii. 19:—see *supra*, Lecture iii. p. 114. S. Thomas Aquinas excellently observes, with reference to Divine communications of this class:—"Si cui fiat divinitus repræsentatio aliquarum rerum per similitudines imaginarias (ut Pharaoni, et Nabuchodonosor), aut etiam per similitudines corporales (ut Balthassar), non est talis censendus Propheta, nisi illuminetur ejus mens ad judicandum."—*loc. cit.* art. 2. Cf. what has been already said, p. 145, and Lecture i. p. 42, as to the necessity of Inspiration even in cases where a revelation had been received. For further instances in which men, who were not Divine agents, in the sense in which Prophets are to be considered as such, have received intimations from God in dreams, cf. Gen. xx. 6 (Abimelech); xxxi. 24 (Laban); xl. 5 (Pharaoh's Butler and Baker); Judges, vii. 13 (the Jewish soldier).

[2] Scripture affords some information as to the personal state of the prophet while in the ecstatic condition, and which may be exemplified by the case of Daniel. (1.) He is overpowered by the Divine influence: "Now as he was speaking with me, I was *in a deep sleep* (נִרְדַּמְתִּי) on my face toward the ground"—Dan. viii. 18. (2.) He is next raised to the state of spiritual intuition: "He touched me, and set me upright."—*ibid.* (3.) The revelation is now communicated: "And he said, Behold I will make thee know what shall be in the last end," &c.—ver. 19, &c. (4.) To this condition of spiritual excitement succeeds a state of bodily exhaustion: "And I. Daniel fainted, and was sick certain days."—ver. 27. See also Dan. x. 7–21: "I retained no strength, yet heard I the voice of his words * * * then was I in a deep sleep (נִרְדָּם) on my face * * * and behold an hand touched me, which set me upon my knees," etc. The account of the Transfiguration presents a remarkable analogy: "While he [S. Peter] yet spake, behold a bright cloud overshadowed them: and behold a voice out of the cloud * * * and when the disciples heard it they fell on their face * * * and Jesus came *and touched them*," etc.—S. Matt. xvii. 5–7: cf. Rev. i. 17. In all such instances the *touch of the hand* acted restoratively in the case of those who had been overpowered by the sight of the Divine glory (cf. Ezek. iii. 23, &c.: see also Lecture iii. p. 129, &c). The suppression of the external senses is referred to more expressly in Gen. xv. 12: "And when the sun was going down, *a deep sleep* fell upon Abraham." On the term here employed (and also, as we have seen, in Dan. viii. 18; x. 9), Feurstius in his Concordance (p. 1043) observes: "תַּרְדֵּמָה—Somnus gravior et profundior, sive naturalis sive supernaturalis, e quo non facile homo expergefieri potest, a v. רדם = רדם, vi dormiendi, non obturandi s. obstruendi, uti nonnulli finxere. LXX. θάμβος, ἔκστασις, κατάνυξις, φόβος. A. καταφορά. S. κάρος. Th. ἔκστασις. Gen. ii. 21. Job, iv. 13; xxxiii. 15. Prov. xix. 15. Isai. xxix. 10. Gen. xv. 12. 1 Sam. xxvi. 12."

received this species of revelation, were employed by the Almighty to furnish *the form* under which His communications were conveyed. S. Peter, we are told, "went up upon the house-top to pray, about the sixth hour: and *he became very hungry, and would have eaten;* but while they made ready, he fell into a trance."[1] We all know the nature of the vision then presented to his mind's view; and how the momentous revelation which the Apostle received, was embodied in a symbolical representation, of which his natural condition at the time supplied the form.

And here the course of our inquiry brings before us the peculiar character of the ecstatic condition. Our ignorance of the manner according to which God acted directly upon the mind of the prophet will, no doubt, always continue: but this no more affects the reality of such operations, than our ignorance of the *modus operandi* in the world of nature affects the reality of the operations of God in it. Assuming, therefore, that certain immediate suggestions have been conveyed to the soul of the prophet, we have to consider in what manner they were received and appropriated by him, in his state of trance or ecstasy.

In this condition the entire vital energy is concentrated on the world within, the activity of the outward senses passing into repose:[2]—for example, S. Paul "cannot tell" whether what took place in his ecstasy, happened while he was "in the body," or

[1] Acts, x. 9–16. Cf. Olshausen, *in loc.* The following words—"Now while Peter doubted in himself what this vision which he had seen should mean" (v. 17)—exemplify in the clearest manner how the prophets were, throughout their ecstasy, conscious of their state; and accurately remembered both the fact of their condition, and what had taken place in it. Hävernick ("Einl.," II. ii. s. 36), alluding to this feature of the case, draws attention to a remark of Tholuck ("Vermischte Schriften," i. s. 87), to the effect that this continued consciousness completely severs the connexion, alleged to exist, between the prophetic ecstasy and (the so-called) facts of somnambulism. Nothing exhibits more fully the prejudices and prepossessions with which some modern writers approach the whole subject, than the remark of Knobel, that prophetic visions cannot have taken place as they are represented, "*because* (!) most of them are described so circumstantially and diffusely, and withal so clearly, accurately, and perfectly, that they cannot possibly have been so seen."—*loc. cit.* Th. i. s. 170. But see *infra*, Lecture v.

[2] On this subject I avail myself partially of the remarks of Knobel ("Der Proph. der Hebräer," Th. i. s. 155 ff.), from whose general principles, however, I totally dissent. He quotes the following apposite passages from S. Augustine: "Quando penitus avertitur atque abripitur animi intentio a sensibus corporis, tunc magis Ecstasis dici solet. Tunc omnino quæcunque sint præsentia corpora, etiam patentibus oculis non videntur, nec ullæ voces prorsus audiuntur: totus animi contuitus aut in corporum imaginibus est per spiritalem, aut in rebus incorporeis nulla corporis imagine figuratis per intellectualem visionem."—*De Genesi*, lib. xii. 25, t. iii. p. 305. And again: "Ecstasis mentis excessus est."—*Enarr. in Ps.* xxxiv.–lxvii. t. iv. p. 242, 683.

"out of the body."[1] The infusion of the spiritual influence suspends, at the same time, the usual succession of ideas and ordinary current of thought; the power of imagination alone remaining active, and the sense of spiritual vision being excited to the highest degree of intensity. As the bodily senses exert their agency impelled by the vital principle which pervades man's animal organization, so the sense of spiritual intuition is called into action by means of the new life poured into the soul. Hence Visions are the result of Ecstasy. Now, as it is only by the creation of *new* ideas and conceptions in the mind, that the mysteries of God, and revelations of things unseen can, in most instances, be conveyed to the soul still fettered by its bodily organization, such ideas and conceptions must receive a certain clothing,—assume certain forms,—be embodied, as it were, in certain shapes,—before they can be apprehended by an understanding, limited to the experience of this life of ours. If this be not effected, such revelation, at the utmost, must be confined to the individual who received it: for, were he even enabled, under the guidance of the Holy Spirit, to comprehend disclosures thus transcending the powers of human thought, and the range of human experience,—human language would obviously be incapable of conveying any representation of those ideas to others.[2] Of this nature, would seem to have been the revelations vouchsafed to S. Paul, when "he was caught up into Paradise, and heard unspeakable words which it is not lawful" (or rather "possible") "for a man to utter."[3] But, if it were designed that the revelation should be communicated to others, the ideas, by which it was conveyed to the prophet's mind, must be there invested with certain forms supplied by such intellectual powers as now possess activity. In dreams and ecstasy, imagination alone is active;[4] and the forms

[1] 2 Cor. xii. 2. *Εἴτε ἐν σώματι οὐκ οἶδα, εἴτε ἐκτὸς τοῦ σώματος οὐκ οἶδα.*

[2] "Per donum prophetiæ confertur aliud humanæ menti supra id quod pertinet ad naturalem facultatem, quantum ad utrumque, scilicet et quantum ad judicium per influxum luminis intellectualis, et quantum ad acceptionem, seu repræsentationem rerum, quæ fit per aliquas species. Et quantum ad hoc secundum potest assimilari doctrina humana revelationi propheticæ, non autem quantum ad primum. Homo enim suo discipulo repræsentat aliquas res per signa locutionum; non autem potest interius illuminare, sicut facit Deus."—S. Th. Aquinas, *Summ. Theol.* 2da 2dæ, qu. clxxiii. art. 2, t. xxiii. p. 305.

[3] 2 Cor. xii. 4. *ἃ οὐκ ἐξὸν ἀνθρώπῳ λαλῆσαι.*

[4] The modern Jewish writers (e. g. Maimonides, R. Joseph Albo, etc.), seem to have had a just apprehension of the manner in which human agency was thus employed. The learned J. Smith of Cambridge thus sums up their views: "They sup-

or symbols created by this faculty, acting according to its natural laws, are presented to the spiritual vision of the prophet, to be gazed at as an object of thought; although, previously, the original of such symbols had been but the subject of thought—or, in other words, mere ideas or conceptions.

The nature of the case, of necessity, imposes the several steps of the process which has here been described; and in it we can trace the source of that human coloring, by means of which the prophets have been enabled to render intelligible to their fellow-men the mysteries of the Kingdom of God,—so far, at least, as God has been pleased to reveal them.

To this origin, therefore, we are to ascribe symbolic actions and symbolic visions.[1] The peculiarity of the former consists in this, that the prophet's own personality is so mingled with the objects which are presented to his spiritual gaze, that he takes an active part in the drama, representing one or other of the parties engaged in all such intuitions,—Jehovah, or the people. The symbolic action, however, was no more intended to facilitate the understanding of the revelation, than were the Parables of the New Testament to elucidate the sense of the doctrines which they convey.[2] Symbolic visions differ from symbolic actions

posed the imaginative power to be set forth as a stage, upon which certain *visa* and *simulacra* were represented to their understandings, just indeed as they are to us in our common dreams; only that the understandings of the prophets were always kept awake and strongly acted upon by God in the midst of these apparitions, to see the intelligible mysteries in them; and so in these types and shadows, which were symbols of some spiritual things, to behold the antitypes themselves; which is the meaning of that old maxim of the Jews which we formerly cited out of Maimonides, 'Magna est virtus seu fortitudo prophetarum, qui assimilant formam cum formante eam," [i. e. "Great is the power of the prophets, who, while they looked down upon these sensible and conspicable things, were able to furnish out the notion of intelligent and inconspicable beings thereby, to the rude senses of illiterate people."] Smith proceeds to observe: "Now these ecstatical impressions, whereby the imagination and mind of the prophet was thus ravished from itself, and was made subject wholly to some agent intellect, informing it and shining upon it, I suppose S. Paul had respect to. 'Now we see δι' ἐσόπτρου ἐν αἰνίγματι, by a glass, in riddles or parables' (1 Cor. xiii. 12); for so he seems to compare the highest illuminations which we have here with that constant irradiation of the Divinity upon the souls of men in the life to come: and this glassing of Divine things by hieroglyphics and emblems in the fancy, which he speaks of, was the proper way of prophetical inspiration."—*Of Prophecy*, ch. ii.

[1] See Hävernick, "Einleit." II. ii. s. 41 ff.

[2] "Ueberhaupt aber darf die symbolische Handlung nicht so zu einem verständig berechneten Mittel herab gedrückt werden, da sie vielmehr die höchste innerlichste Erregung im Gemüthsleben des Propheten voraussetzt. Sie ist also vielmehr der nächstliegende unmittelbare Ausdruck des innerlich Erlebten, ihre Anwendung daher jedesmal von der Individualität des Propheten und seinem Verhältnisse zur Zeit abhängig."—Hävernick, *ibid.* s. 42.

merely in this, that the prophet is no longer an actor in the scenes which he describes: he now regards them simply as a spectator.[1] And here the general question of the symbolism of Scripture suggests itself.

When the ideas, Divinely infused into the prophet's mind, related to things which surpass the bounds of human experience, it is plain, as I have observed, that ordinary language must fail to convey to others what was thus revealed. It was necessary, therefore, that such representations or symbols should be moulded, as it were, for the occasion, which would best conform to those ideas. In this case we may regard the imagination as *productive.* Of this nature, for example, was the symbolism employed by Ezekiel, "as he was among the captives by the river of Chebar, and the heavens were opened, and he saw visions of God."[2] But there were occasions, on which the ideas supplied to the prophet's mind were in some measure related to the world of sense; and here the symbol corresponds to the *form* which such ideas had actually represented. In this case the imagination may be regarded as *reproductive*:[3]—for example, when "the rod of an almond tree" is the object of Jeremiah's vision.[4] In such an instance there is not, necessarily, any essential connexion between the image, and the *idea* represented; there is merely what we

[1] It is not material to the present inquiry to examine whether the symbolic act was, in any case, performed externally, or was (as some maintain) at all times merely exhibited on the scene of the prophet's imagination,—as we know to have been the case in many instances: e. g. "Thus saith the Lord God of Israel unto me: Take the wine-cup of this fury at My hand, and cause all the nations, to whom I send thee, to drink it. * * * Then took I the cup at the Lord's hand, and made all the nations to drink."—Jer. xxv. 15, &c. An analogy to such *inward acts* is afforded by what took place in prophetic vision. Thus God, we are told, "*brought forth* Abraham, *abroad*, and said, Look now toward heaven, and tell the stars, if thou be able to number them."—Gen. xv. 5; while we know from ver. 12, that the stars were then invisible to the eye of sense, for the sun had not as yet gone down. See J. Smith's discussion of this question (*loc. cit.* ch. vi.) Hengstenberg ("Christol," I. i. cap. v. s. 331, and III. s. 14 ff.) maintains that, with a few exceptions, the symbolical act was never performed externally. The obscurity, however (as Hävernick remarks), in which the sacred writers have left this subject, proves of how little real moment the question is: and it is only material to observe, that the prophets have, in either case, equally placed on record a perfect description of their inward intuitions.

[2] "And I looked and behold a whirlwind came out of the north, a great cloud, and a fire unfolding itself, and a brightness was about it, and out of the midst thereof as the color of amber out of the midst of the fire. Also out of the midst thereof came the likeness of four living creatures," &c., &c.—Ezek. i. 4, &c.

[3] See Knobel, "Der Proph. der Hebräer," i. s. 158.

[4] "The word of the Lord came unto me, saying, Jeremiah, what seest thou? And I said, I see a rod of an almond-tree. Then said the Lord unto me, Thou hast well seen; for I will hasten my word to perform it."—Jer. i. 11, 12.

should term a poetical allusion. Thus, in the passage before us, the prophet sees "the rod of an almond tree"[1]—a tree which has received its Hebrew name from its being the first of plants to awake from the sleep of winter. The conclusion to be drawn is, that Jehovah will soon awaken, and hasten to perform His word.[2]

The process by which the imagination was thus called into activity, and the laws according to which it acted, seem here also to have followed the course of nature; and to have been as strictly in conformity with ordinary laws, as in the case of prophetic dreams. This assertion is fully borne out by the striking analogy which a remarkable class of intellectual phenomena affords. To the mental vision of the painter or the poet, certain ideas and conceptions offer themselves *spontaneously*. In this consists his creative genius. The ideas and conceptions thus brought before his mind, the artist then invests with certain forms of beauty, or sublimity, suggested by his imagination,—of which it is the peculiar function to enlist in its service "those mysterious relations, by which visible external things are assimilated with inward thoughts and emotions, and become the images and

[1] שקד—"*Amygdalus*, ita dicta, quia omnium arborum prima e somno hiberno evigilat et expergiscitur, Jer. i. 11 (ubi alluditur ad vim festinationis et studii, quæ in hac rad. inest)."—Gesenii Lex. *in voc.* Somewhat more suggestive of the import of the vision was the symbol of the "linen girdle" which Jeremiah "put on his loins," which he afterwards hid "in a hole of the rock by Euphrates," and which when taken thence "after many days," "was marred and profitable for nothing:"—for God declared, "After this manner will I mar the pride of Judah * * * for as this girdle cleaveth to the loins of a man, so have I caused to cleave unto me the whole house of Israel," &c.—Jer. xiii. 1–11. In this case we perceive how an additional revelation was required in order to explain to the prophet the meaning of the symbol which he employed. Cf. also the symbol of the potter's vessel, ch. xviii. 1–6.

[2] The following ingenious summary of the different elements of which the Divine communications consisted includes the principle which I am anxious to establish; "Repræsentantur autem divinitus menti Prophetæ, quandoque quidem mediante sensu exterius, quædam *Formæ Sensibiles;* sicut Daniel vidit scripturam parietis, ut legitur Dan. v.: quandoque autem *per Formas Imaginarias*, sive omnino divinitus impressas, non per sensum acceptas (puta si *alicui cæco nato imprimerentur in imaginatione colorum similitudines*), vel etiam divinitus ordinatas ex iis quæ a sensibus sunt acceptæ; sicut Hieremias 'vidit ollam succensam à facie Aquilonis,' ut habetur Hier. i.: sive etiam imprimendo *Species Intelligibiles* ipsi menti; sicut patet de his qui accipiunt scientiam, vel sapientiam infusam, sicut Salomon, et Apostoli. *Lumen* autem *intelligibile* quandoque quidem imprimitur menti humanæ divinitus ad dijudicandum ea quæ ab aliis visa sunt; sicut dictum est de Joseph [qui exposuit somnium Pharaonis], et sicut patet de Apostolis, quibus 'Dominus aperuit sensum, ut intelligerent Scripturas,' et dicitur Lucæ xxiv. 45; et ad hoc pertinet interpretatio sermonum: sive etiam ad dijudicandum secundum divinam veritatem ea quæ cursu naturali homo apprehendit; sive etiam ad dijudicandum veraciter et efficaciter ea quæ agenda sunt. * * * Sic igitur patet quod prophetica revelatio quandoque quidem fit per solam luminis influentiam, quandoque autem *per Species de novo impressas, vel aliter ordinatas.*"—S. Th. Aquinas, *Summ. Theol.* 2da 2dæ, qu. clxxiii. art. 2. t. xxiii. p. 306.

exponents of all passions and affections."[1] It is true that in the case which we are considering the conceptions no longer arise spontaneously, but spring from a Divine revelation ;—the Divine Spirit, moreover, guiding the imagination while clothing them with the appropriate symbols :[2] nevertheless, the means employed for this purpose were strictly natural ;—a fact which will appear more clearly when we consider the phenomena which result.

In the first place, we have to notice the peculiar style in which all Visions are described. Compare, for example, the character of those historical pieces which occur in the writings of Isaiah and Jeremiah, with the language of the prophetical portions in which their Visions are related. We have already seen that, in the case of Visions, the imaginative faculty of the prophets was called into play ; and we consequently find here too, as in the purely natural exercise of this faculty to which I have referred, that poetic diction and poetic imagery color all their writings. Thus it is that the treasures of the unseen are poured forth in all the riches of the visible. The jewels of earth, the stars of heaven, sea, fountains and rivers, mountains and hills,—every object of creation, visible and invisible,—all are blended in the sublime poetry of the prophets. In it is interwoven all that can stir the imagination of man ; armies and their array, the battle and the siege :—all that is terrible or imposing in nature ; the dragon and the beast, the lion and the eagle :—the brightest and the fairest of the objects we behold ; the rainbow and the morning star. In the prophetic language, in fine (to borrow a beautiful thought applied to the Revelation of S. John), "we recognise the rapidity of the eagle's wing over earth, heaven, and sea, with plumage catching the varied light without end."[3]

In the next place, the language and style of the prophets vary, not only according to the genius, and character, and edu-

[1] See Jeffrey's Essays, vol. iii. p. 105.

[2] The favorite idea of Philo (see *supra*, Lecture ii. p. 65), that prophets are 'Interpreters' of the inward suggestions which they receive from God, not inaptly expresses this mode of recording their Visions;—whereby the prophets translate, as it were, the Divine communication into symbolical language.

[3] "The Apocalypse," by the Rev. Isaac Williams, Preface, p. vii. In the passage above, which precedes this quotation, I have availed myself, with some slight verbal alterations, of the eloquent language with which Mr. Williams goes on to describe the characteristics of the Revelation of S. John.

cation of each, but also according to the manner in which they received the Divine revelation. In Hosea imagination seems inexhaustible, and picture follows picture without pause or stay. Habakkuk rejects ordinary rules, and is hurried away into varied and lofty imagery ; observing, at the same time, purity of taste and unity of design. When the prophet has been of sacerdotal race, the various features of the Theocracy,—the Temple and the Altar, the Ark and the Cherubim—float before his view, as in the writings of Jeremiah and Ezekiel.[1] The shepherd Amos still wanders in his pastures ; his imagination lingers with his flocks, and dwells on the culture of his fields ; his similitudes are taken from the mildew which blights the vineyard, or the lion which invades the fold.[2] When the revelation, on the other hand, has been given directly, and without the intervention of Visions, all this is changed ; and we observe a serene and unimpassioned course of thought, as in the books of Haggai and Malachi.[3]

[1] Jeremiah was "son of Hilkiah of the Priests that were in Anathoth."—Jer. i. 1. Ezekiel is expressly called "the Priest, the son of Buzi."—Ezek. i. 3. Cf. Jer. iii. 16; xi. 15; xii. 7; xxiii. 11; l. 28; li. 11, and Ezekiel *passim.*

[2] Cf. Amos, iii. 4; iv. 9. See *supra*, p. 162, note [2]. The permanence of the stamp of individual character is particularly remarkable in the case of this prophet. While the writings of Amos present a striking contrast to his humble origin, distinct traces of a harsh and rustic dialect are continually to be met with. E. g. a peculiar orthography; such as מתאב for מתעב, ch. vi. 8: a softening of guttural sounds; סרף for שרף, vi. 10: the contraction כאר, viii. 8, for כיאר, ix. 5, &c., &c. (see Hävernick, Einleit. I. i. s. 218). His imagery, as I have observed, denotes his occupation as shepherd. "Notwithstanding all this, he closely approaches his contemporaries Isaiah, Hosea, Joel, and is not inferior to them in power, beauty, and richness of style. Eichhorn even remarks: 'His language is in many places very learned, and full of allusions to history, geography and antiquities (cf. ch. v. 26, vi. 2, 14; viii. 8; ix. 7).'"—Hävernick, *Einleit.* Th. II. Abth. ii. s. 306. Indeed, it may be said of Amos, as of S. Paul, to whom, as I have already observed, he bears a remarkable analogy (see *supra*, p. 162), that "though he was rude in speech, yet not in knowledge."

I may observe that the idea, embodied by S. Gregory the Great in the words prefixed to this Lecture, may be clearly traced to the following passage from S. Gregory of Nazianzum: *τοῦτο τὸ Πνεῦμα, σοφώτατον γὰρ καὶ φιλανθρωπότατον, ἂν ποιμένα λάβῃ, ψάλτην ποιεῖ * * * ἐὰν αἰπόλον συκάμινα κνίζοντα, προφήτην ἐργάζεται. τὸν Δαβὶδ καὶ τὸν Ἀμὼς ἐνθυμήθητι * * * ἐὰν ἁλιέας εὕρῃ, σαγηνεύει Χριστῷ, κόσμον ὅλον τῃ τοῦ λόγου πλοκῇ συλλαμβάνοντας * * * ἐὰν διώκτας θερμοὺς, τὸν ζῆλον μετατίθησι, καὶ ποιεῖ Παύλους ἀντὶ Σαύλων, καὶ τοσοῦτον εἰς εὐσέβειαν, ὅσον εἰς κακίαν κατέλαβεν.*—*Orat.* xli. c. 14. t. i. p. 742.

[3] These same facts have been noticed by Spinoza, who, as usual, has distorted and misapplied them: "Sic etiam ipsa revelatio variabat, ut jam diximus, in unoquoque Propheta pro dispositione temperamenti corporis, imaginationis, et pro ratione opinionum, quas antea amplexus fuerat. Pro ratione enim temperamenti variabat hoc modo, nempe; si Propheta erat hilaris, ei revelabantur victoriæ, pax, et quæ porro homines ad lætitiam movent: tales enim similia sæpius imaginari solent. Si contra tristis erat, bella, supplicia, et omnia mala ei revelabantur. * * * Pro dispositione imaginationis autem sic etiam variabat, nempe; si Propheta erat elegans, stylo

It remains for us to notice another class of facts which supply, perhaps, the most forcible illustration of the aspect of Prophecy now under consideration : I mean the source of the symbols made use of by the prophets, and the influence which not only the spirit of the Theocracy, but also the scenes among which their lot was cast, exercised upon the imagery which they employ.[1] Thus the imagery of the prophets who shared the exile of their countrymen continually reminds us of the land of their captivity ; and the gorgeous and attractive symbolism of Chaldea is reflected from every page of the books of Daniel and Ezekiel.[2] The influence of Chaldean art in giving a colour to the predictions of Daniel will be at once apparent, when his own visions are compared with the form assumed by the dreams of Nebuchadnezzar, which the prophet has recorded in his second and fourth chapters ;[3] while the language of both Daniel and Ezekiel is abundantly illustrated by the results of those recent investigations which have brought to light the long-buried memorials of Oriental symbolism. Mr. Layard, in his work on Nineveh, thus speaks of the imagery of Ezekiel :—" The resemblance between the symbolical figures I have described, and those seen by Ezekiel in his vision, can scarcely fail to strike the reader. As the

etiam eleganti Dei mentem percipiebat. * * * Si Propheta erat rusticus, boves, et vaccæ, &c. * * * repræsentabantur."—*Tractat. Theol. Polit.* cap. ii.

[1] Hengstenberg has justly observed that the imagery of the prophets must, from the nature of the case, have been borrowed from objects and relations with which they were familiar. Prophecies conveyed in unknown imagery could not have answered any purpose, and would have been unintelligible. Thus, in the Messianic predictions, it seems to be founded in the very essence of Prophecy, that the Messiah's Kingdom should be described in language taken from the earlier Theocracy. And so, speaking of the three Offices of Christ as foreshadowed by the Priests, Kings, and Prophets of Israel, Eusebius (Hist. Eccl. i. 3, p. 12) says: *ὡς τούτους ἅπαντας τὴν ἐπὶ τὸν ἀληθῆ Χριστὸν, τὸν ἔνθεον καὶ οὐράνιον Λόγον, ἀναφορὰν ἔχειν.*—*Christol.* I. i. cap. v. s. 313.

This same fact has been long since noticed by S. Th. Aquinas:—" Species præexistentes in imaginatione Prophetæ sunt quasi elementa illius visionis imaginariæ, quæ divinitus ostenduntur, cum ex iis quodammodo componatur: et exinde contingit quod Propheta utitur similitudinibus rerum in quibus conversatur."—*De Veritate*, qu xii. art. 7. t. xvi. p. 419.

[2] Having alluded to the nature of Ezekiel's prophecy, Hävernick observes: "Dazu trat nun ein äusserer Umstand, die Berührung mit heidnischer Weise und Sitte, insbesondere mit der reichen, üppigen und anziehenden Symbolik Chaldäas. * * * Wie sollten wir es bei Daniel auch anders erwarten, dessen Stellung am chaldäischen Hofe ihm, dem in die Weisheit der Magier eingeweiheten, seiner Ausdrucksweise ein Colorit durchaus verleihen musste, welches von dem der übrigen prophetischen Gesichte bedeutend verschieden ist."—*Comm. üb. das B. Daniel*, Einleit, s. xxxiii. And Hävernick quotes a remark of Eichhorn to the effect that the book of Daniel opens to us an entirely new world, the reflection not of Palestine, but of scenes altogether different from those in which the life of the other prophets was cast.

[3] See Hävernick, *ibid.* s xxxiv.

prophet had beheld the Assyrian palaces, with their mysterious images and gorgeous decorations, it is highly probable that, when seeking to typify *certain Divine attributes*, and to describe the Divine glory, he chose forms that were not only familiar to him, but to the people whom he addressed—captives like himself in the land of Assyria. * * * It will be observed," continues this writer, "that the four forms chosen by Ezekiel to illustrate his description,—the man, the lion, the bull, and the eagle,—are precisely those which are constantly found on Assyrian monuments as religious types."[1]

But even here we are reminded, notwithstanding all such traces of the prophet's own personality, how a higher principle moulds and directs their words. There was one topic which was not submitted to their own style of representation. Amid the copious and varied symbolism of Scripture, we can observe how the pictures of those visions in which Jehovah Himself is revealed always preserve a character quite peculiar; although when describing *certain attributes* of Deity,—which in no case can be described otherwise than by metaphors,—each prophet still employs his wonted imagery. When Jehovah Himself appears, the sacred writers borrow no coloring from external sources;—were they to do so, indeed, they would manifestly abandon the whole genius and spirit of the Theocracy; and this uniformity in describing their visions of God characterizes the compositions of all the prophets, notwithstanding the prominence, in other parts of their writings, of their own individuality.[2] To satisfy ourselves of this fact, it will be sufficient to compare the accounts of the visions of Jehovah vouchsafed to Isaiah, Daniel, and Ezekiel.[3]

[1] "Nineveh and its Remains," vol. ii. p. 464.

[2] See Hävernick, *ibid.* s. xxxv.

[3] "I saw the Lord sitting upon a throne, high and lifted up, and His train filled the Temple. Above it stood the Seraphims. * * * And the posts of the door moved at the voice of him that cried, and the house was filled with smoke."—Isai. vi. 1–4.

"I beheld till the throne was cast down, and the Ancient of Days did sit. * * * His throne was like the fiery flame, and His wheels as burning fire. A fiery stream issued and came forth from before Him; thousand thousands ministered unto Him," &c.—Dan. vii. 9, 10.

"Above the firmament was the likeness of a throne, as the appearance of a sapphire stone: and upon the likeness of the throne was the likeness as the appearance of a man above upon it. * * * I saw as it were the appearance of fire, and it had brightness round about. * * * This was the appearance of the likeness of the glory of Jehovah."—Ezek. i. 26–28. (Cf. "And they saw the God of Israel:

The manner in which the prophets have described those portions of their spiritual intuitions which relate to future events comes next under our notice. This peculiarity of the sacred narrative affords a further example, no less striking than the cases hitherto considered, of the preservation of the natural characteristics of humanity even while the Divine influence was most directly exerted. In no department of the prophetic statements[1] is the supernatural element confessedly so conspicuous as in the predictions of the future. To such Jehovah Himself appeals, as proof of an intervention undoubtedly Divine. "Produce your cause, saith the Lord ; bring forth your strong reasons, saith the King of Jacob. Let them bring them forth and show us what shall happen. * * * Show the things that are to come hereafter, that we may know that ye are gods."[2] If, therefore, in such portions also of the record of Revelation, we can discern traces of the employment, by the Holy Spirit, of the natural capacity of man ; nay more, if it shall appear that the very limitations of the human understanding have been moulded into an agency which most fitly carries out the Divine purpose,—then may this fact too be adduced, as still further attesting the justice of those principles, on which alone, as I submit, can the inspiration of Scripture be explained and defended.

The leading phenomena in all predictions of the future may be reduced to two classes.[3] The first class includes those cases in which the *idea* intended to be conveyed by the revelation is represented under a particular *form* :—for example, the perfection of the Theocracy is described as a return from the Dispersion to Canaan, a judgment of the nations in the valley of Jehoshaphat, and so forth. This phase of Prophecy appertains to that department of Theology, whose function it is to disen-

and there was under His feet as it were a paved work of a sapphire stone," &c.—Exod. xxiv. 10).

See also Micaiah's vision: "I saw Jehovah sitting on His throne, and all the host of heaven standing by Him on His right hand and on His left."—1 Kings, xxii. 19. It is unnecessary to quote from the Apocalypse:—cf. e. g. Rev. iv.

[1] It may not be superfluous to observe, that the idea of Prophecy or prophetic revelation is by no means to be restricted to the announcement of future events. Moses recorded the *past* history of the creation, and Daniel (ch. ii.) recalled to Nebuchadnezzar the dream which he had forgotten. The *present* was revealed to Elisha, as he himself informed his guilty servant, who had received the Syrian's gifts: "Went not mine heart with thee, when the man turned again from his chariot to meet thee."—2 Kings, v. 26.

[2] Isai. xli. 21–23.

[3] Hävernick, "Einleitung," Th. II. Abth. ii. s. 44, ff.

tangle the spiritual *idea* from the *form* in which it is presented, and the *imagery* in which it is clothed. With this branch of the subject we have no immediate concern: it belongs to the interpretation of Prophecy. The second class embraces the phenomena exhibited by the manner in which prophets, in consequence of their vivid intuition of the future, bring remote events before us. The title of "Seer," as well as that of "Watchman," so often applied to the men of God, suggests of itself a comparison with the literal watchmen to whom they are thus likened, who, placed upon some lofty tower, gaze upon the far off distance. From this analogy has been borrowed the appropriate phrase of the 'perspective' character of Prophecy.[1] As to the eye of the watchman upon his eminence nearer objects appear more distinct, while those more remote are wrapped in the haze of distance, and in all cases each point of the landscape is projected on some other,—so, in a similar manner, the prophet's mental vision takes in the varied events of future times to which his spiritual gaze is directed.[2] Thus it is that he describes events yet to come, as if they were present:—"Unto us," said Isaiah of the far remote birth of the Messiah, "a Child *is* born; unto us a Son *is* given."[3] Thus it is that the *order* of events is often

[1] Hävernick *loc. cit.* s. 45, gives a list of writers who have advocated this view. See especially Hengstenberg, "Christologie," I. i. s. 305 ff.; Jahn, "Einleitung," Th. II. Abschn. ii. s. 368 ff.

[2] Hengstenberg (*loc. cit.* s. 306 and s. 308) quotes the following ingenious illustrations of this fact: "Prophetæ, divina luce qua illuminantur, ad futura plerumque prospexerunt, quemadmodum fit, quando cœlum stelliferum intuemur. Videmus enim supra nos sidera; quanto a nobis intervallo absint, necnon quæ propius, quæ remotius distent, non item animadvertimus."—Crusius, *Theol. Proph.* i. p. 622. "Quemadmodum, simili fallacia optica, longissime distans turris domus propinquæ tecto incumbere, aut lunæ discus montibus nemoribusque contiguus videtur."—Veithusen, p. 89.

[3] Isai. ix. 6. So also the future is represented as if already past; and hence the use of what has been termed the "præter. propheticum," which Ewald ("Grammat." § 262, quoted by Hävernick), defines: "die Phantasie des Dichters und Propheten schauet oft die Zukunft schon als ihr klar vorliegend und erlebt." Even Vitringa (on Isai. vii. 14), observes Hengstenberg (*loc. cit.*), seems to have adopted the vulgar notion that the use of the præterite by the prophet was to indicate the certainty of the event. As an example of this principle, Otto Strauss alleges the words, "Art thou better than populous No? * * * yet *was she carried away*, she went into captivity," &c.—Nahum, iii. 8, 10; observing: "Paucos illos sequimur interpretes, qui *futuram* Thebarum fortunam prænunciatam viderunt, Hieron., Theodoretum, Cyrillum, Cocceium; verborum igitur formæ pro *propheticis*, quæ aiunt, *præteritis* habendæ erunt."—*Nahumi de Nino Vaticin.*, p. 101.

This characteristic of Prophecy has not been overlooked by the Fathers: e. g. "Mos iste sit Scripturarum, ut interdum futura tempore præterito declinentur: Verbi causa, de cruce Domini: *Foderunt manus meas et pedes.*"—S. Hieron. *Comm. in Ep. ad Eph.* lib. i. c. ii. t. vii. p. 575. Some of them, moreover, suggest explanations:

neglected; and facts, widely separate, are intermingled in apparent confusion. For example, in the ninth chapter of Zechariah, from the first to the ninth verse, the prophet sees the triumphant march of Alexander through Syria; in the ninth and tenth verses he gazes upon the Person of Christ in the distant future; and then, from the eleventh verse to the end of the chapter, he suddenly reverts to the age of the Maccabees.[1] Thus also it is that events, parted by long intervals of time, are represented as continuous; the prophet beholding the occurrences of future history in juxtaposition, not in succession. For example, in his fiftieth and fifty-first chapters, Jeremiah represents the capture of Babylon by the Persians, and its final overthrow, as a single event; and yet these two occurrences were separated by several centuries.

Such is the 'perspective' character of the predictions of Scripture. In those inspired pictures of the future there is, however, no confused intermingling of foreground and background: and whenever the observer can take his stand at the proper point of view, and at the requisite distance, he may discern how accurately order and proportion have been preserved, amid all the seeming confusion.[2] To an ancient Jew the predictions concerning the

"In Scripturis Sanctis sæpe ea, quæ futura sunt, quasi facta narrantur, sicut est illud: 'Dederunt in escam meam fel, et in siti mea potaverunt me aceto.' Sed cur futura quasi præterita scribuntur, nisi quia ea, quæ adhuc facienda sunt in opere, jam facta sunt in divina prædestinatione?"—S. Isidor. Hispal. *Sentent.* lib. i. c. 18, p. 421.

[1] This is the ordinary and received interpretation (see W. Lowth on Zech. ix. 1). Jahn, in his "Einleitung" (*loc. cit.* s. 370), adds some further examples. In the prophecy to Abraham the *foreground* is quite clear,—the promise of a son, and that son by Sarah; a multitude of descendants countless as the stars of heaven, or the sands of the sea: somewhat more obscurely appears the sojourn of those descendants in a foreign land for four hundred years; their oppression, their deliverance, the punishment of the oppressors, and the possession of Canaan: still more darkly in the *background*, and without any allusion to the far greater distance of time, the blessing to accrue to all nations by the seed of Abraham. (Cf. Gen. xii. 1–4; xv. 1–21; xvii. 18–21; xviii. 10–14; xxii. 16–18). Again, cf. the prediction of Nathan, 2 Sam. vii.; 1 Chron. xvii.—the background being more obscurely supplied by Ps. lxxxix. 20–38.

[2] In the most important of predictions—the Messianic—this want of distinctness is often avoided by the standing formula, באחרית הימים ("in the last days," Isai. ii. 2); a phrase which, while it removes the period predicted to the distant future, yet contents itself with describing it as the close of one epoch, and as the prelude to a new. See Hävernick, *loc. cit.* s. 45. Cf. אחרי־כן, Joel, ii. 28. Hengstenberg observes that, in general, the various parts of a prediction may be arranged in due chronological order. (1.) There are cases in which the revelation itself gives clear intimation as to the time. E. g. the seventy years of the Babylonian Exile, Jer. xxix. 10. (2.) In cases where events are blended together in the prophet's description (e. g. the deliverance by Cyrus, and the Redemption by Christ, Isai. xliv.; xlv.), we can appeal to other passages in which the same events are separated. (3.) We obtain an insight

liberation from exile were blended with those which related to the Messianic age, so as to present a mass, as it were, of undistinguishable tracery: but when the due distance in point of time had been attained, the several outlines of the picture were brought out in true perspective. Seen by the light which the fulfilment of Prophecy affords, the two events exhibit their mutual relations: the return from captivity contains the germ and presents the pledge of the Messianic deliverance; the one being the beginning, the other the completion. Hence, too, we can at once discern how it came to pass that Jeremiah connects in one picture the first conversion of the Jews in the days of Christ, with their general conversion in the ages yet to come, passing over their intervening rejection;—a fact which is referred to by Daniel and Malachi.[1]

into the true sense by considering the point from which the glance of the prophet is directed. Thus Isaiah (ch. liii.) appears to take his stand between the *past* sufferings and the *future* glories of the Messiah; because the former were to be described as the condition of the latter. (4.) We receive aid from knowing that certain parts of the prediction have been fulfilled. Thus, when the deliverance from Exile, and the Redemption by Christ are blended together; the former event having taken place, we can distinguish which relates to each respectively.—*loc. cit.* s. 310 ff.

[1] Jer. xxiii. 5–8. Our Lord's discourse in S. Matt. xxiv. supplies an important illustration of this phase of Prophecy. After He had announced the future triumphs of the Cross, and the consummation of all things ("This Gospel of the Kingdom shall be preached in all the world for a witness unto all nations; and then shall the end come."—ver. 14), there immediately follows a minute account of the destruction of Jerusalem, without any intimation that what related to events close at hand was to be separated from His previous reference to the remote future. Nay, after dwelling upon the horrors of the siege, our Lord, giving up all determination of time, goes on to observe: "Immediately (εὐθέως) after the tribulation of those days shall the sun be darkened * * * and then shall appear the sign of the Son of Man in heaven: and then shall all the tribes of the earth mourn. * * * And He shall send His angels * * * and they shall gather together His elect," &c.—ver. 29–31. In verses 34 and 36, however, He takes care to separate the two epochs which His foregoing prophetic announcement had seemed to place in juxtaposition; fixing the limits of one of them ("Verily, I say unto you, this generation shall not pass, till *all these things* be fulfilled"), while He projects the other to the remoteness of the future ("Of that day and hour knoweth no man, no, not the angels of heaven"). Nor is this the only instance in the New Testament of this characteristic of Prophecy. S. Matthew, in his narrative of our Lord's words, supplies two further examples, viz. ch. x. 23, and xvi. 27, 28. And, not to adduce the various parables relating to the "Kingdom of God," we can refer to 1 Cor. x. 11; 1 S. John, ii. 18; S. James, v. 8; all expressing the same sentiment—"The end of all things is at hand."—1 S. Peter, iv. 7.

[2] These latter texts suggest a few remarks on a common misconception which, from its bearing on the question of Inspiration, demands some notice. I may take Dr. Arnold as a suitable exponent of this misconception. Having alluded to the preeminent inspiration of S. Paul, he goes on to say: "Yet this great Apostle expected that the world would come to an end in the generation then existing * * * Shall we say then that S. Paul entertained and expressed a belief which the event did not verify? We may say so, safely and reverently, in this instance; for here he was most certainly speaking as a man, and not by revelation; as it has been providentially ordered that our Lord's express words on this point have been recorded [S. Matt.

From the consideration of such phenomena, it is not difficult to infer several important results. Without presumption we may fairly assume, that certain portions only of the Divine counsels were unveiled before the view of the individual prophets. "They knew *in part*, and they prophesied *in part*:"[1]—their respective predictions being but fragments of one vast whole; the single lines, as it were, which each prophet has contributed to the sketch of the great picture of the future. In this point of view, therefore, the prophetic descriptions suggest to the mind the comparison of some elaborate picture of which the outlines, indeed, are traced, but of which the details have not as yet been

xxiv. 36]."—*Sermons on the Christian Life, its Course*, &c., p. 489. In the first place, then, it may be urged in reply that it is, of itself, inconceivable that S. Paul should have been ignorant of our Lord's words here quoted by Dr. Arnold; or that, knowing his determination of the matter, he should have hazarded a mere conjecture of his own. Secondly, we are to remember that S. Paul himself has warned the Church against such a misinterpretation of his words, when he writes: "We beseech you, brethren, by the coming of our Lord Jesus Christ * * * that ye be not soon shaken in mind, or be troubled, neither by spirit, nor by word, nor by letter as from us, *as that the day of Christ is at hand*."—2 Thess. ii. 1, 2. The following criticism, too, on Dr. Arnold's statement deserves all attention. Mr. Greg, whom I have already adduced (Lecture ii. p. 72) as denying the possibility of a Revelation from God to man, having quoted the remark of Dr. Arnold—"Most truly do I believe the Scriptures to be inspired; the proofs of their inspiration grow with the study of them," &c. (*loc. cit.* p. 486),—proceeds to comment on it as follows: "Yet he [Dr. Arnold] immediately afterwards says in reference to one of S. Paul's most certain and often repeated statements (regarding the approaching end of the world), 'we may safely and reverently say that S. Paul in this instance entertained and expressed a belief which the event did not justify.'" Again: "It is particularly worthy of remark (and seems to have been most unaccountably and entirely overlooked by Dr. Arnold throughout his argument), that in the assertion of this erroneous belief, S. Paul expressly declares himself to be speaking 'by the word of the Lord' ["This we say unto you by the word of the Lord, that we which are alive and remain unto the coming of the Lord, &c."—1 Thess. iv. 15]."—*The Creed of Christendom*, p. 25. From the further observation of Dr. Arnold—"Can any reasonable mind doubt that in what he [S. Paul] has told us * * * of that Great Day when we shall arise incorruptible, and meet our Lord in the air, he spoke what he had heard from God?"—Mr. Greg draws the irresistible conclusion: "What is this but to say, not only that portions of the Scripture are from God, and other portions are from man—that some parts are inspired, and others are not—but that, of the very same letter by the very same Apostle, some portions are inspired, and others are not—and that Dr. Arnold and every man must judge for himself *which are which*,—must separate by his own skill the Divine from the human assertions in the Bible?"—*Ibid.*

The misconception which we are considering is, however, altogether removed by bearing in mind the characteristic of Prophecy which has been already explained. In fact, the New Testament writers, who have made the statements in question, but reiterate the invariable language of the Old Testament prophets when referring to this same subject: "The day of the Lord is at hand"—קרוב יום יהוה; see Isa. xiii. 6; Ezek. xxx. 3; Joel, ii. 1; Obad. 15. And yet the prophets expressly state that the *time* when their predictions shall be accomplished is not known except to God: "It shall be one day which shall be known to the Lord."—Zech. xiv. 7. They were conscious that this was a portion of the revelation not unveiled for their understanding, and, accordingly, they searched "*what* or *what manner of time*, the Spirit which was in them did signify."—1 S. Pet. i. 11. On this text see Lecture v.

[1] Ἐκ μέρους, 1 Cor. xiii. 9. Cf. Hengstenberg, "Christologie," I. i. s. 303.

completed. In its first stage all appears indistinct and obscure; objects seem crowded together without order or proportion; no correct judgment can be formed as to either magnitude or distance; and the spectator must pause, until the progress of the work gradually unfolds the artist's design. But according as that design *is* unfolded, each former difficulty insensibly fades away. The introduction of light and shadow determines the relative distances which were before undefined. A few strokes of the pencil add form and meaning to certain outlines previously unintelligible. And, at last, the artist affords the highest exhibition and most conclusive evidence of his skill, by adding those touches which give unity to his composition, and spread over his canvass the tokens of a matured and connected plan.

The comparison here instituted is no mere figment of the imagination. A moment's thought will show how completely this similitude is borne out by the expression employed in the New Testament to denote the accomplishment of Prophecy: *πλήρωσις*—the filling up, as it were, by the events of history, and the progress of Revelation, of the outlines of that sketch of the future which the prophets had traced upon the pages of their inspired compositions. Accordingly S. Paul observes, that the Law contained but the *form* or *outline* of Knowledge and of Truth:[1] while S. John declares that both have been introduced really, and no longer by shadows, in the Christian scheme.[2]

[1] Rom. ii. 20. *Ἔχοντα τὴν μόρφωσιν τῆς γνώσεως καὶ τῆς ἀληθείας ἐν τῷ νόμῳ.* Cf. 2 Tim. iii. 5, "Having a *form* (*μόρφωσιν*) of godliness, but denying the *power* (*δύναμιν*) thereof." Although (as S. Paul here teaches) the Law conveyed *Knowledge* and *Truth* but typically, both are *really* imparted in the Gospel; for S. John, ch. xvii. 3, explains how we thence learn *to know* "the only true God;" while he further tells us that "the Law was given by Moses, but Grace and *Truth* came by Jesus Christ."—ch. i. 17. See Olshausen on S. Matt. v., B. i. s. 212.

[2] Tholuck ("Die Berg-predigt," s. 134) calls attention to the fact that two passages in the New Testament suggest the analogy of a *painting* as elucidating the trope of *fulfilling* a prophecy. The ordinances of the Law were but "a *shadow* (*σκιά*) of things to come, but the *body* (*σῶμα*) is of Christ."—Col ii. 17. Again, we read of "the Law having a *shadow* of good things to come, and not *the very image* of the things"—Heb. x. 1; where *σκιά* is contrasted with *αὐτὴ ἡ εἰκών*. Now this metaphor is plainly borrowed from the technical terms of art employed by Greek writers, *ἀπεργασία* ("*ἀπεργάζομαι, to finish off*, esp. of a painter, *to fill up with color*, opp. to *ὑπογράψαι to sketch*," Liddell and Scott); or *ζωγραφία* ("*ζωγραφέω to paint*, esp. from life," L. and S.), in contrast to *ὑπογραφή* ("*a first sketch, design, outline*, Lat. *adumbratio*, opp. to *τελεωτάτη ἀπεργασία*,"—L. and S.) or *σκιαγραφία* ("*a sketching, rough painting*, such as to produce an effect at a distance," L. and S.) This remark Tholuck illustrates by the following passages. Synesius (flor. A. D. 410), commenting on the words "In the hand of the Lord there is a cup, and the wine is red, it is full mixed," &c., explains that this mixture denotes the union of both Old and New Testament: *ἓν γὰρ τὸ ἐξ ἀμφοῖν συνιστάμενον, τελείωσις γνώσεως. ἡ μὲν παλαιὰ τὴν ὑπόσχεσιν*

This view of the subject renders it manifest in what sense only the prophet can be said to have anticipated history. Time and the relations of time are matters quite subordinate in his descriptions: and while the distinct tracery of events yet to come can be discerned in his predictions when illumined by the light of their fulfilment, still his words had previously been invested with a degree of obscurity amply sufficient to allow the free course of history to proceed,—an obscurity, too, which was indispensably necessary in order to secure that object.[1] This, no doubt, was the end which God designed wherever Scripture shrouds prophetic announcements in dark words and mysterious symbols; and, above all, when it leaves the distinctions of time undefined. Now the method adopted by the Holy Spirit, in order to attain this end, consisted, I venture to submit, in the application of natural agencies; and in the employment of even the limitation of the human intellect, so as to subserve His will. For Him, to whom "a thousand years are but as yesterday,"—before Whose eye the past, the present, and the future, alike are ever spread clear and well defined,—the relations of *time* can have no existence. The vision of the Almighty embraces, with-

ἔσχεν· ἡ δὲ νέα τὸν ἀπόστολον ἐξήνεγκε * * * *καὶ τὸ ποτήριον ἕν. ἓν γὰρ ἔπνευσε Πνεῦμα, καὶ εἰς προφήτην, καὶ εἰς ἀπόστολον. καὶ, κατὰ τοὺς ἀγαθοὺς ζωγράφους, πάλαι μὲν ἐσκιαγράφησεν, ἔπειτα μέντοι διηκρίβωσε τὰ μέλη τῆς γνώσεως.*—*Homil. in Ps.* lxxiv. (ed. Petav., p. 295);—the closing words of which passage Petavius translates as follows: "Et quod boni pictores faciunt, olim quidem adumbrate delineavit; postea vero singulas cognitionis partes elaboravit."

The second illustration is from Theophylact: *πῶς δὲ ἐπλήρωσε; πρῶτον μὲν ὅτι, ὅσα εἶπον περὶ αὐτοῦ οἱ προφῆται, ἐποιήσε. διὸ καὶ ὁ Εὐαγγελιστὴς συχνάκις λέγει· ἵνα πληρωθῇ τὸ ῥηθὲν διὰ τοῦ προφήτου. ἀλλὰ καὶ τὰς τοῦ νόμου ἐντολὰς πάσας ἐπλήρωσεν. ἁμαρτίαν γὰρ οὐκ ἐποίησεν, οὐδὲ εὑρέθη δόλος ἐν τῷ στόματι αὐτοῦ. καὶ ἄλλως δὲ ἐπλήρωσε τὸν νόμον, τουτέστιν, ἀνεπλήρωσεν· ὅσα γὰρ ἐκεῖνος ἐσκιαγράφησε, ταῦτα οὗτος τελείως ἐζωγράφησεν. ἐκεῖνος, τὸ, μὴ φονεύσης. οὗτος, τὸ μηδὲ θυμωθῇς εἰκῇ. ὥσπερ καὶ ὁ ζωγράφος οὐ καταλύει τὴν σκιαγραφίαν, ἀλλὰ μᾶλλον ἀναπληροῖ.*—*Comm. in S. Matt.* v. 18, t. i. p. 25.

[1] Any difficulty, connected with the relation of Prophecy to History, is no other than the old question as to how the freewill of the creature can be reconciled with the foreknowledge of the Creator. The obscurity with which prophetical announcements are invested (the existence of which Scripture itself points out), has been clearly designed in order to leave the freedom of human actions undisturbed. "If thou hadst known" (said our Lord, when "He beheld the city, and wept over it") "even thou, at least in this thy day, the things which belong unto thy peace! but now they are hid from thine eyes."—S. Luke, xix. 42. Dr. Arnold has truly observed: "It is a very misleading notion of Prophecy, if we regard it as an anticipation of History. History, in our common sense of the term, is busy with particular nations, times, places, actions, and even persons. If, in this sense, Prophecy were a history written beforehand, it would alter the very condition of humanity, by removing from us our uncertainty as to the future; it would make us acquainted with those times and seasons which the Father hath put in His own power. It is anticipated History, not in our common sense of the word, but in another, and far higher sense."—*On the Interpret. of Prophecy*, Sermon i. vol. i. p. 375.

out separation, events which the intellect of man can only contemplate in succession; and which, if presented to his mind simultaneously, must, from his very nature, become undistinguishable the one from the other. Before the gaze of the Omniscient is unfolded the entire course of future history,—its various agencies defined, its epochs distinguished, its relations fixed. From before certain portions of such a scene the veil is withdrawn at God's pleasure, when He discloses the future in prophetic Vision, and opens to the eye of man the vista of events yet to come. The human understanding, however, fettered by its natural laws, can no more discriminate, when thus presented simultaneously, *events* separated by *time*, than the eye could originally form any judgment, before experience, respecting the distance or relative position of *objects* separated by *space*. In both cases the mind must necessarily regard the objects presented to it as projected the one upon the other: and thus it came to pass, that the prophet beheld future events in his Visions, unconnected by the relations of time.[1]

From this result of the laws of the human mind it follows, that all disclosures which God has vouchsafed of occurrences yet to come must have been expressed (wherever no overruling power had otherwise directed the pen of the sacred writers), with that degree and kind of obscurity, which ensures that the free course of history shall be preserved, notwithstanding such predictions of the future. Hence the very limitations of man's intellectual capacity have become the means—it may, perhaps, without presumption be alleged—whereby His ends have been attained by the Almighty: and thus we are supplied with another striking example of how the peculiar characteristics of humanity have been incorporated in the organism of Inspiration.

[1] Hengstenberg observes, with reference to this 'perspective' character of Prophecy, that its consideration is particularly important in removing objections against the Divine origin of the prophetic statements, founded on their not being fulfilled at the time when the objector fancies that they ought: no *period* having been in reality marked by the prophet. When, in accordance with the nature of prophetic intuition, the prophet refrains from all determination of time, and makes no claim to fix its limits, we can as little take exception, on such grounds, to the Divine source of what he has announced, as object that every prophet has not foreseen every event of futurity. This mode of regarding the nature of Prophecy obviates, moreover, the necessity of the forced interpretations, to which those who maintain its Divine origin have sometimes recourse, when they set out from the principle that each prophetic description must relate to one and the same time, as well as object.—*Christologie*, i. 1, s. 308.

LECTURE V.

REVELATION AND INSPIRATION.

Ἀλλὰ καὶ τὸ εἰς ἔκστασιν καὶ μανικὴν ἄγειν κατάστασιν τὴν δῆθεν προφητεύουσαν, ὡς μηδαμῶς αὐτὴν ἑαυτῇ παρακολουθεῖν, οὐ Θείου Πνεύματος ἔργον ἐστίν * * * Εἰ δὲ ἐξίσταται, καὶ οὐκ ἐν ἑαυτῇ ἐστιν ἡ Πυθία, ὅτε μαντεύεται, ποδαπὸν νομιστέον πνεῦμα, τὸν σκότον κατεχεύαν τοῦ νοῦ καὶ τῶν λογισμῶν, ἢ τοιοῦτον ὁποῖόν ἐστι καὶ τὸ τῶν δαιμόων γένος;

ORIGENES, *Contra Celsum*, lib. vii. 3, 4.

"Aut igitur, juxta Montanum, Patriarchas et Prophetas in ecstasi locutos accipienda n, et nescisse quæ dixerint: aut si hoc impium est (spiritus quippe Prophetarum Prophetis subjectus est), intellexerunt utique quæ locuti sunt. Et si intellexerunt, quæritur quomodo nunc Paulus dicat, quod aliis generationibus non fuit notum, fuisse Christi Apostolis revelatum. * * * Aut ille igitur, de quo jam supra disseruimus, tenendus est sensus, ita Patriarchas et Prophetas, ut nunc Apostolis revelatum est, Christi ignorasse mysterium, quia aliud sit tenere quid manibus, aliud futurum in Spiritu prævidere."

S. HIERON. *Comm. in Epist. ad Eph.* lib. ii. cap. 3.

Ζητήσεως ἄξιόν ἐστι τὸ περὶ τοῦ Ἁγίου Πνεύματος εἰ δύναται εἶναι καὶ ἐν ἁμαρτωλῷ ψυχῇ.

ORIGENES, *Comm. in Joann.* tom. xxviii. 13.

Ἐκεῖνο δὲ προστίθεμεν τῷ λόγῳ, ὅτι οὔτε πᾶς ὁ προφητεύων ὅσιος· οὔτε πᾶς ὁ δαίμονας ἐλαύνων ἅγιος. καὶ γὰρ καὶ Βαλαὰμ ὁ τοῦ Βεὼρ ὁ μάντις προεφήτευσεν, δυσεβὴς ὤν, καὶ Καϊάφας ὁ ψευδώνυμος Ἀρχιερεύς.

S. HIPPOLYTUS, *De Charismatibus.*

LECTURE V.

REVELATION AND INSPIRATION.

"OF WHICH SALVATION THE PROPHETS HAVE ENQUIRED AND SEARCHED DILIGENTLY, WHO PROPHESIED OF THE GRACE THAT SHOULD COME UNTO YOU: SEARCHING WHAT, OR WHAT MANNER OF TIME THE SPIRIT OF CHRIST WHICH WAS IN THEM DID SIGNIFY."—1 *S. Peter*, i. 10, 11.

THE last Discourse was mainly occupied with one only of the two elements which co-exist in the composition of the Holy Scriptures. In it attention was chiefly directed to the phenomena which exhibit the active co-operation of the human agents who have been chosen to convey to us the history of God's Providence, and God's Revelation. It was there shown how the intellectual emancipation of the state of sleep, and the intellectual intensity of the state of ecstasy, have been made use of as the natural means by which was effected the concourse of the spirit of man with the Spirit of God.[1] And although what was said upon this branch of the subject was, I trust, sufficiently guarded, so as to preclude any misconception of the reasons advanced, and to avoid even the semblance of lending support to the error against which these Discourses are principally addressed, —an error of which the source consists in giving undue prominence to the human element of the Bible,—still this department of our inquiry is too important, and too vitally connected with the whole question of Inspiration, to be dismissed by a simple reference to those illustrations of the constant exercise of the

[1] See M. Athanase Coquerel's "Christianity," p. 205; who observes—"The more the means of Inspiration [meaning Revelation—see *supra*, Lecture iv. p. 146, note [2]] are independent of time, space, matter, and death, the more conformable they are to the nature of God. But there are to be met with in our present human existence, our actual phase of progress, momentary conditions of being, which disengage our minds from the bondage of time, space, matter, and death. These accidents of our present state of being are especially sleep and ecstasy."

Divine agency with which the argument was interspersed. It is a duty obligatory above all on the defender of the theory of Inspiration here maintained, to establish the reality not only of that influence which conveyed to man the Revelation of God, or which enabled the Prophet to express what was thus suggested to his mind in human language ; but also of that further agency of the Holy Spirit whereby the sacred writers have been moved to embody Divine communications, history, and doctrine, in one organic whole, of which each member transmits its own heavenly message to every age.

This aspect of our inquiry, moreover, follows, in natural order, the subjects with which the last Discourse was occupied. Certain questions were then considered relating to the form under which revelations of the future were conveyed to the prophets of God, as well as to the manner in which chronological arrangement has been disregarded in their pictures of events yet to come. Attention was also drawn to that obscurity of expression which, as a consequence of such facts, meets us in the prophetic writings ;[1]—an obscurity by means of which the free course of history is maintained,[2] which restrains the rashness of unreflect-

[1] The fact of this obscurity is clearly referred to in the New Testament. The destruction of Jerusalem had been foretold by Daniel (ix. 26; cf. S. Matt. xxiv. 15), and yet the Jewish nation would not see the application of his words. "Thou knewest not the time of thy visitation" was Christ's remark, when he wept over Jerusalem, saying, "If thou hadst known, even thou, at least in this thy day, the things which belong unto thy peace! but now they are hid from thine eyes."—S. Luke, xix. 41–44. So S. Paul tells the "men of Israel"—"They that dwell at Jerusalem, and their rulers, because they knew him not, nor yet the voices of the prophets which are read every Sabbath day, they have fulfilled them in condemning Him."—Acts, xiii. 27. Cf. ch. iii. 17.

[2] A fact related by Josephus supplies an apposite illustration. With the most minute particularity Ezekiel (ch. xii.; cf. 2 Kings, xxv.; Jer. lii.) had foretold the captivity of Zedekiah: "I will bring him to Babylon to the land of the Chaldeans: *yet shall he not see it*, though he shall die there."—ver. 13. Josephus informs us that Ezekiel, who resided in Mesopotamia "among the captives by the river of Chebar," sent a copy of this prediction to Zedekiah, who set about comparing it with the language of Jeremiah (xxxii. 4; xxxviii. 23). Finding, however, that Jeremiah had merely foretold that he should be carried to Babylon, while Ezekiel had affirmed that he should be brought to Babylon, indeed, *but should not see it*, the king drew the inference that the statement of Ezekiel contradicted that of Jeremiah, and consequently rejected both as false.—See Fairbairn's "Ezekiel," p. 87. The words of Josephus are as follows: *ταῖς δὲ προφητείαις αὐτῶν Σεδεκίας ἠπίστησεν, ἐκ τοιαύτης αἰτίας. τὰ μὲν ἄλλα πάντα συμφωνοῦντα τοὺς προφήτας ἀλλήλοις εἰπεῖν συνέβη, ὥστε ἡ πόλις ἁλώσεται καὶ Σεδεκίας αὐτὸς αἰχμάλωτος ἔσται· διεφώνησε δὲ Ἰεζεκίηλος εἰπὼν, οὐκ ὄψεσθαι Βαβυλῶνα τὸν Σεδεκίαν, τοῦ Ἱερεμίου φάσκοντος αὐτῷ, ὅτι δεδεμένον αὐτὸν ὁ Βαβυλώνιος ἀπάξει βασιλεύς. καὶ διὰ τὸ, μὴ ταὐτὸν αὐτοὺς ἑκατέρους λέγειν, καὶ περὶ ὧν συμφωνεῖν ἐδόκουν, ὡς οὐδ' ἐκεῖνα ἀληθῆ λέγεσθαι καταγνοὺς, ἠπίστησε.*—*Antiq.* lib. x. vii. 2, p. 523—"although," adds Josephus, "everything *did* fall out in accordance

ing zeal, leaves full room for the seeds of faith to germinate, and withholds from human presumption the temptatian to oppose the will of heaven. From none of the phenomena presented by the contents of the Bible can we infer more plainly the distinct recognition, by its authors, of the predominating influence of its Divine Element, than from the manner in which such dark allusions to the future became subjects of speculation to the prophets themselves. This is a circumstance which at once suggests several important considerations; and, above all others, it leads naturally to the inquiry—Did the men of God themselves fully comprehend the sense of the revelations to which they gave utterance? That this question must be answered in the negative is so obvious that the fact has furnished sceptics with an argument—superficial, it is true, but still *an* argument—against the evidence which Prophecy supplies. A late writer, for example, of the modern school of disbelievers, observes, with respect to the proof of Christianity founded upon the fulfilment in Christ's Person of predictions uttered long previously to His coming,—"This is true, and the argument would have all the force which is attributed to it, were the objectors able to lay their finger on a single Old Testament prediction clearly referring to

with these prophecies, as we shall in a fitting place make clear." This explanation he appends, as a sort of moral, to the sequel of this narrative: *καὶ ταῦτα μὲν Ἱερεμίας εἶπε· τυφλωθεὶς δὲ καὶ ἀχθεὶς εἰς Βαβυλῶνα, ταύτην οὐκ εἶδε καθὼς Ἰεζεκίηλος προεῖπε.*—*Ibid.* viii. 2, p. 527. It is interesting to notice how the Jewish historian insists upon this illustration of the *harmony* which exists among the sacred writers. We have already seen (Lecture ii. p. 68, note [3]) how he has adduced the absence of *contradictions* as a proof of the Divine origin of the Old Testament: and here he observes how the fulfillment of Prophecy confounds "the ignorance and the faithlessness of men:" *Ταῦτα μὲν οὖν, ἱκανῶς ἐμφανίσαι δυνάμενα τὴν τοῦ Θεοῦ φύσιν τοῖς ἀγνοοῦσιν, εἰρήκαμεν, ὅτι ποικίλη τ' ἐστὶ καὶ πολύτροπος, καὶ πάντα καθ' ὥραν ἀπαντᾷ τεταγμένως, ἅ τε δεῖ γινέσθαι προλέγει· τήν τε τῶν ἀνθρώπων ἄγνοιαν καὶ ἀπιστίαν κ. τ. λ.*—*Ibid.* viii. 3, p. 527. We have, on the other hand, striking proofs that this half light of Prophecy, which thus leaves the freedom of the human will unfettered, has nevertheless been made an instrument for guiding the course of history. There is no room to doubt that Daniel brought before Cyrus the different predictions which foreshadowed his instrumentality as agent of God's will, viz., the capture of Babylon in the height of a festival (Jer. li. 57; cf. ver. 39); how the Assyrian power should be utterly overthrown by the Medes (Isai. xiii. 17–19; cf. ch. xiv.); in fine, how Cyrus should rebuild Jerusalem and the Temple of Jehovah (Isai. xliv. 28; xlv. 13)—and it is to be observed that the edict of Cyrus is drawn up in the language of this latter announcement, see 2 Chron. xxxvi. 23; Ezra, i. 2. Josephus tells us that Cyrus issued a proclamation "throughout all Asia," to the effect that the Supreme God (*ὁ Θεὸς ὁ μέγιστος*) had, by His prophet, foretold his name, and that he should restore the Temple at Jerusalem. This, adds Josephus, Cyrus knew from reading the prediction of Isaiah written 210 years before,—a fact which he acknowledged as an undoubted proof of its Divine origin: *ταῦτ' οὖν ἀναγνόντα τὸν Κῦρον, καὶ θαυμάσαντα τὸ Θεῖον, κ. τ. λ.*—*Antiq.* lib. xi. i. 2. p. 547. See *infra*, p. 212, note [3].

Jesus Christ, *intended by the utterers of it to relate to Him*, prefiguring His character and career, and manifestly fulfilled in His appearance on earth. *This they cannot do.*"[1] The fallacious character of such reasoning has been long since exposed by Bishop Butler :—" To say that the Scriptures, and the things contained in them, can have no other or farther meaning than those persons thought or had, who first recited or wrote them, is evidently saying that those persons were the original, proper, and sole authors of those books ; that is, that they are not inspired : which is absurd, whilst the authority of these books is under examination ; that is, till you have determined they are of no Divine authority at all."[2] Holy Scripture, in short, presents the prophets to our view as human instruments through whom the Spirit of God speaks, and by whose lips He announces the Divine Oracles,—the sense of which, however, the Prophet himself does not always understand, but after which he " diligently seeks" like other men.

Before entering fully upon this topic, it must be disconnected

[1] "The Creed of Christendom," by W. Rathbone Greg, p. 61.

[2] "Analogy," Part ii. chap. 7. The passage to which I here refer is preceded by the remark: " A long series of prophecy being *applicable* to such and such events is itself a proof that it was intended of them: as the rules by which we *naturally* judge and determine, in common cases parallel to this, will show. * * * Now, there are two kinds of writing which bear a great resemblance to Prophecy, with respect to the matter before us: the mythological, and the satirical where the satire is, to a certain degree, concealed. And a man might be assured that he understood what an author intended by a fable or parable, related without any application or moral, merely from seeing it to be *easily capable of such application*, and that such a moral might *naturally* be deduced from it. And he might be fully assured that such persons and events were intended in a satirical writing, merely from its being applicable to them. And, agreeably to this last observation, he might be in a good measure satisfied of it, though he were not enough informed in affairs, or in the story of such persons, *to understand half the satire*. * * * And from these things it may be made appear that the showing even to a high probability, if that could be, that the prophets thought of some other events, in such and such predictions, and not those at all which Christians allege to be completions of those predictions; or that such and such prophecies are *capable of being applied to other events* than those to which Christians apply them,—that this would not confute or destroy the force of the argument from Prophecy, even with regard to those very instances." To the same effect Hengstenberg observes that, when we speak of the fulfilment of Prophecy, two questions must be kept apart,—What meaning did the Prophets attach to their own words? and, What sense has God designed to convey by them? For reasons which will be presently considered, Hengstenberg decides that the answer to the former question is wholly immaterial; while he enters upon the second by observing that the proper author of all Prophecy is God: on which he further remarks: " The hermeneutic rule, that we must always seek for the sense designed and perceived by the author, is not violated thereby. The difference between us and our opponents lies rather in the different answer to the question, Who is to be regarded as the proper author of the prophecies?"—*Christologie*, I. i. s. 317.

from an opinion, condemned by the primitive Church, but revived in recent times by Dr. Hengstenberg, which, from an erroneous conception of the nature of the Divine influence, and an undue depreciation of the human agency employed by the Holy Spirit, goes into another extreme. This opinion has been already touched upon in the second of these Discourses, where it has been shown how the Fathers,—in opposition alike to heathen divination, and the fanaticism of the followers of Montanus,—strenuously insisted upon the fact that the prophets retained perfect consciousness of all that passed within them, although their senses were closed against the impressions of the external world.[1] In that Discourse it has been also pointed out, how the first Christian Apologists employed this same fact as the criterion whereby to distinguish the condition of the prophets of God from the phrensy of the heathen diviners on the one hand, and the hallucinations of the Montanists on the other,[2] in each of which cases the intelligent consciousness of the speaker was suppressed to such an extent, that he was totally ignorant of all that he himself had uttered. The opinion that this was also the condition of the prophets of God is advocated, as I have observed, by Dr. Hengstenberg; who has asserted that the distinction which the primitive Church laid down between true and false Prophecy is unfounded; and who indentifies the ecstatic condition of the prophets with the state of the Pythoness or the Montanist,—so far as relates to the suppression, in both cases, of intelligent consciousness.[3]

[1] See Lecture ii. p. 84, &c.

[2] Cf. Hävernick, "Einleitung," Th. II. Abth. ii. s. 35. The accuracy with which the Fathers, in this case, eliminated truth from error, as well as the difficulty of doing so, is illustrated in an interesting manner by the extreme views put forward by the author of the "Clementine Homilies." There can be little doubt that this apocryphal work (the composition of which the learned place at different periods, from the second to the fourth century,) was one of the many writings elicited by the reaction against Montanism. (See A. Schliemann, "Die Clementinen," s. 185, *u.* 548.) The "Homilies" lay down two criterions of true Prophecy: (1.) The prophet of God has permanent possession of the gifts of the Holy Spirit (*Πνεῦμα ἔμφυτον καὶ ἀένναον*). To suppose him for any interval abandoned by the Divine influence, is to reduce him to the character of a heathen diviner (*τὸ γὰρ τοιοῦτον μανικῶς ἐνθουσιούντων ἐστὶν ὑπὸ πνεύματος ἀταξίας, τῶν παρὰ βωμοῖς μεθυόντων, καὶ κνίσσης ἐμφορουμένων.—Hom.* iii. 13, ap. Coteler. t. i. p. 643). (2.) The consciousness of the true prophet must be so perfectly retained, that his condition admits *neither dreams, nor visions* (*ἄνευ ὀπτασίας, καὶ ὀνείρων μαθεῖν, ἀποκάλυψίς ἐστιν.—Hom.* xvii. 18. *ibid.* p. 743). Cf. Schliemann, s. 186, ff.; Neander, "Kirchengeschichte," i. s. 610. ff.

[3] Hengstenberg, appealing to the facts to which attention has been already drawn (Lecture iv. pp. 165, 166, &c.), concludes that the state of ecstasy (which he represents

This learned writer has misapprehended as well the line of argument pursued by the early Christian writers, as the true nature of the prophetic condition.[1] In the two extreme cases with which the Church had to contend, the individual, for whom the

as involving an entire suppression of consciousness and intellectual activity) is not merely a frequent concomitant, but the necessary and essential condition of Prophecy. His adoption, as we shall see, of the statements of Plato and Tertullian, further shows how strangely this learned writer has failed to appreciate the nature of the difficulties, on either side, with which the early Church had to contend. Hengstenberg's view, as laid down in his "Christologie" (i. 1, s. 294 ff.), is as follows:—In distinguishing between true and false Prophecy, the Fathers have misapprehended the facts as stated in Scripture. From those statements "it appears that true prophets also found themselves in an extraordinary and unusual condition,—in an ἔκστασις,—in which their intelligent consciousness retired, and their entire self-life (Selbstleben) was suppressed by a powerful operation of the Divine Spirit, and rendered passive to such a degree that, as Philo says, they became 'Interpreters,' of whose organs God made use, in order to impart His revelations."—s. 294. "It admits of no doubt," he continues, "that the Hebrew prophets, *just as the heathen seers* (ebenso wie die heidnischen Seher), found themselves in an ecstasy. * * * Even to the true prophets may be applied *what Plato alleges in the Ion and Phædrus*, that with the prophetic gift was joined, *of necessity*, the suppression of human activity, *and of intellectual consciousness.*" He then proceeds to quote, with approval, a passage from Philo to which I have already adverted (Lecture ii. p. 65, note [1]—ἐξοικίζεται γὰρ ἐν ἡμῖν ὁ νοῦς κατὰ τὴν τοῦ θείου πνεύματος ἄφιξιν),—adding: "Since, therefore, we have found the distinction laid down by the Fathers between true and false Prophecy to be without foundation, the question arises, in the next place, *In what does the distinction consist?* Already has Tertullian placed a difference between the ἔκστασις, and the *μανία*, or *furor;* and ascribed the latter to the false prophets. *And this, with justice.* * * * In the heathen seers the ἔκστασις, it is true, also consisted in the suppression of intelligent consciousness, but this was effected by the lower portion of the soul having been excited to a contest against the higher." And he goes on to say: "The state of the prophets was *supernatural*, the state of the heathen seers *unnatural*—a momentary phrensy."—s. 296 ff. In these remarks it is clear that Hengstenberg accepts Tertullian's statement, and identifies the condition of a prophet of God with that claimed by the fanatical followers of Montanus. This view is but a poor substitute for the sound and rational course pursued by the Church. "Wir halten (observes Hävernick of Hengstenberg's theory) dieselbe für keineswegs berechtigt, an die Stelle der alten kirchlichen Ansicht gesetzt zu werden."—*loc. cit.* s. 36. Hengstenberg draws the following distinction (without alleging any reason for it) between the prophets and the Apostles—"All Divine revelations were known by the prophets through an immediate perception (ein unmittelbares Vernehmen). While in the case of the Apostles, the illumination of the Holy Ghost penetrated all the faculties of the soul in an equal manner, and did not exclude the activity of the understanding;—all impressions were made in their case upon the inward sense, which (while reflection and the outward senses were in repose) was impregnated (befruchtet) by the Divine Spirit."—*Ibid.* s. 299. By the absence of intelligent consciousness in the case of the prophets, he accounts for the want of perfect connexion and clearness in Prophecy—s. 302; see *supra*, p. 177, &c.

[1] Compare with the view of this question which I have suggested in Lecture ii. p. 86, note [1], the following remark of S. Jerome: "Simul et hoc attendendum quod hæc ipsa vel 'assumptio,' vel 'onus,' vel 'pondus,' prophetæ visio sit. Non enim *loquitur* in ἐκστάσει, ut Montanus et Prisca Maximillaque delirant; sed quod prophetat, liber est visionis intelligentis *universa quæ loquitur*, et pondus hostium facientis in suo populo visionem."—*In Naum Prophet.* Præfat. t. vi. p. 535. Rudelbach, having quoted this passage, justly observes that the Fathers, by such statements, neither denied the relative obscurity of Prophecy—which had its ground in the Divine economy; nor did they question that the ecstatic condition was a frequent accompaniment of the Divine communications. But they steadily maintained "that it was altogether inadmissible

possession of a Divine afflatus was claimed, communicated his pretended revelations while totally unconscious of what passed around him ; and the intervention of another party was required for the purpose of interpreting what was uttered in his state of phrensied enthusiasm.[1] It was this absence of reason or intelligence, when giving utterance to oracular sayings, which the primitive Christians justly regarded as a token of estrangement from the Divine Spirit. The Fathers never questioned, or thought of questioning, the fact that, in many instances, the prophets received revelations from God while in the state of ecstasy : they did deny, and in strict accordance with the intimations of Scripture,[2]—firstly, that the prophets were at any time bereft of intelligent consciousness ; and, secondly, that they *gave utterance* to the Divine communications while in the ecstatic condition, or while the exercise of their faculties was thereby affected. Eusebius, who enters at considerable length upon the literature of this controversy,[3] refers to a treatise, composed expressly against the

to represent ecstasy as the psychical foundation of Prophecy,—as Hengstenberg has represented it in his Christology of the Old Testament."—*Die Lehre von der Inspir.*, 1840. H. i. s. 30.

[1] As to heathen divination, we are indebted to Plato for our knowledge of the distinction between the *μάντεις* and the *προφῆται*. He says, in a well-known passage: *οὐδεὶς γὰρ ἔννους ἐφάπτεται μαντικῆς ἐνθέου καὶ ἀληθοῦς, ἀλλ' ἢ καθ' ὕπνον τὴν τῆς φρονήσεως πεδηθεὶς δύναμιν, ἢ διὰ νόσον, ἤ τινα ἐνθουσιασμὸν παραλλάξας * * * τὸ τῶν προφητῶν γένος ἐπὶ ταῖς ἐνθέοις μαντείαις κριτὰς ἐπικαθιστάναι νόμος· οὓς μάντεις αὐτοὺς ἐπονομάζουσί τινες * * * καὶ οὔ τι μάντεις, προφῆται δὲ μαντευομένων δικαιότατα ὀνομάζοιντ' ἄν.*—*Timæus*, ed. Bekker. vol. vii. p. 337. Cf. Lecture ii. p. 84, note [1]. Tertullian similarly describes the pretended revelations of the Montanists: "Edat [Marcion] aliquem psalmum, aliquam visionem, aliquam orationem, dumtaxat spiritalem, in ecstasi, id est, amentia, *si qua linguæ interpretatio accessit.*"—*Adv. Marcion.* v. § 8, p. 591. On this passage Neander observes: " 'The interpretation of the tongue,' in Tertullian's sense, can only mean that when a person in such an ecstatic state had spoken in a manner unintelligible to others, he, or another person—a point which we must here leave undetermined—repeated what had been uttered, in language that would be generally understood."—*Antignosticus*, Th. iii. § 2. (Bohn's ed., p. 509).

[2] It has been already pointed out (see Lecture iv. p. 145), how Scripture intimates that the prophets did not commit to writing, or announce the subjects of their visions until some time after they had received the revelations thus imparted: and consequently not until all ecstatic excitement had passed away. E. g. "Then was the secret revealed unto Daniel in a night vision." On this he blessed God, who "revealeth the deep and secret things," and went to Arioch, "and said thus unto him, * * * bring me in before the king, and I will show unto the king the interpretation."—Dan. ii. 19–24. Again: "Daniel, whose name was Belteshazzar, was astonied for one hour, and his thoughts troubled him. The king spake and said, Let not the dream or the interpretation thereof trouble thee. Belteshazzar answered and said, My Lord, the dream be to them that hate thee," &c.—Dan. iv. 19. So, in the New Testament, some time had elapsed before S. Peter, restored to his ordinary condition, related and acted upon the Divine communication made to him in his ecstasy. (Acts, x.)

[3] The writers, to whom Eusebius refers as having composed special treatises

Montanists by a very early writer named Miltiades, entitled "The Prophet may not *speak* in ecstasy;"[1] and the historian further quotes, as the leading authority upon this whole subject, an anonymous author, who wrote at the opening of the third century, by whom a marked distinction was drawn between the true prophetic ecstasy, and the false ecstasy of the Montanists, which he discriminated by a special name.[2] "The pseudo-prophet,"

against the Montanists, are—Apollinaris, Bishop of Hierapolis, A. D. 170 (Eccl. Hist., iv. 27; v. 16); Miltiades (v. 17); Apollonius, who states that he wrote his work forty years after the appearance of Montanus (v. 18); S. Serapion, Bishop of Antioch, A. D. 182 (v. 19); and especially an author whose name he does not give, but whom he quotes at considerable length, and to whose opinions he evidently attaches much importance. There has been great diversity of opinion as to who this writer was. S. Jerome identifies him with Rhodon, who, as he states, composed "adversum Phrygas insigne opus: temporibusque Commodi, et Severi floruit."—*Lib. de Vir. Illustr.*, cap. xxxvii. t. ii. p. 863; cf. cap. xxxix. p. 865. See also Routh, "Reliquiæ Sacræ," t. ii. p. 195, and t. i. p. 437.

[1] The anonymous author, from whom Eusebius derived his information, describes the work of his "brother Miltiades" as one—*ἐν ᾧ ἀποδείκνυσι περὶ τοῦ μὴ δεῖν προφήτην ἐν ἐκστάσει λαλεῖν.*—*Eccl. Hist.*, v. xvii. p. 232. Cf. Lecture ii. p. 86, note [1]. M. Gaussen ("Theopneustia," p. 409) having observed that the ancient Church regarded as of great importance the principle "that it is *not* necessary to attribute to the prophets a state of excitement and enthusiasm which prevented due control of their faculties," refers to this work of Miltiades; adding, "See the same principles in *Tertullianus* (against Marcion, iv. ch. 22); in Epiphanius, Jerome, Basilius the Great, &c." A reference on this head to Tertullian is unfortunate: the passage, too, quoted by M. Gaussen, is perhaps the strongest proof of his Montanist opinions. In it, alluding to S. Peter's words at the Transfiguration, which the Apostle uttered, "not knowing what he said" (S. Luke, ix. 33),—Tertullian asks: "Quomodo nesciens? Utrumne simplici errore, an ratione *quam defendimus in causa novæ prophetiæ*, gratiæ ecstasin, id est, *amentiam* convenire? In Spiritu enim homo constitutus, præsertim quum gloriam Dei conspicit, *vel quum per ipsum Deus loquitur, necesse est excidat sensu*, obumbratus scilicet virtute Divina; de quo inter nos et Psychicos [*scil.* Catholicos] quæstio est. Interim, *facile est amentiam Petri probare.* Quomodo enim Moysem et Heliam cognovisset nisi in Spiritu?"—*Adv. Marcion.*, iv. 22, p. 537. Speaking of Apollonius, to whose work I have referred in the last note, S. Jerome tells us: "Apollonius vir disertissimus, scripsit adversus Montanum. * * * Tertullianus sex voluminibus adversus ecclesiam editis, quæ scripsit *περὶ ἐκστάσεως*, septimum proprie adversus Apollonium elaboravit."—*De Vir. Illustr.*, cap. xl. t. ii. p. 867.

[2] 'Parecstasis.' His words are: *Ἀλλ' ὅγε ψευδοπροφήτης ἐν παρεκστάσει· ᾧ ἕπεται ἄδεια καὶ ἀφοβία· ἀρχόμενος μὲν ἐξ ἑκουσίου ἀμαθίας, καταστρέφων δὲ εἰς ἀκούσιον μανίαν ψυχῆς, ὡς προείρηται. τοῦτον δὲ τὸν τρόπον, οὔ τέ τινα τῶν κατὰ τὴν παλαιὰν, οὔτε τῶν κατὰ τὴν καινὴν πνευματοφορηθέντα προφήτην δεῖξαι δυνήσονται· οὔτε Ἄγαβον κ. τ, λ.*—Eusebius, *Eccl. Hist.*, v., xvii. p. 233; on which words Valesius remarks: "Notandum est hunc anonymum scriptorem *nunquam* ECSTASES *appellare vanos illos mentis excessus Montanistarum, sed semper* PARECSTACES, * * * Quippe ecstases *fere in bonam partem* sumuntur. * * * At 'Parecstasis' semper in malam partem accipitur." This writer constantly employs the term 'parecstasis.' Thus he describes Montanus as *αἰφνιδίως ἐν κατοχῇ τινὶ καὶ παρεκστάσει γενόμενον.* —*Ibid.* v. xvi. p. 229; and he mentions, respecting a certain Theodotus, that he *παρεκστῆναί τε καὶ καταπιστεῦσαι ἑαυτὸν τῷ τῆς ἀπάτης πνεύματι*—*Ibid.* p. 231; on which Valesius again notes: "Male interpretes omnes hunc locum cepere. *Παρεκστῆναι* est falso mentis excessu abripi. Sic *παρέκστασις* supra sumitur, id est falsa ecstasis. *Sunt enim veræ ecstaces in Ecclesia*, cujusmodi fuit Petri Apostoli, in Actibus cap. x. et xi. ubi Petrus vidisse dicitur in ecstasi visionem. Talis item fuit ecstasis Pauli Apostoli, cum ad tertium usque cœlum abreptus est. * * * Sunt

observed this writer, "is sunk in his 'false ecstasy.' Beginning by a voluntary ignorance, he ends by involuntary phrensy: but they will never be able to prove that any prophet in either the Old or the New Testament was hurried away by the Spirit after this manner;" and, as exemplifying the true prophetic state, the case of Agabus is adduced, of whom mention is made on two occasions in the Acts of the Apostles.[1]

Turning, in the second place, to the other misapprehension into which Dr. Hengstenberg has fallen,—namely, as to the true nature of the prophetic condition itself,—it is to be observed that any theory which represents the state of those who have received revelations from God, as offering any real analogy to that of the heathen diviners, or fanatical Montanists, rests upon principles wholly unsupported by facts. Such a theory must confound what is *supernatural*, with what is altogether *unnatural;*[2] or with what, on the most favorable supposition (as will be shown elsewhere), is but a perversion[3] of the Divine influence. The simple fact, that the prophets of God subsequently describe the scenes enacted before the eye of the soul,—even entering with the utmost minuteness upon all the details connected with their visions,[4]—affords the clearest proofs that their powers of memory were retained throughout unimpaired, and of itself precludes the possibility of their having been unconscious. It would be equally inconsistent, indeed, with the character of the Divine influence, and the nature of the human spirit, were we to regard the former as a crushing and disturbing power, instead of one which elevates and calms the soul of man; or, on the other hand, were we to consider the human spirit as so estranged from and unrelated to God, that, in order to become capable of transmitting the revelation from heaven, it must lose its vital power, and remain sunk in its former darkness and inability to comprehend the Divine

item falsæ ecstaces apud hæreticos, quæ παρεκστάσεις eleganter dicuntur ab hoc scriptore. Eodem modo quo παραδιορθώσεις falsæ emendationes dicuntur a Porphyrio in questionibus Homericis."

[1] Acts, xi. 28; xxi. 10.

[2] Hävernick truly remarks that the manner in which Hengstenberg has attempted to distinguish the *supernatural* state of the true prophet from the *unnatural* state of heathen diviners (see *supra*, note, p. 192), altogether fails: "A forcible suppression of the self-life (Selbstlebens) is, and ever remains, an unnatural state."—*Einleit.* II. ii. s. 37.

[3] I refer to S. Paul's remarks on "spiritual gifts," 1 Cor. xii. and xiv. See *infra*, p. 223, note [2].

[4] See Lecture iv. p. 167, note [1].

mysteries, rather than be reanimated, and enlightened, and raised above the limits of earthly experience.

The prophets tell us, it is true, how the energy of the Spirit of God mastered their natural strength; but they also tell us how their souls were supported, and enabled to endure the sublime visions upon which they gazed.[1] This is a fact which, while it proves that the object of their intuitions was no mere creation of their own imagination,—no mere subjective phantasm,—exhibits, at the same time, how their understanding was qualified to apprehend the Divine communication, and enabled to reproduce it for the benefit of others. Strange, above all,[2] would the phenomenon be, to which I have so repeatedly alluded, of the preservation of each writer's peculiar individuality,—an individuality so plainly stamped upon the form of his representations, —had he been deprived of the use of those natural faculties, by means of which he has embodied in suitable language the ideas which were supernaturally infused into his soul, and placed on record the details of the revelation which they conveyed. So far, indeed, are the facts of the case from suggesting a suppression of the Prophet's intelligent consciousness as being essential or even congruous, that we can at once discern how an elevation, rather, of all the powers whereby ideas are apprehended was, of necessity, required for the purpose of enabling him to receive, or to transmit to others, the mysterious truths which were disclosed to him. None felt more sensibly than the men of God themselves how incompetent, without such spiritual support, are the ordinary faculties of man to grasp conceptions so widely transcending the natural limits of the human soul. The prophet Isaiah, in that most sublime of visions recorded in his sixth chapter, thus felt his innate incapacity: "Woe is me!" he exclaims, "for I am undone, because I am a man of unclean lips * * * for mine eyes have seen the King, the Lord of Hosts." But, on a sudden we find his whole being transformed, and his fears dispelled; he comes boldly forward with the words, "Here am I; send me:" for his weakness became strength, and his iniquity was taken away, as soon as the seraph had touched his lips with fire from the Altar of God.[3]

[1] See Lecture iv. p. 166, note [2].

[2] Cf. Hävernick, *loc. cit.*

[3] "Then flew one of the Seraphims unto me, having a live coal in his hand which

From the remarks just made it follows, that the continued preservation of the human agent's intelligent consciousness, and the elevation of his natural faculties for the reception of the Divine suggestions, are the characteristics of true Prophecy. Nor does the opinion, already referred to, which denies the force of the Christian argument from Prophecy derive the least support from such a conclusion. It is no legitimate inference from the facts which have been adduced, that the *understanding* also of the Prophet[1] must have been so far enlightened as to enable him to comprehend the full signification, and to perceive all the bearings of the Oracle which he uttered. The passage which I have quoted from Bishop Butler points out where the fallacy of such a notion lies. But the subject demands some further consideration, inasmuch as there is no feature of our inquiry which, when justly apprehended, exhibits more clearly the Divine element of Scripture.

It was well remarked by S. Irenæus,[2] that "every prophecy is an enigma before its accomplishment." Let us examine on what foundation this principle rests. In the supernatural and natural worlds, Revelation and Prophecy are, in some obvious respects, parallel to knowledge and teaching.[3] In giving utter-

he had taken from off the Altar, and he laid it upon my mouth, and said, Lo, this hath touched thy lips," &c.—Isai. vi. 6.

[1] The following judicious remarks supply an apt illustration: Isaac gave a prophetic blessing to his son, and was therein inspired, and yet mistook as to the person to whom he applied it; wherein the matter was overruled without his privity. * * * Inspiration, therefore, is confined to the purposes which God has to serve by it. On which account we need not wonder that some prophets, though inspired, yet did not understand distinctly their own predictions. Indeed, it was not for God's purpose in those cases that they should understand distinctly. He revealed Himself to them, not so much for themselves, as for others. Much less have we any reason to wonder that some inspired persons should not understand the predictions of other inspired persons, but search diligently into their meaning (Dan. ix. 2: 1 Peter, i. 10, 11)."—Edm. Calamy, *The Inspiration of the Old and New Testament*, p. 127.

[2] He had just observed, that "Christ is the treasure hid in the field, which is the world [S. Matt. xiii. 38, 44]: He was pointed out by types and parables which could not be understood *πρὸ τοῦ τὴν ἔκβασιν τῶν προφητευομένων ἐλθεῖν*, which is the coming of the Lord." S Irenæus then quotes in proof the words of Daniel: "But thou, O Daniel, shut up the words, and seal the book, even to the time of the end," &c. (xii. 4, 7;) and of Jeremiah; "In the latter days ye shall consider it perfectly" (xxiii. 20),—on which follow the words which I have referred to: *πᾶσα γὰρ προφητεία πρὸ τῆς ἐκβάσεως, αἴνιγμά ἐστι καὶ ἀντιλογία τοῖς ἀνθρώποις· ὅταν δὲ ἔλθῃ ὁ καιρὸς, καὶ ἀποβῇ τὸ προφητευθὲν, τότε τῆς ἀκριβεστάτης ἐπέτυχεν ἐξηγήσεως.*—*Cont. Hæres.* IV. xxvi. p. 262.

[3] "When Paul asks, 'What shall I profit you, except I shall speak to you either by revelation or by knowledge, or by prophesying, or by doctrine?' (*ἢ ἐν ἀποκαλύψει ἢ ἐν γνώσει ἢ ἐν προφητείᾳ ἢ ἐν διδαχῇ*—1 Cor. xiv. 6)—'revelation' and 'prophecy' unquestionably correspond to each other, just as 'knowledge' and teach-

ance, however, to miraculous communications from God, it would seem, even *à priori*, to be the more reasonable supposition that the Prophet should not comprehend the mysteries which have been divinely imparted to him, to the like extent, or in the same degree as an ordinary teacher understands the various branches of information which he has acquired by study and meditation, —by the exercise of human intellect and the employment of human industry. The full meaning of the language which he utters must, from the very nature of the case, extend beyond the Prophet's own mental vision. That supernatural intuition in which the present and the future are intermingled,[1] and which has arisen independently of the human agent's own reflection, transcends the power of his understanding, and cannot be analyzed by the discursive faculty of the mind. This analysis, we are told in the words of our text, the prophets attempted to perform. When their spiritual intuitions had ceased, their ordinary powers of reflection came into play; and the subject of their prophetic communications, when presented to the judgment of their understandings, naturally prompted effort and research. "The prophets," writes S. Peter, "have inquired, and searched diligently * * * searching what, or what manner of time the Spirit of Christ, which was in them, did signify." The foundation of this inquiry lay in the *pre-forming* character of Revelation; according to which it ever veiled, in its intimate reference to the present, a constant reference to the future. This peculiar feature of the Divine communications was implied by Christ Himself, when He taught that "the seed is the word of God:"[2] and, according to this principle, the future development of the sense of Prophecy is to be regarded as the product of the germinating power of the "seed," which lies still dormant until the "fulness of time."[3]

That the predictions of Scripture are not to be thoroughly un-

ing;' and are therefore evidently to be distinguished as supernatural information and as natural acquirements."—Ritschl, *Die Entstehung der altkath. Kirche*, s. 489. To the same effect Hengstenberg, having observed, that "What viewed in respect to the manner of receiving it, is 'revelation;' the same, when viewed in respect to the manner of its delivery, is 'prophecy'"—goes on to remark on 1 Cor. xiv. 6: "Here we have a double pair of corresponding parts: revelation and prophecy constitute the one, knowledge and doctrine the other."—*The Rev. of S. John*, Prologue. (Clarke's For. Theol., Lib. i. p. 40).

[1] See Lecture iv. p. 176, &c.

[2] S. Luke, viii. 11.

[3] Cf. Beck, "Propäd. Entwicklung," s. 252; and Lecture iv. pp. 149–154.

derstood before their fulfilment is clearly indicated by our Lord's language when He points out their nature and their object:[1] "And now I have told you before it come to pass, that *when it is come to pass* ye might believe." Thus it is that Prophecy is likened unto the rays of a taper, which glimmers by night, and faintly illumines the darkness, until the appearance of the morning star.[2] The progress of history, meanwhile, enables us to ascertain *what* prophetical announcements have already received their ful-

[1] S. John, xiv. 29. Cf. "And when this cometh to pass (lo it will come), then shall they know that a prophet hath been among them."—Ezek. xxxiii. 33.

[2] 2 S. Pet. i. 16–21. The sense of this much disputed passage which I have here adopted may be thus stated somewhat more fully. S. Peter had summed up for the "brethren," from whom he was about to be parted for ever (ver. 15), the grounds of the Faith: viz., the testimony of the Apostles, and the language of Prophecy. "We have not," he argues, "followed cunningly devised fables, when we made known the power and coming of Christ, but were eye-witnesses of His Majesty * * * when we were with Him in the holy mount." We have also, continues S. Peter, a further reason for our belief,—viz., "the word of Prophecy," which has now been rendered "more sure" and stedfast (*βεβαιότερον*) by those proofs of its fulfilment with which you are acquainted. (Cf. "Verily I say unto you, that many prophets have desired to see those things which ye see, and have not seen them."—S. Matt. xiii. 17). To this "ye do well that ye take heed;" for before its accomplishment—"until the day dawn"—the language of Prophecy is ever obscure, and casts but a feeble light upon the future, as a taper dimly shining where its rays cannot be reflected (*ὡς λύχνῳ φαίνοντι ἐν αὐχμηρῷ τόπῳ*:—*αὐχμηρός*=*ἄνυδρος*). Nor need this cause you surprise. Even the prophets could not expound the revelations which were committed to them;—the meaning which the event fixes upon their language was not a meaning infused into it by their own design;—the sense of their predictions, as it did not proceed from themselves, could not be unravelled by their own powers of interpretation (*ἰδίας ἐπιλύσεως οὐ γίνεται*:—for which sense of *ἐπίλυσις*, cf. S. Mark, iv. 34; Acts, xix. 39):—and the reason is obvious: "Prophecy came not in old time by the will of man [i. e. so that the prophet gave utterance to *his own* thoughts and feelings—*τὰ ἴδια*]: but holy men of God spake as they were moved (*φερόμενοι*) by the Holy Ghost." (Cf. the favorite expression of the Fathers—*πνευματοφόροι*; see Lecture ii. p. 83, and *supra*, p. 194, note [2].) Rudelbach ("Die Lehre von der Inspir." 1842. H. ii. s. 15) justly observes, that this *φορά*, or impulse of the Holy Spirit, is by no means to be confounded with the *ἔκστασις*, or personal condition of the prophet. In confounding these distinct notions consists the error of Hengstenberg on this question; see *supra*, p. 191, note [3]. This explanation of the passage plainly includes that to which I have alluded in Lecture ii. p. 71, note [1].)

Here we see Prophecy illustrated under that aspect according to which the Divine agents appear *passive:* the words of the text (1 S. Pet. i. 10–12) exhibit them, on the other hand, as *active* and *conscious*. We thence learn—(1) that the prophets diligently applied their understandings to ascertain the sense of their predictions (*ἐξεζήτησαν καὶ ἐξηρεύνησαν*). (2) The chief object of their search was, "What, or what manner of time (*εἰς τίνα ἢ ποῖον καιρόν*) the Spirit of Christ which was in them did signify." ("*Quod* innuit tempus per se, quasi dicas æram, suis numeris notatam: *quale* dicit tempus ex eventibus variis noscendum."—Bengel.) (3) The reason is added of the obscurity in which their words were shrouded;—they were not personally concerned in the event: "it was revealed to them that *not unto themselves* did they minister" such things. (4) The Apostle intimates that all this was no accidental mystery, no undesigned form of ambiguous words. Not to prophets alone was this knowledge denied; even the highest of created beings were not admitted to these secret counsels of the Almighty: "which things the angels desire to look into."

filment; and to recognise the bearing upon the future of certain statements of Scripture which we might otherwise regard as unconnected with the Christian scheme, or as merely figurative allusions.[1] For example:—in the twenty-second Psalm, "the

[1] This subject is further elucidated by the nature of Types (Τύπος—*a blow, that which is produced by a blow*, or *its mark* (S. John, xx. 25); *the impress* of a seal; also *a model* or *mold* (e. g. τύπος σκηνῆς,—Hebr. viii. 5); used also of the *resemblance* between two *opposite* things (e. g. Adam by whom came *death* is the τύπος of Christ by Whom came *Life*,—Rom. v. 14.) That a type differs in no essential particular from a prediction, is proved by the application to both of the New Testament formula, ἵνα ἡ γραφὴ πληρωθῇ (e. g. the ordinances which regulated the type of the Paschal Lamb are quoted as constituting, in the most literal sense, a prediction: "These things were done *that the Scripture should be fulfilled*, A bone of Him should not be broken."—S. John, xix. 36.) The only distinction which can be maintained is this, that in Types, whether consisting of words, things, or persons, the concealment, not only of their ultimate design, but even of any further reference beyond the mere representation of each particular type,—was carried to a greater extent than in Prophecy; in which, as we have seen, the prophets were *conscious* that their language had a more extensive application than they could themselves perceive. For example: —the type of the Paschal Lamb was repeated yearly for many centuries, its reference *to the future* being neither understood nor suspected. Referring to this fact, Mr. Davison defines "the genuine Type of the Old Testament" to be "a concealed prophecy, which the completion explains."—*On Prophecy*, p. 275. "The Sense of the [ritual] Types," he observes, "was a *latent* one. It was a Sense not disclosed to the Hebrew worshipper. * * * When those types are instituted, there is no discovery of their principle, nor hint of their interior signification joined with them. * * * Whatever access the Israelite had to the great significations of his sacrificial and ritual worship, he obtained it by the insinuation of Prophecy, by imperfect and partial arguments, which could not go so far as to reveal the truth."—*Ibid.* p. 135. But to take a more extended view of this matter:—Types are usually divided into those which are represented by persons (viz., Melchizedek, David, Jonah, &c.); or by things (viz., the Tabernacle, the Sacrifices, the Brazen Serpent, &c.). To this division Rudelbach ("Zeitschrift," 1842. H. ii. s. 38 ff.) adds what he terms ("on account of their prevailing typical character," s. 46) "verbal types," or typical *prophecies*; of which he gives as examples, Hos. xi. 1 [see *supra*, Lecture iii. p. 109, note [1]]; "Rachel weeping for her children," Jer. xxxi. 15, quoted S. Matt. ii. 18; and the words of Ps. lxix. 25, "Let their habitation be desolate," &c., quoted Acts, i. 20, as predicting the fall of Judas. Considering the question thus generally, we shall perceive a further analogy between Types and Prophecy properly so called. S. Peter (1 Ep. i. 12) expressly tells us, that "it was revealed" (ἀπεκαλύφθη) to the prophets that their words had a significance extending to the future. Now, similar "revelations" were made as to the allusions embodied in Types: e. g. Psalm cx. disclosed the spiritual nature of Melchizedek's Priesthood; while the manner in which the history of David is made use of in the language of Prophecy gave the people clear intimations how closely the Psalmist's person was connected with the development of the Divine Scheme. (Cf. Jer. xxxiii. 26; Ezek. xxxiv. 23, 24; Amos, ix. 11; Zech. xli. 7, 8, &c. &c.) Even where we have not express information of such disclosures, we may safely infer that the pious Jew was not left in ignorance of the true bearing of the system of Types in which his religion was shrouded. Take the single case of the Brazen Serpent. In the Book of Wisdom it is expressly called "a sign of salvation;"—"for he that turned himself toward it was not saved by the thing that he saw; but by Thee, that art the Saviour of all." —Wisd. xvi. 6, 7.

Olshausen does not, perhaps, go too far when he lays down in his first Tract, "On the more profound Sense of Scripture," that "Types, Symbols, Allegory [cf. Gal. iv. 24; Rev. xi. 8], Prophecy, are not to be regarded as differing in essence, but merely with reference to what is externally visible" (s. 70): to which he adds, in his second Tract on the same subject, "What regarded *as an act* is a Type, when expressed *in words*

piercing of the hands and the feet;" Zechariah's description of the Messiah entering Jerusalem riding "upon an ass;" or this same prophet's mention of the "thirty pieces of silver."[1]

Such considerations clearly show how essential it was that the historian of a revelation should have been *inspired;*—or, in other words, that his writings should have been Divinely guarded from all possibility of omission or misstatement. The meaning of the predictions which he has recorded frequently depends upon the turn of a sentence, upon a metaphor, or an expression, which if writing without the guidance of the Holy Spirit, he might have deemed trivial or unnecessary; especially when we know that even the Prophet himself did not, in general, understand how far such features of his announcements were, or might be, of importance.[2] This remark will appear more obvious from an example. In the last chapter of Daniel, the date of a future event is darkly foreshadowed: "It shall be for a time, times, and an half." On

is called an Allegory: but because every word is a spiritual *act*, and every act an embodied *word*, they are to be distinguished only after a human manner, for in their inward nature both are but *one*. And inasmuch as no prophecy is arbitrary or magical, but the spiritual foreshadowing of that which is to be—so far all Prophecy is typical, and every Type a prophecy. And so of the whole: for the entire Old Testament is a great prophecy, because its history is an eternal Type."—s. 19.

[1] Zech. ix. 9; xi. 13. To these examples we may add the prediction of Haggai: "Speak to Zerubbabel saying, I will shake the heavens and the earth. * * * In that day, saith the Lord of Hosts, will I take thee, O Zerubbabel, * * * and will make thee as a signet: for I have chosen thee."—Hagg. ii. 21, 23. "Why" (writes Mr. Davison) "is Zerubbabel so distinguished in the prophecy, when it looks so far beyond him? Why is he characterized as the signet of God? He is so distinguished as being the *Representative* of Christ; and his *fitness* to be that *Representative* is most evident. Of his line and seed was Christ born into the world. When God, therefore, restored His people, and reinstated them in their covenant and their land again, by this prophecy He designated Zerubbabel, and set His choice upon him, as the signet of His hand and purpose, in whom *some* work of His providence and mercy should be accomplished. * * * In Zerubbabel the genealogy of the Messiah, after the restoration from Babylon, begins. Zerubbabel is the head of that genealogy: in him it has its double concourse (S. Matt. i. 12; S. Luke, iii. 27): both lines of the descent of the Messiah *meeting* in his person. * * * Such prediction was the more opportune when we consider the state of doubt and ambiguity which might now seem to attach to the former promises of God, given to the family of David, when that family had been set aside from the throne. * * * To Zerubbabel *no throne* is promised, and *none was given*. Yet he is *chosen*. * * * Whence I infer that that *adoption* or *acknowledgment* of him, in relation to 'the sure' and yet remaining 'mercies of David,' the promises of the Christian Covenant, is the specific point of the prophecy of Haggai. It is not to be maintained that all this force and connexion of the prophecy could be understood from the first utterance of it, but they may be understood now."—*Discourses on Prophecy*, p. 340–342.

[2] Jahn has forcibly urged this fact, as exhibiting the distinct functions of Revelation and Inspiration; the latter being *always* necessary—"weil die Propheten selbst, oft diese göttliche Offenbarungen nicht, oder doch nicht ganz verstanden, und folglich ohne göttliche Verwahrung leicht hätten Irrthümer einmengen, und so die Offenbarung selbst wesentlich entstellen können."—*Einleitung*, Th. i. s. 95.

this the prophet takes occasion to observe: "And I heard, but I understood not: then said I, O my Lord, what shall be the end of these things? And he said, Go thy way, Daniel: for the words are closed up and sealed till the time of the end."[1] Such passages not only illustrate the assertion of S. Peter, in the text, that the prophets "searched diligently" for the meaning of their own words;—they also afford conclusive evidence that as each prediction was uttered, reason continued its habitual efforts to penetrate the unknown; and exhibit the important fact, that, while he was subject to the Divine influence, there was carried on, simultaneously, a parallel exercise of the natural faculties of the human agent, who was thus employed to express the revelations of God in the language of men.[2]

[1] Dan. xii. 7–9. Cf. "It shall be one day which shall be known to the Lord, not day, nor night: but it shall come to pass that *at evening time it shall be light.*"—Zech. xiv. 7. The New Testament affords some striking illustrations of the fact that the full sense of a Divine revelation was frequently unperceived by the person who received it. After the effusion of the Holy Ghost at Pentecost, S. Peter announces to the Jews—"The promise is unto you and to your children, and *to all that are afar off*, even as many as the Lord our God shall call."—Acts. ii. 39. Looking from our point of view, no one can doubt that by those words the admission of the Gentiles to Gospel privileges was plainly intimated: and yet it was not for some time afterwards—and that, too, by aid of a new revelation (Acts, x.; cf. xi. 15–17)—that S. Peter, still fettered by his Jewish creed, fully understood the force of what he himself had uttered. The case of Caiaphas "prophesying," unconsciously, that "one man should die for the people," is still more remarkable, "This *spake he not of himself* (ἀφ' ἑαυτοῦ οὐκ εἶπεν); but, being High Priest that year, *he prophesied* (ἐπροφήτευσεν)."—S. John, xi. 51. Here the Evangelist leaves no room for supposing his own interpretation to be a mere "subjective exposition." The express *denial* that Caiaphas "spake of himself" is introduced in such a manner as to place it beyond any doubt that "he *prophesied*," that is, "spake under the influence of God." The reference to the office of Caiaphas does not imply that S. John considered that every High Priest necessarily prophesied; but merely points out that the High Priest was the natural medium through which God *might* at times reveal Himself. "Fuit, inquam, sacerdos; ὁ δὲ πρὸς ἀλήθειαν ἱερεὺς εὐθὺς ἐστι προφήτης, ut Philo ait."—C. F. Fritzsche, *De Revel. notione Bibl.*, p. 62. Cf. also Olshausen, *in loc.*

In considering the question, "Utrum prophetæ semper cognoscant ea quæ prophetant," S. Thomas Aquinas decides in the negative, by a reference to this case of Caiaphas; laying down the principle: "In revelatione prophetica, movetur mens prophetæ a Spiritu Sancto, sicut instrumentum deficiens respectu principalis agentis:" —from which he infers, "Etiam veri prophetæ non omnia cognoscunt quæ in eorum visis, aut verbis, aut etiam factis, Spiritus Sanctus intendit."—*Summ. Theol.* 2da 2dæ., qu. clxxiii. art. iv. t. xxiii. p. 308.

[2] Before leaving this branch of our subject, a word may be said as to the *numerical* statements of Prophecy. Numbers are sometimes employed, as natural facts or historical events, in their ordinary signification: e. g. Jer. xxviii. 16, 17; Isai. vii. 8. In the great majority of cases, however, they are symbolically significant: e. g. the mystic number *seven*—as in the days of Creation, and throughout the ordinances of the Law; cf. also Dan. ix. 24–27; Rev. xiii. 18. "The *numbers* of Prophecy," observes Beck, "are to it means of representation as essential as its natural and historical characteristics;—only most difficult to be deciphered, because our computations are chiefly dependent on the proportions of the outward world: Die prophetischen Zahlen dagegen sind zusammengesetzt theils aus den innersten Urbestimmungen der

The history of Balaam illustrates still further the principles which I have endeavored to establish. Balaam was, in the strictest sense (although not officially[1]), a prophet, or agent through whom God revealed His will. This may be inferred, partly from the language made use of by the sacred historian when narrating the personal history of Balaam, and recording his predictions ; partly from the nature of the predictions themselves. In the first place, Balaam expressly calls Jehovah his God ;[2] and he nowhere disclaims the justice of the reputation which had attracted the notice of the King of Moab : "I wot," said Balak, "that he whom thou blessest is blessed, and he whom thou cursest is cursed ;"[3]—on the contrary, the phraseology employed throughout denotes his intimate relation to the Supreme God. Thus it is plainly stated that he "heard the words of God ;" that he saw "the vision of the Almighty ;"[4] that "the Spirit of God[5] came upon him ;" that Jehovah "met him," and "put a

aussenweltlichen Maassverhältnisse, heilige Urzahlen, die elementare Welt-Organisation bemessend, zu deren Enträthselung nur die biblischen Aufschlüsse über Schöpfung und Urzeit dienen ; theils aus den Grundbestimmungen der theocratischen Chronologie und Arithmetik (namentlich Festrechnung), heilige Ziffern, geschöpft aus der Zeit-und Maass-Ordnung der Theocratie."—*Propäd. Entwickl.*, s. 201.

[1] See Lecture iv. p. 175, note [2]. That Balaam must be distinguished from the ordinary ministers of the Theocracy, whether officially Prophets, or Seers, may be inferred from the title given to him in Josh. xiii. 22, "the Soothsayer" (הקוסם):—a term which the LXX. render by *μάντις*, and which is usually employed in a bad sense ; e. g. "There shall not be found among you any one * * * that *useth divination*" (קסם קסמים).—Deut. xviii. 10. Balaam himself, too (Numb. xxiii. 23), places "divination" (קסם), together with "enchantment" (נחש), in contrast to true prophecy, as found only in Israel. Compare, however, Prov. xvi. 10—"A Divine sentence (קסם) is in the lips of the king."

[2] "If Balak would give me his house full of silver and gold, I cannot go beyond the word of Jehovah my God (יהוה אלהי) to do less or more."—Num. xxii. 18. Balaam no less plainly asserts the great truth that Jehovah was the God of Israel: "He hath not beheld iniquity in Jacob, neither hath he seen perverseness in Israel: Jehovah his God (יהוה אלהיו) is with him."—xxiii. 21. This use of the term Jehovah is peculiar to those who stood within the sphere of Revelation. See Hengstenberg's "Beiträge," ii. s. 300 *u.* 407 ; as well as his Dissertation on Balaam.

[3] Num. xxii. 6 : see also Balaam's reply : "Lodge here this night, and I will bring you word again, *as* JEHOVAH *shall speak unto me.*"—ver. 8.

[4] שדי. Num. xxiv. 4.

[5] רוח אלהים. *Ibid.* ver. 2. Cf. Lecture iii. p. 128, &c. Deylingius ("Observ. Sacræ," vol. iii. p. 105, &c.) points out some analogies between the expressions employed in this narrative and those which occur in the prophetical writings. E. g. Balaam describes his predictions by the term נאם (ch. xxiv. 4, 16), which is usually employed in the exordiums of prophetic announcements to denote a revelation from God. "Thus, David the son of Jesse *said*" (נאם)—2 Sam. xxiii. 1 ; "*Saith* the Lord God of Hosts"—Isai. iii. 15 ; "I am against the prophets *saith* the Lord, that use their tongues, and say, He *saith*."—Jer. xxiii. 31. So also the term used to signify the ecstatic condition : "He hath said * * * which saw the vision of the Almighty, *falling*" [נפל—the words "into a trance" do not occur in the original], &c. Num. xxiv. 4, 16. Compare Ezek. i. 28 ; iii. 23 ; Dan. viii. 17, &c.

word in his mouth."[1] His sacrifice, too, of seven bullocks and seven rams, was of a form identical with that which Jehovah Himself prescribed in the book of Job ;[2] a form, moreover, which, we are told, was employed on one of the most solemn occasions of Jewish history,—the bringing "up the Ark of the Covenant of the Lord out of the house of Obed-Edom :" "And it came to pass, when God helped the Levites that bare the Ark of the Covenant of the Lord, that they offered seven bullocks and seven rams."[3] In the second place, if we look to his predictions,[4] we shall find that they comprise the entire range of Prophecy: Jewish,--namely, the condition, safety, and conquests of the Hebrews ; Christian,—the dominion of the "Star and Sceptre ;" Pagan,—the visitation of the heathen enemies of Israel.[5] Of one of his predictions, indeed, we ourselves can judge : even in that early stage of their history, Balaam foretold the wonderful isolation of the Israelites among the inhabitants of the earth : "Lo! the people shall dwell alone, and shall not be reckoned among the nations."[6] In fine, the manner in which Jeremiah

[1] Num. xxiii. 16. "And Jehovah met Balaam" (ויקר יהוה). Alluding to this expression, Tholuck ("Vermischte Schriften," i. s. 409) observes that commentators have seldom noticed a feature in this narrative by which Balaam is distinguished from other prophets. It is always said that *he went apart* when he desired to prophesy, and that God *met* him. Thus: "Balaam said unto Balak, Stand by thy burnt-offering, and I will go: peradventure Jehovah will *come to meet* me. * * * And *God met* Balaam."—xxiii. 3, 4. Compare ch. xxii. 19, 20. It may be noticed, that Tholuck is inclined to regard the fact of Balaam's exhibiting no surprise at the miracle of the ass speaking to him (Num. xxii. 29) as a proof that this entire transaction was purely *subjective;* and that there was no *external* reality corresponding to the details narrated. On the other hand, S. Augustine more profoundly observes: "Nihil hic sanè mirabilius videtur, quam quod loquente asinâ territus non est, sed insuper ei, velut talibus monstris assuetus, *irâ perseverante* respondit."—*Quæst. in Num.*, xlviii. lib. iv t. iii. p. 549.

[2] "Jehovah said to Eliphaz the Temanite, My wrath is kindled against thee * * * therefore take unto you now seven bullocks and seven rams, and go to my servant Job, and offer up for yourselves a burnt-offering."—Job, xlii. 7, 8. See Deylingius, *loc. cit.* p. 112.

[3] 1 Chron. xv. 26. Cf. also the solemn sacrifice of Hezekiah: "Then Hezekiah the king rose early, and gathered the rulers of the city, and went up to the house of the Lord. And they brought seven bullocks and seven rams. * * * And he commanded the priests the sons of Aaron to offer them on the altar of the Lord."—2 Chron. xxix. 20, 21.

[4] Gesenius prefaces his comments on Isai. xv. and xvi. by a dissertation on the history of Moab: "Among the oracles, that of Balaam (Num. xxii. xxiv.) is specially remarkable, in which that early, although not Israelitic, prophet—urged by Moab to curse Israel—is moved by the Divine Spirit to bless it, and to announce to Moab its future destruction by a mighty hero in Israel (David), (Num. xxiv. 17, 18; cf. 2 Sam. viii. 2):—a genuinely epic piece, worthy of the greatest poets of all times." —*Der Prophet Jesaia*, i. s. 504.

[5] Davison, "Discourses on Prophecy," p. 290.

[6] Num xxiii. 9.

makes use of Balaam's oracle against Moab[1] affords the fullest sanction to his prophetic authority;—an authority which commands the repeated recognition of the sacred writers; as we learn from the books of Moses, Joshua, Nehemiah, and Micah.[2]

The Divine source of his predictions having been thus pointed out, it is to be remarked, in the next place, how the very defects of Balaam's character were bent to serve the purpose of Jehovah. We see, as subsequently in the history of Jonah,[3] how vain was his opposition to the will of heaven: both cases affording, perhaps, the most striking examples in the sacred narrative, of that 'Law' of Prophecy already dwelt upon at some length,[4] according to which each single prediction attaches itself to certain events or occasions presented at the period of its delivery. The disobedience of Balaam became the occasion of that prediction which filled the Gentile world, at the eve of Christ's Nativity, with the expectation of a Universal Monarch. The flight of Jonah from the presence of the Lord was made the occasion of that marvellous type which symbolically foretold Christ's sojourn in the tomb.[5]

We have further to notice how Balaam (whose visions are so plainly described as the result of genuine prophetic ecstasy), in the midst of his announcements retains his consciousness unimpaired, and exhibits the unclouded exercise of his natural understanding. When about to be dismissed by the King of Moab, he

[1] Cf. Jer. xlviii. 45, with Num. xxiv. 17. See *infra*, Lecture vii.

[2] Deut. xxiii. 4, 5; Josh. xxiv. 9; Neh. xiii. 2; Micah, vi. 5.

[3] "The word of the Lord came unto Jonah, saying, Arise, go to Nineveh, and cry against it. But Jonas rose up to flee unto Tarshish from the presence of the Lord; and he found a ship going to Tarshish. But the Lord sent out a great wind into the sea," &c.—Jonah, i.

[4] Lecture iv. p. 147, &c.

[5] "As Jonas was three days and three nights in the whale's belly; so shall the Son of Man be three days and three nights in the heart of the earth."—S. Matt. xii. 40. The manner in which German writers, even of the school considered pre-eminently "Evangelical," venture, without any *external* evidence whatsoever, to tamper with the text of Scripture, is painfully illustrated by the following remark of Neander on the Type of Jonah: "In Matt. xii. 40, the reference is made to bear upon the *Resurrection* of Christ, which is quite foreign to the original sense and connexion of the passage. * * * A special application of the type in this way would have drawn the attention of the hearers away from the main point of comparison. *For these reasons we think* the verse in question is a commentary by a later hand."—*The Life of Jesus Christ*, § 165. (Bohn's transl., p. 266.) It is well to compare the language of Mr. Davison: "Jonah is in his own person a *Type*, a *prophetic Sign of Christ.* * * * Our Saviour has fixed the truth and certainty of this Type; the correspondence of the miracle has fixed it. * * * Jonah, as I may say, *compensates* for the absence of any direct Christian prediction in what he delivers, by the typical prophecy embodied in his personal history."—*On Prophecy*, p. 275.

again reminds him of his powerlessness in the hands of God: "If Balak would give me his house full of silver and gold, I cannot go beyond the commandment of the Lord to do either good or bad of mine own mind; but what the Lord saith, that will I speak. And now (he continues) behold I go unto my people; come therefore and I will advertise thee what this people shall do to thy people in the latter days;"[1]—words which are followed, in continuation, as it were, of his personal observations, by that grand series of predictions with which his ministry as God's prophet closes.[2]

To the examples already adduced in illustration of the principle which we are considering must be added an incident recorded by Ezekiel. According to that principle, the continued exercise of each prophet's consciousness was preserved unimpaired, and his understanding still reflected upon the visions which his spiritual sense had contemplated, even while his imagination was engaged in embodying them in certain forms or symbols. "The word of the Lord," writes Ezekiel, "came unto me, saying, Son of man, set thy face toward the south * * * and prophesy against the forest of the south field:"—a command which is followed by a representation of the vision, composed in a style so

[1] Numb. xxiv. 12–14. The continued struggle between Balaam's covetousness and the Divine impulse which prompted his words is forcibly described by the inspired historian. At first, having sacrificed, he goes to meet Jehovah (ch. xxiii. 1–3). This he does a second time, at Balak's request: "Come, I pray thee, with me unto another place, and curse me them from thence" (ver. 13). Having again "received commandment to bless," and having said, "He hath blessed; and I cannot reverse it" (ver. 20), he is led "unto the top of Peor," a hill dedicated to the idol of Moab (Deut. iii. 29; iv. 46). Here Balaam "went not *as at other times* to seek for enchantments" (נחשים—of the nature of which nothing is known)—but, urged by an irresistible impulse, he proclaims again his blessing; and even after the indignant remonstrance of Balak (xxiv. 10), he feels himself compelled once more to bless the people of God.

[2] Le Clerc observes, on Numb. xxiv. 2—"The Spirit of God came upon him,"—"Vult Philo hoc et reliqua vota emissa esse a Balaamo invito, et contra animi sententiam loquente, sed Deum non multo aliter organa ejus movisse ac asinæ (lib. i. *De Vita Mosis*). Verum affectio animi vatis hujus verius describetur, si dicatur, phrasi Homericâ, *ἑκὼν ἀέκοντί γε θυμῷ* hæc prolocutus esse; nam voluisset quidem gratificari Balako, ut præmium ab eo auferret, sed subjecta sibi a Deo non audebat subticere, aut iis contraria proferre. *Erat plane compos sui*, nec alienatâ mente vaticinabatur, ut ex tota historia liquet." This narrative is employed by Philo to illustrate his theory of Inspiration already described, Lecture ii. pp. 64–7. He represents the angel who met Balaam on the way as indignant at his dissimulation, and commanding him to proceed; for, the angel assures him, his resistance to God's will would be of no avail: *ὀνήσεις γὰρ οὐδὲν, ἐμοῦ τε λεκτέα ὑπηχοῦντος ἄνευ τῆς σῆς διανοίας, καὶ τὰ φωνῆς ὄργανα τρέποντος, ἡνιοχήσω γὰρ ἐγὼ τὸν λόγον, θεσπίζων ἕκαστα διὰ τῆς σῆς γλώττης οὐ συνιέντος*.—*De Vita Mosis*, ii. p. 124.

abrupt, and conveyed in language so obscurely metaphorical, as to be justly regarded one of the darkest portions of even Ezekiel's writings.[1] Of this the prophet himself was thoroughly conscious. Having received the mysterious communication, he is evidently struck by its enigmatical character; and he at once proceeds to remonstrate, as it were, with the Lord on account of its obscurity: "Then said I, Ah, Lord God, they say of me, Doth he not speak parables?"

In all the cases which we have just considered, it is obvious if any confidence is to be placed in, or value ascribed to, their assertions—that the different sacred writers aver, as a simple matter of fact, that they received certain communications from without which they pointedly distinguish from the suggestions of their own minds, and the results of their own reflection.[2] The two questions, then, arise, by what means were they assured themselves,[3] and how did they convince others, that such communica-

[1] Ezek. xx. 45–49. [xxi. 1–5] "It is written throughout in a style so singularly abrupt, and in some parts so utterly enigmatical, that it may certainly be considered, as a whole, one of the darkest portions of Ezekiel's writings."—"*Ezekiel*," p. 185, by Mr. Fairbairn; who observes that Bishop Horsley ["Bibl. Crit.," vol. ii., 2nd ed. p. 97] "has here simply left a record of his inability to proceed, in the brief note, 'The difficulties of this chapter are to me insuperable.'"

[2] This fact appears most clearly in the contrast which the prophets of God draw between their own words and the predictions of the false prophets. Ezekiel represents that distinction as being threefold: "Son of man, prophesy against the prophets of Israel, and say thou unto them (1) *that prophesy out of their own hearts*, Hear ye the word of the Lord; Woe unto the foolish prophets (2) *that follow their own spirit*, and (3) *have seen nothing*."—Ezek. xiii. 2, 3. On this description of false prophecy Mr. Fairbairn well observes: "Expressed in philosophical language, the whole was *subjective* merely, without any *objective* reality. The true prophet differed in each particular from the false one: He prophesied not from his own heart, but from the heart of God; in conceiving and uttering his message, he followed not his own spirit, but the Spirit of God; and consequently the word he spake contained a true and Divine reality. * * * Hence the peculiar expression which is frequently employed of *seeing* the *word* of the Lord—(Isai. ii. 1; xiii. 1; Amos, i. 1; Mic. i. 1)." *Ezekiel*, p. 96.

[3] With respect to the absolute assurance which the prophets had of the 'objective' reality of the Divine communications, S. Thomas Aquinas argues with great acuteness. (1) He alludes to the conviction of the truth of his message which Jeremiah must have felt when he braved the death to which the Law (Deut. xviii. 20) had condemned the false prophet: "Know ye for certain," said Jeremiah, "that if ye put me to death ye shall surely bring innocent blood upon yourselves: for *of a truth* the Lord hath sent me unto you."—Jer. xxvi. 15. (2) He points out the readiness of Abraham to slay his son: "Signum propheticæ certitudinis accipere possumus ex hoc quod Abraham, *admonitus in prophetica visione*, se præparavit ad filium unigenitum immolandum: *quod nullatenus fecisset, nisi de divina revelatione fuisset certissimus*."—*Summ. Theol.* 2da 2dæ, qu. clxxi. art. 5. t. xxiii. p. 295. We may add the case of S. Paul. Can we feel any doubt as to the force of those proofs which convinced that profound intellect of the truth of the revelations which he received; and which effected a revolution in his nature that impelled him, without "conferring with flesh and blood," to come forward as the most zealous and enlightened promulgator

tions were undoubtedly Divine? As to the manner, indeed, by which the external suggestions were conveyed to the mind, we know nothing. They only who received those revelations from God could have imparted this information,—for they only had experience of the feelings which accompanied the illapse of the Divine energy: and they are silent. Or, if a casual hint be dropped with reference to this action of the Divine influence on the soul, it is simply by employing a material image to express the inward experience. Thus Jeremiah says: "The Lord put forth His hand, and touched my mouth:" and Ezekiel records how "an hand was sent unto me; and lo, a roll of a book was therein; and * * * He said unto me, Son of man, eat this roll, and go speak unto the house of Israel."[1] Respecting this want of information, the defender of Revealed Religion need feel neither concern nor surprise.[2] It is but another example of that ignorance which is the natural condition of humanity. In our intercourse with our fellow-men, we cannot tell how spirit acts upon spirit. In our every-day life, we cannot tell how matter acts upon mind.[3] Persons who are without the sense of sight cannot represent to themselves the perceptions which accompany the

of doctrines which he had hitherto mistaken, and persecuted to the death?—Gal. i. 16–23.

[1] Jer. i. 9; Ezek. ii. 9, iii. 1. Cf. Rev. x. 8–10; and *supra*, p. 196, note [2].

[2] "As our sensations carry the notions of material things to our understandings which before were unacquainted with them; so there is some analogical way whereby the knowledge of Divine Truth may also be revealed to us. For so we may call as well that historical truth of corporeal and material things, which we are informed of by our senses, *truth of revelation*, as that Divine Truth which we now speak of; and therefore we may have as certain and infallible a way of being acquainted with the one, as with the other. And God having so contrived the nature of our souls, that we may converse one with another, and inform one another of things we knew not before, would not make us so deaf to His Divine voice that breaks the rocks, and rends the mountains asunder; He would not make us so undisciplinable in Divine things as that we should not be capable of receiving any impressions from Himself of those things which we were before unacquainted with."—J. Smith (of Cambridge.) *Of Prophecy*, ch. i.

[3] "What are the facts which are the objects of intuition or consciousness, and what are those which we merely infer? But this inquiry has never been considered a portion of logic. Its place is in another and a perfectly distinct department of science, to which the name metaphysics more particularly belongs. * * * To this science appertain the great and much debated questions of the existence of matter; the existence of spirit, and of a distinction between it and matter; the reality of time and space, as things without the mind, and distinguishable from the objects which are said to exist *in* them. For in the present state of the discussion on these topics, it is universally allowed that the existence of matter or of spirit, of space or of time is, in its nature, unsusceptible of being proved; and that if anything is known of them, it must be by immediate intuition."—J. S. Mill, *A system of Logic*, vol. i. 3rd ed. p. 7.

ideas of light and color ; and yet they do not question the existence of those qualities of the material world, convinced by the evidence which the experience of others supply. Shall we, then, ungifted with the power of spiritual vision, deny the reality of that knowledge which God has conveyed by it, while moral evidence equally powerful is at our command ? Or to state the same thing more generally, and with reference to speculative difficulties respecting both the questions above proposed :—we know how the Idealist triumphs in his supposed refutation of the existence of the external world ; and yet men of ordinary understanding still listen to his arguments with wondering disdain, or regard it, at the most, as a clever exhibition of dialectical skill. We live, and act, and think, perfectly indifferent to the arguments which should convince us that the world without is a nonentity. The original reception of Christianity by the Gentile world enables us, here also, to appeal to the common sense of mankind, in reply to an analogous exhibition of mere intellectual ingenuity. Not to dwell upon Hume's notorious argument to show that no evidence can prove a miracle,[1] or upon the practical answer to it which such a fact supplies, the speculations of a writer, to whom allusion has been made more than once in these Discourses, afford an immediate illustration. Schleiermacher argues against the efficacy of miracles, and chiefly against the efficacy of Prophecy, as proofs of Christianity ;[2] and with his de-

[1] The only consistent view is that which denies the *possibility* of a revelation : "If we may be well enough assured of the author of any book, and also of his honesty, yet it was further objected that this author, whoever he was, could not be sure that he himself was not deceived in his opinion of his own inspiration, or of a revelation made to himself. * * * But, *First*, if he could not be sure of his own inspiration, or of a revelation made to himself, how then could *any man* now-a-days be *sure* of the same, if God should vouchsafe to speak to us now, as 'tis said He did in former times to the prophets and other inspired men, by Himself, or an Angel ? So that this objection, if it be well grounded, cuts off not only all reasonable belief of former revelations, but likewise all reasonable belief of any revelation that can now be made to ourselves, or others. And 'tis to no purpose to offer at anything to convince those of the truth of any revelation who are of opinion that even the infinite power and wisdom of God cannot make such a revelation of His will to them as would be credible, such as they should reasonably judge sufficient for their conviction."—*Fourteen Sermons* by Bishop O. Blackall, p. 21.

[2] Schleiermacher sets out from the following proposition: "There is no other means of obtaining a share in the Christian Community, than through Faith in Jesus as the Redeemer." By the expression, "Faith in Christ," Schleiermacher understands "The certainty accompanying a state of the higher self-consciousness ; which consequently is different from, but not therefore inferior to, that which accompanies the objective consciousness. In the same sense Faith in God is used to denote nothing else than the certainty concerning the absolute feeling of dependence as such, i. e. as conditioned (bedingt) by a Being placed without us, and expressing our

nial of the latter is closely connected his rejection of the authority of the Old Testament.[1] But the Christian Apologist will turn from the subtlety of the mere dialectician to the facts of history,

relation to Him. * * * The expression, Faith in Christ (as that of Faith in God) is the reference of the state, as effect, to Christ as cause. * * * Although in Scripture itself arguments, of which the witnesses to the Gospel have availed themselves, are frequently mentioned (Acts, vi. 9, 10; ix. 20–22; xviii. 27, 28), still, it is never maintained that Faith has arisen from the adducing of proofs, but from the announcement." Such proofs, he adds, were solely designed to point out the *applicability* of the prophecies to this Jesus as Redeemer—otherwise the Gentiles must have first become Jews in order to be brought to Christianity by *the authority* of the prophets. Here, therefore, all demonstration must be excluded:—but "Men would fain bring about the acknowledgment of Christ, by means of the Miracles which He has wrought, or the Prophecies which have announced His coming, or the peculiar nature of the evidence originally given concerning Him, that it is a work of Divine Inspiration. The fallacy here (speaking generally) is, that the efficacy of these circumstances always presupposes Faith as already existing, and therefore cannot produce it. As to Miracles, in the strict sense of the word (i. e. excluding Prophecy, Inspiration, &c.), if we confine ourselves to those which Jesus Himself has wrought, or even take in those wrought with reference to Him—these can by no means effect such an acknowledgment. * * * For Scripture itself attests, partly that Faith has been produced without Miracles, partly, that Miracles have not produced it; from which it can be concluded that where Faith has been produced even in connexion with Miracles, it has not been produced *by* them, but in that *original* manner." As to Prophecy, we can easily conceive that a *Jew* might admit its reference to Jesus, and, nevertheless, that he neither had true Faith, nor was a member of the Church, —because he did not yet feel the need of Redemption. And were a *Gentile* even to be convinced that the Prophecies were connected with each other; and that all of them have in view one and the same subject; and, further, that they have been all strictly fulfilled in Christ,—still it must be assumed that Jesus is the Redeemer, because the Redeemer has been predicted by such intimations as the Gentile finds applicable to Jesus. Nay, more—we cannot see how a Gentile could have confidence in the men who uttered the Prophecies, unless we further assume that their inspiration has been proved to him. But further:—since it can never be proved that the prophets have foreseen Christ as He has actually existed, and still less the Kingdom of the Messiah, as it has been actually developed in Christianity, "it must be conceded that a proof of Christ as the Redeemer is impossible by means of Prophecy. * * * We must therefore clearly distinguish between the apologetic use of the Prophecies made by the Apostles in their relation to the Jews, and a general use of them as means of proof."—*Der Christl. Glaube*, B. i. s. 87 ff. (Cf. also Lecture iii. p. 100, note [3].) Schleiermacher next proceeds to the question of Inspiration, for his remarks on which see *supra*, Lecture i. p. 35.

[1] Quinet says of Schleiermacher, that no man has made greater efforts to reconcile ancient faith with modern science. The concessions into which he has been drawn are incredible:—"Comme un homme battu par un violent orage, il a sacrifié les mâts et la voilure pour sauver le corps du vaisseau." At first he gives up the Old Testament; "c'est ce qu'il appelait rompre avec l'ancienne alliance." At a later period, having made an Old Testament without prophecies, he makes a Gospel without miracles: "Encore arrivait-il à ce débris de révélation, non plus par les Écritures, mais par une espèce de ravissement de conscience, ou plutôt par un miracle de la parole intérieure."—*Revue des deux Mondes*, 1838, t. iv. p. 473. In a series of papers published in the "Studien und Kritiken," for 1829, entitled, "Ueber seine Glaubenslehre an Dr. Lücke," Schleiermacher avers that he neither can nor will maintain against external investigation a dominant ecclesiastical doctrine, which, to all who are without, appears an unsubstantial spectre; but that he will avail himself of history as it develops itself, and then will resign much which many are still disposed to consider inseparably connected with the essence of Christianity. "I will not speak," he observes, "of the Six Days' Work; but the very *idea* of Creation, as it is usually con

in whose pages he will read that no evidence has appeared more overpowering to the mind of enlightened Heathenism, than the fulfilment of the predictions of ancient times in the Person of Jesus of Nazareth.[1]

strued—even abstracting from all return to the Mosaic Chronology—how long will it be able still to maintain itself against the power of a cultivated view of the world resulting from scientific combinations which no one can escape?" How long, he asks, will the New Testament miracles,—he will not waste time upon those of the Old,—maintain their place against far weightier objections than those advanced by the French Encyclopedists? "Either the whole history to which they belong must be regarded as a fable, from which what is historical in its foundation can no longer be extricated,—and then Christianity appears no longer to proceed from the Being of God, but from *nothing:* or if they be really regarded as matters of fact, we must grant that so far as they have been produced *in* nature, analogies to them must be also found in nature—and thus the old idea of a miracle must be given up."—(s. 489.) On these remarks Quinet observes: "Je ne crois pas que l'on ait jamais considéré l'abîme avec un plus tranquille désespoir."

[1] In every age of the world the prescience of future contingents has appeared to human reason the most incomprehensible of the attributes ascribed to Deity. Cicero, ridiculing the pretensions of the heathen oracles (he describes the oracles of Apollo as being "partim falsa, partim casu vera, partim flexiloqua et obscura, ut interpres egeat interprete," c. 56), represents the philosophy of his age when he denied the existence of any such power: "Nihil est tam contrarium rationi et constantiæ quam fortuna: ut mihi ne in Deum quidem cadere videatur, ut sciat, quid casu et fortuito futurum sit. Si enim scit, certe illud eveniet: sin certe eveniet, nulla fortuna est. Est autem fortuna. Rerum igitur fortuitarum nulla est præsensio."—*De Divinat.* lib. ii. c. 7. From this we can at once see how forcibly, in those days, the plain fulfilment of an ancient prediction must have told upon an honest mind. Hence the object of the early Apologists, when they insist so repeatedly on the antiquity of the prophetic writings (Cf. S. Justin M. Apol. i. § 31. p. 62; Tatian, Adv. Græcos. § xxxi; p. 268; Clemens Alex. (who quotes Tatian) Strom. I. xxi p. 378, &c.); while they further tell us that the proof of the fulfilment of Prophecy was the chief agent in their own conversion. Such was the statement of S. Justin M. to Trypho. The aged Christian who had instructed him, brought before him the words of the prophets, men—*Θείῳ Πνεύματι λαλήσαντες, καὶ τὰ μέλλοντα θεσπίσαντες, ἃ δὴ νῦν γίνεται.*—§ vii. p. 109. Theophilus of Antioch similarly describes the arguments by which he had been convinced: *Μὴ οὖν ἀπίστει, ἀλλὰ πίστευε· καὶ γὰρ ἐγὼ ἠπίστουν τοῦτο ἔσεσθαι* [*scil. ἀνάστασιν*], *ἀλλὰ νῦν κατανοήσας αὐτὰ πιστεύω, ἅμα καὶ ἐπιτυχὼν ἱεραῖς γραφαῖς τῶν ἁγίων προφητῶν, οἱ καὶ προεῖπον διὰ Πνεύματος Θεοῦ τὰ προγεγονότα ᾧ τρόπῳ γέγονε, καὶ τὰ ἐνεστῶτα τίνι τρόπῳ γίνεται, καὶ τὰ ἐπερχόμενα ποίᾳ τάξει ἀπαρτισθήσεται. ἀπόδειξιν οὖν λαβὼν τῶν γινομένων καὶ προαναπεφωνημένων, οὐκ ἀπιστῶ· ἀλλὰ πιστεύω πειθαρχῶν Θεῷ.*—*Ad Autolyc.* lib. i. § 14. p. 346. The manner in which Tatian states this same fact is peculiarly forcible: *περινοοῦντι δέ μοι τὰ σπουδαῖα, συνέβη γραφαῖς τισὶν ἐντυχεῖν βαρβαρικαῖς, πρεσβυτέραις μὲν, ὡς πρὸς τὰ Ἑλλήνων δόγματα, θειοτέραις δὲ ὡς πρὸς τὴν ἐκείνων πλάνην. καί μοι πεισθῆναι ταύταις συνέβη διά τε τῶν λέξεων τὸ ἄτυφον, καὶ τῶν εἰπόντων τὸ ἀνεπιτήδευτον, καὶ τῆς τοῦ παντὸς ποιήσεως τὸ εὐκατάληπτον, καὶ τ ῶ ν μ ε λ λ ό ν τ ω ν τ ὸ π ρ ο γ ν ω σ τ ι κ ό ν.*—*Adv Græcos*, § 29. p. 267. Paley ("Evidences," part iii. ch. 5) gives another reason why the argument from Prophecy was so much dwelt upon. He quotes S. Irenæus, Tertullian, Origen, Lactantius, who agree in stating that the miracles of Christ were ascribed by the heathen to magic; observing that while these Apologists insist upon the force of the proof of Christianity from Miracles, they were compelled, in consequence of this objection, to rely rather upon the evidence of Prophecy. Strange to say, Paley is inclined to condemn "the judgment of the defenders" of Christianity for taking this course. I may remark that Arnobius (A. D. 298) forms an exception to this exclusive reliance upon the evidence of Prophecy: he lays much stress on Miracles in his work "Adv. Gentes," observing: "Nulla major est comprobatio quam gestarum ab Eo [Christo] fides

This last allusion at once brings before us those proofs by which God's servants, however silent as to their own inward feelings, have convinced the world of their Divine Commission. There must, clearly, be external, sensible proof given that any human being has been selected as a messenger of God. Without such proof we should have no evidence of the fact beyond the assertion of the individual himself who claims our belief.[1] Revelation, therefore, has always been accompanied by certain indications which evince that its source must be attributed to other faculties, and a higher power, than could have naturally characterized the agent by whom it has been conveyed.

Two proofs, only, of this sensible nature are conceivable—Prophecy and Miracles. Prophecy, from its embracing at once events of which living men might judge,[2] and the history of the far distant future, performs the function of a witness to every age. Miracles, by virtue of the Creative and Revealing Presence, apparent in them, offer to all conscientious minds the clearest of proofs. The language of unprejudiced reason must ever be—"We know that thou art a teacher come from God: for no man can do these miracles that thou doest except God be with him."[3]

rerum, quam virtutum novitas," &c.—Lib. i. c. 42, ap. Routh, "Script. Eccl. Opusc." t. ii. p. 277.

[1] Scripture itself acknowledges the justice of this principle: "Long time therefore abode they speaking boldly in the Lord, *Which gave testimony* (τῷ μαρτυροῦντι) *unto the word of His grace*, and granted *signs and wonders* (σημεῖα καὶ τέρατα) to be done by their hands."—Acts, xiv. 3. So also of Prophecy: "When the word of the prophet shall come to pass, then *shall the prophet be known* that the Lord hath truly sent him."—Jer. xxviii. 9. And thus Jeroboam acknowledges the Divine mission of Ahijah: "Behold there is Ahijah the prophet, *which told me that I* should be king over this people."—1 Kings, xiv. 2.

[2] Thus the prediction of "the man of God" that the altar at Bethel should be rent (1 Kings, xiii. 3; cf. ver. 5), was addressed to the generation then living; the announcement of the reign of Josiah (ver. 2) was addressed to generations yet to come. To the same effect were the prediction of the death of Jeroboam's child (1 Kings, xiv. 12; cf. ver. 17), and the announcement of the future destruction of his race (ver. 10). Cf. too, Jer. xxviii. 16, 17. In this sense Origen argued that before the coming of the Messiah the inspiration of the Old Testament could not have been clearly proved; but now the appearance of Christ has dispelled all doubts: *ἐναργῆ παραδείγματα περὶ τοῦ θεοπνεύστους εἶναι τὰς παλαιὰς γραφὰς πρὸ τῆς ἐπιδημίας τοῦ Χρίστου παραστῆσαι οὐ πάνυ δυνατὸν ἦν· ἀλλ' ἡ Ἰησοῦ ἐπιδημία, δυναμένους ὑποπτεύεσθαι τὸν νόμον καὶ τοὺς προφήτας ὡς οὐ Θεῖα, εἰς τοὐμφανὲς ἤγαγεν, ὡς οὐρανίῳ χάριτι ἀναγεγραμμένα.—De Princip.* lib. iv. t. i. p. 161.

[3] S. John, iii. 2: cf. 1 Kings, xvii. 22–24: "And the Lord heard the voice of Elijah, and the soul of the child came unto him, and he revived. * * * And the woman said to Elijah, *Now by this I know* that thou art a man of God, and that the word of the Lord in thy mouth is truth." Bishop Hinds ingeniously observes: "In the case of a person claiming to be commissioned with a message from God, the only proof which ought to be admitted is miraculous attestation of some sort. * * * The miracle, in these cases, is, in fact, a *specimen* of that violation of the ordinary

Miracles both accredit those who work with them, as organs of God; and seal as truth what such organs utter. This demonstrative power abides even in the record of the miracles, the truth of that record being assumed.[1] That our minds can imagine no other species of proof is shown by this circumstance, that these are invariably offered to us as tests, wherever claims, well or ill-founded, are made to Divine Inspiration. S. Paul considers such tokens to be as indispensable a requisite of an Apostle as they had been of the Old Testament prophets. "Truly," he argues, "the signs of an Apostle were wrought among you in all patience, in signs, and wonders, and mighty deeds."[2] And so far is the claim of false prophets to the possession of such gifts from being any objection to their force as proofs, that it rather exhibits more clearly their validity. They are the only proofs given, because they are the only proofs admissible.[3] It is true, that in the case of the authors of Scripture, there are many instances, in which, to our knowledge at least, such sensible proofs were not given. But that proofs were at all times given of a sufficiently overpowering kind to silence every reasonable doubt, and to remove every natural scruple, we have abundant reason to conclude.[4] Should any difficulty arise (on the part either of the

course of nature, which the person inspired is asserting to have taken place in his appointment and ministry; and corresponds to the exhibition of *specimens* and *experiments*, which we should require of a geologist, mineralogist, or chemist, if he asserted his discovery of any natural phenomena—especially of any at variance with received theories."—*Inspiration*, p. 9.

[1] "*Single* miracles are often said to have convinced eye-witnesses on the first publication of the Gospel.—John. vi. 14. 'Then those men, when they had seen *the miracle* which Jesus did, said, This is of a truth that Prophet which should come into the world.'—So ch. ii. 11. The same Evangelist puts the miracles *collectively* for the written evidence to the *future faith* of the world: 'Many other signs truly did Jesus in the presence of His disciples which are not written in this book; but *these are written*, that ye might believe that Jesus is the Christ, the Son of God.'—xx. 30, 31."—Davison, *On Prophecy*, p. 406.

[2] 2 Cor. xii. 12.

[3] See M. Athanase Coquerel, "Christianity," p. 219.

[4] Take, e. g. the important event of the separation of Israel and Judah. Ahijah the Shilonite announced to Jeroboam, "Thus saith the Lord, Behold I will rend the kingdom out of the hand of Solomon, and will give Ten Tribes to thee."—1 Kings, xi. 31. That this prediction became notorious, and obtained general belief, we learn from the statement: "Solomon sought therefore to kill Jeroboam. And Jeroboam arose and fled into Egypt."—ver. 40. After Rehoboam's accession to the throne, "Israel rebelled against the house of David;" and Rehoboam "assembled all the house of Judah, with the Tribe of Benjamin, an hundred and fourscore thousand chosen men which were warriors, to fight against the house of Israel, to bring the kingdom again to Rehoboam." "But the word of the Lord came to Shemaiah the man of God, saying, Thus saith the Lord, Ye shall not go up, nor fight against your brethren: return every man to his house; for this thing is done of Me. And they

agent himself when receiving his powers from God, or of those to whom his commission was addressed), as to whether the announcement were really Divine, we are often informed of the means by which such difficulty was dispelled. To this effect were the signs given to Moses, to Gideon, to Hezekiah.[1] On the other hand, when the sacred writers do not refer to Divine Revelation, or to the means by which it was imparted, we observe how carefully they indicate their clear appreciation of the fact, that *ordinary* dreams or visions are altogether valueless. The Psalmist, for example, writes: "As a dream when one awaketh; so, O Lord, when Thou awakest, Thou shalt despise their image:"[2] while in the case of visions a broad line of distinction is drawn between the real communications which God thus conveyed to the mind, and the hallucinations of false prophecy, the worthlessness of which is pointed out by Ezekiel: "Thus saith the Lord God, Woe unto the foolish prophets that follow *their own* spirit, and *have seen* nothing."[3]

Intimations no less clear are also conveyed to us, from time to time, by the sacred writers, that the Divine Author of Scripture exercised a constant supervision over their acts and words. Such intimations relate either to those cases in which the human agent, trusting to his previous participation in the Divine influence, and relying upon his own judgment, presumes to decide

obeyed the words of the Lord, and returned from going against Jeroboam."—1 Kings, xii. 21; 2 Chron. xi. 4. Speaking of these two predictions Mr. Davison observes: "The agency of man had been prophetically foreshown in the one instance; it was authoritatively suspended in the other. A ferocious and self-willed king, who would take no counsel before the revolt, acquiesced, and all Judah with him, in the dictate of a prophet, after it. Why did he and his people so act except upon a conviction, which they could not resist, of that prophet's authority? * * * I infer that they had reason to know Whose word it was which they obeyed."—*On Prophecy*, p. 236.

[1] Exod. iv. 1–9; Judges, vi. 36–40; 2 Kings, xx. 8–11. Of this nature was the confirmation which S. Peter received as to the source and reality of his trance: "While Peter thought on the vision, the Spirit said unto him, Behold three men seek thee," &c.—Acts, x. 19: cf. xii. 7–11. A striking example is afforded by an incident recorded of Jeremiah. He had predicted, at God's command, the subjection of his country by the Chaldeans. Immediately afterwards he is directed to act in a manner which seems to have excited not unreasonable doubts in his mind. The existence of such doubts he clearly intimates, and he relates, with the most perfect simplicity, the means by which they were dispelled: "And Jeremiah said, The word of the Lord came unto me, saying, Behold, Hanameel the son of Shallum, thine uncle shall come unto thee, saying, Buy thee my field that is in Anathoth, for the right of redemption is thine to buy it. So Hanameel, mine uncle's son, came to me in the court of the prison, according to the word of the Lord, and said unto me, Buy my field, I pray thee, &c. * * * *Then I knew that this was the word of the Lord. And I bought the field*, &c."—Jer. xxxii. 6–9. Cf. Zech. xi. 11.

[2] Ps. lxxiii. 20. Cf. Eccl. v. 7. [3] Ezek. xiii. 3. Cf. *supra*, p. 207, note [2].

without the immediate suggestion of the Holy Spirit; or to those in which a line of action that we should otherwise have looked upon as purely natural, or as dictated by the circumstances of the time, is referred to the direct intervention of God. In such instances the veil is, as it were, withdrawn; and we are permitted to see how the Spirit of God acts upon, and guides the spirit of man. For example, in the Old Testament, when Samuel, in pursuance of the Divine command, was about to select the future king from among the sons of Jesse, following his own judgment, his choice was about to fall upon Eliab. But "the Lord said unto him," "I have refused him." When, at length, David is introduced, "the Lord said, Arise, anoint him, for this is he."[1] Again, we read that David, when the Lord had given him peace from his enemies, called for Nathan the prophet, and said, "Lo, I dwell in an house of cedars, but the Ark of the covenant of the Lord remaineth under curtains. Then Nathan said unto David, Do all that is thine heart; for God is with thee." In this, his natural approval of the pious design of the king, Nathan acted on his own human judgment, and erred; for "it came to pass the same night, that the word of God came to Nathan, saying, Go and tell David my servant, Thus saith the Lord, Thou shalt *not* build me an house to dwell in."[2] Similar instances, in which the human judgment of men, who acted as agents of the Divine commands, was thus controlled, are recorded in the New Testament. We read how S. Paul had laid out for himself a practical field of labor.[3] He would have preached in Galatia, but "was forbidden of the Holy Ghost." He "assayed

[1] 1 Sam. xvi. 6–12.

[2] 2 Sam. vii. 1 Chron. xvii. On this case S. Gregory the Great observes: "Aliquando prophetæ sancti dum consuluntur, ex magno usu prophetandi quædam ex suo spiritu proferunt, et se hæc ex prophetiæ Spiritu dicere suspicantur. Sed quia sancti sunt, per Sanctum Spiritum citius correcti, et ab Eo quæ vera sunt audiunt, et semetipsos, quia falsa dixerint, reprehendunt."—*In Ezekiel*, lib. i. Hom. i. t. i. p. 1180.

[3] Acts, xvi. 6–10. "The manner in which Luke describes this hindrance is well calculated to bring to view the operation of the higher Πνεῦμα in the souls of the Apostles. The ψυχή of him, who had received the Holy Ghost, was in no way so identified with the Spirit as to take away a full consciousness of the distinction which existed; he could, on the contrary, very clearly distinguish the impulses of his own soul from the suggestion of the Spirit. The former often prompted (if not to what was sinful) to what was erroneous or unsuitable [see *infra*, p. 222, &c.]; the latter in such cases checked the soul in its activity, and guided it to what was right * * * In this passage ἐπείραζον describes the natural impulse of the ψυχή; οὐκ εἴασεν αὐτούς the restraining agency of the far-seeing Spirit."—Olshausen, *Comment in loc.* B. ii. s. 829.

to go into Bithynia, but the Spirit suffered him not." And when he paused, doubting where God's will would lead him, "a vision appeared to Paul in the night: There stood a man of Macedonia, and prayed him, saying, Come over into Macedonia, and help us. And after he had seen the vision," continues the sacred historian, "immediately we endeavored to go into Macedonia, assuredly gathering that the Lord had called us for to preach the Gospel unto them." The history of S. Paul affords another instance of the constancy of this Divine supervision;—an instance which, taken in connexion with those already adduced, warrants our concluding, as a just and natural inference, that, in other cases also where such information may not be expressly given, the servants of God were in like manner specially guided and directed by Him. In the account of the controversy respecting circumcision we are told that the Church of Antioch "determined that Paul and Barnabas, and certain other of them, should go up to Jerusalem unto the Apostles and elders about this question."[1] Here everything appears natural, and what might have been expected. There was a division in a certain branch of the Church upon an important question; and it was resolved to refer the matter to the Apostles. Had this entire discussion been conducted by mere human wisdom, this was precisely the course which we should have anticipated. Without some express intimation, therefore, from Scripture itself, we could not, perhaps, have safely ventured to maintain, that each step in this matter was regulated by the *immediate* guidance of the Holy Spirit. But of this *fact* we have special information. S. Paul himself tells us, that his journey to Jerusalem was not the mere result of his or the Church's human judgment. He writes expressly, that he "went up" to Jerusalem "*by Revelation*."[2]

But another topic of the utmost moment must be referred to before we close this branch of our inquiry. In order to preserve the due subordination of the human to the Divine element of the Bible, it is altogether essential that we should bear in mind the distinction between that extraordinary influence under which the

[1] Acts, xv. 2.

[2] Gal. ii. 2. Ἀνέβην δὲ κατὰ ἀποκάλυψιν. Cf. S. Luke, ii 26, 27, where Simeon's presence in the Temple, which from his character (ver. 25) might have appeared a purely natural circumstance, is ascribed to the special guidance of the Holy Ghost "He came by the Spirit (ἐν Πνεύματι) into the Temple."

sacred writers have composed their respective works, and that ordinary actuation by the Holy Spirit, to which in like manner the term *Inspiration*[1] has been assigned. From neglecting or refusing to discriminate between these two aspects of the Divine agency, a greater number, perhaps, of erroneous views with respect to our present subject have taken their rise, than from any other source. In illustration of the importance of attending to the distinction which exists between the two classes of spiritual gifts, I would adduce an observation of a well-known writer, whose statements have been considerably embarrassed by his having continued to regard as identical these *specifically* different phases of the operations of the Holy Ghost. Dr. Arnold, when enumerating certain inferences relating to Inspiration which he considers "unwarranted,"[2] goes on to say: "It is no less an unwarranted interpretation of the term 'Inspiration' to suppose that it is equivalent to a communication of the Divine perfections. Surely, many of our words and many of our actions are spoken and done by the inspiration of God's Spirit, without Whom we can do nothing acceptable to God. Yet does the Holy Spirit so inspire us as to communicate to us His own perfections? Are our best words or works utterly free from error or from sin? All inspiration does not, then, destroy the human and fallible part in the nature which it inspires; it does not change man into God."[3] The result, which legitimately follows from this confusion of the two significations conveyed by the

[1] My object here is to prove that these two significations of the word 'Inspiration' are *specifically* distinct; denoting operations of the same Divine Spirit which differ in *kind*, as well as in *degree*. On the other hand, their *identity in kind* is continually laid down as a great *principle* in treatises on this subject. Thus, in an essay often quoted, entitled "De revelatione Religionis externa, eademque publica," by C. L. Nitzsch (Lipsiæ, 1808), one of the theses maintained is—"Quod inspiratio Apostolorum *ejusdem plane generis* fuit cum revelatione interna, quæ *reliquis omnibus veri nominis Christianis contigisse dicitur*:" where, for "generis," "speciei" should, strictly speaking, be substituted; as appears from the further remark: "Minime negamus *gradu* diversam, sive modo et mensura potiorem fuisse Apostolorum inspirationem."—p. 67. See *infra*, p. 226, note [3].

[2] "If a single error can be discovered [in Scripture], it is supposed to be fatal to the credibility of the whole. This has arisen from an unwarranted interpretation of the word 'Inspiration,' and by a still more unwarranted inference. An inspired work is supposed to mean a work to which God has communicated His own perfections; so that the slightest error or defect of any kind in it is inconceivable, and that which is other than perfect in all points cannot be inspired. This is the unwarranted interpretation of the word 'Inspiration.' "—*Sermons on the Christian Life*, ed. 1841, p. 486.

[3] Sermons on the Christian Life, p. 487.

word 'Inspiration,' is exemplified by Dr. Arnold himself when speaking of the pre-eminent inspiration of S. Paul. He observes —"Yet this great Apostle expected that the world would come to an end in the generation then existing. * * * Shall we then say that S. Paul entertained and expressed a belief which the event did not verify? We may say so, safely and reverently, in this instance."[1]

Another aspect—attended with consequences if possible more important—under which this same misconception presents itself, is that of regarding the degree of authority due to the several parts of Scripture as depending upon the personal qualities of their respective authors, or the opportunities of acquiring information which they possessed. One modern theory of Inspiration, for example, makes the possession of religious Truth by the Apostles to depend on the measure of their sinlessness; while another estimates the Divine character of Scripture by the relation in which its authors stood to Christ. From this latter view it results, we are further told, that a distinction is to be drawn between the different parts of the New Testament; and that higher authority must be ascribed to the writings of the Apostles, than to those portions of it which have been composed by their disciples and assistants:—hence it follows that the Gospels of S.

[1] *Ibid.* p. 488. See Lecture iv. p. 180, note. A still greater degree of confusion is to be traced in the language of Mr. Coleridge. "The main error," according to him, of the principle maintained by the assertors of "Bibliolatry"—"consists in the confounding of two distinct conceptions, revelation by the Eternal Word, and actuation of the Holy Spirit. The former, indeed, is not always or necessarily united with the latter,—the prophecy of Balaam is an instance of the contrary—but yet being ordinarily, and only not always, so united, the term, Inspiration, has acquired a double sense. First, the term is used in the sense of Information miraculously communicated by voice or vision [here Mr. Coleridge confounds Revelation and Inspiration]; and secondly, where, without any sensible addition or infusion, the writer or speaker uses and applies his existing gifts of power and knowledge under the predisposing, aiding, and directing actuation of God's Holy Spirit. Now, between the first sense, that is, *inspired revelation*, and the highest degree of that grace and communion with the Spirit which the Church under all circumstances, and every regenerate member of the Church of Christ, is permitted to hope, and instructed to pray for—there is a positive difference of kind,—a chasm, the pretended overleaping of which constitutes imposture, or betrays insanity. Of the first kind *are the Law and the Prophets.* * * * But with regard to the second, neither the holy writers—the so-called Hagiographi [i. e. Job, David, Solomon, Jeremiah in the Lamentations, Daniel, &c.]—themselves, nor any fair interpretations of Scripture, assert *any such absolute diversity*, or enjoin the belief of *any greater difference of degree*, than the experience of the Christian World grounded on, and growing with the comparison of these Scriptures with other works holden in honor by the Churches, has established."—*Confessions of an Inquiring Spirit*, Letter vii. p. 94.

Mark and S. Luke possess less authority than those of S. Matthew or S. John.[1]

With reference to the principle on which such theories are founded, there is, it is true, a certain sense in which we may

[1] The writer who first suggested this view in modern times was, I believe, Dr. George Benson, in an "Essay concerning Inspiration," to be found in Bishop Watson's collection of Theological Tracts (vol iv. p. 469), and which was received with much applause in Gemany. Cf. Töllner, "Die göttliche Eingebung," s. 69, *u.* s. 127. Dr. Benson considers the degree of Inspiration possessed by the Apostles to have been the highest under the New Testament: it may be called *Gradus Apostolicus*, as the Jews called that which Moses had under the Old Testament *Gradus Mosaicus*. (See *supra*, Lecture ii. p. 61) Hence he infers that the Gospels of S. Mark and S. Luke are inferior in authority to the writings of the Apostles. Schleiermacher and his school have derived the same result from their peculiar principles. Schleiermacher, in his "Critical Essay on the Gospel of S. Luke," objecting to the notion that "the agency of the Holy Spirit in the composition of the Scriptures is of a specific kind, distinct from its working in the universal Church, and from its general agency in the disciples of Christ," draws the following distinction: "There is first the agency of the Divine Spirit in *those who were witnesses of the events, and heard* and reported the speeches of Christ. * * * In the second place, there is the agency of the Spirit in the persons who collected and digested. * * * Now, if the compiler of our Gospel [S. Luke's] was one of whom it may seem doubtful whether, as he does not belong to the number of the Twelve, an extraordinary influence of the Spirit can, with propriety, be attributed to him, it is, at all events, safer that he should appear as the compiler and arranger only, *not as the author*, and that we should have to look for the first and largest portion of the extraordinary agency, *not in him*, but only in those who stood in immediate connexion with the Redeemer."—*Preface*, (Thirlwall's transl., p. iv.) Tholuck describes some other modifications of this view. "If a less degree of authority belong to the writings of the Apostles' disciples than to those of the Apostles themselves, the question arises, what degree of difference exists between the illumination of both? and consequently between their normative authority? * * * A fundamental inquiry concerning this topic must proceed from the determination of the manner in which the consciousness of truth *has existed in Christ Himself.* The dogmatic system (die Dogmatik) of Schleiermacher has placed this question, in a peculiar manner, in connexion with the doctrine of the sinlessness of Christ. * * * Proceeding from Schleiermacher's stand-point, Elwert makes the possession of religious truth in the Apostles, too, to depend on the measure of their sinlessness; while Twesten (in whom the views of Schleiermacher retire before the interest of supernaturalism), proves the Inspiration of the Apostles to be free from error, in consequence of its destination for the Church."—*Comm. zum Br. an die Hebr.*, Einleit. kap. vi. s. 87. The natural remark suggests itself, that if Inspiration, in its only true sense, be confined to the Apostles, why do we not receive many other writings, in addition to those of S. Luke, or S. Mark, or the Epistle of S. James, &c., as in like manner canonical? (Cf. Lecture ii. p. 56, note [2].) Twesten notices this point as follows: "If all Christians have the Holy Ghost (as Scripture teaches), can then every religious statement of a Christian be called inspired? But we make a distinction between Apostolic writings and others,—between Inspiration and Christian illumination; although this, too, must be looked upon *rather as gradual than specific.* For of a specific contrast between the Apostles and other Christians, Scripture says nothing, but only of the distinction between them and the world (John, xiv. 17): so that we shall not go astray if we suppose Inspiration to be something analogous to illumination.—*Vorlesungen*, i. s. 407. Although, he continues, the disciples of the Apostles "stand a degree lower than the Apostles, still we must place them higher, speaking generally, than other enlightened Christians" (e. g. "Clemens, Ignatius, Polycarp, who had seen, no doubt, individuals of the Apostles, but had scarcely associated long with them.")—*Ibid.* p. 412. "The nearer or more remote connexion with Christ, as the centre of our Faith, presents a measure according to which we can distinguish what is to be deemed more or less

say that an *analogy* subsists between the manner in which the Holy Spirit has actuated the sacred writers, and His influence on believers in general: for in neither case are certain attributes, with which man has been gifted, suppressed, or obliterated. Thus, in the case of each inspired penman, as I have repeatedly argued, that type of thought, and those personal characteristics which he inherited from nature, are still retained, and may be traced in every page of his writings. Even when acting *officially* as organs of the Holy Spirit, the agents chosen exhibit styles quite dissimilar,—they pursue different paths of teaching,—they grasp the Truth from different sides: such individual peculiarities being, in fact, the means which God has employed for the purpose of exhibiting and developing the different phases of Divine Truth. Again, in their ordinary life, and when not acting *officially*, there does not appear to have been any distinction (at least *in kind*) between the Divine guidance which the authors of Scripture enjoyed, and that in which all Christians share. We see S. Peter, for example, still ardent and impetuous, still sensitive to the breath of human disapproval; we see S. John still exhibiting the same union of deep love and burning zeal. Here therefore, a certain analogy exists; but here, also, all analogy ceases.[1] When acting directly under the impulse of the Holy Spirit as *official* ministers of the Kingdom of God, we cannot admit that either imperfection in conduct, or fallibility

essential for Christian consciousness, and, therefore, more *mediately*, or *immediately*, under the influence of the Holy Ghost." Hence, argues Twesten, is to be derived the distinction between the *Old and New Testaments*, and also between the writings of the Apostles and *their* disciples,—"between that which has been spoken or written in the name of Christ, in the consciousness of the call received from Him,—and what has been produced, to a certain degree, in the writer's own name, and occasioned by more personal relations and objects."—*Ibid.* s. 421.

It is interesting to observe (as illustrating the fact that Christianity has had to encounter, from the very first, the same difficulties which modern criticism prides itself on having originated), that this objection against the authority of the Gospels of S. Luke and S. Mark was urged by the earliest of heretics—the Marcionites: M. *Μάρκον καὶ Λουκᾶν οὐδὲ ἔσχε μαθητὰς ὁ Χριστός· ἐντεῦθεν ἐλέγχεσθε φάλσα ποιοῦντες. διὰ τί γὰρ οἱ μαθηταὶ, ὧν γέγραπται τὰ ὀνόματα ἐν τῷ Εὐαγγελίῳ, οὐκ ἔγραψαν, ἀλλ' οἱ μὴ ὄντες μαθηταί.—Dial. de recta in Deum fide*, Sect. i. ap. Origenis Opp. t. i. p. 806.) The voice of the Church, in opposition to all such views, may be expressed in the words of S. Augustine: "Divina Providentia procuratum est per Spiritum Sanctum, ut quibusdam etiam ex illis qui primos Apostolos sequebantur, non solum annuntiandi, verum etiam scribendi Evangelium tribueretur auctoritas. Hi sunt Marcus et Lucas."—*De Consens. Evang.*, lib. i. 1. t. iii. pars ii. p. 3.

[1] I have here adopted some remarks of Mr. Alford in the Prolegomena to his edition of the Greek Testament (vol. i. ch. i. sect. vi). I cannot, however, accept many of the observations with which they are accompanied.

in teaching, has adhered to the authors of Scripture. It is true, that to Christ alone was "the Spirit given without measure;" to the sacred writers His influence was communicated but partially:—it was only in their character of official teachers[1] that the Lord promised His Disciples that perfection which the immediate guidance of the Holy Ghost implies. Nor do they themselves ever base their claim to Inspiration upon the degree of sinlessness which they possessed.[2] S. Paul, who, when he speaks as a teacher to the Thessalonians, thanks God "that they received the word of God which they heard of him, not as the word of men, but as it is in truth, the word of God,"[3] speaks to the Philippians of his *personal* attainments with great humility. "He had not already attained, nor was he already perfect."[4] Nay, his remark in this latter epistle as to those who preach Christ of envy and strife—"that whether in pretence or in truth, Christ is preached, and I therein do rejoice; yea, and will rejoice,"[5]—of itself proves that certain truths can come home with convincing and life-imparting power to the souls of men, independently of the personal excellence of him who communicates them.

Hence it was that S. Peter, who, in his vocation as a witness

[1] We are clearly told that, in the discharge of such duties, the influence of the Spirit was felt in a peculiar manner. E. g. when brought before the Jewish Council "Peter *filled with the Holy Ghost* (πλησθεὶς Πνεύματος Ἁγίου), said unto them," &c.—Acts, iv. 8; cf. ver. 31. Again: when rebuking Elymas, S. Paul, "*filled with the Holy Ghost*, set his eyes on him, and said," &c.—xiii. 9; and thus he exhorts the Ephesians to pray for him "that utterance *may be given unto him*."—Eph. vi. 19. "One may find a difficulty in the fact that Paul had certainly received, once for all, the Holy Ghost, and with it also the full power of utterance, so that he needed for this no request of the Church. But the agency of the Holy Ghost in the Apostles is not to be conceived as a permanently operating power, but as a power which revealed itself, at different times, in different degrees and forms of activity."—Olshausen, *Comment. in loc.* B. iv. s. 300. Cf. Acts, xvi. 6, and *supra*, p. 215, note [3]. So, too, in the case of the Apostles' power of working miracles, the manifestation of their supernatural gifts was not left to their own discretion. S. Paul could strike Elymas blind, because, as we have just seen, he was so directed by the Spirit; but he could not miraculously restore to health Epaphroditus, his "brother and companion in labor" (Phil. ii. 25-27): he had the spirit of prophecy as to Antichrist (2 Thess. ii. 3), and he was enabled to predict the safety and fate of his fellow-travellers (Acts, xxvii. 24-26); but he could not foresee what was to befall himself, when about to encounter persecution, or when suffering imprisonment (Acts, xx. 22, 23; Phil. i. 1–25; ii. 17). But see *infra*, Lecture vi.

[2] On this whole question see the very remarkable treatise of Dr. J. C. F. Steudel, entitled "Ueber Inspiration der Apostel," published in the second and third parts of the "Tübinger Zeitschrift für Theologie," for the year 1832; and directed principally against the theory of Elwert already referred to, p. 219, note.

[3] 1 Thess. ii. 13.

[4] Phil. iii. 12, 13.

[5] Phil. i. 15, 18. Cf. Steudel, *loc. cit.* H. iii. s. 18.

[6] "When Peter was come to Antioch, I withstood him to the face, because he was to be blamed. For before that certain came from James (observe τινὲς ἀπὸ Ἰακ.

to Christ, was furnished by successive revelations with unclouded knowledge respecting the relation of Jews and Gentiles, in his vocation as a Christian man could become untrue to his own knowledge and testimony. In that testimony is to be found the condemnation of his *acts ;* although his acts could not overthrow his testimony.[1] Indeed S. Paul, in his whole address on this subject, appeals to the previous conduct of his brother Apostle in opposition to that Apostle's present conduct: "If I build again the things which I destroyed, I make myself a transgressor."[2] It is strange, no doubt, how the Judaizing Christians were able to exercise so great an influence over S. Peter and S. Barnabas : but the fact that the proceedings of all parties are expressly ascribed to "dissimulation,"[3] taken in connexion with the principle laid down on another occasion by S. Paul, "We also are men of like passions with you,"[4]—denotes clearly that the Apostles did not cease, after receiving their spiritual impulse from above, to be frail human beings. Like the "men of God" under the Old Testament, they also carried their treasure "in earthen vessels :"[5] whether Prophets or Apostles, the authority of the doctrines officially declared was independent of the measure of their personal holiness, and rested on the purely objective communication to them of the Truth from on high. The only supposition on which the authority of Scripture could be affected by such facts as the error of S. Peter would be if that error had been inserted as truth. Its exposure, on the other hand, proves the purity of the record ; while it also shows how God has ever provided[6] that His inspired Word should not suffer through the error of an individual ; but

i. e. from the Church at Jerusalem over which S. James presided,—not persons *commissioned by* him, which would require ὑ π ό, or παρά] he did eat with the Gentiles; but when they were come he withdrew and separated himself, fearing them which were of the circumcision."—Gal. ii. 11, 12.

[1] See Beck, "Propäd. Entwicklung," s. 231.

[2] Gal. ii. 18.

[3] "The other Jews *dissembled* likewise with him (συνυπεκρίθησαν αὐτῷ); insomuch that Barnabas also was carried away with *their dissimulation* (αὐτῶν τῇ ὑποκρίσει)."—ver. 13. On this "dissimulation" see *supra*, Lecture ii. p. 76. Olshausen remarks: "Peter *taught* quite correctly, and had not at all misapprehended the decree of the Council [Acts, xv.]; he merely *acted* weakly, because he allowed himself to be intimidated. His error was, therefore, a purely personal one, and one by which his official character as an Apostle was not in the least compromised. With reference to his personal character, it is meanwhile remarkable that he, the Rock (der Felsenmann), could here too be overcome by fear, as formerly when he denied the Lord."—*Comment. üb. Gal.* ii. 11–13, B. iv. s. 46.

[4] 'Ομοιοπαθεῖς—Acts, xiv. 15.

[5] For example, Jonah; "The man of God," in 1 Kings, xiii. 1, &c.

Cf. *supra*, p. 215, the cases of Samuel and Nathan.

that, if the occasion required, a corrective should be supplied by the instrumentality of others. In a word, the promised impartation of the Holy Ghost to the Apostles had not the object of making them morally perfect, but simply that of raising them in their *teaching* to be infallible organs of the Truth. A single remark of S. Augustine, when discussing this very question, contains the pith of the whole matter. In reply to the objection that S. Paul, by circumcising Timothy, had himself committed the error which he censured in S. Peter, S. Augustine observes: "I do not now inquire how he *acted*; I seek what he has *written*."[1]

It seems difficult to understand how the opinion could ever have been entertained that the deference due to the different components of the Bible is to be measured by the personal qualities of their respective authors. That opinion, surely, has no warrant in the language of Scripture. S. Paul interrupts his discourse on the subject of miraculous gifts, contained in the twelfth and fourteenth chapters of the first Epistle to the Corinthians, in order to lay down, in the most express manner, that such gifts could exist *without* "love:"—"Though I have the gift of prophecy, and understand all mysteries, and all knowledge; and though I have all faith, so that I could remove mountains, and have not charity, I am nothing."[2] Christ Himself declares:

[1] S. Paul "took and circumcised Timothy because of the Jews which were in those quarters: for they knew all that his father was a Greek" (Acts xvi. 3). S. Augustine's remark is: "Non est, inquis, credibile hoc in Petro Paulum, quod ipse Paulus fecerat, arguisse. *Non nunc inquiro quid fecerit; quid scripserit quæro.* * * * Si autem verum scripsit Paulus, verum est, quod Petrus non recte tunc ingrediebatur ad veritatem Evangelii. Id ergo faciebat, quod facere non debebat: et si tale aliquid Paulus ipse jam fecerat, correctum potius etiam ipsum credam co-apostoli sui correctionem non potuisse negligere, quam mendaciter aliquid in sua Epistola posuisse; *et in Epistola qualibet:* quanto magis in illa, in qua prælocutus ait, 'Quæ autem scribo vobis, ecce coram Deo quia non mentior'? [*scil.* Gal. i. 20]."—*Ad S. Hieron.* Ep. lxxxii. t. ii. p. 191.

Equally strong is the judicious remark of Tertullian: "Ceterum si reprehensus est Petrus, quod cum convixisset ethnicis, postea se a convictu eorum separabat personarum respectu: utique *conversationis fuit vitium non prædicationis.*"—*De Præscr. Hær.* § 23, p. 239.

[2] 1 Cor. xiii. 2. This is but a single instance of the fact that, although there is but "the same Spirit," there are, at the same time, those "diversities of gifts" (*διαιρέσεις χαρισμάτων*), which S. Paul had just explained in ch. xii. 4–6,—a passage which Mr. Alford thus excellently paraphrases: "But (as contrasted to this absolute unity, in ground and principle, of all spiritual influence), there are varieties of gifts (*χαρίσματα* = eminent endowments of individuals, in and by which the Spirit indwelling in them manifested Himself—the *φανέρωσις τοῦ Πνεύματος* in each man), but the same Spirit (as their Bestower). And there are varieties of ministries (appointed *services* in the Church in which as their channels of manifestation the

"Many will say to Me in that day, Lord, Lord, have we not prophesied in Thy name, and in Thy name done many wonderful works? And then will I profess unto them, I never knew you!"[1]

From what has been just said it will appear that the character of that Divine influence, under which the Bible has been composed, was absolutely unique, and *specifically* different from those preventing and assisting graces of the Holy Ghost which have been the gift of Christ to His Church. I have not, for obvious reasons, thought it advisable to lay aside the established theological term, or to substitute for 'Inspiration' the word 'The-

χαρίσματα would work), but the same Lord (Christ, the Lord of the Church, Whose it is to appoint all ministrations in it); and varieties of operations (effects of Divine *ἐνέργειαι*), and the same God, Who works all of them in all persons (all the *χαρίσματα* in all who are gifted). Thus we have God the Father, the first source and operator of all spiritual influence in all: God the Son, the Ordainer in His Church of all ministries by which this influence may be legitimately brought out for edification: God the Holy Ghost, dwelling and working in the Church, and effectuating in each man such measure of His gifts as He sees fit."

The distribution of those gifts is thus described by the Apostle: "To one is given by the Spirit the word of wisdom; to another the word of knowledge; to another faith; to another the gifts of healing; to another the working of miracles; to another prophecy; to another discerning of spirits; to another divers kinds of tongues; to another the interpretation of tongues. But all these worketh (*ἐνεργεῖ*) that one and the self-same Spirit, *dividing to every man severally* as He will."—ver. 8–11. The case of the Tyrian prophets, already quoted (Lecture i. p. 43), affords a striking illustration of this division of "spiritual gifts." On the other hand, in the persons of the different authors of Scripture, *as such*, those various gifts were combined and cooperated. Cf. their union in the persons of the Apostles after Pentecost, when they spoke with tongues, performed miracles, expounded, taught, &c., &c. In this fact consisted the pre-eminence of such men over all others:—*ὅταν οὖν ἀκούσῃς* (writes S. Chrysostom), *πρῶτον ἀποστόλους, δεύτερον προφήτας, τρίτον ποιμένας καὶ διδασκάλους, χαρίσματα ἰαμάτων, ἀντιλήψεις, κυβερνήσεις, γένη γλωσσῶν, μάθε ὅτι πᾶσα ἡ χορηγία τῶν λοιπῶν χαρισμάτων, ὥσπερ ἐν κεφαλῇ, τῇ Ἀποστολῇ ἐναπόκειται.*—*Homil. de util. lect. Script.* t. iii. p. 77. For some additional remarks on this subject, see Appendix K.

[1] S. Matt. vii. 22, 23. The remarks of S. Thomas Aquinas on this subject are as profound as they are philosophical. He is discussing the question: "Utrum bonitas morum requiratur ad Prophetiam." After stating the arguments urged in support of the affirmative, he adds: "Sed contra est, quod Matt. vii. 22, his qui dixerant: 'Domine, nonne in nomine tuo prophetavimus?' respondetur: 'Nunquam novi vos.' 'Novit' autem 'Dominus eos qui sunt Ejus,' ut dicitur 2 ad Timoth. ii. 19. Ergo prophetia potest esse in his qui non sunt Dei per gratiam. * * * Prophetia potest esse sine charitate: quod apparet ex duobus. Primo, quidem, ex actu utriusque. Nam Prophetia pertinet ad intellectum, cujus actus præcedit actum voluntatis, quam perficit caritas: unde et Apostolus, 1. ad Cor. xiii., Prophetiam connumerat aliis ad intellectum pertinentibus, quæ possunt sine caritate haberi. Secundo, ex fine utriusque: datur enim Prophetia ad utilitatem ecclesiæ, sicut et aliæ gratiæ gratis datæ, secundum illud Apostoli 1 ad Corinth. xii. 7: 'Unicuique datur manifestatio Spiritus ad utilitatem.' Non autem ordinatur directe ad hoc quod affectus ipsius Prophetæ conjungatur Deo, ad quod ordinatur caritas. Et ideo Prophetia potest esse sine bonitate morum, quantum ad propriam radicem hujus bonitatis."—*Summ. Theol.*, 2da 2dæ, qu. clxxii. art. 4. t. xxiii. p. 301.

opneustia,' which many writers seem inclined to prefer.[1] The distinction, however, to which I have adverted must be carefully borne in mind. The inspiration of the authors of the Bible was an energy altogether *objective*, and directed to supply the wants of the Church. The inspiration of the Christian is altogether *subjective*, and directed to the moral improvement of the individual.[2] The sacred narrative decides this question. The histories of David[3] and Solomon, of Balaam[4] and Jonah,[5] of the

[1] The word 'Theopneustia' has been formed from the adjective *θεόπνευστος*, which S. Paul applies to the Old Testament Scriptures—see *infra*, Lecture vi. The term 'Inspiratio' seems to have been used from the earliest times as expressive of the Holy Ghost's agency in the composition of Scripture. Thus the Vulgate translates 2 Tim. iii. 16—"Omnis Scriptura *divinitus inspirata*" (*θεόπνευστος*): and again 2 S. Pet. i. 21—"Spiritu Sancto *inspirati* (*φερόμενοι*), locuti sunt sancti Dei homines." The substantive occurs in its version of Job, xxxii. 8, "Spiritus est in hominibus, et inspiratio Omnipotentis (נשמת שדי) dat intelligentiam;" where the LXX. has *πνοὴ δὲ Παντοκράτορος*. The Vulgate, however, translates the same phrase in Job, xxxiii. 4, by "*spiraculum* Omnipotentis;" by which it also renders נשמה—"*the breath* of life" (Gen. ii. 7). See Töllner, "Die göttl. Eingebung," s. 85 ff.

[2] As further exemplifying this principle, it may not be amiss to observe that the influence of the Holy Spirit, *in this sense*, is represented in Scripture as the distinctive gift of the Christian dispensation. Our Lord has, indeed, expressly declared that the Holy Ghost co-operated in the composition of the Old Testament ("How then doth David *in Spirit*—*ἐν Πνεύματι*—call Him Lord," &c.—S. Matt. xxii. 43); but we also read again: "This spake He of the Spirit (*περὶ τοῦ Πνεύματος*), which they that believe on Him *should receive* (*ὃ ἔμελλον λαμβάνειν*): for the Holy Ghost WAS NOT YET (*οὔπω γὰρ ἦν Πνεῦμα*) *because that Jesus was not yet glorified.*"—S. John, vii. 39. Cf. the saying of Christ: "Verily I say unto you, among them that are born of women *there hath not risen a greater* than John the Baptist ["A prophet? *yea, I say unto you and more than a prophet*"—ver. 9]: notwithstanding, *he that is least in the Kingdom of Heaven is greater* than he."—S. Matt. xi. 11.

[3] Referring to the occasion on which S. Paul had rebuked S. Peter, the question is put hypothetically by S. Augustine: "At enim satius est credere, apostolum Paulum aliquid non vere scripsisse, quam apostolum Petrum non rectè aliquid egisse." To which he replies: "Hoc si ita est; dicamus (quod absit) satius esse credere mentiri Evangelium, quam negatum esse a Petro Christum; et mentiri Regnorum librum quam tantum Prophetam, a Domino Deo tam excellenter electum, et in concupiscenda atque abducenda uxore aliena commisisse adulterium." * * * Immo vero Sanctam Scripturam, in summo et cœlesti auctoritatis culmine collocatam, de veritate ejus certus et securus legam * * * potius quam, facta humana dum in quibusdam laudabilis excellentiæ personis aliquando credere timeo reprehendenda, ipsa divina eloquia mihi sint ubique suspecta.—*Ad Hieron. Ep.* lxxxii. t. ii. p. 191.

[4] S. Augustine observes as to Balaam's character: "Postea illi et angelus loquitur, arguens et improbans ejus viam: quo viso tamen exterritus adoravit. Deinde ire permissus est, ut jam per ipsum prophetia clarissima proferretur. Nam omnino permissus non est dicere quod volebat, sed quod virtute Spiritus cogebatur. Et ipse quidem reprobus mansit."—*Quæst. in Num.* xlviii. lib. iv. t. iii. p. 549. S. Ambrose writes as follows: "Sed non mireris infusum auguri a Domino quod loqueretur, quando infusum legis in Evangelio etiam principi Synagogæ [*scil.* Caiaphæ] uni ex persequentibus Christum, quia oportet unum hominem mori pro populo. In quo non prophetiæ meritum, sed adsertio veritatis est; ut adversariorum testimonio manifestaretur, quo perfidia non credentium vocibus suorum augurum redargueretur."—*Epist.* l. t. ii. p. 994.

[5] The case of Jonah illustrates, in a striking manner, the distinction which our Lord has drawn between "a prophet" and "a righteous man"—the chief forms of

disobedient Prophet[1] and S. Peter himself, all prove that personal excellence is not essential to the due reception, and perfect transmission of God's Revelation. Whatever may have been our anticipations on this subject, such facts cannot be disputed ; and a moment's consideration will show that the fullest recognition of them not only does not derogate from, but, on the contrary, establishes the supreme authority of the Bible. On any other view, however we may exalt the personal excellence of the sacred writers, in that same degree must we diminish the obligation to regard what they have written as infallible. Infallibility does not admit of degrees. Now there was but ONE Who "was in all points tempted like as we are, yet without sin."[2] Whenever, therefore, we attempt to estimate the amount of deference due to Holy Scripture by the amount of moral perfection to which its various authors have attained, we can no longer refuse to admit that imperfect views of doctrine, and partial, if not erroneous, representations of facts may—nay, must—exist in its pages ; for we are at once encountered by the argument, the truth of which experience proves, and Scripture itself teaches, that the brightest purity, if enshrined in merely human form, will yet be clouded by the shadow which still rests upon the gates of Paradise.[3]

Old Testament piety: "He that receiveth a prophet in the name of a prophet shall receive a prophet's reward; and he that receiveth a righteous man, in the name of a righteous man, shall receive a righteous man's reward."—S. Matt. x. 41. Cf. Olshausen, *in loc.*

[1] 1 Kings, xiii.

[2] Hebr. iv. 15.

[3] Mr. Maurice, in his volume of "Theological Essays," has devoted the thirteenth essay to the question of Inspiration. The chief topic there discussed is that distinction between the significations of the word 'Inspiration' which has been now considered; and on this subject Mr. Maurice's opinion is adverse to that which I have advocated. I venture to think that this difference of opinion has arisen from one of those ambiguities of language which have tended to obscure the question of Inspiration to a greater extent, perhaps, than any other within the range of Theology. Mr. Maurice approaches this topic as follows: "Religious men, the most earnestly religious men, speak of themselves as taught, actuated, inhabited by a Divine Spirit. They declare that they could know nothing of the Scriptures except they were under this guidance. Is *this* the Inspiration which we attribute to the writers of the Old and New Testament, or is that different from it in kind?"—p. 321. Mr. Maurice then proceeds to observe that "the Church of England has used this very word 'Inspiration,'"—viz., in the Collect for the Fifth Sunday after Easter, and in the Communion Service, on which he asks: "Are we paltering with words in a double sense? When we speak of Inspiration, do we mean Inspiration? When we refer to the Inspiration of the Scriptures in our sermons, ought we to say, 'Brethren, we beseech you not to suppose that *this* Inspiration at all resembles that for which we have been praying. They are *generically*, essentially unlike.'"—p. 323. The use here of the word '*generically*' indicates, I apprehend, the source of Mr. Maurice's opinion on this subject. He appears to have thought that if the word 'Inspiration' implies two *distinct* kinds of influence, the reference of either

The very manner in which Scripture notices this inherent frailty of even the organs of Revelation, forcibly illustrates how the Divine element engaged in its composition has neutralized every tendency which is merely human. Take the case of S. Peter's denial of his Master. We can find in the Gospel narrative no stern denunciation of the act ; no indignant allusion to its cowardice or its ingratitude : lightly as the glance of the Lord Himself fell upon the Apostle while he disowned Him, the pen of the sacred writers but touches on the occurrence, and passes on.[1] Such failings are, in general, noticed, as we should say, in

to the Holy Ghost must exclude His agency in exercising the other. "Can we conceive," he asks, "any view of the Holy Scriptures which would have seemed to him [S. Paul] more dreadful, than one which, under color of exalting them, *should set aside their own express testimony concerning the unspeakable gift which God had conferred on His creatures?*" * * * "In solitary chambers, among bedridden sufferers, the words of these good men ["our Venns and Newtons"] have still a living force. The Bible is read there truly as an inspired book; as a book which does not stand aloof from human life, but meets it; *which proves itself not to be the work of a* DIFFERENT SPIRIT *from that which is reproving and comforting the sinner, but of the same.*"—p. 333. Here the writer seems to have overlooked the bearing upon this question of S. Paul's express statement: "There are *diversities* of gifts, but THE SAME Spirit" (1 Cor. xii. 4). These words assuredly imply a *specific* difference in the manifestations of spiritual agency; and hence the following alternative does not convey an accurate statement of the opinion on which Mr. Maurice pronounces judgment: "Either we must set at nought the faith of those who have clung to the Bible, and found a meaning in it when the doctors could not interpret it; or we must forego the demand which we make on the consciences of young men, when we compel them to say that they regard the Inspiration of the Bible as GENERICALLY unlike that which God bestows on His children in this day."—p. 334.

Mr. Maurice's motive for dwelling on this question, of itself, accounts for the view which he has propounded: "I have appeared to protest against current theories of Inspiration because they fail to assert the actual presence of that Spirit whom it has been one of the standing articles of his [the Unitarian's] creed *not* to confess. I cannot deny this charge. I do think that our theories of Inspiration, however little they may accord with Unitarian notions, have a semi-Unitarian character; that they are derived from that unbelief in the Holy Ghost which is latent in us all, but which was developed and embodied in the Unitarianism of the last century."—p. 346. Mr. Maurice, in fact, conceives that the theories "about Inspiration current among our Evangelical and High Church teachers," and according to which the agency of the Holy Ghost in the composition of Scripture differs from the influences which He sheds upon Christians in every age,—have tended to prevent "a full assertion of that portion of our creed which refers to the Person of the Comforter." Without considering whether this notion is well or ill founded, I would merely observe that 'the theory' advanced in these Discourses is certainly not obnoxious to the charge of casting a cloud over the Personal agency of the Holy Spirit.

[1] "And the Lord turned, and looked upon Peter. And Peter remembered the word of the Lord, how He had said unto him, Before the cock crow, thou shalt deny me thrice. And Peter went out, and wept bitterly. And the men that held Jesus mocked him," &c.—S. Luke, xxii. 61–63. Compare the *single* remark which the Evangelists make use of when referring *historically* to the name of Judas Iscariot—"who also betrayed Him," (S Matt. x. 4.); or, again, the narrative of the murder of S. John the Baptist (S. Matt. xiv. 3–12) which closes with the simple statement: "His disciples came, and took up the body and buried it, and went and told Jesus." So, too, in the Old Testament, the sin of Lot (Gen. xix. 30–38) is recorded without

the most cursory manner. The sinful act is dwelt upon, and the violation of the command of God by His ambassador is held up as an object of reprobation, in such cases only where there might be danger of misapprehension, or where the moral sense of itself might not at once reconcile the difficulty. Thus, in the thirteenth chapter of the first Book of Kings, we read how the "old prophet who dwelt in Bethel" seduced "the man of God" by whom, in the strength of the Spirit, the King of Israel had been braved beside the altar. At first, indeed, "the man of God" refused to disobey the express command of the Lord; but he is answered by the assertion, "I am a prophet also as thou art, and an angel spake unto me by the word of the Lord." Here there is plainly room for the utmost offence and misapprehension, which, the inspired historian, without any comment, at once dispels by the single phrase, "But he lied unto him."[1]

There are many other characteristics of the sacred volume which cannot fail, in like manner, to impress the mind with the deepest conviction of the unceasing presence and controlling influence of its Divine Author. Consider, for example, the superhuman wisdom with which the language of Scripture touches upon the institutions of the old Gentile world in their relation to Christianity. Need I mention here the often quoted instance of how the New Testament writers abstain from all *direct* reprobation of the great social crime of slavery? They confine themselves to pointing out the source, and inculcating the great prin-

any comment. The incest of Reuben (Gen. xxxv. 22) is noticed with the single remark: "And Israel heard it." In 2 Kings, xvi. 10–16, an act of peculiar impiety is recorded as having been committed by King Ahaz and the High Priest Urijah: we are, no doubt, informed in the beginning of the chapter of the character of Ahaz; but were we unacquainted with the ordinances of the Mosaic Law, we assuredly could not have formed any adequate notion of the nature of his crime, from what the narrative itself unfolds.

[1] Ver. 18. The importance of these facts will be at once seen, if we remember that the manner in which Scripture touches upon the morality of many actions related in its pages has been urged as an objection against a strict view of its inspiration. Thus, alluding to "the *progressive* character of the Scripture morality," and having asserted that an "imperfect morality is plainly discernible throughout the period of the Old Testament dispensation, and frequently embodied, too, in the Old Testament Scriptures," Mr. Morell observes: "These things, it is said, may be explained as being permitted by God for a time on account of the weakness of human nature, or, as our Saviour expressed it on one occasion, 'on account of the hardness of their hearts.' But surely it is one thing to suppose that God would tolerate these things, just as he tolerates sin in His creatures, while the struggle against evil is going on, and quite another thing to have them either justified (?) or spoken of *as matters of moral indifference*, in words dictated immediately by the Holy Spirit."—*Philos. of Religion*, p. 168.

ciple of Christian brotherhood :[1] the result they leave to the fructifying influence of the Holy Spirit, and to time. Again, observe the marked distinction which exists between the Bible and all other writings which relate to the history of man individually or collectively. To take a single illustration :—we may remark throughout the Scripture narrative the absence of personal feeling, and the suppression of personal emotion.[2] Josephus, observes Pascal, conceals the dishonor of his nation : Moses does not conceal his own.[3] What reader has failed to notice how the cold sententiousness of Tacitus expands into tenderness, and warms with passion, when he turns aside to weep over the last moments of Agricola ?[4] But compare with this natural outpouring of feeling the record of the Evangelists. There no expression of human sympathy accompanies the story of the Agony in the Garden,—the awful scene before Pilate,—the horrors of the Cross! No burst of emotion attends their Master's body to the grave, or welcomes His Resurrection :—and yet who has not felt how this treatment of their theme but adds to its pathos and its grandeur ?[5]

[1] "By one Spirit are we all baptized into one body, whether we be Jews or Gentiles, whether we *be bond or free*."—1 Cor. xii. 13. Cf. ch. vii. 20, 21; 1 Tim. vi. 1, 2; 1 S. Pet. ii. 18, &c., &c.

[2] Speaking of the predictions contained in Lev. xxvi. and Deut. xxviii., Mr. Davison observes: "It is a striking fact in the delivery of this prophecy, that it comes from the mouth of Moses, the legislator of the commonwealth whose dissolution he is directed to foreshow. * * * How unlike is it to the ordinary course of man's own spirit or wisdom to dwell upon the downfall of his own works, just at the moment when they come fresh from his hands. * * * The approaching settlement of this chosen people, their first advance to Canaan, is the season when their ruin, and their expulsion from that land, are introduced to view. The prophetic tidings of their distant overthrow are made to sound in our ears as loud as the song of their present victory. A combination of things rarely made, and not conformable to the human feeling left to itself; but which is not without example in other conspicuous parts of Prophecy. For as Moses foretells the desolation of his people at the moment when he reared them into a community, so to Solomon were foreshown the ruins of his Temple at the like season, when he beheld it completed in its magnificence, and bearing upon it the omens of hope and joy in the blessing of its first Inauguration."—*On Prophecy*, p. 164.

[3] "Josèphe cache la honte de sa nation; Moïse ne cache pas sa honte propre."—ed. Faugere, t. ii. p. 193.

[4] Cf. "Julii Agricolæ Vita," cap. xliii.–xlvi. E. g. "Tu vero felix, Agricola, non vitæ tantum claritate, sed etiam opportunitate mortis: ut perhibent, qui interfuerunt novissimis sermonibus tuis, constans et libens fatum excepisti, tamquam pro virili portione innocentiam Principi donares. Sed mihi filiæque, præter acerbitatem parentis erepti, auget mœstitiam, quod adsidere valetudini, fovere deficientem, satiari vultu, complexu, non contigit. Excepissemus certe mandata vocesque, quas penitus animo figeremus. Noster hic dolor, nostrum vulnus:" &c.—cap. xlv.

[5] "On the subject of miracles, the means to this great end, they speak in calm, unimpassioned language; on man's sins, change of heart, on hope, faith, and charity;

And thus it is that human instrumentality, according to the various aspects under which we have considered it, has been moulded by the Holy Spirit into the organism of Revelation. Each ray of the Divine Light has been borne to mankind through the medium best suited for its transmission: and yet, while borrowing, on its course, that particular hue which the medium lends through which it passes, it retains, no less sensibly, the purity of the source from which it streams. In past ages God had spoken unto the fathers by means of sundry partitions of the Truth, and in divers manners.[1] The constituent elements of Revelation were thus conveyed gradually, and under aspects best suited to the time: and this partial communication of His decrees was, no doubt, one consequence of the Fall;—rendered necessary by man's incapacity to receive, and so ordained by God's wise counsel to withhold. But in these "last days" He has spoken to us by His Son.[2] In the language of Christ we can discern no features tinged by human genius, no hues borrowed from human thought. In His words the severed rays of Revelation have been re-combined in one uncolored beam of Truth.

on the objects in short to be effected, they exhaust all their feelings and eloquence. Their history, from the narrative of our Lord's persecutions to those of Paul, the abomination of the Jews, embraces scenes and personages which claim from the ordinary reader a continual effusion of sorrow, or wonder, or indignation. In writers who were friends of the parties, and adherents of the cause for which they did and suffered so great things, the absence of it is, on ordinary grounds, incomprehensible. * * * Had these authors no feeling? Had their mode of life bereaved them of the common sympathies and sensibilities of human nature? Read such passages as Paul's parting address to the elders of Miletus; the same Apostle's recommendation of the offending member of the Corinthian Church to pardon; and, more than all, the occasional bursts of conflicting feeling, in which anxious apprehension for the faith and good behavior of his converts is mixed with the pleasing recollection of their conversion, and the minister and the man are alike strongly displayed—and it will be plain that Christianity exercised no benumbing influence on the heart. * * * Still, is it possible that the natural man should have sustained, without one relapse, one single deviation, a tone of feeling so much beyond man? Could the circumstances of these writers, overpoweringly impressive though they were, have secured them against even an occasional betrayal of wonder, of pity, of indignation, or of sorrow? The more we reflect on the nature of the scenes they describe, the more forcibly will the question be suggested. Must not such emotions have arisen, on some occasions at least, in the breast even of men so circumstanced—men who were still of like passions with ourselves? That the expression of such feelings should nowhere appear, throughout the narratives of each and of all, does certainly seem inexplicable; unless we admit a miraculous control of their authorship,—unless we suppose them, in short, to have been, not merely workers and witnesses of miracles, but miraculously guided in their writings."—Bishop Hinds, *On Inspiration*, p. 83, &c.

[1] *Πολυμερῶς καὶ πολυτρόπως πάλαι ὁ Θεὸς λαλήσας.*—Heb. i. 1.

[2] *Ἐλάλησεν ἡμῖν ἐν Υἱῷ.*—*Ibid.*

The clouds have now parted which once veiled from the eye of fallen man the gracious purpose of his heavenly Father. "God who commanded the light to shine out of darkness hath shined in our hearts, to give the light of the knowledge of the glory of God, in the face of Jesus Christ."[1] The Sun of Righteousness has arisen with healing in His wings :—the Eternal Word has become incarnate, to regenerate, and to redeem.

[1] 2 Cor. iv. 6.

LECTURE VI.

SCRIPTURAL PROOF.

Θαυμαστὴν δὲ λίαν ἐχόντων τῶν ἁγίων Εὐαγγελιστῶν τὴν ἐν τῷ γράφειν ἀκρίβειαν· οὐ γὰρ αὐτοὶ λαλοῦσι, κατὰ τὴν τοῦ Σωτῆρος φωνὴν, ἀλλὰ τὸ Πνεῦμα τοῦ Πατρὸς τὸ ἐν αὐτοῖς.

S. CYRILL. Alex. *Comm. in S. Joan. Evang.*, lib. i. Procem.

"Cedamus igitur et consentiamus auctoritati Sanctæ Scripturæ, quæ nescit falli nec fallere."

S. AUGUST. *De peccator. merit.*, lib. i. c. 22.

Τῷ διορισμῷ χρησάμενος ἀπέκρινε τὰ τῆς ἀνθρωπίνης σοφίας συγγράμματα. θεόπνευστον δὲ γραφὴν τὴν πνευματικὴν ὠνόμασεν. ἡ γὰρ τοῦ Θείου Πνεύματος χάρις διὰ τῶν Προφητῶν καὶ τῶν Ἀποστόλων ἐφθέγξατο. Θεὸς τοίνυν τὸ Πνεῦμα τὸ Ἅγιον, εἴπερ ἀληθῶς κατὰ τὸν Ἀπόστολον θεόπνευστος τοῦ Πνεύματος ἡ γραφή.

THEODORETUS, *In Epist.* ii. *ad Tim.*

LECTURE VI.

SCRIPTURAL PROOF.

WHICH THINGS ALSO WE SPEAK, NOT IN THE WORDS WHICH MAN'S WISDOM TEACHETH, BUT WHICH THE HOLY GHOST TEACHETH.—1 *Cor.* ii. 13.

THE topics which have hitherto chiefly engaged our attention have been the reality of a Divine Revelation, and the nature of the Holy Spirit's agency by means of which that Revelation has been imparted to mankind. The co-operation of the Holy Spirit for such a purpose has been termed 'Inspiration;' and the evidence already adduced, in order to exhibit the character of this peculiar influence, has consisted principally of inferences from certain phenomena presented by the Bible, as well as from the structure of its various parts. An important subject, therefore, still remains untouched, the consideration of which, as stated on a previous occasion, has been necessarily postponed:[1]—I mean the direct evidence which the sacred writers themselves supply. The connexion of this branch of our inquiry with what has preceded is too obvious to require comment: a few preliminary remarks, however, may serve to strengthen the combined force of the two lines of proof, and to illustrate the general tendency of the course of reasoning here pursued.

I would observe, therefore, that if the fact of a Revelation having been given be not questioned; and if the Bible be, confessedly, the repository of such a communication from God,[2]—

[1] See Lecture iv. p. 140.

[2] Even those systems which profess to be founded on a new revelation unite with the Christian in admitting the Divine authority of the Bible. Thus Mohammed was content to appeal to the facts of Scripture as precedents: "Verily we have revealed our will unto thee, as we have revealed it unto Noah, and the prophets who succeeded him, and as we revealed it unto Abraham and Ismael, and Isaac and Jacob, and the tribes, and unto Jesus, and Job, and Jonas, and Aaron, and Solomon; and we have given thee the Koran as we gave the Psalms unto David," &c. &c.—Sale's *Koran*, ch. iv. &c. &c. See Dr. Henderson's work entitled "Divine Inspiration," p. 11

there is the highest possible presumption, *à priori*, that a certain degree of Divine assistance has been superadded, for the purpose of enabling the authors of this record to compose their narratives with perfect accuracy, and to transmit the Revelation to others in its original purity. If this Revelation was intended for men in every age,—and so much, at least, the nature of the case entitles us to assume,—on what grounds can any doubt be cast on the credibility of God's having specially commissioned certain agents to hand down the history of it to future times, or of His having bestowed upon them such aid as would ensure that the knowledge which He had disclosed should be preserved free from all alloy of human imperfection? Such precautions, in fact, are no more than what any man, who has made a great discovery in some department of science, is sure to take, if he only desire that the knowledge of his discovery should not be lost. Nay, when we bear in mind that so many astonishing miracles have been performed in order to convey this Revelation to man, and to bring to pass the system of things which it announces, we feel instinctively inclined to presuppose that God cannot have withheld the far less striking miracle of providing against error in the documents which preserve it.[1] When we remember, too, how vast a space of human history is included in the narratives of which the sacred volume is composed, this presumption becomes still stronger. Without such superhuman guidance, it is

We are told, moreover, that the Mohammedan Doctors teach that both the Gospel and the Koran were predicted in the Old Testament. In the "Specimen Hist. Arabum," by Abul-Faragius, we read: "Porro asserunt Islamitarum docti, factam fuisse mentionem Mohammedis in libris a Deo demissis, sc. in Lege, isto textu; 'Venit Deus a Sina, et ortus est a Sair, et manifestatus est a monte Paranis' (Deut. xxxiii. 2): quibus verbis indicari dicunt descensum Legis ad Mosem, Evangelii ad Jesum, et Alcorani ad Mohammedem."—(Pococke's transl., pp. 14 and 183.) It is, in like manner, one of the articles of the Mormon "Creed:"—"We believe in the word of God recorded in the Bible."

[1] To this effect Bishop Warburton observes: "They [the Apostles] worked miracles, they spake with tongues, they explained mysteries, they interpreted prophecies, they discerned the true from the false pretences to the Spirit: and all this for the temporary and occasional discharge of their ministry. Is it possible, then, to suppose them to be deserted by their Divine Inlightener when they sat down to the other part of their work; to frame a rule for the lasting service of the Church? Can we believe that that Spirit, which so bountifully assisted them in their assemblies, had withdrawn Himself when they retired to their private oratories; or that, when their *speech* was *with all power*, their *writings* should convey no more than the created fallible dictates of human knowledge? To suppose the endowments of the Spirit to be so capriciously bestowed, would make it look more like a mockery than a gift. And to believe all this would be a harder task than what (the Deist tells us) religious credulity imposes on us."—*On the Office of the Holy Spirit:* Works, vol. iv., p. 561.

inexplicable, considering the contents of the Bible, that just so much should have been placed on record, and no more.[1] Were we to admit that any portion of Scripture has resulted from the unaided exercise of human judgment or of human faculties, it would always be possible to argue that the historian has omitted much information which it concerns us to know, or that he has preserved many facts which are trivial or unnecessary; that he has but partially or imperfectly handed down the communication from heaven; that such or such a fact has not been reported with accuracy; or, in fine, that some particular expression or doctrine has not been conveyed to us as God intended:—especially in cases where the subject matter of the narrative appears strange, or opposed to human preconceptions. If we had never heard of the difficulties which have been urged against Inspiration—if we had never opened the Scriptures themselves—could the suspicion have ever occurred to any fair mind, that God may have thus left to all the chances of human fallibility the history of that Revelation which (it is assumed) He has given to His creatures, instructing them in their duties, and unfolding to them His decrees?[2]—above all, when we know, as a matter of fact, that in every age an unhesitating conviction has been expressed by the Jewish, and subsequently by the Christian Church, that the different portions of the Bible have been composed under the immediate direction and impulse of the Holy Ghost. Now if all this must appear highly credible to any unprejudiced inquirer, who had never opened the pages of Scripture, it remains for us to see whether, having opened its several Books, and studied their contents, such credibility either diminishes or disappears.

The value of the inspired writers' own statements is naturally of the highest order.[3] Those statements fully confirm the here-

[1] Take, for example, the Gospel narrative. S. John's account embraces but few of the particulars recorded by the Synoptists; while they, in turn, omit all mention of such facts as the raising of Lazarus, the prophecy of Caiaphas, &c. Indeed we are expressly told that no record has been preserved of "many other things which Jesus did."—S. John, xxi. 25.

[2] Cf. Töllner, "Die göttl. Eingebung der heil. Schrift." s. 148 ff.—"Für Leute, welche nicht nur die Eingebung sondern auch die Wahrheit und Glaubwürdigkeit der heiligen Schrift bestreiten, schreibe ich nicht."—s. 149.

[3] In considering the evidence supplied by the statements of Scripture itself, I would observe that the full bearing of the different texts can only be appreciated when we regard them as combined in one argument—an argument, moreover, which must not be separated from the other proofs adduced. The opponent cannot be permitted to pass judgment upon the several statements of the sacred writers in detail,

ditary doctrines of the Church upon the subject of Inspiration, as well as complete that testimony where it is, of necessity, defective;—for the authors of Scripture alone could bear *direct* evidence to the fact, that they had received revelations from God, or that they had been inspired to compose the sacred narrative. Every other species of evidence must either be traced back to that of the writers themselves, or have been founded partly on the tokens of miraculous power which they displayed, partly on the information supplied by other agents of God, who were similarly endowed. We naturally expect, as I have said, to find information on this matter in the pages of Scripture. When we read this account, so minute and circumstantial, of the various disclosures which God has made to man, we cannot believe[1] that no information has been imparted as to the amount of care taken to ensure the purity of the documents in which they are preserved. Were the Bible altogether silent upon this subject, we can easily picture to ourselves the use which would be made of such a fact; but when the very reverse is the case, as I now proceed to show, the force of the argument which thence results, in proof of the perfect inspiration of all the parts of Scripture,

and to argue that such or such a passage of Scripture does not, taken separately, support the whole weight of the conclusion which it is sought to establish on the basis of all combined. Nor, indeed, can justice be done to the reasoning by which the inspiration of the Bible is proved, were either the force of the direct evidence to be estimated merely by the force which will still be retained, after all evasion, by its constituent parts taken singly; or were such evidence to be considered apart from the many collateral proofs which have been adduced in confirmation. To borrow the admirable illustration of Bishop Butler when speaking of the "evidence of Christianity,"—The evidence for Inspiration combines many things "of great variety and compass * * * making up, *all of them together*, one argument; the conviction arising from which kind of proof may be compared to what they call *the effect* in architecture or other works of art; a result from a great number of things so and so disposed, and taken into one view."—*Analogy*, Part II. ch. vii.

[1] In saying this, I take for granted, as a matter of fact, that we possess in the Bible *a written* narrative of God's Revelation to man;—a narrative, too, which can be shown to have been composed in accordance with a Divine command (see *supra*, Lecture ii. p. 53, &c.; and *infra*, Lecture vii). I do not, therefore, in any way contravene the following important principles laid down by Bishop Butler: "We are in no sort judges by what methods, and in what proportion, *it were to be expected* that this supernatural light and instruction would be afforded us. * * * Nay, we are not in any sort able to judge whether *it were to have been expected*, that the revelation should have been committed to writing; or left to be handed down, and consequently corrupted by verbal tradition. * * * It may be said, 'that a revelation * * * which was not committed to writing * * * would not have answered its purpose.' I ask, what purpose? It would not have answered all the purposes, which it has now answered, and in the same degree; but it would have answered others, or the same in different degrees."—*Analogy*. Part II. ch. iii.

will best be estimated by reflecting upon the desperate efforts which have been made to evade it.[1]

And, first of all, as to the titles which have been appropriated to the sacred writings. This collection of documents is styled, either absolutely and simply "Scripture," in the singular; or "the Scriptures," in the plural:[2]—the term "Scripture," moreover, being on more than one occasion[3] used as if it were synonymous with its Author, where, from the references to the Old Tes-

[1] I cannot avoid alluding to the manner in which Perrone copies, as one may say, the words of the most extreme Rationalists, in his desire to prove that the authority of the Church is the *sole* ground for our belief in the inspiration of Scripture. He argues thus: "Seclusa Ecclesiæ auctoritate nulla alia nobis superest via ad divinam sacrorum librorum inspirationem internoscendam nisi aut Scriptura ipsa, aut antiqua documenta, aut intrinsica quædam librorum illorum proprietas. * * * Porro *nihil horum* ad rem conficiendam valet." In reply to the second and third members of this alternative, see Lecture ii., and Lecture i. p. 46, &c. As to the first, Perrone writes: "Non *Scriptura ipsa;* nuspiam enim Scriptura declarat quinam singillatim libri Spiritu S. afflante conscripti sint, quinam vero nequaquam. Et quamvis nonnulla huc illuc afferantur dicta tanquam oracula a Spiritu S. dictata, hæc præcise non afficiunt integrum librum ex quo peculiaria illa testimonia promuntur, ita ut presse inferri possit ac debeat, librum integrum cum omnibus suis partibus fuisse Spiritu S. afflante conscriptum. Si interdum legitur 'omnem Scripturam esse divinitus inspiratam' ejusmodi effata nonnisi de libris Vet. Test. accipi possunt, idque sane generatim, sic ut semper incertum maneat quinam libri singillatim Spiritu S. afflante, fuerint exarati, seu quinam illam 'omnem Scripturam' Spiritu S. inspiratam revera constituant."—*Prælect. Theol.*, vol. ii. par. ii. cap. 2. p. 89. The resemblance of this passage to the following statement of Bretschneider is very remarkable: "Dasselbe gilt von den Stellen, wo sich die Apostel den Geist zuschreiben, und in seiner Kraft zu lehren versichern, wie 1 Kor. ii. 4 ff. Denn daraus folgt, dass sie den Geist hatten, dass also der Inhalt ihrer Lehre, Lehre des Geistes sei, keineswegs aber, dass ihnen der Geist ihre Schreiben dictire. Noch weniger mag 2 Tim. iii. 16, beweisen, da dort Paulus vom alten Test. spricht, und nicht von seinen eignen oder andern neutestamentlichen Schriften."—*Handb. der Dogmat.*, B. i. s. 393. Indeed the Roman Catholic theologian goes further than the Rationalist; especially when he replies as follows to the argument in support of the inspiration of the Old Testament, derived from the manner in which Christ and His Apostles refer to it: "Formulæ quas Christus et Apostoli adhibuere *vagæ ac generales sunt.* * * * Multo vero minus ex generalibus illis formulis constare nobis poterit singulas uniuscujusque libri partes fuisse inspiratas."—Perrone, *loc. cit.* p. 97.

[2] Ἡ γραφή. S. John, ii. 22; Acts, viii. 32; Rom. iv. 3, &c., &c.; *αἱ γραφαί*, S. Matt. xxii. 29; S. Mark, xiv. 49; S. Luke, xxiv. 27; S. John, v. 39, and *passim.*

[3] "The Scripture (ἡ γραφή), foreseeing that God would justify the heathen through faith, preached before the Gospel unto Abraham, saying, In thee shall all nations be blessed."—Gal. iii. 8; while in Gen. xii. 1–3, we read: "Now the Lord had said unto Abram, Get thee out of thy country * * * unto a land that I will show thee * * * and in thee shall all the families of the earth be blessed." Again, S. Paul writes: "The Scripture saith unto Pharaoh, Even for this same purpose have I raised thee up," &c.—Rom. ix. 17; words which Mr. Alford paraphrases as follows: "*The Scripture* (identified with God, its Author: the case, as Tholuck remarks, is different when merely something *contained* in Scripture is introduced by ἡ γραφὴ λέγει: there ἡ γρ. is merely personified. The justice of Tholuck's remark will be apparent, if we reflect that this expression could not be used of the mere ordinary words of any man in the historical Scriptures, Ahab or Hezekiah,—but only where the *text itself* speaks, or where *God spoke*, or, as here, some man under inspiration of God) *saith to Pharaoh.*" Cf. also the general mode of quoting the Old Testament in the Epistle to the Hebrews.

tament, the Author can be no other than God Himself. As might be expected, the term is generally applied to the Old Testament; the New Testament Canon not having been as yet completed. In one instance, however, S. Paul's Epistles are implicitly referred to by S. Peter under this name,[1] and are, consequently, declared by him to be inspired; since in all the fifty places where the term "Scripture" occurs elsewhere in the New Testament, it is employed solely with reference to that collection of writings which the Jews regarded as the "oracles of God;"[2]—or, to speak more accurately, perhaps, it is applied only to the Old Testament, and to those portions of the New which had been composed at the time; for no argument which has hitherto been advanced explains away the fact that our Lord's words in the Gospel, "the laborer is worthy of his hire," are quoted *verbatim* as "Scripture" by S. Paul, in the same sense as the passage from the Pentateuch which is coupled with them.[3] We also find distinctive epithets added:—"The Prophetic Scriptures;"[4] or "Prophecy of Scrip-

[1] "Even as our beloved brother Paul also * * * hath written (ἔγραψεν) unto you; as also in all his Epistles * * * in which are some things hard to be understood, which they that are unlearned and unstable wrest, as they do also *the other Scriptures* (ὡς καὶ τ ὰ ς λοιπὰς γραφάς)."—2 S. Pet. iii. 15, 16. "Peter reckons Paul's Epistles, while the author was still alive, among the γραφάς, Holy Scriptures."—Hug, *Einleitung*. Th. i. § 17. 4te Aufl. s. 101.

[2] See Wordsworth, "On the Canon," p. 185. Hence, in the language of the New Testament, the term γραφή must be understood, in the strictest sense, *as a proper name*.

[3] S. Paul, referring to the provision which the Church is bound to set apart for its ministers,—a duty to which he has elsewhere (1 Cor. ix. 14) adverted as being what "the Lord hath ordained"—writes: "For the Scripture saith (λέγει γὰρ ἡ γραφή), 'Thou shalt not muzzle the ox that treadeth out the corn' [Deut. xxv. 4]. And, 'The laborer is worthy of his reward' (Ἄξιος ὁ ἐργάτης τοῦ μισθοῦ αὐτοῦ)."—1 Tim. v. 18. The words of the second quotation are nowhere to be found in the Old Testament: but our Lord, *prescribing to the Church the same duty to which the Apostle has here adverted*, on one occasion observes (to the "Twelve"), ἄξιος γὰρ ὁ ἐργ. τῆς τροφῆς αὐτοῦ—S. Matt. x. 10; and on another (to the "Seventy"), ἄξιυς γὰρ ὁ ἐργ. τοῦ μισθοῦ αὐτοῦ—S. Luke, x. 7. It surely will not do to say, with Wiesinger, *in loc.*: "If he [S. Paul] desired to support this dictum by an authority, *he would have appealed*, as in Acts, xx. 35 [where, be it observed, S. Paul adduces *an unwritten* saying of Christ], or 1 Cor. ix. 14, to the Κύριος, and not to the Gospel of his helper Luke [*whose words*, however, S. Paul *literally* copies], including this along with the Old Testament under ἡ γραφή. * * * The words, 'the Scripture saith,' are therefore not to be connected with this citation, and Calvin is right when he says, 'citat * * * quasi dictum proverbiale, quod omnibus dictat communis sensus. Quemadmodum et Christus quum idem dicebat nihil aliud quam sententiam proferebat omnium consensu approbatam.' "—s. 524.

It may be observed, that the Apostle here combines the Old and the New Testament under the title γραφή, when addressing the same person to whom he subsequently writes, πᾶσα γραφὴ θεόπνευστος—2 Tim. iii. 16.

[4] "Made known by the Scriptures of the Prophets (διά τε γραφῶν προφητικῶν)."—Rom. xvi. 26.

ture ;"[1] or the significant phrase "Scripture given by Inspiration of God."[2] In fine, there are the two emphatic expressions "the Holy Scriptures," and "the Hallowed Writings,"[3]—the latter being the technical phrase by which the Jews were wont to designate the Books of the Old Testament.[4] There exists, however, an important distinction between the ideas which these two expressions convey, although our English Version represents them as being equivalent. The epithet "Holy" Scripture intimates the special relation of the Bible to God the Holy Ghost ;[5] and in this sense it is that the Apostle defines "all Scripture" as

[1] *Προφητεία γραφῆς.*—2 S. Pet. i. 20.

[2] *Γραφὴ θεόπνευστος.*—2 Tim. iii. 16,—an expression which may be illustrated by the New Testament phrase, *ἐν Πνεύματι* [Θεοῦ], as denoting the state in which the Divine influence was felt: see *supra*, Lecture iii. p. 129. note. Thus, having quoted our Lord's words: "How then doth David *in Spirit* call Him Lord," &c. (S. Matt. xxii. 43),—S. Gregory of Nyssa observes: *οὐκοῦν τῇ δυνάμει τοῦ Πνεύματος οἱ θεοφορούμενοι τῶν ἁγίων ἐμπνέονται. καὶ διὰ τοῦτο πᾶσα γραφὴ θεόπνευστος λέγεται, διὰ τὸ τῆς θείας ἐμπνεύσεως εἶναι διδασκαλίαν.*—*Cont. Eunom.*, Orat. VI. t. ii. p. 605. We may also compare the words of the text prefixed to the present Lecture (1 Cor. ii. 13) with the statement of David himself: "The Spirit of the Lord spake by me, and His word was in my tongue."—2 Sam. xxiii. 2. Cf. too, *ὑπὸ Πνεύματος Ἁγίου φερόμενοι ἐλάλησαν ἀπὸ* Θεοῦ *ἄνθρωποι.*—2 S. Pet. i. 21. To which illustrations of the force of *θεόπνευστος* may be added the analogy of a similar term likewise employed by S. Paul alone: "Ye yourselves *are taught of God* (*θεοδίδακτοι*) to love one another."—1 Thess. iv. 9. (Cf. *διδακτοὶ* Θεοῦ—S. John, vi. 45.) As further illustrating the signification which such a compound term as *θεόπνευστος* must have conveyed to the mind of a Jew, we may compare the following form of expression: "The holy Law *made* and given by God (*τῆς ἁγίας καὶ θεοκτίστου νομοθεσίας*)"—2 Macc. vi. 23; and also that of Philo—*θεόχρηστα λόγια*—already quoted, Lecture ii. p. 67, note [1]. According to some, who follow the analogy of the word *ἄπνευστος* which has an *active* sense ("*without breath, breathless*, Od. v. 456: hence *lifeless*"—L. and S.), *θεόπνευστος* = *spirans Deum*, or, as we may say, "*plenus Deo*," without much affecting the signification. Baumgarten Crusius considers *analogy* to be decisive in favor of this *active* sense: "Die *active* giebt noch den angemessenen Zusammenhang: was den göttlichen Geist in sich hat, würkt auch durch diesen auf das Leben ein."—*Grundzüge der bibl. Theol.*, s. 235; and he considers that the Apostle in order to express this idea employs *θεόπνευστον*, not *προφητικόν* (Rom. xvi. 26).

[3] *Γραφαὶ ἅγιαι*—Rom. i. 2; and *τὰ ἱερὰ γράμματα*—2 Tim. iii. 15. The English Version translates in both places, "the Holy Scriptures."

[4] See Hävernick, "Einleitung," Th. I. Abth. i. s. 79; who compares "the distinction between *ἱερός* and *ἅγίος*; *sacer* and *sanctus*;" (e. g. "Ἅγιος, Sanctus, ut *ἁγιωτάτη νησάων*, Callim. H. in Del. (275) Plut. in Probl. *Τῇ δὲ τιμῇ ποιοῦσιν αὐτὸν ἱερὸν, καὶ ἅγιον, καὶ ἄσυλον*, ubi *ἱερὸν καὶ ἅγιον*, pro Sacrum et Sanctum ponit, quod vocabulo composito Latini Sacrosanctum appellant."—H. Stephanus, *Thesaur. Gr. Ling.*, ed. Valpy, vol. iii. p. 1331.) Hävernick also calls attention to the following illustrations of the sense in which *Ἱερὰ γράμματα* must have been understood (cf. *supra*, Lecture ii. p. 70, note [1]): Josephus, having quoted Daniel's exposition of Nebuchadnezzar's dream, adds, that if any of his readers desires to know more on the subject: *σπουδασάτω τὸ βιβλίον ἀναγνῶναι τοῦ Δανιήλου· εὑρήσει δὲ τοῦτο ἐν τοῖς ἱεροῖς γράμμασιν.*—*Antiq.*, lib. x. x. 4 t. i. p. 535. Speaking of the Therapeutæ Philo writes *Ἐντυγχάνοντες γὰρ τοῖς ἱεροῖς γράμμασι, φιλοσοφοῦσι τὴν πάτριαν φιλοσοφίαν ἀλληγοροῦντες.*—*De Vita Contempl.*, t. ii. p. 475.

[5] See *supra*, Lecture i. p. 24, &c.

"given by Inspiration of God." The designation "Hallowed Writings" refers to the human recognition of these sacred compositions; which are, accordingly, elsewhere described by the same Apostle as containing "the ancient covenant" between God and man.[1] We are also to note how S. Paul, when about to be withdrawn from the scene of his labors,[2] unites these two senses in his final instructions to his disciple and successor; and how he combines an assertion of the practical value of "the Hallowed Writings," with the statement of the source whence their vitality is derived. "The Hallowed Writings," he argues, "have power to make thee wise unto salvation, *because* Scripture, in all its parts, is given by Inspiration of God."[3]

I do not pause to consider the objections which have been urged against the rendering of this passage.[4] Without entering

[1] "Until this day, remaineth the same vail untaken away in *the reading of* the Old Testament (τῆς παλαιᾶς διαθήκης)"—2 Cor. iii. 14. See Hävernick, *loc. cit.;* who points out the reference to certain *written* documents which is contained in the expression τῇ ἀναγνώσει; to which is added in explanation, ἡνίκα ἂν ἀναγινώσκηται Μωϋσῆς.—ver. 15. Cf. "And he [Moses] took *the Book* of the Covenant"—Exod. xxiv. 7; "And the Lord said unto Moses, *Write thou* these words: for after the tenor of these words I have made a covenant with thee, and with Israel"—xxxiv. 27; together with the phrase βιβλίον τῆς διαθήκης, 2 Kings, xxiii. 2 (LXX.): see also Ecclus. xxiv. 23; 1 Macc. i. 57.

[2] The idea that this passage forms the parting admonition and rule of action bequeathed by S. Paul to Timothy has been beautifully expressed by S. Chrysostom, who explains the connexion of the words as follows:—The Apostle naturally consoles his disciple, since he was about to impart a great sorrow. If Elisha, who to the last had accompanied his master, rent his garments when he beheld him departing, and the glory of his departure,—what must one so beloved, so loving, have suffered, upon hearing that the life of his instructor was drawing to a close,—a life, too, the last moments of which it was not to be his lot to soothe? Therefore, before he announces his approaching death (2 Tim. iv. 6, 7), S. Paul proceeds to administer consolation: "and this in no ordinary way, but in words adapted to comfort him, and fill him with joy. * * * 'For I am now ready to be offered up,' he says. For this reason he writes: 'All Scripture is given by Inspiration of God, and is profitable,' &c. All what Scripture? All that sacred writing, he means, of which I was speaking. This is said of what he was discoursing of; about which he said, 'From a child thou hast known the Holy Scriptures.' All such, then, 'is given by Inspiration of God;' therefore, he means, do not doubt. * * * Thou hast the Scriptures, he says, in place of me. If thou wouldest learn anything, thou mayest learn it from them. ('Α ν τ' ἐ μ ο ῦ, φ η σ ὶ, τ ὰ ς γ ρ α φ ὰ ς ἔ χ ε ι ς· εἴ τι βούλει μαθεῖν, ἐκεῖθεν δυνήσῃ.) * * * And if he thus wrote to Timothy, who was filled with the Spirit, how much more unto us!"—*Homil.* ix. in 2 Tim., t. xi. p. 715. (Oxf. transl., p. 249.)

[3] Τὰ ἱερὰ γράμματα οἶδας τὰ δυνάμενά σε σοφίσαι εἰς σωτηρίαν διὰ πίστεως τῆς ἐν Χ. 'Ι. Πᾶσα γραφὴ θεόπνευστος καὶ ὠφέλιμος πρὸς διδασκαλίαν, κ. τ. λ.—2 Tim. iii. 15, 16.

[4] Thus Bishop Middleton observes:—"This is one of the texts usually adduced in support of the inspiration of the Jewish Scriptures; but it has been doubted whether the rendering of the English Version be the true one. * * * Mr. Wakefield remarks, that the 'Æthiopic alone of the old Versions does not omit καί, and that the Æthiopic is with him equivalent to all the rest in a difficult or disputed passage.' Notwithstanding this declaration, Mr. W., without assigning any reason, renders in

upon the grammatical or other difficulties,[1] it is manifestly impossible, however we translate the words, that S. Paul could have meant by them anything else than the whole body of the Old Testament writings; since no Jew,—and he was addressing a man of Jewish descent, to whom he had just appealed as being versed in the sacred literature of the nation,—could have attached any other meaning to his language, or could have supposed that, in the expressions here employed, some particular writings only, or certain portions of them, were referred to as the work of the Spirit of God.[2] This passage, indeed, does no more than apply the general principle laid down by S. Peter in each of his Epistles, namely, that the Spirit of Christ "was in the prophets;" and that "holy men of God spake as they were moved by the Holy Ghost."[3]

defiance of the Æthiopic, 'every writing inspired by God *is* useful,' &c. I agree, however, with him in his translation of *πᾶσα γραφή* * * * and I take the assertion to be, 'every writing (viz., of the *ἱερὰ γράμματα* just mentioned) is Divinely inspired, and is useful,' &c. I do not recollect any passage in the New Testament in which two Adjectives, apparently connected by the Copulative, were intended by the Writer to be so unnaturally disjoined."—*Doctrine of the Greek Article*, Rose's ed., p. 391. On the other hand, Dr. Pye Smith translates: "Every writing Divinely inspired [is] also profitable for instruction," &c.—on which one may ask how is the absence of *ἐστί* to be accounted for? "It is evident (continues Dr. Smith) that the Apostle, in ver. 16, resumes distributively what he had before advanced collectively: so that 'every writing Divinely inspired' is a description, by which the Apostle designates *each and every one* of the writings comprised under the well-understood collective denomination *τὰ ἱερὰ γράμματα, the holy writings*."—*The Scripture Testimony to the Messiah*, vol i. note, p. 32. 3rd ed.

[1] Winer ("Grammatik," Abschn. iii. § 17, s. 104), lays down the following *general* Canon respecting the use of the article. "The article stands before a substantive connected with *πᾶς* in the singular, when this adjective describes the totality of the object, and is to be translated 'the whole'—e. g. 'the whole city'—*πᾶσα ἡ πόλις*—S. Matt. viii. 34; xxi. 10." Cf. S. Matt. vi. 29; S. Luke, ii. 1. When, on the other hand *πᾶς* denotes some object out of a multitude, and is to be rendered 'every,' the article is wanting"—cf. *πᾶν δένδρον*—S. Matt. iii. 10; *πᾶσα φάραγξ*—S Luke, iii. 5. This Canon does not, however, apply *to the case of proper names:* e. g. Herod "was troubled and *all Jerusalem* (*πᾶσα Ἱερος.*) with him"—S. Matt. ii. 3; "Let the *whole house of Israel* (*πᾶς οἶκος Ἰσραήλ*) know, &c."—Acts, ii. 36 (cf. *ἐπέβλεψε πᾶς οἶκος Ἰσραήλ*—1 Sam. vii. 2, 3; *ὀπίσω παντὸς οἴκου Ἰούδα*—Neh. iv. 16):—where *οἰκ. Ἰσρ.*, according to the Old Testament usage, and the practice of the LXX. (cf. *χαρμοσυνῶν οἴκου Ἰσραήλ*—Judith, viii. 6): takes the nature of a proper name. So also, in the New Testament, in the words *τὰ πρόβατα τὰ ἀπολωλότα οἴκου Ἰσραήλ*—S. Matt. x. 6, and xv. 24. Now if any term can strictly claim the title of a proper name, from its exclusive application to a single object, assuredly *γραφή* is such.—See *supra*, p. 240, note [3].

[2] Töllner ("Die göttl. Eingebung," s. 228) well observes, that S. Paul must have expected that Timothy would understand the terms which he employed in the same sense which the Jews of his time were accustomed to affix to them. If, on the other hand, dissenting from the well-known doctrine of the Jews as to the inspiration of their sacred books, the Apostle nevertheless made use of expressions which they could only understand in a sense different from that which he desired that his words should convey, he has written so as to confirm an error.

[3] The prophets searched "what manner of time *the Spirit of Christ which was in*

The point of view from which the Apostles thus regarded the Old Testament suggests an immediate answer to the questions, How did they judge of their own writings? and, By what prepossessions on the subject of Inspiration were they influenced? While they plainly announced their belief that the Old Testament is the work of the Holy Ghost, they, with equal distinctness, proclaimed, as a leading doctrine of the Gospel, that in their days spiritual gifts were diffused in a greater measure than in any former age. If, therefore, they regarded the Old Testament as authoritative and infallible, *because* it was "given by Inspiration of God," no less authority and infallibility must they have ascribed to the writings composed by themselves—bountifully endowed, as they were, by the same Divine Spirit. This inference would be legitimate, even if we could not point to any express statement respecting that supernatural assistance which they received as authors of the New Testament. Let us merely conceive that they did not depart from the whole frame of thought which prevailed around them, and we can at once confidently pronounce as to their estimate of those portions which they themselves contributed to the Canon of Scripture. But if their express statements on this subject be taken into account, it is of itself manifest that they who, as Jews, well knew what was the signification of the words "the Spirit of the Lord fell upon me," must have apprehended, in a similar manner, the meaning of the promises of Christ which we are about to consider: and we may safely infer that in every exigency they counted upon, and failed not to receive, a degree of aid and guidance corresponding to that by which the prophets had been directed, and of which the prophets also had had previous assurance. Thus, when Moses had pleaded —"O my Lord, I am not eloquent * * * but I am slow of speech, and of a slow tongue;" "the Lord said unto him, Who hath made man's mouth? * * * have not I, the Lord? Now, therefore, go, and I will be with thy mouth, and teach thee what thou shalt say."[1] And that this promise was not to rest

them did signify;" and again, "The things which are now reported unto you by them that have preached the Gospel unto you *with the Holy Ghost* sent down from heaven." —1 S. Pet. i. 11, 12: see also 2 S. Pet. i. 21.

[1] Exod. iv. 10–12. Cf. "My Spirit that is upon thee, and My words which I have put in thy mouth"—Isai. lix. 21; "The Lord said unto me, Say not I am a child * * * whatsoever I command thee, thou shalt speak. * * * Then the Lord put forth His hand, and touched my mouth. And the Lord said unto me, Be-

here, but that it was to apply to the succession also of prophets after Moses, was again expressly declared by Jehovah Himself: "I will raise them up a Prophet from among their brethren like unto thee, and will put My words in his mouth; and he shall speak unto them all that I shall command him:"[1]—words which, as the context proves, must have related in their *primary* sense to the Prophetic Office in general, although they were *fully* realized only in the Person of Christ.

To the New Testament writers similar assurances were given. We are told that Christ, on four distinct occasions[2] previously to His passion, promised His Disciples the assistance of the Holy Ghost;—the promises of Divine aid which He gave them after His Resurrection being altogether subsidiary to His former statements.[3] The first occasion on which such an assurance was given

hold I have put My words in thy mouth."—Jer. i. 7–9. "I am full of power by the Spirit of the Lord * * * to declare unto Jacob his transgression and to Israel his sin."—Micah, iii. 8.

[1] Deut. xviii. 18. It has often been argued that these words refer *exclusively* to a single individual, and consequently to the Messiah alone. But the context seems decisive against this view. The contrast with the false prophets, which is there instituted, requires us to understand a plurality of individuals opposed to them; while, as nothing in the passage points to a single person endowed with special prophetic gifts,—so everything suggests the application to the collective body of the true prophets of Jehovah. The use of the singular number,—נביא "a Prophet,"—has, indeed, been strongly pressed in opposition to the admissibility of this interpretation: but we have an exact parallel in the use of the singular מלך, "a King"—Deut. xvii. 14–20. The occasion, too, on which Moses employed this form of speech at once accounts for it. His design, in the book of Deuteronomy, is to announce each crisis in the future history of his nation: for it is his duty, as Legislator, to provide for each exigency which is to come. He accordingly declares that, whenever need may require, a true prophet shall appear in Israel. The greater the need, therefore, and the longer the interval during which this promise might remain suspended, the more distinguished must be the fulfilment of the prediction; and in this consideration we see the force of the allusions in the New Testament.—Acts, iii. 22; vii. 37. Even without such allusions, indeed, we might of ourselves discern how Christ alone has fully realized this Theocratic ideal of Prophecy,—He who has accomplished for the human race, what the prophets attempted for a single nation: but still the fact of the *primary* reference of the words remains unaffected. The following conclusions result: (1.) All prophecy, which is not of Hebrew origin, is excluded by the Law (cf. ver. 15—"from the midst of thee, of thy brethren"—מקרבך מאחיך). (2.) Every true prophet must resemble Moses ("like unto me"—כמני): i. e. there can be no opposition between the earlier and later revelation of God: the one being a necessary continuation, and development of the other. (3.) The prophet must receive a special call from Jehovah ("The Lord thy God *will raise up*"—יקים);—herein consists the distinction between the Prophet and the Priest. (4.) By virtue of this special appointment, such a Prophet represents Jehovah to the people:—Jehovah "puts His words in his mouth" (ver. 18); and the prophet speaks "in His name," (ver. 20). And thus, as has been already observed (Lecture iv. p. 156), the Law, without calling forth the full activity of Prophecy, recognised its existence, and announced its privileges. See Hävernick, "Einleit," Th. II. Abth. ii. s. 9 ff.

[2] See C. F. Fritzsche, "De Revelat. notione Biblica," p. 54.

[3] E. g. "Behold I send the promise of My Father upon you," &c.—S. Luke, xxiv. 49. Cf. Acts i. 8.

was when He instructed and sent forth the Twelve, as we read in the tenth chapter of S. Matthew's Gospel ;[1] the second was during that discourse to His disciples which has been preserved in the twelfth chapter of S. Luke ;[2] the third was on the third day of the week in which He suffered, "as He sat upon the Mount of Olives ;"[3] and the fourth promise is contained in the discourse which S. John has recorded in the fourteenth and following chapters of his Gospel. These passages are at once reducible to two classes ; the three former being so similar in their import that they may be considered together, and apart from the fourth.

I. Each of the passages of which the first class consists expresses the same idea :—"When they deliver you up, take no thought how or what ye shall speak ; for it shall be given you in that same hour what ye shall speak : for it is not ye that speak, but the Spirit of your Father which speaketh in you."[4] In such

[1] Ver. 19, 20. See, *infra*, note [4].

[2] "When they bring you unto the synagogues, and unto magistrates, and powers, take ye no thought (*μὴ μεριμνήσητε*): for the Holy Ghost shall teach you in the same hour what ye ought to say."—S. Luke, xii. 11, 12.

[3] S. Mark, xiii. 3; see Wieseler, "Chronol. Synopse der vier Evang.," s. 393. The forms of this promise are as follows: "When they shall lead you, and deliver you up, take no thought beforehand (*μὴ προμεριμνᾶτε*) what ye shall speak, neither do ye premeditate: but whatsoever shall be given you (*ὃ ἐὰν δοθῇ ὑμῖν*) in that hour, that speak ye: for it is not ye that speak, but the Holy Ghost."—S. Mark, xiii. 11. "Settle it therefore in your hearts, not to meditate before (*μὴ προμελετᾷν*) what ye shall answer: for I will give you (Ἐγὼ *γὰρ δώσω ὑμῖν*) a mouth and wisdom, which all your adversaries shall not be able to gainsay or resist."—S. Luke, xxi. 14, 15. Cf. "They were not able to resist the wisdom and the Spirit by which he [S. Stephen] spake."—Acts, vi. 10.

[4] *Ὅταν δὲ παραδιδῶσιν ὑμᾶς, μὴ μεριμνήσητε πῶς ἢ τί λαλήσητε· δοθήσεται γὰρ ὑμῖν ἐν ἐκείνῃ τῇ ὥρᾳ τί λαλήσετε· οὐ γὰρ ὑμεῖς ἐστε οἱ λαλοῦντες, ἀλλὰ τὸ Πνεῦμα τοῦ Πατρὸς ὑμῶν τὸ λαλοῦν ἐν ὑμῖν.*—S. Matt. x. 19, 20. Perrone attempts to evade, as follows, the force of these texts; arguing against the method adopted by Michaelis, of inferring the inspiration of the Books of the New Testament from the inspiration of the Apostles: "Sic, e. g. Matt. x. 19, 20, loquitur Christus *de fortitudine* quam, præsidibus coram positi, discipuli Sui essent patefacturi, atque de sapientia qua sua essent daturi responsa: idem dic de Luc. xii. 11, 12; Marc. xiii. 11; et iterum Luc. xxi. 14, 15."—*loc. cit.* p. 98. It is to be noticed, in addition to what I have already said, p. 239, note [1], that this is precisely the argument by which Le Clerc (next to Spinoza, the chief assailant of Inspiration during the 17th century), has attempted to evade these same texts. Having quoted S John, xvi. 13, and S. Luke, xii. 11,—of which he observes, "Ce sont les deux passages les plus formels, que l'on puisse citer sur cette matière,"—Le Clerc proceeds: "Pour commencer par le dernier, je remarque premièrement, qu'il ne promet point une inspiration perpétuelle, mais seulement en certaines occasions, savoir quand les Apôtres seroient conduits devant les tribunaux des juges."—p. 240. In such situations, he adds: "on reconnoît sans peine qu'ils parlent avec beaucoup de pieté *et de courage*, mais il semble qu' ils ne disent rien qu' on ne puisse bien dire sans inspiration. * * * Au reste, on ne peut pas trouver étrange que par le S. Esprit, ou l' Esprit de Dieu, on entende Esprit de sainteté et de constance que l' Evangile inspire," &c.—*Sentimens de quelques Theolog. de Hollande*, Lettre xi., p. 243, &c.

words Christ plainly declared that they should be guided by a real positive influence from without. A marked distinction is drawn between the result of their own judgment and what the Spirit of God was to effect;—the expression "it is not ye that speak" being placed in strong contrast to the assurance that "the Spirit of their Father should speak *in* them." The three promises which we are now considering embrace, moreover, all the public occasions on which the Apostles could be called upon to defend themselves, whether before councils or synagogues, before governors or kings. In every such case the assurance is to the same effect—"Take no thought beforehand what ye shall speak, neither do ye premeditate; but whatsoever *shall be given to you* in that hour, that speak ye: for it is not ye that speak, but the Holy Ghost:" where the *objective* nature of the Divine influence is denoted by the words "it shall be given you," which are continually employed by the New Testament writers to express this fact. Thus, S. Peter subsequently speaks of "the wisdom *given*" to "our beloved brother Paul;"[1] and S. Paul himself writes: "When James, Cephas, and John perceived the grace that *was given* unto me."[2] The practical signification, indeed, of all such assurances may be briefly illustrated by the words with which a New Testament prophet, Agabus, introduced his prediction: "Thus saith the Holy Ghost."[3]

In connexion with this class of promises, and as the fittest explanation of their design, we must bear in mind the language of Christ to the Eleven shortly before His Ascension—"Go ye, therefore, and make disciples of all nations * * * teaching them to observe all things whatsoever I have commanded you: and lo! I am with you alway, even unto the end of the world."[4] The inference from such words, regarded as the sequel of the former passages, is plain. If any confidence is to be placed in the Gospel narratives, repeated pledges were given from the lips of the Son of God Himself, that *no* occasion should arise during the course of their ministerial labors in which the Holy Ghost should not instruct them "how and what they should say:"—in other words, that in every exercise of their Apostolic office, both

1 *Κατὰ τὴν δοθεῖσαν αὐτῷ σοφίαν.*—2 S. Pet. iii. 15.
2 *Γνόντες τὴν χάριν τὴν δοθεῖσάν μοι.*—Gal. ii. 9.
3 *Τάδε λέγει τὸ Πνεῦμα τὸ Ἅγιον.*—Acts, xxi. 11.
4 S. Matt. xxviii. 19, 20.

the *form* and the *substance* of their statements[1] *should be given them* "in that same hour."[2] We know that this was the interpretation which the Apostles themselves placed upon their Lord's words; and hence S. Paul entreats the Ephesians to pray on his behalf "that utterance might be *given* unto him, that he may open his mouth boldly, to make known the mystery of the Gospel."[3] Such assurances of Christ's continued presence with them in their teaching are most conclusive; for it cannot, surely, be regarded as either just or reasonable to maintain that the Divine influence guarded the Apostles from error when *orally* conveying the Truth to their hearers; but that they were left to all the hazard of human fallibility when instructing by letter their converts in Corinth or Colosse,—when writing to the Twelve Tribes "which are scattered abroad," or to "the strangers scattered throughout Pontus and Bithynia."[4]

As to the actual fulfilment of their Master's promises, the sacred narrative enables us ourselves to form an opinion. It has been observed, by one of the chiefs of modern Rationalism, that, "if we embrace in historic glance the record of the origin of Christianity, from the last evening of the life of Jesus, to the close of the fifty days next following, it is undeniable that, in that short interval, something of a nature encouraging beyond what was ordinary must have taken place, to transform the trembling and irresolute Apostles of that evening into men exalted above all fear of death, who could exclaim before the most embittered judges of the murdered Jesus,—'We must obey God, rather than man.'"[5] This remark is as just as it is confirmatory of our

[1] See *supra*, p. 246, note [4]: πῶς ἢ τί—πῶς indicating the *form*, and τί the *substance* of the statements which they were to make.

[2] It is to be remarked that this phrase occurs in each of the three promises:—ἐν ἐκείνῃ τῇ ὥρᾳ—S. Matt. x. 19, and S. Mark, xiii. 11; ἐν αὐτῇ τῇ ὥρᾳ—S. Luke, xii. 12: see also next note.

[3] Ἵνα μοι δοθῇ λόγος ἐν ἀνοίξει τοῦ στόματός μου, ἐν παῤῥησίᾳ γνωρίσαι, κ. τ. λ.—Eph. vi. 19. Cf. Col. iv. 3; 2 Thess. iii. 1; and "Open Thou my lips," &c.—Ps. li. 15. In opposition to a common error,—viz., that the Apostles were distinguished from the Old Testament prophets, by the fact of being *permanently* endowed with the highest gifts of the Spirit,—it appears both from the tenor of Christ's promises, and from S. Paul's practice, as here, of soliciting the prayers of the Church on his behalf, that Inspiration, in its highest sense, and as it related to the promulgation of the Gospel, was not conferred except on special occasions, and for special purposes. Cf. *supra*, Lecture v. p. 221, note [1].

[4] See *supra*, p. 236, note [1], the remarks of Bishop Warburton on this subject.

[5] Dr. Paulus, "Kommentar," Th. iii. s. 867—quoted by Tholuck "Glaubwürdigkeit der evang. Geschichte," s. 371. Tholuck adds that even Strauss admits this transformation in the character and conduct of the Apostles to be *inexplicable*, unless

present argument. A transformation of the whole nature of the Apostles seems to have followed Christ's Ascension, analogous to that described in the words of Samuel to Saul: "The Spirit of the Lord will come upon thee, and thou shalt be turned into another man."[1] We find these poor fishermen of Galilee, whose whole tone of thought and line of conduct before their Lord's departure had remained so true to the character of "unlearned and ignorant men," changed, on a sudden, into the courageous rivals of the philosophers and rhetoricians of their age. We see them, at first restless from doubts and fettered by prejudice, now immovable in their convictions and alive to each new aspect of the Truth. Formerly timid and wavering, they now are fearless and resolved. Their delusive dream of temporal deliverance becomes a real assurance of eternal Redemption. Their narrow estimate of the Divine covenant with their nation expands, under the guidance of the Holy Ghost, into the sublime conception of "the Israel of God."[2]

That this subjection to the Divine influence was no result of their spontaneous efforts, no effect of their own volition, we can collect from the language of those who were the subjects of that influence, under both the Old and the New Testament. Jeremiah tells us that, because the word of the Lord was daily made a reproach unto him, he had said, "I will not make mention of Him, nor speak any more in His name. But His word was in mine heart as a burning fire shut up in my bones, and I was weary with forbearing, and I could not stay."[3] Such, too, is S.

SOMETHING extraordinary be supposed to have occurred during this interval. The Apologists, he observes, with justice insist upon the fact that—"der ungeheure Umschwung * * * *sich nicht erklären* liesse, wenn nicht in der Zwischenzeit ETWAS ganz ausserordentlich Ermuthigendes vorgefallen wäre."—*Ibid.*

[1] 1 Sam. x. 6.

[2] This idea has been finely expressed by S. Gregory the Great: "Tunc Petrus negavit in terra, cum latro confiteretur in Cruce. * * * Ecce gaudet Petrus in verberibus, qui ante in verbis timebat. Et qui prius ancillæ voce requisitus timuit, post adventum Sancti Spiritus vires principum cæsus premit."—*In Evang. Hom.* xxx. lib. ii., t. i. p. 1580.

[3] Jer. xx. 8, 9. See also the seventh verse, the force of which is lost in the English Version: the marginal reading, however, approaches the true meaning—"O Lord, *thou hast deceived me*, (marg. "enticed") and *I was deceived* (marg. "enticed":) thou art stronger than I, and hast prevailed: I am in derision daily," &c.—where the original conveys a sense still stronger than "enticed;" denoting—"Thou hast put forth Thy powers of persuasion (פתיתני), and I have suffered myself to be persuaded (ואפת)," as Gesenius renders:—"פתה, Niph.—*sibi persuaderi passus est; Pi.—persuasit* alicui (πείθω) Jer. xx. 7." Cf. "Is not My Word like a fire, saith the Lord and like a hammer that breaketh the rock in pieces?"—Jer. xxiii. 29. See also Ps. xxxix. 2, 3.

Paul's express assertion with respect to the urgency of the Divine impulse :—" Though I preach the Gospel, I have nothing to glory of: for necessity is laid upon me ; yea, woe is unto me, if I preach not the Gospel !"[1]

II. Those sayings of our Lord recorded by S. John, which conveyed to the Disciples the second class of promises above referred to, come next under consideration. Here too, as in the other passages which have been already dwelt upon, the gift of the Holy Ghost forms the subject of the assurance : " I will pray the Father, and He shall give you another Comforter, that He may abide with you for ever,—even the Spirit of Truth ;"[2] to which it is subsequently added that their Master's presence was to be supplied in such a sense that His departure would prove a real good : " It is expedient for you that I go away ; for, if I go not away, the Comforter will not come unto you."[3] The Apostles who had followed their Divine Teacher during His sojourn on earth were, no doubt, acquainted with the facts of His life : but there was, as yet, no *object* of Christian Faith, in the true sense of the term, until the Lord had been received into glory, and had triumphed over death and the grave. When He was removed from them, and His words no longer served as their guide, it became indispensable that His Presence should be supplied. The suggestions of the Holy Ghost were then required in order to qualify them for their future labors :—to develop the full signification of the great events of which they had been spectators, and which now lay before them as matters of history ; to give them a just insight into the Divine counsels ; to enable them to insert in their teaching, without interweaving any heterogeneous element, each particular circumstance as it contributed to the elucidation of the general scheme ; to remind them of what had passed, without any distortion of the whole series of facts ; and, in fine, to disclose the future so that they might be able to decide, without error, in all the exigencies which should befall the Church. And this, in point of fact, is what the language of Christ

[1] 1 Cor. ix. 16. Compare the language of Amos, the analogy of whose history to that of S. Paul has been pointed out *supra*, Lecture iv. p. 162 : "Surely the Lord God will do nothing, but He revealeth His secret unto His servants the prophets. The lion hath roared ; who will not fear? The Lord God hath spoken ; who can but prophesy ?"—Amos, iii. 7, 8 ; see also ch. vii. 15.

[2] Τὸ Πνεῦμα τῆς Ἀληθείας.—S. John, xiv. 16, 17.

[3] S. John, xvi. 7.

here amounts to. The Holy Spirit, Who was thenceforward to supply His Personal Presence, is emphatically described as "the Spirit of Truth," by Whose agency the most essential features of the Gospel were to be gradually unveiled : "At that day ye shall know that I am in my Father, and ye in Me, and I in you."[1] The influence of their Divine Guide shall be directed, they are told, to the attainment of two separate ends ;—the additional information to be imparted by the Comforter being contrasted with what the Disciples had already learned from their Lord, while "He spake unto them, being yet present with them." "The Holy Ghost," shall not only "bring all things to their remembrance, whatsoever Christ had said unto them ;" He shall also "*teach* them all things :"—thus not only reproducing the doctrines which they had already heard, but imparting fresh knowledge from the treasures of Divine Truth.[2] For the reception of such spiritual gifts, and for the due performance of their future duties, the Disciples had been qualified by having been companions of their Master during His earthly pilgrimage. "When the Comforter is come, Whom I will send unto you from the Father, even the Spirit of Truth which proceedeth from the Father, He shall testify of Me, and ye also shall bear witness, *because* ye have been with Me from the beginning."[3] Here it is manifestly implied that the Holy Ghost was further to testify of Christ ; and, therefore, that the future knowledge of His followers was not to be confined to what they had heard from Himself ; —an inference which is fully established by the additional statement : "I have yet many things to say unto you, but ye cannot bear them now : howbeit, when He, the Spirit of Truth, is come, He will guide you into all truth. * * * He will show you things to come. * * * He shall take of Mine, and shall show it unto you."[4] In these words the Lord plainly intimated that the guidance of the Spirit was designed to supply the need which the Apostles had of still further instruction. The influence

[1] S. John, xiv. 20.

[2] "These things have I spoken unto you, being yet present with you. But the Comforter, which is the Holy Ghost, whom the Father will send in My name, He shall *teach you* all things, and bring all things to your remembrance whatsoever I have said unto you."—*Ibid.* xiv. 25, 26.

[3] S. John, xv. 26, 27.

[4] *Ibid.* xvi. 12–15. Cf. the remarks of Steudel, "Ueber Inspiration der Apostel und damit Verwandtes," published in the Tübingen Journal for 1832 (Heft ii. s. 128 ff).

of the Holy Ghost was to be exerted, not merely in reproducing with infallible accuracy what they had heard from Christ, or in guarding them from all error in their inferences from the facts of His life, but also in suggesting the knowledge of "the many things" which He had still to say to them, but which they could not then "bear." In fact, our Lord here distinguishes the two elements of the Divine agency to which I have so repeatedly called attention, under the names of Revelation and Inspiration. He separates that exercise of supernatural power which is truly *creative* and derived from the Eternal Word, through the Spirit, and which consists in disclosing new truths,—from that distinct agency of the Spirit Himself whereby "all things are brought to remembrance." It is not said, 'the Spirit shall teach you all things which I have told you;'—such matters He was to recall to their recollection; but He was to unfold those new features of the Gospel scheme which had not, as yet, been communicated to mankind. Of this fact we shall presently examine some striking instances: meanwhile, it may be noticed here, that the extent of this latter assurance completely removes the idea that the spiritual aid which it announced was to be confined to such contingencies as might appear to have been more specially implied in the former group of promises; namely, when they should be brought "unto the synagogues, and unto magistrates, and powers."[1] We can also infer from the language of S. John that the additional instructions of the Holy Ghost were to bear the same stamp of infallibility as those which had been imparted by Christ Himself. On no just or reasonable interpretation does this promise lend the slightest color to the notion that the guidance into truth, and preservation from forgetfulness to which it refers, related merely to the 'leading truths' of the Gospel. The plain inference from such expressions as "all the truth,"[2] and "shall

[1] See *supra*, p. 246, note [2].

[2] I have adopted this rendering of *πᾶσαν τὴν ἀλήθειαν* in S. John, xvi. 13 (where Tischendorf and Lachmann, after Codices A and B, read *τὴν ἀλήθειαν πᾶσαν*), instead of that given in our English Version "*all truth*," chiefly for the purpose of noting that the argument which I have founded on the passage is unaffected by the adoption of either translation. Bishop Middleton, who translates "all the truth," does not speak with perfect certainty, observing: "It is frequently difficult, and even impossible, to ascertain where the Article should be used before abstract Nouns; yet there is not *the same difficulty* when such Nouns are preceded by *πᾶς*."—*loc. cit.* p. 258. In whatever manner the words are to be translated, it is manifest, on the one hand, that our Lord assured His Disciples that they should be divinely guided in every particular which related to the preaching of the Gospel; and, on the other hand, that He did

teach you all things," is simply this, that when the Apostles acted in any way as the official teachers of Christianity, not only was every species of error to be excluded, but new truths also were to be unfolded, as need required.

The character and extent of our Lord's assurance in this passage of itself supplies a complete answer to a modern theory of Inspiration which is founded upon a misconception opposed in the last Discourse.[1] According to this theory, there was no *peculiar* spiritual gift conferred upon the sacred writers :—their pre-eminence over others consisting merely in their greater opportunities of becoming acquainted with the facts of their great Teacher's life ; and in their having received the truths of Christianity as they were enunciated by Himself. The spiritual guidance bestowed upon them was, it is maintained, identical with that in which all Christians, less favorably circumstanced, equally share : its effect, in the case of the Apostles, being nothing more than an opening out, and a developing of certain results from their previous experience, and awakened spiritual life.[2] The

not promise to impart to them supernatural information in every department of human knowledge. To draw such an inference from His words would be to violate the most elementary principles of reasoning; and to take in a universal sense a term which, as the whole tenor of the discourse in which it occurs proves, must be understood in a limited sense, and as denoting solely *Evangelical* Truth. Archdeacon Hare has devoted several pages, as I venture to think very unnecessarily, to a refutation of this exaggerated view of the passage ; and I advert to his remark merely for the purpose of drawing attention to the following statement: "Assuredly the misprision of this passage has aided in fostering the delusive notion that the Bible is a kind of encyclopedia of universal knowledge, and that every expression in it bearing however allusively upon astronomy, or geology, or history, has the same Divine attestation of its infallibility as what it reveals concerning God, and concerning man in his relation to God. * * * This notion has ever been still more injurious to Religion than to Science: for Science soon overleaps and treads down the fences which are thus erected to check it; but as Religion cannot possibly maintain the positions, which she is thus engaged to defend, her failure in this field shakes the confidence in her power even within her own province."—*The Mission of the Comforter*, note B. p. 395.

In this passage the writer appears to me to have fallen into another extreme. I must, however, refer the reader to Lecture viii. *infra*, for some remarks in reply to the general idea thus put forward respecting the fallibility of Scripture when alluding to "astronomy, or geology, or history."

[1] See the remarks on the nature of that Scriptural influence which presided over the composition of the Bible, as distinguished from the ordinary graces of the Holy Ghost to which the name Inspiration has also been assigned,—p. 230, &c.

[2] Such is the theory of Elwert, a follower of Schleiermacher, to whose views I have already referred, Lecture v. p. 221, note [2]; and from whose works Steudel, in the treatise quoted above, p. 251, note [4], adduces the following propositions: "The influence of the Holy Spirit, in the case of the Apostles, was not a suggestion of elaborated ideas, and knowledge; still less a dictation of words: but the Spirit wrought in them Faith, by virtue of which they appropriated the revelation of Christ; and from this revelation, by means of Faith, they developed, in the natural way of reflection, their religious ideas and conceptions. * * * Infallibility is not to be

foregoing remarks, of themselves, afford, as I have just observed, a sufficient refutation of this theory; but it is completely subverted by what the New Testament tells us of the two great preachers of Christianity, S. Peter and S. Paul.[1]

The most superficial glance at the history of S. Peter must render it impossible to maintain that his statement of Christian doctrine on the Day of Pentecost was the mere deduction of his own judgment from his previous knowledge of Christ's life and acts. Should it, however, be regarded as a matter of doubt whether his development of the Christian scheme on that occa-

attributed to them in historical matters of a collateral nature, in unessential points of deduction from their ideas, and of statement of doctrine;—and generally, in anything which when compared with the foundation of Faith (regarded as the spirit of Holy Scripture), appears to be *formal*."—*loc. cit.* s. 109. In the following number of his Journal (s. 3 ff.), Steudel proceeds to examine the statement here made, viz., that in the representation of religious truth by the Apostles error could not find room; adducing Elwert's principle, that "Christian knowledge is based upon a Christian frame of mind." Referring to this principle, Steudel shows how the source of this writer's error consists in his confounding the two significations of which the expression "Christian knowledge" is susceptible. This phrase denotes, (1.) the knowledge, obtained by revelation or by personal experience or historically, of what Christianity imports to be; or (2.) it denotes the *manner* in which Christian Truth (when the *historical* knowledge of it has been *already* conveyed to us), has been appropriated by us, and made our own. In this latter sense our Lord observes: "If any man is willing (ἐάν τις θέλῃ) to do His will *he shall know* (γνώσεται) of the doctrine whether it be of God."—S. John, vii. 17. Now when Christ again tells the Apostles, "*I have yet many things to say unto you*, but ye cannot bear them now. Howbeit when He, the Spirit of Truth, is come, *He shall guide you into all truth*,"—He, assuredly, cannot have meant that the *knowledge* to be thus acquired was of the same nature as that resulting from the mode of appropriating Divine Truth of which He had formerly spoken: He must clearly have intended to intimate those new disclosures by the Holy Ghost, which, like His own teaching, could subsequently be brought home to the hearts of believers. S. Paul points out the distinction between these two senses—"*Knowledge* (γνῶσις [i. e. a mere acquaintance with the facts of Christianity] puffeth up, but *charity* edifieth."—1 Cor. viii. 1: in other words, the link that unites both kinds of knowledge, and stamps the former as genuinely Christian, is "love;" or, as S. John declares, "he that loveth not, *knoweth* not (οὐκ ἔγνω) God."—1 S. John, iv. 8. Cf. the language of Eph. i. 17, 18, with the grounds of "ignorance" assigned in ch. iv. 18. From the necessity of the Spirit's influence to evoke in the souls of all Christians,—whether writers of Scripture, or members of the Church at large—the state of feeling here described, the school of Schleiermacher has strangely inferred that no other species of Spiritual influence was required in order originally to communicate "historical Christianity" to the Apostles. Who, for example, can imagine that when S. Paul speaks of "the knowledge of Jesus Christ," and "counts all things but loss" in comparison with "knowing Him, and the power of His resurrection;"—Phil. iii. 8–10—who, I say, can imagine that the Apostle was not already in possession of the whole Gospel scheme? It surely cannot be inferred from the Apostle's fervent prayer for a more *personal* appropriation of the great truths which he had preached, that he had hitherto been but imperfectly acquainted with those truths themselves; or that his knowledge of them could have been intermingled with error. See *supra*, Lecture iv. p. 143, note [2].

[1] Thus passages such as Acts, iv. 8; xiii. 9; clearly imply a *special* illapse of Spiritual influence, distinct from any sense in which Inspiration, as bestowed upon Christians in general, can be understood. Cf. *supra*, Lecture v. p. 221, note [1].

sion were really a direct result from the inward suggestions of the Holy Ghost, such doubt must disappear when the subsequent narrative is considered. Were we ignorant, indeed, of the events which followed, it might have appeared inconceivable that the principle laid down by the Apostle in this his first address after the descent of the Holy Ghost,—"The promise is unto you, and to your children, *and* to all that are afar off, even as many as the Lord our God shall call,"[1] could have left behind any scruple as to the reception of the Gentiles into the Church of Christ. The account, nevertheless, of the ecstatic Vision in the tanner's house at Joppa proves that S. Peter quite misapprehended the bearing of these words. No one can assert for a moment that the knowledge which he derived from that Vision was the result of his previous Christian experience. He expressly states that it was a completely new disclosure, which he could not have elicited of himself, but which God unfolded to his view, in opposition to his former prejudices;[2]—a fact which clearly indicates that, when need required, the Holy Ghost poured new light upon certain of the Apostles' own statements which had not previously been illuminated, even for themselves.[3] We further learn from the sacred historian that even this revelation did not remove all occasion of doubt.[4] It settled, it is true, the controversy as to the reception of the Gentiles into the Church: but the question of discipline still remained open; and this difficulty was only solved after protracted discussion,[5] and by the renewed guidance of the

[1] Καὶ πᾶσιν τοῖς εἰς μακράν.—Acts, ii. 39.

[2] S. Peter said to the company at the house of Cornelius: "Ye know that it is an unlawful thing for a man that is a Jew to keep company, or come unto one of another nation; but *God hath showed me* that I should not call any man common or unclean."—Acts, x. 28; cf. ver. 14, 15. See Steudel, *loc. cit.* s. 7. It may be well to observe, that S. Peter in this memorable discourse conveys in six verses (ver. 36–41) an epitome of the Gospel of S. Mark. In ver. 36, 37, is defined the point of time from which the Synoptical Gospels date the opening of Christ's ministry: ver. 38 details His Unction by the Holy Spirit from which that ministry and its miraculous course proceeded: ver. 39 indicates the events in which the Evangelists were called to bear witness: ver. 40, 41, comprise the Lord's Crucifixion, Resurrection, and how He appeared to the disciples, together with His eating and drinking with them "after He rose from the dead." Cf. Thiersch, "Versuch zur Herstell," s. 111.

[3] See *supra*, Lecture v. p. 202, note [1].

[4] "And certain men which came down from Judea taught the brethren, and said, Except ye be circumcised after the manner of Moses, ye cannot be saved."—Acts, xv. 1, &c.

[5] "And the Apostles and elders came together for to consider of this matter And when there had been much disputing (συζητήσεως), Peter rose up and said," &c.—ver. 6, 7.

Holy Ghost.[1] Thus we see how very gradually the whole truth burst upon the Apostles. Not even S. Peter's Vision displayed it on all its sides; and hence, even of ourselves, we can discern how truly Christ could say of the revelations to be subsequently given, "Ye cannot bear them now."

Fresh light is cast upon the nature of the Spirit's agency in the case of the Apostles by the statements of S. Paul, in his Epistle to the Galatians. In that Epistle he pointedly and repeatedly declares, and, as one might almost say, goes out of his way to insist upon the fact, that never, during many years of his labors as a preacher of the Gospel, had his intimacy with the other Apostles been such as that from it his knowledge of Christian doctrine could, in anywise, be explained.[2] As he dwells, with emphasis, on the additional circumstance that, in his final interview with the chief pillars of the Church, he had proved his perfect agreement with them in doctrine, and that those great Apostles had made no new disclosures to him,[3] it must have been his own peculiar acquirements which caused them to acknowledge him as a person qualified above others for laboring among the Gentiles, and to entrust to him "the Gospel of the uncircumcision." Without a special revelation, the knowledge which S. Paul thus claims for himself could only have been obtained from the most intimate converse with the other Disciples of Christ; we are compelled, therefore, to admit, in the absence of any such converse, that the effect of the Divine influence was far different from that of merely casting new light upon particulars of which he had been previously aware. Had the promised aid of the Holy Ghost been merely designed to unfold the sense of what Christ had taught while on earth;—did the Inspiration of the Apostles, in short, merely consist in

[1] "It seemed good to the Holy Ghost, and to us (Ἔδοξε γὰρ τῷ Πνεύματι τῷ Ἁγίῳ καὶ ἡμῖν)."—ver. 28. See *infra*, p. 268, note [2].

[2] "I certify you, brethren, that the Gospel which was preached of me is not after man: for I neither received it of man, neither was I taught it, but by the revelation of Jesus Christ. * * * When it pleased God * * * to reveal His Son in me * * * immediately I conferred not with flesh and blood: neither went I up to Jerusalem to them which were Apostles before me: but I went into Arabia. * * * Then after three years I went up to Jerusalem to see Peter, and abode with him fifteen days. But other of the Apostles saw I none, save James the Lord's brother. * * * Then, fourteen years after, I went up again to Jerusalem. * * * And when James, Cephas, and John, who seemed to be pillars, perceived the grace *that was given* unto me (τὴν χάριν τὴν δοθεῖσάν μοι)," &c.—Gal. i. and ii.

[3] Ἐμοὶ γὰρ οἱ δοκοῦντες οὐδὲν προσανέθεντο.—Gal. ii. 6.

the fact of the Divine Spirit kindling a *new life* in their souls by which a greater degree of clearness was diffused over their former ideas ;—how can we account for S. Paul's disclaimer of all the human means which alone could have enabled him to acquire any accurate knowledge of our Lord's teaching ? We can only explain this passage in his Epistle, therefore, by admitting that the Apostle had received a direct revelation from Christ, imparting to him new truths, and giving him a more comprehensive insight into the doctrines of Christianity.

S. Paul's express statement to this effect is illustrated, in an interesting manner, by the fact that although he was the bearer of the inspired decree of the Council of Jerusalem to the Churches,[1] —which decree, be it observed, related to the very question discussed in his Epistle to the Galatians,—he never alludes to this decision of the Council ; nor does he, in any part of his writings, appeal to its authority.[2] Of the historical facts made known to S. Paul by immediate revelation, and which enabled him to dispense with the ordinary sources of information, I need only mention the Institution of the Eucharist ; the knowledge of which he expressly tells us he had "received of the Lord."[3]

The facts, to which attention has been drawn in these latter remarks, afford examples of how the promise was accomplished that the "Comforter" was to *teach* the Apostles *all things.* Christ's additional assurance, that all things were to be brought to their *remembrance*, was no less accurately fulfilled. This circumstance the sacred writers expressly take notice of, and intimate by the established formula—*ἐμνήσθησαν*. Thus S. John, having related the question of the Jews, "What sign showest Thou unto us?" and our Lord's reply, "Destroy this Temple, and in three days I will raise it up,"—goes on to explain, "But He spake of the Temple of His Body: when, therefore, He was

[1] Acts, xv. 25.

[2] Thiersch ("Versuch zur Herstell.," s. 81), on the other hand, considers this fact to be merely a proof that the Epistle of the "Council of Jerusalem" was not regarded as conveying permanent commands, or as a sacred document. To which I would answer, that the opposite conclusion seems established by the manner in which "James and all the elders" subsequently appealed to this same Epistle: "As touching the Gentiles which believe, *we have written* (or rather "*enjoined by letter*," *ἐπεστείλαμεν*), and concluded," &c.—Acts, xxi. 25. Cf. *infra*, p. 268, note [2].

[3] "I have received of the Lord, that which also I delivered unto you; that the Lord Jesus, the same night in which He was betrayed," &c.—1 Cor. xi. 23. Cf. ch. xv. 3, &c.

risen from the dead, His Disciples *remembered* that He had said this unto them."[1] Again, as the same Evangelist observes more fully:—"These things understood not His Disciples at the first: but when Jesus was glorified, then *remembered* they that these things were written of Him, and that they had done these things unto Him."[2] Or, to quote a still more apposite example: in the account of another inspired historian we read that S. Peter, when describing to those "that were of the circumcision" the descent of the Holy Ghost in the house of Cornelius, takes occasion to observe,—"Then *remembered* I the word of the Lord, how that He said, John indeed baptized with water, but ye shall be baptized with the Holy Ghost."[3]

It has been already noted, when referring to the accounts transmitted to us in the Synoptical Gospels of the promises of Divine guidance which Christ gave to His disciples, that we are ourselves able to form an opinion as to the manner in which those promises have been fulfilled. The same remark may also be made as to the accomplishment of the assurance recorded by S. John. How aptly each speech or saying, recorded by the different sacred writers, corresponds to the speaker's exact position; how the language of Christ soars above the range of human expression, and is, in all the Gospels, stamped with a unity and a sublimity peculiarly its own;—how, on the other hand, the various traits of individual character are preserved in the case of each personage whose history or words are introduced by the Evangelists, or in the Acts of the Apostles;[4]—all such topics have been often and forcibly dwelt upon. To take a single instance; how completely does that precious fragment of one of our Lord's dis-

[1] S. John, ii. 18–22. Cf. ver. 17, where Ps. lxix. 9 is quoted, with the remark—"His Disciples remembered (ἐμνήσθησαν) that it was written," &c.

[2] S. John, xii. 16. Cf. S. Luke, xxiv. 8.

[3] Acts, xi. 16. See the remark of Tholuck on S. John, ii. 17: "Wie sie bei solchen Anführungen durch die überraschende Ueberstimmung der Sache geleitet wurden, zeigt die Formel ἐμνήσθησαν."—*Comm. zum Ev. Johan.*, s. 87.

[4] A competent judge has observed of the Acts of the Apostles: "It deserves particularly to be remarked that S. Luke has well supported the character of each person, whom he has introduced as delivering a public harangue, and has very faithfully and happily preserved the manner of speaking which was peculiar to each of his orators." J. D. Michaelis, *Introduction to the New Testament* (Marsh's transl., vol. iii. part i. p. 332). Take, as a single example, the often quoted fact by which the Epistle of the Church, Acts, xv. 23–29, is shown to have been the composition of S. James; viz. the occurrence in its superscription of the term χαίρειν which is found in the superscription of the Epistle of S. James, but in none other of the New Testament Epistles.

courses, commencing with the words "Come unto Me all ye that labor and are heavy laden," and which S. Matthew alone of the Evangelists has preserved,[1]—bring before us the whole genius and spirit of those sayings of Christ which are recorded in the narrative of 'the Apostle of Love!' For those, indeed, who question the inspiration of the sacred writers it becomes a duty to explain how men uneducated and unrefined, writing, too, without mutual concert, and harassed as well by internal controversy as by external persecution, could ever have painted such a Character[2] as that of Christ, or how could they have preserved its peculiar features untinged by any colors reflected from their own.[3] Or

[1] S. Matt. xi. 28–30. Cf. also the statement of ver. 27, and of S. Luke, x. 22, with the doctrine which is developed in the opening verses of S. John's Gospel. Numerous instances of this same unity of character may be adduced. Compare, for example, as follows: S. John, xii. 25, 26, with S. Matt. x. 38, 39; S. John, iv. 44, with S. Matt. xiii. 57; S. John, xiii. 20, with S. Matt. x. 40; S. John, xv. 20, with S. Matt. x. 24, &c., &c. Not less remarkable is the agreement of the Evangelists in their narratives of events. E. g. The betrayal of S. Peter; the anointing of Christ's feet (cf. especially S. John, xii. 7, 8, with S. Matt. xxvi. 11, 12); the conduct of Pilate, &c. See Tholuck's "Glaubwürd. der evang. Gesch.," s. 324 ff.; and Gieseler "Die Entsteh. der schriftl. Evang.," s. 137. Hug points out that any apparent difference in the features of our Lord's character, as drawn by S. John and by the other Evangelists, has arisen solely from the different nature of the subjects of their respective Gospels: S. John chiefly referring to Christ's ministry and discourses in Judea among the learned of His nation, to whom it was necessary to expound His high origin, and His future destiny; the Synoptists, on the other hand, confining themselves, in great measure, to a narrative of the events in Galilee, and of our Lord's addresses to the people at large. See his "Einleit." Th. II. § 57, s. 184.

[2] It has been well remarked that no single expression of a trivial character, or which does not convey the most profound truth, has been ascribed to our Lord in the Gospels. Compare, on the other hand, the few sayings attributed to him and preserved by Tradition, which Mr. Jones has collected in his work on the Canon, vol. i. p. 408, &c. The Character of our Lord, as it stands forth in the New Testament narrative, in its unity and its sublimity, is unique in history. Are we to believe, asks Quinet ("Revue des deux Mondes," 1838, p. 495), that the strange mixture of races, Hebrews, Greeks, Syrians, Egyptians, Romans, the Grammarians of Alexandria, and the Scribes of Jerusalem,—the worshippers of Jehovah, of Mithras, and of Serapis,—have all combined, notwithstanding their diverse origin, creeds, institutions, and manners, in inventing, with one spirit, the same ideal? So far, indeed, were the peasants of Palestine from having the capacity to develop this ideal, that we find the great majority of Christ's Parables end with the allegation that His doctrine was too sublime for the people to comprehend.

[3] The truth of this assertion has been denied by Strauss, who alleges that S. John not only makes our Lord speak (e. g. ch. iii. 16–21) in "that metaphysical strain" peculiar to the Evangelist himself; but also S. John the Baptist, "that unmystical Old Testament Prophet" (i. 15–18: iii. 27–36): on which facts Strauss especially insists, terming them, "das Hauptmoment in dieser Sache." In reply Tholuck (*loc. cit.* s. 330 ff.) justly asks, on what ground does Strauss assume that the passage S. John, iii. 16, &c., is anything else than the Evangelist's own inspired comment on his Master's words? It is true that S. John does not mark the transition from ver. 15 to ver. 16; but this is an ordinary feature of his style. Thus, in ch. i. 16–18, the words are assuredly *not* those of the Baptist;—ver. 16 ("Of His fulness have all we received, and grace for grace"), being obviously a continuation of the words πλήρης χάριτος καὶ ἀληθείας in ver. 14, and ver. 15 being inserted parenthetically in order to strengthen

when, in the New Testament history, we find details of events, of discourses, of parables—the significance of which often depends upon the force of a single term—all repeated, after the lapse of so many years, with every internal mark of truthfulness and accuracy,—for example, the discourses preserved in the Gospel of S. John,—our opponents may again be fairly asked, what unassisted human memory could have achieved such a task as this? But here, also, as in the case of the accomplishment of the other promises already referred to, we can summon to our aid a witness whose testimony is unexceptionable; whose testimony, moreover, shows how weighty an argument the fact now before us supplies.

One of the services which Strauss has unconsciously rendered to the Christian cause is the clear light in which he has exhibited the alternatives between which we have to choose. This writer has devoted a considerable portion of his elaborate treatise to a discussion of two classes of opinions which are logical 'opposites;' and between which he considers the opposition to be that technically termed 'contrariety:'—in other words, he considers both opinions to be false.[1] The one class of opinions is that of the Rationalists; the other, that of the Supernaturalists—as Strauss

the Evangelist's statement; for we are to remember that S. John had been the Baptist's disciple. Of this mode of writing, ver. 7 affords another example. As to ch. iii. 27–36: (1.) The form of the passage ver. 31–36, is in obvious contrast with the Baptist's usual mode of expression; and at once leads to the conclusion that the Evangelist himself is the speaker. (2.) This conclusion is supported by the analogy of S. John's style, of which some instances have been just exhibited. (3.) In ver. 26 the Baptist states of Christ—"all men come to Him;" while at ver. 32, the Evangelist, speaking of a different period, alleges that "no man receiveth his testimony:" cf. ch. xii. 37. (4.) If we examine the words which S. John actually *does* ascribe to the Baptist,—viz. ch. i. 19–36, and ch. iii. 27–30—we shall perceive that they either are identical with his language as given in the other Gospels, or contain no more than what is perfectly explicable as proceeding from one who filled the character of an Old Testament Prophet. Mr. Westcott observes: "Though no one will deny that S. John was led by his natural peculiarities to dwell chiefly on a certain form of our Lord's teaching, and to employ a singular phraseology in setting forth its import, yet he nowhere attributes the key-words of his system to others: our Saviour still speaks in his Gospel as the 'Son of God,' or the 'Son of Man,' and not as the 'Word,' or 'God.'"—*Elements of Gosp. Harm.*, p. 68. As to S. John, iii. 10–21, Mr. Westcott, like Tholuck, points out that ver. 16 is a parenthesis suggested by the last words of ver. 15, and ver. 18–21, a similar commentary on ver. 17.—*Ibid.* note.

[1] In the Preface to the first German edition of the "Life of Jesus," Strauss writes: "The exegesis of the ancient Church set out from the double presupposition; first, that the Gospels contained a history, and secondly, that this history was a supernatural one. Rationalism rejected the latter of these presuppositions, but only to cling the more tenaciously to the former, maintaining that these books present unadulterated, though only natural, history. Science cannot rest satisfied with this half measure: the other presupposition also must be relinquished."—Chapman's transl. vol. i. p. x. London, 1846.

terms those who maintain the possibility and the fact of a Divine Revelation. Parallel with his series of assaults upon each particular of the Gospel narrative, Strauss combats separately each of these opinions. The Rationalist—to borrow Strauss's own description—"firmly maintains the historical truth of the Gospel narratives, and he aims to weave them into one consecutive, chronologically arranged, detail of facts; but he explains away every trace of immediate Divine agency, and denies all supernatural intervention."[1] Accepting as perfectly conclusive this writer's refutation of Rationalism,[2] there remain but two systems

[1] *Ibid.* p. 19. Eichhorn and the other Rationalists, continues Strauss, considered "the miraculous in the sacred history as a drapery which needs only to be drawn aside, in order to disclose the pure historic form."—p. 21. Of Rationalism in general, and its source, Quinet pointedly observes: "Ce système conservait fidèlement, comme on le voit, le corps entier de la tradition; il n' en supprimait que l' âme. C'était l' application de la théologie de Spinosa dans le sens le plus borné, à la manière de ceux qui ne voient dans sa métaphysique que l' apothéose de la matière brute."—*loc. cit.* p. 469.

[2] Referring to the efforts of the rationalistic school, and especially of Paulus, Strauss observes: "With regard to this account of the angelic apparition [S. Luke, i. 26] given by Paulus —and the other explanations are either of essentially similar character, or are so manifestly untenable as not to need refutation,—it may be observed that the object so laboriously striven after is not attained. Paulus fails to free the narrative of the marvellous. * * * Paulus has in fact substituted a miracle of chance for a miracle of God. Should it be said, that to God nothing is impossible, or to chance nothing is impossible, both explanations are equally precarious and unscientific. * * * The natural explanation makes too light of the incredibly accurate fulfilment of a prediction originating, as it supposes, in an unnatural, over-excited state of mind. In no other province of inquiry would the realization of a prediction which owed its birth to a vision be found credible, even by the Rationalist. * * * Is biblical history to be judged by one set of laws, and profane history by another?—an assumption which the Rationalist is compelled to make, if he admits as credible in the Gospels that which he rejects as unworthy of credit in every other history:—which is, in fact, to fall back on the supranaturalistic point of view; since the assumption, that the natural laws which govern in every other province are not applicable to sacred history, is the very essential of supranaturalism." Part I. ch. i. § 18 (*loc. cit.* vol. i. p. 110, &c.) Again: "The narrative of the cure of the blind man at Bethsaida, and that of the cure of 'a man that was deaf and had an impediment in his speech,' which are both peculiar to Mark (viii. 22, &c.; vii. 32, &c.), are the especial favorites of all rationalistic commentators. If, they exclaim, in the other evangelical narratives of cures, the accessory circumstances by which the facts might be explained were but preserved as they are here, we could prove historically that Jesus did not heal by His mere word, and profound investigators might discover the natural means by which His cures were effected. [Strauss adds in a note, "These are nearly the words of Paulus, 'Exeg. Hand-buch,' ii. s. 312, 391."] * * * The complacency of the rationalistic commentators in these narratives of Mark, is liable to be disturbed by the frigid observation, that, here also, the circumstances which are requisite to render the natural explanation possible are not given by the evangelists themselves, but are interpolated by the said commentators. For in both cases Mark furnishes the saliva only; the efficacious powder is infused by Paulus and Venturini: it is they alone who make the introduction of the fingers into the ears first a medical examination, and then an operation; and it is they alone who, contrary to the signification of language, explain the words, *ἐπιτιθέναι τὰς χεῖρας ἐπὶ τοὺς ὀφθαλμούς*, 'to lay the hands upon the eyes,' as implying a surgical operation on those organs"—Part II. ch. ix. § 95. (*loc. cit.* vol. ii. p. 293, &c.)

which are, logically speaking, 'contradictory' one to the other; that is, one of which must be false, and the other true: namely, the system of Strauss himself—according to which the Gospel history is a fable,—and that which he justly describes as "the doctrine of the Church." In this point of view, therefore, I adduce Strauss as a witness in support of that argument for Inspiration from which this digression has started. When laying down "criteria by which to distinguish the *unhistorical*[1] in the Gospel narrative," Strauss gives as his *negative* criterion—"That the matter related by an Evangelist could not have taken place in the manner described, when the narration is irreconcilable with the known and universal laws which govern the course of events." Of this dogma he gives the following illustration: "By the same rule it is contrary to all the laws belonging to the human faculty of memory that long discourses, such as those of Jesus given in the fourth Gospel, could have been faithfully recollected and reproduced."[2] All must admit that evidence more unexceptionable as to the fact here stated cannot be adduced; and I build upon it a conclusion which is, as I have observed, the logical 'contradictory' of that of Strauss.

We come next to consider the manner in which the sacred writers express themselves as to the result of the Divine influence by which, as we have seen, they had been so distinctly assured that their words and acts were to be guided. The passages of Scripture which bear upon this branch of the subject may be reduced to two classes. The first class illustrates the harmony which is assumed to subsist between the Divine and the human intelligence; and affords a striking confirmation of the views respecting Inspiration which have been advocated in these Discourses. The second class of passages exhibits the manner in

[1] This is the usual euphemism employed in modern times as a substitute for the more honest adjective—*false*. E. g. Neander writes: "Matthew (iii. 7) *states expressly* that 'many Pharisees and Sadducees came to John's baptism;' and the form of the statement distinguishes these from the ordinary throng. It seems somewhat *unhistorical* that these sects, so opposite to each other, should be named together here. * * * It does not follow, however, that the mention of the Pharisees is in the same predicament: on the contrary, the *historical* citation of the latter, may have given rise to the *unhistorical* mention of the Sadducees."—*Life of Christ*, § 36. (Bohn's transl., p. 51.) Having noticed Neander's assertion, Mr. Westcott acutely points out that in S. Matthew's Gospel alone is the Baptist "particularly described as addressing the several bodies of the Jewish Church;" and observes: "S Matthew gives the relation of each *religious* party of the Jews to Christianity, as S. Luke of each *social* class."—*loc. cit.* p. 97.

[2] *Loc. cit.* § 16, vol. i. p. 89.

which inspired men claim infallible authority for their own words and writings.

I. In the first place, the texts already quoted, and especially those from S. John's Gospel, imply that a Presence of the Lord, by His Spirit, was to abide with his chosen witnesses. In such statements, it is also implied, that there was to be no contrast between the Divine and human principles of life ;—no such contrast, I mean, as subsists (to borrow the language of philosophy) between *object* and *subject :* nor was there to be, on the other hand, a merely 'mechanical,' or a merely ideal intermixture of the two principles ; but a vital 'dynamical' combination, or interpenetration of the human spirit and the Divine. It is to be inferred, therefore, that the effect produced in every such case by the Holy Spirit's influence was a completely harmonious blending of the human and the Divine intelligence ; and that the result of this combination—whether we speak of the Old or of the New Testament—was that distinct energy which has received the name of Inspiration. This fact is clearly exemplified by the manner in which the words of the Old Testament are quoted, and are, at times, attributed to their Divine and their human author, indifferently.[1] For example : Christ, having prefaced His quotation from one of the Psalms[2] with the words, "David himself said by the Holy Ghost," immediately adds : "David, therefore, himself calleth Him Lord, and whence is He then his son ?" Again : S. Matthew writes that Christ on one occasion quoted the Fourth Commandment with the remark, "For God commanded, saying ;"[3] while in the parallel narrative of S. Mark we read : "For Moses said, Honor thy father and thy mother."[4]

[1] See *supra*, p. 239, note [3]. A striking example is supplied by Christ's quotation: "Have ye not read that He, which made them (*ὁ ποιήσας*) at the beginning, made them male and female ; *and said* (*καὶ εἶπεν*), For this cause," &c.—S. Matt. xix. 4, 5, —where *καὶ εἶπεν* must be referred to *ὁ ποιήσας*: while we know from Gen. ii. 24 that Adam was the speaker. The inference is obvious: God, by His Spirit, was the source from which the sentiment proceeded.

[2] Ps. cx., quoted in S. Mark, xii. 36—*Αὐτὸς Δαυὶδ εἶπεν ἐν τῷ Πν. τῷ Ἁγ.* In proof of the assertion that "the Spirit of God and of His Logos spoke in the authors of the Psalms," Sack observes, that "David's own testimony respecting his call to speak through the Spirit of the Lord ['The Spirit of the Lord spake by me, and His Word was in my tongue], 2 Sam. xxiii. 1, 2, is as clear as it is important ; with which agrees Christ's recognition of David having spoken 'in Spirit' (S. Matt. xxii. 43) : and the Apostle Peter's recognition of his being a Prophet in the fullest sense of the word (Acts, ii. 30)."—*Apologetik*, s. 280.

[3] S. Matt. xv. 4 ; or as Tischendorf and Lachmann read, *Ὁ γὰρ Θεὸς εἶπεν.*

[4] S. Mark, vii. 10—*Μωϋσῆς γὰρ εἶπεν.* So also, in S. Luke's account, (xx. 37),

Once more; S. Paul applied to the Jews at Rome the language of Prophecy—"Well spake the Holy Ghost by Esaias the prophet:" the same passage being cited by S. John under the simple form, "These things said Esaias."[1] And this class of illustrations, founded on the manner of quoting the Old Testament, may be summed up by the usage, so striking in the Epistle to the Hebrews,[2] according to which each of the three divisions of the former Scriptures—"the Law, the Prophets, and the Psalms"—is, in express terms, adduced as the language of the Holy Ghost. The Old Testament writings, therefore, with reference to their inward principle, are described as "given by Inspiration of God;" their language being regarded as the language of the Holy Ghost: and thus the Evangelist can say, "All this was done, that it might be fulfilled which was spoken of the Lord by the Prophet."[3]

From all such passages it is clear, that no artificial line of distinction is to be drawn between the human and the Divine

our Lord quotes Exod. iii. 6, with the words "Moses showed at the bush, when he calleth the Lord the God of Abraham," &c.; while in S. Matthew (xxii. 31) the form of citation, "Have ye not read that which was spoken unto you by God," is given as being equivalent.

[1] Τὸ Πνεῦμα τὸ Ἅγιον ἐλάλησεν διὰ Ἡσαΐου—Acts, xxviii. 25. Ταῦτα εἶπεν Ἡσαΐας—S. John, xii. 41; cf. ver. 38. Origen, commenting on the quotation from the Psalms by S. Peter, Acts, i. 16 (τὴν γραφὴν ἣν προεῖπεν τὸ Πν. τὸ Ἅγιον διὰ στόματος Δαυΐδ), profoundly observes: προσωποποιεῖ τὸ Πνεῦμα τὸ Ἅγιον ἐν τοῖς προφήταις. καὶ ἐὰν προσωποποιήσῃ τὸν Θεὸν οὐκ ἔστιν ὁ Θεὸς ὁ λαλῶν, ἀλλὰ τὸ Πν. τὸ Ἅγ. ἐκ προσώπου τοῦ Θεοῦ λαλεῖ· καὶ ἐὰν προσωποποιήσῃ τὸν Χριστὸν, οὐκ ἔστιν ὁ Χριστὸς ὁ λαλῶν, ἀλλὰ τὸ Πν. τὸ Ἅγ. ἐκ προσώπου τοῦ Χριστοῦ λαλεῖ. οὕτω κἂν προσωποποιήσῃ τὸν προφήτην, ἢ τὸν λαὸν ἐκεῖνον, ἢ τὸν λαὸν τοῦτον, ἢ ὅτι δήποτε προσωποποιεῖ, τὸ Ἅγιον Πνεῦμα ἐστὶ τὸ πάντα προσωποποιοῦν. *Homil. in Act. Apost.* t. iv. p. 457.

[2] (1.) The references to the description given by Moses of the Holy of Holies, and of the rites connected with the Temple-ceremonial, are followed by an exposition introduced with the words, "The Holy Ghost this signifying."—Heb. ix. 8. (2.) The words of Jeremiah are applied with the remark, "The Holy Ghost also is a witness to us."—ch. x. 15. (3.) The elaborate argument founded on Ps. xcv. commences thus: "Wherefore (as the Holy Ghost saith), To-day if ye will hear His voice."—ch. iii. 7. "In this remarkable Epistle, God or the Holy Ghost is constantly named as the speaker in the passages which are adduced from the Old Testament; and this not only in regard to those which are accompanied in the Old Testament by the expression, 'God said,' but also to those in which some man speaks,—for instance, David, as author of a Psalm. Herein is clearly exhibited the view of the author in relation to the Old Testament and the writers of it. He considered that God was, by His Holy Spirit, the living agent and speaker in them all: so that, consequently, the Holy Scriptures were to him purely a work of God, although brought forward by men."—Olshausen, *The Genuineness of the N. T. Writings.* (Clarke's For. Theol. Lib, p. cxxv.)

[3] Τὸ ῥηθὲν ὑπὸ Κυρίου διὰ τοῦ προφήτου—S. Matt. i. 22; ii. 15; where ὑπό denotes that the Lord Himself was the source of what had been foretold; and διά, in contrast with ὑπό, points out the Prophet as the instrument, merely, by which the Divine will had been announced.

elements of Scripture ; while the Old Testament itself presents Revelation to our view as it is incorporated with the realities of human life by means of Divine instruction and Divine acts. The language and the conduct of men, therefore, become the channels whereby God communicates His will ; presenting, in some cases, a certain opposition to that will : while in others we find perfect submission to the training and the guidance of Heaven. This relation of mankind to the Divine Revelation the Old Testament exhibits, not only under the form of external events, but also by means of dramatic pictures of the inward life of the soul ;—as in the book of Job, and in the Psalms, where we look, as it were, into the very hearts of our fellow-men : where the Omnipotence of Deity is displayed, not in mastering the phenomena of nature, or controlling the course of history ; but where the strife takes place in the world within, and presents to the gaze of all time the different aspects of human life in conflict with the Spirit of God.[1] Hence the profound remark of S. Athanasius, that the Psalms present to each of us a mirror wherein we can see reflected the emotions of our souls.[2] These inspired pictures of the inward life of man are to be distinguished from what is more properly styled Revelation, partly by the express statements of the sacred writers themselves, partly by the manner in which, on

[1] "The more closely we connect ourselves with them [the Psalms], the more will God cease to be to us a shadowy form, which can neither hear, nor help, nor judge us, and to which we can present no supplication."—Hengstenberg, *Comm. on the Psalms*, App. vii. (Clarke's For. Theol. Lib., vol. iii. p. liv.) "What is there necessary for man to know," writes Hooker, "which the Psalms are not able to teach? * * * Heroical magnanimity, exquisite justice, grave moderation, exact wisdom, repentance unfeigned, unwearied patience, the mysteries of God, the sufferings of Christ, the terrors of wrath, the comforts of grace, the works of Providence over this world, and the promised joys of that world which is to come; all good necessary to be either known, or done, or had, this one celestial fountain yieldeth."—*Eccl. Polity*, B. v. c. 37, vol. ii. p. 159. Keble's ed. Nor is this the language of "mere theologians" alone:—"David's life and history, as written for us in those Psalms of his, I consider to be the truest emblem ever given of a man's moral progress and warfare here below. All earnest souls will ever discern in it the faithful struggle of an earnest human soul toward what is good and best. Struggle often baffled, sore baffled, down as into entire wreck; yet a struggle never ended; ever, with tears, repentance, true unconquerable purpose, begun anew. Poor human nature! Is not a man's walking, in truth, always that: 'a succession of falls?' Man can do no other. In this wild element of a Life, he has to struggle onwards; now fallen, deep abased; and ever with tears, repentance, with bleeding heart, he has to rise again, struggle again still onwards."—*Hero Worship*, by Thomas Carlyle, p. 75.

[2] *Καί μοι δοκεῖ τῷ ψάλλοντι γενέσθαι τούτους, ὥσπερ ἔσοπτρον εἰς τὸ κατανοεῖν καὶ αὐτὸν ἐν αὐτοῖς τὰ τῆς ψυχῆς αὐτοῦ κινήματα * * * καὶ ὅλως οὕτως ἕκαστος ψαλμὸς παρὰ τοῦ Πνεύματος εἴρηται καὶ συντέτακται, ὡς ἐν αὐτοῖς, καθὰ πρότερον εἴρηται, τὰ κινήματα τῆς ψυχῆς ἡμῶν κατανοεῖσθαι.*—*Epist. ad Marcellin.*, t. i. p. 988.

the one hand, the beams of Divine truth penetrate the physiognomy, as it were, of human life ; while, on the other hand (as in the book of Job, where God's Revelation has recognised the great enigma of humanity,[1]) the outlines of that human physiognomy are still retained : the master-hand of the Spirit preserving for our instruction all the features of the portrait ; supplying the lover of truth with an infallible key to human knowledge and experience ; and the most experienced with new pictures of human life, in exhaustless variety.[2]

Turning, in the next place, to the New Testament, this same fact of the harmony of the Divine and the human intelligence is equally clear, although deducible from premises somewhat different. "Ye are *witnesses* of these things," said Christ ; "and behold I send the promise of My Father upon you."[3] Such was the pledge given to the Apostles ; and S. Peter subsequently asserts its fulfilment, in words which supply the strongest proof, perhaps, which the New Testament affords of the point now under consideration :—"We are His witnesses of these things, and so is also the Holy Ghost."[4] By thus conjoining the Holy Ghost as a Witness with themselves, they claim and assert the accomplishment of the promise already quoted ;—"The Comforter whom I will send unto you from the Father * * * shall testify of Me, and ye also shall bear witness ;"[5]—a pledge to which S. Peter again alludes where he speaks of himself and the other Apostles as men who "preached the Gospel with the Holy

[1] To quote again the language of Mr. Carlyle: "Biblical critics seem agreed that our own Book of Job was written in that region of the world. I call that, apart from all theories about it, one of the grandest things ever written with pen. One feels, indeed, as if it were not Hebrew; such a noble universality, different from noble patriotism or sectarianism, reigns in it. A noble Book; all men's Book! It is our first, oldest statement of the never-ending Problem,—man's destiny, and God's ways with him here in this earth. And all in such free flowing outlines; grand in its sincerity, in its simplicity; in its epic melody, and repose of reconcilement. There is the seeing eye, the mildly understanding heart. So *true*, every way; true eyesight and vision for all things; material things no less than spiritual: the Horse,—'hast thou clothed his neck with *thunder?*'—he '*laughs* at the shaking of the spear!' Such living likenesses were never since drawn. Sublime sorrow, sublime reconciliation; oldest choral melody as of the heart of mankind;—so soft and great;—as the summer midnight, as the world with its seas and stars! There is nothing written, I think, in the Bible, or out of it, of equal literary merit."—*Ibid.* p. 78.

[2] Cf. Beck, "Propäd. Entwicklung," s. 250.

[3] *Ὑμεῖς μάρτυρες τούτων. Καὶ ἰδοὺ, Ἐγὼ ἐξαποστέλλω τὴν ἐπαγγελίαν τοῦ Πατρός μου ἐφ' ὑμᾶς.*—S. Luke, xxiv. 48, 49.

[4] *Καὶ ἡμεῖς ἐσμεν μάρτυρες τῶν ῥημάτων τούτων καὶ τὸ Πνεῦμα τὸ Ἅγιον.*—Acts, v. 32.

[5] *Ἐκεῖνος μαρτυρήσει περὶ Ἐμοῦ· καὶ ὑμεῖς δὲ μαρτυρεῖτε.*—S. John, xv. 26, 27.

Ghost sent down from heaven."[1] The New Testament writers, in short, express themselves so as to convey the notion that the Holy Ghost AND the Disciples—in other words, the Holy Ghost by their agency—bore testimony to the Gospel, and made provision for the future fortunes of the Church.[2] The fact moreover, which all such expressions imply, affords a further illustration of an important characteristic of the theory which I advocate: for such statements disclose to us the principle, that God, when bestowing the guidance of the Holy Spirit upon the Apostles, still employed those *natural*[3] means whereby their testimony should acquire the utmost credibility which *uninspired* human testimony could claim. Hence it is that the preaching of the Apostles is invariably represented, throughout the entire New Testament, as a *testimony*, and that peculiar importance is attached to the fact of their having been eye-witnesses of the events of Christ's life. This is a point equally insisted upon in the first discourse after Pentecost,[4] and in the last revelation of the New Testament.[5] Such was the qualification required on the part of the successor to Judas;[6] and such was the proof of his Apostleship to which S. Paul himself appealed.[7] Now, bearing this circum-

[1] 1 S. Peter, i. 12. Cf. also 2 Cor. iii. 8, where their ministry is termed ἡ διακονία τοῦ Πνεύματος.

[2] "Now the Spirit speaketh expressly (Τὸ δὲ Πνεῦμα ῥητῶς λέγει) that in the latter times some shall depart from the faith," &c.—1 Tim. iv. 1. On these words Wiesinger observes: "The expression ῥητῶς, as also the whole tenor of the passage, teaches us that the Apostle appeals to predictions of the Spirit lying before him;" and these Wiesinger considers to have been our Lord's prophecy in S. Matt. xxiv. 11, 24, or S. Paul's own words in 2 Thess. ii. 3, &c., in allusion to Dan. vii. 25; viii. 23; xi. 30. Cf. 1 S. John, ii. 18; 2 S. Pet. iii. 3; S. Jude, 18. Olshausen, on the other hand, considers that S. Paul appeals to a prediction uttered by the prophets of that period,—referring in support of this view to Acts, xi. 28 (Agabus); xiii. 1, 2 ("Now there were in the Church that was at Antioch *certain prophets*. * * * And as they ministered to the Lord and fasted, the Holy Ghost said," &c.); xx. 23 ("The Holy Ghost witnesseth in every city, saying (λέγον) that bonds," &c.); xxi. 11 (Agabus again prophesies: "Thus saith the Holy Ghost," &c).—*Comm.* B. v. s. 469. But why not adopt the simple explanation that S. Paul refers to a revelation which he had himself received?

[3] See *supra*, Lecture iv. p. 147.

[4] Οὗ πάντες ἡμεῖς ἐσμεν μάρτυρες.—Acts, ii. 32. Cf. ch. iii. 15; x. 39; 1 S. John, i. 1–3; 2 S. Pet. i. 16–18.

[5] "Who *bare record* (ἐμαρτύρησεν) of the Word of God, and of the *testimony* (τὴν μαρτυρίαν) of Jesus Christ, and of all things that *he saw* (ὅσα εἶδεν)."—Rev. i. 2; see Lecture iv. p. 163, note [2].

[6] Acts, i. 21, 22.

[7] "Am I not an Apostle, am I not free, *have I not seen* (ἑώρακα) Jesus Christ our Lord."—1 Cor. ix. 1. Sack appears to me to transgress the limits of warrantable speculation in his application of this principle. Having truly observed, "dass der Mangel unmittelbarer Augen- und-Ohrenzeugenschaft an sich nicht von der Inspiration ausschliesst"—he goes on to say: "Auf der anderen Seite *ist es auch klar*,

stance in mind, if we combine the words of S. Peter, "We are His witnesses, and so is also the Holy Ghost," with the suggestive statement of S. James, by which he prefaced the decision of the Council of Jerusalem, "It seemed good to the Holy Ghost AND to US"[1]—our conclusion is still further strengthened. The words "and to us," can never be taken to represent the Apostles as *separated* from the influence of the Spirit: and whether we understand the passage to mean "it seemed good to the Holy Ghost working *in* us;" or, rather, as signifying the employment, by the Spirit, of the *personal* agency of the Apostles, and that His Divine Testimony was conjoined with their human testimony, —we equally see the fact expressed of the harmonious combination of the Divine and the human intelligence. The language, in a word, is that of men who are moved by the Divine impulse; but who do not lay aside their own intellectual individuality, which is made use of by the Supreme Intelligence, in order to shed a human coloring over the truths which He imparts.[2]

dass Mangel an Befähigung, das Thatsächliche zu wissen und zu schreiben, entschieden ausschliesst."—*Apologetik*, s. 421.

[1] Ἔδοξεν γὰρ τῷ Πνεύματι τῷ Ἁγίῳ καὶ ἡμῖν—Acts, xv. 28; "which style," observes Hooker, "they did not use as matching themselves in power with the Holy Ghost, but as testifying the Holy Ghost to be the Author, and themselves but only utterers of that decree."—*Eccl. Pol*, B iii. c. x., vol. i. p. 385.

[2] The unhesitating submission of the *whole* Christian community to this decree of the Council of Jerusalem—which in fact abrogated the literal signification of the Law,—was the clearest proof that the Church could have given of its belief in the inspired authority of the Apostles, and in the justice of the claim, here advanced by them, of combining in their decision their own conclusion with that suggested by the Holy Ghost. A very different interpretation has been given by Bishop Burnet, when arguing that this passage affords no support to the authority claimed for General Councils: "The Apostles here, *receiving no inspiration to direct them in this case*, but observing well what S. Peter put them in mind of, concerning God's sending him by a special vision to preach to the Gentiles, * * * they upon this did by *their judgment* conclude from thence, that what God had done in the particular instance of Cornelius was now to be extended to all the Gentiles. So by this we see that those words 'seemed good to the Holy Ghost' relate to the case of Cornelius; and those words 'seemed good to us' import that *they* [i. e. by their own uninspired judgment] resolved to extend that to be a general rule to all the Gentiles."—*On the XXXIX. Articles*, Art. xxi. The acute writer seems, however, not to have observed that such an interpretation of the passage overturns the conclusion which he sought to build upon it. If the Apostles, assembled in Council at Jerusalem, had "received no inspiration to direct them,"—an assertion which the mere nature of the question they were discussing proves to be wholly gratuitous; if, indeed, this were not a case *per se*, and the Apostles differed in no respect from the members of any future Council in the matter of immediate supernatural aid, then, assuredly, such future Councils must have a perfect right to claim authority equal to that of any other which was similarly without "inspiration to direct" it. Any Council at the present day may, therefore, according to Bishop Burnet's hypothesis, similarly preface its decrees by the formula, "It seemed good to the Holy Ghost and to us"—in whatever sense these words are to be taken, and may fairly demand the same deference for its Canons, as Scripture

II. The second class of passages above referred to, in which inspired men claim infallible authority for their own words and writings, may now be briefly examined. We have just seen how the human testimony of the Apostles was exalted into Divine Testimony by the co-operation of the Spirit of God. The effect of this influence upon their minds cannot be more forcibly illustrated than by the confident tone in which all their statements are advanced. No honest and merely human historian has ever dared to write thus. When recording the minute facts of his history, the greater his honesty the less willing is he to express himself with too great assurance. The writers of Scripture, on the other hand, never admit the possibility of their assertions being erroneous. I need only mention the Preface to S. Luke's Gospel. Although "many had taken in hand" to record the facts of the Life of Christ, this Evangelist takes up his pen to represent them with "unerring accuracy."[1] Modestly though the sacred penmen judged of themselves on other occasions, they never drop the slightest hint that aught which could be regarded as the effect of their former prejudices adheres to their teaching.[2] Nay, if the doctrine imparted by them is assailed in any of its aspects, they reject such opposition with the utmost energy as something perverse, and wholly untenable. This feature of their writings we can trace in the language of S. Paul and S. Peter, of S. James and S. John.[3] S. Paul even pronounces the most fearful malediction upon all who advance doctrines contrary to his own: "Though an angel from heaven preach any other Gospel unto you than that which we have preached unto you, let him be accursed."[4] They neither intimate, as I have already shown, that this infallible doctrine had been derived from previous principles by their own reasoning powers, nor do they ever pride themselves

implies that the Church was bound to pay to the decision of the "uninspired" members of the Council of Jerusalem.

[1] Ἀσφάλεια.—S. Luke, i. 4. Cf. *supra*, Lecture ii. p. 56, note [1].

[2] The argument, derived from the silence of the sacred writers on this head, becomes much stronger when we remember that, as has been proved in the last Discourse (see *supra*, p. 221, &c.), they were perfectly conscious that infallibility did not attach itself to their conduct on those occasions when they did *not* act under the immediate influence of Inspiration.

[3] Cf. Col. ii.; 2 S. Pet. ii.; S. James, ii.; 2 S. John, 9, &c. See Steudel's "Zeitschrift," for 1832. H. iii. s. 13.

[4] Παρ' ὃ εὐηγγελισάμεθα ὑμῖν, ἀνάθεμα ἔστω.—Gal. i. 8. Cf. too, the tone of command so constantly assumed: e. g. "Them that are such we command and exhort by our Lord Jesus Christ," &c.—2 Thess. iii. 12.

upon their disinterested devotion to the service of the Gospel. They refer all to the illuminating influence of God. "Unto me," writes S. Paul, "who am less than the least of all saints, is this grace given, that I should preach among the Gentiles the unsearchable riches of Christ."[1] The obligation under which all men are placed of accepting with entire submission the doctrines thus preached, the sacred writers infer from the fact that their labors had been accompanied by such miracles as attest the authority of an Apostle.[2] This authority, moreover, the New Testament defines as being equal to that of the Prophets: "You are built," declares S. Paul, "upon the foundation of the Apostles and Prophets;"[3] and S. Peter admonishes the Church to be "mindful of the words which were spoken before by the holy Prophets, and of the commandment of us the Apostles of the Lord and Saviour."[4] And when we bear in mind the manner in which the different authors of the New Testament refer to the Prophets, and how they declare the old Testament to have been "given by Inspiration of God;" we cannot escape from the conclusion that they claim for their own teaching the same Divine guidance which they, on all occasions, attribute to those "men of God, who spake as they were moved by the Holy Ghost."

It has been objected, indeed, that the promises of Christ had relation merely to the oral teaching of the Apostles, not to their *written* compositions.[5] Not to insist again upon the obvious remark already made, that if the guidance of the Holy Spirit was needed to direct them when teaching their contemporaries or pleading their cause before rulers, *à fortiori* was similar guidance necessary when they were about to bequeath instruction to every future age;—not to repeat, I say, such an observation, the sacred penmen themselves expressly claim the same authority whether

[1] Eph. iii. 8.

[2] Rom. xv. 19; 2 Cor. xii. 12; Heb. ii. 4.

[3] Eph. ii. 20. The Apostles, observes S. Chrysostom on this passage, are placed first in order, although last in point of time: S. Paul hereby declaring—*ὅτι θεμέλιός εἰσι καὶ οὗτοι καὶ ἐκεῖνοι, καὶ μία οἰκοδομὴ τὸ πᾶν, καὶ ῥίζα μία.*—*Homil.* vi. *in Ep. ad Eph.*, t. xi. p. 39.

[4] 2 S. Pet. iii. 2. Cf. S. Jude, 17, 18.

[5] Mr. Morell seems to consider—no doubt consistently with his general views—that neither the oral nor the written teaching of the Apostles can be regarded as inspired: "We cannot infer that they [the Books of the New Testament] are verbally inspired, any more than were the oral teachings of the Apostles. We cannot infer that they had any greater authority attached to them than the general authority which was attached to the apostolic office."—*Philosophy of Religion*, p. 182. See *supra*, Lecture iv. p. 143, note [2].

they refer to their written or to their oral teaching. S. John declares of his Gospel, "These *are written*, that ye might believe that Jesus is the Christ, the Son of God; and that, believing, ye might have life through His name."[1] S. Paul admonishes the Thessalonians to "stand fast, and hold the traditions which they had been taught, whether by word, *or our Epistle*."[2] Nor are we to imagine that the influence of the Holy Spirit extended merely to the *contents* of the Apostles' writings, suggesting the doctrines which they were to teach, and the facts which they were to record:—we find the same Divine guidance claimed for the *language* also which they employ.[3] The passage selected as the text of this Discourse of itself establishes this fact: "Which things we speak, not in the *words* which man's wisdom teacheth, but which the Holy Ghost teacheth."[4] And to the same effect, S. Paul again thanks God that the Thessalonians received the word of God which they had heard from him, "not as the word of men, but as it is in truth, the word of God."[5]

[1] *Ταῦτα δὲ γέγραπται.*—S. John, xx. 31.

[2] *Εἴτε διὰ λόγου εἴτε δι' ἐπιστολῆς ἡμῶν.*—2 Thess. ii. 15.

[3] Dr. Henderson urges the following curious objection against views of this nature: "A fourth argument against the notion of an entirely literal inspiration of the sacred Scriptures, is its tendency to sink the authority of faithful translations, by depriving them of all claim to that quality."—*Divine Inspiration*, p. 433.

[4] 1 Cor. ii. 13. *Ἃ καὶ λαλοῦμεν οὐκ ἐν διδακτοῖς ἀνθρωπίνης σοφίας λόγοις ἀλλ' ἐν διδακτοῖς Πνεύματος.* If *any* objective truth is to be ascribed to these words, we can entertain but one opinion as to the source and character of the language of Scripture.

[5] 1 Thess. ii. 13. In the neglect of this great truth—viz., that the genuine idea of "the word of God" is not only to be found in the Bible, but that it is the very condition of its existence as Holy Scripture,—consists the grand defect of many modern theories on the subject of Inspiration. That Scripture is "the word of God" to man, conveyed, it is true, at different periods, and with different degrees of clearness—but ever acomplishing the end for which it was designed—was the foundation of the creed of the early Church. Hence the language of the inspired writers has been profoundly termed by Origen, *ἐργατικὸν ῥῆμα*. To this effect he observes: *τι χρὴ νοεῖν περὶ τῶν προφητῶν, ἢ ὅτι πᾶν ῥῆμα λαληθὲν διὰ στόματος αὐτῶν ἐργατικὸν ἦν; καὶ οὐ θαυμαστὸν εἰ πᾶν ῥῆμα τὸ λαλούμενον ὑπὸ τῶν προφητῶν εἰργάζετο ἔργον τὸ πρέπον ῥήματι. ἀλλὰ γὰρ οἶμαι ὅτι καὶ πᾶν θαυμάσιον γράμμα τὸ γεγραμμένον ἐν τοῖς λογίοις τοῦ Θεοῦ ἐργάζεται. καὶ οὐκ ἔστιν ἰῶτα ἕν, ἢ μία κεραία γεγραμμένη ἐν τῇ γραφῇ, ἥτις τοις ἐπισταμένοις χρῆσθαι τῇ δυνάμει τῶν γραμμάτων, οὐκ ἐργάζεται τὸ ἑαυτῆς ἔργον.*—*Homil.* xxxix. *in Jerem.*, t. iii. p. 286. Cf. Rudelbach, "Die Lehre von der Insp." 1840. H. i. s. 7. "'The only-begotten Son, which is in the bosom of the Father, He hath revealed Him.' It is as a Personal Being, therefore, communicating with us through those functions of soul and body, which He has vouchsafed to share with ourselves, that the Eternal Word discovers Himself. But so far as the knowledge which He communicates is clothed in earthly words, it is as capable of being conveyed to those to whom it comes in books, as it was to those to whom it addressed itself through their hearing. Therefore were men who 'had perfect understanding of all things from the very first' moved 'to write in order,' that subsequent generations might 'know the certainty of those things wherein' they had 'been instructed.' Thus did it please Him, who made Himself visible only to the men of

I cannot close this branch of the subject without adverting to the objection usually urged against all arguments such as I have just advanced. If, indeed, the nature of those arguments be kept in view—founded as they are upon the whole tenor of Scripture, and the express statements of the sacred writers—it must surely appear antecedently improbable in the highest degree, that any difficulty, suggested by the language of the inspired penmen themselves, can be either real or valid. The objection, however, to which I allude is founded upon a passage in the New Testament; and it furnishes the ordinary burden of all popular reasoning against any strict view of Inspiration.[1] In the seventh chapter of the first Epistle to the Corinthians, S. Paul writes at the tenth verse: "Unto the married I command, yet not I, but the Lord"[2]—words in which he obviously places his own injunction on a perfect equality with that "of the Lord," and which, therefore, merely supply another proof of his inspired authority in addition to the kindred passages already considered. So far, it is plain, no objection arises. But the Apostle, continuing his subject, shortly afterwards adds, "To the rest speak I, not the Lord;" observing further, with reference to a third class, "I have no commandment of the Lord, yet I give my judgment:"[3]—by which language he is supposed to intimate that, in certain parts

one generation, to 'pour out doctrine as prophecy, and leave it to all ages for ever.'"—Wilberforce, *On the Incarnation*, p. 476.

[1] Thus Perrone writes, in continuation of the passage already cited (p. 239, note [1]): "Quamvis porro videantur apostoli privilegium de quo est sermo sibi tribuere, alibi tamen, si insistas literæ, videntur sibi denegare, ut 1 Cor. vii. 12, 40; xiv. 37, 38 (?), quæ reipsa loca, *una cum pluribus aliis*, nobis objiciuntur a rationalistis ad excludendam divinorum Bibliorum inspirationem." See also Spinoza, "Tract. Theol. Polit., cap. xi.

[2] It must be carefully noted here, that the difficulty which this chapter has suggested to many, does not commence at ver. 6 ("I speak this *by permission*, and not of commandment—*τοῦτο δὲ λέγω κατὰ συγγνώμην, οὐ κατ' ἐπιταγήν*."), as the ambiguity of the English word "permission" by which *συγγνώμη* is rendered, might lead us at first to suppose:—but where *συγγνώμη*, which does not occur elsewhere in the New Testament, can only mean, (1) *forgiveness*; (2) *indulgence*. As Olshausen observes, *συγγνώμη* differs from *γνώμη* (ver. 25) only so far as the "judgment" of the Apostle comprises the additional notion of *a concession*; cf. Vulg., "Secundum indulgentiam." The meaning, then, of ver. 6 is, "But this I say by way of allowance (for you), not by way of command,"—"this" (*τοῦτο*) referring to the whole recommendation given in ver. 5; or, perhaps, as Olshausen thinks, to the preceding verses also. This is proved beyond a question by ver. 7—"For I would that all men were even as I myself," &c. The recommendation, therefore. of ver. 5 is given not "*as a command* in all cases, but *as an allowance* to those to whom he [S. Paul] was writing, whom he knew and assumes to be thus tempted."—Alford, *in loc.* The difficulty first arises at the passage commencing with ver. 10.

[3] Verses 12 and 25

of Scripture, the author may write according to his own uninspired human judgment, although guided in other portions of his work by the Holy Ghost.[1] Such an inference, however, is altogether at variance with S. Paul's design, whose words in this place can only be distorted into the form of an argument against Inspiration by utterly overlooking his object and his meaning. The first of the three expressions which have been quoted, "I command, yet not I, but the Lord,"[2] obviously refers to the reinstitution by Christ (as S. Mark has recorded the circumstance) of the original Law of Marriage, and relates to an ordinance *revealed* from the very first, and obligatory on every occasion, and in every age; while by the two latter passages[3]—on which the

[1] This opinion is sometimes held by persons who love and reverence the Bible, but who conceive that they are required, by the Apostle's language here, to relax their views as to Inspiration. Such persons are surely not aware of the extent of their admission; and in order to show what this opinion really amounts to, I would refer to the unanswerable remark of a writer who denies altogether the authority and truth of Scripture, and which I have already quoted in connexion with a similar admission as to the fallibility of the Apostles:—see the words of Mr. Greg, quoted in Lecture iv. at the close of the note, p. 180.

[2] In this place (ver. 10) S. Paul "is about to give them a command, resting, not merely on *inspired Apostolic authority*, great and undoubted as that was, but on that of THE LORD HIMSELF, so that all supposed distinction between the Apostle's own writing *of himself*, and *of the Lord*, is quite irrelevant."—Alford, *in loc.* The Lord's *command*, to which the Apostle refers, had been already given ("And if a woman shall put away her husband, and be married to another, she committeth adultery," S. Mark, x. 12—in which place only is *the woman's* part brought out).

[3] In ver. 12 ("But to the rest speak I, not the Lord"—Τοῖς δὲ λοιποῖς λέγω ἐγώ, οὐχ ὁ Κύριος) S. Paul for the first time states the result of his own inspired judgment: "I," i. e. "I, Paul, in my own apostolic office, under the authority of the Holy Spirit—'not the Lord,' i. e. *not Christ*, by any direct command spoken by Him; it was a question with which Christ *did not deal*, in His recorded discourses." Again, in ver. 25, ("Now concerning virgins I have no commandment of the Lord—ἐπιταγὴν Κυρίου οὐκ ἔχω—yet I give my judgment (γνώμην), as one that hath obtained mercy of the Lord to be faithful—ὑπὸ Κυρίου πιστὸς εἶναι.") there is no contrast between ὁ Κύριος and ἐγώ; the emphasis is on ἐπιταγήν—" '*command* of the Lord have I none,' i. e. no *expressed* precept." See Mr. Alford's judicious summary. In ver. 25, πιστὸς εἶναι can only mean, says Olshausen: "be worthy of belief, i. e. of confidence. To this there is a reference altogether peculiar, in the mention of his γνώμη. He was, however, worthy of confidence because he had the Spirit of God, which determines all relations correctly, a fact referred to in ver. 40."—*in loc.* B. iv. s. 615. In a word, S. Paul does not distinguish between *his own* commands, and those received by an immediate revelation from Christ, but between *his own* commands, and those which Christ had given when on earth, and which were now *historical.* To *such* injunctions of the Lord, S. Paul more than once refers in this Epistle. Alluding to the provision of Christ for the ministers of the Gospel (S. Matt. x. 10), he writes: "Even so *hath the Lord ordained* (διέταξεν)"—ix. 14; and again: "I praise you brethren, that you keep the ordinances (παραδόσεις—*traditions*, as the margin renders) as I delivered (παρέδωκα) them to you"—xi. 2: cf. ver. 23.

Even rationalistic commentators have been compelled to arrive at this conclusion. Thus De Wette observes: "Hitherto the Apostle has spoken from his own judgment *illuminated by the Holy Ghost* (v. 40); so also in what follows (vv. 12, 25, 40); but here (v. 10) he appeals to an expression of the Lord (Mark, x. 12). The distinction

argument against Inspiration rests—S. Paul, as the context clearly proves, merely intends to convey, that Christ had not *directly* provided for those particular cases in which His Apostle now pronounces his *inspired* and authoritative opinion.

In the former of these passages, the very nature of the question respecting which the Apostle issues his directions, namely, "If any brother hath a wife that believeth not,"—an exceptional case which arose from the state of society then existing, and which could not be of frequent recurrence in after times,—of itself explains why our Lord had not Himself promulgated an express law respecting it. Here, as in other matters of discipline, the Holy Ghost was to guide the Apostles into "all the truth;" and the decisions at which they arrived are therefore equally binding with those of Christ Himself, in every case to which those decisions can apply. This, indeed, is clear from S. Paul's own words when summing up the question: "So ordain I in all churches."[1] And accordingly he is so far from representing his "judgment," delivered in the various aspects of the temporary exigency which he discusses in this chapter, as a mere human and fallible opinion, that he closes his remarks by the apparently uncalled-for assertion, "I think also that I have the Spirit of God."[2]

is not that which subsists between human and Divine Truth, but between immediate revelation and that which has been appropriated and recalled to mind by the assistance of the Spirit—since the Spirit takes from Christ that which He teaches (John, xvi. 14): thus can even the commands of the Apostle be regarded as the commands of Christ (xiv. 37)." And Meyer writes with reference to the contrast between *ἐγώ* and ὁ Κύριος (ver. 10): "As to his *ἐγώ*, the Apostle was conscious that his individuality was under the influence of the Holy Ghost.—ver. 40. He *therefore* distinguishes here and vv. 12, 25 not between *his own* and *inspired* commands, but between those which proceeded *from his own inspired* (theopneusten) *subjectivity*, and those which *Christ Himself maintained by His objective word.*"

[1] Ver. 17—*εἰ μὴ ἑκάστῳ ὡς ἐμέρισεν ὁ* Κύριος, *ἕκαστον ὡς κέκληκεν ὁ Θεός, οὕτως περιπατείτω καὶ οὕτως ἐν ταῖς ἐκκλησίαις πάσαις διατάσσομαι*:—where *διατάσσομαι* in the middle has the force of "to make a decree." Mr. Alford thus accurately points out the connexion with the previous verses: "*εἰ μή* takes an exception, by way of caution, to the foregoing motive for not remaining together (ver. 16). The Christian partner might carry that motive *too far*, and be tempted by it *to break* the connexion *on his own part:* a course already prohibited (vv. 12–14). Therefore the Apostle adds, 'But (i. e. only be careful not to make this a ground for *yourselves* causing the separation) as to each (*ἑκάστῳ ὡς*=*ὡς ἑκάστ.*) the Lord has distributed his lot, as (i. e. *ἡ κλήσει*, ver. 20) God has called each, so (in that state, without change) let him walk.' And so ordain I," &c.

[2] Ver. 40—*δοκῶ δὲ κἀγὼ* Πνεῦμα *Θεοῦ ἔχειν*. Observe, too, that in ch. ii. 16, S. Paul similarly declares: "But we have the mind of Christ." As might be expected, objectors urge the use of *δοκῶ*, in this verse, as a proof that the Apostle felt no *certainty* as to his having spoken under the guidance of the Spirit: in which sense, also, Baur considers the words, "When James, Cephas, and John, *who seemed to* be pillars

If we turn, in the next place, to the other passage on which the objector relies,—"Now concerning virgins I have no commandment of the Lord: yet I give my judgment, as one that hath obtained mercy of the Lord to be faithful"—we again perceive an allusion to the fact that Christ, when laying down His commands, had made no provision for this special exigency. Under such circumstances, therefore, an exercise of apostolic authority was again required: and consequently S. Paul proceeds here also to pronounce his "judgment," introducing his decision with the words: "I suppose (or rather consider), therefore, that this is good *for the present distress.*"

On the whole, then, we observe that three questions are here discussed by the Apostle. The first relates to the Law of Marriage, where both husband and wife were believers: and in this instance, having pointed out that it had been decided once for all by Christ, S. Paul contents himself with simply repeating that decision. The second question has also reference to the marriage state, in cases where one of the parties had not as yet embraced the Christian faith; the third, on the other hand, being "concerning virgins:" and in these latter questions it is expressly pointed out, although the rules laid down did not *directly* pro-

(*οἱ δοκοῦντες στῦλοι εἶναι*)"—Gal. ii. 9, to import "zweideutige ironische Seitenblicke" of S. Paul against the Twelve. Ebrard ("Krit. der evang. Gesch.," s. 702) justly observes that any Lexicon might have taught him that *οἱ δοκοῦντες* means 'those who *are* held in repute (by others),' not 'those who would fain be so esteemed.' For the classical usage, cf. "*οἱ δοκοῦντες εἶναί τι, men who are held* to be something, men *of repute*, Plat. Gorg. 472. A; so *οἱ δοκοῦντες* alone, Eur. Hec. 295."—Lidd. and Scott. As to the usage of *δοκέω* by the Greek Fathers, one of the greatest of patristic scholars observes: "Alia vox est, in qua item Latine transferenda non pauci interpretes labuntur, scil. *δοκεῖν, videri; δοκεῖ, videtur:* quod verbum vulgo usurpatur ad minuendam adfirmationem; ita ut si, verbi causa, de quopiam dicatur *δοκεῖ εἶναι σοφός, videtur esse sapiens*, id ut asseveranter dictum non habeatur, sed dubitationem quamdam præferat. Verum frequentissime apud scriptores bene multos *δοκεῖ nihil minuit adfirmationem;* ut e. g. in his Commentariis, ad Ps. cxviii. p. 729, de Deo dicitur *δικαιότατος εἶναι δοκεῖ*, ubi vertendum sine dubio, *justissimus est.* Innumera proferri possunt cum ex Eusebio, tum ex aliis Scriptoribus exempla. Sic apud Athanasium, *ἵνα τοίνυν καὶ ὧν ἐπιθυμεῖς τετυχηκέναι δοκοίης, ut igitur optata consequaris.*"—Montfaucon, Prælim. in *Euseb. Comm. in Psal.*, c. x. 2. Such a sense is frequent in the New Testament. E. g. "I think (*δοκῶ*) that God hath set forth us the Apostles," &c.—1 Cor. iv. 9. Cf. "From him that hath not, *even that he hath* (*ὃ ἔχει*) shall be taken away from him"—S. Luke, xix. 26 (see S. Matt. xiii. 12), with the parallel words, in the same Gospel, "even that which *he seemeth to have*" (*ὃ δοκεῖ ἔχειν*)—viii. 18. So, also, 1 Cor. xi. 16; Heb. iv. i.

In considering the passage before us we are also to remember that the Apostle was writing to men who would gladly have shaken off his authority, and who continually sought "a proof of Christ speaking in him" (2 Cor. xiii. 3); to whom, moreover, in ch. xii. he adduced the two great proofs of his being God's agent—viz., the working of miracles, and the receiving of revelations.

ceed from Christ, yet that they are prescribed by one who "had the Spirit of God." And not only do we thus see how untenable is this objection which has been founded upon the Apostle's language, but we can also point out the fallacy on which it depends. The objection, in fact, is based upon the assumption—equally opposed to the context, and to the whole tenor of those numerous passages of Scripture considered in this Discourse—that the phrase "the commandment of the Lord"[1] signifies the inward suggestion of the Holy Ghost by which the Apostles were guided and prompted in the discharge of their labors. By pointing out the injunction of Christ to which alone that phrase makes allusion, commentators have proved, that such cannot be the meaning of S. Paul's words; and in doing so they have also proved that nothing could have been further from the Apostle's design than to institute any contrast unfavorable to his own inspired authority. So far, indeed, was he from intending to convey by them the idea that any of his inspired directions to the Church was to be looked upon as of less authority than even those of Christ Himself—that in this same Epistle,[2] having re-

[1] Mr. Westcott is certainly in error when he says: "The reality of an *objective* Inspiration * * * seems to be implied in the Pauline formula *κατ' ἐπιταγήν* (Rom. xvi. 26; 1 Tim. i. 1; Titus, i. 3; 1 Cor. vii. 6, 25; 2 Cor. viii. 8)."—*Elem. of Gosp. Harm.*, p. 11. The import of *ἐπιταγή* in 1 Cor. vii. 6, has been pointed out p. 272, note [2]; and in 2 Cor. viii. 8, its meaning is clearly the same. In neither case is there the slightest allusion to a *Divine* command. The other texts referred to by Mr Westcott have clearly nothing to do with the inspiration of Scripture. In the same *general* sense *ἐπιταγή* is used in Titus, ii. 15, and it is not found again in the New Testament.

[2] 1 Cor. xiv. 37. Olshausen sums up the question as follows: "We find (ch, vii. 10, 12, 25, 40) that the Apostle distinguishes between what *he* says, and what *the Lord* says; between a definite command of Christ (*ἐπιταγή*), and his own subjective judgment (*γνώμη*). * * * Suppose, therefore, that Paul had no traditional command of Christ upon a certain subject, yet we must esteem his inspired conviction equivalent to such a command, for Christ wrought it in him by His Holy Spirit! In ch. xiv. 37, he openly lays claim to this privilege. It is there said: *εἴ τις δοκεῖ προφήτης εἶναι ἢ πνευματικὸς, ἐπιγινωσκέτω ἃ γράφω ὑμῖν, ὅτι Κυρίου εἰσὶν ἐντολαί* [or, adopting the reading which criticism has established, "the things which I write unto you proceed from the Lord (*Κυρίου ἐστιν*)"]. Here no traditional commands of Christ can be intended,—for in order to know such commands one need not be a prophet; but the expressions of Paul are so far called Christ's commands, inasmuch as He wrought them in him by His Spirit."—*loc. cit.*, s. 600.

There are two other passages in the writings of S. Paul which have been sometimes considered to imply that the great Apostle did not always write under the guidance of Inspiration. (1.) "Being then made free from sin, ye became the servants (*ἐδουλώθητε*) of righteousness. I speak *after the manner of men* (*ἀνθρώπινον λέγω*) because of the infirmity of your flesh."—Rom. vi. 18, 19. This passage is well explained by Mr. Alford: "For the expression *ἐδουλώθητε* the Apostle apologises: 'it is not literally so; the servant of righteousness is *no slave*, under no yoke of bondage; but in order to set the contrast between the former and the new state better before

ferred at considerable length to the existence of special miraculous gifts in the Church (of which a prominent gift was the faculty of "discerning of spirits"), he appeals to persons thus endowed in the remarkable words: "If any man think himself to be a prophet, or spiritual, let him acknowledge that the things that I *write* unto you are the commandments of the Lord."

you, I have used this word: 'I speak as a man (according to the requirements of rhetorical antithesis) on account of the (intellectual) weakness of your flesh,' * * * and want such figures to set the truth before you." On such words, therefore, no argument against Inspiration can be founded.

(2.) The next passage is as follows: "I say again, let no man think me a fool (ἄφρονα): if otherwise (εἰ δὲ μή γε) yet as a fool receive me, that I may boast myself a little. *That which I speak, I speak it not after the Lord* (ὃ λαλῶ, οὐ κατὰ Κύριον λαλῶ), but as it were foolishly, in this confidence of boasting."—2 Cor. xi. 16, 17. Here, however, Mr. Alford says: "Proceeding on the ὡς ἄφρονα he disclaims for this self-boasting the character of inspiration—or of being said in pursuance of his mission from the Lord." But there is no question here of the Apostle's "mission." The "false Apostles" (ver. 13) had compelled him to enter upon the subject of his privileges; S. Paul, therefore, considers it prudent, in order to guard against a possible perversion of his words, to point out that the apparent boasting or self-glory to which he is thus compelled is not *in itself* to be approved, or, as a general rule, in accordance with the Lord's will. He accordingly uses the words, "not after the Lord" (ver. 17), in strong contrast to the expression "after the flesh (κατὰ τὴν σάρκα)" in ver. 18. His meaning, therefore, is—"Since many glory after the flesh, I will glory also:—but, in so doing, I am compelled to adopt a course of which, as a general rule, I cannot approve; self-boasting is not after the Lord; and this I forewarn you of, as I do all things, dearly beloved, for your edifying (ch. xii. 19)." "In ver. 16 the Apostle plays on the idea implied by ἄφρων. At first, he requests them not to regard him as such, because he boasts himself (want of understanding is charged against those who really do so out of self-conceit); but if they would not obey him in this instance (εἰ δὲ μή γε), yet they might, if they pleased, look upon him even as ἄφρων—as those vaunting individuals—provided he may pride himself even in a small degree. In these last words, together with a refined irony, is contained a censure of the Corinthians, that they permitted those false prophets so to exalt themselves. In ver. 17 the ὡς ἐν ἀφροσύνῃ shows that the Apostle does not mean to say that he really speaks with a want of understanding, but that his speech has merely a semblance of it."—Olshausen, *Comm.* B. iii. s. 867. Indeed S. Paul expressly declares that it is in this sense only that the charge of "folly" can be brought against him: "For though I would desire to glory, *I shall not be a fool;* for I will say the truth: but now I forbear."—xii. 6.

The passages, "By the grace of God I am what I am: I labored more abundantly than they all: yet not I, but the grace of God which was in me"—1 Cor. xv. 10; and again, "God forbid that I should glory, save in the cross of our Lord Jesus Christ" (Gal. vi. 14), convey the principle against any violation of which S. Paul desires to guard; and hence we can explain his reiteration of the charge of "folly" against himself in that assertion of his privileges to which he next proceeds, viz., ver. 21, 23; and especially, ch. xii. 11, "I am become a fool in glorying; ye have compelled me:" cf. also xi. 30; xii. 1–5.

LECTURE VII.

THE COMMISSION TO WRITE.—THE FORM OF WHAT WAS WRITTEN.

Διόπερ τοῖς πειθομένοις μὴ ἀνθρώπων εἶναι συγγράμματα τὰς ἱερὰς βίβλους, ἀλλ' ἐξ ἐπιπνοίας τοῦ 'Αγίου Πνεύματος βουλήματι τοῦ Πατρὸς τῶν ὅλων διὰ 'Ιησοῦ Χριστοῦ ταύτας ἀναγεγράφθαι καὶ εἰς ἡμᾶς ἐληλυθέναι, τὰς φαινομένας ὁδοὺς ὑποδεικτέον.

ORIGENES, *De Princip.*, lib. IV. ix.

"Duo vero Cherubim pennis suis obumbrant Propitiatorium, id est honorant velando; quoniam mysteria ista ibi sunt: et invicem se adtendunt, quia consonant; duo quippe ibi Testamenta figurantur: et vultus eorum sunt in Propitiatorium, quia misericordiam Dei, in qua una spes est, valde commendant."

S. AUGUSTIN., *Quæst. in Exodum*, lib. II. qu. cv.

"'Vox in excelso audita est lamentationis, fletus et luctus, Rachel plorantis filios suos.' Nec juxta Hebraicum, nec juxta Septuaginta, Matthæus sumsit testimonium * * * Ex quo perspicuum est, Evangelistas et Apostolos nequaquam ex Hebræo interpretationem alicujus sequutos; sed quasi Hebræos ex Hebræis, quod legebant Hebraice, suis sermonibus expressisse."

S. HIERON., *Comm. in Jerem.*, lib. VI.

Τὴν θείαν αἰτιῶνται γραφὴν, μὴ τῷ περιττῷ καὶ κεκαλλωπισμένῳ χρωμένην λόγῳ, ἀλλὰ τῷ ταπεινῷ καὶ πεζῷ.

S. ISIDOR. Pelus., *Epist.* lib. IV. lxvii.

Οἱ θεσπέσιοι καὶ ὡς ἀληθῶς θεοπρεπεῖς, φημι δὲ τοῦ Χριστοῦ τοὺς 'Αποστόλους, ἀρετῇ πάσῃ τὰς ψυχὰς κεκοσμημένοι, τὴν δὲ γλῶτταν ἰδιωτεύοντες, τῇ γε μὴν πρὸς τοῦ Σωτῆρος αὐτοῖς δεδωρημένῃ θείᾳ καὶ παραδοξοποιῷ δυνάμει θαρσοῦντες, τὸ μὲν ἐν περινοίᾳ καὶ [illegible] λόγων τὰ τοῦ Διδασκάλου μαθήματα πρεσβεύειν, οὔτε ᾔδεσαν οὔτε ἐνεχείρουν.

EUSEBIUS Pamph., *Eccl. Hist.*, lib. III. xxiv.

LECTURE VII.

THE COMMISSION TO WRITE.—THE FORM OF WHAT WAS WRITTEN.

YEA, THEY MADE THEIR HEARTS AS AN ADAMANT STONE, LEST THEY SHOULD HEAR THE LAW, AND THE WORDS WHICH THE LORD OF HOSTS HATH SENT IN HIS SPIRIT BY THE FORMER PROPHETS.—*Zechariah*, vii. 12.

HAVING examined those statements of the New Testament which, in express terms, ascribe Inspiration to our sacred books taken collectively, or from which the influence of the Holy Ghost upon their authors may be inferred,—it still remains for us to inquire whether the Old Testament, either by its own intimations confirms, or by the manner in which its language is made use of in the New, tends to support, the views hitherto maintained as to the co-operation of the Divine Spirit in the composition of the Bible. To the consideration of these questions the present Discourse must be chiefly devoted.

The words of the text form a portion of an immediate revelation from God; the passage from which they are taken opening with the customary formula, "The word of the Lord came unto Zechariah, saying, Thus speaketh the Lord of Hosts." In this prophetic announcement two important facts are implied. It is implied, in the first place, that a collection of sacred writings was already in existence when Zechariah received this communication,—for not only "the Law," but also "the words which the Lord of Hosts hath sent by the former prophets," are expressly referred to: and secondly, that those writings had been composed under Divine guidance,—for, with respect to the words of the prophets, Jehovah declares that He had sent them by "His Spirit;" while the Law, strictly so called, is on all occasions represented in Scripture as the voice of God Himself. We meet with statements of a similar character in other portions of the Bible which were written at this same period ;—statements which possess the greater importance from the fact that they proceeded from those men to whom both Jewish tradition, and the most advanced criticism of modern times, unite in ascribing the formation of the Old Testament Canon : I mean Ezra and Nehemiah.[1]

[1] This fact is conclusively established by Hävernick, "Einleitung," Th. I. Abth. i. s. 27 ff. "All reasons," he observes, "if correctly estimated, lead us to the time of Ezra and Nehemiah, as that which can alone accord with the closing of the Canon:"—e. g. the circumstances of Jewish history (see *infra*, p. 284); the reverential allusions *for the first time to the Canon, taken collectively* as a sacred document, in the period which followed Ezra and Nehemiah (see *supra*, Lecture ii. p. 61, &c.); the refusal to receive as canonical such a work as the book of Ecclesiasticus, of which the claims to authority are so prominently advanced (see *supra*, p 55, note [2]); the testimony of Josephus to the failure of a "succession of prophets" (see *supra*, p. 68) &c. Hävernick appeals, in the next place, to the Tradition of the Jews, the importance of which he justly insists upon. This Tradition expressly refers the collection of the sacred books to Ezra, and "the Great Synagogue." (1.) One of the oldest parts of the Talmud, the "Capita Patrum," or "Sayings of the Fathers" (פרקי אבות—see Mischna, ed. Surenhus. iv. p. 409), begins with the words: "Moses received the Law from Sinai, and transferred it to Joshua; Joshua to the Elders; the Elders to the Prophets; *the Prophets to the men of the Great Synagogue*," which consisted of one hundred and twenty Elders in the time of Ezra; among whom were Zerubbabel, Seraiah, the prophets Haggai, Zechariah, and Malachi, &c.: see Surenhusius, *ibid.* (2.) The important passage in the Gemara of Babylon (Tr. Baba Bathra, fol. xv. col. 1), declares that "the Wise Men" "**have** left to us the Thorah, the Prophets, and the Kethubim, *collected into one whole* (מדובקים כאחד)." "Who," asks the Talmudists, "*has inserted these books in the Canon* (ומי כתבן)?" in which phrase, as Hävernick proves conclusively—and here he follows Vitringa ("In lib. Isai." t. i. p. 13) and Gesenius ("Der Proph. Jesaiah," i. s. 16), in opposition to De Wette ("Einleit." § 14, s. 17) and Hengstenberg ("Beiträge," i s. 2),—כתב can only mean "*inserted*" (i. e. in the Canon) or "*edited.*" Thus כתב is employed in this passage to express that "Hezekiah and his College *wrote out* (or formed into one collection) Isaiah, *Proverbs*, Canticles, and Ecclesiastes,"—clearly referring to the statement of Scripture itself: "These are the Proverbs of Solomon, which *the men of Hezekiah King of Judah copied out.*"—Prov. xxv. 1. It surely cannot be imagined that the Talmudists regarded "Hezekiah and his College" as *the authors* of the Book of Proverbs! This extract from the Gemara ends by ascribing to Ezra the book which bears his name, and the genealogies in the books of Chronicles; the completion of the Chronicles it ascribes to Nehemiah. "Jewish Tradition, therefore," concludes Hävernick, "concurs with historical, positive testimony in proving that Ezra, in connexion with other famous men of his time, completed the collection of the Sacred Writings."—*loc. cit.* s. 49. To his labors in arranging the Canon is clearly to be referred the origin of Ezra's title—"A Scribe of the words of the commandments of the Lord and of His statutes to Israel;" "A Scribe of the Law of the God of Heaven."—Ezra, vii. 11, 12; on which passages, taken in connexion with the Jewish Tradition already considered, was founded the opinion of the primitive Church. Thus S. Irenæus writes: [Θεὸς] *ἐνέπνευσεν Ἔσδρᾳ τῷ Ἱερεῖ * * * τοὺς τῶν προγεγονότων προφητῶν πάντας ἀνατάξασθαι λόγους, καὶ ἀποκαταστῆσαι τῷ λαῷ τὴν διὰ Μωσέως νομοθεσίαν.—Contr. Hær.* iii. 21, p. 216; words which have been erroneously understood to imply that S. Irenæus adopted the modern fiction (2 Esdras, xiv. 21) that Ezra "*composed anew*" all the books of the Old Testament which had perished during the Exile. Thus the old Latin version renders *ἀνατάξασθαι* by *rememorare;* and Valesius (Euseb. H. E., lib. v. c. 8, p. 222) by "*denuo componeret.*" D. Massuet (*in loc.*) justly observes: "Verterem ego, *digerere;*" giving to *ἀνατάξ.* its legitimate meaning. To the same effect Feuardentius (*in loc.*) quotes Tertullian: "Hierosolymis Babylonia expugnatione deletis, omne instrumentum Judaicæ literaturæ per Esdram *constat restauratum.*"—*De cultu mulier.*, c. iii. p. 171. Cf. Clemens Al., "Strom.," i. 22, p. 410.

When God again committed to Moses upon Sinai the Law engraved on the two Tables of stone, it had been expressly commanded that the Israelites should not intermarry with the inhabitants of the land.[1] Ezra, when recording how this law had been broken, observes: "Then were assembled unto me every one that trembled at the words of the God of Israel."[2] This, however, as I have just remarked, was but the formal creed of his nation as to the Pentateuch. But Ezra proceeds, in his prayer, to combine the commands of God by His prophets with those which had been enunciated by the Jewish lawgiver: "And now, O our God, what shall we say after this? for we have forsaken Thy commandments which Thou hast commanded by Thy servants the prophets,"[3]—this latter phrase, as we learn from other writers of the Old Testament, embracing the entire body of God's inspired messengers. For example, the Lord declares by the mouth of Jeremiah: "Since the day that your fathers came forth out of the land of Egypt unto this day, I have even sent unto you all My servants the prophets."[4]

The Divine character of the Old Testament is expressed with equal distinctness by Nehemiah. He tells us how Ezra complied with the desire of the people that he should read before them "the Book of the Law of Moses which the Lord had commanded to Israel."[5] And again, in the prayer of the Levites (which is followed by the covenant which Nehemiah, and the Levites, and people, "sealed" "to walk in God's Law which was given by Moses the servant of God"), it is said: "Yet many years didst Thou forbear them, and testifiedst against them by Thy Spirit in Thy prophets;"[6]—expressions which, like those of Ezra, exactly correspond to the statement of our text.

[1] Exod. xxxiv. 16; cf. Deut. vii. 3. [2] Ezra, ix. 1–4.

[3] *Ibid.* ver. 10, 11.

[4] Jer. vii. 25; xxv. 4; cf. 2 Kings, xvii. 6–23; 2 Chron. xxxvi. 14–16.

[5] Neh. viii. 1.

[6] Neh. ix. 30; see ch. x. 29; in which passages the 'Law' and the 'Prophets' only are referred to. In ch. xii., however, Nehemiah further alludes to the *third* division of the Old Testament as forming, with the other parts, an authoritative code. Having spoken of the ordinances of the Law respecting the Priests, he adds that "singers and porters kept the ward of their God * * * according to *the commandment* of David and of Solomon his son. For in the days of *David and Asaph* of old, there were chief of the singers, and *songs of praise* and thanksgiving unto God."—ver. 44–46.

The relation of Nehemiah to the formation of the Canon is confirmed by the author of the second book of Maccabees. Having stated the zeal of Jeremiah for the preservation of the Ark, and of the Law, which the writer tells us that he had

Such allusions to the Law and the Prophets, implying, as they do, that a collection of sacred documents was already in existence, suggest a brief consideration of some circumstances connected with the closing of the Old Testament Canon. Here also, as in those numerous instances so frequently noticed, we can trace the continued use of natural means, and the employment of what, to a human eye, might appear merely natural motives, in securing this permanent record of Divine Revelation. The various incidents of Jewish history, in the age of Ezra and Nehemiah, had a necessary tendency to turn the attention of their countrymen to the books of the prophets. Even so early as the Assyrian period of Prophecy,[1] the calamities which impended over the kingdoms of Israel and Judah had cast their shadows before. In the midst of the gloomy present the future became gradually invested with greater interest. Through the entrance of the penalties which had been foretold, the blessings, of which the chosen people had received an equal assurance, acquired a new significance ; and hence the promissory side of the Law attracted the hopes, as its denunciations awoke the fears, of the nation. The history of Josiah[2] exemplifies the existence of this latter state of feeling ; while the former is accounted for by the light which passing events cast upon the language of the pro-

"found in the records (εὑρίσκεται δὲ ἐν ταῖς ἀπογραφαῖς)"—ch. ii. 1, &c., he adds: "The same things also were reported in the writings and commentaries of Neemias ; and how he, *founding a library* (βιβλιοθήκην), gathered together the Acts of the Kings, and the Prophets, and of David, and the Epistles of the Kings concerning the holy gifts (τὰ περὶ τῶν βασιλέων, καὶ προφητῶν, καὶ τὰ τοῦ Δαυὶδ, καὶ ἐπιστολὰς βασιλ. περὶ ἀναθεμάτων)"—ver. 13. Thus Nehemiah is compared with Jeremiah ; the latter having preserved the Law, the former the other writings, of which he proceeded to form *a collection*—(Hävernick, *loc. cit.* s. 46, shows that βιβλιοθήκη is to be understood in this sense: cf. Maitland's "Dark Ages," p. 194). It is also to be particularly noted that Nehemiah is here said to have "gathered together" (ἐπισυνήγαγε) the different elements of Jewish literature, and thence selected what was to be reckoned as Canonical. As to the principle on which this selection was made see *supra* Lect. ii. p. 54, &c.

[1] The 'prophetic age' of Jewish history commences from Samuel (cf. "All the prophets from Samuel," &c.—Acts, iii. 24 ; "David also, and Samuel, and the prophets"—Heb. xi. 32), and includes about seven hundred years, viz., B. C. 1100–400. It has been thus divided: (1.) The 'early period' (B. C. 1100–800), in which the *collective* activity of the 'Prophetic Order' was conspicuous, and which terminated with the contemporaries of Elijah and Elisha. (2.) The 'Assyrian period' (B. C. 800–700), in which, as in the periods which followed, the agency of *individual* prophets is employed. Here the leading subject is the relation of the Assyrians to the people of God: under this head are included the predictions of Isaiah. (3.) The 'Chaldæan period' (B. C. 625–536). (4.) The period which followed the Captivity, viz., B. C. 536–400. See Knobel, "Prophetismus der Hebräer," ii. s. 18 ff.

[2] 2 Kings, xxii. ; 2 Chron. xxxiv. The thirteenth year of Josiah's reign, in which year Jeremiah's functions commenced (Jer. i. 2), was B. C. 629.

phets respecting the future,—language which was but a devel opment of the predictions of the Law.[1] In proportion to the importance thus attached to the prophetic announcements, was felt to be the need of preserving the records in which they were perpetuated. Such, we cannot doubt, was the *external* motive which occasioned the collection of those sacred writings in which the past glories of Israel were still recalled to mind ; and by which, in the depth of their present humiliation, the children of Abraham were solaced by a series of imperishable Prophecy. Acting, therefore, upon this external impulse, the inspired men,[2] who formed the collection of the books of the Old Testament, were divinely guided to select from the literature of their nation those documents only "which had been written for our learning" at the express command of God. With reference to this subject it has been already shown that in order to give any account of the selection of such books, and such books only, as components of the Canon, their Divine inspiration must be assumed :[3] another feature of the case, however, remains to be examined here.

It is not unfrequently urged by the opponents of a definite theory of Inspiration that, admitting the authenticity and genuineness of the sacred books, we have no evidence which shall entitle us to assert that their authors claimed for themselves any distinct Commission from God to preserve a written record of His successive revelations, or to compose a narrative of the events which marked the development of the Theocracy. Still less, it has been argued, can we maintain that such a Commission was actually given. Hence it follows, we are also told, that a profound sense of the importance of the facts recorded, or of the communications which the prophets had received from heaven, must be regarded as the only motive which caused the composition of the different parts of the Bible.[4] It may be well to examine such a statement with some particularity.

[1] Cf. Deut. xxviii.–xxx.

[2] "The agency of the Holy Spirit has brought into existence the books of the Bible; the agency of the Holy Spirit has also brought them together. The former agency alone is not sufficient to account for all that is peculiar to Scripture; under that influence, which we are accustomed to name Inspiration, we must comprehend both agencies."—Hofmann, *Weissagung und Erfüllung*, s. 49.

[3] See *supra*, Lecture ii. p. 53, &c.

[4] "A third form, in which the mechanical idea of Inspiration has been upheld,' writes Mr. Morell, "is that which asserts a *distinct commission* in respect to the au

Were it possible to prove that God had issued to chosen individuals a special Commission to compose certain narratives, no one, it may be presumed, would venture to assert that the sacred penmen were left unaided in the performance of that duty, or that any imperfection could possibly exist in the work so produced.[1] There are, it is true, many cases in which we have no specific intimation of such a Divine Commission; and yet, even here, the Old Testament writers often employ language which implies that they had abundant reason to believe that they were moved by an impulse from above. Take, for example, the phrase so continually made use of, "Thus saith Jehovah;" or the words of David, "The Spirit of the Lord spake by me, and His word was in my tongue."[2] So also the prophets at times inform us of the manner in which they received their Commission from God. "Gird up thy loins," said the Lord to Jeremiah, "and speak unto them all that I command thee."[3] And to such commands, we are told, was added an inward spiritual impulse: "Truly," said Micah, "I am full of power by the Spirit of the Lord, and of judgment, and of might, to declare unto Jacob his transgressions, and to Israel his sin."[4] Frequent intimations of this nature, clearly denoting their Divine source and their Divine

thorship of each one of the sacred books." * * * "Admitting them [the Sacred Books now constituting the Canon] to be genuine, and admitting them to be inspired, —what did the authors themselves in good faith mean to include under the notion of Inspiration? Did they claim for themselves any distinct commission to pen the works in question? was such a commission at the time awarded to them? or was not the whole of the Inspiration attaching to them rather viewed as resulting simply from the extraordinary intuitions of Divine truth which they had received, and which they were here impelled by a deep sense of their infinite value to depict?" * * * "With regard to the prophetic writings, these certainly occupy a much higher position than the historical books, inasmuch as we learn that the authors actually received a prophetic commission to declare the counsels of God to the people, but this does not necessarily involve any distinct and separate commission to *write* the books in question;—nor have we any reason to regard their writings as inspired in any other sense than as being the rescript of their inward prophetic consciousness."—*Philos. of Religion*, pp. 159–162. See also *supra*, Lecture i. p. 27, note [4].

[1] "Though the origin of the words, even as of the miraculous acts, be supernatural—yet the former once uttered—the latter once having taken their place among the *phænomena* of the senses, the faithful recording of the same does not of itself imply, or seem to require, any supernatural working, other than as all truth and goodness are such [but see *supra*, Lecture vi. p. 236]. In the books of Moses, and once or twice in the prophecy of Jeremiah, I find it, indeed, asserted that not only the words were given, but the recording of the same enjoined by the special command of God, and *doubtless executed under the special guidance of the Divine Spirit. As to all such passages, therefore, there can be no dispute.*"—Coleridge, *Confess. of an Inquiring Spirit*, Letter ii. p. 16.

[2] 2 Sam. xxiii. 2.

[3] Jer. i. 17.

[4] Micah, iii. 8. Cf. Lect. iii. p. 128, &c.

authority, present themselves in various books of Scripture: to which must be added the many external reasons[1] which in like manner guided the Jewish Church to recognise their inspiration. We are not left, however, to such intimations, conclusive as they must appear to every unprejudiced mind: instances of an express command from God to commit to writing various portions of the Bible are far more numerous and significant than may at first sight be supposed.

"The Lord said unto Moses, Write this for a memorial in a book, and rehearse it in the ears of Joshua.[2]" Here we are to observe, that Jehovah commands His servant to place on record, not some revelation of His secret counsels,—not any express prediction of events still future,—not a class of precepts relating to spiritual or ritual worship,—but a simple narrative of an historical fact; namely, the defeat of the Amalekites at Rephidim.[3] It is also to be noticed, that this record was designed to serve for a "memorial:" "for," the Lord further informs Moses, "I will utterly put out the remembrance of Amalek from under heaven:" —words which refer to a people of whom it is afterward said that they "feared not God." Here we see foreshadowed the great truth subsequently enunciated by the Apostle when adducing the facts of Jewish history; "All these things happened unto

[1] E. g. the miracles performed by individual prophets; the accomplishment of their predictions (cf. Lecture v. p. 212, note [1]); such acts as that performed by Isaiah, of which we read in his eighth chapter (see *infra*, p. 291); &c. &c.

[2] Exod. xvii. 14.

[3] Mr. Blunt ("Undesigned Coincidences," § xvi. 3rd ed. p. 69, &c.) has pointed out the connexion of this narrative with the sacred history: "All the congregation of the children of Israel journeyed * * * and pitched in Rephidim: and *there was no water* for the people to drink."—Exod. xvii. 1. On this the people "murmured against Moses" (ver. 3), who entreats the Lord. "And the Lord said unto Moses * * * Behold I will stand before thee there upon the rock in Horeb, and thou shalt smite the rock, and there shall come water out of it. * * * And Moses did so * * * *Then came Amalek* and fought with Israel in Rephidim" (ver. 4–8). In order to perceive the connexion here, it is only necessary to call to mind, on the one hand, the miraculous supply of water in an arid wilderness; and, on the other, the repeated allusions, in the narrative of Moses, to disputes for the possession of a well (e. g. Gen. xxi. 25; xxvi. 22; Exod. ii. 17; Numb xx. 17; xxi. 22; Deut. ii. 6; Judges, v. 11). The sudden gushing of water from the rock conferred upon the Israelites an invaluable treasure; and the sin of Amalek consisted, not in their natural desire to possess or share this unexpected supply, but in their refusing to recognise the Divine intervention; and, by fighting against Israel, fighting against God. "Such," observes Mr. Blunt, "I persuade myself, is the true force of an expression in Deut. xxv. 18, used in reference to this very incident,—for Amalek is there said to 'have smitten them when they were weary, and to *have feared not God*;' that is, to have done it in defiance of a miracle, which ought to have impressed them with a fear of God; indicating, as of course it did, that God willed not the destruction of this people."—p. 74.

them for ensamples ; and they are written for our admonition." From this statement of S. Paul, taken by itself, we might have inferred that Moses received a Commission from God to compose a written narrative of the various historical events which he records: but we are able to appeal to his express announcement of the fact. "These are the journeys of the children of Israel, which went forth out of the land of Egypt with their armies under the hand of Moses and Aaron. And Moses wrote their goings out according to their journeys, *by the commandment of the Lord*."[2] It is needless to dwell upon the motives which led to the composition of those portions of the books of Moses which were not of a strictly historical character ; suffice it to quote the words of the Lord by the prophet Hosea: "*I have written* to Ephraim the great things of My Law, but they were counted as a strange thing."[3]

[1] 1 Cor. x. 11.

[2] Numb. xxxiii. 1, 2.

[3] Hosea, viii. 12. With respect to this portion also of the Pentateuch, we read of various commands which Moses received. Thus in the case of the "Song" contained in Deut. xxxii. 1–43, it is written: "And the Lord said unto Moses * * * Write ye this Song for you, and teach it the children of Israel; that this Song may be a witness for Me against the children of Israel. * * * Moses therefore wrote this Song the same day."—Deut. xxxi. 16–22. Cf. too, *ibid.*, ver. 9–11: "And Moses wrote this Law, and delivered it unto the Priests the sons of Levi," &c.: on which practice see *supra*, Lect. ii. p. 68, the remarks of Josephus. That Moses from time to time committed to writing the words of the Lord as he received them (and we cannot doubt that he did so at God's command, as in the particular case of this "Song"), we learn from Ex. xxiv. 4, where, after Moses had "told the people all the words of the Lord, and all the judgments," we read that he "wrote all the words of the Lord." Then follows the remarkable narrative of the delivery of the Tables of stone: "I will give thee," said Jehovah Himself, "Tables of stone, and a Law, and Commandments *which I have written*" (ver. 12),—of which we further read that they were "written with the finger of God" (Ex. xxxi. 18; Deut. ix. 10); and which when broken by Moses (Ex. xxxii. 19), were renewed by the Lord (see Ex. xxxiv. 1–28; Deut. x. 1–4) on the Mount. On this occasion Moses mentions again that he received a command to write: "The Lord said unto Moses, Write thou these words," &c.—Ex. xxxiv. 27.

Such was the commencement of the Old Testament Canon, for the preservation of which provision was made as follows: "It came to pass when Moses had made an end of writing the words of this Law in a Book until they were finished, that Moses commanded the Levites, saying, Take the Book of the Law and put it in the side of the Ark of the Covenant" (Deut. xxxi. 24–26)—where it was kept with the most holy badges of their faith. To this collection of writings, combining a narrative of historical facts, doctrinal precepts, and predictions of the future, Joshua is referred by God Himself: "This Book of the Law shall not depart out of thy mouth; but thou shalt meditate therein day and night."—Josh. i. 8. And here, considering the hallowed character of the Law, as well as the express statements which have been just quoted, the remark is obvious that, to a collection so made, no Israelite, in future times, could have ventured to add any further documents without a command from Jehovah equally explicit with those which Moses had received. And yet we know that Joshua himself, as well as the successive writers of Scripture, *did* make such additions as if they were performing what was their obvious duty. Thus we read, without a word of comment on the part of the historian, that Joshua "wrote in the Book of the Law of God" (ch. xxiv. 26). Samuel, too, when he "told the people the manner of the kingdom," "wrote in *the Book* (בַּסֵּפֶר), and laid it up before the Lord."—1 Sam. x. 25.

Precise information, as to the manner in which the prophets obeyed the Divine command to place their predictions on record, is supplied in the thirty-sixth chapter of the book of Jeremiah. The chapter opens with the following injunction: "This word came unto Jeremiah from the Lord, saying, Take thee a roll of a book, and write therein all the words that I have spoken unto thee against Israel, and against Judah, and against all the nations." The prophet then proceeds to recount how he dictated his work to his amanuensis;[1] and how it came to pass that no human opposition, or attempt to destroy the document so drawn up, availed to impede the promulgation of the Divine decrees. In this instance we perceive that a Commission to write was given: we are informed of the manner in which the Commission was executed; and also of the means by which God provided that His will thus to transmit to after-times the memorial of His revelations should overrule all resistance whether of king or of people.[2]

"Here [as well as in Exod. xvii. 14; Deut. xxviii. 58] the expression הספר shows that reference is made to a definite Book, already in existence, to which Samuel's document was now added, and thus the previous collection increased."—Hävernick, *loc. cit.*, s. 20. This same proceeding was continued in future ages. Isaiah,—in imagination, regarding his denunciations against Idumea as already fulfilled,—invites all who doubted to compare with this fulfilment *his recorded prediction*: "Seek ye out of the Book of the Lord (דרשו מעל־ספר י״י) and read; no one of these shall fail, none shall want her mate: for My [i. e. Jehovah's] mouth it hath commanded, and [resumes the prophet] His Spirit it hath gathered them."—xxxiv. 16. (Observe the union here of the Divine and human agencies in uttering this prediction.) Isaiah "seems here to refer to the depositing his prophecy in a collection of oracles and sacred writings, from which posterity could judge of the justice of his predictions. Towards the close of the Exile a beginning had, beyond any doubt, been made of a collection, and editing of the national literature,—there was a beginning, in short, of the formation of a Sacred *Codex*. A later trace of this collection occurs in Dan. ix. 2 ["I Daniel understood *by Books* the number of the years, whereof the word of the Lord came to Jeremiah the prophet"], where mention is made of ספרים, "*books*," among which was the book of Jeremiah. The employment of דרש, which approximates to the ἐρευνᾶτε τὰς γραφάς (John, v. 39; cf. vii. 52), presupposes even now a time when men began to study the Holy Scriptures."—Gesenius, *Der. Proph. Jesaia*, i. s. 921 (Cf. Ps. xl. 7; Is. xxix. 18.) See also Jer. xxv. 13: "I will bring upon that land all My words which I have pronounced against it, even all that is written in this book which Jeremiah hath prophesied against all the nations." Cf. Lecture vi. p. 242, note [1].

[1] "Then Jeremiah called Baruch the son of Neriah: and Baruch wrote from the mouth of Jeremiah all the words of the Lord, which He had spoken unto him, upon a roll of a book."—ver. 4.

[2] "Then the word of the Lord came to Jeremiah, after that the King had burned the roll * * * saying, Take thee again another roll, and write in it all the former words," &c.—ver. 27, 28. Cf. "The word that came to Jeremiah from the Lord, saying * * * Write thee all the words that I have spoken unto thee in a book."—Jer. xxx. 1, 2. See also ch. xxii. 30; li. 60: ch. xxix. is clearly of the same class; compare ver. 1 and 4. Commands of the same nature were given to Ezekiel: "The

Nor is this the only information which has been vouchsafed to us on this matter. We are also told by Isaiah what measures were taken to attest for after-times the Divine character of the books thus written. The Law, it is to be remembered, had expressly enjoined that false prophets should be put to death: not only those who should prophesy in the name of other gods, but also those who should presume to speak in Jehovah's Name without His command.[1] To the latest period of Prophecy this injunction was rigidly enforced. God Himself declared, by the mouth of Zechariah, that it was the duty of even parents to inflict this penalty upon the false prophet:—"Then his father and his mother that begat him shall say unto him, Thou shalt not live; for thou speakest lies in the name of the Lord: and his father and his mother shall thrust him through when he prophesieth."[2] The permanent obligation of this precept—a fact which the repetition of it by so late a prophet as Zechariah establishes—enables us clearly to discern the grounds which guided Ezra and Nehemiah in their selection of those books which were

word of the Lord came to me, saying, Son of man, write thee the name of the day," &c.—xxiv. 1, 2; "Thou son of man, show the House to the house of Israel * * * and all the Laws thereof: and write it in their sight, that they may keep the whole form thereof, and all the ordinances thereof, and do them."—xliii. 10, 11. Can we suppose, when we read "Daniel had a dream, and vision of his head upon his bed: then he wrote the dream," &c.—vii. 1, that the prophet placed this revelation on record without the Divine sanction, merely because we are not expressly told that the command was given?

[1] Deut. xiii. 1–3: xviii. 20. "And if thou say in thine heart, How shall we know the word which the Lord hath not spoken? When a prophet speaketh in the name of the Lord, if the thing follow not, nor come to pass, that is the thing which the Lord hath not spoken, but the prophet hath spoken it presumptuously."—ver. 21, 22. Hence, in the case of predictions, the accomplishment of which was reserved for the distant future, some proofs of the nature here promised by Jehovah Himself, or some exhibition of miraculous agency were required, and were given. E. g. Hananiah of Gibeon, in direct opposition to Jeremiah (cf. xxvii. 2, xxviii. 10), had ventured to prophesy: "Thus saith the Lord, Even so will I break the yoke of Nebuchadnezzar within the space of two full years." But Jeremiah immediately declared, "The Lord hath not sent thee. * * * Therefore thus saith the Lord, Behold this year thou shalt die, because thou hast taught rebellion against the Lord. So Hananiah the prophet died the same year."—Jer. xxviii. 11–17. See also Lecture v. p. 214, note [1]. The opposing claims of false prophets were among the most severe trials which the servants of God had to encounter. "Mine heart within me," said Jeremiah, "is broken because of the prophets."—xxiii. 9; and he writes to the captives in Babylon: "Let not your prophets and your diviners * * * deceive you * * * for they prophesy falsely unto you in My Name: I have not sent them, saith the Lord." —ch. xxix. 8, 9. Again: "Because that Shemaiah hath prophesied unto you, and I sent him not, and he caused you to trust in a lie: therefore thus saith the Lord, Behold I will punish Shemaiah and his seed."—ver. 31, 32. See also (ver. 21) the reference to Ahab and Zedekiah. Compare to the same effect Ezek. xiii.

[2] Zech. xiii. 3.

inspired: for, independently of their own inspiration when discharging this function, we at once perceive that no book could have been put forward as Divine had there not been a public recognition that it had been composed at God's command.[1] How this was effected, Isaiah, as I have observed, informs us, when giving a narrative of the manner in which he announced to King Ahaz the approaching conquest of Israel by the Assyrians:—"The Lord said unto me, Take thee a great roll, and write in it with a man's pen concerning Maher-shalal-hash-baz."[2] The brief prediction conveyed by this name is then developed; previously to which the prophet had taken two "faithful witnesses" to attest his words[3] which he commits to a formal legal document; thus ensuring, in opposition to the prevailing incredulity of the

[1] See *supra*, Lecture ii. p. 53, note [1], an important remark quoted from Sack.

[2] Isai. viii. 1: "a great roll"—גליון גדול. Vitringa (*in loc.*, t. i. p. 203) compares the "roll of a book (מגלת־ספר)"—Jer. xxxvi. 4; and explains that there were two modes employed by the prophets for the purpose of recording the Divine communications. (1.) As here, by means of a series of "rolls," or sheets of parchment wrapped round a cylindrical roller, which admitted of being preserved with greater care; and which method was therefore employed for transmitting the prophecy to future times (cf. *supra*, p. 289, note [2]): (2.) By means of tablets of some smooth material (לוחות) which were hung up in some public place so that the people might the sooner become acquainted with the Divine will. Such were the Tables of stone on which the Ten Commandments were first written (Exod. xxxi. 18; Deut. ix. 9); and thus the prophet Habakkuk explains the custom, "The Lord answered me and said, Write the Vision and make it plain *upon tables, that he may run that readeth it.*"—ii. 2. Both methods are described where the Lord tells Isaiah: "Now go, write it before them in a table (כתבה על־לוח), *and* note it in a book (ספר) that it may be for the time to come forever and ever."—xxx. 8:—"Sensus mandati est, ut Propheta suum hunc Elenchum scriberet in *tabula* quam ipsis hoc tempore committeret legendam; et simul exararet in *Libro* in usum et memoriam posterorum."—Vitringa, *in loc.* t. ii. p. 171. (Gesenius, however, observes that in place of גליון the Chaldee reads לוח in Isai. viii. 1.—*Der Proph. Jesaia*, i. s. 324). The theory which Calvin has advanced on this subject is, no doubt, ingenious; but is, as he himself admits, merely conjectural: "Posteaquam prophetæ concionem habuerant ad populum, brevem ejus summam colligebant, quam valvis templi affigerent, ut omnibus pateret ac melius innotesceret prophetia. *Quæ cum per aliquot dies satis patuisset, auferebatur a ministris templi, atque reponebatur in thesaurum, ut perpetuum ejus rei monumentum extaret.* Hinc confectos esse libros prophetarum verisimile est: idque colligi potest ex secundo capite Habac. ver. 2, siquis ipsum rite expendat: atque etiam ex capite octavo hujus prophetæ."—*Comm. in Isai.*, Præf.

[3] "And I took unto me faithful witnesses to record, Uriah the priest, and Zechariah the son of Jeberechiah."—ver. 2. All admit that Uriah was the person mentioned in 2 Kings, xvi. 10–16: "King Ahaz sent to Urijah the priest the fashion of the altar. * * * Thus did Urijah the priest according to all that King Ahaz commanded." Gesenius (*in loc.*, s. 327) thinks that Zechariah was the Levite mentioned in 2 Chron. xxix. 13. On the other hand, Mr. Blunt with great probability conjectures that the father of the wife of Ahaz was the witness thus chosen by Isaiah; inasmuch as we read of "Hezekiah the son of Ahaz," that "his mother's name was Abi *the daughter of Zachariah.*"—2 Kings, xviii. 2. "We can account for the choice of Isaiah, who wished the transaction in which he was engaged to be enforced upon the attention of Ahaz with all the advantages he could command, and so selected two of the King's bosom friends to testify concerning it."—*loc. cit.*, p. 233.

age, that what he had written could not, at a future period, be looked upon as a mere 'prophecy after the event.' As long as the event did not come to pass, Isaiah was prepared to find his announcement disregarded. Before the fulfilment of their predictions, the prophets were continually subjected to scorn and ridicule:—"The word of the Lord came unto me," writes Ezekiel, "saying, Son of man, what is that proverb that ye have in the land of Israel saying, The days are prolonged, and every vision faileth?"[1] The precaution, therefore, taken by Isaiah in the case before us, had reference to the attestation of his words for future ages: and accordingly, having secured witnesses to the date and performance of his Commission, he received another express command from God "to bind up and seal" the document to which he had committed the record of this revelation.[2] The prophet obeys, and, suspending his reputation, and perhaps his life, upon the issue, calmly awaits the accomplishment of his prediction.[3]

From all this we may infer, with a degree of confidence proportional to our trust in the veracity of Scripture, that its several books were designed by their Divine Author to serve as a stand-

[1] Ezek. xii. 21, 22.

[2] "Bind up (צור) the testimony (תעודה—*the attested oracle*, cf. ver, 2), and the Law (תורה) among My disciples."—ver. 16. These words, in which the prophet refers to vv. 21, 22, form part of a new revelation supplementary to the former, and introduced by the phrase: "The Lord spake thus to me with a strong hand."—ver. 11. (See *supra*, Lect. iii. p. 129, note [7].) This prediction, observe Gesenius (*loc. cit.*, s. 341), Isaiah was commanded to secure against every suspicion of falsification by binding it up (צרר, *to wrap in a cloth*), and sealing it till its fulfilment: cf. Dan. xii. 4: "Thou, O Daniel, shut up the words, and seal the book, even to the time of the end," &c.

[3] The intrepid discharge of their duty by the prophets affords a conclusive proof of their conviction that their mission was from God. The danger which they encountered was no imaginary one. The people, writes Nehemiah, "cast Thy Law behind their backs, and slew Thy prophets which testified against them."—ix. 26. Cf. the case of Zechariah the son of Jehoiada, put to death by King Joash, 2 Chron. xxiv. 21; or the statement of Jeremiah: "Then spake the priests and the prophets unto the princes and to all the people, saying, This man is worthy to die: for he hath prophesied against this city. Then spake Jeremiah, The Lord sent me to prophesy against this House, and against this city all the words that ye have heard. Therefore now mend your ways * * * as for me, behold I am in your hand: do with me as seemeth good unto you,"—xxvi. 11–24; see also the account of the murder of Urijah by Jehoiakim, *ibid.*, ver. 20–23. Notwithstanding this certainty of persecution, the prophets fearlessly performed their duty. Amos disregarded the power of Jeroboam (ch. vii. 10, &c.); and Elijah, although he avoided unnecessary danger ("When he saw that, he arose, and went for his life," &c.—1 Kings, xix. 3), did not shrink from denouncing the sins of Ahab (1 Kings, xxi. 17, &c). Even Balaam resisted the solicitation of the King of Moab; and the "disobedient prophet" braved the King beside the altar (1 Kings, xiii).

ing witness and memorial of His Revelation whether declared by the mouth of prophets, or manifested in the history of the covenant-people. Hence it is that Daniel has quoted by name the predictions of Jeremiah, as being contained in the books which he was enabled to understand ;[1] hence, too, the Divine messenger who instructs him declares : "I will show thee that which is noted in the Scripture of Truth."[2] The very phrase "Scripture," indeed, or written document, as employed in this saying,—as made use of also by the various writers of the New Testament, and even by Christ Himself,[3]—of itself proves the justice of the inferences already drawn. S. John, moreover, in the Apocalypse, on *twelve* different occasions, states that he received a command to write the narrative of his visions :[4] and to the narrative thus composed were applied by the angel words which equally describe each portion of the Bible : "He saith unto me, These are the true sayings of God."[5]

That the New Testament, like the Old, was designed as a memorial for after times, S. John has not obscurely intimated when he announced the motive which led to the composition of his Gospel : "These are written that ye might believe that Jesus is the Christ, the Son of God, and that believing ye might have life through His name."[6] Of this destination of the sacred writings for the use of every future age, a striking proof is afforded by the fact that, while combating the errors and heresies of their day, the Apostles never descend into details, neither naming the heresiarchs, nor describing the factions with which they had to contend : the only exception to this reserve occurs

[1] Dan. ix. 2.

[2] בכתב אמת—Dan. x. 21.

[3] "Moses "*wrote* of Me."—S. John, v. 46.

[4] "What thou seest, write in a Book (ὃ βλέπεις γράψον εἰς βιβλίον)"—Rev. i. 11: cf. 19; ii. 1, 8, 12, 18; iii. 1, 7, 14; xiv. 13; xix. 9; xxi. 5.

[5] Rev. xix. 9.

[6] S. John, xx. 31. The fact of S. Luke having addressed each of his writings to an individual may seem inconsistent with this idea; and may appear to prove that they were not intended for general use. The contrary, however, is the case. S. Luke's writings, as internal evidence shows, were designed for Gentile readers; and at this period there was only one channel through which the works *of a Christian* could be published at Rome. By the Roman law literary production, when presented to some man of station, could claim, were the gift ("strena," "munusculum"), accepted, his support as *patronus libri*;—a relation which imposed duties analogous to those of the *patronus personæ*. In the case before us, therefore, S. Luke's dedication imposed upon Theophilus the duty of multiplying copies of the Gospel and of the Acts, and of distributing them to the utmost of his ability:—see Hug, "Einleit.," Th. i. § 13, s. 93

in the *confidential* communications of S. Paul to Timothy.[1] It is not to be denied, that the New Testament affords no *direct* information on this subject, and that it is equally silent as to the collection of its several parts. So far, indeed, are the sacred writers from taking notice of matters respecting which we might beforehand have anticipated some information that, throughout the Acts of the Apostles, which enter with such minuteness into S. Paul's history, we can trace no hint of his ever having written an Epistle.[2] But if we add to the arguments respecting these questions which are founded upon external testimony and internal presumptions, the fact of the existence of "spiritual gifts" in the early Church, especially that of "discerning of spirits" which S. Paul ranks so highly;[3] and if we, at the same time, bear in mind how S. John appeals to this test, and alludes to its necessity: "Beloved, believe not every spirit, but try the spirits whether they are of God, because many false prophets are gone out into the world;"[4]—if these circumstances, I say, be borne in mind, we can feel as little doubt respecting the Divine influence which effected the formation of the New Testament Canon, and designed the composition of its several parts, as the observations already made allow us to entertain with reference to the Old.

The various parts of the Canon having been successively committed to writing at the Divine command, and thus presenting to inspired men in after-times certain records which they also could consult, the question at once suggests itself—How far, and in what sense, have its earlier portions been made use of in those books which are of later date? That the successive authors of Scripture have availed themselves of the works of their predecessors, requires no proof; and we have already considered[5] the *manner* in which the sacred writers, when referring to previous portions of the Bible, have quoted its language as proceeding from God, or from the Holy Ghost. It only remains for us, therefore,

[1] 1 Tim. i. 20; 2 Tim. ii. 17, 18. The fault of Diotrephes (3 S. John, 9) was plainly one of insubordination merely. Cf. Thiersch, "Versuch zur Herstell." s. 255.

[2] Wordsworth, "On the Canon," p. 169.

[3] Διακρίσεις πνευμάτων—1 Cor. xii. 10. "Let the prophets speak two or three, and let the others judge (οἱ ἄλλοι διακρινέτωσαν)."—xiv. 29; cf. ver. 37. See Appendix K.

[4] Δοκιμάζετε τὰ πνεύματα.—1 S. John, iv. 1. See *supra*, Lecture ii. p. 53, note [1].

[5] See *supra*, Lecture vi. p. 263, &c.

now to examine the *form* of the passages in which such quotations occur; to inquire how the frequent deviations from the words of the authors cited are to be explained; and to prove that no conclusion adverse to the perfect inspiration of Holy Scripture can be drawn from any deviations of this nature.

Before entering upon this feature of the question, I would briefly touch upon one of the leading topics of modern criticism, —I mean the relation of the Synoptical Gospels, one to the other. Every reader of the New Testament must have noticed, not merely the similarity of certain sections occurring in the Gospels of S. Matthew, S. Mark, and S. Luke, but also the repetition of whole passages, frequently without the least variation of language or expression. Thus there are forty-two sections common to these three Evangelists: in addition to which there are twelve sections common to the Gospels of S. Matthew and S. Mark; five to those of S. Mark and S. Luke; and fourteen to those of S. Luke and S. Matthew, which in each case are wanting in the third Gospel.[1] To explain these facts three principal hypotheses have been started: Firstly, that there was an original Gospel, no longer extant, which served as the basis of those which have come down to us. Secondly, that among our Synoptical Gospels whichever was of earliest date was made use of by the writer of that which came next in order of time; both having been, in like manner, employed by the author of the third. Thirdly, That a body of oral teaching had been preserved for some years by tradition; and that each Evangelist made use of this tradition as he judged most suitable for the end at which he aimed. It is unnecessary here to dwell[2] upon the numerous variations and combinations of these different hypotheses: their value cannot be better estimated than by keeping in mind what has been justly remarked by the author of the most celebrated of the three:—namely, that in consequence of the insufficiency of historical information, we can *never* possess perfect certainty

[1] I quote here the statement of Gieseler, "Die Entst. der schriftl. Evangelien," § i. s. 3; who adds that five sections are altogether peculiar to S. Matthew, two to S. Mark, and nine to S. Luke. These facts had been already noticed by S. Augustine: "Marcus eum [*scil.* Matthæum] subsecutus, tanquam pedissequus, et breviator ejus videtur. Cum solo quippe Johanne, nihil dixit; solus ipse, perpauca; cum solo Luca, pauciora; cum Matthæo vero, plurima; et multa pene totidem atque ipsis verbis, sive cum sola sive cum cæteris consonante."—*De Consensu Evangelist.*, lib. i. c. 2, t. III. pars. ii. p. 3.

[2] See Appendix L.

on the subject; and that, at most, we can only arrive at that degree of probability attainable, in general, by historical conjectures.[1]

To which observation I would add, that even were certainty attainable in this matter,—were any phase of any of the hypotheses in question capable of demonstration, and we were, therefore, able to point out the external sources by the aid of which, as such hypotheses assume, each Evangelist composed his Gospel,—such a result could, in no particular, invalidate, or weaken, or in any manner affect, the inspired authority of the New Testament. It forms a prominent feature, it will be remembered, of the theory of Inspiration maintained in these Discourses, that each writer of Scripture made use, on all occasions, of such materials as were in his power,[2] whether supplied by his own experience or by the information of others. This principle, as we have seen, forms the foundation of the distinction between Revelation and Inspiration. The particulars recorded in the pages of

[1] "Man muss sich gleich im Anfange bescheiden, dass man, so verschiedene Wege man auch zur Erklärung dieser Dunkelheiten einschlagen mag, bei dem Unzureichenden der historischen Nachrichten doch nie zu vollkommener Gewissheit, sondern nur zu der Wahrscheinlichkeit gelangen kann, welcher historische Conjecturen überhaupt fähig sind."—Gieseler, *loc. cit.* s. 1. Schleiermacher's remark has been often quoted: "For my part I find it quite enough to prevent me from conceiving the origin of our three Gospels according to Eichhorn's theory, that I am to figure to myself our good Evangelists surrounded by five or six open rolls or books, and that, too, in different languages, looking by turns from one into another, and writing a compilation from them. I fancy myself in a German study of the eighteenth or nineteenth century, rather than in the primitive age of Christianity; and if this resemblance diminishes, perhaps, my surprise at the well-known image having suggested itself to the critic in the construction of his hypothesis, it renders it the less possible for me to believe that such was the actual state of the case."—*The Gospel of S. Luke.* (Thirlwall's transl., p. 6.)

[2] As S. Luke tells us, in the Preface to his Gospel (ch. i. 1–3); or, to take the case of the Old Testament, as we learn from the frequent references, by the authors of the Books of Kings and Chronicles, to the public documents from which they derived their information. Thus we read "the rest of the acts of Solomon * * * are they not written in the book of the acts of Solomon?"—1 Kings, xi. 41 Such were the documents entitled "the book of the chronicles of the kings of Israel," or "of Judah," which "are quoted in the Books of Kings *thirty-one* times up to the history of Jehoiakim, inclusive (2 Kings, xxiv. 5)."—Hävernick, *Einleit.*, Th. II. Abth. i. s. 151; while Nehemiah appeals to these same public records in attestation of his own accuracy: "The sons of Levi * * * were written in the book of the chronicles, even unto the days of Johanan the son of Eliashib."—Neh. xii. 23. That Nehemiah does not refer in these words to our Books of Chronicles, is clear from the fact, that while the document quoted by him counts up the High Priests as far as the time of "Darius the Persian" (ver. 22), the catalogue in the Chronicles terminates with Jehozadak, who "went into captivity, when the Lord carried away Judah and Jerusalem by the hand of Nebuchadnezzar."—1 Chron. vi. 15. See Movers, "Krit. Untersuch. üb. die bibl. Chronik," s. 234. For some further remarks as to this branch of Hebrew literature, see Appendix D.

Scripture were not all matters of Revelation ; the sacred writers have touched upon many topics which were not originally communicated to them from heaven : but this circumstance in no respect invalidates the assertion, that the narrative of each and every fact of which the Bible takes notice has been handed down to future ages under the influence of Inspiration. In other words, the Holy Spirit provided that each portion of the Bible should convey such information as best subserved the Divine purpose, irrespectively of any consideration as to the character of that information,—whether it consisted of plain historical facts, or of immediate disclosures of supernatural truths. Hence therefore, any one of the hypotheses proposed in order to explain the origin of the Gospels may be accepted as true, without in the least affecting the force of a single argument put forward in this investigation. Each Evangelist may have borrowed, to the fullest extent, from those sources which modern critics have attempted to define, and yet his entire composition will remain, in the most literal sense, inspired. But however irrelevant to the inspiration of Scripture the fate of all or any of the hypotheses alluded to has thus been shown to be, it would be ungrateful of the Biblical student to deny that the thorough ventilation which this question has received, has been productive of the most beneficial results as regards the elucidation of the New Testament. The mutual connexion of the different portions of the Gospel history has been more fully brought to light ; the phraseology of the sacred writers has been more accurately analyzed ; and the structure of the whole Evangelical record more perfectly exhibited, in consequence of this discussion, than in any previous stage of Biblical exegesis. Without any exaggeration, indeed, we may apply to this subject of modern research Bacon's apposite illustration of the labors of the Alchemists. They sought for a phantom of their own imagining, and their efforts were not rewarded by the prize for which they struggled ; but the results which met them on their progress were neither few nor unprofitable for other times. The buried treasure, it is true, was not discovered in the vineyard, but the toil expended in the search found a rich return.[1]

[1] "Neque tamen negandum est Alchemistas non pauca invenisse, et inventis utilibus homines donasse. Verum fabula illa non male in illos quadrat de sene qui filiis

I. To revert, however, to the facts which have suggested this digression,—I mean the use made by the sacred writers of those books of Scripture which had been already composed, and which lay before them while engaged themselves in drawing up their own portion of the Bible,—we have to notice, in the first place, the constant references by the Old Testament writers to the labors of their predecessors. For example: the prophecy of Jeremiah against Moab is manifestly founded upon the previous prediction contained in the twenty-first chapter of the book of Numbers.[1] Indeed it appears, even from the English Version, how Jeremiah repeats, almost *verbatim*, the words of the Oracle preserved by Moses. We have, in point of fact, but this one prophecy against Moab; and yet in what various forms is it repeated by the prophets! The language of Isaiah, in his fifteenth and sixteenth chapters, as well as that of Zephaniah referring in like manner to this same subject, are equally based upon the original prediction in the Pentateuch.[2] Again: among the an-

aurum in vinea defossum (sed locum se nescire simulans) legaverit; unde illi vineæ fodiendæ diligenter incubuerunt, et aurum quidem nullum repertum; sed vindemia ex ea cultura facta est uberior."—*Nov. Organ.*, lib. i. Aphor. 85.

[1] "A fire shall come forth out of Heshbon, and a flame from the midst of Sihon, and shall devour the corner of Moab, and the crown of the head of the tumultuous ones כי־אש יצא מחשבון ולהבה מבין סיחן ותאכל פאת מואב וקדקד בני שאון. Woe be unto thee, O Moab! the people of Chemosh perisheth: for thy sons are taken captives, and thy daughters captives."—Jer. xlviii. 45, 46. Cf. "There is a fire gone out of Heshbon, a flame from the city of Sihon (כי־אש יצאה מחשבון להבה מקרית סיחן) it hath consumed Ar of Moab, and the lords of the high places of Arnon. Woe to thee, Moab! Thou art undone, O people of Chemosh: he hath given his sons that escaped, and his daughters into captivity, unto Sihon King of the Amorites."—Numb. xxi. 28, 29; cf. also ver. 30, with Jer. xlviii. 18, 22. We see, too, that Jeremiah has also *embodied* here the prediction of Balaam: "There shall come a Star out of Jacob, and a Sceptre shall rise out of Israel, and *shall smite the corners of Moab and destroy all the children of Sheth* (ומחץ פאתי מואב וקרקר כל־בני־שת)."—Numb. xxiv. 17. For some remarks on Jeremiah's substitution of the noun קדקד for the verb קרקר, see Tholuck's "Vermischte Schriften," Th. I. s. 431; where Tholuck also observes: "A second example is supplied by the word שאון, which Jeremiah has employed instead of the archaic term שת. Here also our lexicographers acknowledge that the term used by Jeremiah is to be regarded as an explanatory translation." Thus: "בני שת, *filii tumultus bellici*, i. e. Israelis hostes tumultuantes. Ap. Jeremiam xlviii. 45 (*qui locus ex nostro* [Num. xxiv. 17] *expressus est*), pro eo est: בני שאון."—Gesenii Lex. *in voc.* As we shall have occasion to revert to the principle which these facts embody (see *infra*, p. 308, and p. 325, note [2]), the reader will bear in mind what has been just noticed, viz., the *combination* of two texts (Num. xxi. 28, 29; xxiv. 17) in *one* quotation, and the alteration by Jeremiah of an expression in the passage which he borrows from an earlier writer. Hävernick observes that it is characteristic "of Jeremiah to refer particularly often to earlier writings of the Old Testament, and to copy them."—*Einleit.*, Th. II. Abth. ii. s. 200.

[2] Zeph. ii. 8–10. Cf. "He is gone up to Bajith, and to Dibon, the high places, to weep: Moab shall howl over Nebo, and over Medeba," &c.—Isai. xv. 2, with "Heshbon is perished even unto Dibon, and we have laid them waste even unto Nophah which reacheth unto Medeba."—Numb. xxi. 30. See also Amos, ii. 1–3.

nouncements of Jeremiah we find an epitome of the denunciation of Obadiah against Edom.[1] In all these cases, however, certain points of difference are observable, which prevent such instances of parallelism from degenerating into mere imitation, or becoming simple repetitions. Thus, in the case before us, the allusions contained in the seventh verse of Obadiah, and in the passage from the nineteenth verse to the end of his pre-

[1] Jer. xlix. 7–22: cf. "I have heard a rumor from the Lord, and an ambassador is sent unto the heathen, saying, Gather ye together and come against her and rise up to the battle. For lo! I will make thee small among the heathen, and despised among men. Thy terribleness hath deceived thee, and the pride of thine heart, O thou that dwellest in the clefts of the rock, that holdest the height of the hill: though thou shouldest make thy nest as high as the eagle, I will bring thee down from thence, saith the Lord"—ver. 14–16, with—"We have heard a rumor from the Lord, and an ambassador is sent among the heathen, Arise ye, and let us rise up against her in battle. Behold I have made thee small among the heathen: thou art greatly despised, The pride of thine heart hath deceived thee, thou that dwellest in the clefts of the rock whose habitation is high. * * * Though thou exalt thyself as the eagle, and though thou set thy nest among the stars, thence will I bring thee down, saith the Lord."—Obad. 1–4. Obadiah had "already before him the more ancient predictions of Balaam (Numb. xxiv. 18), of Joel (iii. 19), of Amos (i. 11, 12; ix. 12), on the ground of which he makes this [viz., the eventual triumph of the Kingdom of God (cf. ver. 21) over the powers of this world, as typified by Israel's conquest of Edom] the object of a more detailed prediction."—Hävernick, *Einleit.*, Th. II. Abth. ii. s. 317. The points of agreement between Isaiah and other writers of Scripture are particularly to be noted. Thus we may compare Isai. xii. 2, with Exod. xv. 2; Isai. xiii. with Jer. l. and li. (cf. Isai. xiii. 19–22, with Jer. l. 39, 40); Isai. xiii. 6, with Joel, i. 15. Or, more particularly still, the passage, "The earth shall be full of the knowledge of the Lord, as the waters cover the sea"—Isai. xi. 9, is repeated with the addition of a single term by Habakkuk: "The earth shall be filled with the knowledge of the glory of the Lord, as the waters cover the sea"—Hab. ii. 14: words which are employed by Isaiah to denote the blessings and the peaceful tenor of the Kingdom of Christ; but which are quoted by Habakkuk for the purpose of describing the judgments and the wrath of God:—see Hengstenberg on Rev. i. 7. (Clarke's For. Theol. Lib. i. p. 81.) The importance of this remark will be seen further on, p. 321, note [4]. Cf. again, Isai. v. 14, with Hab. ii. 5; Isai. xiv. 4, 13, &c., with Hab. ii. 6, 9. "The expressions of Habakkuk," writes Hävernick, "rest so obviously upon the predictions of Isaiah, that they may be regarded as their further development."—*loc. cit.* s. 388. O. Strauss observes on the language of Nahum: "Luculentissima vestigia Jesaiæ librum indigitant."—*Nahumi de Nino Vaticin.*, p. xv. E. g. "How beautiful upon the mountains are the feet of him that bringeth good tidings, that publisheth peace," &c.—Isai. lii. 7. "Behold upon the mountains the feet of him that bringeth good tidings, that publisheth peace!"—Nah. i. 15. Cf. also Isai. xlvii. 2, 3, with Nah. iii. 5 (see Jer. xiii. 22); Isai. li. 19, with Nah. iii. 7. So, too, Zeph. ii. 15, repeats almost word for word the expressions of Isai. xlvii. 8; and the words of Amos, ix. 13, are found again in Joel, iii. 18. The well-known relation between Isai. ii. 2–4, and Mich. iv. 1–3, cannot be passed over without notice; especially as the remarks of commentators upon it afford an interesting illustration of the controversy as to the source of the Gospels. Thus Hengstenberg ("Christol.," Th. I. Abth. ii. s. 20) and Gesenius ("Der Proph. Jesaias," i. s. 177) consider that Micah was the first to utter this prediction, and that Isaiah made use of Micah's language when recording his own vision in which the same revelation was conveyed. Abarbanel, on the contrary, held that Isaiah's words were copied by Micah. Others again maintain that both prophets availed themselves of an earlier prediction, of which their writings now afford the only trace: see Gesenius *loc. cit.*

diction, convey sundry particulars which are not touched upon by Jeremiah.[1]

Here, again, as I have observed with respect to the Gospels, the distinction between Revelation and Inspiration comes to our aid in explaining such phenomena. Historical facts formed the basis of the evangelical narrative ; and, under the guidance of the Holy Spirit, those facts were worked up by each writer into his independent statement, which, accordingly, presents certain features of resemblance to the records of his fellow-laborers. In the prophetical books, on the other hand, the basis of the written document was the direct revelation presented to the intuitive faculty of each prophet.[2] Such revelations, when once received, correspond to the facts in the case of historical narratives ;[3] and they, consequently, became, in like manner, the groundwork of the various prophetic announcements, which (under that same guiding influence of the Holy Ghost to which I have restricted the term Inspiration), have assumed the form of prediction, denunciation, didactic statement, or such like phases of Prophecy.

This feature of the question will be brought out more fully by an example. If we compare the opening verses of the seventh chapter of the Book of Amos with the first and second chapters of the Book of Joel, it will at once appear that at the ground of each prophetic warning lies the same Vision of the desolation of the land by locusts.[4] But observe how different is the treatment

[1] See Köppen, "Die Bibel, ein Werk der göttl. Weisheit," B. ii. s. 115. In order to establish the fact in proof of which I have adduced this example,—viz., that the one prophecy was a development of the other,—it would be necessary to show that Obadiah wrote subsequently to Jeremiah: but this has been denied by other writers (e. g. by Hävernick, "Einleit.," *loc. cit.* s 319 ff). Zechariah's prophecy of "the Branch" (Zech. vi. 10–15), however, affords an incontestable illustration. "The title of 'the Branch' had been already consecrated in Prophecy to the Messiah. It is so given once by Isaiah ["Isai. iv. 2. In xi. 1, a *different*, though *equivalent* word, is employed"], twice by Jeremiah (xxiii. 5; xxxiii. 15). * * * Zechariah's prophecy is a *revival* of Jeremiah's; he introduces it as of a person already known: 'Behold the Man whose name is the Branch.' "—Davison, *On Prophecy*, pp. 320–323. See also the remarks of Hengstenberg ("Beiträge," B. ii. s. 48 ff.) on the manner in which Hosea develops the idea, so often repeated in the Pentateuch, according to which the relation of Jehovah to Israel is symbolized by the relation of marriage; and idolatry denounced under the image of whoredom. E. g. "I will set my face against that man * * * and all that go a whoring after him to commit whoredom with Moloch," &c.—Lev. xx. 5. Cf. ch. xix. 29; Numb. xiv. 33, &c., &c. Observe, too, how Hosea's prophecy opens with a literal repetition of the promises contained in Gen. xxii. 17; xxxii. 12: "Yet the number of the children of Israel shall be as the sand of the sea, which cannot be measured nor numbered"—Hos. i. 10; the spiritual import of which allusion is still further explained by S. Paul, Rom. ix. 26.

[2] See *supra*, Lecture iv. p. 162, &c. [3] See *supra*, Lecture iv. p. 146, &c.

[4] "Thus hath the Lord God showed unto me; and behold he formed grass-

of this theme in the two cases. While Amos confines himself to a simple record of the Vision, Joel has given an elaborate description of its details; employing the imagery and style peculiar to his writings, in which his conception of the future and his allusions to the present are combined with threats and exhortations. Each prophet, we can scarcely doubt, had received the same revelation; but see how differently each, under the guidance of the Holy Spirit, has applied the Divine communication.[1]

II. I turn, in the second place, to the quotations from the Old Testament which meet us in the New.[2] Certain aspects of this subject have been already touched upon, not only when it was argued, from the nature of such quotations, that the Old and New Testaments are both portions of one organized whole,—every section of each subserving the accomplishment of the Divine Counsels;[3] but also, as in the last Discourse, where it was shown how the New Testament writers, as well as our Lord Himself, ascribe

hoppers in the beginning of the shooting up of the latter growth. * * * And it came to pass, that when they had made an end of eating the grass of the land, then I said," &c.—Amos, vii. 1, 2.

[1] The assertion that the same Vision was the germ of each prophetic announcement, does not, of course, imply that the perceptions offered to the spiritual sense of Amos were presented under as fully-developed a form as the revelation to Joel. As O. Strauss observes, Joel "*universæ Prophetiæ* brevem quodammodo exhibet conspectum * * * Amos hostium *non* immensas omnino catervas *vidit, sicuti Joël;* verum certam populi speciem, longe remoti cujusdam et ferocissimi, *cujus tamen nomen ignorat* (cf. Amos, vi. 14; v. 27)."—*loc. cit.* p. lxvii. See also Hävernick, *loc. cit.*, s. 43, *u.* 295.

[2] The following remarks will fitly introduce this subject:—"In the freedom of the Spirit of Truth, the question is not whether Divine sayings already promulgated have been quoted with rigid adherence to their mere *letter*, but whether they have been given anew, true to their *spirit:* a repetition which, under different circumstances, takes a direction, towards their spiritual end, both new, and withal appropriate; in which, moreover, the original import is not falsified, and suited to error or prejudice, but, in the sense of its Author, the Spirit, is now developed further and more profoundly—is defined more nearly, and adapted to the new requirements of Truth, to the meaning which is spiritual and not carnal, to the requirements of Divine and not of worldly progress. * * * Such is the manner in which the Holy Ghost, at every higher stage of His communications, acts with respect to what has been already given within the limits of a lower or preparatory stage of Revelation. Such things as could not, as yet, be there expressed, and were still veiled under figure or symbol, are, at a later period, proclaimed without reserve from the house tops. According to this principle are to be estimated the quotations and expositions of the Old Testament sayings, and narratives in the Apostolic writings:—matters which, when handled by men unconsecrated, and endowed with merely human cultivation, are lost in frivolous allegory, as in the expositions of Philo. Such expositions, when proceeding from the Spirit, the authentic Author and Expounder of His own work, become a higher and more profound development of Truth:—that which, were it combined, from a purely human stand-point, out of doctrine and history, would be fiction or conjecture, becomes, in the Divine Author's own representation, an infusion of life, and the completion of His design."—Beck, *Propäd. Entwickl.*, s. 242.

[3] See Lecture i. p. 26, &c.; and Lecture iii. Cf. Appendix B.

the Old Testament to the immediate agency of the Holy Ghost. On these occasions I confined myself either to an examination of the *manner* in which such passages from the former Scriptures are introduced, or to the general points of connexion between the sacred writings which they exhibit : it still remains to consider the *form* and *substance* of the quotations themselves. The importance of this subject arises from the fact that the two divisions of the Bible are composed in different languages ; combined with the parallel fact that, at the period when the New Testament was written,[1] there had already existed, for a considerable time, a translation of the Old Testament into Greek, which, although of great value, is not inspired,[2] but of which the writers of the New Testament have confessedly availed themselves. This fact at once presents a kind of *experimentum crucis* of every theory of Inspiration.[3] Not to dwell upon the extravagant opin-

[1] See the valuable discussion of Hug ("Einleit.," Th. II. cap. i. § 10), as to the language of Palestine in the Apostolic age. Too great importance, he observes, "is attached to the fact that Jesus is represented as speaking in Hebrew (Mark, v. 41—Ταλιθὰ κοῦμι ; vii. 34—'Εφφαθά ; and Matt. xxvii. 46 ; Mark, xv. 34). It might be replied that the Hebrew words in these passages are quoted by the Evangelists as something remarkable, which would not have been the case had Jesus for the most part spoken in Hebrew ; and what could reasonably be objected to this answer ? We will not, however, dismiss the matter so hastily. The Lord may have adddressed the Jewish multitude in their own language, on account of their predilection for it. But how did He address a mixed assembly collected from different regions and cities ? How did He speak to proselytes and pagans, as at Gadaris (Matt. viii. 28, &c., Mark, v. 1 ;. Luke, viii. 26) ? How in the district of Tyre and Sidon (Mark, vii. 24, &c.), where the Syrophenician Greek woman (γυνὴ 'Ελληνίς Συροφοινίκισσα) entered into conversation with Him ? How in Decapolis, which consisted of Greek cities, such as Philadelphia, Gerasa, Gadara, Hippos, and Pella ?"—s. 46.

[2] I do not consider it necessary to discuss the question as to the inspiration of the LXX. The fabulous character of the narrative of Aristeas, to a belief in the truth of which that notion chiefly owes its currency, has been sufficiently exposed by Hody, in his well-known work, "De Bibliorum Text. Originalibus."

[3] Tholuck ("Das A. Test. im N. Test," s. 7) quotes a remark of Billroth on 1 Cor. i. 19,—where S. Paul does not adhere literally to either the Hebrew or the LXX.,—which forcibly expresses the alternative in this question : "According to his wont, the Apostle quotes, in proof, passages of the Old Testament which certainly do not always suit in a strictly historical sense (i. e. so that the respective authors had meant what Paul means in the connexion in which he quotes them), but which, however, so far as regards the words, imply what they are applied to. In order not to accuse Paul (as well as the other writers of the New Testament—nay, Christ Himself) of either ignorance, or even perhaps dishonesty in this point, we must firmly maintain the principle according to which the Old Testament, taken collectively, is a type of the New :—so that the predictions of the prophets (e. g. those relating to the Messiah) are not to be understood as if the writers had *consciously* referred to the historical Christ, who was born under the reign of Augustus (every child perceives that this is not the case, and the fact is one which writers need not make so much of), but so that, in the words which they utter, that same Divine Spirit expresses Itself, which *organically* penetrates the entire history, and which, consequently, has also appeared in Christianity."

ion that the Apostles have often misunderstood[1] or misquoted the Hebrew Scriptures, it is held by an extensive class of modern commentators that the authors of the New Testament, when making use of the Septuagint Version, continually "quote from memory."[2] This assertion can only mean, that the passages adduced by the inspired writers are not cited with as much accuracy, or correctness, as might have been attained had they been at the pains to consult the source from which they have borrowed the form of their quotations. Nay more, such a principle would undoubtedly lend some color to the statement,—which, as we shall presently see, has actually been advanced,—

[1] In the "Studien u. Kritiken" for 1835 a writer of considerable repute, Dr. Bleek, in an essay on "The dogmatic use of Old Testament sayings in the New," proposes the following question:—"If an Old Testament saying is employed in the New Testament, in such a manner that we cannot question the fact that the New Testament writer has referred it to the Messiah,—and this, too, not by way of mere application; while, at the same time, his use of it does not throughout belong strictly to the original sense and original reference,—is, then, such a use of the passage binding upon us; and a rule of itself sufficient to determine us to understand, in the same sense, the Old Testament saying?"—s. 443. This question, in all its generality, Dr. Bleek answers *in the negative*,—adding that he has "on his side the majority of German theologians of the present age,"—on the ground that we cannot imagine the language of the Old Testament to have any other meaning than that which the Old Testament writer himself perceived in it. Thus in the case of the second Psalm, which is applied so frequently to the Messiah in the New Testament (e. g. Acts, iv. 25, 26; xiii. 33; Heb. i. 2; v. 5; Rev. ii. 27; xii. 5; xix. 15), Dr. Bleek considers that there is not the slightest intimation that any other time or person was intended than the time when the Psalmist wrote, and the king then "anointed on Zion" (s. 456). To suppose "that the Holy Spirit so guided the Psalmist in his poetry and his composition, that his words present a second more remote and higher reference extending beyond this *immediate* sense, and of which he himself was unconscious, or at least, not clearly conscious," would be to assume an inspiration by the Holy Ghost of such a nature as Dr. Bleek is not disposed to concede (s. 458). (In reply to this principle, which assumes that the human agents were the sole and proper authors of the Bible, see what has been already said, Lecture v. p. 189, &c.) The use of the Old Testament in the New (chiefly by S. Matthew and S. John), Dr. Bleek describes as resulting from an "earlier exegetical tradition of the Jewish schools; an exegesis, too, which we are not "justified in regarding as founded upon perfectly just principles, or as treated in a perfectly correct manner."—s. 447. Such Jewish views, he adds, we cannot but expect to have had their influence on the New Testament writers; who accordingly have understood sundry texts of the Old Testament "in a sense which would not be received as either correct or accurate had they attained to a greater perfection of exegetical science and skill."—s. 448.

[2] E. g. Olshausen (see *infra*, p. 323, note [4]); Bleek; Mr. Alford (who writes on S. Matt. xxvii. 9: "The citation is not from Jeremiah, and is probably quoted from memory, and inaccurately [but see *infra*, p. 308, note [3]); we have similar mistakes in two places in the apology of Stephen, Acts, vii. 4, 16, and in Mark, ii. 26. * * * The quotation here is very different from the LXX., and not much more like the Hebrew;" cf. also his notes on Rom. xi. 34; and 2 Cor. vi. 17); Tholuck (who observes: "In very many, nay in most cases, in consequence of *quoting from memory* the passage, so far as *the words* are concerned, is altered sometimes to such an extent that the deviation, as is the case in 1 Cor. ii. 9 (Eph. v. 14) [but see *infra*, p. 307, note [2]], has even caused the supposition that the citation belongs to some apocryphal book."—*Das A. Test. im N. Test.*, s. 39.)

that, in consequence of thus citing the Greek translation from memory, the Apostles may, at times, although undesignedly, have missed the sense of the original. Such a doctrine, if capable of proof, is obviously fatal to that view of the inspiration of Scripture which I have endeavored to maintain; according to which each and every portion of the Bible is perfect and Divine. On the other hand, if this latter inference be legitimate, any opinion which ascribes to *the form* in which the Old Testament is quoted a less degree of perfection than might have been secured by a somewhat greater amount of diligence or care on the part of those New Testament writers who adduce it must be radically and essentially unsound; and to establish this conclusion must now be my task.

The references to the Old Testament which meet us in the New may be arranged under two classes.[1] The *first* embraces those passages which are strictly prophetical; and of this class the following subdivisions present themselves:—(1.) Those texts which refer almost exclusively to the Messiah's Personal history or Character; and in which the principle of pointing to Him as their end is clearly intimated:—such texts being brought forward, not as mere illustrations, or by way of adaptation to the events of His life, but as requiring an actual fulfilment in an actual fact. Predictions of this kind are referred to with the words, "That the Scripture might be fulfilled;" or, "Now all this was done that it might be fulfilled;"[2] or, "Then was fulfilled that which was spoken by the prophet:"[3] the New Testa-

[1] In the following discussion I avail myself of the excellent remarks of Rudelbach in his "Zeitschrift" for 1842, H. ii. s. 42 ff.

[2] Ἵνα, or ὅπως πληρωθῇ.—e. g. "I know whom I have chosen: but that the Scripture may be fulfilled (ἀλλ' ἵνα ἡ γραφὴ πληρωθῇ,) He that eateth bread with Me," &c.—S. John, xiii. 18; or "Now all this was done that it might be fulfilled (ἵνα πληρωθῇ) which was spoken of the Lord by the prophet, saying, Behold a Virgin shall be with child," &c.—S. Matt. i. 22, 23. Again: "Without a parable spake He not unto them; that it might be fulfilled (ὅπως πληρωθῇ) which was spoken by the prophet, saying, I will open My mouth in parables," &c.—S. Matt. xiii. 34, 35. "The signification of the oft-recurring phrase, ἵνα πληρωθῇ, as involving a real connexion between Prophecy and its fulfilment, is no longer questioned by the more judicious expositors. The fact that Grammar itself, against the will of those who handle it, is compelled to give at least formal testimony to the Faith, is not to be overlooked as an apologetic element of the Christian Evidences; and indeed it has never, when the occasion offered, been overlooked by the Ancients. The sense, however, of that formula (cf. e. g. in the first Gospel, S. Matt. ii. 15; viii. 17; xii. 17; xiii. 35; xxi. 4; xxvi. 56; xxvii. 35) is plainly nothing else than what lies in the expression itself, viz., that the fulfilment has taken place *in order* to display the truth of Prophecy."—Rudelbach, *Zeitschr.*, 1840. H. i. s. 3.

[3] "Then was fulfilled that which was spoken by Jeremy the prophet (Τότε

ment writers thereby declaring that God had pre-ordained that the prophet's announcement should receive its true accomplishment in the single fact to which it is thus applied. (2.) To this subdivision may be added those which are in the strictest sense typical predictions :—that is, where the words or symbols of the Old Testament are adduced as having conveyed, from the first, an allusion to the particular fact or event in which they are stated to have been now at length realized ; and respecting the true signification of which the fulfilment alone could have given certainty.[1] Although the reference is made under the form of an involved type, its substance is always prophetical, as we learn from the use, here also, of the phrase, "That it might be fulfilled which was spoken by the prophet," or such like expressions. Of this nature was the mention by S. John of the ceremonies connected with the Paschal Lamb, which he represents as being at length truly exhibited in the Sacrifice upon the Cross : "These things were done that the Scripture should be fulfilled, A bone of Him shall not be broken."[2] (3.) There are also those passages

ἐπληρώθη τὸ ῥηθὲν διὰ Ἱερ.), saying, In Rama was there a voice heard," &c.—S. Matt. ii. 17.

[1] See *supra*, Lecture v. p. 200, note [1], where I have differed from Rudelbach ("Zeitschr.," 1842. H. ii. s. 38) in regarding the relation of Types to Prophecy as more intimate than he is disposed to admit. In accordance with his views, instead of referring such quotations in the New Testament to the class of strictly prophetical passages, Rudelbach regards the "vaticinia typica," there adduced by the sacred writers, as forming a distinct class.

[2] *Ἐγένετο γὰρ ταῦτα ἵνα ἡ γραφὴ πληρωθῇ*—S. John, xix. 36 ; and in the same sense another Apostle writes: "Ye were not redeemed with corruptible things * * * but with the precious blood of Christ, as of a *Lamb* without blemish."—1 S. Pet. i. 18, 19 (cf. also ver. 2); S. John, i. 29; 1 Cor. v. 7 ; &c. Quite similar is S. Matthew's allusion, in his account of the rending of the Vail of the Temple (xxvii. 51); on which feature of the Tabernacle S. Paul dwells with such particularity (Heb. ix. 3, 11, 12; x. 20). The following instances may be added: Joseph arose and "took the Young Child and His Mother by night, and departed into Egypt, that it might be fulfilled (*ἵνα πληρωθῇ*) which was spoken of the Lord by the prophet, saying, Out of Egypt have I called My Son"—S. Matt. ii. 14, 15 ; for the sense of which typical prediction see *supra*, Lecture iii. p. 109, note [1]. Still more forcibly illustrative of this class of typical predictions is the manner in which the New Testament teaches that the *entire* course of Jewish history, and not the Exodus merely, pointed to Christ. This we learn from the reference to Ps. lxxviii., by both S. Paul and S. Matthew: the former declaring that "these things were our examples," or rather "*types*"—*Ταῦτα δὲ τύποι ἡμῶν ἐγενήθησαν*—1 Cor. x. 6 ; and the latter quoting its words with the formula, "That it might be fulfilled which was spoken by the prophet." —xiii. 35. On the use of this Psalm see also *supra*, Lecture iv. p. 151, note. Cf., too, the well-known difficulty connected with the words, "He came and dwelt in a city called Nazareth: *that it might be fulfilled* (*ὅπως πληρ.*) *which was spoken by the prophets*, He shall be called a Nazarene."—S. Matt. ii. 23 : where, as Olshausen ("Ein Wort üb. tief. Schriftsinn," s. 64) conjectures, the Evangelist may refer to the saying of Jacob that Joseph "*was separate* from his brethren (נזיר אחיו)—Gen. xlix. 26 (cf. Num. vi. 1–22); considering Joseph as a type of the Messiah,—a character already

which are quoted so that their direct reference to a particular person or event cannot be questioned. Thus Isaiah's prediction that S. John the Baptist should appear in the character of the Messiah's forerunner is introduced by S. Matthew with the words: "This is he that was spoken of by the prophet Esaias."[1] (4.) The last subdivision embraces those texts which are cited so that the causative particle connects the Messianic fact with the prediction,—thus assuring us, in the way of inference, that such was the end at which the prophet's language aimed. For example, S. Peter explains how "it was impossible" that Jesus of Nazareth "should be holden of" death, "*For* David speaketh concerning him" the prophecy which has been handed down as the sixteenth Psalm.[2]

As forming the *second* class of quotations are to be counted those passages in which the language of the Old Testament is incorporated with the body of Christian doctrine; and in which the prophets are represented in the same light as the men who directly announced the New Covenant. In such instances we have a practical illustration of Christ's saying that heaven and earth should disappear rather than "one jot or one tittle pass from the Law till all be fulfilled."[3] In this case the language of the former Scriptures is sometimes introduced without an express reference:—as in the first Epistle of S. Peter, where passages from Isaiah and Ezekiel are embodied in the Apostle's argument,

implied in the name "Saviour of the World" ("Zaphnath Paaneah") assigned to him by Pharaoh (Gen. xli. 45). It is clear that Ναζαρέτ (whence Ναζωραῖος—*the despised one*) cannot, as many writers hold, be derived from נֵצֶר—*a branch* (Isai. xi. 1); since ζ invariably corresponds to ז, not צ. (E. g. in S. Matt. i.; S. Luke, iii. Ἄχαζ = אחז, Ζοροβάβελ = זרבבל, &c.: while Σιδών = צידן, Σιών = ציון.) Cf. the employment by Christ Himself of the type of Jonah: Ὥσπερ γὰρ ἦν Ἰωνᾶς ἐν τῇ κοιλίᾳ * * * οὕτως ἔσται ὁ Υἱὸς τοῦ Ἀνθρ. κ. τ. λ.—S. Matt. xii. 40; as well as that of the "brazen serpent," Καθὼς Μωϋσῆς ὕψωσεν τὸν ὄφιν, οὕτως ὑψωθῆναι δεῖ τὸν Υἱὸν τοῦ Ἀνθρ.—S. John, iii. 14; which latter exposition teaches us how fully our Lord has adopted the typical mode interpretation.

[1] S. Matt. iii. 3; Isai. xl. 3. The purchase of "the potter's field" with "the price of blood," is described as follows: "Then was fulfilled (τότε ἐπληρώθη) that which was spoken," &c.—S. Matt. xxvii. 9. So also S. Peter explains as the fulfilment of the words of Joel, ii. 28, 29, the events on "the Day of Pentecost" (Acts, ii. 16)—ἀλλὰ τοῦτό ἐστιν τὸ εἰρημένον διὰ τοῦ προφήτου Ἰωήλ.

[2] Acts, ii. 24, 25—οὐκ ἦν δυνατὸν κρατεῖσθαι Αὐτὸν * * * Δαυὶδ γ ὰ ρ λέγει. κ. τ. λ. Or again: "Therefore they could not believe, *because that* Esaias said again," &c. (ὅ τ ι πάλιν εἶπεν Ἠσ.).—S. John, xii. 39. Or: "*For it* is written in the Book of Psalms (Γέγραπται γ ὰ ρ ἐν βίβλῳ ψαλμ.) * * * his bishopric let another take. *Wherefore* (δ ε ῖ ο ὖ ν) of these men which have companied, &c. * * * *must* one be ordained," &c.—Acts, i. 20–22. Cf. Eph. iv. 8—Διὸ λέγει.

[3] See *supra*, Lecture iii. p. 104, &c.

unaccompanied by any observation denoting the sources from which they were taken.[1] On the other hand, the reference to the Old Testament is sometimes plainly expressed.[2] Again: a statement of some former inspired writer is employed in such a manner as to connect the prediction which it conveys, with a series of historical facts:—those facts indicating, on some occasions, that the accomplishment of the prediction *had commenced* (thus S. Matthew adduces Isaiah's language, which describes the sufferings of the Messiah, as beginning to receive its fulfilment in Christ's miracles of healing: "Himself took our infirmities, and bare our sicknessess");[3] or at other times signifying the *continuous* accomplishment of the prophetic declaration (as when S. Paul interprets the nineteenth Psalm as having foreshadowed the permanent preaching of the Gospel: "Their sound went into all the earth, and their words unto the ends of the world."[4])

Under this class comes also a series of references by which the writers of the New Testament exemplify, in the plainest manner, their belief in the inspiration of the Old Testament; and from which it obviously results that each portion of Scripture

[1] "Who His own Self bare our sins in his own Body on the tree * * * by Whose stripes ye were healed (Isai. liii. 4, 5). For ye were as sheep going astray (Ezek. xxxiv. 11, 12); but are now returned unto the Shepherd and Bishop of your souls (Ezek. xxxvii. 24)."—1 S. Pet. ii. 24, 25. Cf. also ch. i. 24, 25: "All flesh is as grass, and all the glory of man as the flower of grass. The grass withereth * * * but the word of the Lord endureth for ever,"—words which are incorporated in the Apostle's exhortation from Isai. xl. 6–8. This mode of employing the Old Testament, as Rudelbach observes, "is a surety to us that, in the judgment of the Apostle, there lies in its language a *ῥῆμα Θεοῦ, μένον εἰς τὸν αἰῶνα*."—*loc. cit.*, s. 47. Such also is the mode of referring to Hab. ii. 4, "The just shall live by his faith"—in Gal. iii. 11; and Hebr. x. 38.

[2] E. g. "Dearly beloved, avenge not yourselves * * * for it is written (*γέγραπται γάρ*), Vengeance is Mine," &c.—Rom. xii. 19. Again: "That, according as it is written (*καθὼς γέγραπται*), He that glorieth," &c.—1 Cor. i. 31. Cf. Acts, xiii. 40. A still more striking instance is supplied by the passage: "Wherefore he saith, Awake, thou that sleepest, and arise from the dead, and Christ shall give thee light" —Eph. v. 14—a passage which is not to be found in express words in either the Hebrew or the LXX.; while the formula *διὸ λέγει* (as Olshausen, B. iv. s. 270, truly says) points infallibly to a quotation from Scripture. S. Paul here clearly refers to Isai. lx. 1.

[3] "He cast out the spirits with His word, and healed all that were sick. That it might be fulfilled which was spoken by Esaias the prophet [liii. 4], saying, Himself took our infirmities, and bare our sicknesses."—S. Matt. viii. 16, 17. So also ch. iv 14, 15, the first dawn of the Gospel and the future conversion of the Heathen, when "the people which sat in darkness saw great light"—is inferred from Isai. ix. 1, 2, with the formula of citation, *ἵνα πληρωθῇ*:—the Evangelist adding, "From that time Jesus *began* to preach."—ver. 17.

[4] Rom. x. 18. Compare, too, the reference, in ver. 8, to Deut. xxx. 12–14. From Heb. viii. 8–12, we learn that the days of the Gospel afford the never-ceasing accomplishment of Jer. xxxi. 31–34.

must be regarded as part of one Divine whole :—I mean the system of collective quotations, where a number of passages are brought together, in the same connexion, from various books of the Bible, in order to establish some one point of Christian doctrine.[1] Of this, the Epistle to the Hebrews affords many instances :[2] but the most striking example is, perhaps, supplied by the passage commencing at the tenth verse of the third chapter of the Epistle to the Romans, where five different texts from the Psalms are combined in the same quotation with a text from Isaiah :—the whole series commencing with the formula "As it is written."[3] It is plain that in these collective quotations the

[1] This *fact* affords a satisfactory reply to the opening observations of Mr. Coleridge in the passage quoted *supra*, Lecture ii. p. 53, note [2]. Had the Bible not been *generically* different from "all other writings," such a "practice" would be indeed "unexampled."

[2] In Heb. i. 5–13, the exaltation of Christ above all creatures and angels is inferred from Ps. ii. 7; 2 Sam. vii. 14: Ps. xcvii. 7; xlv. 6. 7; cii. 25–27. In ch. ii. 6–8, 12, 13, the true human nature of Christ is inferred from Ps. viii. 4–6; xxii. 22; xviii. 2. In ch. iv. 4–10, the 'Rest of the people of God' is shown to have been predicted in Gen. ii. 2; Ps. xcv. 7–9. "No more instructive codex of prophetical theology could be presented to us than in these highly fruitful quotations."—Rudelbach, *loc. cit.*, s. 48.

[3] Καθὼς γέγραπται—Rom. iii. 10–18,—where the following passages are combined: Ps. liii. 1; v. 9; cxl. 3; x. 7; Isai. lix. 7, 8; Ps. xxxvi. 1. So also in Rom. x. 19, 20, with reference to the obstinacy of Israel and the call of the Gentiles, we find Deut. xxxii. 21, and Isai. lxv. 1, 2, united. Cf. in Rom. xi. 8–10, the quotations from Isai. xxix. 10; Deut. xxix. 4; Ps. lxix. 22, 23: where also (Rom. ix. 33), Isai. viii. 14, is combined with Isai. xxviii. 16;—the same combination occurring in 1 S. Pet. ii. 6–8, with the addition of a further quotation from Ps. cxviii. 22 (cf. S. Matt. xxi. 42, &c.). In the same manner 2 Cor. vi. 16, is composed of Lev. xxvi. 12, and Ezek. xxxvii. 26, 27; while in ver. 17, to the quotation from Isai. lii. 11, there is added an expression (εἰσδέξομαι ὑμᾶς) from Ezek. xx. 34, which briefly sums up the promise of Isai. lii. 12:—ver. 18 being taken from Jer. xxxi. 1–9, 33; xxxii. 38. Again, the words of S. Stephen (Acts, vii. 7), "and serve me in this place," are not found in either the Hebrew or LXX. of Gen. xv. 14. They are taken from God's words, Exod. iii. 12:—the combination of the two passages pointing out the connexion of the different parts of the Divine Scheme. The following examples of this procedure require some remarks: In S. Mark, i. 2—where the reading adopted in the English Version, "As it is written *in the prophets*" (ἐν τοῖς προφήταις), is certainly incorrect; and where we should read "in Isaiah the prophet" (ἐν Ἠσαΐᾳ τῷ προφήτῃ), —we find the language of Mal. iii. 1, combined with that of Isai. xl. 3. It is obvious that the words of Malachi, "he shall prepare the [a] way before Me" are based upon the expression of Isaiah—"Prepare ye the [a] way of the Lord:" and that this is not a mere undesigned coincidence on the part of the later prophet is proved by Malachi (iii. 2; iv. 5) having similarly incorporated in his own statements the language of another and earlier servant of God, viz., Joel, ii. 11, and 31. The design of Malachi here was to show the Jews who had returned from the Exile, and whose temporal condition seemed to present a contradiction to the promised glories of Messiah's reign, that Isaiah himself had already foretold that the evangelical promises were not as yet at hand; and that "the preparation of the way" must precede Messiah's glory. The passage quoted by S. Mark from Malachi, therefore, is not an *independent* prediction. Malachi is merely the *auctor secundarius*; and the Evangelist points out that this is the case by ascribing both commentary and text to Isaiah, whom he thus represents as the *auctor primarius*,—the commentary being placed

Apostles adduce the several passages as all denoting, and from the first pointing to, one great truth;—although separately, in their *primary* connexion, such statements of the Old Testament had often merely a reference to more special relations.

This review of what are plain matters of fact of itself brings to light the principle which guided the sacred writers, under the Gospel Dispensation, in the use which they have made of the Old Testament. The Holy Spirit, when inspiring God's servants in former times, had infused a deeper significance into their words than the men who uttered them, or who committed them to writing, perceived.[1] The depth of meaning conveyed could only be apprehended, in the fulness of time, by those who, like the authors of the New Testament, "had the mind of Christ;"[2] and who were thereby enabled to unfold the hidden mystery couched under the earlier form.[3] Consider how Christ Himself has exem-

first, as it serves to elucidate the text. S. Mark's exordium, "The beginning of the Gospel," also shows that he had in view the closing book of the Old Testament. That in S. Matt. iii. 1–4, these words of Isaiah are in like manner quoted with reference to Malachi is clear from the use of *μετανοεῖτε*—ver. 2, compared with Mal. iv. 5, 6, where "Elijah the prophet" is described as the preacher of *μετάνοια*. See Hengstenberg, "Christol.," B. iii. s. 398. On the principle here laid down, Hengstenberg (B. ii. s. 259) explains why S. Matthew (xxvii. 9) has ascribed to Jeremiah the words of Zechariah (xi. 13):—the Evangelist desiring to explain that Jeremiah was to be regarded as the *auctor primarius* of a prediction with which his readers were well acquainted, and to whose words (Jer. xviii. 1–3; xix. 2) the expression of Zechariah, "And the Lord said unto me, *Cast it unto the potter*," refers us; Jeremiah standing to Zechariah in the same relation as Ezekiel and Daniel to the Apocalypse. Nor is the reference in such cases to a single prophet unusual. The quotation, "That it might be fulfilled which was spoken *by the prophet*, Tell ye the daughter of Sion, Behold thy king cometh unto thee, meek," &c., in S. Matt. xxi. 4, 5, is taken from Isai. lxii. 11, and Zech. ix. 9; on which Bengel observes: "Hic locus exemplo est multos sermones apud prophetas accipi debere, non solum ut ab illis dictos sed ut ab Apostolis dicendos." Cf. too, our Lord's words, S. Matt. xxiv. 30, with Dan. vii. 13; Zech. xii. 10–12. This combination of different passages meets us even in the Old Testament. Thus Nahum, in the words, "For now I will break his yoke from off thee, and will burst thy *bonds* in sunder."—i. 13, alludes to the expressions of Isai. x. 27 in language differing from them in some respects (e. g. מוסר); *both* statements being combined in Jer. xxx. 8. See O. Strauss, *loc. cit.*, p. 40.

[1] See *supra*, Lecture v. p. 189, &c.

[2] "Who hath known the mind of the Lord (*νοῦν Κυρίου*)? * * * But we have the mind of Christ" (*ἡμεῖς δὲ νοῦν Χριστοῦ ἔχομεν*).—1 Cor. ii. 16.

[3] Rudelbach (following Olshausen) has truly observed that "a *ὑπόνοια*—a deeper sense, intended by the Holy Ghost,—must be allowed, in the interpretation of Scripture, by all who have a clear apprehension of the *objectivity* of the Holy Spirit's influence upon the prophets."—*Zeitschrift*, 1842, H. ii. s. 34. Olshausen ("Ein Wort üb. tief. Schriftsinn," s. 70) establishes the justice of this principle by an appeal to the plain statements of the sacred writers. In this sense S. Paul expounds the history of Hagar and Ishmael (see *supra*, Lecture iii. p. 109),—"which things," writes the Apostle, "*are an Allegory*" (*ἅτινά ἐστιν ἀλληγορούμενα*).—Gal. iv. 24. So also S. John writes: "Their dead bodies shall lie in the street of the great city, *which spiritually is called* (*ἥτις καλεῖται πνευματικῶς*) *Sodom and Egypt*."—Rev. xi. 8. Cf. Rom. ix. 7, 8; 2 Cor. iii. 13, &c.; Eph. v. 32, &c. The classical phrase *ὑπόνοια* is ad-

plified this principle :—His saying, "Blessed are the meek, for they shall inherit the earth,"[1] exhibits the spiritual sense of that inheritance of the promised land which so constantly forms the theme of Old Testament Prophecy ; and in which Canaan, the terrestrial object of the Divine promises, symbolizes every Divine blessing. The argument founded upon these same promises in the Epistle to the Hebrews[2] clearly shows how this idea pervades the entire organism of the Bible, and how it implies the realization of the Kingdom of God even in its earthly form.

But while the authors of the New Testament, by their full appreciation of the deeper meaning conveyed in the words of earlier sacred writers, show how widely they differ from that class of expositors who see no further intent in the language of Inspiration than its naked, literal signification ; they are, at the same time, as widely opposed to that other class which fixes its exclusive attention upon the allegorical or mystical sense of Scripture.[3] From this latter school the inspired penmen are severed by broad lines of distinction. In the first place, they assert unconditionally the literal signification and historical reality of every narrative in the Bible ; insisting, nevertheless, upon the spiritual

mirably suited to express the truth which such texts convey: inasmuch as it implies that under the obvious signification of the words there lies, not indeed a different, but the same signification again, more profoundly apprehended. See also *supra*, Lecture iv. p. 153, note [1].

[1] S. Matt. v. 5—*κληρονομήσουσιν τὴν γῆν*. Cf. "I will give unto thee, and to thy seed * * * all the land of Canaan *for an everlasting possession.*"—Gen. xvii. 8. "Sic ergo et promissio Dei, quam promisit Abrahæ, firma perseverat * * * Repromisit autem Deus hæreditatem terræ Abrahæ et semini ejus: et neque Abraham, neque semen ejus, hoc est, qui ex fide justificantur, nunc sumunt in ea hæreditatem: accipient autem eam in resurrectione justorum. Verus enim et firmus Deus: et propter hoc 'beatos' dicebat 'mites, quoniam ipsi hæreditabunt terram.'"—S. Irenæus, *Cont. Hær.*, lib. v. xxxii. p. 331. See Olshausen *in loc.*

[2] "Seeing, therefore, it remaineth that some must enter therein, and they to whom it was first preached entered not in because of unbelief: again He limiteth a certain day, saying in David, To-day, &c. There remaineth, therefore, a rest to the people of God."—Heb. iv. 6–9. In a similar manner Christ has pointed out the spiritual signification of the Mosaic rites, by referring the ordinance that all sacrifices must be sprinkled with salt (Lev. ii. 13) to the spiritual sprinkling of the soul with the salt of suffering and self-denial: "Every one shall be salted with fire, and every sacrifice shall be salted with salt. Salt is good ; but if the salt have lost his saltness, wherewith will ye season it ? Have salt in yourselves, and have peace one with another." —S. Mark, ix, 49, 50.

[3] Two celebrated names in the early Church may be taken as representing these extreme opinions, Origen, and Theodore of Mopsuestia, the leaders of the schools of Alexandria and Antioch. Assuming alike the Divine origin and inspiration of the Bible, these teachers founded their systems of exposition on principles diametrically opposed; and which, moreover, are equally removed from that line of interpretation which Scripture itself has suggested. For some remarks on these two opposing systems, see Appendix G.

and heavenly import which underlies the earthly record. Secondly, their use of the Old Testament unfolds what the passage to be interpreted, taken in strict connexion with its context, actually does mean ; in no instance exhibiting the capricious and arbitrary subtlety of allegorical expositors—their unnatural applications, or overstrained ingenuity. And, thirdly, their expositions invariably refer to the grand design of promoting the moral welfare of man. They do not strive to point out how far the sense of scriptural expressions may actually extend ; they content themselves with indicating what shall profit those whom they address.[1] Thus S. Paul, when expounding the spiritual significance of the Legal ceremonial, refuses to dwell upon the mysteries of the Cherubim.[2]

Having thus pointed out the principle on which the sacred writers themselves have treated the language of Scripture ; and having shown how, in pursuance of that principle, their system of interpretation attaches equal weight to the historical reality, and the spiritual import,—we are prepared to enter upon the question of *the form* under which quotations from the Old Testament

[1] See the excellent remarks of Olshausen, "Ein Wort," &c. s. 71 ff. Compare, too, the profound remark of S. Jerome, referring to Rev. v. 2: "Leo autem de Tribu Juda, Dominus Jesus Christus est, qui solvit signacula libri, non proprie unius, ut multi putant, Psalmorum David, sed omnium Scripturarum, quæ uno Scripturæ [scriptæ] sunt Spiritu Sancto; et propterea unus liber appellantur. De quo Ezekiel mystico sermone testatur, quod scriptus fuerit intus et foris; *in sensu, et in litera*. De quo et Salvator loquitur in Psalmis: 'In capitulo libri scriptum est de Me;' non Jeremiæ, non Isaiæ, sed in omni Scriptura Sancta, quæ unus liber appellatur."—*Comm. in Isaiam*, lib. ix., t. iv. p. 393.

The following remarks of S. Th. Aquinas, discussing the question, "Utrum Sacra Scriptura sub una litera habeat plures sensus," may serve to connect with the present stage of this inquiry what has been said, *supra*, Lecture iv. p. 153, note [1]; "Auctor Sacræ Scripturæ est Deus, in cujus potestate est ut non solum voces ad significandum accommodet (quod etiam homo facere potest), sed etiam res ipsas. * * * Illa prima significatio qua voces significant res pertinet ad primum sensum, qui est sensus historicus, vel literalis. Illa vero significatio qua res significatæ per voces iterum res alias significant dicitur sensus spiritualis, qui super literalem fundatur, et eum supponit * * * Multiplicitas horum sensuum non facit æquivocationem, aut aliam speciem multiplicitatis: quia sensus isti non multiplicantur propter hoc quod una vox multa significet, sed quia ipsæ res significatæ per voces aliarum rerum possunt esse signa. Et ita etiam nulla confusio sequitur in Sacra Scriptura, cum omnes sensus *fundentur super unum, scilicet literalem, ex quo solo potest trahi argumentum;* non autem ex iis quæ secundum allegoriam dicuntur. * * * Non tamen ex hoc aliquid deperit Sacræ Scripturæ: quia nihil sub spirituali sensu continetur fidei necessarium quod Scriptura per literalem sensum alicubi manifeste non tradat."—*Summ. Theol.* Pars 1ma, qu. i. art. x. t. xx. p. 9. Cf. too, Lecture iii. p. 108, note [5].

[2] "And over it the Cherubims of glory shadowing the mercy-seat; of which we cannot now speak particularly."—Heb. ix. 5. Cf. too, the remark as to Melchizedek: "Of whom we have many things to say, and hard to be uttered, seeing ye are dull of hearing."—*Ibid.*, v. 11.

meet us in the New. On a former occasion I have proved that, in no instance can we account for such quotations by our Lord and His Disciples on the plea of 'accommodation' to the prejudices or errors of the Jews:[1] it is therefore unnecessary again to enter upon that question. I would now observe further, that we must with equal earnestness reject the notion that the facts and statements of the Old Testament are introduced merely by way of 'application,' or as illustrations founded on some features of general resemblance.[2] Were this view correct, the idea that the employment of such passages in the New Testament had been originally designed by the Holy Spirit of itself disappears: nay,

[1] Lecture ii. p. 71–77. The single fact, indeed, that to a great extent the Gospels, as well as the majority of S. Paul's Epistles, were not addressed to Jews but to Gentiles, may of itself suffice to answer those who still maintain that the writers of the New Testament employed, in their citations from the Old, the principle of 'accommodation.' In addition to the answer of Tertullian to Marcion, which I have quoted *supra*, p. 74, note, I may adduce the reply of S. Irenæus to the same argument when advanced by the Gnostics: "Quemadmodum dicunt hi, qui sunt vanissimi Sophistæ, quoniam Apostoli *cum hypocrisi* fecerunt doctrinam *secundum audientium capacitatem*, et responsiones secundum interrogantium suspiciones [i. e. ὑπολήψεις] * * * uti [i. e. adeo ut] non quemadmodum habet ipsa veritas, sed *in hypocrisi*, et quemadmodum capiebat unusquisque, Dominum et Apostolos edidisse magisterium * * * Quis autem medicus volens curare ægrotum, faciat secundum concupiscentias ægrotantium, et non secundum quod aptum est medicinæ? Quoniam autem Dominus Medicus venit [S. Luke, v. 31], * * * non igitur jam *secundum pristinam opinionem* loquebatur eis," &c.—*Cont. Hær.*, lib. III. v. p. 179. Tholuck, therefore, is inaccurate when he observes: "A peculiarity of modern times is the theory of 'accommodation,' according to which all quotations of this class (viz., the entire mode of proof adopted in the Epistle to the Hebrews) are disposed of as an 'argumentatio e concessis'—so Semler, Ernesti, Teller, Griesbach, and also, for the most part, Stuart."—*Das A. Test. im N. Test.*, s. 5.

[2] Tholuck, for example, arranges the quotations to be found in the New Testament under the following classes: (1.) Direct prophecies. (2.) Typical prophecies. (These two classes I have considered already.) (3.) Supports (Anlehnungen), and Adaptations or Applications (Anwendungen). The quotations which he terms 'supports' are the same as those described *supra*, p. 307, notes [1] and [2]. An 'adaptation,' or 'application,' Tholuck defines to be the citation *of a parallel*, with some formula of quotation; of which class he gives the following as examples: S. Matt. xiii. 35 ("That it might be fulfilled which was spoken by the prophet"); xxvi. 31 ("For it is written"); S. John, ii. 17 ("It was written"); Acts, i. 20 ("For it is written"); xiii. 40 ("Is spoken of in the prophets"); Rom. xi. 8 ("According as it is written"); 1 Cor. ix. 9 ("For it is written"); xiv. 21 ("In the Law it is written"); 2 Cor. vi. 2 ("For He saith"); viii. 15 ("As it is written").—*loc. cit.*, s. 26 ff. On which see *infra*. Stuart appears to reduce such passages to the principle of 'accommodation'—an 'accommodation,' however, to *the writer's own views*. "Such cases," he observes, "are frequent in the New Testament. God says by the prophet Hosea, 'When Israel was a child, then I loved him, and called My Son out of Egypt'—ch. xi. 1. Now this is not *prediction*, but *narration*. But when Matthew describes the flight of Joseph and Mary, with the infant Jesus, to Egypt, he says, 'This took place, so that this passage of Scripture [in Hosea] had an accomplishment, ἵνα πληρωθῇ, κ. τ. λ.' Now here is, evidently, nothing more than a *similarity* of events."—*A Comm. on the Hebrews*, p. 600. The remarks already made will, I trust, supply the answer to such a system of exposition.

we could not even reasonably maintain that this alleged 'adaptation' of the language of the earlier writers was made under the Holy Spirit's direction ; and, consequently, the inspiration of those parts of Scripture in which such 'applications' occur is altogether subverted. In addition to what has been already said with reference to the grounds on which the authors of the New Testament rest their system of interpretation, it is a sufficient answer to the allegation which we are considering, that in all the instances of this mere 'application' of the Old Testament which are usually brought forward, we find the quotation introduced by the phrases, "For it is written ;"—"That it might be fulfilled which was spoken by the prophet ;"—or some other expression to the same effect. Thus S. John, when relating how the soldiers cast lots for our Lord's garments, refers as follows to the words of the twenty-second Psalm :—"That the Scripture might be fulfilled which saith, They parted My raiment among them, and for My vesture they did cast lots. These things *therefore* the soldiers did."[1] In the use of this passage by the Evangelist it is impossible to regard the expressions of the Psalmist otherwise than as conveying a strictly typical prophecy ; since even the plain grammatical sense renders it impossible to deny that the passage is represented in the Gospel as a direct prediction, which at this point of time, and at no other, found its perfect accomplishment. Or, to take another example which perhaps of all others might seem most to resemble a mere 'adaptation' of a prophetic saying,—I mean where our Lord quotes the language of Zechariah : "Awake, O sword, against My Shepherd, and against the Man that is My fellow, saith the Lord of hosts : smite the Shepherd, and the sheep shall be scattered."[2] Here it will, no doubt, be admitted that Christ Himself is a competent expositor ; and His allusion to these words is as follows : "All ye shall be offended because of Me this night : *for it is written*, 'I will smite the shepherd, and the sheep of the flock shall be scattered abroad.'"[3] In short, that freedom with which the writers of the New Testament employed the language of the Old,[4] and

[1] *Ἵνα ἡ γραφὴ πληρωθῇ· Διεμερίσαντο τὰ ἱμάτιά μου ἑαυτοῖς * * * οἱ μὲν οὖν στρατιῶται ταῦτα ἐποίησαν.*—S. John, xix. 24.

[2] Zech. xiii. 7.

[3] S. Matt. xxvi. 31—*γέγραπται γάρ.*

[4] It is, perhaps, unnecessary to refer *specially* to such objections as are founded on the absence of the most exact and literal translation, even where no object could be

which we are about to glance at more nearly, was the natural result of the fact that they spoke under the guidance of that same Divine Spirit under Whose inspiration the words which they quoted had been recorded, and under Whose instruction were at length developed the manifold allusions which the sayings of the former Scriptures contained.[1]

On this same principle, indeed, the Evangelists adduced the sayings of Christ. In His prayer to His Father, before His betrayal, occur the words: "Those that Thou gavest Me I have kept, and none of them is lost but the son of perdition."[2] After His betrayal, however, when our Lord gave Himself up to the "band of men and officers from the chief priests and Pharisees,"

attained by such adherence to the original. Such objections, indeed, proceed on the tacit assumption that the writers of the New Testament were bound to act as a translator of the Bible must act now; in other words, on the assumption that they were not inspired. To such arguments the ingenious illustration of S. Jerome supplies a sufficient answer: "Legimus, in Marco, dicentem Dominum, TALITHA CUMI; statimque subjectum est, 'quod interpretatur, Puella tibi dico, surge.' Arguatur Evangelista mendacii, quare addiderit, 'tibi dico,' quum in Hebræo tantum est, 'puella surge.'"—*De opt. gen. interpret.*, Ad Pammach., Ep. lvii. t. i. p. 308. That the object of the New Testament writers was merely to represent with fidelity *the idea* to be conveyed, and not to strive after strict verbal agreement, is clear from another fact analogous to that alluded to by S. Jerome. The constant asseveration of Christ, *Amen*, is to be found in Jer. xxviii. 6; where the LXX. render it by *ἀληθῶς*. Now S. Matt. xvi. 28; xxiv. 47; and S. Mark, xii. 43, give *ἀμὴν λέγω ὑμῖν*: while S. Luke, recording the same sayings of Christ, renders, as do the LXX., *ἀληθῶς λέγω ὑμῖν*.—ix. 27; xii. 44; xxi. 3.

[1] Having alluded to the very accurate citation of Jer. xxxi. 15, in S. Matt. ii. 18, Dr. W. H. Mill observes: "Shall we then call this an *application* or *accommodation* of the Old Testament passage to things beyond its immediate visible occasion? There would be no need to scruple the term, if it were not meant to imply that this accommodation was arbitrary on the part of the Evangelist, or that the mind of the Spirit that spoke by Jeremiah does not most fully include this application. But thus meant, we are concerned to repudiate the proposition; and to appeal to the ample range of the prophecy itself as forbidding this restriction of its import." * * * "We think it most reasonable to believe that the distress of the 15th verse is not necessarily confined to the case of these deported captives of Benjamin, among whom the prophet of Anathoth had lived. And as the coming of the Great Deliverer is the principal end to which all Prophecy is directed, we hold that the afflictions which more immediately preceded Christ's mediation and its results, those especially by which His first manifestation to mankind was signalized, lay entirely within the scope of the Divine Spirit in inditing these consolations. * * * The place which these considerations hold in the argument with objectors like Strauss is this only; to prove that they are simply begging the question, when they treat the prophecies as merely human writings, and, applying the rules of criticism not only to the language of the document, where they are truly applicable, but to the supposed mind of the writer as the sole measure of its import, they denounce every application as false and gratuitous, when it lies beyond the primary or immediate occasion."—*The Christian Advocate's Publication for* 1844, pp. 405–414. Cf., also, *ibid.*, p. 391, &c.

[2] S. John, xvii. 12, where our Lord adds *ἵνα ἡ γραφὴ πληρωθῇ*—with an obvious reference to His previous statement (ch. xiii. 18): "I speak not of you all; I know whom I have chosen: but that the Scripture may be fulfilled, He that eateth bread with Me hath lifted up his heel against Me."

S. John again tells us: "Jesus answered, I have told you that I am He; if therefore ye seek Me let these go their way. That the saying (observes the Evangelist) might be fulfilled which He spake, Of them which Thou gavest Me have I lost none:"[1]—where we perceive that an expression, which the Lord had employed with reference to the preservation of His followers from spiritual loss, is appealed to by S. John as predicting their escape from temporal danger. Hence we clearly see that His Disciples regarded their Master's words as containing manifold allusions: and hence we also derive a most important intimation as to the light in which they must have similarly regarded the Old Testament prophecies.

In entering upon the subject of the *form* under which the Old Testament is quoted, I shall pass over, as not directly bearing upon the present inquiry, the many ingenious explanations, by Oriental scholars, of how the Hebrew text and the New Testament reference may, in several cases, be directly reconciled. The writers to whom I refer have endeavored to attain this object by pointing out the different senses of which the original terms are susceptible;[2]—by adopting some of those various readings which may be suggested in the Hebrew text in consequence of the similarity of several of the Hebrew letters;[3]—or, in fine, by

[1] S. John, xviii. 9—*ἵνα πληρωθῇ ὁ λόγος ὃν εἶπεν.* Cf. Olshausen *in loc.*, B. ii. s. 470; and Tholuck, "Comm. zum Ev. Johan.," s. 299.

[2] For example: In S. Matt. iv. 16, "The people which sat in darkness saw great light"—*φῶς εἶδεν μέγα*—in accordance with the pointing of our present Hebrew text of Isai. ix. 2 [1]—רָאוּ; while the LXX. translate—*ἴδετε φῶς μέγα*, and therefore must have read—רְאוּ. Similarly where the E. V. translates "*From the prey* my son thou art gone up"—Gen. xlix. 9, the LXX. render *ἐκ βλαστοῦ*, the word טרף being susceptible of both meanings. In some cases, even the Massora authorizes us to correct the Hebrew text according to the New Testament. E. g. S. Peter quotes Ps. xvi. 10—"Neither wilt Thou suffer *Thine Holy One* (*τὸν Ὅσιόν Σου*) to see corruption"—Acts, ii. 27, which corresponds to the Massoretic reading—חסידך, in place of חסידיך ("Thy holy ones") which our present Hebrew text presents. On this whole subject see H. Hody, "De Bibl. Text. Original." lib. III. pars i. c. 2, p. 243, &c.

[3] E. g. the quotation, "Behold ye *despisers*, and wonder," &c.—Acts, xiii. 41, where, in place of the version authorized by our present Hebrew text, "Behold ye *among the heathen* (בגוים), and regard and wonder," &c.—Habak. i. 5, S. Paul adopts the translation of the LXX. who render *καταφρονηταί*; reading (with the change of ד for ו) בגדים. This explanation is fully confirmed by the fact that in Habak. ii. 5, the LXX. render this same word בוגד by *καταφρονητής*. See H. Hody, *loc. cit.*, p. 261. Similarly (with the change of ר for ד) in Ps. xix. 13, the LXX. instead of מזדים, *superbi*, read מזרים—*ἀπὸ ἀλλοτρίων*. See *infra*, p. 319, note [1]. Cf. De Wette, "Einleit." § 83, s. 125. An interesting confirmation of the justice of such a method for reconciling difficulties has been lately pointed out. Mr. Layard, in his second work on "Nineveh and Babylon," gives the following note of Mr. Thomas Ellis of the British Museum: "A discovery relating to the Jews of the captivity in Babylon, and con-

showing, from a comparison of certain cognate dialects, that the Hebrew terms actually convey the sense ascribed to them in what the New Testament represents as their Greek equivalents.[1] These are topics on which I shall not pause; because, although throwing much light upon the correct rendering of several parts of Scripture, they do not in any way affect the principle of that free use of the Old Testament on which I am now insisting. Indeed, the Old Testament itself points out that we are not to anticipate in the New that strict, literal subserviency, at establishing which, in all cases, the researches to which I have just

sequently of great interest to Oriental scholars, and especially to Biblical students, was made by Mr. Layard during his second expedition to Assyria. Amongst the various curious objects found on the banks of the Euphrates, and in the ruins of ancient Babylonia, were several bowls or cups of terra cotta, round the inner surface of which were inscriptions in the ancient Chaldean language, written in characters wholly unknown, and, I believe, never before seen in Europe. * * * They must have been written long prior to any existing MSS. of the ancient Hebrew and Chaldean languages that we know of. * * * But the most remarkable circumstance connected with these inscriptions is, that the characters used on the bowl marked No. 1 answer precisely to the description given of the most ancient Hebrew letters in the Babylonian Talmud, which contains an account of the nature and origin of the letters used by the Jews. * * * With respect to the translation, I have only to state that in many passages it is mere conjecture * * * but the difficulty is increased tenfold through there being no distinction between ד, ר, and frequently ל; nor is there any distinction between ו, ז, and medial נ; nor between ה and ח, and sometimes ה is written like ח."—pp. 509–511.

[1] E. g. S. Paul, Rom. x. 18, quotes, according to LXX., "*Their sound* (ὁ φθόγγος αὐτῶν) went into all the earth,"—the ordinary rendering of Ps. xix. 5, being "*Their line* (קוּם) is gone out through all the earth." (Gesenius renders: "(b) *Chorda* citharæ, deinde *sonus*.") On the principle that the original has *both* significations, Dr. Pococke here observes: "Concludunt multi lectum ab illis [*scil.* LXX.] non קום *Kavam*, 'linea eorum,' sed קולם *Kolam*, 'vox eorum.' * * * Quam in sententiam qui descendere recusaverit * * * aliam, si libet, viam mecum experiatur, scil. dictioni קו *Kaw* significatum suum (licet minus notum) restituendo. * * * Fiet id (ni fallor) linguæ etiam Arabicæ ope, &c."—*Porta Mosis*, app. p. 47. Again, Isai. xxviii. 16: "He that believeth, shall not make haste" (לא יחיש) is quoted in Rom. ix. 33, after the LXX., under the form, "Whosoever believeth on Him *shall not be ashamed*" (οὐ καταισχυνθήσεται); and in 1 S. Pet. ii. 6, "*shall not be confounded*" (οὐ μὴ καταισχυνθῇ). "Aliter legisse olim Græcæ Versionis authores quos secutus est Apostolus, asserunt docti, scil. יבוש *Yebosh* vel יביש *Yabish* quod sonat 'erubescet.' * * * Quidni potius et hos et illos יחיש *Yachish* olim, prout nunc habetur, legisse? alios tantum ejusdem significatus quam recentiores prætulisse, quos ambitu suo continere verbum illud suadent, et loci circumstantiæ et interpretum authoritati additus linguæ affinis Arabicæ usus in qua themata *Haush*, et *Hish* quæ Hebr. חוש respondent, tres nobis stos (cum aliis) significatus exhibent * * * scil. *festinare, timere, pudore suffundi*, quorum tertium præferunt LXX., secundum Chaldæus et Syrus, primum recentiores."—Pococke, *loc. cit.*, pp. 10, 11. Once more, Jer. xxxi. 9: "Which My covenant they brake, although I was an Husband (בעלתי) unto them, saith the Lord"—is quoted, according to the LXX., in Heb. viii. 9, "And *I regarded them not* (κἀγὼ ἠμέλησα), saith the Lord." Here the probability certainly is that, by an interchange of נ for ב, the LXX. read נעלתי, which means ἠμέλησα; Pococke, however, writes: "Linguæ Arabicæ ope * * * si quid adhuc restat scrupuli, plane tollitur. In ea enim verbum בעל *Baala* est, non modo *Dominum esse*, et *maritari*, sed et *perturbari, separari, fastidire, nauseare*."—*loc. cit.*, p. 9.

alluded sometimes aim. Consider, for example, how Moses himself, in the book of Deuteronomy gives a version of the Fourth Commandment differing in many respects from its original announcement, as written in the book of Exodus ; and how, at the same time, he enforces by the terms of this second version a new and special admonition.[1]

The quotations, by the New Testament writers, to which it is necessary to call attention, are as follows :—

I. In the first place there are those passages which are taken strictly and literally from the Septuagint Version where it differs from the Hebrew. Thus our Lord Himself adopted and sanctioned the interpretation which the Seventy Interpreters had given of the original institution of marriage by accepting from their translation the important words "and they twain," which do not occur in the Hebrew :[2] and this same rendering is repeated by S. Paul.[3] In all such cases the Greek translation is followed, as exhibiting a true and clear perception of the meaning intended by the language of the Old Testament : the idea which the words of the original had veiled being thus brought to light, in the New Testament, by that same Divine authority whereby, at the first, the form had been suggested under which it was expressed by the Old Testament writers.[4]

1 "Remember the Sabbath Day to keep it holy * * * in it thou shalt not do any work, thou, nor thy son, * * * nor thy cattle, nor thy stranger that is within thy gates: *for in six days the Lord made heaven and earth*, &c. * * * *wherefore* the Lord blessed the Sabbath Day and hallowed it."—Exod. xx. 8–11.

"Keep the Sabbath Day to sanctify it, as the Lord thy God hath commanded thee * * * in it thou shalt not do any work, thou, nor thy son, * * * nor any of thy cattle, nor thy stranger that is within thy gates: *that thy man-servant and thy maid-servant may rest as well as thou.* And remember that thou wast a servant in the land of Egypt, and that the Lord thy God brought thee out hence through a a mighty hand, and by a stretched-out arm: *therefore* the Lord thy God commanded thee to keep the Sabbath Day."—Deut. v. 12–15.

2 "For this cause shall a man leave father and mother, and shall cleave to his wife: and they twain shall be one flesh" (καὶ ἔσονται οἱ δύο εἰς σάρκα μίαν)—S. Matt. xix. 5; S. Mark, x. 8, which *verbatim* agrees with the LXX. rendering of Gen. ii. 24, where the Hebrew has merely—והיו לבשר אחד.

3 Eph. v. 31.

4 The most remarkable instance of this class of quotations is unquestionably the citation of Ps. xl. 6—"Mine ears hast thou opened (אזנים כרית לי)."—in Heb. x. 5, where we read, "A body hast Thou prepared Me" (σῶμα κατηρτίσω μοι); in exact conformity with the LXX. Commentators of the most opposite schools, are singularly unanimous in regarding the New Testament form of exhibiting this passage as a strictly correct representation of *the sense* of the original. Bishop Pearson, referring to Phil. ii. 8, has pointed out one line of exposition: "Being the boring of the ear under the Law (Exod xxi. 6; Deut. xv. 17) was a note of perpetual servitude; being this was expressed in the words of the Psalmist, and changed by the Apostle into the preparing of a body; it followeth that when Christ's Body first was framed, even then

II. On the other hand,—and this constitutes the second class of quotations to be considered,—wherever the Septuagint does not represent the true sense of the Prophet's words, the authors of the New Testament altogether abandon it, and give their own translation of the Hebrew. For example, S. John quotes the prediction, "They shall look on Him whom they pierced,"[1] which presents a literal version of the Hebrew of Zechariah, with the slight but, as S. John quotes, necessary change of "Him" for "Me."[2] These words the Seventy had translated: "They shall look upon Me, because they have mocked Me,"[3]—a translation

did He assume the form of a servant."—*Exposition of the Apostle's Creed*, Art. ii. On a different principle, Rudelbach observes: "The apparent difficulty here is most easily removed by the obvious remark that the 'perfodere aures,' according to Exod. xxi. 5, 6, was the token of servants who from love for their master desired to remain his servants for ever"—*Zeitschrift*, 1841. H. iv. s. 5; the Psalmist contrasting *obedience*, the true sacrifice, with the animal sacrifices of the Law. Thus, as Ebrard *in loc.* ("Der Br. an die Hebr.," s. 331) observes, the LXX. have not altered the real meaning of the original, viz., "Thou desirest not beasts for sacrifice, but Myself." Many modern expositors (Hengstenberg, Stier, Hitzig, Tholuck, Bleek, Stuart), on the other hand, reject the reference to the Law, and take כרה, *fodit*, in the sense of גלה, *retexit*. Thus Hengstenberg translates "Ears hast Thou dug through for me"—"The Psalmist must in these words place the obedience, to which he was internally drawn by God, in contrast to sacrifices, i. e. 'Thou hast made me hearing, obedient.'" In the epistle to the Hebrews the thought is not altered by the LXX. translation, "'Thou hast given me a Body, so that I willingly serve Thee in the execution of Thy will.'"—*Comm. on Psalms* (Clarke's For. Theol. Lib., vol. ii. p. 71). So Tholuck (*in loc.*, s. 350): "'Thou hast prepared for me a body, which I am to consecrate as a sacrifice to Thee;'" and he also observes: "To the difference in Heb. x. 5, particularly great importance has been attached; meanwhile, according to what has been adduced by us on that passage, we venture to consider it as decided, that the sense of the Psalmist has been just as little altered by the Greek translator, as when on Hosea, xiv. 3 ["The calves of our lips"], he translated [see Heb. xiii. 15, "The fruit of our lips"] according to the reading, פרי [καρπόν], where we have פרים."—*loc. cit.* s. 41. And that this opinion has not arisen from any antecedent prejudice on Tholuck's part in favor of the infallibility of the sacred writers, is clear from his remark as to Heb. ii. 7: "In the application which he [the inspired writer] makes of the *παρ' ἀγγέλους*, and *βραχύ τι*, his translation has led him astray (hat ihn seine Uebersetzung irre geleitet)"—s. 34. And again: "In reference to this [the quotation Heb. ii. 7] it must be acknowledged that our author has allowed himself to be guided by his translation to an application which does not correspond to the Old Testament text. According to the principles which we have laid down in general concerning the inspiration of the Apostles, we feel no hesitation in acknowledging this. In the same manner, in Heb. xi. 21, the version of the LXX. which the author follows must be held to be erroneous. In importance, these mistakes (diese Versehen) stand in the same category as when Matthew (ch. xxi. 5) quotes, according to the Hebrew, *ἐπὶ ὑποζύγιον καὶ πῶλον νέον* [LXX.], and refers this to the *two animals* in the entry of Christ."—s. 41. Tholuck's reason for charging S. Matthew with error here appears to be merely the fact that S. John (xii, 14, 15) alludes only to the animal *on which* the Lord sat. But cf. Olshausen, B. i. s. 766: and Hengstenberg, "Christol.," B. II. ii. 132 ff.

[1] *Ἑτέρα γραφὴ λέγει· Ὄψονται εἰς ὃν ἐξεκέντησαν.*—S. John, xix. 37.

[2] והביטו אול את אשר־דקרו.—Zech. xii. 10.

[3] *Καὶ ἐπιβλέψονται πρός με ἀνθ' ὧν κατωρχήσαντο.* It is not necessary to consider whether the LXX. gave this version, because (as Olshausen *in loc.* suggests) the

which not only was unsuited to the Evangelist's object, but is also irreconcilable with our Hebrew text. The principle of this class of quotations is accurately described by S. Jerome when, in his exposition of the passage, he observes: "The Evangelist John, who drank wisdom from the Lord's bosom, a Hebrew of the Hebrews, whom the Saviour dearly loved, has not paid much regard to the import of the Greek Version; but has interpreted word for word as he had read in the Hebrew, and has told us that it was fulfilled at the period of the Lord's Passion."[1]

III. The third class consists of quotations which differ from both the original text and the Septuagint Version, even where, according to our exegesis, the Hebrew and the Greek translation correspond with each other. S. Paul, for example, quotes the sixty-eighth Psalm under the following form: "Wherefore he saith, When He ascended up on high, He led captivity captive, and *gave* gifts unto men,"[2]—which latter words present a meaning apparently the reverse of that conveyed by both the Hebrew and the Septuagint, according to which the sense of the passage is, "Thou hast *received* gifts for men."[3] In this instance Some have pro-
commentators have been singularly perplexed.

original, as applied to God, was to them unintelligible; or whether, as S. Jerome thought (see next note), their copies presented a different reading. It is, however, to be observed, that the later Jewish versions of Aquila, Symmachus, and Theodotion, coincide with S. John, and with each other, in employing the verb ἐκκεντέω. Cf. Rev. i. 7.

[1] "Hebraicæ literæ Daleth (ד) et Res (ר), hoc est D et R similes sunt, et parvo tantum apice distinguuntur. Ex quo evenit ut idem verbum diverse legentes, aliter atque aliter transferant. * * * Si enim legatur DACARU (דקרו) ἐξεκέντησαν, id est 'compunxerunt' sive 'confixerunt' accipitur: sin autem contrario ordine literis commutatis RACADU (רקדו), ὠρχήσαντο, id est, 'saltaverunt' intelligitur, et ob similitudinem literarum error est natus. Joannes autem Evangelista, qui de pectore Domini hausit sapientiam, Hebræus ex Hebræis, quem Salvator amabat plurimum, non magnopere curavit quid Græcæ literæ continerent; sed verbum interpretatus e verbo est, ut in Hebræo legerat, et tempore Dominicæ Passionis dixit esse completum."—*Comment. in Zach.*, lib. iii., tom. vi. p. 903.

[2] Διὸ λέγει· Ἀναβὰς εἰς ὕψος ᾐχμαλ. αἰχμ. καὶ ἔδωκε δόματα τοῖς ἀνθρώποις.—Eph. iv. 8.

[3] לָקַחְתָּ מַתָּנוֹת בָּאָדָם—Ps. lxviii. 18; ἔλαβες δόματα ἐν ἀνθρώπῳ.—LXX. "Thou hast *received* gifts for men."—E. V. The manner in which the Apostle, in the earlier part of the verse (Ἀναβὰς εἰς ὕψος ᾐχμαλώτευσεν αἰχμαλωσίαν), follows, word for word, the version of the LXX. (Ἀναβὰς εἰς ὕψος ᾐχμαλώτευσας αἰχμαλωσίαν), proves to a demonstration that his departure from it, towards the close, was designed. Olshausen, speaking of the difficulties connected with this passage, and having referred to the διό of ver. 8, and the obvious reference of the καὶ αὐτὸς ἔδωκεν, of ver. 11, to the αὐτός ἐστιν καί ὁ ἀναβάς, in ver. 10, as proving that the Apostle *designedly* quoted as he has done,—observes: "The expositor must look for the fault in *himself*, if he cannot point to the connecting links of the argument, rather than in his *author*." It will be well to bear this remark in mind when we proceed to consider the assertion that the New Testament writers quote "from memory."

posed to alter the Hebrew according to S. Paul; others have suggested that there is here no quotation from the Psalmist, but a reference to some unknown Christian hymn; while others, again, favor what has been styled "the milder expedient" of saying that S. Paul has arbitrarily altered the meaning according to his own views, or, undesignedly, when citing from memory, missed the sense. But all such "expedients" are as unnecessary as they are untenable: the context of itself affords the clue to the Apostle's line of argument. In the previous verse he had observed, "Unto every one of us is given grace according to the measure of the gift of Christ:" and this great truth—namely the universality of Christ's gifts, to Jew and Gentile alike,—is what he goes on, in the quotation before us, to prove from the Old Testament itself. By means of the Redemption, argues S. Paul, spiritual gifts have been bestowed on all mankind. We know too—for S. John[1] has fully disclosed the doctrine,—that our Lord's bestowal of the gifts of the Holy Ghost is inseparably connected with the fact of His Ascension. In a word, Christ, by His Ascension, has redeemed the captive human race, and has thereby "*taken*" to Himself (as the Psalmist had *directly* stated the matter) gifts among men. Now it is implied in the mere statement of this fact, that they, whom God thus chooses for Himself must, as such, have been furnished with the necessary qualifications: and this is the aspect of the question which S. Paul desires to render prominent.[2] It is only by attending to the context that we can ever discern the drift of the inspired writers: or discover how justly the Apostle can here attach to the "taking" of the Hebrew and the Septuagint the sense of "giving." That God should "take" to Himself, He must first, from the very nature of the case, "give" certain graces to man.[3]

[1] S. John, vii. 39; xiv. 16; xvi. 7.

[2] I have here adopted Olshausen's excellent remarks on this text (B. iv. s. 226 ff).

[3] So also Hengstenberg observes: "It is evident that by the 'He gave,' which occurs in Eph. iv. 8, instead of 'Thou takest,' the sense is not *altered*, but only brought out: the 'giving' presupposes the 'taking;' the 'taking' is succeeded by the 'giving,' as its consequence * * * We observe, further, that the quotation of our passage in the Epistle to the Ephesians is not a mere accommodation, as the character and manner of that quotation evidently show."—*Comm. on Psalms.* (Clarke's For. Theol. Lib., vol. ii. p 354.) I may add that Dr. Pococke, unable to adduce any authority from the Arabic, brings forward a number of Arabic words which have opposite significations; and then attempts to explain S. Paul's quotation by the *conjecture* that the same holds good here:—"Quam significatuum varietatem et olim apud Hebræos habuisse verbum לקח mihi *plusquam probabile videtur.*"—*loc. cit.*, p. 24.

IV. The last class of quotations to be considered is one which combines some of those just described; namely, when the Septuagint having attached a particular meaning to a passage in the Hebrew, one New Testament writer builds his argument upon the literal sense of the Original, while another adopts for his purpose the sense given to it in the Greek Version; thus affording an additional illustration of the pregnant significance of the Old Testament. For example, S. Matthew adduces, with close adherence to the Hebrew, the words of Isaiah, "Surely He hath borne our griefs, and carried our sorrows;"[1] or as the Evangelist quotes: "That it might be fulfilled which was spoken by Esaias the Prophet, saying, Himself took our infirmities, and bare our sicknesses."[2] Here he quite abandons the Septuagint, which translates "He bears our sins and is pained for us;"[3]—a sense which would plainly not have been appropriate in the passage of the Gospel, but which entirely corresponds to the purpose of S. Peter, when dilating upon the internal maladies of humanity, and the healing of sin. That Apostle consequently accepts the signification ascribed to the original by the Seventy Interpreters, when he quotes, as follows, the prophet's words: "Who His own Self bare our sins in His own Body on the tree * * * by Whose stripes ye were healed."[4] In this case, the seeming difference in the explanation of the same passage, by the two inspired writers, disappears if we remember that physical sufferings (and death is to be placed at their head),[5] present one of the as-

[1] Isai. liii. 4.

[2] *Αὐτὸς τὰς ἀσθενείας ἡμῶν ἔλαβεν, καὶ τὰς νόσους ἐβαστασεν.*—S. Matt. viii. 17.

[3] *Οὗτος τὰς ἁμαρτίας ἡμῶν φέρει, καὶ περὶ ἡμῶν ὀδυνᾶται * * * τῷ μώλωπι αὐτοῦ ἡμεῖς ἰάθημεν.*—ver. 4, 5.

[4] *Ὃς τὰς ἁμαρτίας ἡμῶν αὐτὸς ἀνήνεγκεν * * * οὗ τῷ μώλωπι ἰάθητε.*—1 S. Pet. ii. 24 (see p. 307, note [1]). As exhibiting the use of the *same* passage to illustrate *different* aspects of Christian doctrine, cf. the references to Ps. lxxviii. by both S. Matthew and S. Paul; see *supra*, Lecture iv. p. 151, note. Compare, too (*supra*, p. 299, note), the manner in which Habakkuk (ii. 14) employs the words of Isaiah (xi. 9).

[5] "The wages of sin is death."—Rom. vi. 23. To the same effect Vitringa observes: "Apostolus, spirituali oculo videns, Beneficium illud Christi, quo homines a morbis et ægritudinibus pravisque affectionibus suis liberabat, aut earum auferendarum cura se *fatigabat* ad seram vesperam (de eo enim proprie agitur:), in se habere *typum* et *figuram laboris* quem Dominus sumeret in ferendis et auferendis ægritudinibus spiritualibus, h. e. peccatis, et vera peccatorum pœna: verba Prophetæ eo scopo allegavit, ut apertis oculis ipsum Beneficium peccatorum latorum et ablatorum in ipso hoc typo et figura contemplaremur." * * * "Apostoli et Evangelistæ in explicandis et allegandis dictis Prophetarum, hanc ubique secuti sunt hypothesin; omnem emphasin *quæ in verbis et phrasi latet*, per implementum repræsentandam esse. Quandoquidem vero videret Evangelista voces חלים et מכאבים quoque significare posse *morbos* et

pects under which we are taught in Scripture to regard the consequences of sin.

I have dwelt thus minutely on this question for two reasons: Firstly, because its discussion adds considerably to the amount of proof already advanced in support of the inspiration of Scripture:—the manner in which the words of the Old Testament are employed exhibiting, in the strongest light, the deep and pregnant sense of its most casual expressions; while, conversely, the free use thus made of documents which they firmly believed to be Divine no less clearly denotes the influence by which the authors of the New Testament were themselves guided. And, secondly, because the facts, elicited during its examination, supply a complete answer to the assertion which, I have observed above, must be, in every point of view, repudiated;—namely, that we are to ascribe to errors of memory, on the part of the authors of the New Testament, those variations from the Septuagint translation which the form of their quotations presents. The principles which have been laid down in the preceding remarks, if consistently carried out, must, I submit, ultimately establish the truth of the proposition, that in all cases,—even where the acuteness of expositors has hitherto been at fault, and where they have not as yet succeeded in accounting for the *form* of the New Testament quotation,—the sacred writers, however their language is to be explained, really unfold for us the true import of those words of the Old Testament which they adduce; an import, moreover, which the same Holy Spirit by Whom they too were guided had designed, from the first, that its language should convey. An example will briefly show how weak the reasons are which serve as a sufficient inducement for expositors to ascribe their own ill success in accounting for the difficulty before them to a want of accuracy on the part of the sacred writer.

In the ninth chapter of his Epistle to the Romans, S. Paul, who required a striking fact to illustrate his meaning, has quoted the language which God had addressed to Pharaoh[1] when wilfully

affectiones corporales, *quibus tanquam peccati consequentibus* homines afficiuntur; et in *cura* qua Dominus se fatigabat * * * præludium quoddam esse ejus *laboris*, quem in extremis sustineret * * * locum, oculo Divino inspectum, huc quoque transtulit."—*Comm. in Jesai.*, t. ii. p. 667.

[1] *Λέγει γὰρ ἡ γραφὴ τῷ Φαραώ· ὅτι εἰς αὐτὸ τοῦτο ἐξήγειρά σε, ὅπως ἐνδείξωμαι ἐν σοὶ τὴν δύναμίν μου, καὶ ὅπως διαγγελῇ τὸ ὄνομά μου ἐν πάσῃ τῇ γῇ.*—Rom. ix. 17.

and perversely resisting the continued exhibition of His power, and the repeated announcement of His commands. Of necessity, therefore, the Apostle abandoned the Septuagint Version, which had softened down the force of the original by rendering—"On this account hast thou been preserved;"[1] and supplies his own accurate and literal translation of the Hebrew, "For this same purpose have I raised thee up." In the remainder of this quotation—with one trifling exception, for which, however, commentators have satisfactorily accounted,[2]—S. Paul strictly adheres to the Septuagint. If we now turn to the twenty-fifth and twenty-sixth verses of this same chapter, which consist of two quotations from the prophet Hosea,[3] we are told by the expositor to whom I refer, and whose explanation of the former quotation I have just adopted, that, as the difference does not at all affect the thought, it must only be ranked among those incidental to "quotations from memory:"[4] while in the case of the next three verses, in

[1] Ἕνεκεν τούτου διετηρήθης (העמדתיך—"have I made thee stand") *ἵνα ἐνδείξωμαι ἐν σοὶ τὴν ἰσχύν μου, καὶ ὅπως διαγγελῇ τὸ ὄνομά μου ἐν πάσῃ τῇ γῇ.*—Exod. ix. 16.

[2] The adoption of *δύναμις* by S. Paul in place of *ἰσχύς* is well explained by Mr. Alford *in loc.*: "*τ. ἰσχύν μου* LXX.: *δύν.* is perhaps chosen by the Apostle as more *general*, *ἰσχύς* applying rather to those deeds of miraculous power of which Egypt was then witness."

[3] "As He saith also in Osee, I will call them My people," &c.—*Καλέσω τὸν οὐ λαόν μου λαόν μου, καὶ τὴν οὐκ ἠγαπημένην ἠγαπημένην· καὶ ἔσται ἐν τῷ τόπῳ οὗ ἐῤῥέθη αὐτοῖς· Οὐ λαός μου ὑμεῖς, ἐκεῖ κληθήσονται υἱοὶ Θεοῦ ζῶντος.*—Rom. ix. 25, 26. Which passage the LXX. present under the following version: *ἀγαπήσω τὴν οὐκ ἠγαπημένην, καὶ ἐρῶ τῷ οὐ λαῷ μου Λαός μου εἶ σύ.* (Hos. ii. 23) *καὶ ἔσται ἐν τῷ τόπῳ οὗ ἐῤῥέθη αὐτοῖς· Οὐ λαός μου ὑμεῖς, κληθήσονται καὶ αὐτοὶ υἱοὶ Θεοῦ ζῶντος* (Hos. i. 10.) Here we perceive that the Apostle not only combines two distinct passages; but also inverts the order of one of them, in which, too, he consistently substitutes *καλέσω* for *ἐρῶ*:—the Hebrew verb in both places being אמר. Now if it be borne in mind that *καλέω*, according to the usage of the New Testament, is *the technical term for expressing the Divine 'call' to man*, we can discern, I conceive, an obvious motive as well for the arrangement of the words as for their selection; especially if we admit the justice of the following remarks of Mr. Alford: "It is difficult to ascertain in what sense the Apostle cites these two passages from Hosea as applicable to the Gentiles being *called* to be the people of God. That he does so is manifest from the words themselves, and from the transition to the Jews in ver. 27. In the prophet they are spoken of *Israel*; see ch. i. 6–11, and ch. ii. throughout." Mr. Alford—justly rejecting the notion of a mere 'application'—then explains: "He brings them forward to show that it is consonant with what we know of God's dealings, to *receive as His people* those who *were* formerly *not His people*,—that this may now take place with regard to the Gentiles, as it was announced to happen with regard to Israel,—and even more,—that Israel in this, as in so many other things, was the prophetic mirror in which God foreshowed, on a small scale, His future dealings with mankind."

[4] "Aus dem Gedächtniss-citiren."—Olshausen, *in loc.* B. iii. s. 376. It is strange that in all cases where he feels a similar difficulty, Olshausen should have recourse to this solution: e. g. "This passage of Mark [ch. i. 2, see *supra*, p. 308, note] is an unmistakable indication that he had documents before him of which he made use: he borrowed from Matthew and Luke the formula of citation, but inserted *from memory*

which the words of Isaiah are adduced,[1] this same writer points out how exactly they agree with the Greek Version,—the single exception being no longer ascribed to imperfect recollection, but being justly explained by the requirements of the Apostle's argument.

A direct answer, however, to the assertion that the New Testament writers have quoted the former Scriptures "from memory" is supplied by the striking fact to which a distinguished scholar has drawn attention; namely, that "the verbal agreement of the Evangelists with each other is particularly remarkable in many citations from the Old Testament, in which they follow neither the Hebrew text nor the Septuagint with exactness."[2]

The principle on which I have thus insisted is forcibly illustrated by the only instance where the Greek Version, and not the Hebrew text of a passage in the Old Testament, necessarily supplied the source of the quotation. In the eighth chapter of the Acts of the Apostles, the Ethiopian Eunuch is represented as "*reading*"[3]—of course in the translation of the Seventy—a

(aus dem Gedächtniss) the words out of Malachi without altering the formula."—*Comm.*, B. i. s. 163.

[1] Namely, verses 27 and 28 from Isai. x. 22, 23; and ver. 29 from Isai. i. 9. "The words of the [former of these] quotations follow the LXX. with accuracy up to *ἐπὶ τῆς γῆς* [viz., "Because a short work will the Lord make *upon the earth.*"—ver. 28], for which that version reads, *ἐν τῇ οἰκουμένῃ ὅλῃ*. It may be that Paul selected the former phrase, *because it expresses more definitely the universality of the Judgment.*"—*loc. cit.* B. iii. s. 376. Touching the *latter* quotation (ver. 29), Mr. Alford draws attention to the fact of its literal agreement with the LXX., even in the adoption of the word *σπέρμα* as the equivalent for the Hebrew שריד, *residuum*—"implying *a remnant for a fresh planting.*" In ver. 33 the citation is composed of Isai. viii. 14 (quoted from the Hebrew, and already applied to Christ in S. Luke, ii. 34), and Isai. xxviii. 16:—the "stone of stumbling" of the former, being substituted for the "precious corner-stone" of the latter passage. These texts are again conjoined in 1 S. Pet. ii. 6–8 (cf. Alford *in loc.*)

[2] Gieseler, "Die Entstehung der schriftl. Evangelien," s. 4. E. g. S. Matt. xi. 10, and S. Luke, vii. 27 (see also S. Mark, i. 2), agree verbatim as follows: "This is he of whom it is written, *Ἰδού ἐγὼ ἀποστέλλω τὸν ἄγγελόν μου πρὸ προσώπου σου, ὃς κατασκευάσει τὴν ὁδόν σου ἔμπροσθέν σου.*—while the LXX., which in all points corresponds with the Hebrew, thus renders the words of Mal. iii. 1: *Ἰδοὺ ἐξαποστέλλω τὸν ἄγγελόν μου, καὶ ἐπιβλέψεται ὁδὸν πρὸ προσώπου μου.* "*Remarkable,*" writes Olshausen,—unable to have recourse here to the "quotation from memory" theory,—"is the extremely accurate agreement of the Evangelists in this section, as well in single expressions (e. g. Luke, vii. 23), as particularly (Matt. xi. 10) in the Old Testament quotation from Mal. iii. 1. The LXX. translate the passage accurately according to the Hebrew text,—*both Evangelists, however, deviate uniformly from both translations.*"—B. i. s. 353. Gieseler points out that a similar fact is to be noticed in other parts of the New Testament: "There is also found, in quotations in the Epistles of different Apostles, an equal relation to each other and to their sources" (e. g. 1 Pet. ii. 6, 8; Rom. ix. 33 [see *supra*, p. 316, note [1]]).—*Ibid.*, s. 89.

[3] Acts, viii. 32, 33—Ἡ δὲ περιοχὴ τῆς γραφῆς ἣν ἀνεγίνωσκεν ἦν αὕτη, κ. τ. λ.

passage from the fifty-third chapter of Isaiah. In this case (with the exception of the pronouns "him" and "his;" and even here the reading is not absolutely fixed),[1] the extract is word for word coincident with the Septuagint translation, even where it deviates from the Hebrew text. If, indeed, in this quotation, where no motive for any departure from the original could possibly be assigned, we meet with such deviations as occur elsewhere, the assertion that the sacred writers quote "from memory" could not, perhaps, be justly questioned: but here a literal transcript was to be looked for; and that literal transcript is to be found. The Eunuch had read the passage from the Greek Version, and accordingly the inspired historian accurately copies that translation.[2]

The deviation of the LXX. from the Hebrew text of this passage is notoriously very considerable. Vitringa observes on this place (Isai. liii. 8): "Qui hic pluribus *ἀκριβοῦσι* in Versione Græca cum Hebræa comparanda, nihil agunt, et, ut quod verum est dicam, *ineptiunt. Interpres enim Græcus hujus libri fuit imperitus;* et Lucas recenset verba ab Eunucho ex Græco textu lecta."—*Comm. in Jesai.*, t. ii. p. 673.

[1] Our text reads in Acts, viii. 32—*τοῦ κείραντος αὐτόν*, and *τὸ στόμα αὐτοῦ*. But see Lachman's Apparat. Crit.

[2] An interesting parallel to this fact is found in Jer. xxvi. 18: "Micah the Morasthite prophesied in the days of Hezekiah King of Judah, and spake to all the people of Judah, saying, Thus saith the Lord of Hosts: *Zion shall be plowed like a field, and Jerusalem shall become heaps, and the mountain of the house as the high places of a forest*,"—words which are copied verbatim from Micah, iii. 12. We have seen in the instances already examined that, as in the New Testament, where there was *not* a direct transcript of the words, this literal coincidence was not observed:—here there is a direct transcript, and we have, therefore, a faithful adherence to the original. See *supra*, p. 298, note [1]. This deviation from the LXX. of our Lord's reference to Isai. lxi. 1 (in the Synagogue at Nazareth where He "stood up for *to read* (*ἀναγνῶναι*)"—S. Luke, iv. 16–19), may, at first sight, be regarded as an objection to what I have just advanced: but a moment's attention to the nature of the Synagogue worship (see Jahn's "Archäologie," Th. iii. s. 438 ff.) will show that it is not so. That service commenced with a doxology; a section was next read from the Law, which was followed by a second doxology; then came the reading of a passage from the Prophets. These portions of Scripture were read *from the Hebrew text*, and were immediately translated into the vernacular tongue. On this the reader or some other person present addressed the people. Thus S. Paul went into the Synagogue at Antioch, "and sat down. And after the reading of the Law and the Prophets, the rulers of the Synagogue sent unto them, saying, Ye men and brethren, if ye have any word of exhortation for the people, say on. Then Paul stood up," &c.—Acts, xiii. 15. In the case before us our Lord, who was also *the reader*, addressed the people; and we cannot doubt that the parallel passage from the prophet, which S. Luke has incorporated in his translation of the words which Christ had read, was actually adduced by Him in the course of His exhortation when "He began to say unto them, This day is this Scripture fulfilled in your ears," and when all "wondered at the gracious words which proceeded out of His mouth" (ver. 21, 22). These remarks not only answer the supposed objection which we are considering (since our Lord *read* from the *Hebrew* text), but also show the weakness of Olshausen's observation: "The words, *ἀποστεῖλαι τεθραυσμένους ἐν ἀφέσει*, are found neither in the Hebrew text, nor in the LXX. translation of this passage, and have *therefore* been certainly (wohl) inserted, *from memory*, by the Evangelist. * * * These words, which are altogether wanting in Isai. lxi. 1, have been doubtless taken by Luke from the parallel passage in Isai. lviii. 6, and in-

The foregoing examination of the language of the sacred writers naturally leads to a topic which, from the earliest times, has attracted attention. From the very first, the absence from the diction of Scripture of that rhetorical science which was so carefully studied by the Greeks and Romans has been made a source of cavil against the maintainers of Christianity.[1] If "holy men of God spake as they were moved by the Holy Ghost," why, it has been demanded, do we not find in their writings that perfection of style, or that ornate eloquence, which distinguishes the language of the Orators and Philosophers of ancient times, who thereby acquired their personal influence, and have won imperishable fame?[2] This objection, which has been renewed in

terwoven with the other. Here again he followed the LXX. The writers of the New Testament, therefore, treat the Old with great freedom. Wavering in their memories in a manner altogether human; confounding (verwechselnd) passages, interchanging (vertauschend) words,—everything was so directed, nevertheless, by the higher Spirit of Truth, Who animated and guided them, that nowhere does anything untrue or leading to error result; but even the Truth rather presents itself from a new aspect, and accordingly reveals itself, in its nature, so much the more perfectly."—B. i. s. 461 ff.

[1] Arnobius (flor. A. D. 298) enumerates the ordinary objections of this nature: "Sed ab indoctis hominibus, et rudibus, scripta sunt, et idcirco non sunt facili auditione credenda. * * * Trivialis et sordidus sermo est. * * * Barbarismis, solœcismis, obsitæ sunt, inquit, res vestræ, et vitiorum deformitate pollutæ. Puerilis sane, atque angusti pectoris reprehensio. * * * Cum de rebus agitur ab ostentatione submotis, quid dicatur, spectandum est, non quali cum amœnitate dicatur: nec quid aures commulceat, sed quas afferat audientibus utilitates; maxime cum sciamus etiam quosdam sapientiæ deditos, non tantum abjecisse sermonis cultum, verum etiam, cum possent ornatius atque uberius eloqui, trivialem studio humilitatem secutos, ne corrumperent scilicet gravitatis rigorem, et sophistica se potius ostentatione jactarent."—*Adv. Gentes*, lib. I. c. lviii., lix. (ap. Routh "Script. Eccl. Opusc.," t. ii. p. 291). To the same effect S. Isidore of Pelusium (flor. A. D. 412) defends *the style* of the sacred writers, which had been urged against him as a proof *τοῦ μὴ εἶναι θεῖον κήρυγμα*, by alleging the authority of Plato, who had asserted: *ὅτι φιλοσόφων μὲν ἀνάξιον ἡ εὐγλωττία, μειρακίων δὲ παιζόντων ἡ φιλοτιμία.*—*Epist.*, lib. iv. n. 30, p. 429.

[2] Dr. Conyers Middleton,—who, in his "Essay on the Gift of Tongues," has exaggerated to an absurd degree the peculiarities of the Hellenistic dialect,—having quoted the words of Cicero, "Quis uberior in dicendo Platone? Jovem, quidem, aiunt Philosophi, si Græce loquatur, sic loqui," goes on to represent at some length how the Fathers fully recognised the absence of all such rhetorical ornament in the New Testament; and how they founded upon the fact a powerful argument in support of Christianity. His quotation from S. Chrysostom may serve as an illustration: "That Father tells us 'how he once happened to hear a ridiculous dispute between a Greek and a Christian on this very subject,—the Greek maintained that Paul was utterly illiterate; the Christian, on the other hand, was simple enough to affirm that he was more eloquent even than Plato. By which they each of them, severally, hurt their own cause. For if Paul was really the more learned of the two, the wonder would presently cease how he came to get the better of Plato, and to draw all his followers to himself;—since it would appear to be owing to the superiority of his talents, not to the Divine grace: whereas if Paul, illiterate as he was, could vanquish the learned Plato, such a victory was glorious, and the hand of God manifest in it' [In Ep. i. ad Cor. Hom. iii., t. x. p. 20.]"—*Miscell. Works*, vol. ii. p.

our own day,[1] is based upon a misconception, as well of the nature of Inspiration, as of the ends designed by God in the composition of the Bible. The Holy Spirit, as we have seen, did not employ the human agents whom He had selected to be His organs as mere lifeless machines, but as rational beings whose genius, and natural temperament, and individual characteristics, were penetrated by, and combined with, His guiding influence. Nay, it was only by means of these peculiar attributes of each sacred writer that Divine Truth could have reached the soul of man, as being thus united to a basis which is genuinely human: —by such agencies alone could those mysteries "which the angels desire to look into" have been brought home to the universal consciousness of mankind. If it be argued that, on such a theory, we should still expect to find in Scripture perfection of form and of language as the result of human intelligence thus divinely inspired;[2]—the answer is plain, that here too, as in God's other works, we can never argue from preconceived expectations. The method of *à priori* reasoning, long banished from the science of Nature cannot be permitted still to linger in the domain of Revelation. As the laws, therefore, according to which the Manifestation of God[3] by Nature is unfolded, can only be deduced from the information which Nature's phenomena supply to the observer; so our knowledge as to the method by which His Revelation in Scripture has been recorded can be derived solely from the statements of the sacred writers themselves. If the authors of the Bible inform us that the overruling guidance of the Holy Spirit extended so far, and no further; or that it referred to such and such matters, and not to others;—then is it

99. Cf. also the words of S. Ambrose: "Negant plerique nostros secundum artem scripsisse. Nec nos obnitimur; non enim secundum artem scripserunt, sed secundum Gratiam, quæ super omnem artem est: scripserunt enim quæ Spiritus iis loqui dabat." —*Epist. ad Justum*, t. ii. p. 783.

[1] E. g. in the treatise of Elwert, to which I have already referred (Lecture vi. p. 253, note [2]), published in "Klaiber's Studien der evang. Geistlichkeit," B. III. H. ii. s. 1 ff.—my acquaintance with which is derived from Steudel's essay in the "Tübinger Zeitschrift für Theol." for 1832. In Elwert's treatise, observes Steudel, "the preliminary question is proposed—What expectations are to be formed of a written document, and of its structure, the authors of which were supernaturally guided in the act of writing by the Divine Spirit? In such a document, according to this treatise, we should expect perfection of form (Vollkommenheit der Form)."—*Ueber Insp. der Apostel*, Th. i. s. 116.

[2] This is, indeed, in the words of Bacon, still to argue "Ex analogia hominis, non ex analogia universi."

[3] See *supra* Lecture i. p. 20, &c.

plain that all anticipations which overlook such statements are, in their very nature, without foundation. When S. Paul, in his Epistle to the Corinthian cavillers, concedes that he is "rude in speech;"[1] and at the same time appeals to the fact that, notwithstanding this his want of polished language, his labors had been marked by the Divine favor, and exhibited "all the signs of an Apostle,"[2]—it is clear that he presupposes such an aid of the Holy Spirit, in support of those labors, which did not consist in transforming his speech to suit the demands of grammatical criticism, or the subtleties of a refined elocution; but which, by the very absence of such effects, had exhibited more fully the Divine source of the power that it conferred;—since that power thus proved its independence of all those resources which are essential to the acquiring, by human means, an influence over one's fellow-men. How, then, can we require that a writing composed by S. Paul should not exhibit him as "rude in speech?" or why should the absence of rhetorical embellishment prevent

[1] *Εἰ δὲ καὶ ἰδιώτης τῷ λόγῳ ἀλλ' οὐ τῇ γνώσει.*—2 Cor. xi. 6.

It may be well to notice here the very unjust censure by the learned Cave of S. Jerome's criticisms upon S. Paul's style. Having alluded in strong terms to S. Jerome's well-known vehemence in controversy, Cave proceeds to add: "Et quid mirum? cum in ipsum D. Paulum Apostolum duram nimis et plane insolentem (?) censuram exercere solet. * * * Mitto plura in hominem *θεόπνευστον*, et Apostolorum longe eruditissimum durius dicta, ne viri doctissimi et de Ecclesia optime meriti manes nimis sollicitare videar."—*Hist. Literaria*, Art. 'Hieronymus.' Among the passages which Cave considers deserving of censure are the following. S. Jerome had just quoted 2 Cor. xi. 6; on which he proceeds,—evidently in answer to an objection,—"Nos quotiescunque solœcismos, aut tale quid annotavimus, non Apostolum pulsamus, ut malevoli criminantur, sed magis Apostoli assertores sumus: quod Hebræus ex Hebræis, absque Rhetorici nitore sermonis, et verborum compositione, et eloquii venustate, nunquam ad fidem Christi totum mundum transducere valuisset, nisi evangelizasset eum non in sapientia verbi, sed in virtute Dei. Nam et ipse ad Corinthios ait: 'Et ego, quum venissem ad vos, fratres, veni non in eminentia verbi aut sapientiæ, annuncians vobis testimonium Dei [1 Cor. ii. 1]'"—*Comm. in Ep. ad Eph.*, c. iii. lib. ii. t. vii. p. 587,—a passage obviously identical in spirit with those quoted, p. 326, note [2]. Again: "Non juxta humilitatem, ut plerique æstimant, *sed vere* [Paulus] dixerat: 'Et si imperitus sermone, non tamen scientia.'"—*Comm. in Ep. ad Titum*, c. i. *ibid.*, p. 689. S. Jerome gives an example of what he means when explaining Gal. vi. 1 (*Ἀδελφοί, ὑμεῖς οἱ πνευματικοὶ καταρτίζετε τὸν τοιοῦτον* * * * *σκοπῶν σεαυτόν, κ. τ. λ.*)—"Qui putant Paulum juxta humilitatem, et non vere dixisse, 'et si imperitus sermone non tamen scientia,' defendant hujus loci consequentiam. Debuit quippe secundum ordinem dicere: 'Vos qui spirituales instruite hujusmodi * * * *considerantes vosmet ipsos*,' &c. et non *plurali* inferre *numerum singularem*. Hebræus igitur ex Hebræis, et qui esset in vernaculo sermone doctissimus, profundos sensus aliena lingua exprimere. non valebat, nec curabat magnopere de verbis, *quum sensum haberet in tuto.*"—*Comm. in Ep. ad Gal.*, *ibid.*, p. 520.

[2] "In nothing am I behind the very chiefest Apostles, though I be nothing. Truly the signs of an Apostle were wrought among you in all patience, in signs, and wonders, and mighty deeds."—xii. 11, 12.

our acknowledging the immediate Divine causality under which the Epistles of the great Apostle were composed ?[1]

It has, however, been further objected that this reflection from the pages of Scripture of the peculiar characters and distinct individuality of the various writers leaves ample room for the admission of human fallibility. Such an objection manifestly assumes that the same truth is incapable of being presented under different forms, without contracting thereby a certain coloring of error, or losing its invigorating power. But so far is this assumption from being valid or just, that we are able of ourselves to perceive the obvious fitness and necessity, from the very nature of man, of this variety in the mode of conveying Divine knowledge. We find that Christ Himself communicated, under various aspects, the one Truth which He came to reveal ; and that He imparted to His words that power with which they come home to every heart, by diversifying the form in which He gave them utterance : just as He disclosed His Godhead more fully, by manifesting His Omnipotence in miracles not always the same. So little support, indeed, does this variety of form lend to the notion that there was a corresponding variety in the mode of apprehending Divine Truth by the authors of Scripture, and a consequent possibility of error,—that the contrary inference is the only one admissible. We here perceive each inspired writer, without any toilsome effort after some predetermined type of language or of style, at once bringing home to each conscience his sacred message : the Divine nature of which appears the more plainly from its not being confined to one order of expression, or running in one narrow channel ; but rather in its mastery over all such externals, whereby it has be-

[1] "Divine truth hath its humiliation and exinanition, as well as its exaltation. Divine truth becomes many times in Scripture incarnate, debasing itself to assume our rude conceptions, that so it might converse more freely with us, and infuse its own Divinity into us. God having been pleased herein to manifest Himself not more jealous of His own glory than He is (as I may say) zealous of our good. 'Nos non habemus aures, sicut Deus habet linguam.' If He should speak the language of eternity, who could understand Him, or interpret His meaning? * * * Truth is content when it comes into the world, to wear our mantles, to learn our language, to conform itself as it were to our dress and fashions: it affects not that state or *fastus* which the disdainful rhetorician sets out his style withal, 'Non Tarentinis, aut Siculis hæc scribimus;' but it * * * becomes all things to all men, as every son of truth should do, for their good. Which was well observed in that old cabalistical axiom among the Jews, 'Lumen supernum nunquam descendit sine indumento.' "—J. Smith (of Cambridge), *Of Prophecy*, ch. i.

come the common property of the human race. No truth can be grasped under the same exact form by every intelligence :—witness the varied illustrations, borrowed from every walk of human life, or every line of human industry, or every branch of human science, which a skilful teacher adopts in order to render his meaning intelligible to each class of his hearers. From this common fact we learn how necessary it was that in the instruments selected by the Holy Spirit to convey the Truth to man, an analogous variety of character should prevail. Thus only could provision be made to meet the widely different requirements of human intellect and human susceptibility : thus only could the light of Divine knowledge be brought, in every variety of circumstance, to bear upon the ever-changing aspects of mankind.[1]

[1] In reply to the preceding objection, I have availed myself of the remarks of Steudel, in the second part of the essay already quoted—s. 21 ff.

LECTURE VIII.

RECAPITULATION.—OBJECTIONS CONSIDERED.

"Quam non sibi adversantur iidem Scriptores quatuor ostendendum est. Hoc enim solent (illi, scil., imperita temeritate calumniis appetentes, ut eis veracis narrationis derogent fidem), quasi palmare suæ vanitatis objicere, quod ipsi Evangelistæ inter seipsos dissentiant."

S. AUGUSTIN., *De Consensu Evangelist.*, lib. I. vii.

"Primum te scire volumus, omnem sanctam Scripturam non posse sibi esse contrariam."

S. HIERON., *Paulæ et Eust. ad Marcel.*, Ep. xlvi.

Ὡς γὰρ αἱ διάφοροι τοῦ ψαλτηρίου ἢ τῆς κιθάρας χορδαὶ, ὧν ἑκάστη ἴδιόν τινα φθόγγον καὶ δοκοῦντα μὴ ὅμοιον εἶναι τῷ τῆς ἑτέρας ἀποτελεῖ, νομίζονται τῷ ἀμούσῳ καὶ μὴ ἐπισταμένῳ λόγον μουσικῆς συμφωνίας διὰ τὴν ἀνομοιότητα τῶν φθόγγων ἀσύμφωνοι τυγχάνειν· Οὕτως οἱ μὴ ἐπιστάμενοι ἀκούειν τῆς τοῦ Θεοῦ ἐν ταῖς ἱεραῖς γραφαῖς ἁρμονίας, οἴονται ἀνάρμοστον εἶναι τῇ καινῇ τὴν παλαιὰν, ἢ τῷ νόμῳ τοὺς προφήτας, ἢ τὰ Εὐαγγέλια ἀλλήλοις, ἢ τὸν Ἀπόστολον τῷ Εὐαγγελίῳ, ἢ ἑαυτῷ, ἢ τοῖς Ἀποστόλοις.

ORIGENES, *Comm. in S. Matthæum*, t. ii.

"Ego enim fateor caritati tuæ, SOLIS EIS Scripturarum libris, qui jam Canonici appellantur, didici hunc timorem honoremque deferre, ut nullum eorum auctorem scribendo aliquid errasse f 'missime credam. Ac si aliquid in eis offendero literis, quod videatur contrarium veritati, nihil aliud, quam vel mendosum esse codicem, vel interpretem non assecutum esse quod dictum est, vel me minime intellexisse, non ambigam."

S. AUGUSTIN., *Ad Hieron.*, Ep. lxxxii.

LECTURE VIII.

RECAPITULATION—OBJECTIONS CONSIDERED.

HEAVEN AND EARTH SHALL PASS AWAY, BUT MY WORDS SHALL NOT PASS AWAY.—
S. Matt. xxiv. 35.

In considering the subject of Inspiration in general, a prominent feature of the theory advocated in the preceding Discourses has been the co-existence and combination of the two elements engaged in the composition of the Bible:—the originating influence of God, and the subordinate agency of man. The phenomena which the Universe presents to view have guided the Philosopher to a knowledge of that wondrous mechanism, whereby "seed-time and harvest, and cold and heat, and summer and winter, and day and night," keep the appointed times of their coming: while the daily-advancing labors of Science open new vistas along which the eye can gaze upon the ever active energies of Nature, and discern, more and more clearly, the ends which they respectively subserve. The phenomena which the Bible presents to the Theologian enable him, in like manner, to trace in its pages the course of the Divine operations; and to develop more fully those laws according to which the influence of the Holy Spirit has been exerted in its production. This topic has been discussed at some length, and the results have been stated as the inquiry proceeded.

It has been pointed out how God, from time to time, during the successive stages of Revelation, set apart certain individuals to be the exponents of His will; and how the agents chosen by Him were selected in consequence of such natural characteristics as qualified them for their task, and on account of their peculiar fitness, in other respects, to perform the several duties thus committed to them.[1] We have seen how Scripture, as a document intended for all mankind, has been adapted to the complex susceptibilities of our race, not only by its presenting, under different aspects, the one Great Truth which it unfolds ;[2] but also by that marvellous exclusion of those subjective influences and personal feelings which color the language of profane history :[3]—the sacred writers depicting facts as with the pencil of Nature, and thus bringing home to the mind, as it were, the reality itself. We have noticed too, how the writings which thus convey the Divine Revelation, and perpetuate the history upon which that Revelation rests, have been, in every age, distinctly ascribed to the influence of Inspiration ; and how it results from both internal and external evidence that "holy men of God spake as they were moved by the Holy Ghost."[4] Attention has also been directed to the contents of the Books thus composed ; and the question has been considered why such facts were recorded rather than others, and what was the principle of their selection.[5]

The importance of this last feature of the inquiry is so great, that it will be useful to glance at it once more.

S. Paul, when entering upon his grand exposition of Christian Faith, introduces the statement of Moses, "Abraham believed God, and it was counted unto him for righteousness"[6]—with the explanatory remark, "Now it was not written for his sake alone that it was imputed to him ; but for us also."[7] This illustration of the great doctrine before him, as well as the Apostle's repeated use, for the same purpose, of the words of the prophet Habakkuk, "The just shall live by faith,"[8] denotes how thoroughly the writers of the New Testament believed the former Scriptures to be impregnated with the influence of the Spirit :—a belief which is equally exhibited by their allusions to the Old Testament history ; according to which—to take a single illustration—we find adduced as an element of Christian instruction the events preserved from the circumstances attending the Exodus of the Israelites.[9] On this principle it is that we must ever

[1] Lecture i. pp. 37, 38 ; Lecture iv. ; Lecture vi. p. 265.
[2] Lecture vii. p. 329.
[3] Lecture v. p. 228, &c.
[4] Lecture ii. ; Lecture vi.
[5] Lecture iii. p. 108, &c.
[6] Gen. xv. 6, as quoted Rom. iv. 3 ; Gal. iii. 6.
[7] Rom. iv. 23—*οὐκ ἐγράφη δὲ δι' αὐτὸν μόνον* * * * *ἀλλὰ καὶ δι' ἡμᾶς.*
[8] Hab. ii. 4 ; quoted Rom. i. 17 ; Gal. iii. 11 ; Heb. x. 38.
[9] 1 Cor. x. See *supra*, Lecture iii. p. 109, &c.

regard as both unfounded and superficial that view of Inspiration which distinguishes, in the sacred narrative, between matters of fact and matters of doctrine.[1] In the Christian Faith matters of fact exhibit and convey doctrines ; while doctrines are presented to us as matters of fact. Christ's Birth, Death, and Resurrection, are the most sublime of doctrines. That he is coessential and coequal with the Father ; His atonement, and His bestowal of spiritual gifts, we receive as matters of fact. Nay, Scripture expressly informs us that those features, whether of the Old or the New Testament, which at first sight might seem destitute of doctrinal significance,[2] continually express the highest truths of Revelation. We know, for example, that the record of Christ's

[1] Père R. Simon, speaking of H. Holden's assertion of this theory (see Appendix C), observes: "Il eût eté bon qu' il eût donné quelques exemples de ce qu' il entend *par les matieres qui ne sont point purement de doctrine ;* ou qui n' y ont point une entiere relation."—*Hist. Crit. du N. T.*, ch. xxiv. p. 295. A writer in "The Christian Remembrancer" for July, 1849 (p. 231), acutely observes that this view of the inspired writings "is precisely that which the Roman Church maintains with regard to the authority of the existing Church in successive ages." * * * If, for example, "the Church declares *ex cathedra* that a certain doctrine was maintained by Origen, and that it is heretical: the latter of these declarations rests, according to their belief, upon a Divine, the former upon a merely human, authority. Whether or not it would be consistent with the principles of the Roman Church to extend this distinction to the writers of Holy Scripture, and to maintain as *de fide* that their religion and doctrinal assertions are from God; admitting, meanwhile, that upon other questions they were left to the unaided light of fallible human testimony and human intellect,—we do not here inquire. Such at best must be the view maintained by those Protestant philosophers who reject any fact really recorded by the inspired writers upon any subject whatever, while at the same time they admit their inspiration upon matters of religion." I have already alluded (Lecture iii. p. 108) to Twesten's assertion of this distinction. Having referred to the 'mechanical' theory of Inspiration (see Lecture i. p. 37), the next "excess" which Twesten condemns is that which extends the exercise of the Divine influence, in an equal degree, "to all and everything in Holy Scripture, without making any distinction between the different components;—between Old and New Testament, Law and Gospel, historical and prophetical;—between the writings of the Apostles and those of *their* disciples [see *supra*, Lecture v. p. 218];—between expressions which belonged to the fulfilling of their Commission and which had for their object the promotion of the Kingdom of God, and those which occur merely incidentally and in another view; or, further, without distinguishing between the different elements of each statement;—between words and thoughts;—*between doctrine and history;*—between the religious contents and the garb in which such contents are presented to us."—*Vorlesungen*, B. i. s. 419.

With such a statement may be advantageously contrasted the following remark of Sack: "There can be no mention here of a separation between what is historical and doctrinal, as if the former could not be written by Inspiration. For since Revelation is pre-eminently and always an historical fact [see *supra*, Lecture i, p. 20, note [2]], it could not have been committed to writing at all merely as *doctrine,* and not in connexion with the *history* of the Church."—*Apologetik*, s. 420.

[2] A profound observation of Bishop Butler, which applies to God's Revelation in Scripture as well as in Nature, seems to go to the root of this matter: "We are greatly ignorant how far things are considered by the Author of Nature under the single notion of means and ends; so as that it may be said, this is merely an end, and that merely means, in His regard."—*Analogy*, part II. ch. iv.

acts is as important as that of His words. He taught by the former, not less than by the latter :[1] and for this reason alone, the narrative of His earthly life could not have been excluded from the statement of His doctrines ;—even were it conceivable (which it is not) that an historically faithful account of His sayings could be imparted without including His acts. His miracles are themselves expressions of His dignity and exalted Nature ; and, at the same time, typical representations of His invisible agency. The doctrine of the Redeemer Himself, and of His Kingdom, is involved in them : most of them unfolding, together with their immediate design of being deeds of beneficence, and pledges of his grace and power, the further design of conveying instruction under the form of symbolical acts. Thus S. John explains how the change of water into wine was a "manifestation of the glory" of Jesus ;[2] that the feeding of the "five thousand" was not merely an intimation of His beneficence, but also a token of the grace to be bestowed ;[3] that the healing of "the man born blind" symbolized how "for judgment Christ was come into this world, that they which see not might see ; and that they which see might be made blind."[4] From all this we learn that "the voice from the excellent glory," at the Transfiguration, was not the only Manifestation of His essential Godhead. Each of His miraculous acts was but the natural expression of the higher reality concealed beneath His human form : and hence, in the Epistle to the Hebrews, Miracles in general, whether wrought immediately by Christ Himself, or, after His Ascension, by means

[1] See some remarks of H. W. J. Thiersch, "Versuch zur Herstell. des hist. Standpuncts für die Kritik der N. T. Schriften," s. 123 ; who, having laid down in the first place, the principle—"that an isolation of Christ's sayings from the facts which accompanied them was partly unnatural, partly inconceivable and impracticable"—goes on to give "a special proof" that it was Divinely appointed, and designed by Christ Himself, that the minutest facts connected with the close of His life upon earth should be included in the Gospel narrative. This proof is supplied by the saying recorded in S. Matt. xxvi. 13. When Mary had anointed the Lord in Bethany, and the act was censured by His disciples, His reproof was accompanied with the words: "Verily I say unto you, *Wheresoever this Gospel shall be preached in the whole world*, there shall also this, that this woman hath done, be told for a memorial of her."

[2] "This beginning of miracles did Jesus in Cana of Galilee, *and manifested forth His glory.*"—S. John, ii. 11.

[3] "Ye seek Me, not because ye saw the miracles, but because ye did eat of the loaves, and were filled. Labor not for the meat which perisheth, but for that meat which endureth unto everlasting life, which the Son of Man shall give unto you."—S. John, vi. 26, 27.

[4] S. John, ix. 39.

of His Spirit in His Disciples, are termed "the powers of the world to come."[1]

The principle involved in the foregoing remarks,—namely, that the narrative portion of the Bible, whether contained in the historical books of the Old Testament,[2] or in the Gospels and Acts of the Apostles, is to be looked upon as stamped with the same infallible truth as the account of Christ's discourses, or of what are, strictly speaking, revelations, or of doctrinal teaching in general,—this principle is fully borne out by many characteristics of the inspired record. That even the form and language in which its truths are expressed bear the impress of its Divine origin no less plainly than those truths themselves, may be inferred, with absolute certainty, from the nature of the reasoning employed by our Lord and His Apostles; in which it is invariably assumed that the *words* of Scripture are no less Divine than the doctrines which they convey. The following examples will illustrate this assertion.

Christ proves the great doctrine of the Resurrection of the dead from *the tense* of the substantive verb. Jehovah had declared to Moses, "I AM the God of Abraham, and the God of Isaac, and the God of Jacob;" from which our Lord at once con-

[1] *Δυνάμεις μέλλοντος αἰῶνος*—Heb. vi. 5; "a description (observes Thiersch) which is calculated to serve as a just point of entering upon a genuine Biblical theory of Miracles."—*loc. cit.*, s. 146. In illustration of the use of *αἰὼν μέλλων*, Ritschl ("Die Entst. der altkath. Kirche," s. 56) quotes: "Propalavit Dominus per prophetas, quæ præterierunt; et *futurorum* nobis dedit *initia* scire."—*Ep. S. Barnab.*, cap. i.

[2] Christ (S. Matt. xii. 3–7) argues from the seemingly unimportant incident of David, "when he was an hungred," eating "the shewbread, which it was not lawful for him to eat * * * but only for the priests:"—which allusion he combines (ver. 5) with an inference drawn from the necessary performance of the Sacerdotal functions on the Sabbath-day, "Have ye not read in the Law, how that on the Sabbath days the Priests in the Temple profane the Sabbath, and are blameless?"—and hence proves that the Law and its ordinances possessed a spirtual meaning which the Pharisees, notwithstanding their familiarity with its literal sense, had not as yet apprehended. This lesson He shows here (as He had already done, ch. ix. 13) was contained in the Divine principle enunciated by the prophet of old, "I desired mercy, and not sacrifice."—Hos. vi. 6. (Cf. Butler's Analogy," Part II. ch. i.) Again: He teaches that the grand doctrine of the passing away of the Kingdom of God from the Jews to the Gentiles had been foreshadowed by the exhibition of miraculous power on the part of Elijah and Elisha in the cases of the widow of Sarepta, and of Naaman the Syrian—S. Luke, iv. 25–27. Cf. too, how S. Paul at Antioch reasons from the Old Testament history in general (Acts, xiii. 17–23); how he points out that "God hath not cast away His people whom He foreknew," by adducing an incident in the life of Elijah (Rom. xi. 2–4); and how in Heb. xi. he recapitulates the eventful annals of former days,—even those "of Gedeon and of Barak, of Samson and of Jephtha,"—the foundation of all such reasoning being the great truth, "*Whatsoever things were written aforetime* (*ὅσα προεγράφη*) were written for our learning."—Rom. xv. 4

22

cludes: "God IS not the God of the dead, but of the living."[1] Again, He reasons with the Jews as follows: "Is it not written in your Law, I said ye are gods? If He called them gods unto whom the word of God came,—and the Scripture cannot be broken,—say ye of Him whom the Father hath sanctified and sent into the world, Thou blasphemest; because I said I am the Son of God?"[2]—where our Lord founds His whole argument on the use by the Psalmist of the single term, ELOHIM, "gods." In the Pentateuch also, the representatives of Jehovah had been dignified with this name:—Moses was so called, as representing God to Aaron; he was in like manner called "a god to Pharaoh;"[3] and in this same sense, the title is, more than once, applied to those who filled judicial offices in Israel.[4] From this

[1] S. Matt. xxii. 32; cf. Exod. iii. 6,—where "the addition of the name, 'God of Isaac and God of Jacob,' can only mean that the genuine character of the Abrahamitic life has been transmitted solely through Isaac (not through Ishmael), and through Jacob (not through Esau)."—Olshausen, *Comm.*, B. i. s. 818. Cf. also Gen. xxviii. 13. Even Meyer and De Wette refrain from pressing here their theory of "Rabbinical exposition" (cf. Dr. Bleek's remarks quoted, Lecture vii. p. 303, note [1]). Meyer observes: "The view of Strauss and Hase, that this reasoning contains *merely Rabbinical dialectics*, is in itself arbitrary; mistakes the justice and the truth of the consequence drawn by Jesus from the passage, and is derogatory to His character and dignity." On the contrary, he adds: "The quite similar reasoning of Manasse f. Isr. *De Resurr.* i. 10, 6, seems to have been derived *from our passage*."—*Comm. in loc.*, s. 363, De Wette writes: "Not by means of Rabbinical dialectics, but from a profound apprehension of the sense of Scripture, is the continued existence of the Patriarchs proved * * * Jesus does not go beyond the leading idea; since elsewhere ἀνάστασις=ζωή—Rom. vi. 8, 10; 1 Cor. xv. 21 ff."—*Comm., in loc.*, s. 236.

[2] S. John, x. 34. See Ps. lxxxii. 6—"I have said ye are gods (אלהים); and all of you are children of the Most High (בני עליון)"—the expression, "I have said," referring to that class of passages "in which the magistracy, and in particular the judicial office, is designated by the name Elohim."—Hengstenberg, *in loc.* (Clarke's For. Theol. Lib., vol. iii. p. 37):—see also the following notes.

[3] Exod. iv. 16; vii. 1.

[4] Thus among the laws relating to the Hebrew servant we read: "Then his master shall bring him unto *the judges*—Elohim (והגישו אדניו אל־האלהים)"—Exod. xxi. 6. In this sense the word Elohim occurs three times in ch. xxii. 8, 9; where at ver. 28 we again read, "Thou shalt not revile *the gods*, nor curse the rulers of thy people." Cf. Deut. i. 16, 17 ("I charged your judges (שפטיכם) saying, * * * Ye shall not be afraid of the face of man, for *the judgment is God's*"—לאלהים); Deut. xix. 17; and especially 2 Chron. xix. 6, 7 (Jehoshaphat "said to the judges, Take heed what ye do, for ye judge not for man, but for the Lord, *who is with you in the judgment.*") Hengstenberg further compares 1 Chron. xxix. 23, "Solomon sat *upon the throne of Jehovah*"—adding: "It was in connexion *with the office of judge* that the stamp of Divinity was most conspicuous; inasmuch as that office led the people, under the foreground of an humble earthly tribunal, to contemplate the background of a lofty Divine judgment (p. 31). Hence the reproof of the wicked judges contained in this Psalm is introduced with the words: "God (אלהים) standeth in the congregation of the mighty; He judgeth among the gods (אלהים.)"—ver. 1. Olshausen refers to Exod. xviii. 15, as giving the clearest information on the subject. "In this passage it is said: 'And Moses said unto his father-in-law, Because the people come unto me to inquire of God.' These words are to be understood of the kingly and judicial

derived signification of the word Christ argues by rising to its proper force, and higher import; and He explains the fitness of this His more profound use of the passage by the remark, "The Scripture cannot be broken:"—that is, each expression of Holy Writ must possess a depth of meaning which cannot be reached by confining ourselves to its single primary object, or mere allusive application.[1]

This Divine character of the language which the writers of Scripture have employed is nowhere more clearly denoted than by a passage in the Epistle to the Galatians: "To Abraham and his seed were the promises made. He saith not, And *to seeds*, as of many; but as of one: and to thy seed, which is Christ."[2]

activity of Moses; and we therefore see that God is Himself properly understood, according to the genuine Theocratic view [cf. *supra*, Lecture iv. p. 154], as the true King and Judge of Israel, who merely has His organs through whom He reveals Himself. [Here Olshausen notes: "Magistrates are not called 'gods' because an office has been outwardly entrusted to them by God; but because they are said to be organs of the Divine will, which they must be, even although their disposition be impure (cf. the case of Caiaphas. John, xi. 49–52)"]. "That the Redeemer desires the passage in Ps. lxxxii. 6, to be thus understood, is clearly shown by the words: *πρὸς οὓς ὁ λόγος τοῦ Θεοῦ ἐγένετο*—a formula parallel to the well-known phrase, ויהי דבר יהוה על (cf. *supra*, Lecture iii. p. 130, &c.], by which phrase, as is well known, the point of time is described when communications were received by the prophets from above. * * * All such persons [viz., Magistrates, Prophets, Men illuminated by God] are called *sons of God*, because God's power and Essence wrought in them, and were revealed through them. * * * In order to strengthen the argument, and to make it obligatory on His hearers, Jesus adds: *καὶ οὐ δύναται λυθῆναι ἡ γραφή*. The idea of *λυθῆναι* is to be taken here as in Matt. v. 17, and Gal. ii. 18:—the Scripture, as the expressed will of the unchangeable God, is itself unchangeable and indissoluble."—*Comm. in loc.*, B. ii. s. 278. Rudelbach ("Zeitschrift," 1841, H. iv. s. 27) points out that the conclusion is here drawn from the *improper*, or *allusive*, to the *proper* application (not merely a *minori ad majus*): its force resting on the principle, that "otherwise a single word of Scripture—the אלהים of the Psalmist—would be deprived of its essence and its power."

[1] Analogous to this argument of Christ from the words of Scripture is His mode of reasoning from Ps. cx. 1; "How then doth David in Spirit call Him *Lord*, saying, The Lord [Jehovah] said unto my Lord [לאדני], Sit Thou on My right hand, till I make thine enemies Thy footstool? If David then call Him Lord (*Εἰ οὖν Δαυὶδ καλεῖ Αὐτὸν κύριον*), how is He his Son?"—S. Matt. xxii. 43–45. Here He plainly argues from the use of the word אדון=*lord or master* (e. g. Joseph says that He had been made "lord" of Pharaoh's house, Gen. xlv. 8; and Jacob calls Esau אדני, Gen. xxxiii. 8]. Were it possible that this expression had been, or could have been, employed erroneously or improperly by the Psalmist, any argument such as Christ here urged against the Pharisees would be without point or force. "If David," writes Töllner, "could have erred *in the words* which he employed, no certain conclusion could be thence inferred; it were *possible* that he had falsely described magistrates *as gods*, and the Messiah as his *lord*."—*Die göttl. Eingebung*, s. 419. Cf. also *supra*, Lecture v. p. 201.

[2] *Τῷ δὲ Ἀβ. ἐῤῥέθ. αἱ ἐπαγγ. καὶ τῷ σπέρματι αὐτοῦ. οὐ λέγει· Καὶ τοῖς σπέρμασιν, ὡς ἐπὶ πολλῶν, ἀλλ' ὡς ἐφ' ἑνός· Καὶ τῷ σπέρματί σου, ὅς ἐστιν Χριστός.*—Gal. iii. 16. (Cf. ולזרעך—Gen. xvii. 8; xxviii. 13: LXX.—*καὶ τῷ σπέρματί σου.*) Olshausen refers to Gen. xxii. 18; xxvi. 4; xxviii. 13, 14; making Gen. **xxii. 18**, the special object of the Apostle's allusion.

Here S. Paul, without making an express quotation, confines himself to the exposition of a single word,[1] founding his argument on the force of the singular number. His object is to point out the deep sense concealed under the form of this promise to the Patriarch. As there was but *one* chosen race sprung from Abraham, *one* covenant-people of the promise:—in other words, as not all the offspring of Abraham's body were heirs of the blessing, but the posterity of Isaac alone; on a similar principle, argues the Apostle, "the blessing of Abraham" comes now too, not upon his mere bodily descendants, as such, but upon those who, whether they be "Jews or Greeks," "are One in Christ;" and who, "if they be Christ's are *therefore* Abraham's seed, and heirs according to the promise."[2]

[1] זרע=σπέρμα—a *collective* term, signifying *seed, race, posterity;* and which S. Paul does not mean to contrast with the plural, זרעים,—in which form the word occurs but once in the Old Testament, where it has the determinate sense of "*grain*," "*seeds* of corn:" "He will take the tenth of *your seed;*" (1 Sam. viii. 15—cf. too, Dan. i. 12, 16, where in its Chaldee form it denotes "*pulse*"),—but, on the contrary, founds his argument on the *collective* force of the term in the singular; drawing the distinction between σπέρμα, *posterity*, and σπέρματα, *posterities*. That is, he explains how God's promise applied to the line of Abraham's posterity *through Isaac;* not to his descendants generally, whether derived through Isaac or Ishmael indifferently (cf. *supra*, p. 338, note [1]). In his exposition of this passage, Tholuck ("Das A. T. im N. T." s. 51 ff.) points out that this use of זרע as a *collective* term is one familiar to S. Paul, who explains the words of Gen. xxi. 12, "In Isaac shall *thy seed* be called." as meaning "*the children of* God"—ἐν Ἰσαὰκ κληθήσονταί σοι σ π έ ρ μ α· Τουτ' ἔστιν, οὐ τ ὰ τ έ κ ν α τ ῆ ς σ α ρ κ ό ς, ταῦτα τέκνα τοῦ Θεοῦ—Rom. ix. 7, 8; cf. Heb. xi. 18.

[2] This explanation (that of Tholuck and Olshausen—Bengel's is somewhat different) is founded upon the principle laid down in the words: "There is neither Jew nor Greek * * * FOR YE ARE ALL ONE IN CHRIST JESUS. *And if ye be Christ's*, then are ye Abraham's seed, and heirs according to the promise"—Gal. iii. 28, 29. Hence Χριστός (ver. 16) is put for the community of believers, who are "His body," and of whom He is the Head (cf. "We are members of His Body, of His Flesh, and of His Bones"—Eph. v. 30; see, too, ch. i. 23; iv. 12; and 1 Cor. xii. 12, 27.) This exposition is further confirmed by the continuation of the argument, "Now *we*, brethren, *as Isaac was*, are the children of promise," &c.—Gal. iv. 28, &c,; see last note. The Apostle elsewhere explains the true force of the promises to Abraham. The "seed" are they "who walk in the steps of the faith of our father Abraham;" and "the promise" is "sure to all the seed; not to that only which is of the Law, but to that also which is of the faith of Abraham."—Rom. iv. 12, 16. This exposition, writes Tholuck, "the Jew himself must concede the more willingly, since it would prove too much, even in his view, were the prediction to embrace unconditionally *every* descendant of Abraham:—even he would desire to exclude the line through Ishmael, and that through Esau."—*loc. cit.*, s. 58. With reference to the objection that the force thus given to the *singular* of σπέρμα could not have been designedly attached to it by the author of Genesis, Olshausen observes: "The Apostles, like all the other writers of the New Testament, had, in the illumination of the Holy Spirit, the full authority to pass beyond the standpoint of consciousness in the Old Testament writer [cf. Lecture v. p. 197, &c.], and to unveil the innermost truth of the thought according to the sense of Him Who promised and foretold. If, therefore, Jewish learning also has made similar applications of Old Testament passages, still the distinction of the Apostolic mode of procedure from the Rabbinical always consisted in this, that the learned Jews acted merely according to the arbitrary manner

To the foregoing examples must be added a single illustration of that Divine superintendence which guided the authors of Scripture in their selection of expressions from which, as we have just seen, such important truths could be inferred. Christ's title, "Son of Man,"[1] constantly recurs in each of the four Gospels. It is never applied to Him, however, by any other than Himself, so long as He walked on earth. On one occasion, after He was glorified, it is given Him by S. Stephen;[2] but throughout the Apostolic Epistles the title is not once to be found. The conclusion is obvious: and the marked agreement of the sacred writers, even in this single particular, is a manifest proof that they have written under the same Divine influence.[3] In two passages of the Apocalypse,[4] moreover, the title "Son of Man" is employed; there being in both cases an obvious reference, according to S. John's practice in that book, to the great prediction of Daniel: "I saw in the night visions, and behold one like the Son of Man came with the clouds of heaven." And, in continuation of what has been just said, it particularly is worthy of remark, that while a Hebrew phrase, which the English Version similarly translates, "son of man," is of frequent occurrence (as in the book of Ezekiel), the form of expression employed by Daniel is to be met with in no other portion of the Old Testament.[5]

of human beings by which their acuteness often degenerated into mere conceits;—while the Apostles, guided by the Spirit, ever unveiled infallibly the true sense of the predicting Spirit (2 Pet. i. 20, 21)."—*Comm. in loc.* B. iv. s. 65. Cf. *supra*, Lecture vii. p. 309, &c.

[1] 'Ο Υἱὸς ΤΟΥ 'Ανθρώπου. Bishop Middleton observes on S. John, v. 27, where both articles are omitted: "If it be thought remarkable * * * that *υἱὸς ἀνθρώπου*, as applied to Christ, now *first* occurs without the articles, it is sufficient to answer that now, for the first time, has Christ *asserted* His claim to the title: in all other places He has assumed it." Meyer, *in loc.*, considers that "*υἱὸς ἀνθρ.* ist als *Nomen propr.* behandelt, daher artikellos."

[2] Acts, vii. 56.

[3] "Apostolorum vel in hoc uno idiomate convenientia ostendit eos eodem divino motu scripsisse."—Bengelii *Gnomon*, in S. Matt. xvi. 13.

[4] Rev. i. 13; xiv. 14:—in both cases the articles are wanting.

[5] Dan. vii. 13, where we read—בר אנש. The phrase in Ezekiel is בן־אדם. (In Psalm cxliv. 3, בן־אנש occurs, cf. Ps. viii. 5. We also find בני־איש—e. g. Psalm xlix. 2. The verb אנש=*æger male affectus fuit.* May we not hence ("Ægritudinis et morbi significatu, qui inest in rad. אנש," &c.—Gesenius *in voc.*) infer that this phrase, thus appropriated to the Messiah, conveys the idea of the "Man (איש) of sorrows"—Isai. liii. 3? and therefore conclude that, until *after* His period of humiliation, no one was permitted to apply to the Lord a title thus indicative of his exinanition: but that when He had resumed His own glory, the restriction was removed—as in the cases of S. Stephen and S. John?

To the foregoing examples, which so clearly exhibit the superintendence exer-

Thus far I have endeavored to lay down principles from which the Divine authority, the infallible certainty, and the entire truthfulness, of every part of the Scriptures must necessarily result. To this conclusion many exceptions have been taken ; and with some general observations on the nature and foundation of such exceptions these Discourses shall fitly terminate. From the outset I have endeavoured, as far as it was possible, to keep the inquiry as to Inspiration distinct from the many kindred questions, relating to the Bible, with which it has been so continually interwoven in the course of modern criticism ;[1] and I shall now content myself with stating the grounds on which I conceive the weakness of the objections to which I have alluded may in all cases be exposed :—to enter with any particularity on so vast a field would, it is clear, necessitate a discussion on almost every topic connected with the Evidences of Christianity. In illustration of the grounds on which I thus rely, I purposely select those examples which are the most obvious, and the most fa-

cised over the language of Scripture, the following may be added. In order to prove that through the One Son, others, too, should be exalted to be the sons of God, S. Paul insists upon the single term "brethren" in Ps. xxii. 22: "For both He that sanctifieth, and they who are sanctified, are all of one; for which cause (δι' ἣν αἰτίαν) He is not ashamed [even under the Old Covenant] to call them brethren; saying, I will declare Thy name unto My brethren."—Hebr. ii. 11, 12. Cf. our Lord's argument from Gen. i. 27, and v. 2; in S. Matt. xix. 4, &c. Again, S. Mark and S. Luke thus give the demoniac's address to Christ: "What have I to do with Thee, Jesus, Thou Son of the *Most High God?*" (S. Mark, v. 7; S. Luke, viii. 26; cf. S. Matt. viii. 29). "*In no other part of the Gospels* do we find *the Most High* as an epithet to God: they are used separately as equivalent terms. Why, then, are they united by S. Mark and S. Luke? The man and his friends were Pagans; and he was constrained by an overruling power to confess the true God in this explicit manner: just as the Pythonissa did afterwards at Philippi, by saying, 'These men are the servants of *the Most High God.*'—Acts, xvi. 17. And they [who wrote not as S. Matthew for Jews] retain the very form of words used by the demoniac, for the sake of those who had believed in 'gods many and lords many;' and to whom the bare name of God did not so surely present the proper and sublime notion of the word." * * * "*The most high God* occurs but once more in the New Testament, Heb. vii. 1, and is there taken from Gen. xiv. 18, where Melchizedek is called 'The priest of *the most high God,*' to show that the God whom he served was the true God, and not one of the gods of the nations. * * * And I believe, throughout the Old Testament, *The Most High* is conjoined with the name of God only in the like cases."—Townson, *On the Four Gospels*, Disc. v. p. 156. For additional examples cf. Töllner "Die göttl. Eingebung," s. 17 ff. and M. Gaussen, "Theopneustia," p. 411, &c. As I have adduced some passages from S. Matthew in support of this line of argument, it is obviously necessary (as indeed for other reasons connected with the subject of these Discourses) to advert to the question as to the original language of his Gospel. That it was originally composed in Hebrew cannot, I apprehend, be denied. On this subject some remarks will be found in Appendix M.

[1] "Die Untersuchung über die Theopneustie der heiligen Schrift gehört also nicht in die Einleitung, wohin sie z. B. Bauer, Jahn, u. a. ziehen."—Hävernick, *Einleit.*, Th. i. s. 3. Cf. *supra*, Lecture i. p. 32.

miliar. It will manifestly save us the pains of any collateral controversy if such instances only are brought forward, the difficulties connected with which are generally allowed to have received a satisfactory solution.

I. The objections which first demand our notice are those founded upon the assertion that the sacred writers contradict each other. It is the more necessary to insist upon this topic, since, as it has been well observed, "much of the criticism at the present day seems to assume that there is some resting-place between the *perfect* truthfulness of Inspiration, and the uncertainty of ordinary writing."[1] Of this class of objections the want of harmony alleged to exist among the Evangelists affords the most ordinary (as they are the most important) examples.

That in the Gospel narrative certain statements are to be found which, at first sight, seem at variance, every one is aware. It is also well known that many commentators have not been happy in their efforts to reconcile the seeming discrepancies: and hence[2] it has resulted that some advocates of Christianity have been tempted to make admissions which are gratuitous as they are unwarranted. It is too often conceded to the adversary,

[1] Westcott, "Elements of the Gospel Harmony," p. 131. "A subjective standard is erected, which, if once admitted, will be used as much to measure the doctrines as the facts of Scripture; and while many speculators boldly avow this, others are contented to admit the premises from which the conlusion necessarily follows."—*Ibid.* The most obvious illustration of the truth of this remark is Schleiermacher's theory of the "Christian Consciousness." "As the intuitive consciousness of God indicates to the human mind the existence * * * of a Personal Deity, so does this 'Christian Consciousness' *testify that Christ lived, and that He continues, by His Spirit*, to operate upon mankind. * * * It is only he who has a 'Christian Consciousness' that can recognize Christ in the fragments of tradition, and the manifestations of history."—Neander, *The Life of Jesus Christ*, Introd. § 2 (Bohn's transl. p. 3).

[2] Mr. Coleridge writes: "On what other ground [than on the reception "of the plenary inspiration of the Old and New Testaments"] can I account for the whimsical *subintelligiturs* of our numerous harmonists,—for the curiously inferred facts, the inventive circumstantial detail, the complemental and supplemental history which, in the utter silence of all historians and absence of all historical documents, they bring to light by mere force of logic?—And all to do away with some half score apparent discrepancies in the chronicles and memoirs of the Old and New Testaments * * * discrepancies so trifling in circumstance and import, that, although in some instances it is highly probable, and in all instances, perhaps, possible that they are only apparent and reconcilable, no wise man would care a straw whether they were real or apparent, reconciled or left in harmless and friendly variance."—*Confess. of an Enquiring Spirit*, Letter iv. p. 41. Mankind, unhappily, are not content to regard this subject from the heights of such sublime philosophy. A melancholy page in the history of the Church informs us that, from the earliest period to the days of Strauss, the enemies of Christianity (in the words of S. Augustine prefixed to this Discourse) "hoc solent quasi palmare suæ vanitatis objicere, quod ipsi Evangelistæ inter seipsos dissentiant."

that the discrepancies alleged are, in point of fact, *real*. Truth and candor, we are sometimes told, require that this concession should be made : and since a leading argument against any strict view of Inspiration is based upon this assumed want of harmony, these advocates attempt to evade it either by maintaining that such contradictions (which, as they are willing to allow, really exist) are of a trifling character ; or by alleging that the independence of the sacred writers, as well as the absence of concert among them, is the only thing which the existence of discrepancies proves. Nay, we are sometimes told, that nothing but the force of prejudice, or attachment to some preconceived and erroneous theory, can possibly induce any defender of Christianity to uphold the infallibility of the Evangelists in all the details of their Gospels.[1] I would further premise, that this objection, which we are about to examine more closely, is of no modern date. So early as the middle of the second century the Epicurean philosopher Celsus urged the existence of such apparent contradictions against the truth of the Gospel history :—he argued, for example, that S. Matthew and S. Mark made mention of but one angel at the Sepulchre, while S. Luke and S. John speak of two.[2] On which I would observe in passing, that we learn from

[1] Mr. Alford, in the Prolegomena to his edition of the Greek Testament (vol. i. ch. 1, § 4), observes to this effect; "Christian commentators have been driven to a system of harmonizing which condescends to adopt the weakest compromises, and to do the utmost violence to probability and fairness, in its zeal for the veracity of the Evangelists. It becomes important, therefore, critically to discriminate between *apparent* and *real* discrepancy; and while with all fairness we acknowledge the latter where it exists, to lay down certain common-sense rules whereby the former may be also ascertained. The *real* discrepancies between our Evangelistic histories are very few, and those all of one kind. * * * They consist in different chronological arrangements, expressed or implied. * * * The fair Christian critic will pursue a plan different from both ['the enemies of the faith,' and 'the orthodox Harmonists']. With no desire to create discrepancies, but rather every desire truthfully and justly to solve them, if it may be,—he will candidly recognise them where they unquestionably exist. By this he loses nothing, and the Evangelists lose nothing. * * * *Christianity never was, and never can be, the gainer by any concealment, warping, or avoidance of the plain truth, wherever it is to be found.*" The emphasis which Mr. Alford gives, by his italics, to the truism contained in the closing words of this extract would seem to point to a notorious class of writers, whose principle has been a "concealment, warping, or avoidance of the plain truth." In the absence, however, of any direct mention of such writers, the remark appears, to say the least of it, superfluous. To the same effect Neander writes: "It must be regarded as one of the greatest boons which the purifying process of Protestant theology in Germany has conferred upon Faith, as well as Science, that the old, 'mechanical' view of Inspiration has been so generally abandoned. That doctrine, and the forced harmonies to which it led, demanded a clerk-like accuracy in the Evangelical accounts, and could not admit even the slightest contradictions in them; but we are now no more compelled to have recourse to subtleties against which our sense of truth rebels."—*Loc. cit.* p. 8.

[2] Celsus, writes Origen, objected: *ὅτι καὶ πρὸς τὸν αὐτοῦ τοῦ 'Ιησοῦ τάφον ἱστόρηνται*

the numerous accounts of similar objections that the primitive Church did not receive the books of the New Testament as Divine, without a full appreciation of the difficulties which, from the very first, have been so pertinaciously urged against them.[1] Indeed we have an express intimation to this effect in the celebrated Fragment brought to light by Muratori; which is the earliest document extant, with one exception, in which the Evangelists are named, and which is the first catalogue of the Books of the New Testament.[2] The author of this Fragment, having enumerated the four Evangelists, pauses to observe: "Although sundry articles of belief are announced in the several

ἐληλυθέναι ὑπό τινων μὲν ἄγγελοι δύο, ὑπό τινων δὲ εἷς· ὡς οἶμαι, τηρήσας Ματθαῖον μὲν [xxviii. 5] *καὶ Μάρκον* [xvi. 5] *ἕνα ἱστορηκέναι, Λουκᾶν δὲ* [xxiv. 4] *καὶ Ἰωάννην* [xx. 12] *δύο· ἅπερ οὐκ ἦν ἐναντία· οἱ μὲν γάρ, κ. τ. λ.*—*Cont. Celsum*, lib. v. § 56. t. i. p. 621.

[1] Take, e. g., the difficulty which Gibbon has specially singled out to form the climax of his well-known "fifteenth" chapter: "Under the reign of Tiberius, the whole earth, or at least a celebrated province of the Roman empire, was involved in a preternatural darkness of three hours [S. Matt. xxvii. 45]. Even this miraculous event, which ought to have excited the wonder, the curiosity, and the devotion of mankind, passed without notice in an age of science and history. It happened during the lifetime of Seneca and the elder Pliny, who must have experienced the immediate effects, or received the earliest intelligence, of the prodigy," &c., &c.—*The Decline, &c. of the Roman Empire*, ch. xv. This sarcasm has not even the poor merit of originality. Origen informs us that, in his day, two objections were urged against this portion of the Gospel narrative. (1.) "Quomodo hoc factum tam mirabile, nemo Græcorum, nemo Barbarorum factum conscripsit in tempore illo, maxime qui Chronica conscripserunt, et notaverunt sicubi tale aliquid novum factum est aliquando; sed soli hoc scripserunt vestri auctores?"—*Comm. Series in Matt.*, § 134, t. iii. p. 923. (2.) It was also objected, that the only natural cause by which such a phenomenon could be explained, viz., an eclipse of the sun, is here excluded; because, "in tempore quo passus est Christus, manifestum est quoniam conventus non erat Lunæ ad Solem quoniam tempus erat Paschale." To the former objection Origen replies as follows: "Arbitror ergo, sicut cætera signa quæ facta sunt in Passionem Ipsius, in Jerusalem tantummodo facta sunt. * * * Nec alia terra tremuit tunc, nisi terra Jerusalem * * * ut sentirent (verbi gratia) et qui in Æthiopia erant, et in India, et in Scythia: quod si factum fuisset, sine dubio inveniretur in historiis aliquibus eorum qui in Chronicis scripserunt nova aliqua facta."—*Ibid.* And Origen goes on to adduce in illustration how "there was a thick darkness in all the land of Egypt three days * * * but all the children of Israel had light in their dwellings."—Exod. x. 22, 23;—considering the statement of the Evangelist that there was "darkness over all the land," as parallel to the hyperbole of Obadiah, that there was "no nation or kingdom" in which Ahab had not sought for Elijah.—1 Kings, xviii. 10. The second objection Origen answers by alleging that another natural cause might be assigned, viz.: "Quasdam tenebrosissimas nubes, et forte non unam, sed multas et majores concurrisse super terram Judæam et Jerusalem, ad cooperiendos radios solis, et ideo profundæ factæ sunt tenebræ a sextâ horâ usque ad nonam." For the usual cavil as to the Ark of Noah, cf. "In Genes." Hom. ii., t. ii. p. 61.

[2] Cf. *supra*, Lecture ii. p. 57, note [2]. Dr. Routh observes: "Quum vero ponendus sit auctor ejus [Fragmenti] inter scriptores, qui primi omnium, excepto Papia, de Evangelistis ipsis vel commemoraverint, vel ipsorum scripta adjectis nominibus protulerint, fieri non potest quin primus hic librorum Novi Testamenti Catalogus curis nostris dignus censeatur."—*Reliq. Sacr* t. i. p. 400.

Gospels, there is no difference in the Faith of believers ; since all things relating to the Lord's history have been declared by One overruling Spirit."[1]

There are four points of view from which this subject of the Gospel Harmony has been regarded :—(1.) It was argued by a writer who attracted some notice during the last century, that "the Resurrection of Christ is not true, because the narratives of the Evangelists do not harmonize." (2.) He was met by the reply, "This great doctrine is true because the accounts *do* coincide." (3.) A third opinion was interposed : "It may, after all, be true, *although* discrepancies actually exist in the statements of the Gospels." (4.) But there remains yet a fourth mode of regarding the question: "It is, and must be true, even though *I* should not succeed in bringing the representations of the Evangelists into harmony ; or in solving all the difficulties which an ingenious mind may suggest."[2] This last proposition is obviously the only just or philosophical conclusion for those to arrive at, who ascribe, in any true sense of the word, Divine authority to the Bible. I repeat that if we fully and entirely believe in the Divine origin of Holy Scripture, to assert that its statements do not harmonize is a contradiction in terms. Who but the veriest sciolist would question the universality of one of Nature's Laws, because the powers of Science have not as yet brought into subjection certain phenomena, to which this Law, if true, must extend. There are difficulties, no doubt, in explaining all the phenomena which the Gospels present. Such difficulties, however, arise, not from any real discordance among the Evangelists, but from our not being, as yet at least, in possession of the clue which would reconcile their statements : just as certain difficulties occur in the application of the theory of Gravitation ;—not from any want of universality in the Law, but from our ignorance of the conditions of the problem.[3]

[1] "Et ideo licet varia singulis Evangeliorum libris principia doceantur, nihil tamen differt credentium fides, cum uno ac principali Spiritu declarata sint in omnibus de Nativitate, de Passione, de Resurrectione, de Conversatione Domini cum Discipulis Suis."—ap. Routh., *loc. cit.* p. 394: where Dr. Routh considers "voce *principia*, *capita* seu articulos hic significari, quippe cum in ore omnibus sit, *doceri* principia sive capita fidei."—*Ibid.* p. 411.

[2] See Thiersch, "Versuch zur Herstell," s. 30. The three former opinions Lessing mentions as being held by the author of the "Wolfenbüttel Fragments" (Reimarus), by "the Orthodox," who opposed that writer, and by himself respectively ; the fourth is that which Thiersch maintains.

[3] Cf. the remarks of Mr. Westcott, "Elements of the Gospel Harmony," p. 136.

Let us examine how, in such a case, all sound philosophy proceeds: and let us take for our illustration the late solution of a celebrated astronomical problem. "No sooner," observes one of the distinguished men who have afforded Science this triumph, —"No sooner had astronomers commenced, some years ago, to suspect that the motion of Uranus was modified by some unknown cause, than all possible hypotheses were at once hazarded as to its nature."[1] The writer then proceeds to discuss the merits of these several hypotheses, with the significant exception of that which would explain the phenomenon by asserting that the Law of Gravitation is not universal:—"I will not stop," continues M. Le Verrier, "to consider this idea, that the laws of Gravitation may cease to be rigorous at the great distance of Uranus from the Sun. It is not the first time that, in order to explain inequalities for which they were unable to account, certain persons have betaken themselves to the principle of universal Gravitation. But we also know that these hypotheses have always disappeared before a more profound examination of facts." Let us then apply to the question of the Gospel Harmony the principle which, as we learn from the instance just cited, is recognised as legitimate in the exact sciences. In doing so, let us, for a moment, lay aside the notion that the Evangelical narratives are inspired; and consider them merely as ordinary histories, of which we have no reason to question the general trustworthiness.

The contradictions alleged to exist in the Gospels either are apparent only, or they are assumed to be absolute.[2] In the former case, there is clearly no difficulty at all; and we need only point out that the discrepancy is but apparent. In the latter,

[1] In an essay read by M. Le Verrier before the "Academie des Sciences," June 1st, 1846, an historical account is given of previous investigations relating to the perturbations observed in the motion of the planet Uranus. "A peine avait-on commencé, il y a quelques années, à soupçonner que le mouvement d'Uranus était modifié par quelque cause inconnue, que déja toutes les hypothèses possibles étaient hasardées sur la nature de cette cause. Chacun, il est vrai, suivit simplement le penchant de son imagination, sans apporter aucune considération à l'appui de son assertion. On songea à la résistance de l'éther; on parla d'un gros satellite qui accompagnerait Uranus; ou bien d'un planète encore inconnue, dont la force perturbatrice devrait être prise en considération; on alla même jusqu' à supposer qu' à cette énorme distance du Soleil, la loi de la gravitation pourrait perdre quelque chose de sa rigueur. Enfin, une comète n'aurait-elle pas pu troubler brusquement Uranus dans sa marche?"

[2] For some acute remarks on this aspect of the question, see Mr. Rogers' Essay, "Reason and Faith," p. 69, &c.

where it is objected that an absolute contradiction exists,[1] it is equally plain that any hypothetical, or even possible solution, must, in all fairness, be accepted as a sufficient answer, if we only allow the general truthfulness of the narratives which we compare:—indeed to deny this principle is to assume that there is no single circumstance omitted by the Evangelists which, if known, would harmonize their statements.[2] Even were we unable to adduce any example in which the application of such a principle has been successful, every impartial mind must admit its sufficiency as a reply. Many examples, however, illustrative of this position, may be pointed out; and others are being daily

[1] Köppen observes that, in narratives drawn up by men who wrote like the Evangelists, independently of each other, in different places and at different times, the nature of the case requires that there should be considerable diversity of *manner* in the account which they have given of events. And yet all four perfectly agree as to what constitutes the *essence* of their statements. In no single passage of the Gospel is there a *contradiction in matters of fact;* but there is *variety* in the form of *representation*, and must be so, if everything was honestly set down. The opponents of the Gospels interchange these two features of the case; which are in the nature of things, unquestionably different. They seek out passages in which *variety in the form of representation* is to be found, and these they term *mutual contradictions.*—"Die Bibel ein Werk der göttl. Weisheit," B. ii. s. 117.

[2] With reference to the narratives by S. Matthew and S. Luke of the death of Judas, Mr. Alford (on Acts, i. 18, 19) observes: "The ἐκτήσατο χωρίον does not appear to agree with the account in Matt. xxvii. 6–8; nor, consistently with common honesty can they be reconciled, *unless we knew more of the facts than we do.* * * * Whether Judas, as Bengel supposes, 'initio emtionis facto, occasionem dederit ut Sacerdotes eam consummarent,' we cannot say: *such a thing is of course possible.* * * * With regard to *the purchase of the field*, the more circumstantial account in Matthew is to be adopted; with regard to the *death of Judas*, the more circumstantial account of Luke. The *clue which joins these has been lost to us;* and in this, only those will find any stumbling-block, whose faith in the veracity of the Evangelists is very weak indeed." Ebrard gives a striking example of an apparent contradiction, arising from the manner in which the same fact has impressed itself on different eye-witnesses. On the evening of September 5, 1839, a rumor prevailed in Zurich that an attack was to be apprehended from an armed force of Bernese. The greatest commotion was excited, and a body of men was drawn together in the district of Pfäffikon, to repel the attack. The rumor was soon found to be without any foundation, and means were taken by the Government to allay the popular tumult. On subsequently inquiring as to these events, Ebrard was informed, by one person, that the Government despatched N., one of their number, at a late hour, with a letter, to Pfäffikon: on another occasion, Ebrard was told, by a second informant, that N., after going a short distance, *returned* with the intelligence that the tocsin was already ringing in Pfäffikon. A third related that *two persons* on horseback had been despatched; while a fourth averred that *N. had sent* two messengers on horseback to the disturbed district. "If ever four accounts *appear* irreconcilable, these are so. And if a harmonist were to conjecture that N. had been sent to Pfäffikon; that he had been met on the Zürichberg by two peasants, coming from that place with the intelligence that the people were already on the march; that he had returned with them to Zurich, and, entering the neighboring house of a magistrate, had caused two horses to be at once saddled, and commanded the peasants to ride back in haste, to proclaim peace:—all this would, no doubt, be set down as a highly improbable and artificial conjecture. And yet it is no conjecture, but the simple, true account which *N. himself* gave me, when I asked *him* about that event."—*Kritik der evang. Geschichte*, s. 72.

brought to light by the diligence of the learned.[1] It is by no means uncommon to find in the accounts of two perfectly honest historians, referring to the same event from different points of view, certain peculiarities in the structure of their compositions which, when noticed, at once reconcile the seeming variance which such peculiarities may have occasioned : or some fact may have been omitted which lends an air of opposition to their statements,—an opposition which the mention of the omitted fact by

[1] The account given in Dan. v. 30, of the death of "Belshazzar the king of the Chaldeans" (a name which does not occur except in the Bible), on the night of the conquest of Babylon by Cyrus, seems to present an irreconcilable opposition to that of the Chaldean historians.

Josephus ("Cont. Apion.," lib. i. c. 20, t. ii. p. 452) has preserved a fragment of Berosus, in which it is stated that Cyrus invaded Babylonia in the seventeenth year of the reign of Nabonnedus; that as soon as Nabonnedus was aware of his approach, he assembled his forces to oppose him, but was defeated, and fled with a few adherents to the city of Borsippus (εἰς τὴν Βορσιππηνῶν πόλιν): and, in fine, that Cyrus took that place, treated Nabonnedus with kindness, and provided him with a settlement in Carmania, where he died. The name here given by Berosus to the last Chaldean king is repeated, with immaterial variations, in the Canon of Ptolemy, by Alexander Polyhist. and Abydenus (Euseb. "Chron. Armen.," i. pp. 45, 60), and by Megasthenes (Euseb., "Præpar. Evang.," ix. 41, ed. Gaisford, t. ii. p. 442). Herodotus alone calls him Labynetus ("Clio," 188), adding (191), that the city was stormed by night during a festival; which fact is also vouched for by Xenophon, who states further ("Cyrop.," vii. 5. 30), that the King (whom he merely describes as ἀνόσιος βασιλεύς) then perished. On these facts Winer ("Real-Wörterb.," art. *Belsazzar*) observes: "Berosus is, at all events, more trustworthy than a foreign writer who lived long after the transaction. * * * Concerning the fate, too, of the Babylonian King, Berosus is perhaps in the right; and deserves more credit than Xenophon *and Daniel.*" Hengstenberg, however (although he had just adduced the authority of Berosus to confirm the statement of Dan. iv. 30, in opposition to Ctesias and the Greek historians), "finds no difficulty *in rejecting* the account" of Berosus in the case before us, and in accepting the narrative of Xenophon. ("Beitrage, i. s. 316, *u.* 326.) But another voice is to be heard on this question.

Colonel Rawlinson (dating from Bagdad, January 25, 1854) has communicated to the "Athenæum" (No. 1377, p. 341, March 18, 1854), a discovery which he has "recently made in Babylonian history, and which is of the utmost importance for Scriptural illustration." A number of clay cylinders have been lately disinterred in the ruins of Um-Qeer (the ancient Ur of the Chaldees), two of which contain a memorial of the works executed by Nabonidus (the last king of Babylon) in southern Chaldæa. "The most important fact which they disclose is, that the eldest son of Nabonidus was named Bel-shar-ezar, and that he was admitted by his father to a share in the government. This name is undoubtedly the Belshazzar (בלשאצר) of Daniel, and thus furnishes us with *a key to the explanation of that great historical problem which has hitherto defied solution.* We can now understand how Belshazzar, as joint king with his father, may have been governor of Babylon, when the city was attacked by the combined forces of the Medes and Persians, and may have perished in the assault which followed; while Nabonidus, leading a force to the relief of the place, was defeated, and obliged to take refuge in the neighboring town of Borsippa (or Birs-i-Nimrud), capitulating, after a short resistance, and being subsequently assigned, according to Berosus, an honorable retirement in Carmania. By the discovery, indeed, of the name of Bel-shar-ezar, as appertaining to the son of Nabonidus, we are, for the first time, enabled to reconcile authentic history with the inspired record of Daniel."

a third writer instantly clears up.[1] The following solution of a difficulty in ordinary history, together with the application of the principle on which it rests to a parallel case in the Evangelical record, will amply confirm what has been just stated.

Aristobulus, the friend of Alexander the Great, and who watched by his death-bed, relates that he died on the 30th of the Macedonian month Dæsius. On the other hand, Eumenes and Diodotus, who kept the journal of Alexander, and who recount the progress of his malady, place his death on the evening of the 28th of the same month. Here is an obvious variance in statement; and yet no critic has for a moment considered that there is any real contradiction;—although the solutions which have been given are very different. Thus it is shown by some, how the variance will disappear if we call to mind the manner of counting the days of the month by the Greeks; while the explanation of another writer is founded upon the difference in the point of time from which the beginning of the day was reckoned: —whether from sunrise, as at Babylon, or from sunset, according to Grecian usage.[2] Other explanations are also supplied, and any

[1] To take an instance from the Old Testament: Sennacherib had invaded Judea, and Hezekiah endeavored to buy off the approaching attack upon Jerusalem: "That which thou puttest on me," said he, "will I bear." The sum demanded exhausted the Jewish resources to such an extent, that Hezekiah was reduced to the necessity of cutting off the gold from the doors of the Temple (2 Kings, xviii. 13–16). This cowardly sacrifice was in vain; for we know how the Assyrians broke faith with the Jews, and we are also told of God's miraculous interposition in their favor (Isai. xxxvi., xxxvii). Shortly after this event, however, the ambassadors sent to congratulate Hezekiah found his treasury full to overflowing (Isai. xxxix). The apparent contradiction is at once cleared up by a few lines incidentally introduced in the Second Book of Chronicles: "Thus the Lord saved Hezekiah * * * and *many brought presents* to Hezekiah, so that he was magnified in the sight of all nations from thenceforth,"—2 Chron. xxxii. 22, 23; see Blunt's "Undesigned Coincidences," p. 236, &c.

[1] St. Croix observes, in his "Examen Critique des Historiens d'Alexandre," "Les Ephémérides dont l'autorité est ici d'un grand poids, et qu'on ne peut soupçonner ni Plutarque, ni Arrien, d'avoir falsifiées marquent ce jour au vingt-huit du mois Macédonien Dæsius, et Aristobule fixoit cet événement au trente du même mois. Cette différence n'est peut-être qu'apparente; car, comme il y avoit dans l'année Grecque six mois de 29 jours, et que le dernier de ces mois portoit le nom de 30, quoiqu'il ne fût réellement que de 29, il est possible que la différence des deux dates ne fût que du vingt-huit finissant au vingt-neuf commençant, et comme chez les Grecs le jour commençoit le soir, ainsi que chez presque tous les peuples qui avoient des mois lunaires, ces dates pouvoient ne différer en tout que de quelques heures au plus. Longuerue ("De Epoch. et Ann. vet. Orient.," c. 1) et M. Larcher ("Trad. d'Hérodote," t. vii. p. 709) proposent d'autres moyens de conciliation sur lesquels je ne prononcerai pas, mais qui ne tendent pas moins à résoudre la difficulté" (p. 633). Larcher's explanation is as follows: "Mort d'Alexandre le 29 du mois Macédonien Dæsius, qui répond au 30 Thargélion des Athéniens et au 2 Juin.—(*Plutarch. in Alexand*, p. 706; *Arrian.*, lib. VII. cap. xxviii. p. 309). Il se présente ici une difficulté que je crois devoir éclaircir. Aristobule, ami d'Alexandre, et qui ne l'avoit pas quitté pendant sa

one among them is considered to remove every appearance of contradiction. The history of the Gospel Harmony supplies an example exactly parallel. The case is one of peculiar interest; and from a very early period it has presented a difficulty to Christian Apologists. I allude to the statements of S. Mark and S. John, as to the hour of Christ's Passion:—"A question," says S. Augustine, "which, above all others, is wont to stir up the shamelessness of the contentious, and to disturb the unskilfulness of the weak."[1] S. Augustine himself proposed two methods whereby the accounts might be reconciled; and, while admitting the difficulties with which his suggestions were encumbered, he lays down the principle for which I now contend. Referring to a supposed objection to one of his solutions, he asks: "If we both alike believe the Evangelists, do you point out how their accounts can be otherwise reconciled, and I will acquiesce most cheerfully; for I love not my own opinion, but the truth of the Gospel. Until some other explanation is discovered, this of mine shall suffice; and when that other is demonstrated, I too will adopt it."[2] It has been reserved for modern times to suggest a solution which has been almost universally accepted, and which removes every shade of difficulty from the case. S. Mark asserts that our Lord was crucified at "the third hour," or at

maladie, dit qu'il mourut le 30 Dæsius Τριακάδι, tandis que le journal de la maladie de ce prince porte qu'il mourut le 28 sur le soir—Τῇ δὲ τρίτῃ φθίνοντος πρὸς δείλην ἀπέθανεν. Cette contradiction n'est qu'apparente. 1°. Le mois Dæsius avoit 31 jours; par conséquent le troisième du mois finissant répondoit au 29 Thargélion. 2°. Celui qui tenoit le journal de la maladie étant à Babylone, suivoit l'usage des Babyloniens, qui comptoient le jour depuis le lever du soleil jusqu'au lever du jour suivant. Alexandre étant mort sur les huit à neuf heures du soir, c'étoit encore pour eux le 29 Thargélion. Mais Aristobule, qui écrivoit pour les Grecs, suit l'usage de ces peuples, qui commençoit le jour au coucher du soleil et le finissoient le lendemain au coucher. Alexandre, étant mort après le coucher du soleil. étoit mort réellement le 30, selon leur manière de calculer les temps, c'est-à-dire, le 2 juin." This example is referred to by Tholuck, in his "Glaubwürd. der evang. Geschichte," s. 447.

[1] Quæstio de hora Dominicæ Passionis, quæ maxime solet et contentiosorum concitare impudentiam, et infirmorum imperitiam perturbare."—*De Consens. Evangelist.* lib. iii. § 13, t. iii. pars ii. p. 127.

[2] "Unde, inquis, probas horam tertiam fuisse? Respondeo, *Quia credo Evangelistis:* quibus et tu si credis, ostende quemadmodum et hora sexta et hora tertia potuerit Dominus crucifigi? De sexta enim, ut fateamur, narratione Johannis urgemur; tertiam Marcus commemorat: quibus si uterque nostrum credit, ostende tu aliter quemadmodum fieri utrumque potuerit, libentissime adquiescam. Non enim sententiam meam, sed Evangelii diligo veritatem. Atque utinam etiam plures ab aliis inveniantur hujus exitus quæstionis: quod *donec fiat*, utere mecum isto si placet. Si enim nullus alius exitus potuerit inveniri, solus iste sufficiet: si autem potuerit, cum demonstratus fuerit, eligemus. Tantum non putes consequens esse, ut quilibet omnium quatuor Evangelistarum mentitus sit, aut in tanto et tam sancto culmine auctoritatis erraverit."—*Ibid.* p. 123.

nine o'clock in the forenoon; while according to S. John, Pilate "about the sixth hour" was still sitting in judgment. The explanation of this apparent discordance in time—an explanation which even Strauss, while exaggerating "the difficulty" to the utmost, allows to be "possible"[1]—is, that S. John has given the hour according to the Roman calculation of time, which counted as we do, from midnight; while S. Mark adheres to the Jewish custom of counting from sunrise.[2]

The principle, therefore, pointed out by S. Augustine is, I submit, the only one admissible by those who do not deny the Divine origin of the Bible altogether. Any solution, which affords a *possible* mode of harmonizing those statements of the sacred writers which present a semblance of opposition, is to be admitted before we can allow the existence of a contradiction: and it is a circumstance deserving of all attention, that for every example of such variance in the narratives of the Evangelists, no matter how carefully sought out, some solution offers itself as

[1] "According to Mark, it was *the third hour* (*ὥρα τρίτη*) (nine in the morning) when Jesus was crucified (xv. 25). On the other hand, John says (xix. 14) that it was about the sixth hour [*ὥρα ἦν ὡς* (or *ὡσεὶ*) *ἕκτη*], (when, according to Mark, Jesus had already hung three hours on the cross), that Pilate first sat in judgment over him. Unless we are to suppose that the sun-dial went backward, as in the time of Hezekiah, this is a contradiction which is not to be removed by a violent alteration of the reading, nor by appealing to the *ὡσεί* (*about*) in John, or to the inability of the disciples to take note of the hours under such afflictive circumstances: *at the utmost it might, perhaps, be cancelled*, if it were possible to prove that the fourth Gospel throughout proceeds upon another mode of reckoning time than that used by the Synoptists."—*The Life of Jesus*, part iii. ch. 3, § 132 (Chapman's transl. vol. iii. p. 276).

[2] For a full discussion of this question see the eighth of Townson's "Discourses on the Four Gospels;" where it is shown that S. John has, on all occasions, "reckoned the hours as we do, from midnight to noon, and again from noon to midnight:" and also that the interval of time between the "sixth hour" of S. John, and the "third hour" of S. Mark (i. e. between *six* and *nine* o'clock in the forenoon), must have been fully occupied by the vacillation of Pilate, in consequence of his wife's message (S. Matt. xxvii. 19),—by the trial and condemnation of the two malefactors,—and by the procession to Calvary. Adopting this view, Rettig, in the "Studien und Kritiken" for 1830 (s. 103), quotes the words of Pliny: "Ipsum diem alii aliter observavere. * * * Sacerdotes, et qui diem definiere civilem, item Ægyptii et Hipparchus a media nocte in mediam."—*Hist. Nat.*, lib. ii. 77; and Le Clerc (by whom this solution was first suggested), quotes the question of Plutarch—*διά τι τὴν τῆς ἡμέρας ἀρχὴν ἐκ μέσης νυκτὸς λαμβάνουσι*;—*Quæst. Rom.*, lxxxiii. Tholuck ("Glaubwürd. der ev. Gesch." s. 306) shows that the time of sunrise at the vernal equinox, taken in connexion with the rules of Roman jurisprudence, fully confirms the explanation thus given of S. John's expression, "*about the sixth hour.*" He also quotes Macrobius, "Magistratus post mediam noctem auspicantur; et *post exortum solem* agunt"—*Saturnal.* i. 3; and Aulus Gellius, "Senatus-consulta *ante exortum solem*, aut post solis occasum facta, rata non esse."—*Noct. Att.* xiv. 7.

It is strange that the latest English commentator, Mr. Alford, should have taken no notice of this celebrated solution. He writes: "There is *an insuperable difficulty* as the text now stands. * * * We must certainly suppose that there has been some very early erratum in our copies."

being possible—possible I say, since the nature of the case, at times, admits of no more than suggesting such an explanation as may not be improbable.[1] In apparent discrepancies of this kind, the difficulty often arises from the simple fact, that we have altogether lost the clue which unites the different statements. Sometimes, it is true, that difficulty may arise from misconception of what has been written,—a misconception which patient study may, and frequently does, clear up:—as, for example,

[1] Cf. Steudel, "Ueber Inspir. der Apost.," H. ii. s. 72. For example: "As He was come nigh unto Jericho," our Lord restored sight to "a certain blind man" who "sat by the wayside begging," and who "cried, saying, Jesus, thou Son of David, have mercy on me."—S. Luke, xviii. 35–43. In S. Mark, x. 46–52, we read that "as *He went out of Jericho*," He performed the same miracle on "blind Bartimæus, the son of Timæus," who also "sat by the highway side begging," and who addressed the Lord in the very same words as the blind man in S. Luke's account. But where is the contradiction here? What is there improbable or overstrained in supposing that a blind man may have sat "by the wayside begging," *on both occasions;—on the road leading to, as well as that leading from, Jericho?* Assuming this, what can be thought more probable (as Origen has already suggested—"Comm. in S. Matt.," t. iii. p. 732) than that the news of the former miracle should have reached "blind Bartimæus;" and that he too should have placed himself in the way of the great Prophet, and supplicated Him in language which had already arrested His attention, and won His pity? Ebrard (*loc. cit.*, s. 469), moreover, points out that the accounts of the Evangelists themselves intimate that the two transactions were different. Bartimæus, at the mere sound of Christ's voice, comes *himself* without any one to lead him; while the other blind man must have been at some distance; for Jesus "commanded him to be brought unto Him,"—ver. 40 (cf. also ἐγγίσαντος δὲ αὐτοῦ).

Again, what real difficulty arises here from the fact of S. Matthew (xx. 29–34), when relating Christ's departure from Jericho, *having combined facts so strikingly similar* in one summary: "Behold *two blind men* sitting by the wayside, when they heard that Jesus passed by, cried out, saying, Have mercy on us, O Lord, thou Son of David?" There can clearly be no exception taken to the general assertion, that events, strikingly analogous, may have happened on different occasions:—for (not to mention the similarity between the miracles performed by Elijah and Elisha), Christ Himself refers to the *two* instances of His feeding the multitude (see S. Matt. xvi. 9, 10; S. Mark, viii. 19, 20); and S. John, (ii. 14, 15) relates that He cast "the money-changers" out of the Temple at the opening of His ministry; while the other Evangelists tell us that He repeated the same act towards its close (S. Matt. xxi. 12; S. Mark, xi. 15; S. Luke, xix. 45). Cf. also the repetition of the same command, S. Matt. v. 32, and xix. 9. We learn incidentally, from the manner in which S. Augustine employs this principle, the nature of the arguments with which, even in his time, this truth of the Gospel history was assailed. In one of the miracles of feeding the multitude, S. Mark (vi. 40) tells us that "they sat down *by hundreds and by fifties*." According to S. Luke (ix. 14), our Lord said, "Make them sit down *by fifties*." Had S. Mark, observes S. Augustine, *omitted* the "fifties," it would be called a contradiction. And, as to the repetition of the miracle itself, "Hoc sane non ab re fuerit admonere in hoc miraculo de *septem* panibus, quod duo Evangelistæ Matthæus Marcusque posuerunt; quia si aliquis eorum id dixisset, qui de illis *quinque* panibus non dixisset, contrarius cæteris putaretur. Quis enim non existimaret unum idemque factum esse * * * sed aut illum pro quinque panibus septem dum falleretur commemorasse, aut illos pro septem quinque, aut utrosque mentitos, vel oblivione deceptos? * * * Hoc ideo diximus ut *sicubi simile invenitur factum* a Domino, quod in aliquo alteri Evangelistæ *ita repugnare videatur ut omnino solvi non possit*, nihil aliud intelligatur quam utrumque factum esse."—*De Consensu Evang.*, lib. ii. § 50, *loc. cit.* p. 77. Schleiermacher calmly observes: "I cannot prevail on myself to believe the second feeding."—*Essay on S. Luke*, p. 144.

where Neander (who does not, in general, scruple to impeach the accuracy of the Evangelists) observes, with reference to the return of the Holy Family to Nazareth after the flight to Egypt: "It was *formerly* thought that Matthew and Luke contradicted each other here. * * * Both accounts may be equally true, and harmonize well with each other, although those who put them imperfectly together may not perceive the agreement."[1] But there are instances over which it is conceivable, from the nature of the case, that some obscurity must for ever rest. Let any single event be described by different eye-witnesses, and their accounts will present variations, and apparent contradictions, simply because each of them seizes strongly upon some one salient point, which serves to elucidate his purpose, and leaves the rest comparatively in the background. In entering upon the subject of the Gospel Harmony, we must ever remember that our four Evangelists regarded the facts of the Saviour's history each under a different aspect. The essential point of difference between S. John and the others[2] lies in his having in view the opponents of the Gospel within the Church: while the Synoptical writers mainly addressed themselves to the wants of those who stood without its pale, whether Jews or Gentiles. S. Matthew's aim is to establish the identity of the New Testament Revelation with that of the Old; and to prove to the people of Israel that in Jesus, as the Christ, were fulfilled the promises to Abraham and to David. S. Mark desires to exhibit the sublime facts of Christianity, in opposition to the degraded supestitions of heathenism. The narrative of S. Luke, commencing at Jerusalem with the Vision of the Priest in the Sanctuary, closes with S. Paul's address in his prison at Rome;—the design of the inspired historian being to describe the several stages by which the message of Salvation advanced, from the Temple of Jehovah, to the metropolis of the Gentile world.[3] In narratives composed with objects thus

[1] "The Life of Jesus Christ," Book i. ch iii. § 21 (Bohn's transl. p. 31). Neander had immediately before (§ 19) stated: "We cannot vouch with equal positiveness for the accuracy of Matthew's statement of the means by which the Sages learned, after their arrival in Jerusalem, that the chosen Child was to be born in Bethlehem."

[2] See Ebrard, *loc. cit.*, s. 143.

[3] Cf Hofmann, "Weissagung u. Erfüllung," s. 48; and Luger, "Die Rede des Stephanus," s. 2, who refers to the commission given by Christ at the close of S. Luke's Gospel: "That repentance and remission of sins should be preached in His name among all nations, *beginning at Jerusalem*"—xxiv. 47; observing that the address of the Lord (Acts, i. 8), before His Ascension, supplies an index to the con-

distinct, we can feel no surprise at the absence of sundry particulars which, if known to us, would at once clear up many of those obscurities that afford so great a source of perplexity to several minds. Nor should the silence of the Evangelists as to such particulars in any wise disconcert us; unless we impose other rules on them than those by which we are content to test the fidelity of ordinary writers. The omission of a contemporary author to notice a fact which *we*, from whatever reason, may consider of the greatest moment, is a case by no means unusual. The younger Pliny,—although giving a circumstantial detail of so many physical facts, and describing the great eruption of Vesuvius, the earthquake, and the showers of ashes that issued from the volcano,—makes no allusion whatever to the sudden overwhelming of two large and populous cities, Herculaneum and Pompeii.[1]

In illustration of the foregoing observations I would further add, that what we know of the motives which led to the composition of our Gospels renders the existence of contradictions antecedently improbable in the very highest degree. Eusebius, in his chapter "On the order of the Gospels," ratifies the concurrent voice of earlier history which is to the effect that S. John's narrative was the last in point of time; and that he gave his testimony to the truth of what had been previously written.[2]

tents of the Acts of the Apostles regarded as a continuation of the former narrative: —the substance of the first seven chapters being described in the words, "Ye shall be witnesses unto Me in Jerusalem;" of the eighth and ninth chapters in the words, "And in all Judea and Samaria;" while chapters x.-xxviii. are summed up in the words, "And unto the uttermost parts of the earth."

[1] See Lyell's "Principles of Geology," 8th ed., p. 348. The principle on which the omission has been explained, viz., that Pliny's "chief object was simply to give Tacitus a full account of the particulars of his uncle's death,"—suggests, in like manner, the explanation of the Evangelists' silence respecting subjects not connected with *their* "chief object."

[2] *Τῶν προαναγραφέντων τριῶν εἰς πάντας ἤδη καὶ εἰς αὐτὸν* ['Ιωάννην] *διαδεδομένων, ἀποδέξασθαι μὲν φασὶν, ἀλήθειαν αὐτοῖς ἐπιμαρτυρήσαντα.*—*Eccl. Hist.*, lib. III. c. xxiv. p. 116. The earlier writers by whom this fact has been stated are, the author of Muratori's Fragment (ap. Routh, "Reliq. Sacr.," t. i. p. 394); Clemens Alex. in his "Hypotyposes" (ap. Euseb., "Eccl. Hist.," lib. VI. c. xiv. p. 274—*Τὸν μέντοι 'Ιωάννην ἔσχατον, κ. τ. λ.*); S. Victorinus ("qui sub finem sæculi tertii floruit; ita enim ille de Joanne Apostolo in 'Commentario' ei adscripto in Apocalypsim, p. 1253, in 'Biblioth. Parisinæ PP.,' t. i."—Routh. *ibid.*, p. 408); S. Epiphanius, "Hæres." li. § 12, p. 434. S. Jerome sums up the earlier testimonies with the words: "Joannes Apostolus * * * novissimus omnium scripsit Evangelium, rogatus ab Asiæ Episcopis, adversus Cerinthum, aliosque hæreticos * * * sed et aliam causam hujus scripturæ ferunt. Quod cum legisset [Joannes] Matthæi, Marci, et Lucæ volumina, probaverit quidem textum historiæ, et vera eos dixisse firmaverit," &c. *De Vir. Illustr.*, c. ix. t. ii. p. 829. "In ancient times," writes Gieseler, "they

The great historian of the Church then goes on to point out how S. John has supplied details which the other Evangelists had omitted; and he concludes with the remark: "One who attends to these circumstances can no longer entertain the opinion that the Gospels are at variance with each other."[1] It is interesting to observe from what a very early period this entire question has been discussed. It was impossible, indeed, not to have noticed the remarkable omission by S. John of those facts which the Synoptical writers had recorded, but which, at the same time, his whole line of argument perpetually assumes to be well known.[2] It was equally impossible to have overlooked the solicitude with which he often obviates,—by the introduction of a sentence,[3] or even of a single word, occurring, as one might at first sight imagine, without design,—some difficulty likely to

regarded this Gospel as a supplement to the three former, as is expressed in the tradition that John tested, and approved, and completed them by his own."—*Die Enst. der schriftl. Evang.*, s. 133. And Hug concludes, from both internal and external evidence: "John, therefore, saw the others; and this was one of the circumstances on which the plan and tendency of his own Gospel depended; and the selection of the facts to be introduced in it."—*Einleit.*, Th. ii. c. i. § 56. s. 183. I profess myself quite unable to understand how Dr. Davidson, who has fairly stated the evidence, can consider himself "justified in pronouncing the hypothesis in question [viz., that S. John had seen the Synoptical Gospels] unsupported either by external tradition or internal grounds."—*An Introd. to the New Test.*, vol. i. p. 324.

[1] *Οἷς καὶ ἐπιστήσαντι, οὐκέτ' ἂν δόξαι διαφωνεῖν ἀλλήλοις τὰ εὐαγγέλια.—Ibid.* p. 117.

[2] E. g. the Transfiguration; the *fact* of the descent of the Holy Ghost at Christ's baptism,—the Baptist being introduced as referring to that fact in words which, without a previous knowledge of it, would have been, at least, exceedingly obscure (S. John, i. 32–34). Especially remarkable is this Evangelist's silence as to Christ's miracles, on which his argument so constantly depends (e. g. ch. iii. 2; v. 36, and *passim*); but of which he has detailed only five. Who (remarks Hug, "Einleit.," *loc. cit.* § 53, s. 176) was better fitted to describe the particulars with which the institution of the Eucharist was accompanied than the disciple who, during the Supper, lay on Jesus' bosom? And yet he alludes to it only to show that he *designedly* passed over the narrative because it needed no mention; while he recounts other incidental circumstances which are not found elsewhere: "Now before the feast of the Passover, *supper being ended* (*δείπνου γινομένου*), He riseth, and took a towel, and girded Himself. After that He poureth water into a basin, and began to wash the Disciples' feet. So after He had washed their feet, and *was set down again—ἀναπεσὼν πάλιν*," &c.—ch. xiii. 1–12.

[3] Compare the remark, "For neither did His brethren believe on Him" (vii. 5), with the statement, "And when His friends (*οἱ παρ' Αὐτοῦ*) heard of it, they went out to lay hold on Him: for they said, He is beside Himself" (S. Mark, iii. 21). So also the particularity in S. John's account of the raising of Lazarus from the dead—a miracle which was performed in the immediate neighborhood of Jerusalem, and in presence of a large assembly (ch. xi 18, 19)—was clearly designed to explain the Synoptists' account of the rejoicing with which the people celebrated Christ's entry into Jerusalem (S. Matt. xxi.; S. Mark, xi.; S. Luke, xix.); as well as the sudden determination of the Council to put Him to death (ch. xi. 47–53),—a resolution from which their fears seem to have frequently deterred them on former occasions: cf. ch. vii. 25; see also S. Matt. xxi. 46.

arise from a comparison of the narratives of his predecessors. To give an example :—According to S. Matthew it was "another maid ;" according to S. Mark, "a maid ;" and a man, according to S. Luke, whose questioning led S. Peter, on the *second* occasion, to deny his Master. S. John, by means of a single expression, reconciles at once what might have appeared a contradiction in these statements. He tells us,—and we are to remember that he was an eye-witness of what passed,—that, at this moment, *several persons together* interrogated the Apostle : his description of the circumstance is, "*They said*, therefore, unto him."[1] Thus we see that S. John has, in certain cases, solved difficulties which, without his comment, might have been suggested by the narratives of the Synoptists : and surely we cannot believe that had any statements fairly open to objection really existed, they would have been permitted by him to remain without some similar explanation. We cannot doubt, therefore, that the contemporaries of the Evangelists were altogether unconscious of such discordance ; and that they possessed the clue to those difficulties which to us appear so perplexing. Indeed the captious spirit of the Jews[2] must necessarily have compelled the writers of the

[1] Εἶδεν αὐτὸν ἄλλη—S. Matt. xxvi. 71; ἡ παιδίσκη ἰδοῦσα—S. Mark, xiv. 69; ἕτερος ἰδὼν αὐτόν—S. Luke, xxii. 58; while S. John writes εἶπον οὖν αὐτῷ—xviii. 25. Hug observes: "Matthew (xxvi. 69–75) describes the denial by Peter, relating simply the fact, but not dwelling upon the place or persons who occasioned it; in his footsteps Mark (xiv. 66–72) and Luke (xxii. 54–63). John, on the other hand, states very accurately the place of the transaction. *It commenced* in the palace of the High Priest Annas [xviii. 16]. There, in the court into which John had procured him admission, Peter denied our Lord, *for the first time*, to the woman who kept the door (ver. 17). John then *changes the scene* to the presence of Caiaphas, where the other three Evangelists *first take up the narrative*, and begin the story of Peter's denial of his Master [by no means implying, however, even by a casual phrase, that the first denial had *not* taken place previously]; while, according to John, he only finished, in this place, what he began in the house of Annas, and for the second and third time disowned acquaintance with Jesus (ver. 25–27)."—*loc. cit.* § 54. s. 180. If we attend to the language of the context in this place, the explanation suggested by the English Version (viz. translating the ἀπέστειλεν [οὖν] Αὐτὸν ὁ Ἄννας, κ. τ. λ.—ver. 24, by, "Now Annas *had sent* Him bound unto Caiaphas") seems wholly untenable; especially if we observe the impossibility of identifying the examination of our Lord which S. John relates (ver. 19–23), with that before Caiaphas, as recorded by the Synoptists; and which S. John has altogether omitted. Compare Ebrard, *loc. cit.* s. 535 ff.

[2] Gieseler, having quoted the testimony of S. Justin M. as to the exhibition of this spirit by the Jews (ὥσπερ γὰρ αἱ μυῖαι ἐπὶ τὰ ἕλκη προστρέχετε καὶ ἐφίπτασθε. κἂν γὰρ μυρία τὶς εἴπῃ καλῶς, ἓν δὲ μικρὸν ὁτιοῦν εἴη μὴ εὐάρεστον ὑμῖν, ἢ μὴ νοούμενον, ἢ μὴ πρὸς τὸ ἀκριβὲς τῶν μὲν πολλῶν καλῶν οὐ πεφροντίκατε, τοῦ δὲ μικροῦ ῥηματίου ἐπιλαμβάνεσθε, κ. τ. λ.—*Dial. cum Tryph.* § 115, p. 209), goes on to say: "It is clear that, under these circumstances, the strictest agreement alone could secure the Apostles from the reproach of contradicting each other; and that an exact selec-

Gospels of themselves to avoid even the semblance of any contradiction in records the design of which was to overthrow the exclusive claims of the children of Abraham. Nay, the established principles of Judaism must have rendered an avoidance of even seeming discrepancies essential to the acceptance of any historical narrative as deserving of belief:—for, as a well-known argument of Josephus informs us, a Jew considered no proof of the Divine origin of the Old Testament more conclusive, in controversy with a Gentile, than the absence of any contradictions in the several books of which it is composed.[1]

II. The question just examined refers to the supposed want of harmony between one sacred writer and another. The objection which demands our notice in the next place is founded upon the alleged collision between the statements of Scripture and those of profane history. And here that want of argumentative fairness, so often pointed out in the reasoning employed by the impugners of Revealed Religion, cannot be passed over. In ordinary writings, when one author disagrees with another, the most captious critic contents himself with comparing the probabilities on both sides; and, if he can discern no prospect of reconciling the conflicting accounts, he decides without hesitation in favor of that party whose veracity appears the more unexceptionable. In the case of the Bible, however, the course pursued is very different. Should any statement of the Old, or of the New Testament, seem to be at variance with that of an ordinary historian, it is taken for granted, without further inquiry, that the sacred narrative is false. Every presumption in favor of the accuracy of the uninspired writer is brought prominently forward; nor are *his* statements, as to matters of fact unnoticed by others, thought to require corroboration: while the assertion of a Prophet, or of an Evangelist, if similarly unsupported, is

tion of language was requisite in order to afford the malicious no opening for attack in this respect."—*Die Entst. der schriftl. Evang.* s. 101.

[1] See Lecture ii. page 68, note [3]; cf. too, Lecture v. p. 188, note. In addition to the "Contradictions" of Scripture, its alleged "Immoralities" (e. g. Jael's putting Sisera to death; the command to Abraham to slay his son; the extermination of the Canaanites, &c.,) have supplied a fruitful source of objections, not, indeed, so much against the *Inspiration* of the Bible, as against its *truth*;—professing, as it does, to give an account of God's dealings with man. In addition to Bishop Butler's conclusive argument on this subject ("Analogy," Part II. ch. iii.), see the excellent remarks of Dr. Arnold in his "Essay on the right Interpretation of the Scriptures" ("Sermons," 4th ed., vol. ii. p. 390, &c.); and of Mr. Rogers, in "The Eclipse of Faith," p. 148, &c.

immediately subjected to an unscrupulous or prejudiced criticism. This is a species of unfairness to which the Bible, above all other books, affords an opportunity: for it is remarkable with what uniformity the sacred writers abstain from directly touching upon topics of common history, except in cases where their narrative absolutely requires it. There are, however, such points of contact with the ordinary events of the world; and on these sceptics are never slow to fasten. For example:—S. Luke, in the opening verses of the second and third chapters of his Gospel, alludes to external history. In the former passage[1] the Evangelist, when enumerating the circumstances connected with the birth of Christ, dwells with much particularity on the fact that a general census had been decreed by the Emperor Augustus; adding that this census "was first made when Cyrenius was governor of Syria." Against the truth of this statement Strauss argues, in the first place, that no author, except S. Luke, makes mention of such a general census having been prescribed by the Emperor:[2] and, secondly, that Tacitus informs us that Cy-

[1] Ἐξῆλθεν δόγμα παρὰ Καίσαρος Αὐγούστου, ἀπογράφεσθαι πᾶσαν τὴν οἰκουμένην. Αὕτη ἡ ἀπογραφὴ πρώτη ἐγένετο ἡγεμονεύοντος τῆς Συρίας Κυρηνίου.—S. Luke, ii. 2. The objections urged against this statement are as follows: (1.) There was no census of the 'Orbis Romanus' under Augustus. (2.) As *πᾶσα ἡ οἰκουμένη* refers merely to Judea (cf. Acts, xi. 28), *such* a census could not have been held in what was not as yet a Roman Province; and which did not become so until Archelaus, Herod's son, had been deposed by Augustus, after a reign of ten years. Herod, therefore, as "Rex Socius," would have conducted the census by his own authority, without the intervention of the Emperor. (3.) According to Tacitus, P. Sulp. Quirinius was first sent from Rome eleven or twelve years *after* the birth of Christ, to form Judea into a Roman Province; Sentius Saturninus being the Governor at the time of our Lord's birth. From which premises it follows, that (4.) Joseph and Mary cannot have come to Bethlehem for the purpose stated by S. Luke; and, consequently, this portion of his narrative is "unhistorical." Although many, observes Tholuck, have adopted a theory of Inspiration, according to which the credibility of the *religious contents* of the Bible is not weakened by the *historical* mistakes of its authors; still "were we to admit here such a nest of the rudest blunders, it may well be doubted whether the canon of credibility can apply to such an extent. Give up the occasion and the truth of the journey to Bethlehem, and the truth of the Miraculous Birth at Bethlehem become equally mythical."—*Glaubwürd.*, s. 158. As to objections (1.) and (3.), see *infra:* with reference to (2.), it is to be observed that Herod was no "Rex Socius;" but merely a Governor, with a kind of regal authority, whom Augustus, notwithstanding Herod's fidelity to M. Antonius, had, in an exceptional manner, and with his usual astute policy, continued to entrust with authority in Palestine. See W. Hoffmann's "Das Leben Jesu," s. 233.

[2] Hoffmann (s. 231) replies with great force to this objection: "Passages from Livy, Dio Cassius, Tacitus, &c., prove to the celebrated Savigny ["Zeitschrift für geschichtl. Rechtswissenschaften," vi. s. 350], who has collected them, that 'at the very commencement of this Emperor's reign an effort was made to introduce a uniform system of taxation into the Provinces.'" S. Isidore of Seville, in a treatise compiled from historical sources extant in his time, and without any design of supporting S. Luke's statement, tells us: "Era singulorum annorum constituta est a

renius was for the first time sent from Rome, as Proconsul of Syria, eleven or twelve years after the birth of Christ.[1] In the second passage, S. Luke mentions that when S. John the Baptist entered on his ministry Lysanias was Tetrarch of Abilene. Here, again, Strauss objects that Josephus, it is true, speaks of a Lysanias as governor of Abilene, but that the Jewish historian further states that this Lysanias had been put to death thirty-four years before the birth of Christ; while neither Josephus,

Cæsare Augusto, quando primum censum exegit, ac Romanum orbem descripsit."—*Originum*, lib. v. c. 36, p. 41. So also Cassiodorus, one of the most learned men of his age (born *circ.* A. D. 469. He filled successively the highest civil and judicial offices, and was appointed Consul by Theodoric, A. D. 514), has preserved an Epistle, entitled "Consulari Viro Illustri, Theodoricus Rex," appointing an umpire in a dispute relating to the division of certain lands. In this Epistle the passage occurs: "Augusti siquidem temporibus Orbis Romanus agris divisus, censuque descriptus est; ut possessio sua nulli haberetur incerta, quam pro tributorum susceperat quantitate solvenda."—*Variarum*, lib. iii. Ep. 52, t. i. p. 57. The very nature of these quotations refutes the evasion of Strauss and Bauer:—viz., that the information which they convey respecting this census was borrowed from S. Luke. According to Suetonius ("Augustus," c. 27), "Censum populi ter egit [Augustus] primum ac tertium cum collega, medium solus;" and the monument of Ancyra indicates that the census which was carried into effect by himself alone fell in the year before the birth of Christ (Ideler, B. ii. s. 380, quoted by Hoffmann). These latter references, no doubt, refer in the first instance to the city of Rome; but they prove the Emperor's solicitude on the subject: and although S. Luke states that the "Decree" related to "all the world," he does not state that it was everywhere carried out at the same time. Ebrard (s. 170) appeals to the "Breviarium Imperii" (Tac. "Ann." i. 11; Suet. "Octav." ci.) detailing the "tributa aut vectigalia" "civium *sociorumque*" which Augustus left at his death.

[1] Ussher reconciles these statements ("Annal. Vet. Test." Elrington's ed., vol. x. p. 471) by quoting the reference of Tacitus ("Aunal.," lib. iii. c. 48) to P. Sulpicius Quirinius (the Cyrenius of S. Luke): "Impiger militiæ et acribus ministeriis Consulatum sub D. Augusto; *mox expugnatis per Ciliciam* Homonadensium castellis, insignia triumphi adeptus." Cyrenius had been Consul A. U. C. 742 (see Hoffmann, s. 236); and, therefore, according to the system of Augustus (cf. Dio Cassius, lib. liii. 14), could not have gone to his Proconsulate in Cilicia until A. U. C. 747. From Cilicia he might readily have been sent to *the neighboring district of Syria*, either to conduct the census with extraordinary powers; or, as the Emperor's Procurator, with ordinary:—Cyrenius himself still retaining the Proconsulate of Cilicia, and Sentius Saturninus that of Syria. Josephus more than once, in a similar manner calls both Volumnius and Saturninus *ἡγεμόνας* of Syria, although Volumnius was merely *ἐπίτροπος*, or Procurator (B. J. lib. I. xxvii. 2. t. ii. p. 124):—and thus we can at once explain Tertullian's statement ("Adv. Marcion.," lib. iv. c. 19, p. 532): "Census constat actos sub Augusto nunc in Judæa per Sentium Saturninum." S. Luke has preferred to bring forward the part taken in this transaction by Cyrenius, since he desired to combine it with his subsequent allusion (Acts, v. 37) to the second *ἀπογραφή* carried out by Cyrenius ten years later; his object being to point out that, of the two *ἀπογραφαί* conducted by the same magistrate, that connected with the birth of Christ was the earlier:—which exactly agrees with the statement of S. Justin M.—*ἀπογραφῆς οὔσης ἐν τῇ Ἰουδαίᾳ τότε πρώτης ἐπὶ* Κυρηνίου, *κ. τ. λ.*—*Dial. cum Tryph.* § 78, p. 175. In confirmation of this view, Hoffmann (*loc. cit.*) draws attention to the information, given by Suidas ("Lexicon," s. v. *ἀπογραφή*), that twenty Commissaries had been appointed by Augustus to carry out the census through the whole Empire. Ὁ *δὲ* Καῖσαρ Αὔγουστος *εἴκοσιν ἄνδρας τοὺς ἀρίστους τὸν βίον καὶ τὸν τρόπον ἐπιλεξάμενος, ἐπὶ πᾶσαν τὴν γῆν τῶν ὑπηκόων ἐξέπεμψε δἰ ὧν ἀπογοαφὰς ἐποιήσατο τῶν τε ἀνθρώπων καὶ οὐσιῶν.*

nor any author of that time, alludes to the existence of a second ruler of Abilene who bore[1] this name. As I have already observed, it does not lie within my province to examine these objections in detail; I must confine myself to suggesting certain principles which may enable us to form a just estimate of similar exceptions, when urged against the veracity or the accuracy of the sacred writers.

In the cases before us, we may fairly demand for S. Luke—waiving, as before, his claim to Inspiration—the same justice which all persons yield to any ancient historian whose facts are doubted or denied. When instances of such assumed inaccuracy aré alleged, two simple questions are proposed. In the first place, does what we know of the external relations of the author to the events which he records render it probable that he could have committed, in a single passage of his narrative, two such

[1] Tholuck (*loc. cit.* s. 200), admitting the accuracy of Strauss's historical representation, naturally asks, where is the difficulty of supposing the existence of a second Lysanias, who was also Tetrarch of Abilene at the time assigned by S. Luke? And he quotes the still stronger case afforded by Tacitus (writing of A. D. 36), where he speaks of "Clitarum natio, Cappadoci *Archelao* subjecta" ("Annal." vi. c. 41), while he also states ("Annal." ii. c. 42; cf. too, Suetonius "Tiberius," cap. viii.) that Archelaus had died, A. D. 17; and that Cappadocia had then become a Roman Province. See, to the same effect, Winer, "Real-Wörterb.," art. "Abilene." Strauss, however, refuses to accept this reply of Tholuck, alleging that the nature of Tacitus' statements of itself supplies "a clear historical datum that there were two such persons:" but that "it is quite otherwise when, as in the case of Lysanias, *two writers* have each one of the same name, but assign him distinct epochs."—*The Life of Jesus*, part ii. ch. i. § 44 (vol. i. p. 302). Ebrard, however ("Kritik der ev. Gesch.," s. 180 ff.), proves that this entire objection is nothing more than an historical blunder on the part of Strauss himself. The statements of Josephus, on which the objection is founded, are as follows: Ptolemæus, son of Mennæus, ruled over *Chalcis* ("Ant.," XIV. vii. 4, t. i. p. 696); and was succeeded by his son Lysanias ("Bel. Jud." I. xiii. 1, t. ii. p. 83). This Lysanias of *Chalcis* was put to death (B. C. 34) by Antonius, at the instigation of Cleopatra ("Ant.," XV. iv. 1, t. i. p. 749). Seventy-five years later (viz. A. D. 41) Agrippa I. was restored by Claudius to the kingdom of his ancestors, and received in addition an "Abila of Lysanias"—Ἄβιλαν τὴν Λυσανίου ("Ant.," XIX. v. 1, t. i. p. 943; "Bel. Jud." II. xi. 5, t. ii. p. 172). This Lysanias is assumed by Strauss to have been the same person as the Lysanias of Chalcis, who had been put to death by Antonius; and on this assumption, which, however, is utterly subverted by another statement of Josephus, his objection rests. This additional statement of Josephus is to the effect that Claudius *removed* Agrippa II. (A. D. 52) "*from Chalcis* [the kingdom, be it remembered, of Strauss's Lysanias] to a greater kingdom, giving him, in addition, *the kingdom of Lysanias* (ἐκ δὲ τῆς Χαλκίδος Ἀγρίππαν εἰς μείζονα βασιλείαν μετατίθησι * * * προσέθηκε δὲ τήν τε Λυσανίου βασιλείαν)."—*Bel. Jud.* II. xii. 8, t. ii., p. 176,—words which, according to Strauss, must mean "Agrippa was deprived of Chalcis, receiving in exchange a larger kingdom, *and also Chalcis!*" Hence, therefore, Josephus *does* make mention of a later Lysanias; and, by doing so, fully corroborates the fact of S. Luke's intimate acquaintance with the tangled details of Jewish history in his day. Even Meyer (*in loc.*) fully accepts this conclusion of Ebrard: "So wird die Notiz des Luk. durch Joseph. nicht als *Irrthum* dargestellt, sondern bestätiget.

blunders as are charged against our Evangelist; especially when writing of facts notorious at the time? And, secondly, is his historical inaccuracy, elsewhere, so patent that such anachronisms cannot surprise us? If each of these questions must be answered in the negative, then the objector's interpretation of the passages on which he insists would at once, in the case of a profane historian, be set aside as being utterly improbable *à priori:* and if we cannot point out the fallacy of the objection by translating the historian's words differently,[1] we forthwith enter on the path of historical inquiry in order to arrive at the author's real meaning. Now S. Luke's 'Preface' supplies a sufficient answer to the former of the questions just proposed. There he explicitly lays down, not only that the details of his narrative "were delivered" to him by those who "from the beginning were eye-witnesses;" but also that he had "perfect understanding of all things from the very first." A review of his allusions, in the Acts of the Apostles, to the particulars of the Roman Govern-

[1] The following modes of translating S. Luke, ii. 2, have been suggested: (1.) *πρώτη* stands for *προτέρα*; and *ἡγεμονεύοντος* depends on the comparative. Thus we should render "This *census* took place before Cyrenius was Prætor of Syria"—words which are added in order to obviate the possibility of misconception—just as S. John (xiv. 22) has inserted the parenthesis, "not Iscariot." For the use of *πρώτη* for *προτέρα*, cf. S. John, i. 15, 30; and for the use of the participle (as if S. Luke had written *πρὸ τοῦ ἡγεμονεύειν*), Jer. xxix. 2 (LXX.): *οὗτοι οἱ λόγοι τῆς βίβλου, οὓς ἀπέστειλεν Ἱερεμίας * * * ὕ σ τ ε ρ ο ν ἐ ξ ε λ θ ό ν τ ο ς Ἰεχονίου, κ. τ. λ.*—i. e. "after Jechonias had departed," instead of *ὕστέρον τοῦ ἐξελθεῖν*.

(2.) *Πρώτη* is to be taken in connexion with the verb *ἐγένετο*; and stands in place of the adverb—"This census took place for the first time under Cyrenius"—a parenthetical clause, denoting that the Emperor's decree was first carried out under Cyrenius, and that then for the first time was taxation imposed upon the Jews:—the *ἀπογραφή*, at first imperfect, being at length completed, and rendered an actual *ἀποτίμησις*.

(3.) By changing the accents; if in place of *αὔτη* we read *αὐτή*:—rendering, "In the days of Herod the decree went forth, but the taxing *itself* took place for the first time under Cyrenius." Strauss admits that by this translation the chief difficulty is "most easily" removed; but he strongly protests against such an arbitrary alteration in the text! "It is well known," observes Tholuck, (s. 186) "that, with the exception of the single codex D. Claromontanus, our uncial-codices are written without accent and spiritus; and even as to this codex, connoisseurs decide that, in the great majority of passages, the accents have been added by a later hand. Griesbach, Symb. Crit. ii. s. 82." So also Hofmann, "Weissagung und Erfüllung," ii. s. 54.

(4.) S. Luke desired to show that the birth of the Messiah coincided with the political slavery of his nation which now, *for the first time*, was practically exhibited in consequence of the Emperor's edict: "The taxing itself [see (3.)] took place—and this, too, the first unheard-of insult of the kind!—when Cyrenius, &c.,"—the *census* at our Lord's birth being regarded merely as the preliminary stage of the *taxing* (*ἀπογραφή* being susceptible of this double sense) conducted by Cyrenius (Acts, v. 37):—both events being necessarily known to, and thus distinguished by S. Luke. Cf. Ebrard, *loc. cit.* s. 175 ff.

ment, and to other circumstances of the time, in like manner, affords an answer in the negative to the second question.[1]

Of S. Luke's minute accuracy I proceed to give a well-known instance; which I would preface by a parallel example illustrative of the apparent contradictions so constantly to be met with in ordinary history.[2] The medals struck for the coronation of Louis XIV. gave a different day from that which all contemporary historians agree in fixing for the date of that event. Of all these writers one only has noticed a circumstance which accounts for this discrepancy: for he alone mentions that the coronation had been appointed to take place on the day given by the medals, —which were accordingly prepared,—but that circumstances caused a delay till the date assigned by the historians. Nothing can be more simple than this: and yet in a thousand years, had no such explanation been given, antiquarians would have been sadly perplexed in their efforts to reconcile the contradiction. Let us now turn to the parallel case in the Acts of the Apostles: —S. Luke in the thirteenth chapter gives the title of Proconsul[3] to the Governor of Cyprus. In the division, however, of the Roman Empire by Augustus, this island had been reserved for his own jurisdiction: and consequently its Governor must have borne the rank of Procurator;—that of Proconsul being appropriated to those who ruled the provinces which the Emperor had ceded to the Senate. The title here assigned by S. Luke to Sergius Paulus had for a long time perplexed commentators; who knew not how to reconcile the statement of the sacred historian with the assumed facts of the case. Some coins, however, were found bearing the effigy of the Emperor Claudius; and in the

[1] In illustration of the perplexity of Jewish history at this period—not to mention the frequent redistribution of territory—consider the mistakes likely to occur in the case of writers imperfectly informed as to the family of Herod, arising from the identity of the name Herod for the father and all his descendants: e. g. S. Epiphanius ("Hæres." xxx. 13, t. i. p. 138) quotes a passage from the Gospel of the Ebionites, in which Herod the Great is confounded with Herod Antipas. Cf. Tholuck, *loc. cit.* s. 159, *u.* 162.

[2] "Apparent contradictions, indeed, must meet us in every part of history; the difficulty is where to lay the blame. The medals struck for the coronation of Louis XIV. give a different day from that which all contemporary historians accord in fixing for the date of that event. Of them all, one only, D. Ruinart, has noticed a circumstance which reconciles this discrepancy. For he alone has recorded," &c. Wiseman, *Lectures on the Connexion between Science and Revealed Religion*, &c., vol. ii. p. 125.

[3] Ἀνθύπατος, Acts, xiii. 7. See Tholuck, *loc. cit.* s. 172 Paley, "Evidences," Part II. ch. vi.

centre of the reverse occurs the word ΚΥΠΡΙΩΝ, while the surrounding legend gives the title in question of Proconsul to an individual who must have been the immediate successor or predecessor of Sergius Paulus.[1] In addition to this evidence, a passage has been pointed out in the writings of Dio Cassius who mentions that Augustus, subsequently to his original settlement, had changed Cyprus and Gallia Narbonensis into Senatorial Provinces; the historian adding, as if with the design of establishing S. Luke's accuracy, "And so it came to pass, that Proconsuls began to be sent to these nations also."[2] Had the writings of Dio Cassius perished amid the wreck of ancient literature, and the coins alluded to never been found, we should, unquestionably, have seen this hypothetical blunder of the inspired historian foremost among the array of cases adduced by such writers as Strauss. Is not the Christian Apologist therefore fully justified in deprecating the precipitancy of criticism? Has he not ample grounds for maintaining that difficulties, such as those which we have considered, arise from our ignorance of the whole of the case; and that we have good reason to expect that they eventually will disappear as similar evidence accumulates?[3]

[1] ΕΠΙ ΚΟΜΙΝΙΟΥ ΠΡΟΚΛΟΥ ΑΝΘΥΠΑΤΟΥ. Hug, "Einleit.," i. § 4. s. 21.

[2] *Καὶ οὕτως ἀνθύπατοι καὶ ἐς ἐκεῖνα τὰ ἔθνη πέμπεσθαι ἤρξαντο.*—Dio Cassius, liv. 4. So also, the title *ἀνθύπατος* is assigned with the strictest propriety to Gallio (Acts, xviii. 12, &c.). Achaia had been a "Provincia Senatoria" (Dio Cassius, liii. 12) but it had been changed by Tiberius into a "Provincia Imperatoria" (Tacitus, "Annal.," i. 76), and was, therefore, governed by Procurators. It had, however, been again restored to the Senate by Claudius (Suetonius, "Claudius," xxv.), on which its rulers resumed their title of Proconsuls. Again: in Acts, xxviii. 7, the ruler of Melita is styled *ὁ πρῶτος τῆς νήσου*—an appellation in itself suitable, since Malta was a dependency on Sicily (Cicero, 4. "Verr.," c. xviii.). A coin, however, has been found on which a Roman knight Prudens is styled ΠΡΩΤΟΣ ΜΕΛΙΤΑΙΩΝ: cf. Tholuck, *loc. cit*, s. 172. Again: in Acts, viii. 26, the city Gaza is described as being "desert." "It is true," observes Hug (*loc. cit.* s. 39), "this was often its fate; but it was invariably rebuilt, and was so in the days of Herod the Great, not long *before* the event here related. Uncommon erudition has been employed to solve this difficulty; but there are two words in Josephus which have escaped the learned, from which we learn how well Luke was acquainted with an event concerning which all history else is silent." During the commotions which preceded the siege of Jerusalem, the Jews laid waste many towns in Syria and the vicinity; and among these was Gaza: *ἐπὶ ταύταις πυρπολῃθείσαις 'Ανθηδόνα καὶ Γάζαν κατέσκαπτον.*—*Bel. Jud.*, II. xviii. 1, t. ii. p. 197; and in this state S. Luke describes it.

[3] Under the head of "contradictions" or "real discrepancies," some writers place those seeming variations of statement, which are at once accounted for by errors in the transcription of the early Hebrew MSS., in which *letters* or *cyphers* have been made use of to express *numbers*. E. g., in the account of the plagues between which God commanded David to choose, we read of "three [3 = ג] years' famine,"—1 Chron. xxi. 12; for which the transcriber of 2 Sam. xxiv. 13, has substituted "seven" (7 = ז): the LXX., in both places, having read 3. Again: according to 2 Chron. viii. 10, the number of "Solomon's officers that bare rule over the people" was

III. Having thus referred to the arguments against the inspiration of Scripture, founded upon the supposed fact that its authors contradict each other, and that they advance statements at variance with the accounts of profane history,—it remains to examine the assertion, that the language of the Bible is opposed to many truths which the progress of Philosophy has brought to light in unveiling the secrets of Nature. The rapid strides with which the material sciences have advanced in our own age render an examination of this objection more than ever necessary:

250 = רנ; for which we now read ךנ = 550, in 1 Kings, ix. 23. In 2 Kings, viii. 26, it is said that Ahaziah was 22 (כב) years old when he began to reign; in 2 Chron. xxii. 2, the present Hebrew text gives his age as 42 (מב)—an evident oversight of the transcriber; since from ch. xxi. 20, we know that his father died when only 40 years old. Here for כ (20) has been substituted מ (40), which was formerly shaped מ (see Montfaucon's "Prælim. in Origenis Hexapla," p. 22). This same interchange of כ = 20, for מ = 40, may be noticed again in Neh. vii. 44, where the number of the children of Asaph is given as 148, instead of 128, Ezra, ii. 41.

To take another class of examples:—In 2 Sam. viii. 4, David took from Hadadezer 700 horsemen: for which we read 7000 in 1 Chron. xviii. 4. Here there is an obvious interchange by the transcriber of ז (700), for ז̈ (7000); cf. the same interchange of 700 and 7000 in 2 Sam. x. 18, and 1 Chron. xix. 18. Again:—in 1 Sam. vi. 19, we read that the Lord smote 50,070 of the men of Bethshemesh; while in the Syriac and Arabic Versions the number is stated to be 5070. In 1 Kings, iv. 26, "Solomon had 40,000 stalls of horses;" in 2 Chron. ix. 25, we read of but 4000. Let us now consider a case which has supplied Mr. Coleridge with an objection ("Confess. of an Enquir. Spirit," Letter vi.):—"Abijah set the battle in array with an army of 400,000 chosen men: Jeroboam also set the battle in array against him with 800,000 chosen men"—2 Chron. xiii. 3; and "there fell down slain of Israel 500,000 chosen men."—ver. 17. Does not the analogy of the cases last cited at once suggest that here, too, each number has been multiplied by ten? Dr. Kennicott ("Dissert. on the state of printed Hebrew Text," p. 533) observes that the smaller numbers are given in the old Latin translation of Josephus; and we may fairly presume that the Greek text formerly gave the same, from the fact that "Abarbanel [see Meyer's "Chronicon," p. 797] accuses Josephus of having made Jeroboam's loss no more than 50,000, contrary to the Hebrew text." "An Arabic cipher," adds Dr. Kennicott, might very easily be added or omitted, because it is nothing more than our period (.)." "That the Hebrews," writes Movers, "had certain signs to denote numbers is undeniable. * * * The ancient Phœnicians and Aramæans had also a system of ciphers, in all essentials the same; and since the Hebrews had constant intercourse especially with the latter, they must have been acquainted with it." —*Krit. Untersuch. üb. die bibl. Chronik*, s. 54. These remarks are fully confirmed by the existence of numeral letters on the coins of the Maccabees.—(*Ibid.* s. 60.)

The remark of Mr. Rogers on this subject is open to serious objection:—"We are fully disposed to concede to the objector that there are in the books of Scripture, not only *apparent* but *real* discrepancies,—a point which many of the advocates of Christianity are indeed reluctant to admit, but which, we think, no candid advocate will feel to be the less true. * * * The discrepancies to which we refer are just those which, in the course of the transmission of ancient books, Divine or human, through many ages,—their constant transcription by different hands,—their translation into various languages,—may not only be expected to occur, but which *must* occur, unless there be a perpetual series of most minute and ludicrous miracles."—*Reason and Faith*, p. 72. This sense of the phrase "real discrepancies" is certainly not that in which it is generally understood: and the employment of it is unquestionably calculated to mislead.

and I feel particularly called upon to consider what force it may possess, because, as I conceive, the answers usually given to it concede almost everything for which one need care to contend. The objection may be stated as follows :—The language of Scripture, when touching upon topics which involve allusions to the results of Science, is expressed so as to betray complete ignorance of those laws of Nature which modern researches have brought to light : and consequently (it is argued) the Book in which such ignorance is displayed cannot have been inspired by the Holy Ghost. The popular form under which the objection is commonly urged will fairly exhibit the force of this argument against Inspiration. In this form it was, I believe, first suggested by Spinoza ;[1] and it is founded on a principle to which, somewhat differently applied, Galileo was the victim. We read in the book of Joshua, "Then spake Joshua to the Lord * * * and he said in the sight of Israel, Sun, stand thou still upon Gibeon ; and thou, Moon, in the valley of Ajalon. And the Sun stood still, and the Moon stayed, until the people had avenged themselves upon their enemies. * * * So the Sun stood still in the midst of heaven, and hasted not to go down, about a whole day :"[2]—of which passage it is said, that the motion ascribed by its writer to the Sun is in manifest contradiction to an established law of Nature.

The usual reply to this objection is as follows :—'Your remark is, in point of fact, well founded ; the contradiction which you urge does really exist : but Scripture was not intended to teach mankind the conclusions of Natural Philosophy ; and you are not entitled to expect that its statements on such topics shall be found in accordance with the results of scientific discovery.' To a certain extent, all will admit the force of such an answer : for, as it has been justly said, "to seek for an exposition of the phenomena of the natural world among the records of the moral destinies of mankind, would be as unwise as to look for rules of

[1] "Multi, quia nolunt concedere in cœlis aliquam posse dari mutationem, illum locum ita explicant, ut nihil simile dicere videatur; alii autem qui rectius philosophari didicerunt, quoniam intelligunt terram moveri, solem contra quiescere, sive circum terram non moveri, summis viribus idem ex Scriptura, *quamvis aperte reclamante*, extorquere conantur."—*Tract. Theol. Pol.*, cap. ii.

[2] Josh. x. 12–14. Cf. "It shall come to pass in that day, that I will cause the Sun to go down at noon, and I will darken the earth in the clear day"—Amos, viii. 9; "The Sun and Moon stood still in their habitation."—Hab. iii. 11.

moral government in a treatise on chemistry."[1] But I altogether deny that the concession implied, at the same time, in such an answer,—namely, that there does exist a *real* contradiction between this statement of the book of Joshua and the results of Science,—is justified by anything in the sacred narrative. Let us examine more nearly the bearing of the objection, as well as the cause which has produced in the language of Scripture even a semblance of opposition to physical facts.

Now, at the outset, I would observe,—and this no one can deny who admits, in any degree, the force of what the objector has here urged against the accuracy of the sacred writers,—that there are very many passages in the Bible, in addition to the one before us, which are equally obnoxious to the same exception. In the account of Abraham's sacrifice, for example, we read, "It came to pass that when the Sun went down."[2] So also, in the Gospels, our Lord Himself has spoken in a similar manner. He tells us that our "Father which is in Heaven maketh His Sun to rise on the evil and on the good."[3] In all such instances the alleged "contradiction" to scientific truth is, to the fullest extent, as patent as in the case of "Joshua's miracle :" and it cannot be too frequently repeated, that they who press the argument which we are considering must not be allowed to pause at the example

[1] "Allusions and facts relating to the material world are, indeed, incidentally introduced into this Spiritual Revelation, both in the way of historical record, and apt moral illustration; and when so introduced, bearing as they do the direct impress of Divine Inspiration, they are religiously to be received as undoubted facts; but as facts, nevertheless, to be read, and understood by the light of that other more express and explicit revelation of Himself in *the ways of His natural operations*, which God additionally, but equally under the sovereign impress of His hand, has opened to us in the unfolded volume of His Works."—Gray, *Harm. of Scripture and Geology*, 2d ed., p. 23. An interesting example of such allusions by the sacred writers to the facts of the natural world has been pointed out by one of the most distinguished geologists of the day. It has been found that the distribution of gold in its original veinstone, or parent rock, differs from that of every other metal in the superficial range of its particles or threads. Lodes of iron, copper, and argentiferous lead ores, when followed downwards, generally become more and more productive—the reverse being the case with gold. "Such has been the loss attending deep gold mining," observes Sir R. Murchison, "that it has passed into a proverb with the Spaniards. * * * In Europe also the same law has been found to prevail, of the deterioration of the quality of gold veins in depth * * * showing how modern researches sustain the truthfulness of the words of Job—'Surely there is a vein for the silver,' and the earth 'hath dust of gold' (Job, xxviii. 1, 6)."—*Athenæum*, March 9, 1850, No. 1167, p. 266.

[2] Gen. xv. 17; cf. ver. 12. See also: "And as he passed over Penuel the Sun rose upon him."—xxxii. 31. "The Sun also ariseth, and the Sun goeth down, and hasteth to his place where he arose."—Eccl. i. 5; cf. Ps. xix. 5, 6; &c., &c.

[3] S. Matt. v. 45.

which serves as its popular representative. It would not be difficult, indeed, to multiply illustrations : for there are numerous instances in which the language of Scripture presents difficulties precisely analogous. The sacred writers describe God as " sitting upon His throne :" they tell us of the pleasures which are at "His right hand ;" and how " His eyes behold the children of men." But that all such expressions are employed solely through condescension[1] to human imperfection, will assuredly be hereafter *perceived* as vividly, as all now *feel* them to be inadequate,—for then " we shall know, even as also we are known." And yet, who that believes does not gratefully accept, as the clearest intimation of the Divine benignity, such language of Inspiration ; by means of which He, Whom " Heaven, and the Heaven of Heavens, cannot contain," becomes a possible subject of human thought ? while, on the other hand, they who now venture to take exceptions against its use must confess that they are incapable of forming an adequate conception of even a single attribute of God.

These considerations being premised, the objection before us is, I submit, on two distincts grounds, untenable. In the first place, it is to be borne in mind, that whatever difficulty the case presents arises altogether from the necessity of making human language the vehicle of communication to human beings. It is conceivable that the writers of Scripture should have made use of one or other of two languages :—that of Sense, as objects appear to the beholder on this earth ; or that of Science. Now it is obvious that the language of Science would have been, in every point of view, unsuited for their purpose. " Science is constantly teaching us to describe known facts in new language ; but the language of Scripture is always the same. And not only so, but the language of Scripture is necessarily adapted to the common state of man's intellectual development, in which he is supposed not to be possessed of Science. Hence, the phrases used by Scripture are precisely those which Science soon teaches man to consider as inaccurate. Yet they are not, on that account, the less fitted for their proper purpose : for if any terms had been used, adapted to a more advanced state of knowledge, they must have been unintelligible among those to whom the

[1] Cf. *supra*, Lecture ii. pp. 71–77.

Scripture was first addressed."[1] The only language which is fixed is that of ordinary life; whereby phenomena are described as they appear to Sense. The terms used in Science change as each new system is proposed:—in Botany the classification of Jussieu differs from that of Linnæus; in Optics the nomenclature of Newton differs from that of Fresnel. It is plain, therefore,—and the very design of Scripture proves it to be necessary, that the language of Inspiration must have been the language of all mankind. To press as an objection the original and literal sense of particular words and phrases, may, no doubt, exhibit the only channel of conveying knowledge, language, as being, like all else that is human, alloyed with imperfection:[2] we must remember, however, that the earth is our habitation; and that Scripture was composed as a record for man. The sacred historian, consequently, has drawn up his narrative, as a narrative of facts can only be drawn up, in the language of those for whom he writes. The Judge of Israel addresses his prayer to God;

[1] Whewell, "Philosophy of the Inductive Sciences," vol. i. p. 686. Again:—"The meaning which any generation puts upon the phrases of Scripture depends, more than is at first supposed, upon the received philosophy of the time. Hence, while men imagine that they are contending for Revelation, they are, in fact, contending for their own interpretation of Revelation, unconsciously adapted to what they believe to be rationally probable. And the new interpretation, which the new philosophy requires, and which appears to the older school to be a fatal violence done to the authority of religion, is accepted by their successors without the dangerous results which were apprehended. When the language of Scripture, invested with its new meaning, has become familiar to men, it is found that the ideas which it calls up are quite as reconcilable as the former ones were with the soundest religious views. And the world then looks back with surprise at the error of those who thought that the essence of Revelation was involved in their own arbitrary version of some collateral circumstance. At the present day we can hardly conceive how reasonable men should have imagined that religious reflections on the stability of the earth, and the beauty and use of the luminaries which revolve round it, would be interfered with by its being acknowledged that this rest and motion are apparent only."—*History of the Inductive Sciences*, Book v. vol. i. p. 424.

[2] Bishop Butler, when developing his remark, that "we are not in any sort competent judges, what supernatural instruction *were to have been* expected," observes in illustration: "So likewise the imperfections attending *the only method* by which nature enables and directs us to communicate our thoughts to each other, are innumerable. Language is, in its very nature, *inadequate, ambiguous,* liable to infinite abuse," &c.—*Analogy*, Part ii. ch. iii. And Dugald Stewart writes: "I cannot help pausing a little to remark how much more imperfect language is than is commonly supposed, when considered as an organ of mental intercourse. * * * Even in conversing on the plainest and most familiar subjects, however full and circumstantial our statements may be, the words which we employ, if examined with accuracy, will be found to do nothing more than to suggest *hints* to our hearers, leaving by far the principal part of the process of interpretation to be performed by the mind itself. In this respect the effect of *words* bears some resemblance to the *stimulus* given to the memory and imagination by an outline or a shadow, exhibiting the profile of a countenance familiar to the eye."—*Philosophical Essays*, v. ch. 1.

and that prayer is recorded in the form in which it was uttered A miracle is wrought for the deliverance of the people ; and that miracle is recorded as human Sense discerned it :—and it is manifest that no other language than that of the sacred writer could have been employed, even by a historian of our own day,[1] without disclosing *the manner in which the miracle had been effected.*[2]

In the second place, this objection, as employed in the case before us, is altogether set aside by attending to that distinction between Revelation and Inspiration to which I have so often adverted ; and of which this example of Joshua's miracle is perhaps

[1] Historians of the present age can describe the brilliant rising of "the Sun of Austerlitz" without being considered ignorant of the laws of nature: nay, the most celebrated astronomers, even when explaining the principles of their own science, employ the language of Sense. Sir J. Herschel tells his readers that "the Sun, which at a considerable altitude always appears round, assumes, *as it approaches the horizon*, a flattened or oval outline."—*Outlines of Astronomy*, p. 34. Again: on crossing the equator the stars which at the spectator's "original station described their whole diurnal circles above his horizon, and never set, now describe them entirely below it, and never rise."—*Ibid.*, p. 46;—so universal, when touching upon the province of phenomena, is the employment by all writers of the language of Sense. In the words of Kepler (quoted by Mr. Gray, *loc. cit.*, p. 28): "Astronomy unfolds the causes of natural things; it professedly investigates optical illusions. For even we astronomers do not pursue this science with the design of altering common language. We say with the common people, the planets stand still, or go down; the Sun rises and sets. These forms of speech we use with the common people: meaning only, *that so the thing appears to us*, although it is not truly so, as all astronomers are agreed. How much less should we require that the Scriptures of Divine Inspiration, setting aside the common modes of speech, should shape their words according to the model of the natural sciences; and by employing a dark and inappropriate phraseology about things which surpass the comprehension of those whom it designs to instruct, perplex the simple people of God, and thus obstruct its own way towards the attainment of the far more exalted end at which it aims."

[2] The reserve (involved in the very nature of a *Miracle*) with which the Scripture narrative has treated the *modus operandi* here, as in the case of all other exhibitions of Divine power, has not been respected by either the assailants or the defenders of Inspiration. Thus, a very amiable writer, M. Gaussen, undertakes to explain the miracle before us: "It is easy to understand that if God, in the day of the battle of Beth-horon, had employed two-thirds of a minute to arrest, by brief and successive retardations, the rotation of our globe," &c. On which he adds, "It will, perhaps here be objected that the rotation of the earth at Beth-horon is twenty-seven times more rapid than that of a steam-carriage on a railroad. It is true;—but since the force of retardation necessary to overcome a given impulsion, is in inverse proportion to the time it occupies, the miracle would be accomplished in eighteen minutes. Let us suppose, then, eighteen minutes, instead of forty seconds, to completely arrest the movement of the earth at the voice of Joshua; and then 'the warring armies, instead of being swept as chaff before the tempest,' would no more feel what was going on than do, at present, thousands of railroad travellers, when stopping at the assigned stations." M. Gaussen enters still more deeply into the successive steps of the procedure: "Let us suppose a double concussion communicated to the earth, above and below its centre, in two opposite and parallel directions; and it will be explained how rotation on its axis may have been suspended, without its progressive motion being at all affected."—*Theopneustia*, p. 174, &c.

the most striking illustration.[1] It is assumed by the objector,—and in this assumption lies the whole strength of his argument,—that the inspired language of Scripture was directly communicated to its writers by the Holy Ghost: that is to say, its several statements, whether historical or doctrinal, are assumed to be the result of an immediate infusion of both words and thoughts into the minds of the human agents who composed the different parts of the Bible. In short, the objection before us rests upon the supposition that the passage against which it is directed is not the *inspired* narrative of an historical event faithfully related as an eye-witness *must* have related it; but that it was designed to be an express impartation of scientific knowledge *revealed* by the Most High. Here the remark above adverted to, that Scripture does not teach matters of science, comes in with all its force:—not, indeed, to explain how the language of Joshua may be reconciled with the language of Philosophy; but to explain why we are not to regard his language as a special revelation, communicating the results of future discoveries.[2]

[1] See *supra*, Lecture iv. p. 146, note 3.

[2] There is yet another class of "discrepancies" which Spinoza was, I believe, the first to urge against the authority of Scripture; and the same objection has been lately pressed, with the same object, by Mr. F. W. Newman ("Phases of Faith," p. 147). It has been even advanced by Mr. Morell, who thus states his views: "Once more we may refer to *discrepancies* in reasoning, in definition, and in other purely formal and logical processes. By those who have most closely analyzed the trains of thought which we have in the Apostolic writings, and especially those of S. Paul, it is well understood how great the difficulty often is to reconcile particular definitions, and passing arguments, with logical order and consistency. To some it might, doubtless, seem very irreverent to speak of errors in reasoning as occurring in the sacred writings; but the irreverence, if there be any, really lies on the part of those who deny their possibility. We have already shown that to speak of Logic, as such, being inspired, is a sheer absurdity. The process either of defining or of reasoning requires simply the employment of the formal laws of thought, the accuracy of which can be in no way affected by any amount of inspiration whatever."—*Philosophy of Religion*, p. 173. The distinction between Revelation and Inspiration indicates one of the mistakes involved in this statement. On Mr. Morell's principles it must be equally absurd to speak of "inspired history" as of "inspired logic." It may, with equal truth, be said of one, as of the other, that its accuracy "can be in no way affected by any amount of inspiration whatever." But the following profound remarks point out the radical fallacy of any attempt to analyze the reasoning of Scripture by the ordinary rules of Logic: "Inspired teaching (explain it how we may) seems comparatively indifferent to (what seems to us so peculiarly important) close logical connexion, and the intellectual symmetry of doctrines. * * * The necessity of confuting gainsayers at times forced one of the greatest of His [Christ's] inspired servants, S. Paul, to prosecute continuous argument; yet even with him how abrupt are the transitions, how intricate the connexion, how much is conveyed *by assumptions such as Inspiration alone can make*, without any violation of the canons of reasoning—FOR WITH IT ALONE ASSERTION IS ARGUMENT. * * * The same may be said of some passages of S. John, supposed to have been similarly occasioned. Inspiration has ever left to human Reason the filling up of its outlines, the careful connexion of its more isolated truths. The two are as the lightning of Heaven, bril-

I have paused upon this particular objection longer, perhaps, than its intrinsic weight may have appeared to demand or deserve, because it has enabled me to introduce some observations which will facilitate the just apprehension of a topic of growing importance, and to which every year that passes by adds a graver interest: I mean the connexion, in general, between the results of scientific discovery, and the statements of Scripture. It is a fact of common notoriety, that men have not yet ceased to feel alarm for the truths of Religion. Let us only bear in mind the spirit with which any progress in the Philosophy of Nature is received. Take, for example, the case of Astronomy, which opens to our view the boundless regions of space; or of Geology, which discloses to our understanding the boundless regions of time. The history of Galileo illustrates the difficulties with which the former has had to struggle. The memory of living men attests the opposition encountered by the latter;[1] an opposition which —it is not going too far to aver—has not as yet disappeared. Strange, indeed, that such misconceptions should still prevail as to the respective provinces of Science and Religion! The great founder of the Inductive Philosophy has from the first raised his warning voice in deprecation of the error: "The unskilfulness of certain Theologians," observed Lord Bacon, "would exclude the study of all Philosophy, however guarded. Some entertain a latent fear lest they may intrude into Divine Mys-

liant, penetrating, far-flashing, abrupt—compared with the feebler but *continuous* illumination of some earthly beacon."—Professor Archer Butler, *On Development*, p. 245. In other words, Mr. Morell's criticism on the Logic of Scripture assumes that Scripture is *not* inspired. But see *infra*, Appendix N, the truly philosophical principles laid down on this subject by Mr. J. S. Mill.

[1] It is important, however, to bear in mind that objections to Geology *as a science* have not originated with the friends of Religion. Voltaire denied *the existence* of fossils, lest he should be compelled to admit the fact of the Deluge:—"As the readiest way of shaking this article of faith, he endeavored to inculcate scepticism as to the real nature of such shells, and to recall from contempt the exploded dogma of the 16th century, that they were sports of nature."—Lyell's *Principles of Geology*, 8th ed., p. 56. Or, shifting his ground to suit the apprehension of the vulgar, he maintained that the shells collected in the Alps were no doubt real shells, but that they were "Eastern species which had fallen from the hats of pilgrims coming from Syria."—*Ibid.* "It is interesting and instructive to observe," remarks an able writer in the "Christian Remembrancer" for July, 1849, "how speedily and entirely unbelievers changed their views of Geology. It was soon whispered that geological phenomena seemed to indicate that the antiquity of the globe was much greater than that attributed by the Mosaic account to the human race. * * * In Mr. Brydone's 'Tour through Sicily and Malta in 1770,' eight years before the death of Voltaire, the immense antiquity of the globe, as proved by the geological phenomena of Ætna, is treated of with a radiant satisfaction which is hardly exceeded when he descants upon the profligacy of the Sicilian monks or knights of Malta."—p. 228.

teries by penetrating too deeply into the secrets of Nature. Others conceive that, by remaining ignorant of the means, the effects can be more easily ascribed to the agency of God. Others, again, apprehend that changes in Philosophy may produce results injurious to Religion. While a fourth class seems alarmed lest researches into Nature's laws shall bring to light what may subvert or weaken their faith. These two latter apprehensions," continues this great writer, "appear to us to savor of a wisdom altogether animal:—as if, in the recesses of their breasts, men mistrusted the certainty of Religion; and, therefore, feared that danger impends from a search after Truth."[1]

With reference to this supposed variance between the conclusions of Science and the received interpretation of Scripture, it is entirely overlooked by those to whose minds such a result presents a difficulty, that the constant recurrence of apparent contradictions between the observed facts of every progressive science, and the sense which we are in the habit of attaching to the statements of the Bible, seems, beforehand, almost a matter of certainty. This has already been the case with Astronomy, Geology, Ethnology:—we may expect it in the continued investigation of these sciences; and, no doubt the same will occur in other cases also. There are some—and these persons Bacon has described—who take alarm at every investigation in Natural Philosophy. To the minds of such men, the theory of Nebulæ, started by philosophers, suggests a doubt of the creation of the world by God; the truth of the Mosaic narrative appears to waver before the facts of Geology; the descent of man from one original stock seems impugned by an examination into the history of nations.[2] To all such apprehensions one only answer can be given. "No one Truth can be contradictory to any other Truth." The question which we must settle, in the first instance, *and on its own peculiar evidence*, is—Does the Bible

[1] "Novum Organum," lib. i. aphor. 89.

[2] "When men had conceived the occurrences of the Sacred Narrative in a particular manner, they could not readily and willingly adopt a new mode of conception; and all attempts to recommend to them such novelties, they resisted as attacks upon the sacredness of the Narrative. They had clothed their belief of the workings of Providence in certain images; and they clung to those images with the persuasion that, without them, their belief could not subsist. * * * The most memorable instance of a struggle of this kind is to be found in the circumstances which attended the introduction of the Heliocentric Theory of Copernicus to general acceptance."—Whewell, *Phil. of the Induct. Sciences*, vol. i. p. 685.

come from God? And if it be Divine (and therefore true), "then is it certain, demonstrably certain—that no fact in the universe,—in heaven above, or earth beneath, or in the waters or the rocks under the earth,—can by possibility be really inconsistent with it."[1] Hence, the conclusion which Theologian and Philosopher alike must admit is simply this :—Let each inquirer produce his results ; the one from God's words in His Scriptures, the other from God's acts in His Creation ; and should any inconsistency present itself, it is either because the pages of Inspiration do not really say what the former supposes : or else because the theory of the latter is founded upon an imperfect or erroneous induction. On such a principle the Philosopher may be invited to collect his facts, and to build up his theory, undismayed by any alarm lest his conclusions shall contravene a single truth of Religion : while it becomes the duty of Divines—a duty increasing in its obligation as Science advances,—in the first place, to qualify themselves to understand and appreciate such conclusions ; and, when the evidence on which they rest is weighed and accepted, the next duty of Theology is to compare the results with the preconceived opinions of religious men, and, should they be found not to agree, to examine how this discrepancy is to be set right, and to teach in what other way the face of the world and the words of God may be shown to be,—as when rightly understood, they must, of necessity be,—perfectly harmonious.[2]

[1] I here avail myself of the very forcible argument of the writer in the "Christian Remembrancer," *loc. cit.*, pp. 232–234.

[2] "Other apparent difficulties arise from the accounts given in the Scripture of the first origin of the world in which we live: for example, Light is represented as created before the Sun. With regard to difficulties of this kind, it appears that we may derive some instruction from the result to which we were led in the last chapter;—namely, that in the sciences which trace the progress of natural occurrences, we can in no case go back to an origin, but in every instance appear to find ourselves separated from it by a state of things, and an order of events, of a kind altogether different from those which come under our experience. The thread of induction respecting the natural course of the world snaps in our fingers, when we try to ascertain where its beginning is. Since, then, Science can teach us nothing positive respecting the beginning of things, she can neither contradict nor confirm what is taught by Scripture on that subject; and thus, as it is unworthy timidity in the lover of Scripture to fear contradiction, so is it ungrounded presumption to look for confirmation in such cases."—Whewell, *loc. cit.* p. 687. In one of Mr. Chapman's publications, entitled "The Hebrew Cosmogony," the author, drawing all his inferences from the most literal construction of the English translation of the Hebrew text, observes: "Thus, between indolent surmises and absurd theories, the world has (with few exceptions) permitted itself to be blind to the fact that Moses' narrative is entirely at variance with existing phenomena; and that that error is one of the most vital importance, affecting the proof of his inspiration"—p. 9; and the writer concludes with the re-

Nor can it for a moment be maintained that such endeavors to readjust our interpretation of the language of Holy Scripture can derogate from its supreme authority. A remark of Bishop Butler with reference to "the scheme of Scripture," holds equally true with reference to its interpretation,—if we only substitute the facts of Science for the events of History: "Nor is it at all incredible, that a Book which has been so long in the possession of mankind should contain many truths as yet undiscovered. For all the same phenomena, and the same faculties of investigation from which such great discoveries in natural knowledge have been made in the present and last age, were equally in the possession of mankind several thousand years before. And possibly it might be intended that events, as they come to pass, should open and ascertain the meaning of several parts of Scripture."[1] It may be well, too, to note that the same objections which have been advanced against inquiring into the laws of Nature have been equally urged even against inquiries into the text of Scripture. When Dr. Kennicott commenced his labors on the text of the Old Testament, all the world was in commotion; and it was apprehended that Christianity itself would be sorely shaken. But men's fears were soon appeased;

mark: "Whether these objections affect the evidence for the inspiration of the preceptive and prophetic portions of the Old Testament is quite another question." Or, to take the less offensive statement of Mr. Morell: "Under this head we may refer to the acknowledged (?) discrepancies between some of the Scriptural statements and scientific truth. The account of the Creation, for example, as given in the Book of Genesis, is by no means exactly reconcilable (viewed as a scientific account) with the most palpable facts of Geology. We do not doubt but that ingenuity may smooth down one expression, and give a broad meaning to another, and after all may bring out a tolerable case of consistency; but still it is impossible to say that, as a scientific view of the creation of the world, the Book of Genesis would convey at all the same impression to the mind of any ordinary reader as do the results of geological research."—*Philosophy of Religion*, p. 170. To this class of objections the following remarks suggest the true answer: "The Sacred Narrative, in some of its earliest portions, speaks of natural objects and occurrences respecting them. In the very beginning of the course of the world, we may readily believe (indeed as we have seen in the last chapter, our scientific researches lead us to believe) that such occurrences were very different from anything which now takes place;—different to an extent and in a manner which we cannot estimate. Now the narrative must speak of objects and occurrences in the words and phrases which have derived their meaning from their application to the existing natural state of things. When applied to an initial supernatural state, therefore, these words and phrases cannot help being to us obscure and mysterious, perhaps ambiguous and seemingly contradictory."—Whewell, *loc. cit.*, p. 684.

[1] "Analogy," Part ii. ch. iii. Cf. the remark of Cassiodorus: "Nequaquam vobis modernos expositores interdico. Caute tamen quærendos esse Catholicos; quoniam accessu temporum multis noviter gratia Divinitatis infunditur, quæ forsitan priscis doctoribus cælata monstratur."—*De Instit. Div. Liter.*, c. viii. t. ii. p. 544.

and they were amazed at the trivial and easily explicable variations which the Hebrew manuscripts presented :—so trivial indeed are they, that they have almost ceased to possess any interest in the eyes of critics.[1]

What Religion, then, has to fear is not the most searching criticism of the contents of Scripture ; not any fundamental inquiry into the laws of physical phenomena ; not the fullest examination of every vestige upon the field of Nature left by the footsteps of Time :—her true source of alarm is the danger to their faith which those persons must encounter who content themselves with superficial information, or partial knowledge. Scripture has never anything to apprehend from the results of any branch of Science ; a semblance of investigation and half-learned sciolism alone can represent its great truths in a disadvantageous light. They who seek in the announcements of Scripture for positive information on matters appertaining to Natural Science will, indeed, ever seek in vain. For those, on the other hand, who, while they venture not to deliver physical doctrines as the teaching of Revelation,[2] recognise the undoubted supremacy

[1] Dr. Moses Stuart observes: "In the Hebrew MSS. that have been examined, some 800,000 various readings actually occur as to the Hebrew consonants. How many as to the vowel-points and accents, no man knows. But at the same time it is equally true, that all these taken together do not change or materially affect any important point of doctrine, precept, or even history. A great proportion, indeed the mass, of variations in Hebrew MSS. when minutely scanned, amount to nothing more than the difference in spelling a multitude of English words [e. g. קֹל or קוֹל ; as *honour* or *honor*]. * * * "Indeed one may travel through the immense desert (so I can hardly help naming it) of Kennicott and De Rossi, and (if I may venture to speak in homely phrase) not find game enough to be worth the hunting. So completely is this chase given up by recent critics on the Hebrew Scriptures, that a reference to either of these famous collators of MSS. who once created a great sensation among philologers is rarely to be found."—*On the Old Test. Canon*, p. 169.

"When the very erudite and truly pious Professor Bengel of Tübingen published his New Testament, with all the various readings which he had been able to discover, many minds were filled with anxiety, thinking that an entirely New Testament would be the result in the end, if all the various readings were hunted up. They thought it would be better to leave things as they were. But mark:—although 40,000 various readings were discovered in the ancient MSS., the New Testament was hardly at all altered thereby."—Olshausen, *The Genuineness of the N. T. Writings* (Clarke's For. Theol. Lib. p. vii).

[2] "By delivering physical doctrines as the teaching of Revelation, Religion may lose much, but cannot gain anything. This maxim of practical wisdom has often been urged by Christian writers. Thus S. Augustine says (lib. I. "De Genesi," c. xviii.): 'In obscure matters and things far removed from our senses, if we read anything, even in the Divine Scripture, which may produce diverse opinions without damaging the faith which we cherish, let us not rush headlong by positive assertion to either the one opinion or the other; lest when a more thorough discussion has shown the opinion we had adopted to be false, our faith may fall with it: and we should be found contending, not for the doctrine of the Sacred Scriptures, but for our

of that Revelation in its own province;—for those who thus take up the "Oracles of God" with integrity and honesty (and, again to use the words of Bishop Butler, "Religion presupposes this as much, and in the same sense, as speaking to a man presupposes he understands the language in which you speak")—for all such inquirers the Bible will ever possess the peculiarity of meeting every want, and appeasing every difficulty. In its pages every longing of our nature, the most superficial and the most profound, will find satisfaction. Here provision has been made alike for the tender susceptibility of the child, and the mature intellect of manhood: and whatever shadow our imperfect knowledge may allow, for the present, to rest upon certain of its statements, the Mourner will still find solace in the songs of Sion, and Philosophy still drink wisdom from the parables of Galilee. It is true, as I have said, that all difficulties may not have been removed which the enemies of Christianity have started: nevertheless, the marvellous success with which most of them have already been met must convince any fair mind that such as still remain are not insurmountable; and that here, if anywhere, it befits our weakness "to be thankful and to wait."[1] The supercilious philosophy which refuses to Religion this justice,—which scorns "to conciliate the finger and the tongue of God, His works and His word,"[2]—must answer, as best it may, the demand of the Most High: "Where wast thou when I laid the foundations of the earth? Declare if thou hast understanding."[3] The Christian, on the other hand, fearlessly accepts the source of Divine knowledge which has been vouchsafed to him. In the pages of Scripture he recognises the record of imperishable Truth; and as he shrinks from no inquiry, so he chal-

own; endeavoring to make our doctrine to be that of the Scriptures, instead of taking the doctrine of the Scriptures to be ours.' "—Whewell, *loc. cit.* p. 693.

[1] Mr. Westcott, *loc. cit.*, p. 133, quotes the words of Origen: *ἀσφαλὲς οὖν τὸ περιμένειν τὴν ἑρμηνείαν τοῦ σαφηνιστοῦ λόγου.—Philocalia.*

[2] "We may add, as a further reason for mutual forbearance in such cases, that the true interests of both parties are the same. The man of Science is concerned, no less than any other person, in the truth and import of the Divine dispensation; the religious man, no less than the man of Science, is, by the nature of his intellect, incapable of believing two contradictory declarations. Hence they have both alike a need for understanding the Scripture in some way in which it shall be consistent with their understanding of Nature. It is for their common advantage to conciliate, as Kepler says, the finger and the tongue of God, His works and His word."—Whewell, *loc. cit.* p. 695.

[3] Job, xxxviii. 4.

lenges all examination. His sole demand is, justice in the conduct of this inquiry, and due qualifications on the part of those who enter on this examination. He knows that every assault which has marked the course of nineteen hundred years has but served to strengthen the bulwarks of his belief; and that above the chaos of human systems, and the wreck of philosophical speculation, the light of Inspiration shines more brightly than ever. Earthly dynasties have passed away, while the Kingdom of Christ has but enlarged its borders. Empires have crumbled into ruins, but the Religion of the Cross shows no symptoms of decrepitude. Under the banner of that Cross will yet be signalized the further triumphs of the Church of God: and, unfailing as that Church Herself, are those Divine Institutes which are entrusted to Her charge, and which contain Her Commission. "Heaven and earth shall pass away, but My words shall not pass away,"—is the assurance of the Church's Head. And although philosophers object, or critics cavil, or unbelievers scorn, the Christian calmly abides the issue, with a confidence "strong as Faith, and patient as Time."

APPENDIX.

APPENDIX

APPENDIX A.

FICHTE.

(LECTURE I.—PAGE 19.)

"IT is needless," observes a rationalistic writer, "to prove the *necessity* of a Revelation. For, if Reason allow that a Revelation is *possible*, Theology has merely to adduce the *historical* proof that God has revealed Himself."[1] To prove the *possibility* of such a communication from the Divine Being is the problem which Fichte undertakes to solve; and, in entering upon his "Attempt at a Criticism of all Revelation," he sets out from an analysis of the *actual state* and constitution of man—his faculties and his susceptibilities.

The result of this analysis differs but little, if at all, from the following description given by Bishop Butler:—"Together with the general principle of moral understanding we have, in our inward frame, various affections towards particular external objects. These affections are naturally, and of right, subject to the government of the moral principle, as to the occasions upon which they may be gratified; as to the times, degrees, and manner, in which the objects of them may be pursued: but then the principle of virtue can neither excite them, nor prevent their being excited. On the contrary, they are naturally felt when the objects of them are present to the mind, not only before all consideration whether they can be obtained by lawful means, but after it is found they cannot."—*Analogy*, Part i. ch. v.

Fichte opens his "Criticism" by laying down a "Theory of the Will as preparation, in general, for a deduction of Religion" (§ 2). "The determining one's self, with the consciousness of our own activity, to produce a conception is called *will* (Wollen): the power to determine one's self, with this consciousness of the self activity, is called *the power of desire* (Begehrungs-Vermögen). The will is distinguished from the power of desire, as the *actual* from the *possible*." "There must be a *medium* which is capable of being determined, on the one hand, by the conception to which the subject is but passively related; and, on the other, by spontaneity, the consciousness of which is the exclusive character of all will. This *medium* we name *propension* (den Trieb)." "That which existing in the subject-mat-

[1] Bretschneider, "Handbuch der Dogmatik," B. i. s. 210.

ter of the sensation determines the propension we name *agreeable;* and the propension, so far as it is thereby determined, we name the *sensuous* (sinnlichen) propension" (s. 5).

The *higher* power of desire—the object of which is the idea of what is *absolutely right*—is to be distinguished from the *lower*. To the *former* no object is *given*,—it *gives* to itself its object: to the *latter* its object must be given. The *former* is absolutely independent; the *latter* is, in many respects, merely passive. That this higher power of desire, which is merely *a power*, should produce *a willing* as an actual process of the mind, something further is required; and that the determination of the will in finite creatures should be possible, a certain *medium* must be pointed out. This is called the *feeling of respect* (das Gefuhl der Achtung), which is, as it were, the point in which the rational and sensuous natures of finite beings inwardly combine. It is therefore a perfectly just maxim of morality, "Respect thyself:" and hence we see why minds which are not ignoble prize the approval of their own hearts far higher than the plaudits of a universe. This self-respect, as an *active* propension determining the will is called *moral interest:* which must necessarily be accompanied by a feeling of pleasure. *Respect* (Achtung) is the earliest feeling which, displaying itself in every man, is not to be explained by his whole sensuous nature, and immediately points to his connexion with a higher world. The sensuous propension on the one hand, and the purely moral propension, on the other, hold the scales in the human will; the pleasure arising from the submission of the former to the Law imposed by the latter is a spark of the Deity within us, and a pledge that we are of His race (s. 25).

The Moral Law demands supremacy within us. According to its prohibition, or non-prohibition, a propension is allowable or the reverse. "The Moral Law, if it shall not contradict itself, and cease to be a Law, must maintain the rights imparted by itself:—it must, consequently exercise not only command, but absolute rule over Nature. This cannot take place in beings who are themselves passively affected by Nature,—but in a Being only Who, in all respects independently, determines Nature: in Whose Person are united moral necessity, and absolute physical freedom. This Being we name God" (s. 41). By virtue of the demands of the Moral Law, God must produce perfect congruence between morality and the happiness of finite rational beings. "The determinations in the idea of God (which Reason, practically determined by the injunctions of morality, has laid down) are—(1.) Those presented by His very idea: viz. that He is determined wholly and solely by the Moral Law (i. e. the demand of the practical Reason on Him is not a *command*, but a *Law;*—it is with respect to Him not *imperative*, but *constitutive*): and—(2.) Those which belong to Him, so far as relates to the possibility of finite moral beings; on account of which possibility we were just now obliged to assume His existence. The *former* represent God as the most perfect *Holiness:*—as the Alone-Happy, because He is the Alone-Holy. Hence He represents the *Highest Good*—the attained end of practical Reason—the possibility of which was Reason's postulate. The *latter* represent Him as the Supreme Ruler of the world by moral laws; the Judge of all rational spirits. The *former* regard Him in, and for, Himself, according to His Being; and He thereby appears the most perfect observer of the Moral Law: the *latter*, according to the operations of this Being upon other moral natures, and by virtue of which He is the highest executor of the requirements of the Moral Law; and therefore a Legislator. Hence we get a Theology (which we must have in order not to place in contradiction our theoretical convictions and the practical determinations of our will); but not as yet a Religion, which itself, in turn, might, as Cause, exert an influence upon this determination of the will. Theology is mere Science: Religion, as its very name imports (*religio*), is that which *binds* us; and this, too, more powerfully than we were bound without it" (s. 46). Theology becomes Religion, when the propositions assumed to determine our will by means of the Law of Reason operate practically upon us, in consequence of the further motive that such is God's command.

The Moral Law *in* us contains the law of God *to* us; and is, according to its *matter*, His Law. We have still to inquire whether it is also His Law, according to its *form*: i. e. whether it has been promulged by Him, and as His. In other words:—"Has God really promulged His Law to us? Can we point out a fact which proves itself to be such a promulgation?" (s. 71). The problem to be solved, therefore, is—"Has God announced Himself to us as a Moral Legislator? and, *how* has He done so?" This is conceivable in two ways. God has promulged His Law either *in* us, as moral beings, in our rational nature; or in a way exterior to that nature. There are, therefore, two principles of Religion:—the principle of the supernatural *within* us; and the principle of the supernatural *without* us. A Religion based upon the former is called Natural Religion: if based upon the latter it is called Revealed Religion. "According to the second principle, the announcement of the Legislator without us either sends us back to our rational nature, and the entire Revelation, expressed in words, merely says: 'God is the Legislator; the Law written in your hearts is His;'—or, it prescribes to us, in a special manner, God's Law once more, in the same way in which it makes Him known as Legislator. In the case of a Revelation given *in concreto*, there is no reason why both may not take place" (s. 79). (Cf. Butler's "Analogy," Part ii. ch. i.)

"Revelation, according to its form, is a kind of *making known* (eine Art von *Bekanntmachung*); and every thing which holds good of this its species holds good also of it. Of all "making known" there are two *internal* conditions: viz. (1), the something which is made known, *the subject matter* (der *Stoff*); and (2) the manner in which it is made known, the *form* of the "making known." The *external* conditions are also twofold:—a person who makes known, and one to whom it is made known. That which is made known is *made* known only because I knew it not before. Knowledge which is *à priori* possible is developed, or pointed out, not *made known*: it is only knowledge which is possible *à posteriori* that is made known." Hence it follows that we must exclude from the idea of Revelation all possible instruction and knowledge derived from a contemplation of the world of sense. "Revelation is therefore a perception which is wrought in us by God, in conformity with the idea of some instruction to be given us thereby, as its *end* or object." As to the logical possibility of this notion there can be no doubt. Its physical possibility is founded upon the postulate of the Moral Law that a free intelligent being can be a cause in the world of sense, in conformity with an idea of the end to be effected. But how shall we know that God has thus wrought a certain perception in us?

Although we cannot penetrate the notion of a Revelation on the side of its *form;* the idea of Religion enables us to attain to it on the side of its *matter* (s. 96).

If the existence of finite moral beings—i. e. beings who besides the Moral Law are likewise subject to laws of Nature—be assumed, we may anticipate that the operations of these two causalities (whose laws are reciprocally quite independent of each other) will fall into collision in determining the will of such beings. "If such beings shall not in this case become quite incapable of morality, their sensuous (sinnliche) nature must be determined by impulses of sense to allow itself to be determined by the Moral Law." The sole purely moral impulse is the inward holiness of Right (des Rechts). This holiness, by virtue of a postulate of the pure practical Reason, exists in God *in concreto:* He is, therefore, the Legislator of all rational beings; and must, therefore, announce Himself to them, and His will as their law, in the world of sense. Now the world of sense does not contain an announcement of this *law-giving* holiness. God must, therefore, announce Himself to those beings in the world of sense as Legislator, by means of a special phenomenon expressly designed for this purpose and for them. And since God is determined by the Moral Law to forward by all moral means the highest possible morality in all rational beings, we may expect, if such beings exist, that He will avail Himself of those means, if they be physically possible. This deduced idea is really the idea of Revelation:—i. e. the idea of a phenomenon produced in the world of sense by the causality of God, whereby He announces Himself as moral Legislator" (s. 106).

"In deducing the notion of Revelation from the practical principles of Reason, the fact was assumed *à priori* that there *can* be moral beings in whom the Moral Law loses its casuality *for ever*, or only in *certain cases.* The Moral Law claims a casuality over the *higher power of desire*, in order to determine the will; and over the *lower*, in order to produce the perfect freedom of the moral subject from the constraint of the impulse of Nature. If the *former* kind of causality be removed, the *will* to recognise and obey the Law is wanting: if the latter only be hindered, man, however good his will may be, is too weak *actually to practise* the good that he wills. The empirical possibility of this hypothesis, if proved, answers the question, Why was a Revelation needed? and why could not man make shift with Natural Religion alone?" (s. 112). The *highest* moral perfection of man (impossible to be determined *à priori* as existing in any individual man, and in the present state of humanity *improbable*) is that pure religion of Reason which waits for no demand of God to obey Him; but only for permission to look up to Him with willing obedience. The *second* degree of moral perfection (and which is the foundation of Natural Religion), is that in which Reason seeks for proof of the notion of God, as moral Legislator; and finds it in the idea of Him as Creator of the world. The *lowest* fall of rational beings with respect to morality, is when not even the *will* exists to recognise and obey a moral law.

In each of these cases Religion is required. In the *first*, to satisfy the emotion of reverence and gratitude towards the Supreme Being; in the *second*, to add a new weight to the authority of the Moral Law; in the *third*, to produce the *will* to acknowledge that Law. This Religion can attain to humanity thus constituted, only by the way in which everything reaches it which it conceives, or by which it allows itself to be determined:—viz., by the senses. "Humanity may fall so deeply into moral degradation, that it is not to be brougnt back to morality by any other means than by Religion; and to Religion by any other means than by *the senses.* A religion which shall take effect upon such men can no otherwise be founded than immediately upon Divine authority. Since God cannot will that any moral being should forge (erdichte) such an authority, He Himself, it must be, who confers it upon such a religion" (p. 134). But upon what can God found this authority? Clearly not upon a Sublimity for which men have no sense and no reverence; nor yet upon His Holiness, which were to presuppose a moral feeling already existing in them, which Religion has yet to develop; but upon that which they *are* capable of marvelling at on natural grounds—His greatness, and power, as Lord of Nature, and as their Lord. Hence results merely *attention* on man's part to the motives to obedience which are at a later period to be laid before him. The demand, therefore, of God, in a possible Revelation, that we should *hearken* to Him is founded upon His Omnipotence: His demand that we should *obey* Him can only be founded upon His Holiness; but the notion of Holiness, as well as of reverence for it, must have been already developed by means of Revelation. We have a sublime expression which explains this: "Be ye holy, for I am Holy, saith the Lord" (p. 136).

But, before the moral feelings are excited, how are men to judge if it can be God that speaks?"

The counterpoise to those determinations that resist duty and have strength sufficient to suppress altogether the voice of Reason, is the *power of imagination* (die Einbildungs-kraft); which, on the one hand, appertains to *sense* (and is thus capable of a determination to work in opposition to the sensuous nature of man); on the other, is determinable by *freedom*, and has spontaneity. By means of it, therefore, must the sole possible motive of morality—viz., the *conception* of the legislation of the Holy One—be brought before the soul. In Natural Religion this conception is founded on principles of Reason; but if this Reason (as we assume) is completely suppressed, then its results appear dark, uncertain, insecure. The principles therefore of this conception also should be capable of representation by the power of imagination. Now principles of this class would be facts in the world of sense,—or a Revelation. In such moments man must be able to say to himself: "It is God, for He has spoken, and acted: He wills that I should *not* act so now, for He has expressly forbidden it, in such words, and under such circumstances," &c. If conceptions of this nature shall make an impression upon him, he must be able to assume as perfectly true, and just, the facts which lie at their foundation; they must, therefore, not be anything feigned by his own power of imagination, but be *given* to it.

Is it, in general, possible—is it, in general, conceivable—that anything *without* Nature, should have a causality *in* Nature? That this must be, in general, possible, is the first postulate which the practical Reason makes

25

à priori, when it determines the supernatural element *within us* (our higher power of desire) to be a cause *without* itself in the world of sense whether *within* us or *without* us. The entire philosophy of Nature knows nothing of a causality by means of freedom: so long, therefore, as we speak of the mere determining by the higher power of desire, it is needless to pay any regard to the existence of Nature. These two causalities, viz., of Nature, and of the Moral Law, are infinitely different as well in the kind of their causality, as their objects. The Law of Nature ordains with absolute necessity; the Moral Law commands freedom: the former rules Nature; the latter the world of spirits. Their operations in the world of sense, however, come in contact, and may even not be contradictory. Their harmony may be conceived possible by their mutual dependence on a higher legislation, which lies at the foundation of both; which is, however, for us quite inaccessible. Were we able, indeed, to place such a principle at the basis of our view of the Universe, the same effect which appears to us when referred to the world of sense according to the Moral Law as *free*, and in Nature as *contingent*, would be recognised as altogether *necessary*. But since we cannot do so, it follows plainly that so soon as we pay regard to a causality by means of freedom, we must not assume all phenomena in the world of sense as necessary, according to mere laws of Nature, but many merely as contingent: and that we may not, therefore, explain them all *from* the laws of Nature, but many merely *according* to such laws:—by which latter phrase is meant that we are to assume the causality of the *matter* of the operation to be *without* Nature, and the causality of its *form* to be *within* Nature.

In God, Who determines Nature according to the Moral Law, the two legislations spoken of unite. We are compelled by our Reason to derive the whole system of phenomena—the entire world of sense—from a causality by means of freedom, according to laws of Reason; and that, too, from the causality of God. The whole world is for us this supernatural operation; and it is conceivable (1) that God, from the first, has interwoven in the plan of the Universe the first natural cause of a phenomenon, which was in conformity with one of His moral designs. (The objection that this is to do in a roundabout way (durch einen Umweg) what could be done directly, is based upon a gross *anthropomorphosis*, as if God stood under the conditions of time). In this case the phenomenon might be perfectly explicable from the laws of Nature, up to the supernatural origin of all Nature itself, were we able to take a connected survey of it;—and yet it must be also regarded as effected by the causality of a Divine idea of the moral end to be attained thereby. Or, again, (2) we might assume that God has actually interrupted the series of causes and effects already commenced and proceeding according to natural laws; and that by the immediate causality of His moral idea He has brought to pass an effect different from what would have followed by means of the mere causality of the course of Nature according to its laws: still we have not determined at *what* link of the chain He should interfere;—whether at that immediately preceding the designed effect, or whether He might not do so at a link, perhaps, very far removed from it in time, and intermediate effects. In this latter case (if we are thoroughly acquainted with the laws of Nature) we shall at length ascertain, by a progress *in infinitum*, that a certain effect is to be explained not *from* but *according* to natural laws. Suppose, however, we were unable, or unwilling, to trace the series of natural causes beyond a certain point, it might be very possible that the effect, no longer to be explained naturally, did not fall within these limits placed by us—still we should not yet be justified in concluding that the phenomenon in question could *not* have been effected by a supernatural causality. In the first case only would we at once infer from the phenomenon a causality not to be explained from natural laws, and which rendered it theoretically possible to assume for it a supernatural cause. Since all that is required is to afford grounds, not of conviction, but of *attention* to the Moral Law, this theoretical possibility is quite sufficient; and for this nothing more is required than that *we* see no natural causes of this phenomenon. Suppose, however, it could be shown by means of an exalted insight into the laws of nature, that certain phenomena, on which this Revelation is founded, and which had been regarded as supernatural, were perfectly explicable from the laws of nature, no conclusion can be drawn from this against the possible Divine character of such a Revelation; inasmuch as an operation—especially if it be ascribed to the original Source of all laws of Nature—may be wrought in a perfectly natural manner, and yet, at the same time, supernaturally; i. e. by the causality of His freedom, in conformity with the idea of a moral design. Hence, therefore, little though it can be permitted the dogmatic defender of the notion of Revelation to infer a supernatural causality from the *inexplicability* of a certain phenomenon by natural laws, and thence directly inferring the causality of God: just as little is it allowable for the dogmatic opponent of this notion to infer from the *explicability* of these same phenomena by natural laws, that they are possible neither by means of supernatural causality in general, nor, in particular, by means of the causality of God" (s. 157). "By this criticism," concludes Fichte, "the possibility of a Revelation in itself, and the possibility of a belief in a given definite Revelation in particular, is rendered perfectly certain; all objections against it are set at rest for ever; and all controversy on the subject eternally removed."—(s. 233.)

Such, briefly stated, is Fichte's "Criticism of all Revelation;" and it requires but little attention to perceive how far it *assumes* some of the most profound of those truths which, as experience has taught, Revelation alone has been able to convey to man:—the perfect holiness of God, the depravation of human nature, the supremacy of the Moral Law (Rom. ii. 14, 15). In such inquiries, as Twesten[1] has remarked, the error has generally prevailed "of wishing to explain and found Revelation in a purely speculative manner, and from a merely philosophical point of view, without any regard to the system to which it belongs. And yet it is impossible for the man who proceeds from a view so opposed to the Christian (as, e. g. Fichte, the author of the 'Versuch einer Kritik aller Offenbarung') to arrive at the Christian idea of Revelation. If, however, he find it on his path, *perhaps only through an inconsequence*, yet it has for him a different meaning." A single example will show the nature of such "inconsequences" in this attempt of Fichte. Having inferred from his views respecting the mutual relation of "the sensuous propension" and "the

[1] "Vorlesungen über die Dogmatik," B. i., 340.

Moral Law," that "he who has not sacrificed his life at the demand of the Law is unworthy of life; and must lose it, if the Moral Law is to have force for the world of phenomena,"—he adds in a note, "What a curious coincidence!—'He that loveth his life shall lose it; and he that loseth his life in this world shall keep it unto life eternal' [S. John, xii. 25,] said Jesus; a sentiment which has precisely the same import as the above"[1].—(s. 36.)

The manner in which Kant has availed himself of the *actual* Divine Revelation is far less disguised. In the Preface to the second edition of his treatise—"Die Religion innerhalb der Grenzen der blossen Vernunft," he states that his design is, assuming Revelation as an historical system, to see if it does not lead back to a pure religion of Reason. "If this attempt succeeds, then can we say that there is to be found not merely a compatibility between Reason and Scripture, but also unity; so that whoever (under the guidance of the moral idea) follows the one shall not fail to meet with the other."—(s. xxiii.)

Referring to that view which allows Revelation to be no more than "a public and actual introduction, and exciting cause of rational religion confined to the world," Nitzsch observes: "With regard to this element of the idea of Revelation—which we call historical,—Lessing and Kant, who are opposed to naturalism, as well as supernaturalism, deserve more credit than has yet been acknowledged. * * * Kant, who at all times seizes on the practical point of view, requires, in order to maintain a good fight against the evil principle, an ethical commonwealth. Now he deems it a weakness that this commonwealth cannot be realized by pure religious faith alone; but, notwithstanding, he esteems it a proportional gain, that there should exist a reuniting Church Faith. It is a direct consequence of his hypothesis, that in the sense in which contemporary theologians spoke of Revelation, he could neither discern its necessity nor its reality. Proceeding, however, from the undisputed fact, that pure morality never possessed a firmer basis than the monotheism of the Biblical Church Faith, he insisted on its records and its use of the idea of Revelation being so treated as that the combined effect of the mysteries, which otherwise were passive and indifferent or even injurious, might be accommodated to ethico-theistical decisions. His doctrine was, that we should avail our-

[1] In the "Studien u. Kritiken" for 1832 (s. 378 ff.), Ullmann has given an essay, entitled, "Parallels from the writings of Porphyry to passages from the New Testament, as proof of the remarkable influence of Christianity upon one of its opponents." Porphyry was born A.D. 233, and according to Socrates ("Hist. Eccl." iii. 23) had been originally a Christian. Although one of the most bitter foes of Christianity, he could not divest himself of its influence, or refrain from accepting the truths for which human Reason, however unconsciously, is indebted to it.

Ullmann, in proceeding to cite his parallels which he takes from the epistle of Porphyry to his wife Marcella, first published by Cardinal Mai (Milan, 1816), observes: "Even that truth which is opposed exerts a quiet and involuntary influence upon its opponents. While Porphyry resisted the light, its beams unceasingly forced themselves upon his vision." E. g. S. Paul writes: "Know ye not that ye are the temple of God."—1 Cor. iii. 16; a saying which Porphyry imitates in the words: *Σοὶ δὲ, ὥσπερ εἴρηται, νεὼς μὲν ἔστω τοῦ Θεοῦ ὁ ἐν σοὶ νοῦς.*—*Ad Marcellam*, c. xix. Again we read: "Let no man say when he is tempted, I am tempted of God."—S. James, i. 13; with which cf.—*τῶν δὲ κακῶν αἴτιοι ἡμεῖς ἐσμὲν οἱ ἑλόμενοι· Θεὸς δὲ ἀναίτιος.*—*Ibid.* c. xii.

selves of the Son of God, and His atoning death, &c., as historical expressions, as active types and pledges of practical and rational truths; and thus he sketched out a philosophy of Christianity, which comprehended the nature of the subject matter as truly as it ever possibly could do from that point of view."[1]

The value of the speculations to which allusions have now been made is in one point of view, by no means inconsiderable. It may safely be maintained, to borrow a profound remark, that "even in the assertion that the most important truths of Religion belong not to Revelation but to Reason, the Christian perceives an indirect proof of the reality of the former idea. Such an assertion testifies of the power which Revelation has exercised over the world; since it has effected that what was formerly hidden from even the wisest of our race appears now as the common possession of all rational men."[2] Or, as Mr. Davison has forcibly expressed the same idea, —"the fact is not to be denied; the Religion of Nature *has* had the opportunity of rekindling her faded taper by the Gospel light, whether furtively or unconsciously taken. Let her not dissemble the obligation and the conveyance, and make a boast of the splendor, as though it were originally her own, or had always, in her hands, been sufficient for the illumination of the world."[3]

APPENDIX B.

SCRIPTURE AN ORGANIZED WHOLE.

(Lecture I.—Page 30.)

To enter, at any length, upon the mutual relation of the different portions of Scripture is of course impossible here: such a subject would occupy volumes. A few instances, however, may be stated :—

I. The Book of Job[4]. Before Christ had brought "life and immortality to light," to those only who had drunk deeply of the sources of Revelation, and had formed the true idea of the Deity (which of itself implies future union with Him "in Whom we live, and move, and have our being,")—to such persons only was a future state an object of Faith. To the mass of mankind this world was their abiding place; and therefore, with those on whom Religion exerted its sway, it was a main object to exhibit virtue ever triumphant, and vice undergoing the merited penalties :—in fact to deny, as an article of their belief, the disorders which the government of the world presents to view. How profoundly this principle was implanted in the Jewish mind we learn from the Gospels themselves. "Hath this man sinned, or his parents, that he was born blind?" asked the Jew in the days of Christ: and such, too, was the opinion, which He refutes, as to the guilt of those upon whom the Tower of Siloam fell, and of those Galileans

[1] "System der christl. Lehre," § 25 (Montgomery's transl., p. 69).

[2] Twesten, *loc. cit.* s. 342.

[3] "Discourses on Prophecy," Introd. p. 7.

[4] I have compressed under this head some suggestions of a very able article in the "Christian Remembrancer" for January, 1849, entitled "The Book of Job."

whom Pilate had slain when in the act of worship. This sentiment—the natural result of man's innate sense of justice—appears to be the ground of the reasoning of Job's friends. Anxious to maintain that this world is a scene of satisfactory Divine justice, they argue that, pre-eminently devout, holy, and charitable though Job to all appearance had been, some secret iniquity, some weighty sin close locked in his bosom, must have been cherished amidst all the goodness of his outward life. "Doth God pervert judgment?" reasoned Bildad the Shuhite, "or doth the Almighty pervert justice? If thou wert pure and upright, surely now He would awake for thee, and make the habitation of thy righteousness prosperous."—viii. 3-6. Against the principles and conclusion alike of such reasoning Job utters his protest. He maintains that this visible system of things is irregular and unjust. He insists upon facts, and demands their recognition, whatever difficulties may ensue. He therefore steadily asserts his own righteousness, from which fact, combined with that of his affliction, he draws a conclusion the very opposite to the favorite one which his "friends" maintained.

Such is the process by which the Book of Job opens at length upon that great question which has grieved, and perplexed, and embittered men from the beginning of the world. The entire tone of the popular literature of every age re-echoes the same sentiment; and in the same words have Poet and Philosopher alike sighed over the grand problem of humanity—*ἐν δὲ ἰῇ τιμῇ ἠμὲν κακὸς, ἠδὲ καὶ ἐσθλός.*

We might have expected from the mere fact of its being a Book intended for the consolation and instruction of the human race, that the Bible should touch upon this feeling; and this would of itself account for an ample recognition in its pages of the difficulty which impelled the Psalmist to exclaim, "My feet were almost gone; my steps had well nigh slipped, for I was envious at the foolish when I saw the prosperity of the wicked." But a further end is to be pointed out, which the Book of Job accomplishes in the Divine Scheme.

The Jew expected a temporal deliverer; and "his hopes and aspirations in behalf of his nation and race combined with his previous prejudice in favor of present rewards in committing him to the confident expectation of a visibly prosperous and glorious Messiah. It is evident that to resist such a traditional notion of a Messiah some book would be serviceable which would specially resist that view of this world upon which such a notion was founded. If the Jew was to accept a Messiah who was to lead a life of sorrow and abasement, and to be crucified between thieves, it was necessary that he should be somewhere or other distinctly taught that virtue was not always rewarded here, and that therefore no argument could be drawn from affliction and ignominy against the person who suffered it. The Book of Job does this. It spoke things *φωνᾶντα συνετοῖσιν*, in describing the afflictions of one, whom when the ear heard, it 'blessed him, and when the eye saw, it gave witness unto him; who delivered the poor that cried, the fatherless and him that had none to help him.' And thus it stood in a particular relation to the prophetic books of Scripture—a kind of interpretative one; supplying a caution where they raised hopes, suggesting suspicions of apparent meaning and conjectures as to a deeper one, and drawing men from a too material to a more refined faith. Accordingly, all the Fathers agree in declaring that Job prefigured Christ that as David typified the Conqueror, he typified the Victim; and that, put before us in the one special character of an undeserving sufferer, he foreshadowed the great undeserving Sufferer of all, the Sufferer upon the Cross."[1]

These principles have been well summed up by the latest writer on the subject:—"The Book of Job has for its strictly elaborated theme, a problem which, as the ample discussion of it proves, impressed most profoundly the religious life of men under the Theocracy: the question, namely, how the sufferings of the righteous are related to the Divine justice; or 'the Mystery of the Cross.'"[2]

II. The Book of Esther. Difficulties have been raised with respect to the *fitness* of this Book to form an element of the Canon of Scripture; but as to the *fact* of its recognition as Canonical no doubt can be entertained: from the first it has ever stood in the highest estimation among the Jews.[3] As to its relation to other parts of the Divine Scheme, it may be observed that from this Book only can we answer the question, Did God confine to the one or two Tribes that returned to Jerusalem the many promises which He had given to the people of Israel in general, that when they turned to Him again, they should find Him in the hour of their need?

[1] See *loc. cit.* p. 208. I do not, of course, mean to imply that this is the *only* object designed by the Holy Spirit in the composition of the Book of Job. See, for example, the very interesting (and to the present view by no means inappropriate) remarks of Mr. De Burgh, in his lately published "Donnellan Lectures," on the title "Redeemer" (גֹּאֵל, Job, xix. 25), "here first given to the Saviour * * * but applicable to redemption only in a special sense, and literally denoting an 'Avenger'" (cf. Num. xxv.; Josh. xx.) * * * "When redemption by *sacrifice* or *atonement* is spoken of, a different term is invariably employed (פדה): as in Ex. xiii. 13." * * * "'I know that my AVENGER liveth, and that He shall stand at the latter day upon the earth,' Who in that day, as 'the righteous Judge' should vindicate him [Job] from the unjust judgment of his persecutors; and also avenge him of that which is the great power of the spiritual adversary—Death, with its forerunner, Disease, and its follower, the Grave" (pp. 64–66). Nor, again, do I mean to imply that, although Scripture, at the close of the Book, in passing judgment upon the whole discussion between Job and his friends, definitely declares that he "had spoken the thing that was right," whereas his friends, who had taken the opposite line to him, had offended,—I do not mean to imply, I say, that Job's treatment of the subject is, in all respects, unexceptionable. Indeed, that his feelings hurried him away, and required correction, we learn not only from the rebuke which Jehovah administered ("The Lord answered Job out of the whirlwind, and said, * * * Shall he that contendeth with the Almighty instruct him? he that reproveth God, let him answer it"—xl. 2), but also from Job's own retractation:—"I know that Thou canst do everything, and that no thought can be withholden from Thee. * * * I uttered that I understood not; things too wonderful for me, which I knew not. * * * Wherefore I abhor myself, and repent in dust and ashes."—xlii. 2–6. That such an admission does not, however, involve anything in the least derogatory to the inspired character of the Book will at once appear from attending to the true idea of Inspiration, as laid down in the preceding pages. —Cf. *supra*, p. 41, note [1].

[2] C. F. Keil, in his continuation of Hävernick's "Einleitung," B. iii. s. 300.

[3] In proof of its *historical* character it is unnecessary to say more than that the institution of the Feast of Purim (ch. ix. 21, &c.)—founded upon the fact which forms the entire theme of the Book—can receive no other possible explanation than by admitting the reality of that fact. This is granted in substance even by De Wette (§ 198, b.). In proof of its *inspiration*, it need only be said that it was received into the Canon (see Lecture ii. p. 43, &c).

or had the Israelites who continued to dwell in the land of the Gentiles any share in those promises? The Book of Esther affords one great proof,—from which many others may be inferred,—that even in the Dispersion the children of Abraham, if they only sought their God, ever experienced His support; if not, as in other days, by manifestations of miraculous power, yet an assistance which proved that His word had not been spoken in vain.[1] "The manner in which the deliverance, at that time, ensued, affords, next to the history of Joseph, the greatest proof which the Bible contains, of how God, in the ordinary course of His Providence, with quiet, noiseless rule, connects, ordains, guides the most minute circumstances:—everything appearing to come to pass as if by chance; and everything, at the same time, contributing to His ends as certainly as by means of a manifestly miraculous dispensation."[2]

One word as to the popular objection, that the absence of the name of God from the Book of Esther deprives it of a religious character. It might be sufficient to reply, that were this conclusion just, it would never have been received into the Canon by the Jews of Palestine:—but a full answer is supplied by that portion of the narrative which describes *the cause* of the calamity which threatened the Jews—ch. iii. 1, &c. The occasion from which it arose was in the strictest sense a *religious* question: namely, the refusal to perform an act of heathen adoration, *because* the Law of the Jews did not permit it. The author points out this fact in the clearest manner: "The King's servants that were in the King's gate *bowed and reverenced Haman: for the King had so commanded concerning him.* But Mordecai bowed not. * * * And Haman said unto King Ahasuerus, There is a certain people scattered abroad and dispersed among the people in all the provinces of thy kingdom; and their laws are diverse from all people, neither keep they the King's laws."—iii. 2–8[3]. This conduct of Mordecai, in fact, is an exact parallel to what is recorded of Daniel (ch. iii. and vi.): all such instances exhibiting on the part of the different individuals, the same intense devotion to the Law, and the institutions of the Theocracy.[4]

[1] That such was the impression produced by this narrative upon the Jewish mind, is plain from the traditional statements preserved in the apocryphal additions to the Book: "Then Mardocheus said, God hath done these things. * * * My nation is this Israel which cried to God and were saved: for the Lord hath saved His people. * * * God remembered His people, and justified his inheritance."—ch. x. 4–12 (after the Greek). Is what Bishop Butler calls "The appearance of a standing miracle in the Jews remaining a distinct people in their dispersion," notwithstanding their almost uninterrupted persecution, anything else than a perpetuated repetition of the events of this history?

[2] Köppen "Die Bibel ein Werk der göttl. Weisheit," B. ii. s. 102.

[3] This fact is again confirmed by the tradition:—"Then Mardocheus thought upon all the works of the Lord, and made his prayer unto Him, saying, Thou art Lord of all things, Thou knowest, Lord, that it was neither in contempt nor pride, nor for any desire of glory, that I did not bow down to proud Aman. For I could have been content with good will for the salvation of Israel to kiss the soles of his feet. But I did this that I might not prefer the glory of man above the glory of God: neither will I worship any but Thee, O God."—ch. xiii. 8–14. Mordecai's conduct is explained on the same grounds by Josephus, Ant. XI. vi. 5.

[4] See Hävernick, "Einleitung," Th. II. Abth. i. s. 360. To the same effect also is the tone of Esther's prayer, which the tradition has also preserved, and which ends thus: "O Thou mighty God above all, hear the voice of the forlorn."—ch. xiv. 19. Cf. also the prayers preserved by Josephus. See Köppen, *loc. cit.* s. 107.

III. The Books of Chronicles.[1] Even a rapid survey of the Books of Chronicles will exhibit their object as both strictly defined, and of the most profound importance.

On the return of the Jews from their Captivity not only the means of reviving the spirit of the nation, crushed by a protracted exile, but also the renewal of the ancient sacred institutions and a fundamental reform of the abuses that had crept in, were the subjects which occupied all minds. Hence, the promises to the dynasty of David, the restoration of the Temple, and the details of public worship, were topics of absorbing interest. The contents of the Books of Chronicles exemplify this state of feeling:—The section 1 Chron. i.–ix. is devoted to genealogies; ch. x.–xxix. to the history of David; 2 Chron. i.–ix. contain the history of Solomon,—and this chiefly as regards his part as builder of the Temple; ch. x.–xxxvi. embrace the events of the Kingdom of Judah, with special reference to the worship of Jehovah. As to the historical details, it may be observed, in general, that their bearing upon other parts of the Old Testament, and their relation to the Divine Scheme, as there exhibited, do not yield in point of interest or importance to any other portion of Scripture. To prove this latter assertion I must restrict myself to a single example elucidating a principle already pointed out,[2]—viz., that God's Revelation has been, for the most part, conveyed according to the remarkable Law that "each prediction proceeds from, and attaches itself to, some definite fact in the historical present."

The twentieth chapter of the second Book of Chronicles contains an account of Jehoshaphat's victory over the Moabites, Ammonites, and other tribes. "A brilliant confirmation of this account is afforded by the prediction (without this information quite unintelligible) contained in Joel, iii. The entire form of the prophetic intuition rests upon the ground of this narrative: it is the *substratum* of the great judgment pronounced by God upon the enemies of the Theocracy. In the valley of Jehoshaphat the heathen are gathered to be judged (Joel, iii. 2). As in that war, so here also Jehovah leads His heroes ('Thither cause Thy mighty ones to come down, O Lord,'—ver. 11). Hosts upon hosts have assembled (ver. 14.—המנים המנים; cf. 2 Chron. xx. 2, 15—המון רב). It is not now "the valley of blessing" (עמק ברכה—2 Chron. xx. 26), but "the valley of decision" (עמק החרוץ—Joel, iii. 14). A time still more happy, and incomparably more glorious than that under Jehoshaphat, (2 Chron. xx. 27, &c.) follows the victory of the Lord (Joel, iii. 18, &c.)[3]"

To return to the genealogies. The account of the genealogy of the

[1] See Hävernick, "Einleitung," Th. II. Abth. i. s. 174 ff. Dr. Moses Stuart—having enumerated, *without annexing any refutation*, most of the strong points which De Wette and others conceive that they have established against the inspiration of these books,—observes: "The devout and reverential reader of the Old Testament has, it must be confessed, some difficulties of a serious nature to encounter in regard to such things in the Chronicles as have been pointed out. The tyro in matters of sacred criticism must certainly feel that he has a formidable task before him; specially if he adopts the theory of plenary *verbal* inspiration."—*On the O. T. Canon*, p. 142. On the consideration of so extensive a subject I cannot enter here; but would refer to Hävernick's admirable criticism, which, I should observe, Dr. Stuart states (p. 146) that he has not seen.

[2] Lecture iv. p. 147, &c.

[3] Hävernick, *loc cit.* s. 216.

Patriarchs is followed by that of the Tribe of Judah, and of the house of David—1 Chron. ii.–iv. 23. Compared with this statement, the genealogical notices relative to Simeon, Reuben, Gad, and Manasseh (iv. 24–v. 26) are exceedingly brief; and these again are followed by the particularly copious genealogies of the Levites (vi. 1–18). The Tribe of Benjamin is mentioned at great length (vii. 6–12; viii. 1–40; ix. 35–44); but the Tribes of the Kingdom of Israel are either glanced at cursorily (as Naphtali, ch. vii. 13), or passed over in silence (as Zebulon and Dan): while, on the other hand, the sacred writer comes back once more to the families of the Levites in ch. ix. 1–34. Two important features of the case thus present themselves:—(1) We know that on the return from the Exile in Babylon all persons were excluded from the sacerdotal office who were unable to prove their Levitical descent (Ezra, ii. 61, 62; Neh. vii. 64, 65); and we learn from Josephus ("Cont. Apion.," lib. I. vii., and "Vita," §1) that this strictness was never relaxed. Josephus also tells us the motive of such precautions: to this chosen family was committed *the custody of the Sacred Books;* and the accurate preservation of the genealogies he considers "both natural and necessary," in order to secure more perfectly a deposit so precious.[1] Hence, therefore, we clearly discern the importance of this portion of the genealogical records of the Books of Chronicles. But (2) we can at once perceive how the family annals of David's line are inseparably connected with the whole scheme of Redemption. The manner in which this record is inserted (see 1 Chron. iii.) is particularly striking. "In communicating the genealogy of the Davidic family alone the author makes an exception, and continues it to his own time. Not without just grounds. In the period that followed the Exile the Messianic hopes, awakened by the subjection of the people, were again excited: the Messiah Himself, in accordance with a promise recently given, was to adorn by His Presence the Temple which had been erected anew. It must have been a matter of importance for the writer's contemporaries to find collected here the names of the still remaining descendants of the ancient reigning house; who, although little celebrated, and even otherwise unknown to us from the Books of Ezra and Nehemiah, were yet to be the ancestors of the longed-for Deliverer. He therefore continues the genealogy of the line of Solomon up to two generations after the Exile—i.e., perhaps up to his own time. Thus, ch. iii. 19, 20, the sons of Zerubbabel are named:—Meshullam, Hananiah, &c; to which are added the names of two sons of Hananiah, Pelatiah and Jesaiah, with whom the genealogy terminates—the author then proceeding to enumerate some of the posterity of David."[2]

[1] See Lecture ii. p. 68, and *infra*, Appendix F.

[2] Movers, "Kritische Untersuch," s. 29. Hävernick confirms the justice of this remark by pointing out that, in a similar period of humiliation,—"in which but the faintest traces of the Messianic idea can be pointed out," viz., the age of the Maccabees,—the idea of the permanence of the royal line of David was still vividly cherished: "David for being merciful possessed *the throne of an everlasting kingdom.*"—1 Macc. ii. 57; cf. Ecclus. xlvii. 11; and as to the future glories of Jerusalem, see Tobit, xiii. 7–18; xiv. 4–7—*καθῶς ἐλάλησαν οἱ προφῆται*;—see his "Neue kritische Untersuch. üb. das B. Daniel," s. 34.

APPENDIX C.

MODERN THEORIES OF INSPIRATION.

(LECTURE I.—PAGE 34.)

ANY account of the theories of Inspiration which have been put forward in modern times naturally commences with the period of the Reformation. In the general religious commotion of that epoch, it could scarcely have been expected that the heat of party controversy should not have prompted men of the most opposite views to hazard opinions respecting the authority of Scripture, which in a cooler frame of mind they would have wholly disavowed. And, accordingly, we find both Protestants and adherents of the Church of Rome equally obnoxious to such a charge. In proof of this assertion one can appeal to the writings of Luther and of Erasmus.

I. The opinions of Luther with respect to Scripture,—the Divine character of which, it is, perhaps, needless to remark, he resolutely and consistently maintained,—had relation to two distinct subjects: the canonical authority of certain portions of the Bible, and the nature of Inspiration in general. It has been already observed that these two questions, although continually confounded, are wholly distinct; and attention has been drawn to the fact—exhibited by every page of his writings—that Luther's rejection of particular Books arose, not from his refusing to acknowledge the Divine origin and character of the Bible, but from his venturing to lay down a certain standard by which to test the claim of *any* composition to have proceeded from God. The natural result of such a procedure on his part—and the same must necessarily happen in every similar case—was the rejection of those writings which failed, in his estimation, to satisfy the criterion by which he assumed that they must be judged.[1]

"These views of Luther," writes H. W. J. Thiersch, "of which the subordinate position occupied in our German editions of the Bible by the Epistle of the Hebrews, the Epistles of James and Jude, together with the Apocalypse, is a permanent memorial,—were either upheld for a period by his successors, the orthodox Lutherans (although in a milder form), or, at least, were judged very leniently."[2]

[1] See *supra*, Lect. i. p. 47, and Lect. ii. p. 79. The criterion which Luther proposed will be seen from the following extract from his Preface to the Epistles of S. James and S. Jude: "Das Amt eines rechten Apostels ist, dass er von Christi Leiden, und Auferstehung, und Amt predige, und lege desselbigen Glaubens Grund, wie er selbst saget, Joh. xv. 27: 'Ihr werdet von mir zeugen.' Und darinne stimmen alle rechtschaffene heilige Bücher überein, dass sie allesammt Christum predigen und treiben. *Auch ist das der rechte Prüfestein aller Bücher zu tadeln, wenn man siehet,* OB SIE CHRISTUM TREIBEN ODER NICHT. * * * Was Christum nicht lehret, das ist noch nicht Apostolisch, wenne gleich Sanct Petrus oder St. Paulus lehrete. Wiederum, was Christum prediget, das wäre Apostolisch wenns gleich Judas, Hannas, Pilatus, und Herodes thät."—*Werke* (Walch's Aufg., B. xiv. s. 149).

[2] "Versuch zur Herstell," s. 17. Of the evil consequences of Luther's rash decisions on this subject, every one who has looked into the writings of neologists, of whatever school, must be painfully aware. His expressions are invariably brought

With respect to the other subject touched upon by Luther—viz., the *nature* of Inspiration itself,—the following passage from the "Elementa Theologiæ Dogmaticæ" of the learned Mosheim gives a succinct and just account:—

"Duæ sunt sententiæ de vocabulo Sacræ Scripturæ. Multi, in primis doctores ecclesiæ nostræ, hoc vocabulum sensu latissimo sumunt, et per id intelligunt omne quod scriptum est, ut non modo veritates, sed etiam formam Spiritui S. tribuant. Duo nempe sunt in Sacra Scriptura: materia, et forma. Materia sunt ipsæ veritates; forma est stilus, vocabula, phrases, et constructiones, &c. At sunt tamen in ecclesia nostra nonnulli qui secus sentiunt, et docent Spiritum S. tantum materiam Sacræ Scripturæ inspirasse, sed non formam. Esto propositio: Fides sola justificat; hæc veritas a Spiritu S. proficiscitur, et forma ejus a sancto Paulo. Hujus sententiæ in nostra ecclesia auctor est ipse Lutherus, qui in nonnullis locis scriptorum suorum clare fatetur Spiritum S. modo materiam inspirasse. Præcipue Theologi Sæc. xvi. hanc sententiam habuere. Sed hæc sententia a Pontificiis in defensionem propositionum suarum trahebatur. Hanc enim Pontificii conclusionem fecerunt:—Si Spiritus S. materiam tantum inspiravit, fieri potuit ut Prophetæ et Apostoli in enunciando et scribendo erraverint, et satis luculenter propositiones et veritates a Spiritu S. inspiratas non proposuerint. Inde concludebant: necessarium ergo est, ut Scripturæ Sacræ aliud principium adjungatur. Quum ita concluderent Pontificii, Theologi nostri deserebant Lutheri sententiam, et sub fine Sæc. xvi. et sub initium Sæc. xvii. hanc sententiam assumserunt: Sacram Scripturam non modo quoad materiam, sed etiam quoad formam a Spiritu S. inspiratam esse. Hæc sententia primo in Saxonia oriebatur, et deinde per totam fere ecclesiam dilatata est. At supersunt tamen quidam Theologi, qui sententiam Lutheri dimittere nolunt."—pp. 111, 112.

The reaction to which Mosheim here refers may be exemplified by the theory of the younger Buxtorf, who went so far as to maintain the inspired authority of even the Hebrew vowel-points and accents:[1] and the strict 'mechanical' theory itself of Inspiration (cf. *supra*, p. 21, &c.), in which that reaction terminated, is accurately laid down by Carpzovius, in his "Critica Sacra Veteris Testamenti:"—

"Plura involvit Inspiratio momenta. (1) Nihil hic tribuendum esse hominibus præter operam solum ministerialem, qua illapsum divinum percipientes, prompte ac alacriter mentem manumque Deo commodarent, qui

forward, however unjustly, as a justification of any amount of scepticism or disrespect to which such writers think fit to subject Holy Scripture. As examples I may refer to the complacency with which Bretschneider ("Handb. der Dogmatik," B. i. s. 342) alludes to Luther's opinions; as well as to the remark of Mr. Greg ("The Creed of Christendom"): "Luther, in the Preface to his translation, inserted a protest against the inspiration of the Apocalypse, which protest he solemnly charged every one to prefix who chose to publish the translation. In this protest one of his chief grounds for the rejection is the suspicious fact that this writer alone blazons forth his own inspiration," p. 19.

[1] "Si Punctatio, et Accentuatio Biblica non profecta esset a Viris Propheticis, et extraordinariis Spiritus S. instructis donis; sed a sapientibus vulgaribus, quales seu his nostris temporibus, seu superioribus sæculis, post Prophetarum tempora, imo post absolutum et obsignatum Talmud, fuerunt; nullo modo ita παμψήφει et ἀναντιῤῥήτως a gente Judaica esset acceptata," &c.—*Tract. de Punct. Vocal.*, Pars II. c. v. p. 335.

utramque pro libitu suo ageret, moveret, ac dirigeret. (2) Ad unum solumque Deum quicquid est Scripturæ S., tanquam ad causam principem, referri debere, ita quidem, ut non modo mysteria scripta, inde divina, sed ipsa quoque γραφή (tam scribendi actio transiens, quam ejus effectus, voces, apices, ac literæ) θεόπνευστος esset, ac ἱερὰ γράμματα prodirent. (3) Idque propter immediatum et singularissimum cum amanuensibus, ad scribendi ministerium excitatis, concursum, quo eorum et voluntatem impulit ut prompte scriberent, et mentem illuminavit, ac *suggestione rerum vocumque consignandarum* replevit, ut intelligenter scriberent, et manum direxit, ut infallibiliter scriberent, neque tamen plus conferrent ad Scripturam, quam calamus velocis scribæ (Ps. xlv. 1)."—Pars I. p. 43.

II. The opinions of Erasmus may be inferred from an Epistle written to him by Eckius, dated "Ingolstadt, 2 Feb. A.D. 1518 :"—"Primo autem omnium, ut hinc exordiar, plures moleste ferunt, te in Annotationibus Matthæi capite secundo sic scripsisse : 'Sive quod ipsi Evangelistæ testimonia hujusmodi non e libris deprompserint : sed memoriæ fidentes, ita ut fit, lapsi sint.' Istis enim verbis innuere videris, Evangelistas more humano scripsisse : et quod memoriæ confisi hæc scripserint, quod libros videre neglexerint, quod ita, hoc est, ob eam causam lapsi sint. Audi, mi Erasme, arbitrarisne Christianum patienter laturum, Evangelistas in Evangeliis lapsos? Si hic vacillat Sacræ Scripturæ auctoritas, quæ pars alia sine suspicione erroris erit? ut pulcherrimo argumento A. Augustinus colligit."—(*ap. Erasmi opp.*, Epist. 303, Lugd. Bat. 1703, t. iii. p. 296.)

These views of Erasmus were chiefly assailed by the church of Spain; and the excitement which they occasioned he himself describes in his address, "Candido Lectori," at the close of the writing entitled, Desid. Erasmi Apologia adv. articulos aliquot per Monachos quosdam in Hispaniis exhibitos" (Opp. t. ix. p. 1015). "Quid hic commemorem quos tumultus excitarint primum in aula Cæsaris, deinde Salamanticæ ; quoties palam ac publice vociferati sint hæreticum et Luthero deteriorem Erasmum?"—(p. 1092). As an example of the objections of the Spanish Monks, may be taken the following, as stated under the heading, "Contra auctoritatem Sacræ Scripturæ, Evangelistarum, et Apostolorum :"—"Objectio 45. In annotationibus Matthæi cap. ii. in editione 3tia manifeste labitur Erasmus, si quis Christiana pietate rem consideret, non contentus verborum implicamentis. Nam et Evangelistas errasse, lapsosque esse memoria contendit. Asserit item ex uno errore in Sacris Literis non derogari totius Scripturæ auctoritati."—(*Ibid.* p. 1070.) Erasmus replied that he had not himself maintained this opinion, but had proposed it "adversus morosos et impios calumniatores," in order to defend the authority of Scripture; so that, even had its writers erred in unimportant matters, the whole structure might not be thereby overturned. Explanations of this nature, he adds, had been introduced by him "per fictionem ;" and he obviously submits to the objections urged against him, when he says, "Responsio 45 :"—"Et tamen quod ad meum sensum attinet, magis eorum sententiæ faveo qui credunt Apostolos in Scripturis canonicis duntaxat, nec sententia nec verbo lapsos fuisse." The objectionable passages, too, appear to have been erased from subsequent editions of his Commentary.

The next appearance of any controversy upon this question within the

Church of Rome was during the Jansenist dispute. In 1586 the Jesuits, Leonard Less, and John Hamel, in their public lectures in the University of Louvain, on "Scripture, Grace, and Predestination," advanced, among others, the following propositions:—(1) "Ut aliquid sit Scriptura Sacra, non est necessarium singula ejus verba inspirata esse a Spiritu S." (2) "Non est necessarium ut singulæ veritates et sententiæ sint immediate a Spiritu S. ipsi scriptori inspiratæ." (3) "Liber aliquis (qualis forte est secundus Machabæorum) humana industria, sine assistentia Spiritus S. scriptus, si Spiritus S. postea testetur nihil ibi esse falsum, efficitur Scriptura sacra." These propositions were at once condemned. The Archbishops of Cambray and Mechlin submitted them to the University of Douai; and the learned Estius[1] having drawn up a severe criticism, in the name of the Theological Faculty, the Propositions were publicly censured by both Universities[2] (A. D. 1588). The third "Proposition" was specially condemned:—the "Censura" of Douai[3] declaring, "Multo magis hæc quam duæ superiores improbanda est assertio, tanquam manifesti erroris periculum continens." This "Censura" also justly argues that, on such a principle, *any* writing of which the truth has been proved (e. g. the Athanasian Creed, or a book of Livy or Thucydides of which the facts are admitted), might be classed with Scripture: adding, "Non enim ideo inspiratum aliquid divinitus est, quia *postea* sit approbatum, sed ideo est approbatum quia *fuerat* divinitus inspiratum." The "Censura" of Louvain compares the doctrine maintained in the objectionable propositions[4] to the heresy of the Anomœans (see *supra*, Lecture ii. p. 87).

[1] The opinions of Estius as to Inspiration may be estimated from the following remarks on 2 Tim. iii. 16; where, having quoted the Vulgate, he states that the passage may be more clearly understood from the Greek:—

"'Omnis Scriptura divinitus inspirata, et utilis:'—Subaudi *est.* Itaque duo affirmantur:—omnem Scripturam esse divinitus inspiratam; et, eandam esse utilem ad ea quæ sequuntur. *Scripturam* intelligit sacram, de qua dixerat: *Sacras literas nosti.* Nam Scripturæ nomine passim in Bibliis Sacra Scriptura, per antonomasiam significatur: ut Matt. xxii. 29, John, v. 39, et x. 35. Recte igitur et verissime, ex hoc loco statuitur omnem Scripturam sacram et canonicam Spiritu Sancto dictante esse conscriptam; ita nimirum ut non solum sententiæ, sed et verba singula, et verborum ordo, ac tota dispositio sit a Deo, tanquam per Semetipsum loquente, aut scribente. Hoc enim est 'Scripturam esse Divinitus inspiratam.'"—*Comm. in D. Pauli Epist.*

[2] See Schröckh, "Kirchen-Geschichte seit der Reformation," B. iv. s. 293.

[3] "Censuræ Facultatum Sacræ Theologiæ Lovaniensis ac Duacensis, super quibusdam articulis de Sacra Scriptura, Gratia, et Prædestinatione, A. D. 1586. Lovanii scripto traditis."—Paris, 1641.

[4] Rudelbach ("Die Lehre von der Inspir.," Zeitschr. 1840, H. ii. s. 40) makes the judicious remark that the view advanced in Proposition (3) is plainly founded upon an incapacity to regard the Word of God *as one organized whole.* He also draws attention to an article in Bayle's "Dictionary" on Father Adam, a Jesuit, who in 1650 published a sermon against the Jansenists, in which, according to Bayle, he spoke very freely of the Inspiration of both the Old and the New Testament. The Jansenists replied in a pamphlet entitled "Defense de S. Augustin contre le Père Adam," in which they appealed to the "Censuræ" of Louvain and Douai in the case of Less and Hamel. Rudelbach states that he has been unable to see this pamphlet. I have myself been equally unsuccessful; a circumstance not unusual in any matter connected with the Jansenist controversy.

In Doddridge's "Dissertation on the Inspiration of the New Testament," a curious opinion is advanced, in some respects analogous to the Jesuits' Proposition (3): "Should God miraculously assure me that any particular writing contained nothing but the truth; and should He, at the same time, tell me it had been drawn up with-

The Jesuits having appealed to the Sorbonne, and to the Universities of Treves and Mayence, forwarded a copy of the "Propositions" to their General at Rome. The dispute was, however, terminated by an "Apostolical Breve," dated April 15, A.D. 1588, in which Pope Sixtus V. enjoined silence on all parties until the affair should be decided by the Holy See. In this state it still remains.

In Calmet's "Dissertation sur l'Inspiration des Livres Sacres"[1] mention is made of a treatise by Claude Frassen, a Franciscan monk (A. D. 1662), in which three kinds of Inspiration are distinguished: "antecedent," "concomitant," "consequent"—the last being identical with the Jesuit's third Proposition already referred to.

The following opinion was maintained by Henry Holden, a Doctor of the Theological Faculty of Paris (A. D. 1650):—

"Auxilium speciale, divinitus præstitum authori cujuslibet scripti quod pro verbo Dei recipit Ecclesia, ad ea solummodo se porrigit quæ vel sint pure doctrinalia, vel proximum aliquem aut necessarium habeant ad doctrinalia respectum. In iis vero quæ non sunt de instituto scriptoris, vel ad alia referuntur, eo tantum subsidio Deum illi adfuisse judicamus, quod piisimis cæteris authoribus commune sit."—*Divinæ Fidei Anal.*, lib. i. c. v. P. R. Simon, having quoted this passage, and having stated that Holden's work had been approved by the Chancellor of the University of Paris, adds:—"Je me contente d'exposer l' opinion de ce Docteur de la Faculté de Theologie de Paris sans oser la combattre, la voyant autorisée par de si sages Maitres. Je n' ose pourtant pas l'appuyer dans toute son étendue. *Il eût été bon qu'il eûs donné quelques exemples* de ce qu' il entend par les matieres qui ne sont point purement de doctrine, ou qui n'y ont point une entiere relation."—"*Hist. Critique du texte du N. T.*," ch. xxiv. p. 295.

The view maintained, at present, in the Church of Rome, may be gathered from Perrone, the latest writer of authority in that Communion: "Jure merito Concilium Tridentinum docet unum Deum esse librorum canonicorum utriusque Testamenti auctorem, seu eos esse libros sacros, utpote Spiritu S. afflante, *saltem quoad res et sententias*, conscriptos. * * * Diximus *saltem quoad res et sententias*, quia cum noluerit Ecclesia definire, seu dirimere quæstionem inter scholasticos agitatam, utrum præterea Deus verba ipsa dictaverit, nexumque verborum et periodorum; ideo ne controversiam domesticam cum Ecclesiæ doctrina temere permisceremus, coarctavimus propositionis sensum ad rei substantiam, sine qua vera Inspiratio Divina neque est, neque intelligi quidem potest."[2]

out any miraculous assistance at all,—though I could not then call it inspired, I should be as much obliged to receive and submit to it, on its being thus attested by God, as if every single word had been immediately dictated by Him."—*Works*, vol. v. p. 346, ed. 1804.

[1] "Commentaire sur la Bible," t. viii. p. 741.

[2] "Prælectiones Theologicæ," vol. ii. pars ii. p. 71. The opinion of Maldonatus is hardly reconcilable with such a conclusion:—"Marcus iisdem quibus Matthæus [c. xxvi. 28] verbis scribit, 'Hic est Sanguis Meus Novi Test.;' Lucas vero 'Hic est calix Novum Test. in Meo Sanguine.' Paulus autem 'Hic calix N. T. est in Meo Sanguine. * * * *Nego Christum hæc verba dixisse.* Cum enim Matthæus, qui aderat, et Marcus, qui ex Matthæo didicerat, scribant Christum his verbis Sanguinem Suum tradidisse: 'Hic est Sanguis Meus, N T.' * * * æquum est credere Mat-

Meanwhile a systematized opposition to the inspiration of Scripture was growing up in another quarter; suggested by the writings of an individual through whom, as will presently be seen, the source of every hue and shade of modern scepticism on this question may be ultimately traced. Quinet has truly said: "L'homme qui de nos jours a fait faire le plus grand pas à l'Allemagne, ce n'est ni Kant, ni Lessing, ni le grand Frédéric; c'est Benedict Spinosa." Benedict (or Baruch) Spinoza was born in 1632, and died in 1677. He was the first, observes Töllner, "who made a tolerably complete collection of the objections against Inspiration. The result was curious. Some theologians gave up the cause as entirely lost; while others attempted still to maintain it, according to the usual theory."[1] The subject, thus placed upon a new footing, was soon taken up in a kindred spirit by Le Clerc, whose celebrated Letters, entitled "Sentimens de quelques Theologiens de Hollande," were first published in 1685. These Letters excited an immense sensation, especially in England;[2] but they were after all a mere reflexion of the ideas of Spinoza. As P. R. Simon truly observed: "En effet, ces Theologiens [from whom Le Clerc's work purported to have proceeded] n' ont fait autre chose pour combattre l' Inspiration de l' Ecriture Sainte, que de mettre en un plus grand jour les raisons de Spinosa, qui a outré cette matière sur de faux prejugés dont il etoit preoccupé."[3] It is unnecessary to give a particular account of Le Clerc's system. Suffice it to say, that he denied the fact of any Divine assistance in the composition of the Bible; maintaining that the ordinary powers of memory were sufficient to enable the authors of Scripture to record any communications from God which the prophets might have received, or the facts of history. His interpretation of some of the promises of Christ to His Disciples has been already quoted (Lecture vi. p. 246, note [4]); in addition to which he further asserted that S. Peter's Vision (Acts, x.), and the controversy respecting Circumcision, proved that Christ's promises that they should be guided into "all truth" were *not* fulfilled. From this period the works of Semler (A. D. 1771–1773), and the treatise of Töllner[4] (A. D. 1772), may be said to form the transition

thæi potius et Marci, quam Lucæ et Pauli, verbis Christum usum fuisse. * * * *Credendum igitur est, verbis potius Matthæi et Marci, quam Lucæ et Pauli usum esse.*"—*Comm. in Matth.* c. xxvi., ed. Mogunt. t. i. p. 314.

[1] "Die göttliche Eingebung," s. 453.

[2] A few of the works which were published in reply may be mentioned:—"A Vindication of the Divine Authority and Inspiration of the writings of the Old and New Testament. In answer to the 'Five Letters concerning the Inspiration of Scripture,'" by W. Lowth, B. D.: Oxford, 1692.—"The Inspiration of the New Testament asserted and explained in answer to some modern writers," by C. J. Lamothe: London, 1694; the occasion of which the author states (Pref. p. 3) to have been Le Clerc's "Letters," to which replies had already appeared from "M. Witsius of Holland, Mr. Lowth, a divine of Oxford, Father Simon, and Father Le Vassour."—"The Inspiration of the Old and New Testament," by Edm. Calamy, D. D.: London, 1710; who observes in his Preface: "There is more of subtilty and artifice in those Letters than in anything of that kind I ever yet met with."

[3] "Histoire Critique du Nouv. Test.," ch. xxv. p. 303. To the same effect Töllner writes: "Spinoza und Le Clerc begegnen hier einander."—*loc. cit.* s. 314.

[4] The unsatisfactory character of this work is well described by Rudelbach: "Töllner stellt uns klar die Fraction in der Zeit dar: viele schöne apologetische Reminiscenzen; daneben aber ein wüstes Streben, alle Gewissheit bis auf einen gewissen Grad zu verflüchtigen, um nachher gerade so viel in seine Construction

to the systems of more modern times;—times in which, as De Maistre has remarked with too great truth: "Un savant, en commentant Anacréon ou Catulle, trouvera l' occasion *naturelle* d' attaquer Moïse."

But I have said that the writings of Spinoza point out the source to which the several varieties of modern errors respecting Inspiration may be traced. Spinoza, in a word, by bringing the opinions of his nation under the notice of subsequent writers, has introduced into Christian theology the speculations of the mediæval Jews, and more particularly the philosophy of Maimonides, the master spirit of his race during the Christian era.[1] To such speculations are to be referred, I conceive, each of the three classes of opinions under which the various theories of Inspiration that exaggerate the *human* element of Scripture, may, speaking generally, be arranged:[2]

I. The two leading representatives of the views held by the first class of writers—those, viz., "Who have changed the formula 'The Bible *is* the Word of God,' into 'The Bible *contains* the Word of God,'"—are, Le Clerc (whose connexion with Maimonides through Spinoza has been already traced), and Grotius, who may be regarded as the representative of the Arminian school. Grotius openly avows the source of his opinions:—

"Vere dixi non omnes libros qui sunt in Hebræo Canone dictatos a Spiritu Sancto. Scriptos esse cum pio animi motu, non nego: et hoc est quod judicavit Synagoga Magna, cujus judicio in hac re stant Hebræi. Sed a Spiritu Sancto dictari historias nihil fuit opus: satis fuit scriptorem memoria valere circa res spectatas, aut diligentia in describendis Veterum commentariis. Vox quoque Spiritus Sancti ambigua est: nam aut significat, quomodo ego accepi, afflatum Divinum, qualem habuere tum Prophetæ ordinarii, *tum interdum David et Daniel;* aut significat pium motum, sive facultatem impellentem ad loquendum salutaria vivendi præcepta, vel *res politicas et civiles*, quomodo vocem Spiritus Sancti *interpretatur Maimonides* ubi de scriptis illis aut historicis, aut moralibus agit. Si Lucas, Divino afflatu dictante, sua scripsisset, inde potius sibi sumsisset auctoritatem, ut Prophetæ faciunt, quam a testibus quorum fidem est secutus. Sic in iis quæ Paulum agentem vidit scribendis, nullo ipsi dictante afflatu opus. Quid ergo est, cur Lucæ libri sint Canonici? Quia pie ac fideliter scriptos, et de rebus momenti ad salutem maximi, Ecclesia primorum temporum judicavit."—*Votum pro pace Ecclesiastica*, Opera, ed. 1679, t. iii. p. 672.

The parentage, therefore, of this class of opinions is clear. Grotius, however, received his principles *directly* from the Jewish Doctors.

II. The origin of the second class, comprising those hypotheses "which assume various *Degrees* of Inspiration," is no less obvious. I have already alluded (Lecture ii. p. 62, note [1]) to the three "Degrees of Inspiration"

aufzunehmen, als ihm wahrscheinlich dünkte; als eine zweite Penelope zerstört er das Tagsgewebe um Nachtzeit wieder, nur dass er keinen heimkehrenden Herrn erwartet."—*loc. cit.* s. 61.

[1] Baumgarten Crusius ("Bibl. Theol." s. 220) having alluded to the notion of the "intellectus agens" put forward by Maimonides, truly says: "Maimonides ist in diesem Artikel, *und überhaupt*, die Quelle des Spinoza."

[2] See Lecture i. p. 34, &c. It is, of course, to be understood that any one of these three classes may be held in combination with either or both of the others.

ascribed by the Jewish Doctors to the writers of the Old Testament; but some additional remarks on the subject are necessary here.

The Old Testament, from a period long anterior to the birth of Christ, has been divided into three parts, the Kethubim or Hagiographa (including the Psalms, Proverbs, Job, the Song of Solomon, Ruth, Lamentations, Ecclesiastes, Esther, Daniel, Ezra, Nehemiah, and the Chronicles); the Law (including the five Books of Moses); and the Prophets (including the remaining books). This division our Lord Himself recognised, when He spoke of "The Law of Moses, the Prophets, and the Psalms."—S. Luke, xxiv. 44. To explain this fact, of which no account altogether satisfactory has ever been assigned,[1] the Jews have invented the notion of *three* Degrees of Inspiration; of which hypothesis Hävernick truly says: "This asserted diversity of Inspiration appears, even its definitions, to be so vague and so inexact, that one can hardly form any regular conception of it. Of Biblical grounds it is wholly deficient:—nay, the New Testament rather decides quite against it, from the manner in which it speaks of David, Daniel," &c. [cf. e. g. Lecture vi. p. 263, note [2].]—*Enleitung*, Th. I. Abth. i. s. 67.[2]

[1] Hengstenberg, who accepts and defends the Jewish tradition that this "threefold division rests upon the different relations in which the authors of the Sacred Books stood to God," attempts to explain, as follows, the obvious difficulty of such a position. He is speaking of the place of Daniel among the Hagiographa: "The name נביא was the *official* title of the Prophets [see *supra*, Lecture iv. p. 158, and *infra*, Appendix J]; and the more ancient and more general meaning (Gen. xx. 7) received, in the Theocracy, a closer limitation, and appears only once in poetry (Psalm cv. 15), and this, too, applied to those who lived before the age of Theocratic Prophecy. On the supposition that all the authors of Scripture could be called נביאים, it remains inexplicable why the Books of Ruth and Ezra, which were generally received, and which were extant at the time of the second collection, were not admitted into it. This *fact* proves, that in separating the historical books into two divisions, they were guided by definite reasons. It remains inexplicable why they parted the Lamentations of Jeremiah from his Predictions, and took them into the third collection. The reason of which can be nothing else than the opinion that the Divine influence which the author received in this Book—bearing as it does a character predominantly subjective—was not the same as in his Predictions. * * * In determining the second division the collectors could not possibly receive Daniel into it. He had not (like the other prophets in Palestine, and Ezekiel in the Exile) labored among his own people *as a Prophet*."—*Die Authentie des Daniels*, s. 25 ff. Hävernick truly observes with respect to this attempt to solve the problem: "Einen neuen Erklärungsversuch macht Dr. Hengstenberg; doch, wie es scheint, auch nicht genügend."—*Comm. üb das B. Daniel*, Einleit. s. xl.

[2] Hävernick observes, in his introduction to the Book of Daniel (s. xxxix.):—"The motives which floated before the collectors of the Canon, in their threefold division of it, are, for the most part, altogether unknown to us; and the knowledge of the reasons which influenced them seems to have been lost at a very early period. Josephus is altogether silent on the subject. Jerome notes the position of our Book [Daniel] as being something remarkable, but can give no explanation of it. Theodoret makes it a matter of reproach to the Jews, that they have placed Daniel in this [third] division." And yet, in his "Einleitung," he accepts, with some modifications, the explanation proposed by Hengstenberg,—observing, however:—"There is *no distinction between the Inspiration of the Prophets, and the writers of the Hagiographa;* any distinction that exists consists merely in the peculiar Theocratic position of the authors" (s. 65). Thus it is easy to understand why the Books of Moses formed by themselves a distinct class. The Books composed by those who were *officially* Prophets were placed in a second division: the third consisting of "the remaining' Books,—as they are called in the Prologue to the Book of Ecclesiasticus (τοῦ νόμου

Let us see, however, what Maimonides says on this subject. This earned Rabbi was born at Corduba in Spain, A.D. 1131. He was the pupil, Brucker tells us ("Hist. Phil." vol. ii. p. 857), according to L. Africanus, of Ibnu Thophail, Ibnu Saig, and Averroes, the Arabians. Hence his knowledge of the writings of Aristotle, of whom Averroes was the ardent disciple; and hence also the justice of Hävernick's remark as to the source of his notion respecting the "degrees" of Inspiration (See Lecture ii. p. 62, note[1]). The Jews say of him, "A Mose ad Mosen, non surrexit sicut Moses." In accordance with the general opinion of his nation, he held that a supereminent degree of Inspiration must be ascribed to Moses, who is to be distinguished from all other prophets by four peculiar characteristics:—

(1) "All the other prophets saw the prophecy in a dream or in a vision; but our Rabbi Moses saw it whilst he was awake." (2) "To all the other prophets it was revealed through the medium of an angel, and therefore they saw that which they saw in an allegory or enigma, but to Moses it is said, 'With him I will speak mouth to mouth' (פה אל־פה, Num. xii. 8); and 'face to face'" (פנים אל־פנים, Ex. xxxiii. 11).[1] (3) "All the other prophets were terrified, but with Moses it was not so; and this is what the Scripture says: 'As a man speaketh unto his friend'" (Ex. xxxiii. 11). (4) "All the other prophets could not prophesy at any time that they wished: but with Moses it was not so; but at any time when he wished for it, the Holy Spirit came upon him; so that it was not necessary for him to prepare his mind, for he was always ready for it, like the ministering angels" (מלאכי השרת).—*Yad Hachazakah*, c. vii. (Bernard's transl. p. 116.) With special reference to this superiority of Moses, Maimonides proceeds in his other great work, the "Moreh Nebochim," to lay down *eleven* distinct "Degrees of Prophecy," from which Abarbanel has deduced the modern Jewish notion as to the *three* "Degrees of Inspiration" under which the Old Testament was written:[2]—

καὶ τῶν προφητῶν, καὶ τῶν ἄλλων,—or, ὁ Νόμος, καὶ αἱ προφητεῖαι, καὶ τὰ λοίπα τῶν βιβλίων). Daniel was placed in this last class, merely because he does not appear to have been a נביא, but simply a חוזה (see Appendix J). The Book of Lamentations Hävernick admits to present an exception to this rule: but he thinks that, from its character as a collection of poetical dirges, it was placed among the Hagiographa, just as Psalm xc., which was written by Moses, was also included in the third division.

[1] I have suggested (*supra*, Lecture iii. p. 128) what appears to be the true meaning of the remarkable prerogatives ascribed to Moses in these passages; and have also drawn attention (Lecture i. p. 41) to the *unimportance* of such prerogatives, as bearing upon the Inspiration of Scripture.

[2] The younger Buxtorf has translated "Is. Abarbenelis [nat. A. D. 1437] aliquot Dissertationes" (Basil. 1662); of which the eighth (p. 496), taken from the preface to his Commentary on Joshua, commences thus: "Quæritur quare veteres Libros sacros diviserint in Legem, Prophetas, et Hagiographa, et quæ sit harum trium appellationum ratio?" One only of our wise men, says Abarbanel, has alluded to this question, Ephodeus, who attempts to explain it from the analogy of the three divisions of the Sanctuary; but this does not meet the difficulty. "Mihi ergo videtur sapientes nostros voluisse nominibus istis monere de *perfectione* singularum harum partium, et *gradu supremo quo unaquæque alteram superat.*" The superiority of the Thorah consists in its being the Law of God. As to the other two divisions, in the one case the authors of the books were *prophets;* while the authors of the Hagiographa were not *prophets*,—" sed 'Loquentes per Spiritum Sanctum,' unde et illorum libri non vocan-

I. "Cum quis auxilio Divino ita instructus est et præditus ut eo moveatur et animetur, ad magnum et heroicum aliquod facinus perpetrandum. Hoc donum vocatur *Spiritus Domini.* Et hic est gradus Judicum Israelis omnium." II. "Cum homo in se sentit rem vel facultatem quampiam exoriri et super se quiescere, quæ eum impellit ad loquendum vel de scientiis et artibus, vel Psalmos et Hymnos. Et hic est de quo dicitur, quod loquatur *per Spiritum Sanctum.* Hac specie Spiritus Sancti instinctus, Psalmos suos scripsit David; Proverbia, Ecclesiasten, et Cant. Canticorum, Salomon. Hoc afflatu scripti sunt Danielis, Jobi, et Chronicorum Libri, et reliqua Hagiographa, unde etiam Kethubim appellantur, quia scripta sunt per Spiritum Sanctum. De libello Esther palam dicunt sapientes nostri: 'Libellus Esther per Spiritum Sanctum dictatus est'" [" Primus et secundus sunt gradus *ad Prophetiam*, unde ii, qui ad duos illos gradus pervenerunt, non numerantur inter prophetas illos, de quibus egimus hactenus" (p. 315).] III. "Qui est primus Prophetiæ veræ, est eorum qui dicunt: 'Et fuit verbum Domini ad me.'" IV. "Cum Propheta verbum aliquod clare et distincte audit in somnio Prophetiæ, sed non videt loquentem illud." V. "Quando Vir aliquis in somnio loquitur cum propheta." VI. "Quando Angelus cum ipso loquitur in somnio." VII. "Cum Propheta existimat Deum secum loqui in somnio." VIII. "Cum offertur ipsi Visio in Visione prophetica, et cum Parabolas videt." IX. "Quando audit verba in Visione." X. "Quando videt Virum secum loquentem in Visione." XI. "Quando videt Angelum loquentem secum in Visione."—Pars ii. cap. 45 (Buxtorf's transl. p. 316, &c.).

By virtue of the principle, "Omnis sermo qui *auditur*, quocunque etiam modo id fiat, in *Somnio* auditur," Maimonides reduces these degrees to *eight* ("Nam si falsum sit, in *Visione* audiri sermonem, concident *tres ultimi gradus.*"—*Ibid.* p. 321.

To this source, therefore, may at once be traced the modern theory of various "degrees" of Inspiration. An example of such a theory has been given in Lecture i. p. 34, note[3]; where the obvious objection to which the entire view is obnoxious has also been stated,—not to mention the fact that the opinion is, at the most, a mere hypothesis, without the slightest warrant in Scripture. Nor are the writers who maintain the theory even agreed as to *the number* of these "degrees." Thus Doddridge, in his "Dissertation on Inspiration" (Works, vol. v. p. 346)—from whom Dr. Dick ("Lectures on Theology," vol i. p. 195, &c.) does not materially differ—*omits*,[1] from the *four* "degrees" usually defined as I have given them in the place cited, the "degree" denominated "the Inspiration of Direction" On the other hand, Dr. Henderson, in his "Lectures on Inspiration," (p. 364, &c.) lays down *five* "degrees:" viz. (1) A Divine *Excitement*; (2) An *Invigoration* (usually called *Elevation*); (3) *Superintendence*; (4) *Guidance*; (5) Direct *Revelation*. Among the advocates

tur prophetiæ." The books, written by those "qui locuti sunt per Spiritum Sanctum, vocarunt, כתובים, *scripta, Hagiographa* * * * *a gradu quem habuerunt ratione influentiæ Divinæ in illis;* hoc est, quia gradus scriptorum illorum non fuit quod viderint formas propheticas, nec quod audiverint verba Dei Vivi, sed quod fuerint in gradu Spiritus Sancti:"—for an account of which influence he appeals to the "More Nebochim" of Maimonides, pars ii. cap. 45.

[1] Doddridge (*loc. cit.* p. 347, note), expressly refers to the authority of Maimonides, and this may account for his reducing the number of "degrees" to three.

of this theory is to be reckoned Professor J. T. Beck of Basle, a writer to whose treatise, entitled "Einleitung in das System der christl. Lehre; oder propädeutische Entwicklung der christl. Lehr-Wissenschaft," I have already acknowledged my many obligations. According to this view the Old and New Testaments each exhibit *three* 'degrees' of Inspiration. The 'degrees of Theopneustia' in the New Testament are as follows:—(1) "The *pisteo-dynamical:* or the concentration of the universal spirit of Christian faith in particular organs, distinguished by the power of faith, for the authentic reproduction of doctrine and history already revealed." To this 'degree' belong the Gospels of S. Mark and S. Luke, and the Acts; and with this influence the Deacons and some others, e. g. S. Barnabas, were endowed:—cf. Acts, vi.–viii.; xi. 22–26; 1 Tim. iii. 9. (2) "The *charismatical:* or the distribution of the miraculous power of the Spirit in extraordinary gifts, extending to ecstasy." This 'degree' distributed over the first community of believers (Rom. xii. 5 ff; 1 Cor. xii. 4, 7), unites itself to the first 'degree of Theopneustia' "according to its more spontaneous side, γνῶσις and σοφία; while its more receptive side, ἀποκάλυψις and προφητεία, joins on to the third degree of Theopneustia:" —(3) "*The apocalyptic,*" which was combined with the two former, in the persons of the Apostles:—men called and set apart for the work, in order to transmit to all the world, by means of written documents, the announcement of the mystery of God:—cf. Rom. i. 1; Eph. iii. 2–10; Col. i. 25–29. The "degrees of Theopneustia" in the Old Testament are:—(1) "Where, in order to present with fidelity the Revelation which had already become positive in history and doctrine, there was need of certain organs in which the general covenant-spirit was energetically concentrated." *It is difficult to point out what books belong to this 'degree;'* there are, perhaps, few in which the *second* does not enter. (2) "The Spirit of special illumination, where, by the moulding energy of the Spirit, a certain virtuosity (Virtuosität) appears developed for the further dissemination of truth revealed in doctrine and history:—such are most of the Psalms." Here also there is a transition to the third 'degree,' (3) which "combines and perfects both the former 'degrees' in the spirit of the progressive Revelation." Thus the prophets wrote of history, and of doctrine, whether relating to the past, the present, or the future; and the Pentateuch "appears as a combination of the entire spiritual activity of the Old Testament."—§ 90–96, s. 235 ff.

III. We now come to the third class of modern theories of Inspiration, of which Schleiermacher may be taken to be the representative, and the opinions of whose school have been discussed, Lecture iii. p. 100, &c.; Lecture v. p. 219; Lecture vi. p. 253; and Lecture vii. p. 326, &c. According to this school, "The idea of Inspiration is of quite subordinate importance in Christianity;" the statements of the sacred writers being in fact nothing more than the results of the *natural* faculties of the human mind, exercised in reflecting upon the revelation exhibited in the Person of Christ (see Lecture vi. p. 253, note [2]). The connexion of this system with Judaism is remarkable.

There are three opinions, writes Maimonides, as to Prophecy. "1ma. Sententia est vulgi et imperitæ multitudinis quod Deus Opt. Max. aliquem ex hominibus, qui ipsi placuerit, eligat eumque mittat, nulla habita ratione, an sit sapiens et eruditus, an vero indoctus et imperitus, senex an juvenis! Tantum hoc requirunt, ut sit vir probus, bonus, honestus."

"2da. Sententia est sententia Philosophorum, qui dicunt: Prophetiam esse perfectionem quandam *in natura hominis.* Hanc autem perfectionem, dicunt, neminem adipisci, nisi studio, industria, et diligentia, quæ id quod in potentia speciei inest, in actum educat; nisi impediatur vel ab impedimento aliquo interno proveniente a temperamento hominis. * * * Juxta hanc opinionem fieri non potest, si quis idoneus sit ad Prophetiam, et prout decet se ad illam præparaverit, *ut actu ipso non prophetet.*"

"3tia. Sententia est Legis nostræ. Fundamentum enim Legis nostræ *plane cum sententia Philosophorum convenit*, unicâ tantum re excepta, hac videlicet, quod credimus fieri posse, ut quis sit idoneus ad Prophetiam, et se ad illam decenter præparet, et tamen non prophetet, propter voluntatem et beneplacitum Divinum. Meo itaque judicio res hîc se habet sicut in Miraculis. Ratio enim naturalis postulat, ut qui a natura sua idoneus est ad Prophetiam, prophetare deberet: qui autem id non potest facere, similis est ei, qui nequit movere manum suam, sicut Jeroboam. *Fundamentum namque hujus rei et præcipuum*, quod nos quoque requirimus, est *dispositio vel dexteritas naturalis*, et perfectio tam in moribus et qualitatibus externis, quam in rationalibus et intellectualibus."[1]—*Moreh Nebochim*, Pars II. cap. xxxii. (Buxtorf's transl. p. 284.)

The chief element among the natural faculties from which Prophecy is thus said to result, viz. the "intellectus agens," has been borrowed from the Peripatetics. As the learned John Smith (of Cambridge) explains the language of Maimonides, "The true essence of Prophecy is nothing else but an influence from the Deity upon the *rational* first, and afterwards the *imaginative* faculty by the mediation of *the active intellect*,"[2]—("On Prophecy," ch. ii.) And this doctrine Maimonides proceeds to apply as follows:—

"Si influentia ista intellectualis influat in facultatem rationalem solum nihilque in facultatem imaginatricem destillet, inde oriri sectam sapientum, *speculatorum* seu *theoricorum.* Quando vero influentia illa in utramque facultatem, rationalem nempe et imaginativam, easque ab illarum creatione in summo gradu perfectas influit, exinde fit secta *prophetarum.* Quando

[1] It should be added here that Abarbanel rejects this theory of Maimonides:—"Mens mihi hoc loci non est, de preparatione loquenti, istas dispositiones prædicare, quas vel ex naturâ homo possederit vel acquisiverit studio, uti factum R. Maimonidi, dum vias recenset per quas ad Prophetiam necessario perveniatur; nam illis (uti Legis nos scientia docet) nulla necessitas adest, conferens ipsam Prophetiam. Verum enim vero præparationes seu dispositiones hæ plurimum valent, &c."—*Comm. in* xii. *Proph. Min.*, Præf. (Husen's transl. p. 16).

[2] "Veritas et quidditas Prophetiæ nihil aliud est, quam influentia, a Deo Opt. Max., mediante *intellectu agente*, super facultatem rationalem primo, deinde super facultatem imaginatricem influens." It is not to be found in every one, no matter what his other perfections may be, "nisi simul conjuncta sit summa facultatis imaginatricis, inde ab ipsa hora nativitatis, perfectio." * * * "Has autem tres perfectiones quod attinet:—perfectionem videlicet facultatis rationalis in studendo; perfectionem facultatis imaginatricis in nativitate; et perfectionem morum seu qualitatum in puritate cogitationum * * * has inquam quod attinet, notum est magnam earum inter perfectos esse differentiam et præcellentiam. Et secundum illam differentiam distincti quoque sunt prophetarum gradus."—*Mor. Neb. Ibid.* c. xxxvi. p. 292, &c.

denique influentia illa influit solum in facultatem imaginatricem; et in facultate rationali imperfectio aliqua existit, exsurgit inde secta *Politicorum, Jurisperitorum, Legislatorum, Divinatorum, Incantatorum, Somniatorum, et Præstigiatorum.*"—*Ibid.* cap. xxxvii. p. 296. "It is needless to remark," writes Rudelbach, "that this psychical founding of Prophecy, according to which the leading idea is the 'natural disposition,' in no sense comes up to the idea of the 'Servant of God,' which, according to Holy Scripture, is common to all prophets; still less to the idea of 'the word of God' which called them, prepared them, and was the principle of their life. It is, perhaps, worth observing that one of the latest dogmatic writers is quite in accord with the Jewish teachers as to this fundamental view. Schleiermacher does not even conceal his belief 'that the idea of Inspiration appears, in this same sense, in every pious community which has a scriptural basis; nay, even in the origin *of civil government.*'"—*Zeitschrift*, 1840, H. i. s. 51. And again: having referred to Spinoza as confessedly the leader of all modern opposition to Inspiration; and having quoted his principle,—"Merito mentis *naturam*, quatenus talis concipitur. *primam Divinæ Revelationis causam* statuere possumus" (*Tract. Theol.*, *Pol.* cap. i.), borrowed from Maimonides,—which refers Revelation to *merely natural causes*, he observes that such opinions "deserve attention were it merely to recall to mind the essential elements of the system canonized by the modern pantheists." On which he notes: "It is well known that Schleiermacher, in his 'Discourses concerning Religion' (3rd edit., 1821), has completed the apotheosis of Spinoza; but certainly in a heathenish manner, by sacrificing on his grave a lock of his hair (indem er eine Locke opfert an seinem Grabe)."—*Loc. cit.*, H. ii. s. 48.

It is needless to refer, with any greater particularity, to the numerous varieties of opinion into which the theories of Inspiration, which have been now considered, may be subdivided. Nor, with respect to the distinction between Revelation and Inspiration, is it necessary to add anything to what has been already said in the foregoing pages. It has, however, been observed (Lecture i. p. 40, note [1]) that Origen noticed this distinction. The occasion on which he has done so is the following:—He had just applied to the Law of Moses the title of πρωτογέννημα of Scripture; and to the Gospels that of ἀπαρχή; the meaning of which terms he thus explains: μ ε τ ὰ γὰρ τοὺς πάντας καρποὺς ἀναφέρεται ἡ ἀπαρχή· πρὸ δὲ πάντων τὸ προτογέννημα—and he goes on to anticipate the objection, that as the Acts and the Epistles were disseminated *after* the Gospels, his use of the word ἀ π α ρ χ ή is objectionable. To which he replies:—Λεκτέον ἤτοι νοῦν εἶναι σοφῶν ἐν Χριστῷ, ὠφελημένων [μὲν] ἐν ταῖς φερομέναις ἐπιστολαῖς, δεομένων [δὲ] ἵνα πιστεύωνται μαρτυριῶν τῶν ἐν τοῖς νομικοῖς καὶ προφητητικοῖς λόγοις κειμένων, ὥστε σοφὰ μὲν καὶ πιστὰ λέγειν καὶ σφόδρα ἐπιτεταγμένα τὰ ἀποστολικὰ, οὐ μὴν παραπλήσια τῷ· τάδε λέγει Κύριος Παντοκράτωρ· καὶ κατὰ τοῦτο ἐπίστησον εἰ ἐπὰν λέγῃ ὁ Παῦλος, πάσα γραφὴ θεόπνευστος καὶ ὠφέλιμος, ἐμπεριλαμβάνει καὶ τὰ ἑαυτοῦ γράμματα, ἢ οὐ τό· κἀγὼ λέγω καὶ οὐχ ὁ Κύριος, καὶ τό· ἐν πάσαις ἐκκλησίαις διατάσσομαι, καὶ τό· οἷα ἔπαθον ἐν Ἀντιοχείᾳ, ἐν Ἰκονίῳ, ἐν Λύστροις καὶ τὰ τούτοις παραπλήσια, ἐνίοτε ὑπ' αὐτοῦ γραφέντα καὶ κ α τ' ἐ ξ ο υ σ ί α ν, οὐ μὴν τὸ εἰλικρινὲς τῶν ἐκ θείας ἐπιπνοίας λόγων.—*Comm. in Johann.*, t. iv. p. 4.

Here it is clear that the distinction is drawn not between one portion of Scripture which is inspired, and another portion which is not inspired; but between words which had been uttered by "the Lord Almighty" (2 Cor. vi. 18), and those which were spoken in the persons of the sacred writers themselves (observe that in each of the three quotations S. Paul speaks *in the first person*):—*both* classes of passages having been written under "Divine Inspiration," but the *former* being, as it were, "unmixed" with human agency. And, on this principle, he goes on to consider S. John's to be the ἀπαρχή of the Gospels. Cf. Cassiodorus, "In Psalter" cap. i., t. ii. p. 3; and S. Basil,[1] "Adv. Eunom." lib. v., t. i. p. 319, who refers to 1 Cor. vii. (cf. Lecture vi. p. 272, &c).

APPENDIX D.

THE "LOST" BOOKS OF THE OLD TESTAMENT.

LECTURE II.—PAGE 55.

WE meet with frequent reference in the Old Testament to a class of writings devotional and historical—writings, too, in many cases composed by the authors of inspired books,—which were never received into the Canon of Scripture. Of such compositions, some (1) are quoted to a greater or less extent in different parts of the Old Testament; or, without any express quotation, are alluded to as being extant; while others (2) are plainly spoken of as the sources from which the sacred writers derived, in certain cases, their information as to historical facts. (Cf. Lecture vii. p. 296, note [2].)

(1) "The Book of the wars of Jehovah," quoted Numbers, xxi. 14, 15, appears to have been one of the earliest instances of a collection of the popular lyrical poetry of the Hebrews (cf. Lecture iv. p. 160, note [2]); and the hymn, quoted in the same chapter (vv. 17, 18), seems to have been also taken from that collection In such poetical pieces was re-echoed the impression which the Lord's dealings with His people were fitted to produce; and from them was reflected the spirit of the Pentateuch, where Jehovah is represented fighting for Israel, as "a Man of war," Exod. xv. 3; cf. xiv. 14, 25. To this collection may, perhaps, also be referred the prophetic sayings (otherwise forming a distinct work) which are described as having been delivered by them "that speak in proverbs" (Num. xxi.

[1] Melchior Canus, who, so far as I am aware, was the first to state expressly this distinction between Revelation and Inspiration (see *supra*, p. 40), appears to have inferred it from these statements of the Fathers. Thus he observes, with reference to this passage from S. Basil:—"Quæ sacri auctores scripsere, hæc in duplici sunt differentia. Quædam, quæ supernaturali solum revelatione cognoscebant: et ea Basilius tradit a Spiritu Sancto esse. Alia vero naturali cognitione tenebant, quæ scilicet aut oculis viderant, aut manibus etiam attrectaverant. Atque hæc quidem, ut paulo ante diximus, supernaturali lumine et expressa revelatione, ut scriberentur, non egebant, sed egebant tamen Spiritus Sancti præsentia et auxilio peculiari, ut licet humana essent, et naturæ ratione cognita, Divinitus tamen sine ullo errore scriberentur. Hæc vero illa sunt, quæ, juxta Basilium, Paulus et Prophetæ de suo loquebantur."—*De Locis Theolog.* lib. ii. c. xviii., p. 127.

17); and with which many of the predictions of the future prophets are so intimately connected (Lect. iv. p. 160, note [2]; cf. Lect. vii. p. 298, &c.) "By the side of the objective statements of the Pentateuch," observes Hengstenberg, "proceeded the subjective in 'the Book of the wars of the Lord.' How they were related to each other, with respect to the preceding historical narrative, we perceive from Exod. xv."—*Beiträge*, B. iii. s. 226.

As the "Book of the wars of Jehovah" contained the praises of the Lord for the wonders wrought by Him for Israel, so, as a continuation, it may be, of that collection, but certainly not identical with it, "the Book of Jasher" ("the upright,"—ספר הישר, i. e. of the ideal true Israel), Josh. x. 13;[1] 2 Sam. i. 18, contained odes in honour of God's distinguished servants. It was so called, perhaps, with a reference to the passages where Israel is described as "Jeshurun" (ישרון, or ישרים—Deut. xxxii. 15; xxxiii. 5, 26; Numb. xxiii. 10)—see Keil's continuation of Hävernick's "Einleitung," s. 8.

In 1 Chron. xxviii. 11–19, we read that "David gave to Solomon the pattern of the porch * * * and the pattern of all that he had, by the Spirit, of the courts of the House of the Lord. * * * Also for the courses of the Priests and the Levites. * * * All this, said David, the Lord made me understand in writing by His hand upon me, even all the works of this pattern." That this document was the recognised guide in the ritual worship of the Temple, we learn from the words of Josiah to the Priests and Levites: "Prepare yourselves by the houses of your fathers, after your courses, *according to the writing of David* King of Israel, and according to the writing of Solomon his son."—2 Chron. xxxv. 4.

In 1 Kings, iv. 32, we read that Solomon "spake three thousand proverbs, and his songs were a thousand and five:" and yet only two of his Psalms are in the Canon—viz. Psalm lxxii. and cxxvii.

It seems clear from 2 Chron. xxxv. 25, that Jeremiah composed a dirge on the death of Josiah: "Jeremiah lamented for Josiah, * * * and behold they are written in the Lamentations."[2]

(2) To turn, in the next place, to those prophetical and other writings which are appealed to by the authors of the Old Testament, as the sources from which their statements have been taken.[3] The division of the land, described by Joshua in the section ch. xiii.–xxii., is founded upon a document drawn up by the "three men for each tribe" "who passed through the land, and described it by cities, into seven parts, *in a Book* (על-ספר)." —Josh. xviii. 9. And here a remark may be made, the importance of

[1] It is curious to observe what slender grounds are sufficient for an assault upon the integrity of Scripture:—"It is worthy of remark that the Book of Joshua (x. 13) quotes the book of Jasher which must have been written as late as the time of David (2 Sam. i. 18). See De Wette, ii. 187."—Greg, *The Creed of Christendom*, p. 38. The bare mention of the fact that this work consisted of *a collection* of popular poetry,—to which, of course, additions were made from time to time,—exposes the weakness of this cavil.

[2] To this class of writings some add "The manner of the kingdom" which Samuel "wrote in a book."—1 Sam. x. 25. This does not appear, however, to have been a *distinct* work: see Lecture vii. p. 289, note.

[3] For the remarks which follow, cf. Hävernick, "Einleitung," Th. ii. Abth. i.

which will presently appear, that the author of the Books of Chronicles had other sources of information with respect to such facts, than the Book of Joshua. Thus the account of the possessions of the Levites in 1 Chron. vi. 54–81, differs from that given in Josh. xxi. The progress of time, indeed, must necessarily have rendered the former description inexact: e. g. Ziklag (Josh. xix. 5) was assigned to the Tribe of Simeon; but we learn from 1 Sam. xxvii. 6, that it afterwards "pertained unto the Kings of Judah."

The author of the Books of Samuel, on one occasion only (namely, 2 Sam. i. 18, already noticed) makes express *mention* of documentary sources. The frequent insertion, however, of poetic pieces plainly intimates that such sources were at his command:—viz. the Song of Hannah, 1 Sam. ii. 1–10; the Hymn of Victory, xviii. 6, &c.; the Lament of David for Saul and Jonathan, 2 Sam. i. 17–27, and for Abner, iii. 33, 34; David's Psalms, contained in ch. xxii. and in xxiii. 1–7. Hence we may not unfairly form a conjecture as to the source of such quotations; and conclude that these poetic pieces were selected from the "Book of Jasher." We read, too, in 1 Chron. xxix. 29, that "the acts of David are written in the Book of Samuel, and in the Book of Nathan, and in the Book of Gad;" any or all of which may have been the author's sources:—for it is clear that these *were distinct works*, since the "Book of Nathan" alone is referred to in 2 Chron. ix. 29 ("The acts of Solomon, are they not written in the Book of Nathan, and in the prophecy of Ahijah, and in the visions of Iddo.") without any allusion to the Books of Samuel or Gad.

The author of the Books of Kings on one occasion appeals to "the Book of the acts of Solomon (ספר דברי שלמה)"—1 Kings, xi. 41: the other sources to which he has referred being "The Book of the Chronicles (ספר דברי הימים) of the Kings of Judah," or of "Israel:"—writings which are quoted thirty-one times up to the history of Jehoiakim, 2 Kings, xxiv. 5. That a *selection* only was made from such documents is obvious from the use, in all cases, of the phrase "*the rest of* (יתר) the acts," &c.; while it is also plain that our books of Chronicles are *not* the sources employed. The documents in question were the public records of the kingdom, which the sacred historians of the Hebrews, like other Oriental annalists, were accustomed to adduce as their authorities (cf. Ezra, iv. 15; Esther, vi. 1; x. 2.) The passage Neh. xii. 23, is conclusive on this point, as has been already proved, Lecture vii. p. 296, note [2].

That the documents thus made use of were in most, if not all, instances, composed by Prophets, will be seen farther on.

In the Books of Chronicles, with the exception of the section 1 Chron. i.–ii. 2,—and even here the facts borrowed are compressed as much as possible (cf. i. 24–27, with Gen. xi. 10–26; and i. 32, 33, with Gen. xxv. 1–4),—the canonical Books of Scripture *are not employed as the sources*: this assertion, however, must be proved. The Books of Chronicles may be divided into the following sections:—

I. The Genealogies, 1 Chron. i.–ix.:—(1) The author gives ample information as to the authorities to which he refers. He appeals to the public register of the Tribes, of which Nehemiah writes:—"I found a register of the genealogy (ספר היחש) of them which came up at the first, and found written therein," &c.—vii. 5. See 1 Chron. iv. 33; v. 1, 7, 17;

vii. 7, 9, 40 ; ix. 1.[1] To the *collection* of such registers he refers ch. ix. 1; and we learn from ch. v. 17, that we are to refer the origin of census-lists of this nature to the times of Jotham and Jeroboam II. (2) He does *not* borrow from the other canonical books. This appears, speaking generally, not only from the absence of any such striking agreement with those books, as must have existed had the Chronicler taken them as his sources; but also from the *additional* information which his statements so often supply: e. g. 1 Chron. ii. 13–17 (cf. 1 Sam. xvi. 6, &c.) ; iii. 20–24 ; iv. 1–23 ; v. 16–34.[2] But this feature of the case must be examined somewhat more particularly, namely,—Has the author, or has he not, made use of the Books of Samuel and the Books of Kings ? a question with which the present inquiry, as to the existence of a *distinct* branch of Hebrew literature is essentially connected. The reply to this question will inform us of the authorities from which the Chronicler has actually derived his facts.

II. In the section 1 Chron. x.–xxix., which contains the history of David, the sources appear to have been (1) works written by early *prophets*, and contemporaneous with the events which they record; together with (2) a book of later date, compiled from the annals which the author had employed in the opening chapters. (1) The account of David's reign closes with the words: "Now the acts of David the King, first and last, behold, they are written in the book of Samuel the Seer, and in the Book of Nathan the Prophet, and in the Book of Gad the Seer"—1 Chron. xxix. 29 :—we have already seen that these were separate, independent works.

(2) The lists of David's heroes (ch. xi. 10, &c.), and of those who came to him to Ziklag (ch. xii. 1–22) ; the information as to the Levites (ch. xv. 17, &c.), and as to Divine worship (ch. xxii. xxvi) ; &c. &c.—all such statements point to the use of a document analogous to those employed in the opening chapters. But we are also informed of the exact nature of this document. We read, "The Levites were numbered from the age of thirty years and upward. * * * By *the last words of David* the Levites were numbered from twenty years old and above."—1 Chron. xxiii. 3, 27 : we are told, moreover, that its author, "Shemaiah the son of Nethaneel the scribe, one of the Levites, wrote them before the King and the Princes, &c."—xxiv. 6. To this document the reader is more than once referred for special information, when the Chronicler speaks of classes of persons who were "expressed by name"—(cf. xii. 31 , xvi. 41); its nature being more explicitly declared in the statement:—"Joab began to number, but he finished not, because there fell wrath for it against Israel; neither was the number put in the *account of the Chronicles of King David*."—xxvii. 24.

III. In 2 Chron. i.–ix. is contained the history of Solomon. We have

[1] The facts borrowed from these documents often afford occasion for explanatory remarks:—e. g. on the transfer of Reuben's Birthright to the sons of Joseph—ch. v. 1.

[2] One example may be given of the light which the Books of Chronicles cast upon other obscure portions of Scripture. 1 Chronicles, iv. 23, we read: "These were *the potters*, and those that dwelt among plants and hedges: there they dwelt with the king for his work." Thus we learn that there was a well-known family of potters, of the tribe of Judah, set apart to labor for the kings. To these the passages, Jer. xviii 1, 2; xix. 1, 2; Zech. xi. 13, evidently refer.

seen to what source the author of the Books of Kings referred on this subject (1 Kings, xi. 41); but here other authorities are adduced: "The rest of the acts of Solomon, first and last, are they not written in the Book of Nathan the Prophet, and in the Prophecy of Ahijah the Shilonite, and in the Visions of Iddo the Seer against Jeroboam the son of Nebat"—2 Chron. ix. 29:—the silence of the Books of Kings with respect to any "Vision of Iddo against Jeroboam," proving that the Chronicler does not refer to them.

IV. In the Section 2 Chron. x.–xxxvi., which contains the succeeding history of the kingdom of Judah, the document most frequently quoted is "the Book of the Kings of Judah and Israel"—(xvi. 11; xxv. 26; xxvii. 7; xxviii. 26; xxxii. 32; xxxv. 27; xxxvi. 8). In xx. 34 we meet with "the Book (ספר) of the Kings of Israel;" and in xxxiii. 18 "the דברי of the Kings of Israel"—which latter work, however, was clearly not confined to the Ten Tribes, as it contained the history *of Manasseh.* These documents are not the Books of Kings. This is proved by the fact that, in many instances, the Books of Kings do not contain the information for which the Chronicler refers to his sources:—e. g. 2 Chron. xxvii. 7; xxxiii. 18. From considering the nature of his references it will appear that the Chronicler has borrowed here from *three* separate authorities:—(1) From a distinct compilation, which contained genealogical details (cf. xxxi. 16, &c.), and also *writings composed by prophets*—e. g.: "The rest of the acts of Jehoshaphat are written in the Book of Jehu, the son of Hanani"—xx. 34 (Jehu is called a *prophet*, 1 Kings, xvi. 7); and, again: —"The rest of the acts of Hezekiah are written in the Vision of Isaiah the Prophet, the son of Amoz, in the Book of the Kings of Judah and Israel"—xxxii. 32. That the different elements thus referred to formed one compilation is confirmed by the title given in ch. xxiv. 27,[1] to the work which the Chronicler had before him, viz. "the *Story* [or *Commentary*] of the Book of the Kings (מדרש ספר המלכים),"—i. e. *an historical commentary* or accurate account of Jewish history, gathered out of the writings of the prophets; a sense which is further confirmed by the passage: "The rest of the acts of Ahijah are written in the *Story or Commentary* (מדרש) of the prophet Iddo."—xiii. 22. The other element of this compilation is referred to in the words: "The acts of Rehoboam, are they not written in the book of Shemaiah the prophet, and of Iddo the Seer, concerning genealogies?"—xii. 15.

(2) The second authority referred to is expressly distinguished from the compilation just spoken of in the following manner. We read: "The rest of the acts of Manasseh, and his prayer unto his God, and the words of the Seers [cf. ver. 10 and 2 Kings, xxi. 10, &c.] that spake to him in the name of the Lord God of Israel, behold they are written in the book (words) of the Kings of Israel."—xxxiii. 18. But in ver. 19, the Chron-

[1] "Now concerning his [Joash] sons, *and the greatness of the burdens laid upon him* (ורב המשא עליו), and the repairing of the house of God, behold they are written in the story of the Book of the Kings"—where, as Hävernick suggests, in place of the words in Italics, we should read "the number of the prophetic denunciations against Joash" (see Lecture iv. p. 163, note, on משא)—spoken of in ver. 19. The different subjects which this passage embraces show how the whole compilation could receive the name of מדרש,—"Commentary," or "Prophetical illustrations of History.'

icler proceeds: "His prayer also, and how God was entreated of him, &c., behold they are written *among the sayings of the Seers*:" or,—as the margin correctly renders—"the sayings of Hosai (דברי חוזי):" in which words the writer clearly refers to a distinct document.

(3) Isaiah's biography of Uzziah: "The rest of the acts of Uzziah, first and last, did Isaiah the Prophet, the son of Amoz, write"—xxvi. 22; but which work was not, like Isaiah's history of Hezekiah, inserted in the "Book of the Kings."—xxxii. 32.

Here, then, may be repeated the questions already proposed in Lecture ii. p. 55:—Why do we not find in the Old Testament Canon the documents which have been enumerated in the preceding remarks? And again:—Why do we not find placed on a par with the inspired writings, such works as the Book of Ecclesiasticus, and the other components of the Apocrypha, which, it is on all hands admitted, the *Jewish Church* never received as Canonical? Only one answer, I conceive, can be given to such questions, viz.: "That the collection of Sacred Books was defined under the Divine guidance, and closed at the Divine command" (see *supra*, p. 61).

It is unnecessary to enter here upon the modern phase of the question relating to the Apocrypha. Suffice it to say, that the Community which has exalted these writings to the dignity of Canonical Scripture, has, nevertheless, been compelled to place them in a lower rank than the Books acknowledged by all to be inspired. How a member of the Church of Rome can draw such a distinction, consistently with the Tridentine Decrees, it is needless to inquire: the agreement, however, of both Roman Catholics and Lutherans in their estimate of the Apocrypha is remarkable;—one party desiring to *exalt* the Apocrypha, the other to *lower* the authority of portions of the New Testament. Perrone—having quoted the Canon of Trent (Sess. iv.), in which both the Canonical and Apocryphal Books of the Old Testament are enumerated, and which concludes with these words: "Si quis libros ipsos *cum omnibus suis partibus*, prout in Ecclesia Catholica legi consueverunt, et in veteri Vulgata Editione habentur *pro Sacris et Canonicis* non susceperit * * * anathema sit" —proceeds to say: "Ex his porro *tum Veteris tum Novi* Test. libris alii dicuntur 'proto-canonici,' alii 'deutero-canonici' * * * Libri 'proto-canonici' Vet. Test., *auctore Josepho Flavio*, xxii. sunt; nempe omnes enumerati præter Baruch, Tobiam, Judith, Sapientiam, Ecclesiasticum, ac duos Machabæorum, *qui serius in Canonem ab Ecclesia relati sunt*, adeoque 'deutero-canonici' nuncupati. Libri 'proto-canonici' N. T., sunt pariter omnes recensiti, *exceptis Epistola B. Pauli ad Hebræos*, 2 *Ep. B. Petri, duabus posterioribus S. Joannis, Ep. S. Jacobi, item Ep. S. Judæ, et Apocalypsi B. Joannis*: ut nonnullas quorumdam librorum partes omittamus," (viz.: "quod attinet ad V. T., sunt hymnus trium puerorum, Dan. iii. 24–90; historia Susannæ, cap. xiii; ac destructio Beli et Draconis, cap. xiv.; septem postrema capita libri Esther, nempe a cap. x. 4 et xvi. 24. *Quod vero spectat ad libros N. T.*, sunt (1) posteriores versiculi cap. xvi. S. Marci, nempe a ver. 9 ad finem; (2) historia sudoris Christi sanguinei quæ legitur ap. S. Lucam cap. xxii. 43, 44; (3) historia mulieris adulteræ Joan. viii. 2–12")—*Prælect Theol.*, t. ii. pars 2, p. 12.

Tholuck accepts this statement as follows: "Auf diese Weise bildete sich *auch unter den neutestamentlichen Schriften*, wie unter den alttestamentlichen, *der Unterschied aus zwischen kanonischen im engeren Sinne, und apokryphischen.* Diesen letzteren Namen gebraucht Hieronymus geradezu von den Antilegomenen, und bezeichnet sie dadurch als solche, 'quæ Ecclesia legit ad ædificationem plebis,' welche aber die Kirche nicht gebraucht 'ad auctoritatem ecclesiasticorum dogmatum confirmandam.' *Eben dieser Unterschied der neutestamentlichen Schriften* ist nun auch *von der lutherischen Kirche angenommen worden*, welche ebenso im N. T., *wie die katholische im A. T.*, 'libri proto-canonici,' und 'deutero-canonici' unterscheidet."—*Der Br. an die Hebr.*, Einleitung, kap. vi., s. 86.

In concluding this subject an observation must be made with reference to the remark of Hug, quoted p. 59, note [1], to the effect that the primitive practice of publicly reading in the Christian assemblies the Books of the New Testament was the mark of distinction by which the Church formally declared its belief in their inspired authority. When such an argument is employed, we are of course to understand the practice of the Church, *in general*, as that to which the appeal is made: for it is well known that there were some exceptions to this principle. When it can be proved, however, that the use, in public worship, of any books which were not inspired was, at the utmost, only partial; and that, in the most remarkable case, such use can be at once accounted for from local causes; the argument for the inspiration of the Canonical Books only which is founded upon the general practice of the Church, is strengthened rather than diminished by the knowledge of such exceptions. Thus the Epistle of S. Clement of Rome, written in the name of the Roman Church to the Church of Corinth, was occasioned by a division which had arisen among the members of the latter, and which was healed by the wise admonitions of S. Clement. What more natural than that the Church of Corinth should continue publicly to read a document with which its history was so closely connected? Accordingly, S. Dionysius, bishop of Corinth (*circ.* A.D. 170), wrote to Soter, bishop of Rome, informing him, among other matters, that it had been the practice of his Church, from the first, to read this Epistle. As Eusebius interprets his meaning:—*τῆς Κλήμεντος πρὸς Κορινθίους μέμνηται ἐπιστολῆς, δηλῶν ἀνέκαθεν ἐξ ἀρχαίου ἔθους ἐπὶ τῆς ἐκκλησίας τὴν ἀνάγνωσιν αὐτῆς ποιεῖσθαι.*—*Hist. Eccl.* iv. c. 23, p. 187. Considering the person by whom this Epistle had been written, we should rather feel surprise that the practice had not become universal (see *supra*, p. 57, &c.); but that it had not, we again learn from Eusebius, who, when desiring himself to express the great estimation in which S. Clement's Epistle was held, can say no more than that it was read *ἐν πλείσταις ἐκκλησίαις* (H. E., iii. c. 16, p. 108). The "Shepherd of Hermas," too, was held in the greatest veneration by so high an authority as S. Irenæus (cf. e. g. "Cont. Hær.," lib. IV. c. XX. p. 253); and yet, the "Fragment of Muratori" expressly mentions it as a book which was *not* publicly read as Scripture:—see *supra*, p. 57, note. It is thus referred to by S. Athanasius:—*ἐν δὲ τῷ Ποιμένι γέγραπται· ἐπειδὴ καὶ τοῦτο καίτοι μὴ ὂν ἐκ τοῦ κανόνος προφέρουσι· πρῶτον κ. τ. λ.*—*De Decr. Nic. Syn.*, t. i. p. 223.[1] The case of the Epistle of S. Barnabas has been considered already, p. 57, note [2].

[1] Bishop Beveridge's assertion, therefore, as to the universal practice of reading

APPENDIX E.

THE EPISTLE OF S. BARNABAS.

(LECTURE II.—PAGE 58.)

OUR information, as to the personal history of S. Barnabas,[1] is very scanty. According to Acts, iv. 36, he was a "Levite of the country of Cyprus." Clemens Al. ("Strom." II. xx. p. 489) and Eusebius ("H. E.," i. 12; ii. 1) tell us that he was one of the Seventy Disciples. This statement fully accords with the inspired historian's account of his early attachment to the Church, and zeal in its cause; for S. Barnabas was the first who "having land sold it, and brought the money, and laid it at the Apostles' feet."—Acts, iv. 37. We next find him introducing the lately converted S. Paul to the Apostles (ix. 27); and subsequently journeying from Antioch "to Tarsus for to seek Saul" (xi. 25), whom he accompanied on his first mission as an Apostle (xiii). In consequence of the dispute respecting his kinsman "John, whose surname was Mark," he was for a time separated from S. Paul (xv. 36–39); and we learn from Gal. ii. 13, that S. Barnabas, in common with S. Peter, was led astray by the dissimulation of the Jews.

Referring to the early records of the Church, we learn further that an Epistle was generally received as proceeding from the pen of S. Barnabas, which is frequently quoted in the writings of Clemens Alexandrinus and Origen. Its existence is also mentioned by Eusebius, S. Jerome, and Nicephorus. For many centuries all knowledge of this Epistle was confined to such allusions. It was for the first time printed in 1643 by Archbishop Ussher, at Oxford; but the entire of this impression was destroyed during a great fire in that city. The first edition, therefore, actually published was that of Hugo Menardus, in 1645; and it was followed in the next year by another, edited by Is. Vossius. Ussher and Menardus were inclined to doubt the genuineness of this composition, which, on the other hand, Vossius defended: and thus the controversy on the subject commenced. This controversy is free from one difficulty, which, in such cases, is usually the most formidable: all parties admitting that, were we to confine ourselves to EXTERNAL EVIDENCE, there can be no doubt that S. Barnabas was the author.[2] The manner in which early writers accepted this Epistle as the

these three writings in the Church is, I venture to think, unsupported by sufficient evidence. (See his "Codex Canonum," lib. II. cap. ix. § 11.)

[1] Ullman ("Studien u. Kritiken," 1828, s. 378 ff.) identifies S. Barnabas with Barsabas (Acts, i. 23); on the grounds that the Peschito and some MSS., in Acts, i. 23, for 'Ιωσήφ read 'Ιωσῆς (who "was surnamed *Barnabas*"—Acts, iv. 36); and that, for Βαρσάβᾶς, Cod. D and the Ethiopian Version read Βαρνάβας. With this agrees the statement of Clemens Al. and Eusebius, that S. Barnabas was one of the Seventy; for *Barsabas* is described as having been an eye-witness of the Life of Christ. Although not elected into the place of Judas, he is called an Apostle (Acts, xiv. 4). How does it happen, also, that we hear no more of Barsabas? Cf. the curious statement of the "Recogn. S. Clementis" (ap. Coteler., t i. p. 507):—"Post quem Barnabas, *qui et Matthias*, qui in locum Judæ subrogatus est Apostolus," &c.

[2] Even Ullman, who, in the essay alluded to, attempts in vain to weaken the external evidence admits: "Das Höchste, was wir den Verfechtern der Aechtheit

work of S. Barnabas, has been already pointed out (Lecture ii. p. 58, and p. 58, note [2]); and so high an authority as Bishop Pearson can be appealed to as deciding "hanc Epistolam eandem esse quam veteres in manibus habuerunt."[1] Nor is this fact, that all external evidence is decisive in support of its genuineness, questioned by its leading opponent in modern times, the historian Neander, who does not, however, condescend to discuss this branch of the question. In his remarks on the most distinguished teachers of the Church, he writes :—"We must mention here, in the first place, Barnabas, the well-known companion of the Apostle Paul, if an Epistle really belonged to him, *which was known in the second century*, *in the Church of Alexandria*, *under his name*, and which bore the superscription of a Catholic Epistle. But we cannot possibly recognise in it the Barnabas who was worthy to be a companion of the apostolic labors of Paul, and who had received his name in the Church from the power of his inspired elocution (*υἱὸς παρακλήσεως*, *υἱὸς προφητείας*). There floats before us here a spirit altogether different from that of such an apostolic man. We here remark an educated Alexandrian Jew, who had gone over to Christianity; who, by his Alexandrian education, was prepared for a more spiritual apprehension of Christianity, but who laid too great stress upon an untenable Alexandrian, artificial Jewish, gnosis; who, in a mystical exposition,—which plays upon the words of the Old Testament, and which seems to resemble the spirit of Philo rather than the spirit of Paul, *or even of the Epistle to the Hebrews*,—sought for special wisdom, and therein idly indulged himself."[2] This statement of the case involves two assumptions, neither of which appears capable of support. (1) It is assumed, in the first place, that an Epistle proceeding from a companion of the Apostles, who, on certain occasions, was inspired in his preaching, must of necessity have been written under the influence of Inspiration. This assumption, however, is founded upon the twofold error,—that the gift of Inspiration was permanent (in answer to which compare the Scriptural facts brought forward, p. 221, note [1]); and that Inspiration itself is of such a nature as the school of Schleiermacher has defined it to be (see also p. 34, and p. 219, note [1]). (2) The second principle assumed by Neander, or, at least, by the majority of writers who agree with him in his argument against this Epistle,—is that the system of allegorical exposition, which is there carried to such an extent, was unsuited alike to the age, and the object, of S. Barnabas, supposing him to have been the author. But both branches of this assumption also are again unfounded. That the principle of spiritually expounding the events and language of the Old Testament was *not* unsuited to the Apostolic *age*, we learn from the fact of the frequent adoption of such a system of interpretation by the New Testament writers

zugeben, ist, dass der Brief, sofern wir bloss die Tradition [i. e. historical evidence], ins Auge fassen, von Barnabas seyn *kann*."—*Loc. cit.* s. 387.

[1] "Minor Theol. Works"—"Lect. in Acta Apost. ii."—ed. Churton, vol. i. p. 335. As J. C. Rördam observes: "Unam eandemque esse Epistolam Barnabæ dubitari nequit; hoc enim satis probant loci ii, quos ex epistola Barnabæ laudarunt Patres ecclesiastici, qui verbo tenus in epistola nostra extant; *quod neque inficias quisquam ivit* præter Abr. Calovium, qui conjecturæ vento leviori obtemperans, Epistolæ hujus consarcinatorem fragmenta illa Barnabæ ex Clemente Alex. et Origene suo figmento inseruisse suspicatur."—*De Authent. Ep. Barnabæ*, Hafn. 1828. p. 9.

[2] Allgem. Gesch. der christl. Kirche," B. i. s. 1133. 2te Aufl.

themselves (e. g. Gal. iv. 22, &c.; Rom. ix. 8; 2 Cor. iii. 13, &c.; Eph. v. 32; Heb. vii.; ix.; x. 1; xi. 19—cf. Lecture vii. p. 318, &c.): as well as from its use by S. Clement of Rome in his Epistle.[1] Any objection, therefore, founded upon the exaggeration of this principle by S. Barnabas (an exaggeration which I am not prepared to deny), rests upon the assumption, already shown to be without foundation, that any composition of his must have been free from defects; i. e. that it must have been inspired. Equally untenable is the objection that an allegorical exposition of the Old Testament was not suited to the writer's *object*. The Epistle, as all critics (except Lardner,—*Works*, vol. ii. p. 19,—who thinks it was written *to Gentiles*) allow, was addressed to Jewish Christians; for whom the author was bound to prove that the "Old Testament was not contrary to the New." Accordingly, S. Barnabas argues (ch. i.–ix.), that, in the prophecies and types of the Old Testament sufficient is contained, relating to Christ and His death, to serve as the foundation of the New Covenant: and hence that the Jews cannot argue against Christianity from their own inspired writings. He then goes on to show that the Old Testament, *as the Jews understood it*, was but an *external* system; and, consequently, was to be done away by means of a system of *internal* religion which was to be perfected (ch. x.); that both Christian Baptism, and the manner of the Messiah's death, were predicted in the Old Testament (xi.; xii.); and therefore that not Jews but Christians are the people of the inheritance. From which it follows (ch. xiii.–xviii.) that neither was the Jewish Sabbath the true day of rest, but merely a type of the great Day of Rest at the end of the world; nor was the Temple of Jerusalem the true dwelling of God, for *It* is in the hearts of believers (*Λαβόντες τὴν ἄφεσιν τῶν ἁμαρτιῶν, καὶ ἐλπίσαντες ἐπὶ τῷ ὀνόματι τοῦ Κυρίου, ἐγενόμεθα καινοί,* * * * *διὸ ἐν τῷ κατοικητηρίῳ ἡμῶν ἀληθῶς ὁ Θεὸς κατοικεῖ ἐν ἡμῖν*—c. xvi). From ch. xviii. to xxi., the contents of the Epistle are hortatory.[2]

It is to be added, that neither in the salutation nor elsewhere does the author name himself; nor does the Epistle appear to have had any title originally (see Wake's "Prel. Disc.," § 35):—facts which, coupled with the frequent citation of it by Clemens Al. as the production of S. Barna-

[1] E. g. his exposition of the "line of scarlet thread," given by the spies to Rahab (Josh. ii. 18; cf. Heb. xi. 31), as symbolizing "the Redemption by the Lord's Blood (*ὅτι διὰ τοῦ αἵματος τοῦ Κυρίου λύτρωσις ἔσται*)"—*Ep. ad Cor.* c. xii.:—see Rördam, *loc. cit.* pp. 33, 86.

[2] See the essay by C. E. Francke in Rudelbach and Guerike's Journal for 1840, H. ii. s. 67 ff. In ch. xv., speaking of the Lord's rest on the Seventh Day (Gen. ii. 2); S. Barnabas says: "We are greatly deceived if we imagine that any one can now sanctify that day which God has made holy, without having a heart pure in all things. * * * He saith unto them, Your new moons and your sabbaths, I cannot bear them (Isai. i. 13);—the sabbaths, says He, which ye now keep, are not acceptable unto Me, but those which I have made; when resting from all things, I shall begin the Eighth Day, that is the beginning of the other world. For which cause we observe the eighth day with gladness, in which *Jesus rose from the dead*; and having manifested Himself to His Disciples, *He ascended into Heaven* (*ἐν ᾗ καὶ ὁ Ἰησοῦς ἀνέστη ἐκ νεκρῶν, καὶ φανερωθεὶς ἀνέβη εἰς τοὺς οὐρανούς*)" ("Wake's transl.) On this passage Rördam ingeniously observes: "Crediderim pæne, haud veri absimilem esse conjecturam, vestigium quoddam *certæ cujusdam et universalis* de ultimis Jesu fatis loquendi rationis, forsan *Symboli Apostolici elementum in hoc loco inesse.*"—*Loc. cit.* p. 60.

bas, at once meet any allegation as to the work being an *intentional* forgery. Hefele, who, on the usual grounds, refuses to acknowledge the authorship of S. Barnabas, thus speaks of its date:—"Revera primis seculi secundi temporibus 107–120 epistolam nostram exaratam esse putem." —*Proleg.* ed. altera.

Whatever decision the reader may arrive at, from considering the foregoing observations, it is plain that the argument, which I have founded upon the admitted fact of the recognition, by the early Church, of this Epistle as the composition of S. Barnabas, remains altogether unaffected—(see *supra*, p. 58). One of the leading arguments of Ullmann is consequently proved to be altogether destitute of weight:—

"Wenn der Brief aus dem Kanon ausgeschlossen wurde, so war *eben hiermit* auch seine Aechtheit geleugnet; denn Kanonicität und Authentie fallen *hier* zusammen:"—*because*, he adds, had the Epistle proceeded from the pen of S. Barnabas, the Church would have felt no scruple as to receiving it into the Canon!—*Loc. cit.* s. 385. It has been shown, however, that Clemens Al., who expressly states that it proceeded from "the companion of S. Paul," did not regard this Epistle as a portion of Scripture.—See Lecture ii. p. 58, note [2].

APPENDIX F.

PHILO AND JOSEPHUS.

(LECTURE II.—PAGE 64, &c.)

THE following extracts, in addition to those which have been already given from the writings of Philo and Josephus, may in each case be ranged under two heads;—namely, those which express (1) their opinions with respect to Inspiration in general; and (2) those which contain references to the separate books of the Old Testament.

I. The *locus classicus* ("Vita Mosis," lib. III. t. ii. p. 163), in which Philo's theory of inspiration is conveyed, and which has been already dwelt upon (see *supra*, p. 64), as follows:—

Οὐκ ἀγνοῶ μὲν οὖν, ὡς πάντα εἰσὶ χρησμοὶ ὅσα ἐν ταῖς ἱεραῖς βίβλοις ἀναγέγραπται, χρησθέντες δι' αὐτοῦ. Λέξω δὲ τὰ ἰδιαίτερα, πρότερον εἰπὼν ἐκεῖνο. τῶν λογίων γὰρ, τὰ μὲν ἐκ προσώπου τοῦ Θεοῦ λέγεται δι' ἑρμηνέως τοῦ θείου προφήτου· τὰ δὲ ἐκ πεύσεως καὶ ἀποκρίσεως ἐθεσπίσθη· τὰ δ' ἐκ προσώπου Μωϋσέως ἐπιθειάσαντος, καὶ ἐξ αὐτοῦ κατασχεθέντος. Τὰ μὲν οὖν πρῶτα ὅλα δι' ὅλων ἀρετῶν θείων δείγματ' ἐστὶ, τῆς τε ἵλεω καὶ εὐεργέτιδος, δι' ὧν ἅπαντας μὲν ἀνθρώπους πρὸς καλοκαγαθίαν ἀλείφει· μάλιστα δὲ τὸ θεραπευτικὸν αὐτοῦ γένος, ᾧ τὴν πρὸς εὐδαιμονίαν ἄγουσαν ἀνατέμνει ὁδόν. Τὰ δὲ δεύτερα μίξιν ἔχει καὶ κοινωνίαν, πυνθανομένου μὲν τοῦ προφήτου περὶ ὧν ἐπεζήτει, ἀποκρινομένου δὲ τοῦ Θεοῦ καὶ διδάσκοντος. Τὰ δὲ τρίτα ἀνατίθεται τῷ νομοθέτῃ, μεταδόντος αὐτῷ τοῦ Θεοῦ τῆς προγνοστικῆς δυνάμεως, ᾗ θεσπιεῖ τά μέλλοντα. Τὰ μὲν οὖν πρῶτα ὑπερθετέον· μείζονα γάρ ἐστιν ἢ ὡς ὑπ' ἀνθρώπου τινὸς ἐπαινεθῆναι, μόλις ἂν ὑπ' οὐρανοῦ τε καὶ κόσμου, καὶ τῆς τῶν ὅλων φύσεως ἀξίως ἐγκωμιασθέντα, καὶ ἄλλως λέγεται ὡσανεὶ δι' ἑρμηνέως

Ἑρμηνεία δὲ καὶ προφητεία διαφερουσι. Περὶ δὲ τῶν δευτέρων αὐτίκα πειράσομαι δηλοῦν, συνυφήνας αὐτοῖς καὶ τὸ τρίτον εἶδος, ἐν ᾧ τὸ τοῦ λέγοντος ἐνθουσιῶδες ἐμφαίνεται, καθ' ὃ μάλιστα καὶ κυρίως νενόμισται προφήτης.

On this statement I have already commented. From it we learn the views of Philo as to the source of the "Sacred Books," and the relations in which their different writers stood to God. His opinion, also, as to the personal state of the Prophets while subject to the Divine influence is laid down in the words which immediately precede the passage quoted p. 65, note [1]:—

Ἕως ἔτι περιλάμπει καὶ περιπολεῖ ἡμῶν ὁ νοῦς, μεσημβρινὸν οἷα φέγγος εἰς πᾶσαν τὴν ψυχὴν ἀναχέων, ἐν ἑαυτοῖς ὄντες, οὐ κατεχόμεθα· ἐπειδὰν δὲ πρὸς δυσμὰς γένηται, κατὰ τὸ εἰκὸς ἔκστασις ἡ ἔνθεος ἐπιπίπτει, κατοχωτική τε καὶ μανία. Ὅτε μὲν γὰρ φῶς ἐπιλάμψει τὸ θεῖον, δύεται τὸ ἀνθρώπινον, ὅτε δ' ἐκεῖνο δύει, τοῦτ' ἀνίσχει καὶ ἀνατέλλει. Τῷ δὲ προφητικῷ γένει φιλεῖ τοῦτο συμβαίνειν· κ. τ. λ.—where Philo is speaking of Gen. xv. 12 [LXX.]: περὶ δὲ ἡλίου δυσμὰς ἔκστασις ἐπέπεσε τῷ Ἄβραμ,—and where he understands by ἥλιος the human spirit, and explains δυσμή by ἐκστῆναι.

Philo's opinion, too, as to the *result* of the influence (Inspiration—which he names προφητεία, in its general sense), under which the "Sacred Books" were written, as distinct from the reception and promulgation by their writers of new truths from God (Revelation—ἑρμηνεία), is clearly intimated by the language in which he adopts the tradition as to the manner in which the Seventy Interpreters translated the Hebrew Scriptures:—viz., that each, in his separate cell, completed the whole work; and that the seventy translations thus produced agreed even in the most minute particulars. He writes ("De Vita Mosis," lib. II. t. ii. p. 140):—Καθίσαντες δ' ἐν ἀποκρύφῳ, καὶ μηδενὸς παρόντος ὅτι μὴ τῶν τῆς φύσεως μερῶν, γῆς, ὕδατος, ἀέρος, οὐρανοῦ, περὶ ὧν πρῶτον τῆς γενέσεως ἔμελλον ἱεροφαντήσειν· κοσμοποιΐα γὰρ ἡ τῶν νόμων ἐστὶν ἀρχή· καθάπερ ἐνθουσιῶντες προεφήτευον οὐκ ἄλλα ἄλλοι, τὰ δ' αὐτὰ πάντες ὀνόματα καὶ ῥήματα, ὥσπερ ὑποβολέως ἑκάστοις ἀοράτως ἐνηχοῦντος.

His previous account, too (*ibid.* p. 139), of the notion which the translators entertained as to what was required in a correct Version of the Divine Oracles, exhibits in the clearest manner the opinion which the Jews held as to the original Scriptures themselves:—λογισάμενοι παρ' αὐτοῖς ὅσον εἴη τὸ πρᾶγμα θεσπισθέντας νόμους χρησμοῖς διερμηνεύειν, μήτ' ἀφελεῖν τι, μήτε προσθεῖναι, μήτε μεταθεῖναι δυναμένους, ἀλλὰ τὴν ἐξ ἀρχῆς ἰδέαν καὶ τὸν τύπον αὐτῶν διαφυλάττοντας, κ. τ. λ. Believing the history of this miracle to be true, Philo naturally regarded the LXX. as inspired; and his opinion as to the nature of *its* Inspiration (and therefore of Inspiration in general), we can infer from the fact that he constantly founds his reasoning on the language employed in the Greek Version:—e. g. on the insertion or omission of the article before Θεός; as well as upon the mere selection of the words employed by the translators. Thus, in his Treatise "De Somniis," lib. i. (t. i. p. 655), he argues:—ὁ ἱερὸς λόγος (i. e. the Old Testament) τὸν μὲν ἀληθείᾳ Θεὸν διὰ τοῦ ἄρθρου μεμήνυκεν, εἰπών· Ἐγώ εἰμι ὁ Θεός [e. g. Ex. xx. 2]. τὸν δ' ἐν καταχρήσει χωρὶς ἄρθρου. (See Gfrörer, "Philo," s. 51 ff.) And again, in his treatise "De Confus. Linguar." (t. i. p. 434), having quoted Gen. xi. 7 (LXX.), Συγχέωμεν ἐκεῖ αὐτῶν τὴν γλῶτταν κ. τ. λ.—he proceeds to argue from these words "tropologically" (ἐπὶ τὰς τροπικὰς ἀποδόσεις); observing, τὰ μὲν ῥητὰ τῶν χρησμῶν σκιάς τινας ὡσανεὶ σωμάτων εἶναι: his argument resting solely on the use in this place, by the LXX., of σύγχυσις instead of διάκρισις: and he goes on (*ibid.*) to reason similarly from the use (ver. 8) of the word διέσπειρεν.

II. In addition to the references to the Books of the Old Testament, given *supra*, pp. 66, 67, may be cited the following:—Ps. xx. 22 is quoted with the phrase τῶν Μωϋσέως γνωρίμων τις ἐν ὕμνοις εὐχόμενος εἶπεν—*De Confus. Ling.*, t. i. p. 410; and David is elsewhere styled ἑταῖρος Μωϋσέως—*Quod a Deo Somnia*, t. i. 691.

The Proverbs are quoted in the treatise "De Ebrietate," t. i. p. 369; and Solomon is called a member ἐκ τοῦ θείου χοροῦ (*ibid.* p. 362); and τις τῶν φοιτητῶν Μωϋσέως.—"*De Congr. quær. Erud. Grat.*," t. i. p. 544.

The words of Jeremiah (ii. 3) are introduced as uttered by "the Father of the Universe:"—ὁ Πατὴρ τῶν ὅλων διὰ προφητικῶν ἐθέσπισε στομάτων.—*De Profugis*, t. i. p. 575.

Philo quotes Hosea (see p. 65, note [4]) and Zechariah alone of Minor Prophets. Hos. xiv. 24, is referred to with the words;—στόματι προφητικῷ θεσπισθέντα διάπυρον χρησμόν.—*De Mutat. Nom.*, t. i. p. 599. And Zech. vi. 12, is thus introduced:—ἤκουσα μέντοι καὶ τῶν Μωϋσέως ἑταίρων τινὸς ἀποφθεγξαμένου τοιόνδε λόγον· Ἰδοὺ ἄνθρωπος ᾧ ὄνομα ἀνατολή.—*De Confus. Ling.*, t. i. p. 414.

Philo refers to several of the other Books without any distinctive epithet; but, as Eichhorn observes ("Einleit. in das A. T.," B. i. s. 135), since he nowhere quotes any part of the Apocrypha, although necessarily, and, from his allusions, obviously, familiar with this portion of the LXX., it clearly follows that the mere reference to a Book of Scripture, although unaccompanied by any title of respect, exhibits its pre-eminence, in Philo's opinion, above all other writings; and is equivalent to a full recognition of its inspiration. E. g. he quotes Job, xiv. 4, with the simple phrase, ὡς ὁ Ἰώβ φησί.—*De Mut. Nom.*, t. i. p. 585.

In the writings of Josephus, the *locus classicus* alluded to *supra*, p. 68, occurs in his treatise against Apion, and is as follows:—

I. Josephus had just alluded to the contradictions to be continually met with in the Greek historians. The Egyptians and Babylonians, indeed, paid great attention to the composition of their records; but the Jews excel all others:—Περὶ δὲ τῶν ἡμετέρων προγόνων, ὅτι τὴν αὐτήν, ἐῶ γὰρ λέγειν εἰ καὶ πλείω τῶν εἰρημένων ἐποιήσαντο τὴν περὶ τὰς ἀναγραφὰς ἐπιμέλειαν, τοῖς ἀρχιερεῦσι καὶ τοῖς προφήταις τοῦτο προστάξαντες. καὶ ὡς μέχρι τῶν καθ' ἡμᾶς χρόνων πεφύλακται μετὰ πολλῆς ἀκριβείας, εἰ δὲ θρασύτερον εἰπεῖν, καὶ φυλαχθήσεται, πειράσομαι συντόμως διδάσκειν. Οὐ γὰρ μόνον ἐξ ἀρχῆς ἐπὶ τούτων τοὺς ἀρίστους, καὶ τῇ θεραπείᾳ τοῦ Θεοῦ προσεδρεύοντας κατέστησαν, ἀλλ' ὅπως τὸ γένος τῶν ἱερέων ἄμικτον καὶ καθαρὸν διαμένῃ, προυνόησαν. Δεῖ γὰρ τὸν μετέχοντα τῆς ἱερωσύνης ἐξ ὁμοεθνοῦς γυναικὸς παιδοποιεῖσθαι, καὶ μὴ πρὸς χρήματα, μηδὲ τὰς ἄλλας ἀποβλέπειν τιμὰς, ἀλλὰ τὸ γένος ἐξετάζειν, ἐκ τῶν ἀρχαίων, λαμβάνοντα τὴν διαδοχὴν, καὶ πολλοὺς παρασχόμενον μάρτυσας. Καὶ ταῦτα πράττομεν οὐ μόνον ἐπ' αὐτῆς 'Ιουδαίας, ἀλλ' ὅπου ποτὲ σύστημα τοῦ γένους ἐστὶν ἡμῶν. κἀκεῖ τὸ ἀκριβὲς ἀποσώζεται τοῖς ἱερεῦσι περὶ τοὺς γάμους· * * * Τεκμήριον δὲ μέγιστον τῆς ἀκριβείας. οἱ ἀρχιερεῖς οἱ παρ' ἡμῖν ἀπὸ δισχιλίων ἐτῶν ὀνομαστοὶ παῖδες ἐκ πατρὸς εἰσὶν ἐν ταῖς ἀναγραφαῖς. Τοῖς δὲ τῶν εἰρημένων ὅ τι οὖν γένοιτο εἰς παράβασιν, ἀπηγόρευται μήτε τοῖς βωμοῖς παρίστασθαι, μήτε μετέχειν τῆς ἄλλης ἁγιστείας. Εἰκότως οὖν, μᾶλλον δὲ ἀναγκαίως, ἅτε μήτε τοῦ ὑπογράφειν αὐτεξουσίου πᾶσιν ὄντος, μήτε τινὸς ἐν τοῖς γραφομένοις ἐνούσης διαφωνίας· ἀλλὰ μόνων τῶν προφητῶν τὰ μὲν ἀνωτάτω καὶ τὰ παλαιότατα, κατὰ την ἐπίπνοιαν τὴν ἀπὸ τοῦ Θεοῦ μαθόντων, τὰ δὲ καθ' αὐτοὺς ὡς ἐγενετο σαφῶς συγγραφόντων. Οὐ γὰρ μυριάδες βιβλίων εἰσὶ παρ' ἡμῖν ἀσυμφώνων καὶ μαχομένων· δύο δὲ μόνα πρὸς τοῖς εἴκοσι βιβλία, τοῦ παντὸς ἔχοντα χρόνου τὴν ἀναγραφὴν, τὰ δικαίως θεῖα πεπιστευμένα. Καὶ τούτων πέντε μέν ἐστι τὰ Μωϋσέως, ἃ τούς τε νόμους περιέχει, καὶ τὴν τῆς ἀνθρωπογονίας παράδοσιν, μέχρι τῆς αὐτοῦ τελευτῆς. Οὗτος ὁ χρόνος ἀπολείπει τρισχιλίων ὀλίγον ἐτῶν. 'Απὸ δὲ τῆς Μωϋσέως τελευτῆς μέχρι τῆς 'Αρταξέρξου τοῦ μετὰ Ξέρξην Περσῶν βασιλέως ἀρχῆς, οἱ μετὰ Μωϋσῆν προφῆται τὰ καθ' αὐτοὺς πραχθέντα συνέγραψαν ἐν τρισὶ καὶ δέκα βιβλίοις. Αἱ δὲ λοιπαὶ τέσσαρες ὕμνους, εἰς τὸν Θεὸν καὶ τοῖς ἀνθρώποις ὑποθήκας τοῦ βίου περιέχουσιν. 'Απὸ δὲ 'Αρταξέρξου μέχρι τοῦ καθ' ἡμᾶς χρόνου γέγραπται μὲν ἕκαστα· πίστεως δὲ οὐχ ὁμοίας ἠξίωται τοῖς πρὸ αὐτῶν, διὰ τὸ μὴ γενέσθαι τὴν τῶν προφητῶν ἀκριβῆ διαδοχήν. Δῆλον δ' ἔστιν ἔργῳ πῶς ἡμεῖς τοῖς ἰδίοις γράμμασι πεπιστεύκαμεν. Τοσούτου γὰρ αἰῶνος ἤδη παρῳχηκότος, οὔτε προσθεῖναί τις οὐδὲν, οὔτε ἀφελεῖν αὐτῶν, οὔτε μεταθεῖναι τετόλμηκεν. Πᾶσι δὲ σύμφυτόν ἐστιν εὐθὺς ἐκ τῆς πρώτης γενέσεως 'Ιουδαίοις, τὸ νομίζειν αὐτὰ Θεοῦ δόγματα, καὶ τούτοις ἐμμένειν, καὶ ὑπὲρ αὐτῶν, εἰ δέοι, θνήσκειν ἡδέως."—*Cont. Apion.* lib. i. § 6–8, t. ii. p. 440.

In this same treatise (lib. ii. t. ii. p. 472), speaking of the origin of the LXX., Josephus styles the Old Testament "Holy Scripture;" Ptolemy Philadelphus, he observes, ἐπιθυμητὴς ἐγένετο τοῦ γνῶναι τοὺς ἡμετέρους νόμους, καὶ ταῖς τῶν ἱερῶν γραφῶν βίβλοις ἐντυχεῖν. (Cf. *supra*, p. 212.)

That the views of Philo and Josephus, as to Inspiration, agree in all essential particulars appears (1) from the fact that Josephus also has used the term ἑρμηνεύς in the sense in which it is employed by Philo (see Lecture ii. p. 64, &c.), although he has not developed his meaning so fully. Thus ("Ant." III. v. 3, t. i. p. 128) Moses is introduced as addressing the people previously to giving them the Ten Commandments. He declares that it is not Moses, the son of Amram and Jochebed, from whom these precepts proceed: they have come from Him Who made the Nile run with blood; Who brought water from the rock; and Who preserved Noah from the Deluge—Οὗτος ὑμῖν τούτους χαρίζεται τοὺς λόγους δι' ἑρμηνέως ἐμοῦ. Cf. also his opinion as to the meaning of προφήτης.—Lecture ii. p. 67, note [2]. (2) Their agreement may also be inferred from the description which Josephus has given of the effects of the Divine influence, as exemplified in the case of Balaam:—

Καὶ ὁ μὲν τοιαῦτα ἐπεθείαζεν, οὐκ ὢν ἐν ἑαυτῷ, τῷ δὲ θείῳ πνεύματι πρὸς αὐτὰ κεκινημένος. Τοῦ δὲ Βαλάκου δυσχεραίνοντος. * * *

ὦ Βάλακε, φησὶ, περὶ τῶν ὅλων λογίζῃ καὶ δοκεῖς ἐφ' ἡμῖν εἶναί τι περὶ τῶν τοιούτων σιγᾷν ἢ λέγειν, ὅταν ἡμᾶς τὸ τοῦ Θεοῦ λάβῃ πνεῦμα, φωνὰς γὰρ ἃς βούλεται τοῦτο, καὶ λόγους, οὐδὲν ἡμῶν εἰδότων, ἀφίησιν. * * * παντελῶς γὰρ ἀσθενεῖς οἱ προγινώσκειν περὶ τῶν ἀνθρωπείων παρ' ἑαυτῶν λαμβάνοντες, ὥστε μὴ ταῦθ' ἅπερ ὑπαγορεύει τὸ θεῖον λέγειν, βιάζεσθαι δὲ τὴν ἐκείνου βούλησιν. Οὐδὲν γὰρ ἐν ἡμῖν ἔτι φθάσαντος εἰσελθεῖν ἐκείνου ἡμέτερον.—*Ant.* lib. IV. vi. 5, t. i. p. 216. With this passage we can compare not only the statement of Philo when referring to this same subject (see Lecture v. p. 206, note [2]); but also his general opinion as to the personal condition of the Prophets, already quoted Lecture ii. p. 70, note [5].

II. As to the opinion of Josephus with respect to the Old Testament, it is sufficiently indicated in the passage, from his work against Apion, quoted above; and, therefore, special reference to his manner of citing the several books is not necessary here. The twenty-two books, there spoken of, comprise the Five books of Moses; the following thirteen written "by the Prophets after Moses:"—viz., (1) Joshua, (2) Judges and Ruth, (3) 1 and 2 Samuel, (4) 1 and 2 Kings, (5) 1 and 2 Chronicles, (6) Ezra and Nehemiah, (7) Esther, (8) Isaiah, (9) Jeremiah and Lamentations, (10) Ezekiel, (11) Daniel, (12) The Twelve Minor Prophets, (13) Job; while the λοιπαὶ τέσσαρες consist of the Books of Psalms and Proverbs, Ecclesiastes, and the Song of Solomon (see De Wette on the passage, "Einleit.," § 15, s. 20). It is needless, after so explicit a statement, to enter into particulars:—one may refer either to his manner of appealing to Isaiah and the Twelve Minor Prophets, as adduced in Lecture ii. p. 68, note [1]; or to his allusions to Isaiah, Jeremiah, and Ezekiel, as cited Lecture v., p. 188, note [2]. It has been also pointed out (Lecture vi., p. 256, note [2]) that he places the Book of Daniel among the ἱερὰ γράμματα; to which statement the following remarkable passage may be added ("Ant." x. xi. 7, t. i. p. 543):—ἅπαντα γὰρ αὐτῷ παραδόξως ὡς ἑνί τινι τῶν μεγίστων εὐτυχήθη προφητῶν * * * τὰ γὰρ βιβλία, ὅσα δὴ συγγραψάμενος καταλέλοιπεν, ἀναγινώσκεται παρ' ἡμῖν ἔτι καὶ νῦν· καὶ πεπιστεύκαμεν ἐξ αὐτῶν, ὅτι Δανιῆλος ὡμίλει τῷ Θεῷ. οὐ γὰρ τὰ μέλλοντα μόνον προφητεύων διετέλει, καθάπερ καὶ οἱ ἄλλοι προφῆται, ἀλλὰ καὶ καιρὸν ὥριζεν, εἰς ὃν ταῦτα ἀποβήσεται· καὶ τῶν προφητῶν τὰ χείρω προλεγόντων, καὶ διὰ τοῦτο δυσχεραινομένων ὑπὸ τῶν βασιλέων καὶ τοῦ πλήθους, Δανιῆλος ἀγαθῶν ἐγίνετο προφήτης αὐτοῖς, ὡς ἀπὸ μὲν τῆς εὐφημίας τῶν προλεγομένων εὔνοιαν ἐπισπᾶσθαι παρὰ πάντων, ἀπὸ δὲ τοῦ τέλους αὐτῶν [i. e. "ex eventuum certitudine"] ἀληθείας πίστιν, καὶ δόξαν ὁμοῦ θειότητος παρὰ τοῖς ὄχλοις ἀποφέρεσθαι. κατέλιπε δὲ γράψας, ὅθεν ἡμῖν τὸ τῆς προφητείας ἀκριβὲς αὐτοῦ καὶ ἀπαράλλακτον ἐποίησε δῆλον [he quotes Dan. viii.] * * * ταῦτα πάντα ἐκεῖνος, Θεοῦ δείξαντος αὐτῷ, συγγράψας κατέλειψεν· ὥστε τοὺς ἀναγινώσκοντας, καὶ τὰ συμβαίνοντα σκοποῦντας θαυμάζειν ἐπὶ τῇ παρὰ τοῦ Θεοῦ τιμῇ τὸν Δανιῆλον.[1] From this we learn that Josephus considered

[1] We learn from this passage that the fulfilment of an ancient prediction was the criterion, to a Jew, of the Divine mission of the Prophet—a principle, indeed, which the Old Testament itself had laid down: cf. Deut. xviii. 22. See also the passages quoted from Josephus, p. 68, note [1], and at the close of the note, p. 189. In the same manner Philo represents Moses as announcing before his death the future

a Book which has been placed among the Hagiographa (see App. C) equal to any production of the greatest Prophets: while we learn from other passages in his writings, that he regarded the second division of the Old Testament—"the Prophets"—as undistinguishable from "the Law." E. g. he mentions the Translation of Elijah, and that of Enoch, as being alike contained in the "Sacred Books:—"περὶ μέντοι Ἡλία, καὶ Ἐνώχου τοῦ γενομένου πρὸ τῆς ἐπομβρίας, ἐν ταῖς ἱεραῖς ἀναγέγραπται βίβλοις. Ant. IX. ii. 2, t. i. p. 475.

APPENDIX G.

THE JUDGMENT OF THE FATHERS.

(Lecture II.—Page 77, &c.)

Before entering fully upon the opinions of the Fathers, it may be useful to point out the critical spirit with which they approached the discussion of all questions connected with the Bible; whether relating to the authenticity of its several parts, its text, or its interpretation. These three particulars may be briefly illustrated.

(*a*) Julius Africanus (A.D. 220), whose critical acumen has been already exemplified (Lecture ii. p. 89), argues, in an epistle addressed to Origen, against the canonical authority of the History of Susanna. The learned, to the present day, have accepted his reasoning as conclusive; and have contented themselves with repeating his proof that this Apocryphal book must have been written originally in Greek, and not in Hebrew. One of his arguments is founded on the paronomasias which occur in the language ascribed to Daniel (Susan. 51–59). Thus on the mention of a "mastick tree" (σχῖνος), Daniel replies that the angel shall "cut thee in two" (σχίσει σε μέσον); and on the "holm tree" (πρῖνος) being named, he replies, with a similar allusion, that the angel waits "to cut thee in two" (πρίσαι σε μέσον). Here Julius Afr. observes:—ἐν μὲν οὖν Ἑλληνικαῖς φωναῖς τὰ τοιαῦτα ὁμοφωνεῖν συμβαίνει, παρὰ τὴν π ρ ί ν ο ν τὸ π ρ ί σ α ι, καὶ σ χ ί σ α ι, παρὰ τὴν σχίνον· ἐν δὲ τῇ Ἑβραΐδι τῷ παντὶ διέστηκεν.—(ap. Routh. "Reliq. Sacr.," vol. ii. p. 226.)

(*b*) Cassiodorus (see Lect. viii. p. 359, note[2]), in his treatise "De Institutione Divinarum Literarum," speaking of the order to be observed in conducting the studies of youth, directs, "Ut tirones Christi, postquam Psalmos didicerint, auctoritatem divinam in *codicibus emendatis* jugi exercitatione meditentur." He states as follows the manner in which his own labors were conducted:—

"Sed quamvis omnis Scriptura Divina supernâ luce resplendeat, et in ea virtus Spiritûs Sancti evidenter irradiet, in Psalterio tamen, et Prophetis, et Epistolis Apostolorum studium maximum laboris impendi. * * * Quos ego cunctos *novem codices* auctoritatis divinæ (ut senex potui) *sub collatione priscorum codicum*, amicis ante me legentibus, sedulâ lectione transivi. Ubi me multum laborasse, Domino adjuvante, profiteor; qua-

destinies of Israel:—ἄν τὰ μὲν ἤδη συμβέβηκε, τὰ δὲ προσδοκᾶται. διότι πίστις τῶν μελλόντων ἡ τῶν προγεγονότων τελείωσις.—*De Vita Mosis*, lib. III. t. ii. p. 179.

tenus nec eloquentiæ modificatæ deessem, nec libros sacros temeraria præsumptione lacerarem."—*Præf.*, t. ii. p. 538.

(*c*) S. Augustine, in his treatise "De Consensu Evangelistarum," compares the accounts, given by S. Mark and S. Luke, of the words from heaven at our Lord's Baptism:—

"Illud vero quod *nonnulli codices* habent secundum Lucam, hoc illa voce sonuisse quod in Psalmo scriptum est: 'Filius meus es tu, ego hodie genui te;' *quamquam in antiquioribus codicibus Græcis non inveniri perhibeatur, tamen si aliquibus fide dignis exemplaribus confirmari possit*, quid aliquid quam utrumque intelligendum est quolibet verborum ordine de cælo sonuisse?"—Lib. II. c. xiv. t. iii. pars ii. p. 46.

Again: discussing the well-known difficulty as to the quotation ascribed, in S. Matt. xxvii. 9, to Jeremiah, S. Augustine objects to the explanation which considers our present text incorrect:—

"Mihi autem cur non placeat hæc causa est, quia et *plures codices* habent Jeremiæ nomen; et qui diligentius in Græcis exemplaribus Evangelium consideraverunt, *in antiquioribus Græcis* ita se perhibent invenisse: et *nulla fuit causa* cur adderetur hoc nomen, ut mendositas fieret: *cur autem de nonnullis codicibus tolleretur, fuit utique causa*, ut hoc audax imperitia faceret, cum turbaretur quæstione quod hoc testimonium apud Jeremiam non inveniretur."—*Ibid.* lib. III. c. vii. p. 114.

The profound scholarship of S. Jerome has been sufficiently illustrated by those remarks respecting the relation of the LXX. to the Hebrew text of the Old Testament, which have been quoted from his writings in Lecture vii.

Similar illustrations of the critical spirit with which the Fathers conducted their theological investigations might be multiplied to any extent. The foregoing remarks have been introduced merely for the purpose of drawing attention to the fact, that the judgment of the Church on the subject of Inspiration—pronounced, as we shall see, in every age, with such decision, and with such unanimity,—has not been formed under the influence of blind prejudice, or in consequence of an ignorant and unreasoning submission to a mere traditional dogma.

The following inquiry will be most fitly conducted according to the method laid down in Lecture ii. p. 81; the quotations being arranged under the heads which have been there adopted.

I. Testimonies relating to the Divine influence exerted in the composition of the Bible. These, again, may be divided into the following classes:

(1) The Article of the Creed—"We believe in the Holy Ghost, Who spake by the Prophets."

S. Irenæus (A. D. 167): Ἡ μὲν γὰρ Ἐκκλησία * * * παρὰ τῶν Ἀποστόλων * * * παραλαβοῦσα τὴν εἰς ἕνα Θεὸν * * * πίστιν * * * καὶ εἰς Πνεῦμα Ἅγιον, τὸ διὰ τῶν προφητῶν κεκηρυχός.—*Cont. Hær.*, lib. I. cap. x. p. 48.

Origen (A. D. 230) lays down the articles of the Faith in the opening of his treatise "De Principiis." Redepenning (*in loc.* p. 90) justly observes: "Inter omnes Fidei regulas, Niceno Symbolo priores, nulla hâc, quam Origenes hoc loco, xi. capitibus sive articulis comprehensam, exhibet, uberior est." Origen there states: "Species eorum, quæ per prædicationem Apostolicam manifeste traduntur, istæ sunt. * * * Sane quod Iste Spiritus unumquemque sanctorum, vel Prophetarum, vel Apostolorum inspiraverit, et non alius Spiritus in veteribus, alius vero in his qui in adventu Christi inspirati sunt fuerit, manifestissime in Ecclesiis prædicatur."—Lib. i. § 4, t. i. p. 48.

S. Epiphanius (A. D. 368), at the close of his "Ancoratus," gives two formulæ of Faith (t. ii. p. 122, *sqq.*), in accordance (as he himself states, *ibid.* p. 123) with that which had been laid down at Nicæa. In the former he recites the words of the Symbol of Constantinople quoted *supra*, p. 81, note [1]. In the second his definition is as follows:—*εἰς τὸ Ἅγ. Πν. πιστευομεν, τὸ λαλῆσαν ἐν νόμῳ, καὶ κηρύξαν ἐν τοῖς προφήταις καὶ * * * λαλοῦν ἐν Ἀποστόλοις, κ. τ. λ.*

And S. Cyril of Jerusalem (A. D. 350) declares: Ἡ *καθολικὴ* Ἐκκλη*σία, παρέδωκεν ἐν τῇ τῆς πίστεως ἐπαγγελίᾳ, πιστεύειν εἰς ἓν Ἅγιον* Πνεῦ*μα, τὸν* Παράκλ*ητον, τὸ λαλῆσαν ἐν τοῖς προφήταις.—Catech.* xvii. § 3, p. 265.

This doctrine was not denied even by the heretics. In Theodoret's (AD. 423) "Dialogues," the answer of the heretic Eranistes (quoted *supra*, Lecture ii. p. 79, note [2]) is preceded by the following question and the answer to it by the representative of the Church:—ΕΡΑΝ. *Τί οὖν, ψεύδεται ὁ προφήτης;* ΟΡΘ. *Μὴ γένοιτο· τοῦ Θείου γὰρ Πνεύματος καὶ ταῦτα κἀκεῖνα τὰ ῥήματα.—Eranistes*, Dial. i. t. IV. p. 12.

Hence the title *προφητικόν* so frequently given to the Holy Ghost; and this even with reference to His *ordinary* operations upon all Christians. S. Justin M. (A.D. 140) writes (cf. too, *supra*, p. 81, note [2]):—*ἐξ ὧν μαθεῖν ὑμῖν πάρεστι, πῶς προτρέπεται ζῆν τοὺς ἀνθρώπους τὸ π ρ ο φ η τ ι κ ὸ ν* Π ν ε ῦ *μ α.—Apolog.*, i. § 40, p. 67.

Nor was this expression used merely in the case of *prophets*, strictly so called. S. Justin M. again writes: *Ἐρῶ ὑμῖν καὶ ἄλλους λόγους τοὺς εἰρημένους διὰ Δαβὶδ τοῦ μακαρίου· ἐξ ὧν καὶ* Κύριον *τὸν* Χριστὸν *ὑπὸ τοῦ* Ἁγίου *π ρ ο φ η τ ι κ ο ῦ* Π ν ε ύ *μ α τ ο ς λεγόμενον νοήσετε.— Dial. cum Tryph.*, § 32, p. 129.

Thus, too, where he adduces Prov. viii. 22, it is employed by Athenagoras (A.D. 177) in a passage which should be taken in conjunction with his words quoted *infra*, No. (7), p. 431:—Συν*άδει δὲ τῷ* Λόγῳ *καὶ τὸ π ρ ο φ η τ ι κ ὸ ν* Πνεῦμα· Κύριος *γάρ, φησίν, ἔκτισέ με ἀρχὴν ὁδῶν αὐτοῦ εἰς ἔργα αὐτοῦ. καί τοι καὶ αὐτὸ τὸ ἐγεργοῦν τοῖς ἐκφωνοῦσι προφητικῶς* Ἅγιον Πνεῦ*μα, ἀπόρροιαν εἶναι φαμὲν τοῦ* Θεοῦ, *ἀπορρέον καὶ ἐπαναφερόμενον, ὡς ἀκτῖνα ἡλίου.—Leg. pro Christ.*, § 10, p. 287.

See also the words of S. Hippolytus quoted under the second head, No. (1) class (*a*), p. 432.

(2.) The *general* manner of alluding to the Holy Spirit's influence upon the writers of Scripture, founded upon the principle laid down in the passages just considered, will appear from the following statements. The result of the Spirit's influence S. Justin M. terms "Divine Inspiration:"— Παντ*αχόθεν τοίνυν εἰδέναι προσήκει, ὅτι οὐδαμῶς ἑτέρως περὶ* Θεοῦ *ἢ τῆς ὀρθῆς θεοσεβείας μανθάνειν οἷόν τε, ἢ παρὰ τῶν προφητῶν μόνον, τῶν δ ι ὰ τ ῆ ς θ ε ί α ς ἐ π ι π ν ο ί α ς διδασκόντων ὑμᾶς.—Cohort. ad Græc.*, § 38, p. 35.

And as to the Old Testament writers in general:—*Ἐγένοντό τινες* πρὸ πολλοῦ χρόνου πάντων τούτων τῶν νομιζομένων φιλοσόφων παλαιότεροι, μακάριοι, καὶ δίκαιοι, καὶ θεοφιλεῖς, θείῳ Πνεύματι λαλήσαντες * * * προφήτας δὲ αὐτοὺς καλοῦσιν * * * μόνα ταῦτα εἰπόντες ἃ ἤκουσαν καὶ ἃ εἶδον, Ἁγίῳ πληρωθέντες Πνεύματι. Συγγράμματα δὲ αὐτῶν ἔτι καὶ νῦν διαμένει.—*Dial. cum Tryph.*, § 7, p. 109.

Clemens Alex. (A.D. 192), speaking of those heretics (especially the Gnostics) who had excluded the prophetical books from their Canon, observes:—Ταύτῃ οὖν οὐκ εὐσεβεῖς, δυσαρεστούμενοι ταῖς θείαις ἐντολαῖς, τουτέστι τῷ Ἁγίῳ Πνεύματι.—*Strom.* vii. c. 16, p. 893.

The passage from Tertullian (A.D. 692) prefixed to Lecture i. continues as follows:—"Viros enim justitia et innocentia dignos Deum nosse et ostendere a primordio in sæculum emisit *Spiritu Divino inundatos* quo prædicarent Deum unicum esse."—*Apolog.*, § xviii. p. 18.

Similarly S. Augustine (A.D. 396): "Si igitur, ut oportet, nihil aliud intueamur in Scripturis illis, nisi quid per homines dixerit Dei Spiritus"—*De Civit. Dei*, xviii. § 43, t. vii. p. 526.

And again:—"Hic insinuatur nobis, ea loqui prophetas Dei quæ audiunt ab Eo, nihilque aliud esse prophetam Dei, nisi enunciatorem verborum Dei hominibus."—*Quæst. in Ex.*, lib. ii. qu. 19, t. iii. p. 426.

Such statements, indeed, are merely developments of the doctrine laid down from the first, by the Apostolic Fathers, as to both the Apostles and the Prophets. S. Clement of Rome (A.D. 65) introduces a quotation from Ezekiel (xxxiii. 11) with the words:—Οἱ λειτουργοὶ τῆς χάριτος τοῦ Θεοῦ διὰ Πνεύματος Ἁγίου περὶ μετανοίας ἐλάλησαν.—*Ad Corinth.*, § viii. Of Jer. ix. 23, he writes:—Ποιήσωμεν τὸ γεγραμμένον, λέγει γὰρ τὸ Πνεῦμα τὸ Ἅγιον.—*ibid.*, § xiii. Of Isai. liii.:—Καθὼς τὸ Πν. τὸ Ἅγ. περὶ Αὐτοῦ ἐλάλησεν.—*ibid.*, § xvi. And of the New Testament writers he observes:—Οἱ Ἀπόστολοι * * * πιστωθέντες ἐν τῷ λόγῳ τοῦ Θεοῦ, μετὰ πληροφορίας Πνεύματος Ἁγίου.—*ibid.*, § xlii.

So also S. Ignatius (A.D. 101) writes:—Οἱ γὰρ θειότατοι προφῆται κατὰ Χριστὸν Ἰησοῦν ἔζησαν. Διὰ τοῦτο καὶ ἐδιώχθησαν, ἐμπνεόμενοι ὑπὸ τῆς χάριτος Αὐτοῦ.—*Ep. ad Magnes.*, c. viii. (Cf. the passage quoted Lecture iii. p. 120, note.[3]) And as to the New Testament, he refers to 1 Cor. iii. 16; vi. 19, with the words:—Τὸ δὲ Πνεῦμα ἐκήρυσσεν.—*Ad Philadelph.*, § vii.

(3.) Hence the Fathers, in opposition to the Gnostic heresy, infer the co-ordinate authority of the Old and the New Testament.

Tertullian writes: "Hæ sunt antitheses Marcionis, id est, contrariæ oppositiones; quæ conantur discordiam Evangelii cum Lege committere, ut ex diversitate sententiarum utriusque Instrumenti, diversitatem quoque argumententur Deorum."—*Adv. Marcion.*, lib. i. § 19, p. 443.

S. Irenæus argues to the same effect:—"Unde autem poterant prædicere prophetæ Regis adventum * * * si ab altero Deo *propheticam Inspirationem* acceperunt?"—*Cont. Hær.*, lib. IV. cap. xxxiv. p. 275.

So also Origen: "Si qui sunt qui Spiritum S. alium quidem dicant esse qui fuit in Prophetis, alium autem qui fuit in Apostolis Domini nostri Jesu Christi, unum atque idem delictum impietatis admittunt, quod illi qui, quantum in se est, naturam Deitatis secant, et scindunt unum Legis et Evangeliorum Deum."—*In Titum*, iii. 10, t. iv. p. 695.

The doctrine of the primitive Church is thus summed up by S. Cyril of Jerusalem :—Μηδεὶς οὖν χωριζέτω τὴν παλαιὰν ἀπὸ τῆς καινῆς διαθήκης. μηδεὶς λεγέτω ὅτι ἄλλο τὸ Πνεῦμα ἐκεῖ, καὶ ἄλλο ὧδε * * * οἴδαμεν τὸ Πνεῦμα τὸ Ἅγιον, τὸ λαλῆσαν ἐν προφήταις· καὶ ἐν τῇ Πεντηκοστῇ κατελθὸν ἐπὶ τοὺς Ἀποστόλους.—*Catech.*, xvi. § 4, p. 244.

And this doctrine, as it has ever been maintained in the West, so it has been expressly repeated by that Father to whose opinions the Eastern Church pays the highest deference, S. Joannes Damascénus (A.D. 730); who concludes, as follows, an enumeration of the Books of Scripture identical with the Canon of the Anglican Church: Εἷς ἐστιν ὁ Θεὸς, ὑπό τε παλαιᾶς διαθήκης καὶ καινῆς κηρυττόμενος, ὁ ἐν Τριάδι ὑμνούμενός τε καὶ δοξαζόμενος, τοῦ Κυρίου φήσαντος, οὐκ ἦλθον καταλῦσαι τὸν νόμον, ἀλλὰ πληρῶσαι * * * καὶ τοῦ Ἀποστόλου εἰπόντος [*scil.* Heb. i. 1] * * * διὰ Πνεύματος τοίνυν Ἁγίου, ὅ τε νόμος καὶ οἱ προφῆται, Εὐαγγελισταὶ καὶ Ἀπόστολοι, ἐλάλησαν. Πᾶσα τοίνυν γραφὴ θεόπνευστος, πάντως καὶ ὠφέλιμος. ὥστε κάλλιστον καὶ ψυχοφελέστατον ἐρευνᾷν τὰς θείας γραφάς.—*De Fide Orthod.*, lib. iv. § 17, t. i. p. 282.

(4.) The manner in which the Fathers *specially* quote or refer to Scripture will appear from the following illustrations (cf. Lecture ii. p. 84, notes [3], [4], [5]) :—

S. Clement of Rome thus quotes 1 Cor. i. 10: Ἀναλάβετε τὴν ἐπιστολὴν τοῦ μακαρίου Παύλου * * * ἐπ' ἀληθείας πνευματικῶς ["certe divinitus inspiratus."—*Vet. Lat. Int.*] ἐπέστειλεν ὑμῖν.—*Ad Corinth.*, § xlvii.

Tertullian, having quoted 1 Cor. iv. 9, with the words, "Providentia Spiritus Sancti demonstravit," proceeds to comment on it with the prefatory remark: "Verebatur nimirum tantæ constantiæ vir, *ne dicam Spiritus Sanctus*," &c.—*Adv. Marcion.*, lib. v. § 7, p. 587. And he thus quotes 1 Tim. vi. 10 : "Spiritus Domini per Apostolum pronuntiavit."—*De Patientia*, § 7, p. 163.

Theophilus of Antioch (A.D. 168) refers ἐπὶ τὴν ἀρχὴν τῆς τοῦ κόσμου κτίσεως, ἣν ἀ ν έ γ ρ α ψ ε Μωσῆς ὁ θεράπων τοῦ Θεοῦ, διὰ Πνεύματος Ἁγίου.—*Ad Autolyc.*, lib. iii. § 23, p. 395.

Clemens Al. writes: Διὰ τοῦτο ἄρα μυστικῶς τὸ ἐν τῷ Ἀποστόλῳ Ἅγιον Πνεῦμα, τῇ τοῦ Κυρίου ἀποχρώμενον φωνῇ, Γάλα ὑμᾶς ἐπότισα [1 Cor iii. 2], λέγει.—*Pædagog.*, lib. i. § 6, p. 127.

S. Hippolytus, Bishop of Portus (A.D. 220), in a remarkable manner ascribes *the quotation* of the words of Isaiah in the New Testament, immediately to the Holy Ghost :—Τὸ Πνεῦμα τὸ Ἅγιον [ἵνα φοβήσῃ,] ἐκ προσώπου των Ἀποστόλων διεμαρτύρατο, λέγων· καὶ τίς ἐπίστευσεν τῇ ἀκοῇ ἡμῶν [Isai. liii. 1; S. John, xii. 38; Rom. x. 16.]—*Cont Hær. Noeti*, § 17 (ap. Routh. "Script. Eccl. Opusc.," t. i. p. 75.)

S. Cyprian (A. D. 248): "Loquitur in Scripturis Divinis Spiritus Sanctus."—*De Opere et Eleemos.*, p. 237. Again :—"Item beatus Apostolus Paulus Dominicæ inspirationis gratia plenus: 'Qui administrat' (2 Cor. ix. 10), inquit," &c.—*Ibid.*, p. 240. So also :—"Denunciat Spiritus S. in Psalmis dicens: 'Deus qui inhabitare' (Ps. lxviii. 6)," &c.—*De Unitate Eccl.*, p. 196. And, "Per Apostolum præmonet Spiritus S., et dicit: 'Oportet et hæreses esse' (1 Cor. xi. 19)," &c.—*Ibid.*, p. 111.

Eusebius Pamph. (A.D. 315) :—Τὸ Πνεῦμα τὸ Θεῖον ἐν προφητείαις, τὴν γενεὰν Αὐτοῦ, φησὶ, τίς διηγήσεται [Isai. liii.]; * * * καὶ ὁ μέγας Μωϋσῆς, ὡς ἂν προφητῶν ἁπάντων παλαιότατος, Θείῳ Πνεύματι ὑπογράφων, κ. τ. λ.—*Eccl. Hist.*, lib. I. cap. ii. p. 4.

And to add the testimony of both East and West :—"How often," asks S. Ephræm Syrus (A.D. 370) have we despised the warnings of Holy Scripture :—"Ω, πῶς τῶν γραφῶν ἀκούοντες ἐχλευάζομεν; ἐκεῖ ὁ Θεὸς ἐλάλει διὰ τῶν γραφῶν, καὶ οὐ προσείχομεν.—*In secundum Domini Advent.*, t. ii. p. 201. And S. Jerome (A.D. 378) writes: "Hæretici quum ante crediderint in Scripturis, quæ a Spiritu S. conscriptæ sunt et editæ, transferunt se ad novas doctrinas," &c.—*Comm. in Mich.*, cap. VII. lib. ii. t. vi. p. 520.

(5.) The epithets applied to Scripture (see Lecture ii. p. 82) are next to be considered :—

a. "Scripture given by Inspiration of God" (2 Tim. iii. 16.) From the countless passages in which this expression is employed, by all the Fathers, the following may be cited :—

Πᾶσαι αἱ θεόπνευστοι γραφαὶ Θεὸν τὸν Υἱὸν τοῦ Θεοῦ μηνύουσιν.—*Syn. Antioch adv. Paulum Samosat.* (A.D. 270). (ap. Routh. "Rel. Sacr.," t. iii. p. 292.)

S. Athanasius (A.D. 325) :—Πᾶσα μὲν, ὦ τέκνον, ἡ καθ' ἡμᾶς γραφὴ, παλαιά τε καὶ καινὴ, θεόπνευστός ἐστι, καὶ ὠφέλιμος πρὸς διδασκαλίαν, ὡς γέγραπται.—*Epist. ad Marcellin.*, t. i. p. 982.

And S. Basil :—Πᾶσα γραφὴ θεόπνευστος καὶ ὠφέλιμος, διὰ τοῦτο συγγραφεῖσα παρὰ τοῦ Πνεύματος, ἵν' ὥσπερ ἐν κοινῷ τῶν ψυχῶν ἰατρείῳ, πάντες ἄνθρωποι τὸ ἴαμα τοῦ οἰκείου πάθους ἕκαστος ἐκλεγώμεθα.—*Hom. in Psal.* i., t. i. 90. Cf. the words of S. Gregory of Nyssa, quoted *supra*, Lecture vi. p. 241, note [2].

β. Scripture is styled "Spiritual;" or "the words of the Spirit." S. Irenæus writes :—Ὅλων τῶν γραφῶν πνευματικῶν οὐσῶν.—*Cont. Hæres.*, lib. ii. cap. 28, p. 156. And Origen eloquently asks :—"Vis tibi ostendam quomodo de verbis Spiritûs S. ignis exeat, et accendat corda credentium? Audi dicentem David in Psalmo; 'Eloquium Domini ignivit eum.' * * * Tu ergo unde ardebis? Unde invenientur in te carbones ignis, qui nunquam Domini igniris eloquio, nunquam verbis Spiritûs S. inflammaris?"—*In Levit.*, Hom. ix. § 9, t. ii. p. 243.

And again: "Sed non possumus hoc dicere de S. Spiritûs literis, quod aliquid in eis otiosum sit aut superfluum, etiamsi aliquibus videntur obscura. Sed hoc potius facere debemus, ut oculos mentis nostræ convertamus ad Eum, qui hæc scribi jussit."—*Homil. in Num.* xxvii., t. ii. p. 375.

Or, as Clemens Al. expresses it: Τὰ ὑπὸ τοῦ Ἁγίου Πνεύματος σωτηρίως εἰρημένα.—*Strom.*, vi. § 15, p. 803.

To the same effect Rufinus writes: "Milites diviserunt sibi vestimenta Jesu: hoc etiam curæ fuit Spiritui S. prophetarum vocibus protestari, *cum dicit:* 'Diviserunt sibi,' &c. [Ps. xxii. 18]."—*Expos. in Symb. Apost.* (ad calc. opp. S. Cypriani, p. ccxvi). He also refers those who desire to inquire particularly as to the doctrine of the Resurrection, "ad ipsos fontes Divinorum Voluminum."—*Ibid.*, p. ccxviii.

γ. The epithet "Divine" is used in different forms. The Presbyter Caius (A.D. 211), a leading opponent of Montanism, writes in a remark-

… le passage :—Κἂν αὐτοῖς προτείνῃ τὶς ῥητὸν γραφῆς θ ε ι κ ῆ ς * * * καταλιπόντες δὲ τὰς ἁ γ ί α ς τοῦ Θεοῦ γραφὰς * * * ἢ γὰρ οὐ πιστεύουσιν Ἁγίῳ Πνεύματι λελέχθαι τὰς θ ε ί α ς γραφὰς, καὶ εἰσὶν ἄπιστοι· ἢ ἑαυτοὺς ἡγοῦνται σοφωτέρους τοῦ Ἁγίου Πνεύματος ὑπάρχειν· καὶ τί ἕτερον ἢ δαιμονῶσιν.—*Parv. Labyrinth.* (ap. Routh. "Rel. Sacr.," t. ii. p. 132.)

Origen's fourth book, "De Principiis," is entitled—Περὶ τοῦ θεοπνεύστου τῆς θείας γραφῆς. The question of Inspiration itself, however, he regards as so completely settled that he declines to dwell upon it at any length :—Μετὰ τὸ ὡ ς ἐ ν ἐ π ι δ ρ ο μ ῇ εἰρηκέναι περὶ τοῦ θεοπνεύστους εἶναι τὰς θείας γραφὰς, ἀναγκαῖον ἐπεξελθεῖν τῷ τρόπῳ τῆς ἀναγνώσεως καὶ νοήσεως αὐτῶν.—cap. viii. t. i. p. 164.

S. Cyprian writes : "In Apocalypsi Scriptura Divina declarat."—*Epist.* lxiii., p. 108.

Tertullian, interpreting 1 Cor. xi. 5, observes : "Nec mirum, si Apostolus eodem utique Spiritu actus, quo cum omnis Scriptura Divina, tum et illa Genesis (c. ii. 23) digesta est, eadem voce usus est mulierem ponendo ; quæ exemplo Evæ," &c.—*De Oratione*, cap. xxii. (ap. Routh. "Script. Eccl. Opusc.," t. i. p. 114).

"Crescens a Cirta [ap. Concil. Carthag.,[1] vii.] dixit : In tanto cœtu sanctissimorum consacerdotum lectis literis Cypriani * * * quæ tantum in se sanctorum testimoniorum descendentium ex *Scripturis Deificis* continent," &c. (ad calc. opp. S. Cypriani, p. 331). Cf. the use of the title "*Deificæ*" by the Martyr Felix, as well as of "*Dominicæ*" by the Pagan Proconsul (proving the universality of such expressions), quoted Lecture ii. p. 93, note [1].

Again : we find the expressions "Heavenly Scriptures :"—"Non utique ex Scripturarum *cœlestium* vitio, quæ nunquam fallunt," &c.—Novatianus (A.D. 251), *De Trinitate*, cap. xxx. (ed. Welchman) ; and "Scriptures of the Lord." Clemens Al., speaking of those auditors who had been attracted from the schools of the Greeks, observes : ἥτε τῶν γραφῶν τ ῶ ν Κ υ ρ ι α κ ῶ ν ἀνάγνωσις εἰς ἀπόδειξιν τῶν λεγομένων ἀναγκαία.—*Strom*. vi. § ii., p. 786

S. Jerome writes : "Non adeo me hebetis fuisse cordis, et tam crassæ rusticitatis ut aliquid de *Dominicis* verbis aut corrigendum putaverim, aut non divinitus inspiratum."—*Ad Marcellam*, Ep. xxvii. t. i. p. 132.

So also Tertullian : "Evolverem Prophetias, si Dominus ipse tacuisset, nisi quod et Prophetiæ, *vox erant Domini*."—*De Resurr. Carn.*, § xxii. p. 394.

And to the same effect :—"Qui ergo putaveris nihil nos de salute Cæsarum curare, inspice *Dei voces, literas nostras* * * * 'Orate,' inquit, 'pro regibus, et pro principibus, et potestatibus,'" &c.—*Apolog.*, § xxxi. p. 30.

And again : "Communes sententias ab argumentationibus philosophorum liberare * * * revocando quæstiones ad *Dei literas*."—*De Anima*, § ii. p. 306.

[1] Mr. Westcott, in the "Catena" appended to his "Gospel Harmony," has collected the following expressions employed in this Council : "Scripturæ Sanctæ" (5, 6, 74); "Scripturæ Deificæ" (8); "Sancta et admirabilia Scripturarum verba" (31); "Divinæ Scripturæ" (33).

In like manner, Lactantius (A.D. 303) arguing that Vespasian had fulfilled Prophecy by destroying Jerusalem: "Confirmata sunt, quæ falsa et incredibilia putantur ab iis, quos vera *cœlestium literarum* doctrina non imbuit."—*Inst. Div.*, lib. IV. cap. xxii.

All which passages but express the following thought of S. Gregory of Neocæs. (A.D. 254): Οὐ γὰρ ἐστὶ χωρὶς Νόμου καὶ Προφητῶν, ἢ Εὐαγγελιστῶν καὶ Ἀποστόλων ἔχω [ἔχειν], τὴν ἀκριβῆ τῆς σωτηρίας ἐλπίδα. διὰ γὰρ τῆς τῶν ἁγίων Προφητῶν, καὶ Ἀποστόλων γλώττης ὁ Κύριος ἡμῶν φθέγγεται * * * ὅταν δὲ ἀναγινώσκεται τὸ Εὐαγγέλιον, ἢ Ἀποστολικὸν, μὴ προσεχῇς τῇ βίβλῳ, ἢ τῷ ἀναγινώσκοντι· ἀλλὰ τῷ ἀπ' οὐρανοῦ φθεγγομένῳ Θεῷ.—*Sermo* ii. *in Annunc.*, p. 19.

δ. Still more strongly the Books of Scripture are termed "Epistles from God to man." In addition to the passage from S. Gregory the Great (A.D. 590), prefixed to Lecture ii., the following words of S. Macarius Ægypt. (A. D. 373) may be quoted: Ὥσπερ βασιλεὺς γράψας ἐπιστολὰς, οἷς βούλεται κωδικέλους καὶ δωρεὰς ἰδίας χαρίσασθαι, σημαίνει πᾶσιν, ὅτι ταχέως σπουδάσατε πρός με * * * οὕτως καὶ τὰς θείας γραφὰς ὥσπερ ἐπιστολὰς ἀπέστειλεν ὁ Βασιλεὺς Θεὸς τοῖς ἀνθρώποις.—*Homil.* xxxix. p. 203.

(6.) As the result of such principles, the Church inferred, as I have already observed (Lecture ii. p. 83), "the sufficiency, the infallible certainty, and the perfection of Scripture." In addition to the opinions there adduced (notes [2] and [3]), the following may be cited:—

Tertullian writes: "Adoro Scripturæ plenitudinem, qua mihi et Factorem manifestat et facta. * * * Scriptum esse doceat Hermogenis officina. Si non est scriptum, timeat Væ illud, adjicientibus aut detrahentibus destinatum."—*Adv. Hermogen.* § 22, p. 277.

S. Hippolytus enforces the same lesson: Εἷς Θεὸς, ὃν οὐκ ἄλλοθεν ἐπιγινώσκομεν, ἢ ἐκ τῶν ἁγίων γραφῶν. Ὃν γὰρ τρόπον ἐάν τις βουληθῇ τὴν σοφίαν τοῦ αἰῶνος τούτου ἀσκεῖν, οὐκ ἄλλως δυνήσεται τούτου τυχεῖν, ἐὰν μὴ δόγμασι φιλοσόφων ἐντύχῃ, τὸν αὐτὸν δὴ τρόπον ὅσοι θεοσέβειαν ἀσκεῖν βουλόμεθα, οὐκ ἄλλοθεν ἀσκήσομεν ἢ ἐκ τῶν λογίων τοῦ Θεοῦ * * * Μὴ κατ' ἰδίαν προαίρεσιν, μηδὲ κατ' ἴδιον νοῦν, μηδὲ βιαζόμενοι τὰ ὑπὸ τοῦ Θεοῦ δεδομένα. ἀλλ' ὃν τρόπον Αὐτὸς ἐβουλήθη διὰ τῶν ἁγίων γραφῶν δεῖξαι, οὕτως ἴδωμεν.—*Cont. Noeti. Hær.*, § ix. (ap. Routh. "Script. Eccl. Opusc.," vol. i. p. 64).

S. Hilary of Poitiers (A. D. 354): "Quid enim infidelibus stultius est, qui præter illum communem irreligiosorum errorem etiam hoc adjiciunt piaculi, ut Divina Scripturarum eloquia putent *perfectæ doctrinæ* carere ratione? * * * Verum quamvis * * * his qui sapientiam Dei sequuntur cognitam *dictorum cœlestium perfectionem* existimem, nihilque eorum esse, quod non *consummatum* atque omni ex parte *perfectum* sit," &c.—*Tract. in Psal.* cxviii., t. i. p. 314.

Novatianus: "Scriptura cælesti abundans plenitudine."—*De Trinitate*, cap. xxiv.

The following is the conclusion of S. Joannes Damascen.:—Διὰ νόμου δὲ, καὶ προφητῶν πρότερον, ἔπειτα δὲ καὶ διὰ τοῦ μονογενοῦς αὐτοῦ Υἱοῦ, Κυρίου δὲ, καὶ Θεοῦ, καὶ Σωτῆρος ἡμῶν Ἰησοῦ Χριστοῦ, κατὰ τὸ ἐφικτὸν ἡμῖν τὴν ἑαυτοῦ ἐφανέρωσε γνῶσιν· πάντα τοίνυν τὰ παραδεδομένα ἡμῖν διά τε νόμου, καὶ προφητῶν, καὶ Ἀποστόλων, καὶ

Ευαγγελιστῶν δεχόμεθα, καὶ γινώσκομεν, καὶ σέβομεν, οὐδὲν παρ αιτέρω τούτων ἐπιζητοῦντες.—*De fide Orthodoxa*, lib. i. cap. 1, t. i. p. 123.

(7.) In fine, "the joint participation of the Eternal Word and of the Holy Spirit in bringing the Scriptures into being, was a truth fully appreciated by the Fathers" (see Lecture ii. p. 83).

The principle on which such statements were founded is thus laid down by S. Athanasius:—

Καὶ ὅτε μὲν λέγει ἡ γραφὴ, ὅτι Πνεῦμα Ἅγιον ἐλάλει ἐν τοῖς προφήταις, ἀλλαχοῦ λέγει ὁ μακάριος Παῦλος, ὅτι ὁ Πατὴρ ἐλάλει ἐν τοῖς προφήταις [Heb. i. 1] * * * καὶ ἀλλαχοῦ λέγει, ὅτι ὁ Υἱὸς λαλεῖ [2 Cor. xiii. 3] * * * ὁ δὲ Υἱὸς, τὸ Πνεῦμα εἶπε το λαλοῦν ἐν τοῖς ἀποστόλοις [S. Matt. x. 20, and S. Luke, xii. 12] * * * ὁρᾷς ὅτι ἅπερ ἐστὶν ἔργα τοῦ Πατρὸς, ταῦτα λέγει ἡ γραφὴ τοῦ Υἱοῦ εἶναι, καὶ τοῦ Ἁγίου Πνεύματος.—*De Incarnat.* cap. xiv., t. i. p. 881. (Cf. also the similar statements *ibid.*, cap. xviii. p. 884; and the words quoted *supra*, p. 83, note [2].)

According to Tertullian: "Regula est autem fidei * * * qua creditur: Unum omnino Deum esse * * * qui universa de nihilo produxerit, per Verbum Suum * * * Id Verbum, Filium Ejus appellatum, in nomine Dei varie visum a patriarchis, *in prophetis semper auditum*," &c.—*De Præscr. Hæret.* § 13, p. 235 (cf. Lecture iii. p. 118, &c.) So also: "Nos quidem certi, Christum semper in prophetis locutum."—*Adv. Marcion.* lib. iii. § 6., p. 481. (Cf. *ibid.*, lib. iv. § 13, p. 519.) While, at the same time, he writes: "De illuminatione mundi, quis Christo ait, 'Posui Te in lumen nationum,' &c. * * * Cui *respondet Spiritus* in Psalmo," &c.—*Ibid.* lib. v. § 11, p. 598.

S. Irenæus writes: "Est autem Hic, Verbum Ejus, Dominus noster Jesus Christus * * * Et propterea prophetæ ab *eodem Verbo propheticum accipientes Charisma*, prædicaverunt Ejus secundùm carnem adventum * * * Quoniam ergo *Spiritus Dei per prophetas futura significavit*," &c.—*Cont. Hær.* lib. IV. cap. xx., p. 254. (Cf. the words prefixed to Lecture i.; and Lecture iii. p. 118, note [2]. See also p. 120, note [3].

Clemens Alex. refers to Jer. l. 20, with the words: ἀφίησί τε τὰς ἁμαρτίας ὁ φωτίζων Λόγος· Καὶ ἐν τῷ καιρῷ ἐκείνῳ, φησὶν ὁ Κύριος, ζητήσουσιν κ. τ. λ.—*Strom.* ii. § 14, p. 463. While, quoting Jer. xxiii. 23, 24, he equally represents the Holy Ghost as the speaker: Μᾶλλον δὲ ἐν Ἱερεμίᾳ τὸ Ἅγ. Πνεῦμα.—*Cohort. ad Gent.* cap. viii., p. 66. Again: Ὁ νόμος διὰ Μωσέως ἐδόθη· οὐχὶ ὑπὸ Μωσέως, ἀλλὰ ὑπὸ μὲν τοῦ Λόγου, διὰ Μωσέως δὲ θεράποντος Αὐτοῦ.—*Pædag.* lib. i. cap. vii., p. 134. While he also writes, quoting Deut. xxxii. 10–12: Λέγει δέ που διὰ τῆς ᾠδῆς τὸ Πνεῦμα τὸ Ἅγιον· κ. τ. λ.—*Ibid.* c. 7, p. 131.

Origen argues that Celsus should in fairness have stated the very expressions of the prophecies:—Εἴτ' ἐν αἷς Θεὸς παντοκράτωρ ἐπηγέλλετο εἶναι ὁ λέγων, εἴτ' ἐν αἷς ὁ Υἱὸς τοῦ Θεοῦ, εἴτε καὶ ἐν αἷς τὸ Πνεῦμα τὸ Ἅγιον λέγον εἶναι ἐπιστεύετο.—*Cont. Celsum*, lib. vii. § 10, t. i. p. 700. And he elsewhere writes: "Christus, Dei Verbum, in Moyse atque prophetis erat. Nam *sine Verbo Dei quomodo poterant prophetare de Christo?* Ad cujus rei probationem non esset difficile ex Divinis Scripturis ostendere, quomodo vel Moyses vel prophetæ *Spiritu Christi repleti*, vel locuti sunt vel gesserunt," &c.—*De Princip.* lib. i. § 1, t. i. p. 47.

Hence were derived the titles Χριστοφόροι and Πνευματοφόροι applied, indifferently, to the sacred writers (see *supra*, p. 83, note [4]). It may be well to add that S. Ephræm Syrus, enumerating the different sacred writers, refers to them as *οἱ θεοφόροι*: and that he calls David *ὁ θεόφατος*. *In secundum Domini Advent.*, t. ii. p. 202.

Compare, too, the language of Athenagoras :—*Δι' αὐτῶν τῶν δογμάτων οἷς προσέχομεν οὐκ ἀνθρωπινοῖς οὖσιν, ἀλλὰ θ ε ο φ ά τ ο ι ς καὶ θ ε ο δ ι δ ά κ τ ο ι ς*.—*Leg. pro Christ.* § xi., p. 288. (see, *supra*, p. 429).

II. The second division of the subject embraces the allusions, by the Fathers, to "the effect of the Divine influence upon the intellectual faculties of the prophets." The notion that, while giving utterance to their predictions, the prophets were sunk in a state of unconsciousness, has been shown, in the Fifth of the preceding Discourses, to have been repugnant to the general teaching of the primitive Church. Nothing more, therefore, is necessary here than (1) to give a Catena of those passages in which the Fathers have employed a material similitude to illustrate the effect of the Divine influence upon the souls of those "holy men of old, who spake as they were moved by the Holy Ghost;" and (2) to adduce some examples which exhibit the Church's belief in the coexistence of the human with the Divine Intelligence. (See Lecture vi. p. 263, &c.)

(1) The similitudes employed may be arranged under two classes: (*a*) those founded upon the analogy of a musical instrument, and obviously suggested by the primary sense of the word "Spirit," ("breath," *πνεῦμα*): and (*b*) material similitudes of any kind.

(*a*) Similitudes, founded upon the analogy of a musical instrument, and suggested by the etymology of the word "Inspiration :"—

S. Justin Martyr :—*Οὔτε γὰρ φύσει, οὔτ' ἀνθρωπίνῃ ἐννοίᾳ οὕτω μεγάλα καὶ θεῖα γινώσκειν ἀνθρώποις δυνατόν· ἀλλὰ τῇ ἄνωθεν ἐπὶ τοὺς ἁγίους ἄνδρας τηνικαῦτα κατελθούσῃ δωρεᾷ, οἷς οὐ λόγων ἐδέησε τέχνης * * * ἀλλὰ καθαροὺς ἑαυτοὺς τῇ τοῦ Θείου Πνεύματος παρασχεῖν ἐνεργείᾳ, ἵν' αὐτὸ τὸ θεῖον ἐξ οὐρανοῦ κατιὸν π λ ῆ κ τ ρ ο ν, ὥ σ π ε ρ ὀ ρ γ ά ν ῳ κ ι θ ά ρ α ς τ ι ν ὸ ς ἢ λ ύ ρ α ς, τοῖς δικαίοις ἀνδράσι χρώμενον, τὴν τῶν θείων ἡμῖν καὶ οὐρανίων ἀποκαλύψῃ γνῶσιν.* —*Cohort. ad Græc.* § viii., p. 13.

Athenagoras expressly develops the idea suggested by the term Πνεῦμα :—*Νομίζω καὶ ὑμᾶς φιλομαθεστάτους καὶ ἐπιστημονεστάτους ὄντας, οὐκ ἀνοήτους γεγονέναι οὔτε τοῦ Μωσέως, οὔτε τοῦ Ἡσαΐου, καὶ Ἱερεμίου, καὶ τῶν λοιπῶν προφητῶν, οἳ κατ' ἔκστασιν τῶν ἐν αὐτοῖς λογισμῶν κινήσαντος αὐτοὺς τοῦ Θείου Πνεύματος, ἃ ἐνηγοῦντο ἐξεφώνησαν· σ υ γ χ ρ η σ α μ έ ν ο υ τ ο ῦ Π ν ε ύ μ α τ ο ς ὡ σ ε ὶ κ α ὶ α ὐ λ η τ ὴ ς α ὐ λ ὸ ν ἐ μ π ν ε ῦ σ α ι*.—*Leg. pro Christianis*, § ix. p. 286. To which statement may be added the following, where the same comparison is given under the form of a musical instrument (*ὄργάνον*) in general (cf. the quotations of class (*b*)) :—*Ἡμεῖς δὲ, ὧν νοοῦμεν καὶ πεπιστεύκαμεν, ἔχομεν προφήτας μάρτυρας, οἳ Πνεύματι ἐνθέῳ* [*ἔνθεοι*] *ἐκπεφωνήκασι καὶ περὶ τοῦ Θεοῦ, καὶ περὶ τῶν τοῦ Θεοῦ. εἴποιτε δ' ἂν καὶ ὑμεῖς, συνέσει καὶ τῇ περὶ τὸ ὄντως Θεῖον εὐσεβείᾳ τοὺς ἄλλους προὔχοντες, ὡς ἔστιν ἄλογον, παραλιπόντας πιστεύειν τῷ παρὰ τοῦ*

Θεοῦ Πνεύματι, ὡ ς ὄ ρ γ α ν α κεκινηκότι τὰ τῶν προφητῶν σ τ ό μ α τ α, προσέχειν δόξαις ἀνθρωπίναις.—*Ibid.* § vii., p. 285. (See *supra*, p. 86, note [4].)

Clemens Alex.:—Ὁ δὲ ἐκ Δαβὶδ, καὶ πρὸ αὐτοῦ, ὁ τοῦ Θεοῦ Λόγος, λύραν μὲν καὶ κιθάραν, τὰ ἄψυχα ὄργανα, ὑπεριδών· κόσμον δὲ τόνδε, καὶ δὴ καὶ τὸν σμικρὸν κόσμον, τὸν ἄνθρωπον, ψυχήν τε καὶ σῶμα αὐτοῦ, Ἁγίῳ Πνεύματι ἁρμοσάμενος, ψάλλει τῷ Θεῷ, διὰ τοῦ πολυφώνου ὀργάνου, καὶ προσᾴδει τούτῳ τῷ ὀργάνῳ, τῷ ἀνθρώπῳ· σὺ γὰρ εἶ κιθάρα, καὶ αὐλὸς καὶ ναὸς Ἐμός· κιθάρα, διὰ τὴν ἁρμονίαν· α ὐ λ ὸ ς, δ ι ὰ τ ὸ Π ν ε ῦ μ α· ναὸς, διὰ τὸν Λόγον· ἵν' ἡ μὲν, κρέκῃ· τὸ δὲ, ἐ μ π ν έ ῃ· ὁ δὲ χωρήσῃ τὸν Κύριον.—*Cohort. ad Gentes*, c. i. p. 5. And to the same effect:—Αἰνεῖτε αὐτὸν ἐν ψαλτηρίῳ· ὅτι ἡ γλῶττα τὸ ψαλτήριον Κυρίου. καὶ ἐν κιθάρᾳ αἰνεῖτε αὐτον· κ ι θ ά ρ α ν ο ε ί σ θ ω τ ὸ σ τ ό μ α, ο ἱ ο ν ε ὶ π λ ή κ τ ρ ῳ κ ρ ο ύ ο μ ε ν ο ν τ ῷ Π ν ε ύ μ α τ ι.—*Pædagogus*, lib. II. c. iv. p. 193.

S. Hippolytus Portuens. (see, *supra*, p. 425):—Οὗτοι γὰρ Π ν ε ύ μ α τ ι π ρ ο φ η τ ι κ ῷ οἱ πατέρες κατηρτισμένοι, καὶ ὑπ' Αὐτοῦ τοῦ Λόγου ἀξίως τετιμημένοι, ὀργάνων δίκην ἑαυτοῖς ἡνωμένοι, ἔχοντες ἐ ν ἑ α υ τ ο ῖ ς ἀ ε ὶ τ ὸ ν Λ ό γ ο ν ὡ ς π λ ῆ κ τ ρ ο ν, δ ι' ο ὗ κ ι ν ο ύ μ ε ν ο ι ἀπήγγελλον ταῦτα, ἅπερ ἤθελεν ὁ Θεὸς, οἱ προφῆται. οὐ γὰρ ἐ ξ ἰ δ ί α ς δ υ ν ά μ ε ω ς ἐ φ θ έ γ γ ο ν τ ο, μὴ πλανῶ [al. ὡς πλάνοι] οὐδὲ ἅπερ αὐτοὶ ἐβούλοντο, ταῦτα ἐκήρυττον, ἀλλὰ πρῶτον μὲν διὰ τοῦ Λόγου ἐσοφίζοντο ὀρθῶς, ἔπειτα δι' ὁραμάτων προεδιδάσκοντο τὰ μέλλοντα καλῶς· εἶθ' οὕτω πεπεισμένοι ἔλεγον ταῦτα, ἅπερ αὐτοῖς ἦν μόνοις ἀπὸ τοῦ Θεοῦ ἀποκεκρυμμένα.—*De Antichristo*, cap. ii. p. 5.

S. Ephræm Syr.:—"Praise thou the Lord of all, Who fashioned and strung for Himself two lyres, that of the Prophets, and also of the Apostles. Thus one finger struck the two distinct sounds of the two Covenants. And yet, though the lyre hath different sounds, it is the same lyre and the same player; the lyres of Truth also, my son, have different sounds, though the Truth be one."—*Rythm*, xxii. ("Select Works, transl. out of the original Syriac," by the Rev. J. B. Morris, Oxf. 1847, p. 178).

S. Macarius Ægypt., having treated allegorically the history of the deliverance from Pharaoh's bondage, proceeds to say:—Τὸ Πνεῦμα ὅπερ ἔλαβε [*scil.* ἡ ψυχή] καινὸν ᾆσμα τῷ Θεῷ ᾄδει διὰ τοῦ τυμπάνου ἤγουν τοῦ σώματος, καὶ τῶν τῆς κιθάρας ἤτοι ψυχῆς λ ο γ ι κ ῶ ν χορδῶν καὶ λεπτοτάτων λογισμῶν, καὶ τ ο ῦ π λ ή κ τ ρ ο υ τ ῆ ς θ ε ί α ς χ ά ρ ι τ ο ς, καὶ ἀναπέμπει αἴνους τῷ ζωοποιῷ Χριστῷ. ὡ ς γ ὰ ρ δ ι ὰ τ ο ῦ α ὐ λ ο ῦ, τ ὸ Π ν ε ῦ μ α δ ι ε ρ χ ό μ ε ν ο ν λ α λ ε ῖ· οὕτω διὰ τ ῶ ν ἁ γ ί ω ν κ α ὶ π ν ε υ μ α τ ο φ ό ρ ω ν ἀ ν θ ρ ώ π ω ν τὸ Πνεῦμα τὸ Ἅγιόν ἐστιν ὑμνοῦν, καὶ ψάλλον, καὶ προσευχόμενον τῷ Θεῷ ἐν καθαρᾷ καρδίᾳ.—*Homil.* xlvii., p. 232.

S. Chrysostom repeats the title, the "Lyre of the Spirit," by which, as already quoted (Lecture ii. p. 88, note [6]), he was wont to designate S. Paul. His Homily on 1 Tim. v. 23 ("Drink no longer water, but use a little wine, for thy stomach's sake and thine often infirmities") commences with words in which the same simile is combined with one still more closely allied to the idea of *Inspiration:* Ἠκούσατε τῆς ἀποστολικῆς φωνῆς, τ ῆ ς σ ά λ π ι γ γ ο ς τῆς ἐκ τῶν οὐρανῶν, τ ῆ ς λ ύ ρ α ς τῆς πνευματικῆς; * * * οὐ γὰρ ἡμέτερα τὰ λεγόμενα, ἀλλ' ἅπερ ἂν ἡ τοῦ Πνεύματος ἐμπνεύσῃ χάρις * * * Μὴ τοίνυν μηδὲ τὰ νομιζόμενα εἶναι ψιλὰ τῶν γραφῶν νοήματα παρατρέχωμεν.—*Ad pop. Antioch.* Hom. i., t. ii. p. 1. And elsewhere, with another form of illustration, he enters more fully into the grounds of such comparisons:—Τούτου τοῦ στόματος ἐβουλόμην τὴν κόνιν ἰδεῖν, δι' οὗ τὰ μεγάλα καὶ ἀπόῤῥητα ὁ Χριστὸς ἐλάλησε, * * * δι' οὗ τὸ Πνεῦμα τῇ οἰκουμένῃ τοὺς θαυμαστοὺς ἐκείνους χρησμοὺς ἔδωκε. * * * Ἄρα Ἐκείνου [*scil.* τοῦ Χριστοῦ] καρδία ἦν ἡ Παύλου καρδία, καὶ τοῦ Πνεύματος τοῦ Ἁγίου πλάξ.—*In Epist. ad Rom.* Hom. xxxii., t. ix. p. 758. The following words apply this principle to the sacred writers in general:—Ὅταν δὲ Παῦλον εἴπω, οὐ τοῦτον μόνον λέγω, ἀλλὰ καὶ Πέτρον, καὶ Ἰάκωβον, καὶ Ἰωάννην, καὶ πάντα αὐτῶν τὸν χορόν. Καθάπερ γὰρ ἐν λύρᾳ μιᾷ διάφοροι μὲν αἱ νευραὶ, μία δὲ ἡ συμφωνία· οὕτω καὶ ἐν τῷ χορῷ τῶν Ἀποστόλων διάφορα μὲν τὰ πρόσωπα, μία δὲ ἡ διδασκαλία, ἐπειδὴ καὶ εἷς ὁ τεχνίτης ἦν τὸ Πνεῦμα τὸ Ἅγιον τὸ κινοῦν τὰς ἐκείνων ψυχάς.—*Hom. in S. Ignat. M.*, t. ii. p. 594.

A comparison of the illustrations thus employed by S. Chrysostom, according to which the sacred writers may appear to have been regarded by him as merely passive instruments, with his remarks on their unadorned style of writing (quoted, *supra*, Lecture vii. p. 326, note [2]), clearly exemplifies his appreciation of that co-existence of the human and the Divine Intelligence, to be presently considered, which forms so important an element of any just view of Inspiration.

(*b*) The comparisons employed by Theophilus of Antioch are founded upon the general idea of a musical instrument:—

Οἱ δὲ τοῦ Θεοῦ ἄνθρωποι, πνευματοφόροι Πνεύματος Ἁγίου καὶ προφῆται γενόμενοι, ὑπ' Αὐτοῦ τοῦ Θεοῦ ἐμπνευσθέντες, καὶ σοφισθέντες, ἐγένοντο θεοδίδακτοι, καὶ ὅσιοι, καὶ δίκαιοι· διὸ καὶ κατηξιώθησαν τὴν ἀντιμισθίαν ταύτην λαβεῖν, ὄργανα Θεοῦ γενόμενοι.—*Ad Autolyc.* lib. ii. § ix., p. 354.

And again:—Οὗτος οὖν ὢν Πνεῦμα Θεοῦ, καὶ ἀρχὴ καὶ σοφία, καὶ δύναμις ὑψίστου, κατήρχετο εἰς τοὺς προφήτας, καὶ δι' αὐτῶν ἐλάλει * * * καὶ διὰ Σολομῶνος προφήτου οὕτω λέγει· ἡνίκα δὴ ἡτοίμασε τὸν οὐρανὸν, συμπαρήμην Αὐτῷ. κ. τ. λ. [Prov. viii.]. Μωσῆς δὲ ὁ καὶ Σολομῶνος πρὸ πολλῶν ἐτῶν γενόμενος μᾶλλον δὲ ὁ Λόγος ὁ τοῦ Θεοῦ ὡς δι' ὀργάνου δι' αὐτοῦ, φησίν· ἐν ἀρχῇ κ. τ. λ. [Gen. i. 1.] —*Ibid.* § x., p. 355.

S. Basil:—Ὁ μὲν γὰρ παρέχων ἑαυτὸν ἄξιον ὄργανον τῇ ἐνεργείᾳ τοῦ Πνεύματος, προφήτης ἐστίν.—*Comm. in Esai.* Procem. § i., t. i. p. 378.

The important adjective "rational" (λογικός) is added by the author of a treatise, entitled "Synopsis Prophetiarum," published by D. Hœschelius in his edition (Aug. Vind. 1602) of "Adriani Isagoge" (A. D. 433):—Κυρίως προφῆται καὶ ἀληθῶς, οἱ πάλαι παρὰ τοῖς Ἑβραίοις, ὡς τοῦ ἀληθινοῦ Πνεύματος λογικὰ καὶ προαιρετικὰ ὄργανα,—p. 29. Compare also the use of the same term by S. Macarius in the passage quoted under class (*a*), p. 433, *supra*.

The expression of the Psalmist, "My tongue is the pen of a ready writer"—Ps. xlv. 1, affords a constant illustration.

Theodoret:—Προφήτου δὲ ἴδιον, τὸ τὴν γλῶτταν ὑπουργὸν παρέχειν *τῇ τοῦ Πνεύματος χάριτι, κατὰ τὴν ἐν τοῖς ψαλμοῖς φερομένην φωνὴν, ἡ γλῶσσά μου, φησὶ, κάλαμος γραμματέως ὀξυγράφου.—Protheoria in Psalm.*, t. i. p. 396.

Procopius Gazæus[1] (A. D. 520):—*ὥσπερ γὰρ ὑπηρέτης βασιλικὸς βασιλέως φωνὴν ὑποκρίνεται, ἐκέλευσα λέγων, ἐδωρησάμην, οὕτως οἱ προφῆται καθάπερ κάλαμον τὴν γλῶτταν ὀξυγράφῳ παρέχονται γραμματεῖ, κατὰ τὸν μέγαν Δαβίδ.—Præf. in Genes.* (ap. A. Mai, t. vi. p. 2).

S. Gregory the Great writes in continuation of the words cited, *supra*, p. 82, note [4]:—"Ipse igitur hæc scripsit, qui scribenda dictavit. Ipse scripsit, qui et in Illius opere Inspirator extitit, et per scribentis vocem imitanda ad nos ejus facta transmisit. Si magni cujusdam viri susceptis epistolis legeremus verba, sed quo calamo fuissent scripta, quæreremus; ridiculum profecto esset, epistolarum auctorem scire, sensumque cognoscere, sed quali calamo earum verba impressa fuerint indagare. Cum ergo rem cognoscimus, ejusque rei Spiritum S. auctorem tenemus, quia scriptorem quærimus, quid aliud agimus nisi legentes literas, de calamo percontamur?"—*Præf. in Moral. in Job*, t. i. p. 7.

Other comparisons are instituted, of which the following instances must suffice:—S. Augustine, answering the objection, "Cur Ipsius Christi nulla scripta?" says, in conclusion: "Itaque cum illi scripserunt, quæ Ille ostendit et dixit, nequaquam dicendum est quod Ipse non scripserit: quandoquidem *membra Ejus* id operata sunt, quod *dictante Capite* cognoverunt. Quidquid enim Ille de Suis factis et dictis nos legere voluit, hoc scribendum Illis *tamquam Suis manibus* imperavit. Hoc unitatis consortium et in diversis officiis concordium membrorum sub uno capite ministerium quisquis intellexerit, non aliter accipiet quod narrantibus Discipulis Christi in Evangelio legerit, quam si *ipsam manum* Domini, quam in proprio Corpore gestabat, scribentem conspexerit."—*De Consens. Evang.* lib. i. cap. xxxv., t. iii. par. ii., p. 26. The following, not unusual, simile may be added:—"Has Domini *sanctas Quadrigas*, quibus per orbem vectus subigit populos leni suo jugo et sarcinæ levi," &c.—*Ibid.* lib. i. cap. vii., p. 6.

And S. Jerome writes:—"Matthæus, Marcus, Lucas, et Joannes, *Quadriga Domini* et verum Cherubim. * * * Tenent se mutuo, sibique perplexi sunt, et quasi rota in rota volvuntur, et pergunt quocumque eos flatus S. Spiritus perduxerit."—*Ad Paulinum*, Ep. liii. t. i. p. 278.

(2.) The co-existence of the human and the Divine Intelligence is

[1] A curious example of the manner in which a translator sometimes improves upon the sense of his author is supplied by the remains of Procopius. Quenstedt ("Theologia Didactico-Polemica," cap. iv. § 2, p. 55) quotes the following passage from the "Comment. in Octateuchum" of Procopius, with which he was acquainted only through the Latin Version ("ap. Gesneros fratres," *s. a.*):—"Oportet eum, qui operam daturus est Scripturæ Sacræ, non accipere illa quæ ibi traduntur, quasi proveniant ex hominibus: altius initium sive principium spectandum reor: firmiter credat necesse est, illa sacrosancta dogmata ex Ipso originem sumere Deo, et inde *per homines quasi canales* seu instrumentum ad nos promanare."—*Præf. in Genes.* p. 1. This language, so utterly foreign from the style and tone of thought of any other writer of that age, is at once shown to be solely attributable to the translator by the publication, in the original Greek, of the "Comm. in Ges." of Procopius, as far as ch. xviii., in Card. Mai's edition, "Classicorum Auctorum" (Romæ, 1834, t. vi.);—where the original of the entire passage, just quoted, is simply as follows:—*Δεῖ τὸν προσιόντα τῇ θείᾳ γραφῇ, μὴ ὡς ἀνθρώπων εἰπόντων, ἀλλ' ὡς Θεοῦ δι' αὐτῶν φθεξαμένου τῶν εἰρημένων ἀκούειν.—Loc. cit.* p. 2—in which the words "per homines quasi canales" are represented merely by *δι' αὐτῶν*.

clearly implied in numerous passages, as examples of which the following *general* statement may be cited :—

Ἱερεμίας δὲ ὁ προφήτης, ὁ πάνσοφος, μᾶλλον δὲ ἐν Ἱερεμίᾳ τὸ Ἅγιον Πνεῦμα, ἐπιδείκνυσι τὸν Θεόν· κ. τ. λ.—Clemens Al., *Cohort. ad Gentes*, c. viii. p. 66. Such, also, is the language in which Origen expresses his belief that S. Matthew's account of the healing of the *two* blind men at Jericho (ch. xx. 30) is not in contradiction to the accounts of S. Mark and S. Luke :—Εἴπερ ἀκριβῶς πιστεύομεν ἀναγεγράφθαι, σ υ ν ε ρ γ ο ῦ ν τ ο ς καὶ τοῦ Ἁγίου Πνεύματος, τὰ Εὐαγγέλια.—*Comm. in Matthæum*, t. iii. p. 732. Compare, too, the words of Eusebius, which form the continuation of the passage prefixed to Lecture vii. :—Τῇ δὲ τοῦ Θείου Πνεύματος τ ο ῦ σ υ ν ε ρ γ ο ῦ ν τ ο ς αὐτοῖς ἀποδείξει, κ. τ. λ.—*loc. cit.* p. 116.

But this conclusion is brought out still more plainly by the manner in which the Fathers reject the idea, that the condition of the sacred writers, when under the influence of Inspiration, at all resembled that state of unconsciousness which the Montanists represented as the essence of true Prophecy. In addition to the passages cited in Lecture v. p. 191, &c., the following may be given :—

S. Basil (if, indeed, the commentary on Isaiah be his) writes of the notion, put forward, by some, as to the ecstatic state of Isaiah and Ezekiel :—Φασὶ δέ τινες ἐξεστηκότας αὐτοὺς προφητεύειν, ἐπικαλυπτομένου τοῦ ἀνθρωπείου νοῦ παρὰ τοῦ Πνεύματος. τοῦτο δὲ παρὰ τὴν ἐπαγγελίαν ἐστὶ τῆς θείας ἐπιδημίας, ἔκφρονα ποιεῖν τὸν θεόληπτον, καὶ ὅτε πλήρης γέγονε τῶν θείων διδαγμάτων, τ ό τ ε κ α ὶ τ ῆ ς ο ἰ κ ε ί α ς ἐ ξ ί σ τ α σ θ α ι δ ι α ν ο ί α ς.—*Comm. in Esai.*, t. i. p. 381.

S. Chrysostom briefly, but completely, points out the distinction :—Τοῦτο γὰρ μάντεως ἴδιον, τὸ ἐξεστηκέναι, τὸ ἀνάγκην ὑπομένειν, τὸ ὠθεῖσθαι, τὸ ἕλκεσθαι, τὸ σύρεσθαι ὥσπερ μαινόμενον. Ὁ δὲ προφήτης οὐχ οὕτως, ἀλλὰ μετὰ διανοίας νηφούσης, καὶ σωφρονούσης καταστάσεως, κ α ὶ ε ἰ δ ὼ ς ἃ φ θ έ γ γ ε τ α ι, φ η σ ὶ ν ἅ π α ν τ α.—*In Epist. ad* 1 Cor. xii., Hom. xxix., t. x. p. 259.

The condition of the Prophets is thus clearly described by S. Gregory the Great :—"Scriptores igitur sacri eloquii, quia impulsu S. Spiritus agitantur, sic de se in illo testimonium tanquam de aliis proferunt. Ergo S. Spiritus per Moysen locutus est de Moyse : S. Spiritus per Johannem locutus est de Johanne. Paulus quoque quia non ex se ipso loqueretur, insinuat dicens : 'An experimentum quæritis Ejus qui in me loquitur Christus.' [2 Cor. xiii. 3.] * * * Itaque scriptores sacri eloquii, quia repleti S. Spiritu super se trahuntur, QUASI *extra semetipsos* fiunt : et sic de se sententias, quasi de aliis, proferunt. Unde et beatus Job S. Spiritu afflatus, potuit sua gesta, quæ erant videlicet supernæ aspirationis dona, quasi non sua scribere : quia eo alterius erant quæ loquebatur, quo homo loquebatur quæ Dei sunt : et eo alter quæ erant illius loquebatur, quo Spiritus S. loquebatur quæ hominis sunt."—*Præf. in Moral. in Job* t. i. p. 8.

The opinions of S. Jerome are well known, and are to be seen in his different "Prefaces," usually prefixed to the editions of the Vulgate :—cf. e. g., his words quoted, *supra*, p. 192, note [1].

The following statement of the same principle occurs in the "Synopsis Prophetiarum" already quoted (p. 484) :—

Πολλάκις δὲ καὶ διὰ τὴν τοῦ λέγοντος περὶ τὸ ἀγγέλλειν ἰδιότητα, γίνεται ἀσάφεια. ὡς καὶ ἐνταῦθα· [*scil.* Ex. xxv.; Ezek. xl.] τὸ μὲν Πνεῦμα τὰ νοήματα ὑ π έ β α λ ε ν ἑκάστῳ τῶν προφητῶν, αὐτοὶ δὲ λοιπὸν ἀπήγγελλον, ὡς ἕκαστος ἠδύνατο, τὰ τοῦ Πνεύματος. οὐ γὰρ ὡς ἀκινήτοις αὐτοῖς ἐχρήσατο, καθάπερ ἡ τῶν δαιμόνων ἐπίπνοια· ἀλλ' ἐβούλετο αὐτοὺς καὶ γινώσκειν τὰ παρ' αὐτοῦ ἐμπνεόμενα, καὶ μετὰ τῆς οἰκείας γνώμης ἅπαντα λέγειν. μὴ γὰρ δὴ τοὺς τοῦ ἀθέου Μοντανοῦ λήρους παραδεξαίμεθα, φήσαντος· τοὺς προφήτας κατεχομένους παρὰ Θεοῦ μὴ εἰδέναι ἃ λέγουσι.[1]—*Loc. cit.*, p. 31.

III. The third division of the subject may now be considered; viz.—"Those testimonies of the Fathers which relate to the nature of the Bible as a written document, the joint product of the Holy Spirit and the men of God" (see, *supra*, p. 88). The uniform manner in which even the language employed by the sacred writers is ascribed to the suggestion of the Divine influence,—and this, too, by those who, like S. Jerome (see, *supra*, p. 328, note [1]), fully recognised the *human* element of Scripture,—affords unquestionable evidence as to the doctrine of the Church respecting the written document itself.

Tertullian, having quoted 1 Thess. iv. 14, 16, proceeds:—"Et ideo majestas Spiritus S. perspicax ejusmodi sensuum, et in ipsa ad Thessalonicenses epistola *suggerit*: 'De temporibus autem et temporum spatiis,' &c. (c. v. 1)."—*De Resurrectione Carnis*, c. 24, p. 396.

S. Irenæus: "Non enim solo sermone prophetabant Prophetæ, sed et Visione, * * * secundum id quod *suggerebat* Spiritus."—*Cont. Hæres.* lib. IV. xx., p. 255.

Origen:—Τὸ δ ι δ ά ξ α ν Μωϋσέα Πνεῦμα τὴν πρεσβυτέραν αὐτοῦ ἱστορίαν * * * τοῦτ' ἐ δ ί δ α ξ ε καὶ τοὺς γράψαντας τὸ Εὐαγγέλιον.—*Cont. Celsum*, lib. i. § 44, p. 360.

S. Cyprian:—"Per Hieremiam quoque hæc eadem Spiritus S. *suggerit*, et docet, dicens," &c.—*De Orat. Dominic.*, p. 205.

S. Jerome:—"Pharisæi stupent ad doctrinam Domini; et mirantur in Petro et Johanne quomodo legem sciant, quum literas non didicerint. Quidquid enim aliis exercitatio et quotidiana in Lege meditatio tribuere solet, illis Spiritus S. *suggerebat*; et erant, juxta quod scriptum est, θεοδίδακτοι."—*Ad Paulin.* Ep. liii., t. i. p. 271. Cf. also the passage quoted,

[1] The cases in which the Fathers *do* ascribe unconsciousness to the utterer of a Divine revelation confirm what has been said. This they considered to have been the state of such agents of God only as were Balaam and Caiaphas; whose unconsciousness is attributed to their personal unworthiness. S. Ambrose (A. D. 374), writes: "Sed non mireris infusum auguri a Domino quod loqueretur; quando infusum legis in Evangelio etiam principi Synagogæ uni ex persequentibus Christum (Joan. xi. 50). * * * Indignatus Dominus per angelum dixit: 'Vade, sed quæcumque tibi inspiravero, hac dices,'—id est, non quæ vis, sed quæ cogêris loqui. Quasi *organum inane* sonum Meis præbebis sermonibus: Ego sum, qui loquar, non tu qui ea quæ audieris, resultabis, et quæ non intelliges. * * * Balac indignatus est. * * * Respondit ille [Balaam], 'Calumniam patior de eo, quod nescio; ego enim nihil meum loquor, *sed quasi cymbalum tinniens sonum reddo.*' "—*Ad. Chromat.*, Ep. 1., t. ii. p. 994. And Theodoret repeats this statement, assigning as a cause the unworthiness of the recipient:—τὸ δὲ, ἐ π ο ρ ε ύ θ η ἐ π' ε ὐ θ ε ί α ν [Num. xxiii. 4], δηλοῖ ὅτι ἀληθῶς τὸ πρακτέον ἠβουλήθη μαθεῖν. τούτου χάριν τὸ ἀκάθαρτον στόμα τοῦ παναγίου Πνεύματος ἐδέξατο τὴν ἐνέργειαν, καὶ φθέγγεται ἃ μὴ βούλεται.—*Quæst.* xlii. *in Num.*, t. i. p. 161.

supra, p. 311, note [1], adopting the *varia lectio*, "scriptæ," given in the "edit. Bened.," Paris, 1704, t. iii. 246.

S. Augustine, referring to the events which followed the "Sermon on the Mount" (S. Matt. viii. 1, 2), observes:—"Hujus leprosi etiam Lucas meminit (v. 12, 13), *non sane hoc ordine*, sed ut solent prætermissa recordari, vel posterius facta præoccupare, sicut *divinitus suggerebantur*, quæ antea cognita, postea recordando conscriberent."—*De Consens. Evang.* lib. ii. c. xix., *loc. cit.* p. 51.

The following expressions of Origen, founded upon the saying of our Lord, that "one jot or one tittle (*ἰῶτα ἓν ἢ μία κεραία*) shall in no wise pass from the Law" (S. Matt. v. 18),—words which convey an idea to which he repeatedly recurs (cf. *supra*, p. 89, note [1], and p. 271, note [5]), and in which he is followed by many other Fathers,—connect the foregoing passages with those which still more directly point to the language of Scripture:—

Εἰ δὲ τὰ λόγια Κυρίου λόγια ἁγνά. * * * καὶ μετὰ πάσης ἀκριβείας ἐξητασμένως τὸ Ἅγιον Πνεῦμα ὑποβέβληκεν αὐτὰ διὰ τῶν ὑπηρετῶν τοῦ λόγου, μήποτε καὶ ὑμᾶς διαφεύγῃ ἡ ἀναλογία, καθ' ἣν ἐπὶ πᾶσαν ἔφθασε γραφὴν ἡ σοφία τοῦ Θεοῦ θεόπνευστον μέχρι τοῦ τυχόντος γράμματος· καὶ τάχα διὰ τοῦτο ὁ Σωτὴρ ἔφη· ἰῶτα ἓν ἢ μία κεραία οὐ μὴ παρέλθῃ ἀπὸ τοῦ νόμου, ἕως ἂν πάντα γένηται. * * * οὕτως ἡμεῖς ὑπολαμβάνομεν περὶ πάντων τῶν ἐπιπνοίας τοῦ Ἁγίου Πνεύματος ἀναγεγραμμένων, ὡς τῆς * * * προνοίας * * * λόγια σωτήρια ἐνεσπαρκυίας, ὥς ἐστιν εἰπεῖν, ἑκάστῳ γράμματι κατὰ τὸ ἐνδεχόμενον ἴχνη τῆς σοφίας.—*Sel. in Psalm.*, t. ii. p. 527.

This principle he applies as follows:—"Sacra volumina Spiritûs plenitudinem spirant; nihilque est sive in Prophetia, sive in Lege, sive in Evangelio, sive in Apostolo, quod non a plenitudine majestatis descendat. * * * Neque vero dixit [Jer. li. 6], *salvare*, sed *resalvare. Appositio syllabæ significat sacramentum.*"—*Hom.* xxi. *in Jerem.*, t. iii. p. 282.

And again: God said to Jeremiah (ch. i. 5)—Πρὸ τοῦ με πλάσαι σε ἐν κοιλίᾳ, and not, πρὸ τοῦ με ποιῆσαί σε:—for, adds Origen, ἀναγνοὺς τὴν Γένεσιν, καὶ τηρήσας τὰ εἰρημένα περὶ τῆς κτίσεως τοῦ κόσμου, εὑρήσεις ὅτι ἡ γραφὴ πάνυ διαλεκτικωτάτη.—*Hom.* i. *in Jerem.*, t. iii. p. 131.

On such principles was founded Origen's allegorizing system of interpretation. This he states in the following words, which are important as proving both that his exalted idea of Inspiration was the established doctrine of the Church, and also that he never abandoned the truth of the *literal sense* of Scripture:—"Est præterea et illud IN ECCLESIASTICA PRÆDICATIONE quod mundus iste factus sit, * * * tum demum quod per Spiritum Dei Scripturæ conscriptæ sint, et sensum habeant, NON EAM SOLUM qui in manifesto est, sed et alium quemdam latentem quamplurimos."—*De Princip.* lib. i. § viii., t. i. p. 48. These words are particularly interesting as having been already quoted by S. Pamphilus, Mart. (A. D. 294.—"Apol. pro Origene," ap. Galland., t. iv. p. 11), in reply to the charge brought against Origen of denying the literal truth of Scripture:—a charge to which he certainly left himself open in some unguarded statements. But see the additional remarks at the close of this Appendix. Although departing from the chronological order hitherto followed, it may be well to quote here the views of so sober a commentator as S. Chrysostom, in order to prove that such opinions, as to the profound meaning latent in every word of Scripture, were not confined to the school of the Allegorists.

S. Chrysostom observes that some surprise may have been felt at the frequency of the Salutations in the Epistles of S. Paul. He proposes, therefore, to point out their utility; laying down the proposition—*Ὅτι τῶν θείων γραφῶν οὐδὲν περιττὸν, οὐδὲν πάρεργόν ἐστι, κἂν ἰῶτα ἓν, κἂν μία κεραία ᾖ, ἀλλὰ καὶ ψιλὴ πρόσρησις πολὺ πέλαγος ἡμῖν ἀνοίγει ὀνομάτων. Καὶ τί λέγω, ψιλὴ πρόσρησις; πολλάκις καὶ ἑνὸς στοιχείου προσθήκη ὁλόκληρον νοημάτων εἰσήγαγε δύναμιν. καὶ τοῦτο ἐπὶ τῆς τοῦ Ἀβαὰμ προσηγορίας ἐστὶν ἰδεῖν.—In illud, 'Salut. Priscil. et Aquil.'* Hom. i., t. iii. p. 172.

And to the same effect:—"Certain illiterate persons (*τινές εἰσιν ἄνθρωποι βάναυσοι*) taking up the Divine Books and perceiving statements as to chronology, or catalogues of names, pass such matters by with the remark,—*Ὀνόματα μόνον ἐστὶ, καὶ οὐδὲν χρήσιμον ἔχει. Τί λέγεις; Ὁ Θεὸς φθέγγεται, καὶ σὺ τολμᾷς εἰπεῖν, οὐδὲν χρήσιμον τῶν εἰρημένων ἐστίν;"—In illud, 'Vidi Dominum'* (Esai. vi. 1) Hom. ii., t. vi. p. 109. (Cf. also his remarks, to the same effect, on Rom. xvi. 5: "Salute Epænetus."—Homil. xxxi. in Ep. ad Rom. t. ix. p. 745.)

The principle of the foregoing statements is contained in the following explanation:—*Οὐ γὰρ ῥήματα ἐστιν ἁπλῶς, ἀλλὰ τοῦ Πνεύματος τοῦ Ἁγίου ῥήματα, καὶ διὰ τοῦτο πολὺν ἐστι τὸν θησαυρὸν εὑρεῖν καὶ ἐν μιᾷ συλλαβῇ. Προσέχετε οὖν, παρακαλῶ, μετὰ ἀκριβείας * * * μηδεὶς ἔξω ῥεμβέσθω τὸν λογισμόν * * * ἀλλ' ἐννοῶν * * * ὅτι διὰ τῆς τῶν προφητῶν γλώττης τοῦ Θεοῦ πρὸς ἡμᾶς διαλεγομένου ἀκούομεν * * * Ὅρα τὴν ἀκρίβειαν τῆς διδασκαλίας. Ἀμφότερα τέθεικεν ὁ μακάριος οὗτος προφήτης, μᾶλλον δὲ τὸ Πνεῦμα τὸ Ἅγιον διὰ τῆς τούτου γλώττης, παιδεῦον ἡμᾶς τῶν γεγενημένων τὴν ἀκολουθίαν.—In Gen.* ii., Hom. xv., t. iv. p. 115. (Cf. Hom. xlii., in Gen. xviii., *Ibid.*, p. 425.)

To return, however, to earlier writers. Alluding to our Lord's words when He wept over Jerusalem, "How often (*ποσάκις*) would I have gathered," &c. (S. Matt. xxiii. 37), Clemens Al. asks,—*Τί οὖν; ἠθέλησε μὲν, οὐκ ἠδυνήθη δέ· ποσάκις δὲ, ἢ ποῦ; δίς, διά τε προφητῶν, καὶ διὰ τῆς παρουσίας. πολύτροπον μὲν οὖν τὴν σοφίαν ἡ Ποσάκις ἐκδείκνυται λέξις.—Strom.* i. p. 332. Having observed that Pythagoras held him to be the wisest of men who gave names to things, he adds:—*Δεῖ τοίνυν τὰς γραφὰς ἀκριβῶς διερευνομένους, ἐπειδὴ ἐν παραβολαῖς εἰρῆσθαι ἀνωμολογηνται, ἀπὸ τῶν ὀνομάτων θηρωμένους τὰς δόξας ἃς τὸ Ἅγιον Πνεῦμα περὶ τῶν πραγμάτων ἔχον, εἰς τὰς λέξεις, ὡς εἰπεῖν, τὴν αὐτοῦ διάνοιαν ἐκτυπωσάμενον διδάσκει, ἵνα ἡμῖν ἀκριβῶς ἐξεταζόμενα διαπτύσσηται μὲν τὰ ὀνόματα πολυσήμως εἰρημένα.—Prophet. Eclogæ*, § xxxii. p. 998.

And again, in language subsequently employed by Origen:—*Καὶ μυρίας ἂν ἔχοιμί σοι γραφὰς παραφέρειν, ὧν οὐδὲ κεραία παρελεύσεται μία, μὴ οὐχὶ ἐπιτελὴς γενομένη· τὸ γὰρ στόμα Κυρίου, τὸ Ἅγιον Πνεῦμα, ἐλάλησεν ταῦτα.—Cohort. ad Gentes*, § ix. p. 68.

S. Athanasius:—Τινες μὲν γὰρ τῶν παρ' ἡμῖν ἀκεραίων, καίτοι πιστεύοντες εἶναι θεόπνευστα τὰ ῥήματα, ὅμως νομίζουσι διὰ τὸ εὔφωνον, καὶ τέρψεως ἕνεκα τῆς ἀκοῆς μελῳδεῖσθαι τοὺς ψαλμούς. οὐκ ἔστι δὲ οὕτως· οὐ γὰρ τὸ ἡδὺ καὶ πιθανὸν ἐζήτησεν ἡ γραφή· ἀλλὰ καὶ τοῦτο ὠφελείας ἕνεκα τῆς ψυχῆς τετύπωται.—*Epist. ad Marcellin.* § xxvii., t. i. p. 999.

S. Gregory, of Nyssa (A. D. 370):—Ὅσα ἡ θεία γραφὴ λέγει, τοῦ Πνεύματός εἰσι τοῦ Ἁγίου φωναί. καλῶς γὰρ προεφήτευσε τὸ Πνεῦμα τὸ Ἅγιον· τοῦτο πρὸς τοὺς κατὰ Ῥώμην Ἰουδαίους εἰπὼν τὰς Ἡσαίου φωνὰς ἐπιφέρει. καὶ πρὸς Ἑβραίους τὸ Πνεῦμα προτάξας, ἐν οἷς φησίν, ὅτι διὸ καθὼς λέγει [Heb. iii.] τὸ Πνεῦμα τὸ Ἅγιον, ἐπάγει τὰ τῆς ψαλμῳδίας ῥήματα, τὰ ἐκ προσώπου τοῦ Θεοῦ διεξοδικῶς εἰρημένα. καὶ παρὰ αὐτοῦ δὲ τοῦ Κυρίου τὸ ἴσον ἐμάθομεν, ὅτι Δαβὶδ οὐκ ἐν ἑαυτῷ μένων, τοῦτ' ἔστιν οὐ κατὰ τὴν ἀνθρωπίνην φύσιν φθεγγόμενος, τὰ οὐράνια διεξῄει μυστήρια [*scil.* S. Matt. xxii. 43].—*Cont. Eunom.* Orat. vi., t. ii. p. 604.

S. Gregory, of Nazianz. (A. D. 370):—Let us not suppose that Scripture has been written without design (εἰκῇ); or that it presents an idle crowd of words and facts to amuse the hearers,"—Ἡμεῖς δὲ οἱ καὶ μέχρι τῆς τυχούσης κεραίας καὶ γραμμῆς τοῦ πνεύματος τὴν ἀκρίβειαν ἕλκοντες, οὐ γὰρ ὅσιον, οὐδὲ τὰς ἐλαχίστας πράξεις εἰκῇ σπουδασθῆναι τοῖς ἀναγράψασι, καὶ μέχρι τοῦ παρόντος μνήμῃ διασωθῆναι· ἀλλ' ἵν' ἡμεῖς ἔχωμεν ὑπομνήματα καὶ παιδεύματα τῆς τῶν ὁμοίων διασκέψεως.—*Orat. Secunda*, t. i. p. 60.

S. Jerome:—"Ego enim non solum fateor; sed libera voce profiteor, me in interpretatione Græcorum, *absque Scripturis Sanctis* UBI ET VERBORUM ORDO MYSTERIUM EST, non verbum e verbo, sed sensum exprimere de sensu." —*Ad Pammachium*, Epist. lvii. t. i. p. 306. Again:—"Patet Exodus cum decem plagis, cum Decalogo, cum mysticis divinisque præceptis. In promtu est Leviticus liber, in quo singula sacrificia, immo *singulæ pæne syllabæ*, et vestes Aaron, et totus ordo Leviticus, *spirant cælestia sacramenta.*"—*Ad Paulinum*, Ep. liii. t. i. p. 274. (See also S. Jerome's words quoted, *supra*, p. 78, note [1]).

S. Augustine, speaking of "the waters which were above the firmament"—Gen. i. 7, observes: "Quoque modo autem, et qualeslibet aquæ ibi sint, esse eas ibi minime dubitemus: major est quippe Scripturæ hujus auctoritas, quam *omnis humani ingenii capacitas.*"—*De Genesi ad. lit.* lib. ii. c. 5, t. iii. p. 135.

To this division of the subject belong the following passages, where the principle is stated on which the harmony of the different parts of Scripture depends. Theophilus of Antioch:—

Πόσῳ οὖν μᾶλλον ἡμεῖς τὰ ἀληθῆ εἰσόμεθα, οἱ μανθάνοντες ἀπὸ τῶν ἁγίων προφητῶν, τῶν χωρησάντων τὸ Ἅγιον Πνεῦμα τοῦ Θεοῦ. διὸ σύμφωνα καὶ φίλα ἀλλήλοις οἱ πάντες προφῆται εἶπον.—*Ad Autol.* lib. iii. c. xvii., p. 390. (Cf., also, *Ibid.* lib. ii. c. xxxv., p. 374.)

S. Epiphanius:—Οὐχὶ ἑκάστῳ ἐμερίσεν ὁ Θεὸς, ἵνα οἱ τέσσαρες Εὐαγγελισταὶ ὀφείλοντες κηρύξαι, εὕρωσιν ἕκαστος τὶ ἐργάσωνται; καὶ τὰ μὲν συμφώνως καὶ ἴσως κηρύξωσιν· ἵνα δειχθῶσιν, ὅτι ἐξ αὐτῆς τῆς πηγῆς ὥρμηνται· τὰ δὲ ἑκάστῳ παραληφθέντα, ἄλλος διηγήσεται, ὃς ἔλαβε παρὰ τοῦ Πνεύματος μέρος τῆς ἀναλογίας.—*Adv. Hær.* lib. ii. Hæres. li., t. i. p. 427.

Origen states the result:—Τρίτος εἰρηνοποιὸς, ὁ τὴν ἄλλοις φαινομένην μάχην τῶν γραφῶν ἀποδεικνὺς εἶναι οὐ μάχην, καὶ παριστὰς τὴν συμφωνίαν καὶ τὴν εἰρήνην τούτων, ἤτοι παλαιῶν πρὸς καινὰς, ἢ νομικῶν πρὸς προφητικὰς, ἢ εὐαγγελικῶν πρὸς ἀποστολικὰς, ἢ ἀποστολικῶν πρὸς ἀποστολικάς.—*Comm. in Matth.*, t. iii. p. 441.

That such statements by no means imply that the Fathers held the 'mechanical' theory of Inspiration, in its modern sense, is obvious from the passages already quoted in Lecture vii. p. 326, &c. The principles there laid down had been already defined by Origen, whose views as to the Divine authority of even the words of Scripture, were, as we know, so rigid:—

Οἱ Ἀπόστολοι * * * φασὶν ἰδιῶται εἶναι τῷ λόγῳ, ἀλλ' οὐ τῇ γνώσει· νομιστέον γὰρ αὐτὸ οὐχ ὑπὸ Παύλου μόνον, ἀλλὰ καὶ ὑπὸ τῶν λοιπῶν Ἀποστόλων λέγεσθαι ἄν. In illustration of which fact, he quotes the saying of S. Paul: "We have this treasure in earthen vessels (ἐν ὀστρακίνοις σκεύεσιν), that the excellency of the power may be of God, and not of us."—2 Cor. iv. 7; explaining, ὀστρακίνων δὲ σκευῶν τῆς εὐτελοῦς καὶ εὐκαταφρονήτου παρ' Ἕλλησι λέξεως τῶν γραφῶν ἀληθῶς ὑπερβολῆς δυνάμεως τοῦ Θεοῦ ἐμφαινομένης, ὅτι ἴσχυσε * * * ἡ δύναμις τῶν λεγομένων οὐκ ἐμποδιζομένη ὑπὸ τῆς εὐτελοῦς φράσεως, φθάσαι ἕως περάτων γῆς:—and he concludes by the argument, which appears to have been an established principle in the Church (see, *supra*, p. 326, note [2]), that, had the sacred writers exhibited that rhetorical style and diction which the Greeks cultivated with such care, their success in converting the world might have been ascribed not to the truth of their doctrine, but to the eloquence with which it had been enforced.—*Comm. in Joann* (t. iv.), t. iv. p. 93.

The absence of exact definitions on the subject is at once accounted for by the fact, that no party, or even individual writer, denied or questioned the perfect Inspiration of Scripture (see, *supra*, p. 79, where also the only exceptions to this statement are noticed). The single occasion, too, on which any controversy seems to have arisen respecting the result of the Divine influence fully confirms so wide an assertion; and also shows that the Church was in possession of principles which, had the occasion presented itself, would at once have led to the most accurate dogmatical definitions. It may be well briefly to state the leading facts as to this controversy; both because the opinions that were then elicited form the natural point of transition between the views of the early Church, and those which have been considered in Appendix C; and also because they exhibit the exact agreement existing, as I venture to think, between the doctrine of Inspiration maintained in the present work, and that which has been inculcated by the Church Catholic from the earliest times.

The controversy to which I refer took place between S. Agobard, Archbishop of Lyons (A. D. 841), and the Abbot Fredegisus, Chancellor of the Emperor Ludovicus Pius, and pupil of Alcuin. Fredegisus had accused S. Agobard of asserting "that the Apostles and Evangelists, the translators of Scripture and its Catholic expositors," had committed grammatical errors.[1] In reply to this charge S. Agobard commences by stating his opinion as to Scripture:—

"Ista tamen inconcussa et firma auctoritas illorum auctorum est, per quos Spiritus S. Novi et Veteris Testamenti volumina confecit; de quibus *nulli unquam homini licuit aut licet cogitare vel unam literam aliter eos dicere debuisse quam dixerunt*, quoniam eorum auctoritas firmior est cælo ac terra, secundum quod Dominus ait: 'Facilius est cœlum et terram transire, quam de Lege unum apicem cadere.' "—*Adv. Fredegisum*, cap. ix. ed. Baluz., t. i. p. 174.

The case, he adds, is altogether different with respect to *translators*, whose errors S. Jerome censures in his Prefaces; or *expositors*, of whom S. Augustine, in his book against Faustus the Manichæan (and this "non solum de illis qui reprehensi sunt a Doctoribus, *etiam de probatissimis*"), writes as follows:—"Quod genus literarum, id est expositionum, non cum credendi necessitate, sed cum judicandi libertate, legendum est. *Soli namque Divinæ auctoritatis libri* legendi sunt non cum judicandi libertate, sed cum credendi necessitate." Hence S. Agobard argues:—You, Fredegisus, have acted far more erroneously, inasmuch as "quoscumque interpretes atque expositores coæquatis Apostolis et Evangelistis; cum Symmachum et Paulum, et Didymum et Johannem, unâ defensione indifferentique laude dignos ducitis" (p. 176). The next charge of Fredegisus which he notices, is the following—"Turpe est enim Spiritum S. qui omnium gentium linguas mentibus Apostolorum infudit, rusticitatem potius per eos quam nobilitatem uniuscujusque linguæ locutum esse." S. Agoburd denies, with much solemnity, the charge of having ascribed "rusticitas" to the Holy Spirit; but he retorts again upon Fredegisus:—"Extra hoc autem quod tale sacrilegium nobis impingere videmini, apparet etiam in his verbis vestris quod ita sentiatis de Prophetis et Apostolis, ut non solum sensum prædicationis, et modos, vel argumenta dictionum, Spiritus S. eis inspiraverit, sed *etiam ipsa corporalia verba extrinsecus in ora illorum* Ipse formaverit. Quod si ita sentitis quanta absurditas sequetur quis dinumerare poterit?"—*Ibid.* c. xii. p. 177. In proof of this statement he quotes Moses' assertion, that he was "slow of speech," and the fact that God admitted its truth (Ex. iv.; vi.); adding:—"Restat ergo ut sicut ministerio angelico vox articulata formata est in are asinæ, ita dicatis formari in ore Prophetarum. Et tunc talis etiam absurditas sequetur, ut si tali modo verba et voces verborum acceperunt, sensum ignorarent. Sed absit talia deliramenta cogitari." In illustration, he refers to S. Jerome's remarks on 2 Cor. xi. 6 (quoted, *supra*, p. 328, note [1]); and also to his Prefaces:—"Qui etiam in præfationibus Esaiæ, Hieremiæ, et Ezekielis quid de differentia locutionis Prophetarum eorum dixerit, diligenter perpendite; et invenietis nobilitatem divini eloquii, non secundum vestram assertionem, more Philosophorum, in tumore et pompa esse verborum, sed in virtute sententiarum, secundum

[1] In the conduct of this controversy Neander observes that S. Agobard "nahe daran anstreifte, in dem Inspirations-begriffe das Göttliche und das Eigenthümlich-Menschliche schärfer zu sondern, wenn gleich er nicht dazu gelangte, dies vollständig zu entwickeln."—*Allg. Gesch. der christl. Kirche*, B. iv. s. 388. It will be seen with what injustice Dupin adduces S. Agobard as an authority to prove that *translations* of Scripture have as full a claim to be considered inspired as the original.—See his "Hist. of the Canon," Book i. ch. ii. § 6.

quod ipse Apostolus ait: "Non enim in sermone est regnum Dei, sed in virtute.' "—*Ibid.* p. 178.

The opinion that Theodore of Mopsuestia affords the example of an early opposition to the Church's doctrine of Inspiration (see *supra*, p. 78, &c.), is next to be considered.

Theodore was born about the year 350, and died about 428.[1] S. Chrysostom was the friend of his youth; and he was one of the most distinguished ornaments of the celebrated school of Antioch. It is unnecessary to add anything, in proof of Theodore's literary merit, to what has been already quoted, p. 79, note [1]. The unquestionable tendency, however, of his writings to support those views which were subsequently developed in the heresy of Nestorius, led to Theodore's condemnation by the Fifth General Council (A. D. 553). He was likewise assailed with great bitterness some years later by Leontius, an advocate of Byzantium (*circ.* A. D. 590). Previously to the condemnation of his opinions by the Council, there appears to have been a warm discussion on the subject: and Theodore was ardently defended by Facundus, Bishop of Hermiane, in Africa (A. D. 540), in a work entitled "Pro Defensione Trium Capitulorum Concilii Chalcedonensis" (ed. Sirmondi, Paris, 1629), and addressed to the Emperor Justinian. In addition to what may be gathered from his own writings, the opinions of Theodore with respect to Inspiration may be inferred not only from the recorded opinions of his defender on the subject,—who assuredly would not have upheld the cause of one who, in any sense, questioned the authority of Scripture; but also from the nature of the charges which were urged against him.[2]

The views of Facundus himself may be collected from the following words —"Nam si obstinatus ille dicendus est, qui non cedit Ecclesiæ constitutis, earundem Scripturarum auctoritate firmatis, quanto deterioris obstinationis dicendus est, qui ipsis Divinis Scripturis dedignans acquiescere, *inviolabili earum plenitudini* aut abrogat veritatem, aut aliquid deesse putat quod propria debeat adinventione supplere?"—*Loc. cit.* lib. xii. p. 514.

The error of Theodore, with respect to Scripture, was twofold. (1) The extreme into which he was led by his opposition to the principles of the Allegorists, against whom he wrote a special treatise; and (2) his rejection from the Canon of portions of the Old and New Testaments.

(1) Theodore seems to have borrowed his system of interpretation from his teacher, Diodorus of Tarsus,—a name unhappily too notorious in the controversies of that age,—whose principle it was to pay regard to the mere *letter* of Scripture (ψιλῷ τῷ γράμματι τῶν θείων προσέχων γραφῶν.—Socrates, *Hist. Eccl.* lib. vi. cap. 3, p. 311). Hence resulted the method of *typical*, as opposed to *allegorical* exposition; a method which is thus described by Theodore himself:—

"All things in both the Old and the New Testament have been ordained by one and the same God, intent upon one end (πρὸς ἕνα σκοπὸν ὁρῶν). Having of old determined with Himself to make known the constitution

[1] See O. F. Fritzsche, "De Theodori Mopsuest. Vita et Scriptis," Halæ, 1836.

[2] A valuable result will follow from this inquiry, namely, that we shall learn the opinion of an Œcumenical Council on the important question which we are considering.

of the Future (τὴν μέλλουσαν ἐκφῆναι κατάστασιν), the commencement of which He has exhibited in the economy introduced by the Lord Christ; and considering it necessary that we should first exist in this present state of things, and be afterwards transferred to that other, by means of the Resurrection from the dead, * * * in order that this might become manifest, and that it might not be thought that He had afterwards determined anything new concerning us,—by many and different means He already suggested (ἐναπέθετο) to men the Advent of the Lord Christ." The promises to Abraham and to David have been fulfilled in the dispensation introduced by Christ; in Whom all nations have been truly blessed, and Whose kingdom shall not be moved. For this purpose, God preserved with care His people, who waited for the coming of the Lord Christ. For this cause He disposed most things under the Old Covenant in such a manner that they might not only afford the greatest profit to those who then lived, but might also indicate what was to be manifested afterwards: and thus the things of old were a type of what was to come:—εὑρίσκετό τε κατὰ τοῦτον τὸν τρόπον τύπος τίς τὰ παλαιὰ τῶν ὕστερον, ἔχοντα μέν τινα μίμησιν πρὸς ταῦτα.—*Proœm. in Jonam* (ap. A. Mai., "Script. Vet. Nova Coll.," t. vi. p. 114). E. g. God released Israel from Egypt and from all that bitter bondage; He saved them by the death of the first-born; and by anointing the door-posts with blood distinguished between His people and the Egyptians: *by types* (ἐν τύποις), denoting beforehand that the Lord Christ would so deliver us, not from the bondage of Egypt, but from that of death and of sin.

Theodore divided the Psalms into four classes,[1] Historical, Prophetical, Moral, and Messianic. According to his disciple, Cosmas Indicopleustes (A. D. 535), the school of Theodore regarded *four* Psalms only as Messianic,[2] i. e. as applicable *throughout to Christ alone:* ὁ Δαυὶδ ἠξιώθη ἐκ Πνεύματος προειπεῖν περὶ τοῦ Δεσπότου Χριστοῦ ψαλμοὺς δ΄., τὸν β΄. καὶ τὸν ή. καὶ τὸν μδ΄. καὶ τὸν ρθ΄., ὅλους τοὺς δ΄. δι' ὅλου εἰς Αὐτὸν εἰρηκώς.—*Christian. Opinio de Mundo*, lib. v. ("Collect. Nov. Patr." ed. Montfauc., t. ii. p. 224.) Without dwelling upon the fact that Facundus (*loc. cit.*, lib. iii. p. 130) quotes a statement of Theodore to the effect that his Commentary upon the Psalms was no more than a crude production of his pen in early youth; or adducing the case of many other writers who have equally limited the number of the Messianic Psalms (e. g. Hengstenberg, see *supra*, p. 151, note), but who have never been regarded, on that account, as opponents of Inspiration;—it will be sufficient, in proof of Theodore's profound sense of the Divine nature of Scripture, to quote two passages from his Commentary on the Minor Prophets, selected almost at random. Explaining Hos. i. 1 ("The word of the Lord that came unto Hosea"), he writes:—Λόγον δὲ Κυρίου τὴν ἐνέργειαν ἀπανταχοῦ λέγει τὴν θείαν τὴν ἐφότῳ δήποτε γιγνομένην * * * θείαν δὲ ἐνέργειαν κἀνταῦθα λέγει, καθ' ἣν ἀποκάλυψις τῶν ἐσομένων ἐγίνετο τῷ προφήτῃ·

[1] See Fritzsche, *loc. cit.* p. 32.

[2] Leontius has charged Theodore with allowing only *three* Psalms to be Messianic, referring the others, in a *Judaizing* manner, to Zorobabel and Hezekiah:—τοὺς πάντας ψαλμοὺς ἰουδαϊκῶς τοῖς περὶ τὸν Ζοροβάβελ καὶ Ἐζεκίαν ἀνέθηκε τρεῖς μόνους τῷ Κυρίῳ προσρίψας.—*Adv. Nestorian.*, § xv. (ap. A. Mai., "Spicileg. Rom." t. x., par. ii. p. 73).

ἀφ' ἧς περ αὐτῷ καὶ τὸ λέγειν τὰ καὶ μηνύειν τὰ ἐσόμενα δύναμις ὑπῆρχεν.—*Comm. in Oseam* (*loc. cit.*, p. 2).

Again:—Τῆς αὐτῆς τοῦ 'Αγίου Πνεύματος χάριτος οἵ τε πάλαι μετεῖχον καὶ οἱ τῷ τῆς καινῆς διαθήκης ὑπηρετούμενοι μυστηρίῳ.—*Comm. in Nahum*, i. 1 (*loc. cit.*, p. 163). (The discussion which follows here, on the ecstatic condition of the prophets, and founded on 1 Cor. xii., is full of interest.)

The Books of Scripture which Theodore rejected were, in the Old Testament, the writings of Solomon, the Chronicles, Job, Ezra; and in the New, as Leontius (*l. c.* p. 73) states, the Catholic Epistles. The principle on which he did so,—at least in some of these cases, as appears from his own words quoted at the Council of Constantinople,—was not founded upon a denial of Inspiration, but (as I have already observed) upon his attempt to lay down a criterion which all inspired books must satisfy:—"His quæ pro doctrina hominum scripta sunt, et Salomonis libri connumerandi sunt, id est, Proverbia et Ecclesiaste; quæ ipse ex sua persona ad aliorum utilitatem composuit, *cum Prophetiæ quidem gratiam non accepisset, prudentiæ vero gratiam*, quæ evidenter altera est præter illam, secundum beati Pauli vocem."—*Art.* lxiii. (ap. Mansi, t. ix. p. 223).

The following extracts exhibit not only the opinion of that Council on the subject of Inspiration, but also the nature of the error respecting Scripture for which Theodore was condemned. A series of "Articles" selected from his writings was recited before the Council,—throughout which, as, indeed, throughout all his writings, the title "Divine Scripture" repeatedly occurs,—each Article being preceded by a brief statement of its contents.

Art. lxiii. is headed "Ejusdem Theodori reprobantis et librum Job, et contra Conscriptorem ejus, *id est Sanctum Spiritum*, dicentis," &c. And again: Art. lxvi. is headed—"Per omnia reprobans Scripturam Job, et Conscriptori maledicens (*idem autem est dicere Sancto Spiritui*)," &c.

The Council next proceeded ("Collatio 5ta," *ibid.*, p. 230, &c.) to read over "ea quæ contra Theodorum Mopsuestenum et ejus blasphemias sancti patres scripserunt;" in which, however, no mention whatever is made of Theodore's having questioned the authority or Inspiration of Scripture, the whole controversy turning upon his *interpretation* of it. That interpretation was obviously founded upon his exalted estimate of the *letter* of Scripture; an estimate which, by a different process, led Origen into an opposite extreme. And here the subject of these two opposite schools of expositors, to which reference has been made in Lecture vii. (p. 310), must be briefly considered.

The light in which Origen regarded the language of Scripture, and which may be inferred from his words already quoted, is laid down in the following striking passage:—"Videtur mihi unusquisque sermo Divinæ Scripturæ similis esse alicui seminum, cujus naturæ hæc est, ut cum jactum fuerit in terram, regeneratum in spicam, * * * multipliciter diffundatur; et tanto cumulatius, quanto vel peritus agricola plus seminibus laboris impenderit, vel beneficium terræ fœcundioris indulserit."—*In Exod.* Hom. i. § i., t. ii. p. 129.

Origen had also a clear apprehension of the still more important principle, that the Bible must be regarded as one organic whole, not as a fortuitous assemblage of independent writings: but he does not seem to have been capable of grasping the great truth which he thus perceived. He observed, that as man consists of body, soul, and spirit, so Scripture consists of the *letter*, the *sense contained under* the letter, and a certain *shadow* of heavenly things (Heb. viii. 5). Thus he writes:—"Triplicem in Scripturis Divinis intelligentiæ inveniri sæpe diximus modum,—historicum, moralem, et mysticum. Unde et corpus inesse ei, et animam, ac spiritum intelleximus."—*In Levit.* Hom. v. § 5, t. ii. p. 209. And again:—*Ὥσπερ γὰρ ὁ ἄνθρωπος συνέστηκεν ἐκ σώματος καὶ ψυχῆς καὶ πνεύματος· τὸν αὐτὸν τρόπον καὶ ἡ οἰκονομηθεῖσα ὑπὸ τοῦ Θεοῦ εἰς ἀνθρώπων σωτηρίαν δοθῆναι γραφή.*—*De Princip.* lib. iv., t. i. p. 168.[1] Now it is plain, if this analogy is to be carried out, that, in order to form a just conception of what Scripture means, due value must be assigned to each of its three elements; and the relation to each other which they respectively hold must be maintained. The *spirit* of man confers its vital power upon the material substance into which it has been infused: while the soul, the product, as it were, of this union of the spiritual and the corporeal,[2] is that in which consists the *real* existence of the living man. To consider the material substance alone, or the spirit alone, is at once to abandon the region of actual being. We should then contemplate an inanimate mass; or speculate respecting the nature of an immaterial element which transcends the limit of all human experience. While if we grasp the full idea of the living man, his material substance becomes the outward, but necessary, garb of the spiritual essence; the union of both being expressed by the Soul, which derives its vital principle from what is spiritual, and the *condition* of its existence from the bodily organization—an organization which (as we learn from the doctrine of the Resurrection of the body), is as essential to its future as to its present being. The fixed relation of these three components was what Origen failed to maintain when he proceeded to apply the analogy which he so acutely pointed out. Neglecting, and at times appearing even to deny, the historical sense of Scripture, he dwelt exclusively upon its spiritual element: nay, so far did his one-sided system

[1] It is interesting to observe how Origen follows here in the footsteps of Philo. Philo having said that "he, to whom God has granted to be, as well as to seem, honorable and virtuous, is truly happy," continues:—*Εἰσὶ γάρ τινες οἳ τοὺς ῥητοὺς νόμους σύμβολα νοητῶν πραγμάτων ὑπολαμβάνοντες, τὰ μὲν ἄγαν ἠκρίβωσαν, τῶν δὲ ῥαθύμως ὠλιγώρησαν, οὓς μεμψαίμην ἂν ἔγωγε τῆς εὐχερείας.* We are not, he goes on to say, to omit the actual observance of a festival because it symbolizes (*σύμβολόν ἐστι*) joy of soul, and thanksgiving to God. Nor because Circumcision denotes (*ἐμφαίνει*) the *excision* (*ἐκτομήν*) of pleasures and affections, must we therefore abrogate the law which commands the rite itself. On such a principle we should do away with the Temple-worship, and innumerable other ceremonies, if we shall attend merely to what the latent sense denotes (*εἰ μόνοις προσέξομεν τοῖς δι' ὑπονοιῶν δηλουμένοις*). He then proceeds to anticipate Origen in his analogy, using almost the same words:—*Ἀλλὰ χρὴ ταῦτα μὲν σώματι ἐοικέναι νομίζειν, ψυχῇ δὲ ἐκεῖνα· ὥσπερ οὖν σώματος ἐπειδὴ ψυχῆς ἐστιν οἶκος προνοητέον, οὕτω καὶ τῶν ῥητῶν νόμων ἐπιμελητέον.*—*De Migr. Abr.*, t. i. p. 450.

[2] "The Lord God formed man of the dust of the ground, and breathed into his nostrils the *breath* [or *spirit*, נשמה,—cf. Lecture v. p. 225, note [1]] of life, and man *became* a living *soul* (נפש)."—Gen. ii. 7. Cf. "I pray God your whole *spirit, and soul, and body* (*τὸ πνεῦμα, καὶ ἡ ψυχή, καὶ τὸ σῶμα*) be preserved blameless," &c.—1 Thess. v. 23. See Mr. Westcott's remarks on this subject, "Elem. of Gosp. Harmony," App. B, p. 207.

of interpretation lead him, that he ventured to assert—ᾠκονόμησέ τινα οἱονεὶ σκάνδαλα καὶ προσκόμματα καὶ ἀδύνατα. * * * ὁ τοῦ Θεοῦ Λόγος. ἵνα. * * * μὴ κινούμενοι ἀπὸ τοῦ γράμματος, μηδὲν θειότερον μάθωμεν.—*De Princip.* lib. iv., t. i. p. 173.[1]

From the natural reaction against such exaggerated allegorizing arose the school of Theodore; which, from an undue depreciation of the spiritual element, and an exclusive assertion of the mere literal sense, fell into the opposite extreme. In consequence of this error, Theodore regarded the primary application (see Lecture iv. p. 153, note [1]) of the Old Testament prophecies as their complete and sole meaning; and hence he was charged with "Judaizing"[2] by the different writers, who opposed his views. E. g. the prediction as to our Lord's triumphant entry into Jerusalem, which the Evangelists (S. Matt. xxi. 4; S. John, xii. 14) quote from Zechariah (ix. 9), Theodore considered as designed to point out Zorobabel alone; alleging that it is referred in the Gospels to Christ, solely because He, too, was great, and just, and a deliverer. The principle according to which part of the prediction applies to Zorobabel, and part to our Lord, in Theodore's judgment, ψυχρολογίας ἐστι περιττῆς καὶ ἀπειρίας τῶν θείων γραφῶν.—*Comm. in Zach.* (*loc. cit.* p. 255).

It is not difficult to perceive how the analogy suggested by Origen, if consistently applied, leads to the true principle of interpretation. The "Soul" of the sacred writings can never be appreciated by fixing our whole

[1] As might naturally be supposed, the passages in which such statements occur have been laid hold of by Strauss ("Introduct." § 4); and with his usual unfairness. Origen's principle was that every isolated phrase and expression of Scripture is replete with profit and instruction: even the ordinances of the Jewish Law, *apart from the great Scheme of which they formed an element*, abound with instruction for Christians. Hence, speaking of the Law as to "the sin-offering," Lev. vi. 24, &c., he argues that the passage must be expounded spiritually, since to announce *to a Christian assembly* the benefit of animal sacrifices as an atonement for sin must lead to offence and to error:—"Hæc omnia nisi alio sensu accipiamus, quam literæ textus ostendit, sicut sæpe jam diximus, *cum in Ecclesia recitantur*, obstaculum magis et subversionem Christianæ religioni, quam hortationem ædificationemque præstabunt."—*In Levit.* Hom. v., t. ii. p. 205. "*What edification* (he asks, in a passage quoted by Strauss) shall *we* derive from the history of Abraham and Abimelech (Quæ *nobis* ædificatio erit)?" "Hæc Judæi *putent*, et si qui cum eis literæ amici non Spiritus."—*In Genes.* Hom. vi., § 3, t. ii. p. 78.—"Origen by no means requires that we should not *believe* this narrative (*πιστεύειν, credere*); but only that we should not *think* (*νομίζειν, putare*) that it so conveyed edification, or that it was written for the sake of its merely *verbal* sense. This latter view is Jewish or literal."—Hoffman *Das Leben Jesu*, s. 42. As Origen himself observes:—"Hæc interim propter eos qui amici sunt literæ. * * * Sed nos qui omnia quæ scripta sunt non pro narrationibus antiquitatum, sed pro disciplina et utilitate nostra didicimus scripta," &c.—*In Exod.* Hom. ii., t. ii. p. 133.

[2] As the extreme maintained by Theodore arose from the reaction against the excessive allegorizing of Origen, so Origen's excesses may, not unfairly, be attributed to *his* opposition to the Chiliasts, or Millenarians (see Neander, "Kirchen-Gesch," B. i. s. 1125), whom he describes as "solius literæ discipulos. * * * Christo quidem credentes, *Judaico autem quodam sensu* Scripturas Divinas intelligentes."—*De Princip.* lib. ii., t. i. p. 104. (See, also, his "Comm. in Matt.," t. iii. p. 827; "Prolog. in Cantic.," t. iii. p. 28; "Sel. ad Psal.," t. ii. p. 570). Eusebius has preserved the account given by S. Dionysius of Alex. of his controversy, at a later period in the third century (A. D. 255), with the Millenarian bishop, Nepos, who was also obnoxious to this charge of "Judaizing:"—Ἰουδαϊκώτερον τὰς ἐπηγγελμένας τοῖς ἁγίοις ἐν ταῖς θείαις γραφαῖς ἐπαγγελίας ἀποδοθήσεσθαι διδάσκων.—*Hist. Eccl.* lib. VII. c. xxiv., p. 349). Cf. Olshausen, "Ein Wort üb. tief. Schriftsinn," s. 13 ff.

attention, with Origen, upon their purely spiritual application; or, with Theodore, upon their merely literal sense. The true signification of Scripture results from the due combination of both the spiritual idea, and the historical fact: and this, as I have shown in the Seventh of the preceding Discourses, is the method which the inspired writers themselves prescribe.

APPENDIX H.

THE ADDRESS OF S. STEPHEN.[1]

(LECTURE III.—PAGE 103.)

IT has been often, and with too little consideration, assumed that S. Luke, in the Book of the Acts, has selected for his theme, through preference merely, the labors of Apostles; and especially of S. Peter and S. Paul. And yet with what particularity does he record the preaching of the other ministers of the Gospel:—e. g. of S. Philip (ch. viii. 5, &c.), and S. Stephen (ch. vi., vii.); the history and martyrdom of the latter being described with such minuteness, while the death of the Apostle James is barely touched upon (ch. xii. 2). To which when we add the obvious design of S. Luke, in each of his writings, to supply instruction for *Gentile* readers,—a design to be inferred from his language and style, and choice of subjects, as well as from the care with which he relates not merely how the preachers of the Gospel, to a great extent abandoning Jerusalem, turned to the heathen world; but also how in each heathen city they turned from the Jews to the Gentiles,—we cannot doubt that he has composed the Acts of the Apostles, not under the influence of mere *subjective* preference; but, impelled by the *objective* necessity of the Divine Scheme, in order to represent the passing of the message of Salvation from the people of Israel to the Pagan world (cf., *supra*, p. 354). We at once perceive the importance of the history of S. Stephen for such an object. His death was the event by which the Jews once more publicly showed themselves to be unworthy of the Gospel; and which, at the same time, not only led to its diffusion, through Samaria, among the Gentiles (ch. viii. 4, &c.; ix. 32, &c.; xi. 19, &c.), but also conduced immediately to the conversion of S. Paul.

Attention has been already drawn (*supra*, p. 103, notes [1] and [3]), to the repeated and emphatic mention of S. Stephen's Spiritual Gifts; and also to the three subjects of which he has treated in his review of Jewish history. These three subjects are not introduced in succession, but are intermingled with each other; the history supplying the different links of the argument. Special pains, too, are taken to point out that that peculiar characteristic of Revelation which consists in the *repetition* of Divine acts[2] is reflected from the entire history of the people; and that its principle of *repetition*

[1] "Ueber Zweck, Inhalt, und Eigenthümlichkeit der Rede des Stephanus, Ap. Gesch. cap. vii.," von Friedrich Luger, Lübeck, 1838.

[2] E. g., Divine Revelation was not restricted to the Law and the Temple; but was perfected only in a *repeated* act of Revelation—viz., in the *accomplishment* of the promise which accompanied the Law.

is to be found visibly stamped upon events seemingly the least important. Thus, Abraham "came out of the land of the Chaldeans and *dwelt* (κατῴκησεν) in Charran: and from thence He [i. e. God] *removed* (μετῴκισεν) him," &c.—ver. 4. God gave him no inheritance in the land which he showed him; but promised its possession "to his seed *after him* (μετ' αὐτόν)."—ver. 5. This seed should be in bondage 400 years; "and *after that* (μετὰ ταῦτα) shall they come forth."—ver. 7. Jacob sent the patriarchs to Egypt *first* (πρῶτον); "and at the second time (ἐν τῷ δευτέρῳ) Joseph was made known to his brethren."—ver. 12, 13. Joseph sent and called (μετεκαλέσατο) his father to him; "so Jacob went down (κατέβη) unto Egypt, and died, he and our fathers, and were carried over (μετετέθησαν) into Sychem."—ver. 14, 16. "*Another* king arose," &c.—ver. 18. "*The next day* Moses showed himself unto them."—ver. 26. *Another* leader, Joshua, conducted the people into the promised land—ver. 45, &c., &c.

In speaking thus, S. Stephen clearly adopted that view of the Old Testament which regards no expression of Scripture, no event which it records, as superfluous or unimportant. In this treatment of his subject he is closely followed by S. Paul:—compare, for example, the Apostle's use of Jewish history in Gal. iv., and 1 Cor. x., to which allusion has so often been made (see *supra*, p. 104, note [2]; p. 109, note [2]); consider, also, how he argues from the most casual expressions (see Lecture viii. p. 339), and even *omissions* of the Old Testament (e. g. Heb. vii. 3, 8). Is it unreasonable to suppose that this address of S. Stephen, of which S. Paul was a hearer,—and which appears to have roused him, at the moment, to frenzy in his zeal for the Law and the Temple (cf. vii. 58; viii. 1, 3),—was not the least among the providential means by which his mind was prepared for his miraculous conversion? Compare, too, the whole tenor of his first address (ch. xiii. 16, &c.), which, equally with the discourse of S. Stephen, is based upon the Old Testament; and, especially, the nature of the reproach brought against him by the Jews, "This is the man that teacheth all men everywhere, against the people, and *the Law, and this place*."—xxi. 28; a charge which presents an exact parallel to that brought by the "false witnesses" against S. Stephen, "This man ceaseth not to speak blasphemous words against *this* (1) *holy place, and* (2) *the Law*. For (3) we have heard him say that *this Jesus of Nazareth* shall destroy this place, and shall change the customs which Moses delivered us."—vi. 13, 14.

I. Here the three subjects of this discourse are imposed, by the necessity of the case, upon S. Stephen:—(1.) The Temple of Solomon, as he proves from Isaiah, lxvi., was not a dwelling worthy of the God "Who inhabiteth eternity."—ver. 47, 49. Indeed, the previous history of Israel had shown that wherever God appeared, were it even "in the wilderness," was "holy ground" (ver. 33, cf. ver. 30, 31): and this not merely in the promised land; for "the God of glory appeared unto our father Abraham when he was in *Mesopotamia*."—ver. 2. (2.) From these latter words, "The God of glory appeared unto our father Abraham," the entire argument starts. The Law was merely an *additional* element in the fulfilment of the promise then made (cf. Rom. v. 20; Gal. iii. 19):—this *fulfilment* being the essential circumstance, not the Law. Nay, even Moses, by whom God accomplished the deliverance promised to Abraham (ver. 36), wrote of the new promise added to the fulfilment of the former: "A prophet *shall* the Lord *raise up* unto you, like unto me."—ver. 37. (3.) It was the chief ground of reproach against S. Stephen that he had taught that "Jesus *of Nazareth*" was to be the subverter of Temple and Law. In his reply S. Stephen does not expressly mention our Lord until the close of his address, where he announces the principle on which he had throughout encountered this charge: "Ye do *always* resist the Holy Ghost, *as your fathers did*, so do ye."—ver. 51. Thus, "the patriarchs *moved with envy* sold Joseph."—ver. 9. Moses "supposed his brethren would have understood how that God by his hand would deliver them: *but they understood not*."—ver. 25. It was said to him, "Who made thee a ruler and a judge over us?"—ver. 27. "This Moses, whom they refused, did God send to be a ruler and a *deliverer*" (λυτρωτής) (ver. 35); "to whom our fathers would not obey, but thrust him from them."—ver. 39. In fine, S. Stephen asks, "Which of the prophets have not your fathers persecuted? *They* have murdered those who announced the Messiah's coming; *you* have betrayed and murdered Him when He came."—ver. 52. Hence therefore his reply to the scorn exhibited against the despised Nazarene. The patriarchs sold Joseph, "but God was with him" (ver. 9); our fathers would not obey Moses, and yet Jehovah "had sent him as a ruler and deliverer." Now, too, exclaims S. Stephen, the people have rejected the Prophet of the Law written in the heart;[1] they have not understood, in His High Priesthood, the fulfilment of the design of the Temple; and yet, behold! I see Him now "standing at the right hand of God."—

"En a dextris Dei stantem
Jesum pro te dimicantem,
Stephane considera.
Tibi cælos reserari
Tibi Christum revelari
Clama voce libera."[2]

II. To turn, in the next place, to the historial objections[3] which have

[1] Cf. ver. 51,—*Σκληροτράχηλοι καὶ ἀπερίτμητοι τῇ καρδίᾳ*, with the exhortation of Moses, *καὶ περιτεμεῖσθε τὴν σκληροκαρδίαν ὑμῶν, καὶ τὸν τράχηλον ὑμῶν οὐ σκληρυνεῖτε.*—Deut. x. 16.

[2] Adam of S. Victor. Bengel well explains:—"*ἑστῶτα* (*stantem*), quasi *obvium Stephano*, cf. ver. 59. Nam alias ubique, *sedere*, dicitur. Egregie Arator:—

'Lumina cordis habens cælos conspexit apertos,
Ne lateat, quid Christus agat: *pro Martyre surgit.*
Quem nunc *stare* videt, confessio nostra *sedentem*
Cum soleat celebrare magis. Caro juncta Tonanti
In Stephano favet Ipsa Sibi.' "

[3] It is scarcely necessary, perhaps, to allude to the following objection. S. Stephen says:—"The God of glory appeared unto our father Abraham, *before He dwelt in Charran*, and said unto him, Get thee out of thy country, and from thy kindred," &c. (vv. 2, 3); while in Gen. xii. 1, it is said (we are told) that God appeared for the first time to Abraham *in Haran*, after he had left Ur of the Chaldees. The English Version avoids the force of this by translating, "Now God *had said* unto Abraham." The words of Genesis, however, at once afford the answer. God commands, לך־לך מארצך וממולדתך; where,—although it cannot, perhaps, be *proved* that מולדת can only be taken in the sense given by the LXX., *συγγένεια*,—the only meaning that ארצך can possibly have is Ur of the Chaldees, the native country of Abraham: in which place, therefore, and *not*, as the objection assumes, *in Haran*, God must have appeared.

been urged against this address. "In the last apology of Stephen," writes Mr. Alford, "which he spoke being full of the Holy Ghost, and with Divine influence beaming from his countenance, we have at least *two demonstrable historical mistakes*."—*The Greek Test.*, vol. I. Proleg., ch. i. § 6. These cases must be considered in order. On the words, "Then came he [Abraham] out of the land of the Chaldeans, and dwelt in Charran: and from thence *when his father was dead* he removed him into this land." (Acts, vii. 4),—Mr. Alford notes as follows: "In Gen. xi. 26, we read that Terah lived 70 years, and begat Abram, Nahor, and Haran; in xi. 32, that Terah lived 205 years, and died in Haran; and in xii. 4, that Abram was 75 years old when he left Haran. Since then 70 + 75 = 145, Terah must have lived 60 years in Haran after Abram's departure. It seems evident that the Jewish chronology, which Stephen follows, was at fault here, owing to the circumstance of Terah's death *being mentioned*, Gen. xi. 32, *before* the command to Abram to leave Haran;—it not having been observed that the mention is *anticipatory*. And this is confirmed by Philo *having fallen into the same mistake*:—*Πρότερον μὲν ἐκ τῆς Χαλδαϊκῆς ἀναστὰς γῆς 'Αβραὰμ ᾤκησεν εἰς Χαῤῥάν· τελευτήσαντος δὲ αὐτοῦ τοῦ πατρὸς ἐκεῖθε κἀκ ταύτης μετανίσταται.*—*De Migr. Abr.*, t. i. p. 463.

Now, without going any further, the remark is obvious, that for critics of the present day to convict S. Stephen of historical inaccuracy,—a man so versed in the sacred literature of his nation as to vanquish in argument the most learned of the Jewish Synagogue, who "were not able to resist the wisdom and the Spirit by which he spake" (Acts, vi. 10); and whose possession of Spiritual Gifts S. Luke has brought so prominently forward,—must be regarded, to say the least of it, as a judgment somewhat precipitate. Such a mode of evading a difficulty in the work of an ancient writer would assuredly be tolerated in no other province than that of religion. But let the objection itself be considered.

The statement of Genesis is, that "Terah lived seventy years, and begat Abraham, Nahor, and Haran."—xi. 26.

From the single fact that Abraham's name occurs first in this passage it is inferred by commentators that he must have been the eldest son. On the other hand, Philo and S. Stephen, as we have seen, agree in a statement which, if they understood the words of Moses, is not easily reconcilable with such an assumption. But is it very unreasonable to assume, in turn, that they *did* understand the language of the Old Testament; and that the opinion of such men may be better founded than the conclusions of modern critics? Now the analogy of the whole Patriarchal history intimates that it was *not* the first born who, in those days, succeeded to the inheritance. We read that "Noah was 500 years old, and begat *Shem*, Ham, and Japhet."—Gen. v. 32, &c. (cf. also vi. 10; x. 1); while we are expressly told in ch. x. 21, that *Japhet was the eldest son.* Compare also the cases of Seth, Isaac, Jacob, and Judah. Josephus, moreover, fully confirms the inference that Abraham could not have been the first-born. We know from Gen. xvii. 17, that he was but ten years older than Sarah; and although she is called "the daughter of his father" (xx. 12), it is plain that, according to Hebrew usage, the phrase would be fully as applicable to the grand-daughter, as to the daughter of Terah.[1] Josephus, moreover, ex-

[1] E. g. Gen. xxix. 5, Laban is called the "son of Nahor;" but we know from ch.

plicitly states that Sarah *was* his grand-daughter,—the daughter of Haran, and sister of Lot and Milcah,—and that Abraham married his niece; a fact which, taken in connexion with their relative ages, demonstrates that Haran must have been many years older than Abraham. The words of Josephus are: Ἀράνης μὲν καταλιπὼν υἱὸν Λῶτον καὶ Σάῤῥαν καὶ Μελχὰν θυγατέρας * * * γαμοῦσι δὲ τὰς ἀδελφιδάς· Μελχὰν μὲν Ναχώρης, Σάῤῥαν δὲ Ἄβραμος.—*Ant.* lib. i. vi. 5, p. 27.

Ussher writes as follows: "1948 [A. M.]—Postquam Thara 70 vixisset annos, natus est ætate primus trium ipsius filiorum. *Non Abram quidem* (*quem post* 60 *demum annos natum infra videbimus*), sed Haran * * * 2008.—Abram natus est: quippe 75 annorum existens, quum pater Thara moreretur, annum agens ætatis 205. (Acts, vii. 4), 2018.—Sarai, *quæ et Iscah*, Haranis fratris Abrami filia, nata est: utpote decennio, marito suo Abramo ætate minor."—*Annales Vet. Test.*, Works, Elrington's ed., vol. viii. p. 21.

Accepting this fact, viz. that Abraham was not Terah's eldest son, Luger (§ 41 ff.) considers another element necessary to explain S. Stephen's allusion. He adopts Bengel's remark: "Abram, dum Thara vixit in Haran, domum quodammodo paternam habuit in Haran, in terra Canaan duntaxat peregrinum agens: mortuo autem patre, plane in terra Canaan domum unice habere cœpit;"—which, however, he explains to mean (rightly translating μετοικίζειν, "to lead to another *domicile*," not, "to emigrate," a sense which would require *the passive*), that, according to the Patriarchal relations, and nomadic usage, the dwelling-place of the head of the Tribe alone could be regárded as the *domicile* of the members of the Tribe: and that although Abraham may have commenced his wanderings before his father's death, yet that he did not receive another *domicile* (as S. Stephen states) *until after the death of Terah:* Terah's name being introduced by S. Stephen merely to denote that he was the first member in the series of the disobedient (cf. Josh. xxiv. 2).

The second "historical mistake" which Mr. Alford ascribes to S. Stephen is founded on ver. 16: "Jacob died, he and our fathers, and were carried over into Sychem, and laid in the sepulchre that Abraham had bought for a sum of money of the sons of Emmor, the father of Sychem." Luger refers here to Calvin's comment, "In nomine Abrahæ erratum esse palam est. * * * quare hic locus corrigendus est;" and adds: "Stier, on the other hand, justly remarks that to ascribe to Stephen an error of memory in the statement of a fact so well known, may be named almost a piece of infatuation (fast thöricht)" (s. 45). Mr. Alford thus states the difficulty: "The facts, as related in the Old Testament, were these:—Jacob, dying in Egypt, was (Gen. l. 13) taken into the land of Canaan, and buried in the cave of Macpelah, before Mamre: Joseph, dying also in Egypt, was taken in a coffin (Gen. l. 26), at the Exodus (Exod. xiii. 19), and finally buried (Josh. xxiv. 32) at Shechem. Of the burial of the other patriarchs the

xxviii. 5, that he was the son of *Bethuel*, who was the son of Nahor (ch. xxiv. 15; xxii. 20–23). Cf. also 1 Kings, xix. 16, with 2 Kings, ix. 2; 2 Sam. ix. 6, with 2 Sam. xix. 24; Josh. vii. 1, 18, with ver. 24; 1 Chron. i. 17, with Gen. x. 23, &c., &c. Nor was Sarah's having two names (viz. Sarai and Iscah, Gen. xi. 29) at all unusual. Thus the name of Samuel's eldest son is Joel, in 1 Sam. viii. 2; and Vashni, in 1 Chron. vi. 28.

sacred text says nothing, but by the specification in Exod. xiii. 19, leaves it to be inferred (?) that they were buried in Egypt. Josephus (Ant. II. viii. 2) relates that they were taken and buried in *Hebron:* * * * the Rabbinical traditions mentioned by Wetst. and Lightf. report them to have been buried in *Sychem.* * * * These traditions probably Stephen followed; and in haste or inadvertence classed *Jacob* with the rest. The burying-place which Abraham bought was not at *Sychem*, but (Gen. xxiii. 3–20) at *Hebron*, and was bought of *Ephron the Hittite.* It was *Jacob* who (Gen. xxxiii. 19) bought a field where he had pitched his tent, near *Sychem*, of the *children of Hamor*, Shechem's father: and no mention is made of its being for a *burying-place*. The two incidents are certainly here *confused;* and no ingenuity of the commentators has ever devised an escape from the inference." Luger answers this common objection by pointing to the peculiar manner in which, as we have already seen, S. Stephen alludes to the national history. Abraham bought the sepulchre near Mamre, and there *Jacob* was buried (Gen. l. 13); Jacob bought "a parcel of a field" at Sychem, and there *Joseph* was buried (Josh. xxiv. 32). That is, Abraham purchased a grave for Jacob; and so did Jacob for Joseph; and thus we have an additional instance of the law of *repetition* above alluded to. These two facts S. Stephen *combines in a single phrase;* and this same system of combination is constantly repeated throughout his address:—e. g. cf. ver. 7, with Gen. xv. 13, 14, and Ex. iii. 12 (see, *supra*, p. 308, note); cf., too, the statement of ver. 9. Compare, especially, the reference of ver. 43,[1] "I will carry you away *beyond Babylon*," with the denunciation of Amos (v. 27) against *the Ten Tribes:* "Therefore will I cause you to go into captivity *beyond Damascus;*"—in which words the deportation to *Assyria* (2 Kings, xvii. 6), is alone spoken of. *Babylon*, however, as the Prophets declared, was to be the exile of disobedient *Judah;* and *both* denunciations are here *combined* by S. Stephen. So also in the passage before us, it is, with similar brevity, implied that Jacob was laid in the grave which Abraham had purchased in Hebron,[2] Gen. xxiii. 19; l. 13;

[1] It may be well to allude to the substitution of Remphan, or Rephan (Ῥεφάν), in this verse, for the "Chiun, כיון" of Amos, v. 26. Of this, two explanations are given:—(1) Chiun=Saturn; Kircher ("Œdip. Ægypt," t. i. p. 384) having proved the existence of a Coptic word, Ῥηφὰν or Ῥεφάν (by which *all Versions* render the "Chiun" of Amos), which also stands for Saturn. (2) Ῥηφάν=ריון; and the LXX., who give Ῥαιφάν, had this reading instead of כיון,—ר standing for כ. See Hengstenberg, "Beiträge," ii. s. 110 ff., and Winer, "Real-Wörterb.," art. *Saturn.*

[2] This explanation has been given, in substance, by Bishop Kidder, in his "Demonstration of the Messias," Part ii. p. 86, &c.; where he also answers another objection hinted at by Mr. Alford, who writes on ver. 14:—"In the Hebrew text, Gen. xlvi. 27; Exod. i. 5; Deut. x. 22, *seventy* souls are reckoned, viz., sixty-six born of Jacob, Jacob himself, Joseph, and his two sons born in Egypt. So also Josephus, Ant. II. vii. 4; VI. v. 6. But the LXX., whom Stephen follows, insert in Gen. xlvi. 20 an account of the children and grandchildren of Manasseh and Ephraim, five in number; and in ver. 27 read *ψυχαὶ ἑβδομηκονταπέντε*—reckoning, as it appears, *curiously enough, among the sons of Joseph, Joseph himself, and Jacob;* for these are required to make up the nine according to their ver. 20." Bishop Kidder considers "that Moses designs to give an account of Jacob's whole family, or such as 'came out of his loins,' Gen. xlvi. 6–8, and ver. 26; in order that by comparing the small number who went down to Egypt, with the great number who came out of that land, the protection of God might be the more manifest. Hence he does not include *the wives of Jacob's sons*, enumerating merely Jacob, his sons, and also Joseph's sons, which were born him in

and Joseph in the possession which Jacob had purchased at Sychem, Gen. xxxiii. 19; Josh. xxiv. 32.

APPENDIX I.

"THE CAPTAIN OF THE LORD'S HOST."

(LECTURE III.—PAGE 127.)

DR. MILL's note on "The Captain of the Lord's Host" (Josh. v. 13–15) is as follows:—

"The question now proposed is this. Whether of these two, the Uncreated or the created Angel, the Angel of Exod. xxiii. 20, or that of xxxiii. 2, is he who appeared to Joshua on the plain of Jericho, and announced himself as come to him in the character of 'Captain of the host of the Lord?' This is stated with other biblical questions by Theodoret, in the fourth century, as one debated among Christians: and he answers, on the ground of the last-cited passage of Exodus, on the latter side, against some, apparently a minority in the Church, who asserted the former. Quæst. IV. *in Jesum filium Naue.* Τίνα νοητέον τὸν Ἀρχιστράτηγον τῆς δυνάμεως Κυρίου; τινές φασι, τὸν Θεὸν Λόγον ὀφθῆναι. Ἐγὼ δὲ οἶμαι Μιχαὴλ τὸν Ἀρχάγγελον εἶναι· ἡνίκα γὰρ ἐπλημμέλησαν, ὁ τῶν ὅλων ἔφη Θεός· οὐ μὴ συναναβῶ μετὰ σοῦ διὰ τὸ τὸν λαὸν σκληροτράχηλον εἶναι· ἀλλ' ἀποστελῶ τὸν ἄγγελόν μου πρὸ προσώπου σου προτερόν σου. Τοῦτον οἶμαι νῦν ὀφθῆναι τῷ Ἰησοῦ παραθαῤῥύνοντα καὶ τὴν θείαν βοήθειαν προσημαίνοντα. [Opera, ed. Schulze, tom. I. p. 308.] What Theodoret here expresses as his own opinion, is that which (with two remarkable exceptions which shall be presently noticed) has received the sanction of the ancient Church."

"The same is also the oldest tradition of the Jews, as exemplified in Jonathan's Chaldean paraphrase of the passage in Joshua, where the Captain of God's host is twice termed מלאך שליח מן קדם י״י 'an Angel sent from the presence of the Lord,' an expression incompatible with the belief that he comprised that Presence in his own person." * * *

"Agreeably to this view, we do not find that the Christian Fathers, when speaking, as they frequently do, of the Son of God as appearing in

Egypt" (see vv. 26 and 27). But take now the words and the design of S. Stephen. He does not confine himself to those who came "out of Jacob's loins:"—he plainly includes all those whom *Joseph called into Egypt.* "Then sent Joseph and called his father to him, and *all his kindred,* threescore and fifteen souls." "Moses tells us how many Jacob and his seed amounted to; *omitting his sons' wives.* Stephen tells us how many *they were that Joseph called into Egypt.*" Some, therefore, in the list of Moses, must be left out of the number given by S. Stephen. Joseph and his two sons could not be said to *be called into Egypt;* still less could Hezron and Hamul, the sons of Phares (Gen. xlvi. 12), who were not yet born. Besides, Jacob too must be considered apart. Hence *six* persons are *to be deducted* from the number of Moses (viz. Jacob, Joseph and his two sons, with Hezron and Hamul), in order to find those who are reckoned by S. Stephen:—and hence sixty-four only are common to both. Add now the *eleven wives of the sons of Jacob,* and we get the number seventy-five given by S. Stephen.

the Old Testament, and as the special object of the provocation of the Israelites,—include this appearance to Joshua among the θεοφάνειαι. But to this there are two distinguished exceptions. The one is Justin Martyr, who, after describing the appearance to Moses in the bush, says [Dial. cum Tryphone, p. 183, ed. Jebb], Μαρτύριον δὲ καὶ ἄλλο ὑμῖν, ὦ φίλοι, ἀπὸ τῶν γραφῶν δώσω, ὅτι ἀρχὴν πρὸ πάντων τῶν κτισμάτων ὁ Θεὸς γεγέννηκε Δύναμιν τινὰ ἐξ ἑαυτοῦ λογικὴν, ἥτις καὶ Δόξα Κυρίου ὑπο τοῦ Πνεύματος τοῦ ἁγίου καλεῖται, ποτὲ δὲ Υἱὸς, ποτὲ δὲ Σοφία, ποτὲ δὲ Ἄγγελος, ποτὲ δὲ Θεὸς, ποτὲ δὲ Κύριος καὶ Λόγος· ποτὲ δὲ Ἀρχιστράτηγον ἑαυτὸν λέγει, ἐν ἀνθρώπου μορφῇ φανέντα τῷ τοῦ Ναυῆ Ἰησοῦ.—The other is Eusebius, who, in the second prefatory chapter to his Ecclesiastical History, 'concerning the preexistence and Divinity of our Lord and Saviour Jesus Christ,' adds to the indubitable instances of His manifestation as the sole image of God to man, this revelation of himself as Leader of the Army of God: relating the appearance at length from the LXX. version of Joshua, and arguing the identity of the person manifested with Him who appeared to Moses, from the command to both to loose the sandals from their feet, because the place on which they stood was sanctified by that Presence. Against this sentiment of Eusebius an ancient annotator has inserted in the margin this remarkable protest, preserved on account of its antiquity and its elegance of style by Valesius *ad loc.* Ἀλλ' ἡ ἐκκλησία, ὦ ἁγιώτατε Εὐσέβιε, ἑτέρως τὰ περὶ τούτου νομίζει καὶ οὐχ ὡς σύ· τὸν μὲν γὰρ ἐν τῇ βάτῳ φανέντα τῷ Μωυσῇ θεολογεῖ· τὸν δὲ ἐν Ἱεριχῷ τῷ μετ' αὐτὸν ὀφθέντα, τὸν τῶν Ἑβραίων ἐπιστασίαν λαχόντα, μάχαιραν ἐσπασμένον, καὶ τῷ Ἰησοῦ λῦσαι προστάττοντα τὸ ὑπόδημα, τοῦτον δέ γε τὸν ἀρχάγγελον ὑπείληφε Μιχαήλ· καὶ δῆλον ὅτι κρεῖττον ὑπείληφε σοῦ· πόθεν; ἐρωτηθεὶς παρὰ τῇ βάτῳ φανεὶς ὁ Θεὸς ἐν εἴδει πυρὸς τῷ ἑαυτοῦ θεράποντι Μωυσῇ, καὶ δηλῶν ὅστις εἴη, τοῦτο αὐτῷ τρανώτατα παριστᾷ, ὅτι δὴ ὁ Θεὸς ἐστίν. ὁ δὲ τῷ Ἰησοῦ φανεὶς, οὐδὲ Θεὸν ἑαυτὸν, ἀλλ' Ἀρχιστράτηγον ὠνόμασε τοῦ Θεοῦ· τοῦτο δὲ τὸ ἀξίωμα τῆς ἀνωτάτω δυναστείας τε καὶ θεότητος ὑποδεέστερον ὂν, καὶ οὐκ ἀρχικὸν ἀλλ' ὑπαρχικόν. [Euseb. H. E. Tom. I. pp. 17, 18, ed. Heinichen.]"

"The interpreter of Scripture has to choose between the reasons of this anonymous writer, supported as they are by the unquestionably true allegation of general Catholic consent, and those of the learned historian on whom he is commenting. That this Angel, in describing his name and dignity to Joshua, so far from exhibiting any analogy with the assertion of Supreme Deity in Exod. iii. 6, gives a name implying only a ministerial superintendence, is undeniable: (for to say that the chief of the army of the LORD must be the LORD Himself is the same as saying that the captain of the guard, the chief of the butlers and of the bakers, all denoted by the same word שׂר in Gen. xxxix., xl., must mean Pharaoh the sovereign of all.) And the impression of this signal difference can only be removed by the most distinct proof that the act commanded severally in Exod. iii. 5, and Josh. v. 15, was in both instances *similarly referred to the immediate speaker*, and that an honor and obeisance were rendered to the latter by Joshua, beyond what is allowed to any created being. * * * But as, with the example of all the earlier as well as the later Scriptures before us, it seems most natural and obvious to conceive that the LORD sent this message to

Joshua (cf. vi. 2) by the mouth of his Archangel, so there seems no derogation to the Divine honor in believing, with the Fathers of old, that the ground was hallowed which was trodden by such an exalted servant of God,—and that the prostrate adoration of Joshua, like that of Daniel before the angel in Dan. x. 15[1] (if it were such), was directed, not to the Captain of the LORD's host, but to the LORD of Hosts who sent him.

"With respect to the identity of this שַׂר־צְבָא־יְהוָֹה with Michael, to whom the same title of שַׂר is given in Dan. x. 13, 21, xii. 1 (*there* translated Prince), it is sufficiently established by the functions ascribed to the latter in that book and in the Apocalypse, as well with respect to the celestial host, as to the people of God whom he defends. But there is one species of testimony to this identity too remarkable to be overlooked, though not proposed to be followed or imitated. The same divines of the foreign reformation, who contend for the Prince of the LORD's host in Joshua being no less than the Second Person of the Ever-blessed Trinity, are most commonly impelled by the same process of argument to predicate the same of the Archangel Michael also. The process may be seen by consulting the notes of Masius and Drusius on this place of Joshua; the latter of whom however shrinks, as he well may, from asserting that Michael (called in Dan. x. 13, *one of the Primary chiefs*, אחד השרים הראשנים), *always* denotes the Uncreated Word."

APPENDIX J.

NABI,—ROEH,—CHOZEH.

(LECTURE IV.—PAGE 158.)

THERE is, perhaps, no single point in the exegesis of the Old Testament respecting which the information to be gleaned from critics is so meagre, and so unsatisfactory, as that relating to the distinction which subsists between the terms חזה, ראה, נביא. That a distinction does exist is unquestionable. This we learn chiefly from the Books of Chronicles; in which the author has on all occasions assigned, with such particularity, his official title to each person named. E. g., "The acts of David *the king*, first and last, behold they are written in the book of Samuel *the seer* (הראה); and in the book of Nathan *the prophet* (הנביא), and in the book of Gad *the seer* (החזה)."—1 Chron. xxix. 29. Cf. also, Nathan "the *prophet*," and Iddo "the *seer*."—2 Chron. ix. 29. Shemaiah "the *prophet*" and Iddo "the *seer*."—2 Chron. xii. 15. Isaiah "the *prophet*, the son of Amoz."—2 Chron. xxvi. 22.

Witsius observes:—"Quænam ergo inter hæc tria nomina significationis est diversitas? Enimvero fateor me ignorare."[2] Carpzovius contents himself with stating that the learned profess ignorance on the subject quoting a conjecture of Vitringa which explains nothing, and which is des-

[1] "But respecting the quality of this obeisance, see Mr. Todd's remarks in p. 138, not. [c] of his fourth Lecture on Antichrist."

[2] "Miscell. Sacra," lib. i. cap. 1, § 19.

titute of support. Winer merely says:—"All three names, Nabi, Roeh, Chozeh, occur together, but applied *to different individuals*, in 1 Chron. xxix. 29. In the Books of Chronicles this distinction is, in general, observed, and Samuel is named Roeh; Gad, Chozeh; and Nathan, Nabi."[2] Dr. Moses Stuart has thought fit to speak contemptuously of any attempt to explain the use of any of these terms, and denies the existence of any distinction at all![3] The following remarks may, perhaps, serve to express how the case really stands.

Hävernick[4] (who considers that Roeh and Chozeh have the same signification) clearly proves that Nabi has a meaning peculiar to itself, and that it invariably expresses the *official* title of the prophets of God. On the other hand, the word חזה (and, according to Hävernick, ראה), denotes "the *act* of receiving a single revelation (cf. the New Testament phrase ἀποκάλυψιν ἔχειν—1 Cor. xiv. 26), but not the particular *function*." Of this distinctive use of Nabi he gives the following examples. In 2 Kings, xvii. 13, we read: "The Lord testified against Israel and against Judah by the hand of all His Prophets (נביאו), *and* of every kind of seers (כל־חזה):" —i. e. the prophets, as public teachers of the people, gave their testimony in Israel; but, at the same time, other private individuals also received communications from God,—the personal pronoun pointing out the distinction between the *official* prophets and ordinary seers. ("Here the words are rendered according to the 'kethib.' The Masorets omitted the pronoun because חזה has no suffix; and they were either ignorant of, or did not observe, the distinction between the two ideas.") Again, 1 Sam. xxviii. 6, the Lord answered Saul, "Neither by dreams [i. e.—employing part of the idea for the whole—by the non-official seers, חזים], nor by Urim [i. e. by the High Priest; cf. the case of Caiaphas, *supra*, p. 202, note [1]], nor by prophets [i. e. by the *official* agents of the Theocracy]." Isaiah, too, has no less clearly pointed out the distinction: "The Lord hath poured out upon you the spirit of deep sleep, and hath closed your *eyes*,

[1] "Quanquam autem nonnihil discriminis inter hæc tria vocabula intercedere, ex 1 Chron. xxix. 29, satis appareat * * * quod sane casu, aut temere factum, nemo facile dixerit: ipsum tamen discrepantiæ momentum, in quo versetur cardine, doctissimi virorum se ignorare fatentur. * * * Vero itaque paulo videtur similius חוזה proprie esse ἐκστατικόν, qui oculos mentis in rem, contemplationi suæ oblatam, alte defigit, et vultu immoto in ejus intuitu hæret, 2 Reg. vi. 11; quæ omnis vis non est in voce ראה, quippe quæ simpliciter notat qualemcunque rei speciem in phantasia descriptam videre, non in ecstasi tantum, sed et per quietem Gen. xxxi. 10; xli. 22, vocisque adeo ראה, latiorem esse significationem; quæ Vitringæ erudita est hariolatio *in 'Typo doctrinæ propheticæ,'* cap. i. § 3, p. 4, quod tamen discrimen in Scriptura ubivis servari, ipse vir clariss. *pro certo affirmare non audet.* * * * Unde satis, opinor, constat esse quidem aliquod inter hæc vocabula æque ac munia discrimen, *quod tamen, quale sit, hodie ignoretur.*"—*Introd. ad Libros Canon. V. T.*, par. iii. cap. i. § 2.

[2] "Real-Wörterbuch," art. *Propheten.*

[3] "Hävernick," writes Dr. Stuart, "has labored at length to show that even the Scriptures themselves make a distinction—a palpable one—between נביא, *a prophet,*—ראי or חוזה, *a seer.* Labor surely bestowed in vain. * * * How easy to have prevented such a mistake as he has made, by duly consulting a Hebrew Concordance. Had he done this, he must have seen that Nabi, and Roeh, or Chozeh are undistinguishingly (!) used to designate the very same individuals."—*The Old Test. Canon*, p. 254.

[4] "Einleitung," Th. I. Abth. i. s. 56 ff.

the prophets (הנביאים); and hath veiled your *heads*, the seers (החזים)."—xxix. 10; where Isaiah, as appears from the principle of "parallelism," has clearly two *distinct* classes of persons in view; the seers being termed "heads," inasmuch as they were usually leading personages in the Theocracy, either kings or priests. Observe, David "the *king*" is never called Nabi.[1]

Now, while fully adopting the principle that נביא is a distictintive term, denoting those "men of God" who were *officially* prophets, and, therefore, conveying an idea altogether different from that expressed by חזה,—I must dissent from the other branch of Hävernick's conclusion, viz., that ראה and חזה are synonymous. On the contrary, the term ראה, is, I submit, simply equivalent to נביא, and, consequently, as distinct from חזה as נביא itself. This appears from the statement of 1 Sam. ix. 9, where the term Roeh first occurs as applied to an agent of God:—"Beforetime in Israel, when a man went to inquire of God, thus he spake, Come, and let us go *to the seer: for he that is now called a prophet* (נביא) *was beforetime called a seer* (ראה)."—words which expressly state that *Roeh* was merely the ancient title assigned, in popular usage, to the *official Nabi*. The usage of the Old Testament fully confirms this view. Samuel (to whom the title נביא is given, 1 Sam. iii. 20;[2] 2 Chron. xxxv. 18) calls himself "the seer" (הראה) in 1 Sam. ix. 19; and such, in general, is his title throughout the Books of Chronicles, viz., 1 Chron. ix. 22; xxvi. 28; xxix. 29. The term חזה is nowhere applied to him. The only other individual to whom the title Roeh is given in the Old Testatament is Hanani, who is called הראה in 2 Chron. xvi. 7, 10.

Let us now turn to the term חזה. In the first place, Roeh is distinguished from it precisely in the same manner as Nabi: "Which say *to the seers* (לראים), See not; and to *the prophets* (לחזים), Prophesy not (לא־תחזו) unto us right things," &c.,—Isaiah, xxx. 10, a passage where the distinction is quite lost in the English Version, but which is exactly parallel to Isaiah xxix. 10, already quoted. In the next place Chozeh and Nabi are both applied to Jehu, the son of Hanani; who is called Nabi in 1 Kings, xvi. 7, 12, and Chozeh in 2 Chron. xix. 2. The only other instance in which these titles are interchanged is that of Gad, who is called Nabi in 1 Sam. xxii. 5; while he is described as "the *prophet* (Nabi) Gad, David's *seer* (Chozeh)," in 2 Sam. xxiv. 11. Gad is in like manner called "David's seer," 1 Chron. xxi. 9; and "the King's seer," 2 Chron. xxix. 25. In 1 Chron. xxix. 29, he is simply styled "the seer." With respect to these ap-

[1] This official position seems also indicated by the duties which the prophet (נביא) discharged. Thus, at stated times, the people were wont to assemble to hear his words and admonitions. The Shunamite's husband said to her, "Wherefore wilt thou go to him [Elisha] to-day? it is neither new moon, nor sabbath."—2 Kings, iv. 23. We are told that "Elisha sat in his house, and the elders sat with him."—vi. 32. The "Elders of Judah," and the "Elders of Israel" came to Ezekiel and "sat before him."—viii. 1; xiv. 1. We also read:—"And they come unto thee as the people cometh, and they sit before thee as My people, and they hear thy words, but they will not do them."—Ezek. xxxiii. 31. Cf. too, the obvious reference to the *official* position of the נביא in the following passages:—Jer. xiv. 18; Amos, vii. 14; Ps. lxxiv. 9; Dan. ix. 24; and in many other places.

[2] "All Israel, from Dan even to Beersheba, knew that Samuel was established to be a Prophet (לנביא) of the Lord."

parent exceptions, adopting Hävernick's premises, I again dissent from his inference as to the manner in which they are to be explained. The case of Gad affords the clue to the difficulty; as it clearly indicates that, attached to the royal establishment, there was usually an individual styled "the king's seer" (who might at the same time be a Nabi), by whom the Lord was wont to reveal His will on any emergency, and by whose instrumentality the king could seek for the Divine assistance. Thus we read of "the seers (החוזים) that spake to Manasseh, in the name of the Lord God of Israel."—2 Chron. xxxiii. 18. With respect to the application of the title Chozeh to Jehu, son of Hanani, everything, as in the case of Gad, denotes that it was in his capacity of "king's seer" that he went out to meet Jehoshaphat: "And Jehu, the son of Hanani, *the seer* went out to meet him, and said to *king* Jehoshaphat, Shouldst thou help the ungodly? Nevertheless there are good things found in thee," &c.—2 Chron. xix. 2. Hence, therefore, I infer that both Gad and Jehu were *officially* prophets: and that each also filled the office of Chozeh in the royal household. (Hävernick considers that Gad was not, properly speaking, a Nabi at all: he does not consider the case of Jehu.[1])

If the foregoing remarks have any weight, the titles Roeh and Nabi equally point out the *official* prophet (the former term being merely the archaic and popular designation of an *office* which had been defined from the very first by Moses,—see, *supra*, p. 156, note [2]): while by Chozeh are indicated those individuals who occasionally, or for some specific purpose, were chosen to convey a communication from God; and, who possessed the *prophetic gift*, but not the *prophetic office*:—e. g. the authors of sacred poetry, such as Asaph (2 Chron. xxix. 30) are so called. And hence the Nabi might be styled Chozeh, but not conversely.

APPENDIX K.

"SPIRITUAL GIFTS," I. COR. xii.–xiv.

(LECTURE V.—PAGE 224.)

IN the following remarks it is not by any means intended to enter upon a minute inquiry into the nature of those Spiritual Gifts, or Charismata, so often referred to in the New Testament, and especially in 1 Cor. xii., and xiv. My object here is merely to illustrate the fact that there *are* such "diversities of gifts,"—even of the extraordinary gifts of the Holy Ghost, —a fact which fully confirms, *a fortiori*, the conclusion that there also exists an absolute difference *in kind* between the Inspiration of Scripture, and that ordinary operation of the Holy Spirit on the hearts of all Christians to which the name Inspiration has likewise been assigned.

In the Apostolic age two contrary tendencies exhibited themselves, which were afterwards developed into the Gnostic,[2] and Montanist systems. The former resulted from that effort of the mind of the ancient world, in

[1] Hävernick proves that "Iddo the seer,"—2 Chron. xii. 15, and "the prophet Iddo,"—2 Chron. xiii. 22, are different persons.—*loc. cit.* s. 59.
[2] Cf. ἀντιθέσεις τῆς ψευδωνύμου γνώσεως.—1 Tim. vi. 20.

its yearnings after knowledge and dissatisfaction with the present, to appropriate the treasures which the Gospel proffered to mankind;[1] it consequently aimed at incorporating into Christianity the existing elements of mental culture. The tendency of the latter system, on the other hand, was to repel and abjure what was *natural: its* aim was to retain for ever in the Church, in their primitive energy, all the elements of the *Supernatural.* The germs of this latter extreme are prominent in that abuse of Spiritual Gifts against which S. Paul directs his warning in the chapters under consideration. Everything connected with the operation of these Spiritual Gifts is now involved in the darkest obscurity. S. Chrysostom, who lived so many centuries nearer the Apostolic age than we do, confesses his ignorance on the subject. His exposition of 1 Cor. xii. opens with the remark:—"This entire passage is exceedingly obscure; an obscurity which is caused as well by our ignorance of the facts, as by the circumstance that what then took place happens no longer."[2] He proceeds, however, to point out, with great acuteness, some particulars which may guide us in applying the Apostle's words. The abuse of Spiritual Gifts arose, he suggests, not only from a spirit of envious rivalry among those who possessed the different Charismata,—an abuse not peculiar to the Corinthians, as we learn from Rom. xii. 6,—but also from the fact that the system of heathen divination prevailed extensively in Corinth, with which the converts to Christianity had been tempted to compare the Gifts of the Spirit of God. Hence,[3] the Apostle commences (xii. 1):—"Concerning the endowments imparted by the Spirit (*τῶν Πνευματικῶν*) I would not have you ignorant. Ye know that ye were Gentiles carried away unto these dumb idols. *Wherefore* I give you to understand," &c. The Apostle, adds S. Chrysostom, does not broadly state his purpose, because he wrote to persons who clearly understood his allusions: and to this absence of detail, throughout, the obscurity of the passage is chiefly owing.

The nature of a "Spiritual Gift" (*χάρισμα*), in general, has been well defined by Neander to be "that predominant endowment (Tüchtigkeit) of an individual in which the power and working of the Holy Ghost, Who animates him, manifest themselves:—the *φανέρωσις τοῦ Πνεύματος* (1 Cor. xii. 7) peculiar to each."[4] The comparison of the members of the human body, of which the Apostle avails himself (1 Cor. xii. 12–27), points out, moreover, that there was no capricious or arbitrary distribution of these qualifications, but a "regulated development of the New Creation in a sanctified natural order." In ch. xii. 4–6, before proceeding to enumerate the distinct Charismata, S. Paul guards himself against any possible misconception by expressly laying down that, distinct and diverse though the Gifts may be, their source is still the same (see, *supra*, p. 223, note [3])—viz., the Godhead Itself, to each Person of Which each particular Charisma can be referred, under whatever external form it may have appeared to the observer.[5] This being premised, he proceeds, ver. 8–10, to

[1] See Neander's "Anti-Gnosticus," Einleit.

[2] "In Epist. i. ad Cor. Homil. xxix.," t. x., p. 257.

[3] *Διὸ καὶ ἀρχόμενος, πρῶτον τὸ μέσον μαντείας καὶ προφητείας τίθησι.*—*loc cit.* p. 258.

[4] "Geschichte der Pflanzung der christl. Kirche," B. i. s. 233, 4te. Aufl.

[5] On ver. 4, "Now there are diversities of Gifts, but the same Spirit," S. Chrysostom writes:—"And first he attends on him that had the lesser Gift, and was grieved

give a definite enumeration of *nine distinct Gifts* which he classifies under *three* heads (which, however, by no means correspond to the three διαιρέσεις of ver. 4–6; since there, *each* member comprehends, as has been said, *all* the Gifts):—the distinction being marked (1) ver. 8, by ᾧ μέν; (2) ver. 9, by ἑτέρῳ δέ; (3) ver. 10, again by ἑτέρῳ δέ. The change from ἄλλῳ to ἑτέρῳ, whereby each new catagory is introduced, places this beyond doubt. Meyer (*in loc.*) clearly exhibits this classification:—

I. Gifts which are to be referred to the intellectual powers:—(1) λόγος σοφίας; (2) λόγος γνώσεως.

II. Gifts of which the condition is the zealous exhibition of Faith:—(1) πίστις itself. (2) The efficiency of this Faith in *acts*, viz., *a.* ἰάματα; *b.* δυνάμεις. (3) The efficiency of this Faith in *words*, viz., προφητεία. (4) Its efficiency in power of *discernment*, viz., διάκρισις πνευμάτων.

III. Gifts of tongues:—(1) speaking with tongues; (2) interpretation of tongues.

This enumeration is preceded by the emphatic statement of the principle that "the manifestation of the Spirit is given to every man *to profit* withal"—ver. 7: a statement which enables us to turn to ch. xiv., in which S. Paul discusses the *violation* of this principle.[1]

Let us consider, for a moment, the manner in which one of the Gifts, the Gift of Tongues, had been abused. An instance of this is given in ch. xiv. 14, a verse which Mr. Alford well explains:—

"Τὸ πν. μου, 'my (own) spirit,' taking himself as an example, as above, ver. 6: a use of the word familiar to our Apostle, and here necessary on account of ὁ νοῦς μου following. 'When I pray *in a tongue*, my higher being, my *spirit*, filled with the Holy Ghost, is inflamed with holy desires, and rapt in prayer: but my *intellectual* part, having no matter before it on which its power can be exercised, bears no fruit to the edification of others.'"[2] The Gift of Tongues had a twofold object:—the edification of

on this account. 'For wherefore,' saith he, 'art thou dejected? because thou hast not received as much as another?' * * * Wherefore he added, 'but the same Spirit.' So that even if there be a difference in the Gift, yet is there no difference in the Giver. For from the same Fountain ye are drawing, both thou and he. * * * Seest thou (ver. 5, 6), that he implies there being no difference in the Gifts of the Father, and the Son, and the Holy Ghost? * * * For that which the Spirit bestows, this he saith that God also works; this, that the Son likewise ordains and grants."—*loc. cit.* p. 261. (Oxf. transl. p. 401.)

[1] The possibility of such abuse of Spiritual Gifts is declared by S. Paul himself where he tells us that "the spirits of the prophets are subject to the prophets."—xiv. 32. "Consider," observes Bishop Butler, "a person endued with any of these Gifts; for instance, that of tongues: it is to be supposed that he had the same power over this miraculous Gift as he would have had over it had it been the effect of habit, of study, and use, as it ordinarily is; or the same power over it as he had over any other natural endowment."—*Analogy*, Part II. ch. iii.

[2] Meyer correctly observes, that, as this passage proves, πνεῦμα in ver. 2 "is not to be understood of the *objective* Holy Spirit, but of the higher spiritual being *of man* (opposed to the νοῦς [cf., *supra*, Appendix G, p. 446, note [2]]); which, however, in those who are inspired is filled by the Holy Spirit (Rom. viii. 16): and thus πνεύματι λαλεῖν (ver. 2), means—"to speak by means of the activity of the higher consciousness raised above all concerns of life (überweltlichen) without the intervention of reflection." What is uttered, therefore, is termed μυστήρια,—i. e. its sense is hidden from the hearers. On the other hand, Olshausen (*in loc.* s. 713) and Beck ("Propäd. Entwickl.," s. 232) consider that the state of ecstasy, proceeding from the impulse of the Holy Spirit (cf. 2 Cor. xii. 2; Acts, xxii. 17), is intended:—πνεῦμά μου (writes

the individual who possessed the gift (ver. 4); and to serve "for a sign to them that believe not" (ver. 22). In the case described by the Apostle, neither end was attained: the speaker's "understanding was unfruitful" (ver. 14); and the Church was not edified (cf. ver. 5): "If, therefore, there come in those that are unlearned (*ἰδιῶται*—'plain believers,' i. e. not endowed with the Gift of Tongues, see ver. 16), or unbelievers, will they not say that ye are mad?"—ver. 23. As at Pentecost the charge of drunkenness had been brought, so the *γλῶσσαι* must sound to hearers now, as an unmeaning jargon. It is only when the Gifts of Class I. (ch. xii. 8, viz., "the word of wisdom" and "the word of knowledge") are possessed that any *communication* of religious truth can take place.

The Apostle, in short, teaches that general edification could only be obtained when several of the single Gifts *co-operated:* either by their combination in the same individual[1] (ver. 5 and 13); or when the Gift possessed by *one* individual *completed* those possessed by others, as we learn from ver. 26, &c. Finally, the principle, according to which all Scriptural Gifts should be employed, is defined in the words, "God is not the author of confusion but of peace" (ver. 33); and on it is founded the general regulation, "Let all things be done unto edifying" (ver. 26), which S. Paul, in the verses that follow, applies to the case before him.[2]

Olshausen on ver. 14)=*τὸ Πν. Θεοῦ ἐν ἐμοί:*—and these writers compare *λαλεῖ μυστήρια* with *ἄῤῥητα ῥήματα*—2 Cor. xii. 4.

[1] "Let him that speaketh in an unknown tongue pray that he may interpret" (ver. 13), i. e. pray for the *Gift* of interpretation,—*ἵνα διερμηνεύῃ*. Meyer, on the other hand, appealing to the connexion of *προσεύχεσθαι* (ver. 14), by *γάρ*, to *προσευχέσθω* in ver. 13, translates, "Let him pray with the view afterwards to expound what he had spoken with the tongue."—"*For if I pray* with a tongue, my spirit prayeth, but my understanding is unfruitful" (ver. 14). Mr. Alford thus explains ver. 15: "'I will pray with the (my) spirit; I will pray also with my mind' (i. e. will interpret my prayer for the benefit of myself and the Church), &c. This resolution or expression of self-obligation evidently leads to the inference by and by clearly expressed, ver. 28, that *if he could not* pray *τῷ νοΐ*, he would *keep silence. ψαλῶ*] hence we gather that the two departments in which the Gift of tongues was exercised were *prayer and praise.* On the day of Pentecost it was confined to the latter of these." (Observe that Tischendorf here *omits γάρ*; and also reads simply *ἑτέρῳ*, in xii. 9, 10.)

[2] Mr. Alford explains this application:—"Ver. 26, *ψαλμόν*] most probably a hymn of praise, to sing in the power of the Spirit, as did Miriam, Deborah, Simeon, &c., see ver. 15. *Διδαχήν*] an 'exposition of doctrine' or moral teaching: belonging to the Gift of *prophecy*, as indeed do also *ψαλμ.* and *ἀποκάλυψιν*, the latter being something revealed to him to be prophetically uttered." The general rule, ver. 26, "Let all things be done unto edifying" is applied to the several gifts:—In ver. 27, 28, to *the speaking with tongues.* [Meyer explains ver. 27:—"*κατὰ δύο*) &c. sc. *λαλείτωσαν* (as v. 11, 16);—'Let him know that in any assembly two, or at the most three, are to appear speaking with tongues:'—*καὶ ἀνὰ μέρος*)—'and this, too, in succession, one after the other, not several at once:'—*καὶ εἷς διερμ.*) 'and let *one* (not several) state the exposition:' 'unus aliquis, qui *id donum* habet' (Grotius); and it appears from ver. 13, that the speaker with a tongue might himself interpret. Ver. 28, 'but in case no interpreter is present, let the speaker with tongues keep silence; *in private devotion*, let him speak to himself and to God.' "] Ver. 29–33 give the regulations as to *prophecy.* [Meyer on ver. 29.—" 'Let the prophets speak two or three' (the *ἀνὰ μέρος*, ver. 27, is rendered specially prominent, ver. 30), (*καὶ οἱ ἄλλοι διακρ.*) 'and let the *other prophets* (i. e. who do not come to speak) judge' (i. e. whether what has been said proceeds or not from the Divine Spirit). Thus we see that the Charisma of 'discerning of Spirits' (with which even those who were *not* prophets might be endowed),

In the case of the Apostles this end was attained in the highest degree. All possibility of abuse was precluded by *the union, in their persons, of the several Charismata.* In their inward life personal consciousness (νοῦς), and spiritual activity (πνεῦμα) co-operated. S. Paul, who says that he spoke with tongues more than all the others (ver. 18), had already stated, "I will pray with the (my) spirit, and I will pray with the (my) understanding also" (ver. 15). In the Apostles their spontaneous feelings, and their reception of the several Spiritual Gifts, were harmoniously and mutually balanced. The full energy of the Spirit was infused into each element of their being, and was, therefore, apprehended with a clear consciousness. Consequently, when they acted as instruments of God for the edification of the universal Church, they were supplied with every needful qualification. To adopt S. Paul's own conclusion (xiv. 18, 19), their *understanding* (νοῦς) was enlightened so as to be in perfect accordance with the Spiritual influence. For the attainment of this end the following gradation in the conferring of Spiritual Gifts had been (as he points out in ver. 6) necessarily observed:—*Revelations*, or new communications of Divine Truth (ἀποκαλύψεις) had been conveyed to their minds; *unclouded insight*, and clear perception (γνῶσις) had next been granted; the power of *expounding* (προφητεία)[1] had also been conferred, and of *expressing* what others could only utter in an unknown tongue; to all which had been added the Gift of *doctrinal application* (διδαχή).[2] (See Beck, *loc. cit.*, s. 234.)

Hence we perceive that, while in those who received the Gifts of the Spirit *in* and *for themselves*, the separate Gifts ("the Spirit dividing to every man severally as He will"—xii. 11) appeared singly, or two or more combined (xii. 8–10);—nevertheless, in order to secure that such Charismata should be productive, *in any degree*, for general edification, several of them *must* have co-operated. Taken *singly*, they were not designed to propagate the Gospel; but, under due restrictions, to adorn it before the world, and to support individual members of the Church during her early struggles. Such was the case of the Tyrian prophets (Acts, xxi. 4), who had not "the word of knowledge" (cf. what has been said on this subject, *supra*, p. 43); or of S. Philip who had "the Gift of healing" (Acts, viii. 6), but who could not confer the Holy Ghost by the "laying on of hands"

(xii. 10), was in certain cases *combined* with the Gift of *prophecy*"]. Ver. 30.] "'But if a Revelation shall have been made to another (prophet) while sitting by, let the first (who was prophesying) hold his peace' (give place to the other: but clearly not as ejected by the second in any disorderly manner: probably, by being made aware of it, and ceasing his discourse). Ver. 31, 32.] He shows that the ὁ πρῶτος σιγάτω is no impossibility, but in their power to effect: 'For ye have the power, one by one, all to prophesy (i. e. you have power to bring about this result—you can be silent if you please), in order that all,' &c. 32.] 'And' (not, *for:* but a parallel assertion to the last, 'Ye have power, &c., *and*') the spirits of (the) prophets (i. e. their own *spirits* filled with the Holy Spirit) are subject to (the) prophets.'" (See, *supra*, p. 461, note [1].)

[1] Cf. S. Chrysostom's remark, quoted above, respecting the question which S. Paul here discusses, with what we know of the nature of heathen divination (see, *supra*, p. 84, and p. 193, note [1]); and we can feel little doubt as to the sense in which the Corinthians must have understood the word προφητεία:—for to the mind of the Gentile world the προφήτης was no more than the *interpreter* of the inspired μάντις.

[2] See, *supra*, p. 197, on the relation between Revelation and Prophecy, knowledge and teaching.

(ver. 14, 15); or, again, of the other inferior teachers "Judas and Silas, who being *prophets* also themselves, exhorted the brethren with many words and confirmed them."—Acts, xv. 32. With respect to this last Gift, special care was requisite:—so much so that the distinct Charismà of "discerning of spirits" was added for the purpose of checking any abuse. Thus S. Paul wrote to the Thessalonians: "Quench not the Spirit: despise not *prophesyings: prove* all things—πάντα δὲ δοκιμάζετε." (1 Thess. v. 19–21); words which, as the context shows, can only refer to the *διάκρισις πνεύματων* of 1 Cor. xii. 10; and to which S. John also alludes: "Beloved, believe not every spirit; but try (*δοκιμάζετε*) the spirits whether they are of God; because many *false prophets* are gone out into the world." —1 S. John, iv. 1. "It was only *in the Apostles*," writes Olshausen on 1 Cor. xiv. 29, "that the power of the Spirit revealed itself with an energy so mighty, and of so many aspects, that all error was removed. In their case alone *one Gift immediately completed another*, so that *their* expressions were subjected to no further *διάκρισις*."—*Commentar*, B. iii. s. 728.

It follows from the foregoing remarks as an additional, and no less important, result, that, notwithstanding the preservation of the *human element* in the composition of the different portions of Scripture, ample provision was made for securing to the sacred writers perfect freedom from error of every kind. And this was effected by means of the principle that the distinct Charismata co-operated, whenever the *general edification* of the Church required. See, *supra*, Lecture vii. p. 329.

APPENDIX L.

THE ORIGIN OF THE SYNOPTICAL GOSPELS.

(Lecture VII.—Page 295)

The following statement of the different theories which have been proposed for the purpose of accounting for the "origin" of the Gospels, unaccompanied as it is by any comment, will, perhaps, of itself justify the remarks in which I have alluded (p. 295, &c.) to this branch of criticism. I am far from insinuating that the several hypotheses are on a par in point of ingenuity, or of literary merit; but it can scarcely be asserted that any among them possesses much superiority over its fellows on the score of probability.

I. The hypothesis that the Evangelists made use of a common document or common documents.[1]

Without dwelling upon the various hints thrown out in the different works which have appeared between more recent times and the days of Le Clerc, who first suggested the idea of a common *Greek* source of the Syn optical Gospels; or of Lessing, who (in 1778) conceived the idea of a common *Syriac* or *Chaldaic* original,—it will be sufficient to start from the

[1] See Marsh's "Dissertation on the Origin and Composition of our three first Gospels," to be found in vol. iii. part 1, of his translation of Michaelis' "Introduction to the New Testament." Also Ebrard's "Wissenschaftliche Kritik der evang. Geschichte," s. 5 ff.

hypothesis of Eichhorn, with whom the modern aspect of the question may be fairly said to have commenced.

Eichhorn at first assumed the existence of an "Original Gospel" in the Aramaic dialect. A particular recension of this document (which he named A) was the basis of the Gospel of S. Matthew. To a second recension, B, S. Luke's Gospel owes its origin. A third, C, arising from a comparison of A and B, was employed by S. Mark. In fine, S. Mark and S. Luke, in addition to these distinct sources, both made use of a fourth recension, D, with which S. Matthew had not been acquainted.

According to this hypothesis, A, B, C, and D, were written in Aramaic; it afforded, consequently, no explanation of the agreement of the Evangelists in single *Greek* expressions (e. g. πτερύγιον τοῦ ἱεροῦ, S. Matt. iv. 5; S. Luke, iv. 9; ἐπιούσιος, S. Matt. vi. 11; S. Luke, xi. 3, &c.) To meet this difficulty, Bishop Marsh[1] suggested another hypothesis "compared with which the former appears as an innocent child." (Ebrard.) He assumed (1) an Aramaic original document ℵ. (2) A translation of this into Greek, ℵ̄. (3) This latter document with certain additions (ℵ̄+A+a). (4) A variation of this (ℵ̄+B+β). (5) A combination of Nos. (3) and (4) was the foundation of S. Mark's Gospel (ℵ̄+A+B+a+β). (6) No. (3), with other additions, was the foundation of S. Matthew's (ℵ̄+A+Γ+a+γ). (7) No. (4), with other additions, was the foundation of S. Luke's (ℵ̄+B+Γ+β+γ). (8) An auxiliary document ב was employed by S. Matthew and S. Luke. "The genealogy, when simplified," writes Ebrard, "appears thus:"

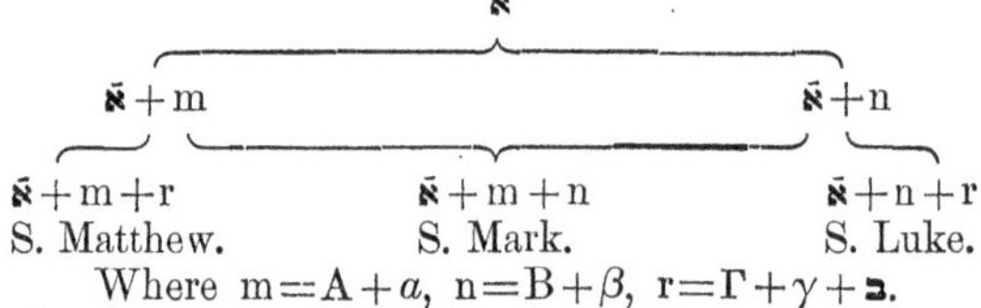

"Since this hypothesis," continues Ebrard, "was evidently still *far too simple*, Eichhorn devised a second:"

1. An Aramaic document.
2. Its Greek translation (=a).
3.=A. A recension of 1.—*S. Matthew.*
4.=A Greek translation of 3, in which 2 was made use of (=a').
5.=B. Another recension of 1.—*S. Luke.*
6.=C. A document resulting from A and B.—*S. Mark.*
7.=D. A third recension of 1.—*S. Matthew and S. Luke.*

[1] "Let ℵ denote all those parts of the XLII. general sections, which are contained in all three Evangelists [see, *supra*, p. 295]. Let a denote the additions made to ℵ in the Gospels of S. Matthew and S. Mark, but not in that of S. Luke. β. The additions made to ℵ in the Gospels of S. Mark and S. Luke, but not in that of S. Matthew. γ. The additions made to ℵ in the Gospels of S. Matthew and S. Luke, but not in that of S. Mark. A. Whole sections found in the Gospels of S. Matthew and S. Mark, but not in that of S. Luke. B. Whole sections found in the Gospels of S. Mark and S. Luke, but not in that of S. Matthew. Γ. Whole sections found in the Gospels of S. Matthew and S. Luke, but not in that of S. Mark."—Marsh's *Dissertation*, p. 148.

8.=A translation of D, in which 2 was made use of (=δ).
9.=E. An Aramaic Gospel of S. Matthew (A+D).
10. *The Greek form of S. Matthew*, arising from E, with an abridgment of 4 and 8.
11. *S. Mark*, arising from C; use having been made of 4 and 5.
12. *S. Luke*, the result of B and 8.

Simplified, the matter stands thus:—

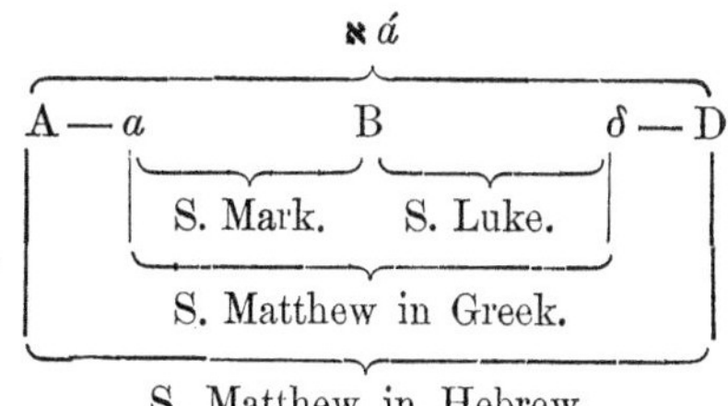

II. Such views having soon lost favor with critics, it was next attempted to explain the convergence of the Gospels by assuming that each Evangelist was acquainted with, and made use of, the Gospel or Gospels which had been written earlier than his own. The question, however, at once arose, *in what order* did this take place? and hence, from the very nature of the case, this hypothesis branched into *six* divisions, each of which has had its advocates:—

1.	S. Matt., the first.	S. Mark, the second.	S. Luke, the third.[1]
2.	S. Matt., " "	S. Luke, " "	S. Mark, " "
3.	S. Mark, " "	S. Matt., " "	S. Luke, " "
4.	S. Mark, " "	S. Luke, " "	S. Matt., " "
5.	S. Luke, " "	S. Matt., " "	S. Mark, " "
6.	S. Luke, " "	S. Mark, " "	S. Matt., " "

III. The third hypothesis, although suggested at an earlier period, owes its celebrity chiefly to the learned essay of Gieseler, so often quoted in the preceding pages—"Historisch-kritischer Versuch über die Enstehung und die frühesten Schicksale der schriftlichen Evangelien," Leipzig, 1818. In it Gieseler maintained that, for several years after our Lord's death, the Apostles,—at least the majority of them,—lived together at Jerusalem. The events of their Master's life, as well as his discourses, naturally formed a constant subject of their conversation; and thus, mutually aiding each other's reminiscences, facts and doctrines became fixed in their memory. Hence arose a *permanent type of oral teaching*, diversified by the private recollections of the different Apostles: and from this traditional source the Gospels in process of time were reduced to their present written form.[2]

It is unnecessary to recount how later writers (e. g. Olshausen, "Bibl.

[1] Townson and Hug advocate this aspect of the present hypothesis.

[2] It may be well to mention here the just remark of Thiersch ("Versuch der Herstell.," s. 120), that this theory of Gieseler, according to which the composition of the Gospels has been brought down to the latest possible period consistently with historical statements, has formed the point of transition to the mythical hypothesis of Strauss.

Comment." B. i. Einleit., § 3) have combined this "Tradition-theory" with that of the successive use, by the Evangelists, of the earlier written Gospels.

In addition to the preceding, the following theory has lately been proposed:—

"1st. Several of the Apostles, including Matthew, *Peter*, and John, committed to writing accounts of the transactions of our Lord and his Disciples in the language spoken by them, i. e. Syro-Chaldaic or Aramaic, known in the New Testament and the works of the Fathers as Hebrew.

"2d. When the Apostles were driven by persecution, from Judea, a history of the life of our Lord was drawn up from the original memoirs, in Hebrew and in Greek, by the Apostle Matthew, for the use of the Jewish converts—the Greek being the same as the Gospel according to Matthew.

"3d. S. Luke drew up, for the use of Theophilus [but see, *supra*, Lecture vii. p. 293, note [6]], a new life of our Lord, founded upon the authority of eye-witnesses and ministers of the Word,—including the Hebrew memoir of Peter, and the Greek Gospel of Matthew.

"4th. After Peter's death, or departure from Rome (ἔξοδον), S. Mark translated the memoir, written by Peter, into Greek.

"5th. John, at a still later period, composed his Gospel from his own original memoirs, omitting much that was already narrated by the other Evangelists, for reasons assigned by himself (xxi. 25)." [1]

APPENDIX M.

DID S. MATTHEW WRITE IN GREEK?

(Lecture VIII.—Page 342.)

"If any statement of the ancients," observes Thiersch,[2] "can lay claim to our confidence as being primitive, universal, and never contested, it is this—that Matthew wrote his Gospel in the *Hebrew* language. On this point all writers, including those best informed, are agreed: but as to how the *Greek* copy, received in the universal Church, has come into existence, they leave us (to all appearance at least) strangely in the dark. In its place the Apocryphal Gospel of the Hebrews—that Proteus of criticism—lets itself be seen in enigmatically changing forms, and is by many of the Hebrew Christians asserted to be the original document written by Matthew."

Such appears to be the natural result to which external evidence leads when we inquire as to the *original* form of our Gospel; ond which, notwithstanding the ingenious efforts of Hug[3] to prove that S. Matthew never wrote in Hebrew, is generally received by critics as the only legitimate conclusion.

The evidence may be briefly stated:—We learn from Eusebius (iii. 39), that S. Papias, bishop of Hierapolis, (*circ.* A. D. 110—Ἰωάννου μὲν

[1] "Dissertation on the Origin and Connexion of the Gospels," by James Smith, Esq. of Jordan Hill, F. R. S., p. xxv. London: 1853.

[2] "Versuch der Herstell.," s. 185.

[3] "Einleitung," Th. ii. s. 14 ff.

ἀκουστής, Πολυκάρπου δὲ ἑταῖρος—S. Irenæus, lib. v. xxxiii. p. 333) was the author of a work wherein several particulars were detailed respecting the contemporaries of the Evangelists, and the composition of the Gospels; and in which "John the Presbyter"[1] was referred to as the chief authority. The statement of S. Papias commences thus, Καὶ τοῦθ' ὁ πρεσβύτερος ἔλεγε, and it proceeds to describe the origin of S. Mark's Gospel. Ταῦτα μὲν οὖν, adds Eusebius, ἱστόρηται τῷ Παπίᾳ περὶ τοῦ Μάρκου. περὶ δὲ τοῦ Ματθαίου ταῦτ' εἴρηται· Ματθαῖος μὲν οὖν Ἑβραΐδι διαλέκτῳ τὰ λόγια συνετάξατο. ἡρμήνευσε δ' αὐτὰ· ὡς ἦν δυνατὸς [ἠδύνατο] ἕκαστος.—(ap. Routh. "Rel. Sacræ," vol. i. p. 13.) This passage,[2] which must be regarded as the keystone of the controversy, may be designated (A).

S. Irenæus writes:[3]—Ὁ μὲν δὴ Ματθαῖος ἐν τοῖς Ἑβραίοις τῇ ἰδίᾳ διαλέκτῳ αὐτῶν, καὶ γραφὴν ἐξήνεγκεν Εὐαγγελίου, τοῦ Πέτρου καὶ τοῦ Παύλου ἐν Ῥώμῃ εὐαγγελιζομένων, καὶ θεμελιούντων τὴν ἐκκλησίαν.—*Cont. Hær.* lib. III. c. i., p. 174.

There are many other vouchers for this fact. E. g. Origen (ap. Euseb. "Hist. Eccl.," lib. vi. c. 25, p. 290.; cf. Origen's "Comm. in Joann.," t. iv. p. 132); Eusebius himself ("Hist. Eccl.," lib. iii. c. 24, p. 116); and S. Jerome in several places, of which the following must for the present suffice:—"Matthæus * * * primus in Judæa propter eos, qui ex Circumcisione crediderant, Evangelium Christi *Hebraicis literis verbisque* composuit:[4] quod quis postea in Græcum transtulerit, non satis certum est."—*De Vir. Illustr.* cap. iii., t. ii. p. 819. This passage I shall call (B).

To the foregoing passages must be added the strictly independent, and, therefore, from the nature of this controversy, most important, testimony of S. Pantænus (A. D. 181). Eusebius tells us that S. Pantænus preached the Gospel as far as India; and that he there found some persons acquainted with S. Matthew's Gospel, to whom S. Bartholomew the Apostle

[1] "Halloixius, 'Vit. S. Papiæ, p. 661, Vitt. P. P. Oriental." qui ait, hunc Joannem unum fuisse e LXX. discipulis. * * * Nec amplius habeo, præter 'Constit. Apost.' illud in lib. vii. c. 46, quod tradit constituisse Joannem Apostolum cognominem hunc suum Ephesi episcopum."—Routh. *Rel. Sacr.*, vol. i. p. 36.

[2] Hug, who considers the testimony of S. Papias to be of no value, but who cannot reject that of John the Presbyter, admits that we must ascribe to John the statement of this passage as to S. Mark; he attempts to show, however, that we are not authorized to understand it as implying that S. Papias derived from the same source the information which it gives with reference to S. Matthew.—*loc. cit.* s. 16.

[3] Hug endeavors to evade the force of these words by arguing that this statement is but a repetition of that of S. Papias, whom S. Irenæus venerated (which of itself is surely some reason why the testimony of S. Papias should be regarded of weight); and, therefore, that it cannot be considered as *independent* evidence (s. 17). It is curious to notice, however, that, when subsequently quoting the words *with which the passage in the text concludes*, viz., μετὰ δὲ τῶν τούτων [*scil.* S. Paul and S. Peter] ἔξοδον, Μάρκος ὁ μαθητὴς καὶ ἑρμηνευτὴς Πέτρου, κ. τ. λ.,—Hug should write: "This witness (S. Irenæus), whose veracity has never been impeached, informs us as follows respecting Mark's Gospel," &c.—*Ibid.*, § 16, s. 61.

[4] S. Jerome founded upon this fact an important apologetic argument. Julian had urged as an objection against Christianity, that "quod de Israel scriptum est [Hos. xi. 1, cf. S. Matt. ii. 15], *Matthæus Evangelista* ad Christum transtulit, ut simplicitati eorum *qui de Gentibus crediderant*, illuderet." S. Jerome replies:—"Cui nos breviter respondebimus; primum Matthæum Evangelium Hebræis literis edidisse, quod non poterant legere nisi hi, qui ex Hebræis erant, &c."—*Comm. in Osee*, t. vi. p. 123.

had already preached, *αὐτοῖς τε Ἑβραίων γράμμασι τὴν τοῦ Ματθαίου καταλεῖψαι γραφήν· ἣν καὶ σώζεσθαι εἰς τὸν δηλούμενον χρόνον.*—*Hist. Eccl.* lib. v. c. 10, p. 223.

The evidence, of which a sketch has thus been given,[1] must be held to establish the fact that S. Matthew *originally* wrote in Hebrew, or rather Syro-Chaldaic; on which the important question arises:—Whence the Greek form of the Gospel which bears his name? Now, while it must be admitted that Hug has altogether failed in shaking the evidence which has been adduced on this subject, he has, at the same time, urged with great force many considerations which prove that *our* Gospel of S. Matthew is itself an original work; *and that S. Matthew was its author.* As Townson has truly observed: "There seems more reason for allowing *two originals* than for contesting either." The following arguments, in support of this opinion, may be assigned:—

Olshausen has drawn attention to the fact that: "While all the Fathers of the Church declare Matthew to have written in Hebrew, they all, notwithstanding, make use of *the Greek text*, as of genuine Apostolic origin, without remarking what relation the Hebrew Matthew bore to our Greek Gospel:—for that the oldest Fathers of the Church did not possess Matthew's Gospel *in any other form than that in which we now have it*, is fully settled."[2] A few illustrations of this important fact may be given:—[3]

Origen, who, in the passage referred to above, had stated that "Four Gospels only are admitted without controversy by the Church of God" (cf. *supra*, Lecture ii. p. 56, note [1]), and had described S. Matthew as *γράμμασιν Ἑβραϊκοῖς συγτεταγμένον*—"seems in his book 'On Prayer,' to suppose it published by him in Greek too; for, in discoursing on the word *Ἐπιούσιον*, he considers it as a word formed by the Evangelist himself."[4]

S. Cyril of Jerus., when arguing with the Jews in proof of the Resurrection, having observed that the Apostles were all Jews, asks:—*Διὰ τί οὖν τοῖς Ἰουδαίοις ἀπιστεῖτε;* Nay, he adds, *Ματθαῖος, ὁ γράψας τὸ Εὐαγγέλιον, Ἑβραΐδι γλώσσῃ τοῦτο ἔγραψε.*—*Catechesis*, xiv. § 15, p. 212. But, within a few pages, he quotes the *Greek* Gospel under S. Matthew's name: *Ἐν μὲν γὰρ τῷ κατὰ Ματθαῖον Εὐαγγελίῳ γέγραπται· πλὴν λέγω ὑμῖν, ἀπ' ἄρτι ὄψεσθε τὸν Υἱὸν τοῦ Ἀνθ. κ. τ. λ.* [S. Matt.

[1] A complete summary of the evidence on this subject will be found in Michaelis' "Introd. to the N. T.," Marsh's ed., vol. iii. part i. page 116, &c.

[2] "The Genuineness of the New Testament writings" (Clarke's For. Theol. Lib. p. xxviii).

[3] Cf. the following testimonies from the first two centuries:—Clemens Alex. quotes S. Matt. i. 17, with the words:—*ἐν τῷ κατὰ Ματθ. Εὐαγγελίῳ.*—*Strom.* i. p. 409. S. Irenæus quotes *verbatim* S. Matt. i. 1, and 18, as follows:—*Ματθαῖος δὲ τὴν κατ' ἄνθρωπον αὐτοῦ γέννησιν κηρύττει, λέγων· κ, τ. λ.*—*Cont. Hær.* III. c. xi., p. 191 (cf. *supra* p. 90, note [1]). So also Tertullian:—"Ipse in primis Matthæus, fidelissimus Evangelii commentator * * * ita exorsus est; 'Liber genituræ Jesu Christi, Filii David, Filii Abraham.'"—*De Carne Christi*, § 22, p. 376.

[4] Townson, "Discourse" ii. § 2, p. 29. The words of Origen are:—*Τί δὲ καὶ τὸ ἐπιούσιον, ἤδη κατανοητέον * * * συνηνέχθησαν γοῦν ὁ Ματθαῖος καὶ ὁ Λουκᾶς περὶ αὐτῆς μηδαμῶς διαφερούσης, αὐτὴν ἐξενηνοχότες.*—*De Oratione*, t. i. p. 245.

xxvi. 64].—*Ibid.* § 29, p. 220 (cf. too his literal transcription of S. Matt. i. 1, "Catech." xi. § 5, p. 151).

Eusebius, commenting on Ps. lxxviii., observes that the phraseology of the LXX. is different from *that employed by S. Matthew*, who, himself master of the Hebrew language, has cited the words *according to his own translation*:—Ὁ δὴ διδάσκει καὶ ἡ τῶν ἱερῶν Εὐαγγελίων γραφὴ, δι' ἧς εἴρηται, ὅτι πάντα ταῦτα ἐλάλησεν ὁ Ἰησοῦς ἐν παραβολαῖς τοῖς ὄχλοις, κ. τ. λ. [S. Matt. xiii. 35]. * * * Ἀντὶ γὰρ τοῦ, φθέγξομαι προβλήματα ἀπ' ἀρχῆς, Ἑβραῖος ὢν ὁ Ματθαῖος, οἰκείᾳ ἐκδόσει κέχρηται εἰπών· ἐρεύξομαι κεκρυμμένα ἀπὸ καταβολῆς· ἀνθ' οὗ ὁ μὲν Ἀκύλας, ὀμβρήσω αἰνίγματα ἐξ ἀρχῆθεν, ἐκδέδωκεν· ὁ δὲ Σύμμαχος, ἀναβλύσω κ. τ. λ.—*Comm. in Psalm.* (ed. Montfaucon, p. 463).[1]

Having quoted this statement, Hug[2] refers to the objection that, as S. Matthew had written *in Syriac*, the version of the Psalmist's words given in our Greek Gospel is made not from the Hebrew, but from the Syriac: and he appeals, in reply, to the manner in which Eusebius compares this version with that of Aquila; adding:—"Did Matthew then write his Gospel in Syriac, and cite passages in it from the Old Testament *in the Greek language?*"—*loc. cit.* s. 19.

In connexion with the argument founded upon this passage from Eusebius, and still more unambiguously intimating that S. Matthew himself translated the Hebrew text of the Psalm *into Greek*, cf. the quotation from S. Jerome prefixed to Lecture vii. S. Jerome, it is true, says in the passage (B) that it is not quite *certain* who was the translator of the Hebrew Gospel. It would appear, too, from many parts of his writings, that he

[1] The following remarks of Eusebius have also been quoted. He is discussing the relation of S. Matt. xxviii. 1, to S. John, xx. 1:—Ὁ μὲν γὰρ Εὐαγγελιστὴς Ματθαῖος Ἑβραΐδι γλώττῃ παρέδωκε τὸ Εὐαγγέλιον· ὁ δὲ ἐπὶ τὴν Ἑλλήνων φωνὴν μεταβαλὼν αὐτὸ, τὴν ἐπιφώσκουσαν ὥραν εἰς τὴν κυριακὴν ἡμέραν, ὀψὲ σαββάτων προσεῖπεν. On this, he proceeds to argue as if the Greek term ὀψέ had proceeded from S. Matthew; as well as from the use of the *plural*, σαββάτων:—οὕτως οὖν ὁ Ματθαῖος τὸν καιρὸν τὸν ἐπιφαύσκοντα εἰς τὴν ἕω τῆς κυριακῆς ἡμέρας, σαββάτων ὀψὲ ὠνόμασεν· οὐκ εἰπὼν ἑσπέραν τοῦ σαββάτου, οὐδὲ ὀψὲ σαββάτου.—*Quæst. ad Marin.* (ap. A. Mai, "Script. Vet. Nova Coll.," t. i. pp. 64–66).

[2] On Hug's inference from this passage,—to which he considers it "hardly necessary to allude,"—Dr. Davidson (and here he follows Meyer, "Evang. des Matt.," Einleit., s. 7) observes: "But the term ἔκδοσις does not signify *translation*. It denotes *recension*. The phrase Ἑβραῖος ὢν indicates the native country of the Apostle, and so determines the sense of οἰκεῖος. Matthew, being a Hebrew, used *that recension* of the Old Testament text, which was current in his native land; and had the Hebrew words to which ἐρεύξομαι κεκρυμμένα, κ. τ. λ., and not φθέγξομαι, κ. τ. λ. correspond."—*Introd. to the New Test.*, vol. i. p. 12. Were such a principle indeed true, or capable of even probable proof, it would afford a simple means of accounting in all cases for the form in which quotations from the Old Testament meet us in the New. It would at once entitle us, on the authority of the inspired writers of the New Testament, to alter the Hebrew text in conformity with the "recension" to which our Lord and his Apostles must (on Dr. Davidson's supposition) have given their sanction. The existence of such "recension," however, has yet to be proved: and I do not find that Dr. Davidson has availed himself of this principle in his useful discussion of "Quotations from the Old Testament in the New." ("Sacred Hermeneutics," ch. xi. pp. 334–515.) But the matter is placed beyond discussion by the use of ἐκδέδωκεν in this very passage, to signify the manner in which Aquila ***interpreted*** or *rendered* the same words.

regarded S. Matthew's *Hebrew* Gospel as agreeing substantially with that received by the Nazarenes and Ebionites, and which *he himself had translated.* E. g.—"In Evangelio, quo utuntur Nazaræni et Ebionitæ (quod nuper in Græcum de Hebræo sermone transtulimus, et quod vocatur a plerisque Matthæi authenticum) &c."—*Comment. in Matt.* xii. 13, t. vii, p. 77.[1] On all such statements two remarks are to be made:—(1) S. Jerome would surely not have translated this document into Greek, had it not differed considerably from the Canonical Gospel. (2) Whenever S. Jerome refers to the Gospel of S. Matthew, he quotes it according to our present Greek text; and when he introduces diverging statements of the "Hebrew Gospel," he does so in a manner which proves that he regarded *it* as of no authority whatsoever. Thus, when alluding to the difference between S. Matthew's mode of giving an Old Testament passage and *the translation of the LXX.* (e. g. ch. ii. 6) he writes: "Quanta sit inter Matthæum et LXX. verborum ordinisque discordia, magis admiraberis, si Hebraicum videas, in quo ita scriptum est," &c.—*Ad Pammach.*, Ep. lvii. t. i. p. 311. And again, discussing what the rending of the Veil of the Temple might mean, he incidentally alludes to a statement of the "Hebrew Gospel,"—of which he takes no further notice; and then proceeds with his examination of the Greek text: "In Evangelio autem quod Hebraicis literis scriptum est, legimus, non velum Templi scissum; sed superliminare Templi miræ magnitudinis corruisse."—*Ad Hedibiam*, Ep. cxx. t. i. p. 825.

To which considerations if we add the fact that all Versions, even the ancient Syriac (in which dialect, be it observed, the Gospel is said to have been originally written),[2] are taken from the present Greek text of S. Matthew, and not from an unknown Aramaic original,—it clearly follows, (1) that the Hebrew Gospel can never have been regarded as Canonical; (2) that it belonged to that class of writings to which I have referred, *supra*, Lecture ii. p. 54, &c., which, although composed by inspired men, were never *designed* to form part of the Bible; and (3) that, since the concurrent voice of antiquity declares the first of our four Greek Gospels to have proceeded from S. Matthew, we are justified in assuming that it actually *has* proceeded, *in its present form*, from the pen of that Apostle. But—

II. This inference is strongly confirmed by the admitted fact that, "our

[1] A writer in "The Edinburgh Review" (July, 1851, p. 39), observes:—"Jerome himself at first thought that it was the authentic Matthew, and translated it into both Greek and Latin from a copy which he obtained at Berœa in Syria. This appears from his Catalogue of Illustrious Men, written in the year 392. Six years later, in his Commentary on Matthew, he spoke more doubtfully about it,—'quod vocatur *a plerisque* Matthæi authenticum.' Later still, in his book on the Pelagian heresy, written in the year 415, he modifies this account still further, describing the work as the 'Evangelium juxta Hebræos, quod Chaldaico quidem Syroque sermone, sed *Hebraicis literis* scriptum est, quo utuntur usque hodie Nazareni, secundum Apostolos, sive, *ut plerique autumant* juxta Matthæum, quod et in Cæsariensi habetur Bibliotheca.'"

[2] This fact is the more to our purpose when we call to mind the nature of the Syrian tradition on this subject. Assemanni ("Bibl. Orient.," vol. iii. p. 8) thus translates a passage in Ebedjesu's "Catal. Libror. Syrorum:" "Cujus [*scil.* Novi Testamenti] caput est Matthæus, *qui Hebraice in Palæstina scripsit.*" On which Assemanni notes:—"*Hæc est communis Syrorum sententia* de sermone, quo primum Evangelia conscripta dicuntur," &c.

Greek Gospel of Matthew is of such a peculiar character, that it is impossible for us to regard it as a mere version. Does a man who is translating an important work from one language into another allow himself to make alterations in the book which he is translating, *to change the ideas it presents?* Something of the kind must be supposed to have been done in the Greek Gospel of Matthew with regard to the Hebrew. * * * Now as sometimes *the argument is wholly based on this independent character of the text in the citations from the books of the Old Testament*, and could not have accorded at all with the Hebrew Gospel of Matthew, it is clear that our Greek Gospel must be something else than a mere version."—Olshausen, *loc. cit.*[1] This *independent character* of our Greek Gospel, as inferred from its manner of quoting the Old Testament, is allowed almost universally by critics.[2] (I should add that Ebrard questions the force of this argument; on the ground that the Greek Gospel is but the translation of an Aramaic original, in which the Hebrew texts *had been already translated.* No *independence*, therefore, he argues, can be ascribed to the Greek:—see his "Krit. der ev. Gesch.," s. 766.)

III. But the most important branch of the argument remains:—"The idea that some unknown individual translated the Hebrew Gospel of Matthew, and that this translation is our Canonical Gospel, is, in the first place, contradicted by the circumstance *of the universal diffusion of this same Greek Gospel* of Matthew, which makes it absolutely necessary to suppose that the translation was executed by some one of acknowledged influence in the Church, indeed, of Apostolic authority. In any other case, would not objections to this Gospel have been urged in some quarter or other, *particularly in the country where Matthew himself labored*, and where his writings were familiarly known? There is not, however, the slightest trace of any such opposition to it."[3] Let some particular features of the case be here glanced at. All are agreed that S. Matthew was the first to write. The passage from S. Irenæus, quoted above (p. 526), places the date of S. Matthew's (Hebrew, Gospel between the years 60–70: and Eusebius states what he had ascertained as to the occasion of its composition;—viz., that when S. Matthew (who alone had remained up to this date at Jerusalem) "was on the point of going to preach elsewhere, he left the Church his Gospel, written in his native tongue, in order to supply the want of his presence (ὡς ἔμελλε καὶ ἐφ' ἑτέρους ἰέναι, πατρίῳ γλώττῃ γραφῇ παρα-

[1] A translator, in short, would either have borrowed from the LXX. its version of the Hebrew quotations inserted in the Aramaic original; or he would have himself supplied a translation according to the *Hebrew*:—in no case would he have ventured to alter the literal meaning by a free translation. The cases in which the author of our Greek Gospel has freely used the Hebrew text of the Old Testament, and departed from the LXX., are, S. Matt. xii. 19; xiii. 35; viii. 17 (cf., *supra*, p. 321); xxvii. 9, 10 (cf., *supra*, p. 309, note); xv. 9. See Hug, *loc. cit.* § 12, s. 52.

[2] De Wette observes: "On account of its relation to the other Gospels,—partly in its use of the LXX., partly in Greek expressions,—so much is certain, that we by no means have in it the simple translation of an Aramaic original composition proceeding from an Apostle"—*Einleit.*, Th. ii. s. 166. And he quotes Credner, who has proved ("Einleit.," s. 94) that all the quotations from the Pentateuch evince, by the form in which they are cited, their Greek origin; especially ch. xix. 5; xv. 4; xviii. 16, &c. The Greek foundation, too, of the form in which the Prophets are quoted is no less unmistakeable.—(*ibid.* s. 168.)

[3] Olshausen, *loc. cit.*

δοὺς τὸ κατ' αὐτὸν Εὐαγγέλιον κ. τ. λ.)"—(H. E. iii. c. 24, p. 116). Here comes in the important testimony of S. Papias (A); which, as Thiersch shows, directs us to the author of the Greek Gospel, and which he translates as follows: "Matthew *had* composed the sacred traditions in the Hebrew language, and each interpreted them as best he could," ["if we thus," writes Thiersch, "translate his words (the aorist as pluperfect), they point—if they are not to be considered as fragmentary to the extent of being unintelligible—to the following thought as their completion"]—until *Matthew himself* published the Greek document, which is read in the whole Church as his Gospel." [1] If mere natural capabilities be looked for, who more competent to undertake such a translation than "Matthew the Publican," who, *from his office*, was necessarily acquainted with the Greek language, so generally spoken in Palestine? And as to the solicitude of the Apostles for the Hellenistic Jews, we have a sufficient proof in the case where "there arose a murmuring of the Grecians against the Hebrews," in a matter of ordinary detail (Acts, vi. 1).[2] We cannot doubt, therefore, that, as soon as the want was felt of a Greek translation of the Hebrew Gospel, means were taken to supply it: to which the additional motive was added of providing a work profitable for the Church universal, which day after day was taking deeper root among the Gentiles as it was spurned by the Jews. The Hebrew Gospel, therefore, was at once supplanted by its Greek successor, which from the earliest times has occupied the first place in the New Testament Canon. On no other hypothesis, indeed, than that of S. Matthew himself having supplied the present form of his earlier work, can we account either for the profound silence of ancient writers respecting the translator[3]—whose version, as we

[1] "Versuch der Herstell.," s. 193. Thiersch explains the meaning of the word "interpreted" (*ἡρμήνευσε*) in this place, by assuming that in this Christian community of native-born Jews, the established custom of the Synagogue worship (see, *supra*, Lecture vii. p. 325, note [2]) had been adopted; and that the *reading* of the Hebrew document was followed by an "interpretation" for the benefit of those who understood only Greek. He refers to Neander "Kirchen-Geschichte," B. i. s. 522) who states that "in many Egyptian and Syrian towns, there were ecclesiastics, *as in the Jewish Synagogues*, who forthwith translated what was publicly read into the vernacular tongue, in order that it might be generally intelligible,—quoting the words of S. Epiphanius when enumerating the different ecclesiastical offices: *Ἑρμηνευταὶ γλώσσης εἰς γλῶσσαν, ἢ ἐν ταῖς ἀναγνώσεσιν, ἢ ἐν ταῖς προσομιλίαις.*—*Expos. Fid. Cathol.*, c. xxi. ("Adv. Hær." lib. iii., t. i. p. 1104).

[2] That the publication of such a translation *by the author himself* was nothing unusual, Townson proves by the evidence of Josephus; who states, in the preface to his narrative of the Jewish War, that his Greek work is but the translation of an earlier composition in Hebrew; which he translates from motives nearly the same as those that have been suggested in the text as likely to have given rise to the Greek form of our Gospel.

[3] When I say that we have no *early* information as to the translator, of course I do not mean to ignore the existence of the following hypotheses, which have been started by later writers:—E. g. In the "Synopsis Scripturæ Sacræ," to be found among the works of S. Athanasius (t. ii. p. 202), (but which Credner "Zur Geschichte des Kanons," s. 127 ff., proves to be, at the earliest, a work of the tenth century), the ingenious conjecture is offered that it was translated by S. James, "the Lord's brother, and first Bishop of Jerusalem." (Cf. what has been said in the text as to the solicitude of the Church for the Hellenizing Christians *at Jerusalem*.) In the "Chronicon" of S. Isidore of Seville, S. Barnabas is named (p. 272): Theophylact. ("Comment in Matt." Præf., t. i. p. 2) is followed by Euthymius Zigabenus ("Comm. in. Evang. Matth.," t. i. p. 15, ed. Matthæi Lips. 1792) in representing S. John as the translator.

have seen (p. 469), was everywhere received and quoted as if it actually proceeded from S. Matthew himself; or for the absence of the least trace of *any other* Greek translation of the Hebrew original. John the Presbyter (to whom unquestionably the statement of S. Papias (A) must be traced) clearly represents the time as past, when each used to interpret for himself the Hebrew Gospel. He evidently implies that our present Greek Gospel was the element of the Canon contributed by S. Matthew; and he states the fact of its original form merely as a piece of casual information, likely to interest those who inquired respecting the origin of the Gospels. The same may be said of all succeeding writers, who repeat that information; but who quote, as we have seen, the Greek Gospel as an original work of S. Matthew.

Should this conclusion not be received, no one, at least, can refuse to accept the conclusion of Ebrard, "that the translation was prepared during the lifetime of the Apostles; unquestionably, too, under their inspection, and by their commission" (*loc. cit.* s. 786). It is only by means of these facts—viz. the early composition, and Apostolic recognition of our Greek Gospel—that we can account for the disappearance of the Hebrew original, or explain the absence of any satisfactory information respecting it. And this is all that is required, in order to remove every difficulty as to the Inspiration of the Greek form of S. Matthew's Gospel.

APPENDIX N.

"INSPIRED REASONING."

(LECTURE VIII.—PAGE 372.)

I HAVE selected Mr. Morell as the exponent of this opinion, merely because his statement of it is characterized by considerable ability, and is advocated with more than usual force. In general the character of Inspiration has been denied to the Reasoning of the sacred writers for the sole purpose of evading the force of certain passages in Scripture, which could not be reconciled with some favorite theory. Thus Bishop Burnet, in his remarks on the sixth Article of the Church of England, observes:—"When Divine writers argue upon any point, we are always bound to believe the conclusions that their reasonings end in, as parts of Divine Revelation: but we are not bound to be able to make out, *or even to assent to*, all the premises made use of by them." Paley, who quotes and adopts this statement, adds:—"In reading the Apostolic writings, we distinguish between their doctrines and their arguments. Their doctrines came to them by Revelation, properly so called; yet in propounding these doctrines in their writings or discourses, they were wont to illustrate, support, and enforce them, by such analogies, *arguments*, and considerations, as their own thoughts suggested. * * * The doctrine [of the call of the Gentiles] itself must be received; but *it is not necessary in order to defend Christianity* to defend the propriety of every comparison, or *the validity of every argument*, which the Apostle has brought into the discussion.

The same observation applies to some other instances." [1]—*Evidences of Christianity*, part iii. ch. 2.

The form in which Mr. Morell has stated this objection is plainly founded upon that particular view of syllogistic Reasoning according to which, when you admit the major premiss, you assert the conclusion either directly, or by implication; [2]—in other words, the view which represents the conclusion as an inference from the major premiss. [3] If this doctrine of the syllogism be received, the reply to the objection may be briefly stated. The major premiss being allowed (as by Mr. Morell) to be some truth divinely revealed, the objector argues that, as the human mind by its own powers can proceed according to the rules of Logic, no Inspiration was required to draw the conclusion; which, according to the doctrine assumed, is but an inference from the one admitted truth. Is it, however, so very obvious a fact, that human Reasoning proceeds in such an orderly and undeviating a course as to require no guidance? Do the opinions of mankind, deduced from facts universally received, or from principles which the understanding, of necessity, acknowledges,—present a unanimity so striking as to justify the assertion that an *inspired* development of that Truth which God has *revealed* is either superfluous, or unnecessary? Of course no one will maintain such an assertion for a moment: and, accordingly, the objection, as I have already observed (see, *supra*, p. 371, note [2]), is at once removed by referring to the distinction between Inspiration and Revelation; as well as to the importance of the former in relation to the

[1] Bishop Hinds justly points out that to suppose the writers of the New Testament "left *liable* to any false reasoning or to any mistaken application of old prophecy," is simply to theorize gratuitously: "because the question is not really one of fact, as the Bible may be confidently defended against the charge of actual error of either kind."—*Inspiration*, p. 162.

[2] Thus Archbishop Whately ("Logic," 9th ed, p. 239), states that "the object of all Reasoning is merely to expand and unfold the assertions wrapt up, as it were, and implied in those with which we set out, and to bring a person to perceive and acknowledge the full force of that which he has admitted." Mr. J. S. Mill illustrates as follows, the nature of his objections to this theory: "I do not say that a person who affirmed, before the Duke of Wellington was born, that all men are mortal, *knew* that the Duke of Wellington was mortal; but I do say, that he *asserted* it: and I ask for an explanation of the apparent logical fallacy of adducing, in proof of the Duke of Wellington's mortality, a general statement which presupposes it. Finding no sufficient resolution of this difficulty in any of the writers on logic, I have attempted to supply one."—*A System of Logic*, vol. i. ch. iii., 3d ed., p. 207, note.

[3] Under this aspect the subject is discussed by S. Th. Aquinas, when considering the question, "Utrum Sacra Doctrina sit argumentativa:"—"Sicut aliæ scientiæ non argumentantur ad sua principia probanda, sed ex principiis argumentantur ad ostendendum alia in ipsis scientiis; ita hæc doctrina non argumentatur ad sua principia probanda, quæ sunt articuli Fidei; sed ex iis procedit ad aliquid ostendendum: sicut Apostolus 1 ad Cor. xv. ex Resurrectione Christi argumentatur ad resurrectionem communem probandam. * * * Utitur Sacra Doctrina etiam ratione humana, non quidem ad probandam Fidem *sed ad manifestandum aliqua alia quæ traduntur in hac Doctrina.* Cum igitur *gratia non tollat naturam, sed perficiat*, oportet quod naturalis ratio subserviat Fidei, sicut et naturalis inclinatio voluntatis obsequitur caritati. Unde et Apostolus dicit 2 ad Cor. x. 5: 'In captivitatem redigentes omnem intellectum in obsequium Christi.' Et inde est quod etiam auctoritatibus Philosophorum sacra doctrina utitur, ubi per rationem naturalem veritatem cognoscere potuerunt, sicut Paulus, Act. xvii. 28, inducit verbum Arati, dicens: 'Sicut et quidam poetarum vestrorum dixerunt: Genus Dei sumus.' "—*Summ. Theol.*, pars 1 ma, qu. i. art. viii., t. xx. p. 7.

latter (see, *supra*, p. 145). Of the neglect of this distinction no clearer illustration can be given than the remark of Paley just quoted:[1] what I have already said, therefore (p. 371), is of itself sufficient to meet this aspect of the question.

A still more complete answer, however, is supplied, and this whole subject has been placed in its true light, by the profound theory of syllogistic Reasoning lately put forward by Mr. J. S. Mill;[2] of which the following is a rapid sketch:—

Ordinarily the major premiss of a syllogism may be regarded as a general proposition or formula which records or registers the inferences already made from particular cases; and "the conclusion is not an inference drawn *from* the formula, but an inference drawn *according* to the formula: the real logical antecedent, or premisses being the particular facts from which the general proposition was collection by induction." According to the indications of this record we draw our conclusion: and the rules of the syllogism are a set of precautions to ensure our reading the record correctly. In this view of the question we assume that our knowledge has been derived from observation; but there are other sources from which we may also suppose it to come. It may present itself as coming from testimony, and it may present itself as coming from Revelation; and this latter species of knowledge, "thus supernaturally communicated, may be conceived to comprise not only particular facts but general propositions, such as occur so abundantly in the writings of Solomon and in the Apostolic Epistles.[3] Or the generalization may not be, in the ordinary sense, an assertion at all, but a command; a law, not in the philosophical, but in the moral and political sense of the term: an expression of the desire of a superior, that we, or any number of persons, shall conform our conduct to certain general instructions. So far as this asserts a fact, namely, a volition of the legislator, that fact is an individual fact, and the proposition, therefore, is not a general proposition. But the description therein contained of the conduct which it is the will of the legislator that his subjects should observe, is general. The proposition asserts *not* that all men *are* anything, but that all men *shall* do something." "These two[4] cases, of a truth re-

[1] Compare also Spinoza's representation of this objection:—"Si ad modum etiam attendamus, quo in his Epistolis Apostoli doctrinam Evangelicam tradunt, eum etiam a modo Prophetarum valde discedere videbimus. Apostoli namque ubique ratiocinantur, ita ut non prophetare sed disputare videantur. Prophetiæ vero contra mera tantum dogmata et decreta continent, quia in iis Deus quasi loquens introducitur, qui non ratiocinatur, sed ex absoluto suæ naturæ imperio decernit. Et etiam quia Prophetæ auctoritas ratiocinari non patitur; *quisquis enim vult sua dogmata ratione confirmare, eo ipso ea arbitrali uniuscujusque judicio submittit.* * * * Itaque tam modi loquendi quam disserendi Apostolorum in Epistolis clarissime indicant easdem non ex revelatione et divino mandato, sed tantum ex ipsorum naturali judicio scriptas fuisse." —*Tract. Theol. Polit.*, cap. xi.

[2] *Loc. cit.* 216, &c.

[3] These latter words are taken from the first edition of Mr. Mill's work (vol. i. p. 260). In the third edition the passage stands thus, more *generally* expressed, but equally conveying the same sense:—"It may present itself as coming from *testimony*, which on the occasion and for the purpose in hand, is accepted as of an authoritative character: and the information thus communicated may be conceived to comprise not only particular facts, but general propositions, as when a scientific doctrine is accepted without examination on the authority of writers."—p. 217.

[4] This statement is omitted in the third edition: cf. the first ed. vol. i. p. 260.

vealed in general terms, and a command intimated in the like manner, might be exchanged for the more extensive cases of any general statement *received upon testimony*[1] and any general practical precept. But the more limited illustrations suit us better, being drawn from subjects where long and complicated trains of ratiocination have actually been grounded upon premisses which came to mankind *from the first* in a general form, the subjects of Scriptural Theology, and of positive Law."[2] "In both these cases the generalities are the original data, and the particulars are elicited from them by a process which correctly resolves itself into a series of syllogisms. * * * The only point to be determined is whether the authority which declared the general proposition *intended to include this case in it*:"—and this "operation is not a process of inference, *but a process of interpretation*." "When the premisses are given by authority, the function of Reasoning is to ascertain the testimony of a witness, or the will of a legislator, by interpreting the signs in which the one has intimated his assertion, and the other his command. In like manner, when the premisses are derived from observation, the function of Reasoning is to ascertain what we (or our predecessors) formerly thought might be inferred from the observed facts, and to do this by interpreting a memorandum of ours or of theirs."

Now, were we to pause here, it would of itself be obvious how essential it was that the sacred writer, when interpreting the divinely revealed Truth from which his Reasoning flows, should have been himself divinely guided, in order to ensure certainty, or even to obtain an insight into the applicability of the Divine command to any particular instance: but we must go a step farther. There are cases, it is true, in which *the minor premiss* (which "always affirms a resemblance between a new case, and some cases previously known")[3] is obvious to the senses, or at once ascertainable by direct observation: it may not, however, be thus intuitively evident, but may itself be known only by inference. It may itself be the conclusion of another argument; and must, therefore, be inferred from some other general proposition, which presents the record of a class of observations that may be totally different.[4] This clearly may take place many times in succession; and hence arises a train of Reasoning.

Under this form almost every instance of Reasoning in Scripture presents itself. The sacred writer, desiring to apply some one proposition that

[1] See note [3] page 476.

[2] On this theory of Mr. Mill, Dr. Whewell observes:—"I say, then, that Mr. Mill appears to me especially instructive in his discussion of the nature of the proof which is conveyed by the syllogism; and that his doctrine, that the form of the syllogism consists in an *inductive assertion, with an interpretation added to it*, solves very happily the difficulties which baffle the other theories of this subject. I think that this doctrine of his is made still more instructive by his excepting from it the cases of Scriptural Theology and of Positive Law, as cases in which general propositions, not particular facts, are our original data."—*Of Induction*, p. 85.

[3] See Mr. Mill's remarks, *loc. cit.* ch. iv. p. 233, &c.

[4] Mr. Mill gives the follow example:—"All arsenic is poisonous; the substance which is before me is arsenic; therefore it is poisonous." Here to prove the minor, viz., "the substance which is before me is arsenic," we proceed thus:—"Whatever forms a compound with hydrogen, which yields a black precipitate with nitrate of silver, is arsenic: the substance before me conforms to this condition; therefore it is arsenic."—*Ibid* p. 234.

expresses the Revelation from which he proceeds, introduces a second proposition in order to exhibit its applicability. Now, this second proposition may be merely the *result* of some other Divine Truth; or be itself a revealed proposition. In such a train of Reasoning each new premiss may have been supernaturally communicated (cf. the remark of Professor Butler quoted, *supra*, p. 369, note [2]); and thus, in point of fact, the inspired reasoner but connects the different threads of the Divine Counsels, exemplifies how "deep answereth to deep" in the mysteries of Revelation, and presents in one connected train of argument those words of God which had been uttered "at sundry times and in divers manners."[1]

[1] E. g. the reasoning of S. Paul, 1 Cor. iii. 16, is plainly a case of this kind. His argument may be thus stated:—"The habitation of the Spirit of God becomes thereby the Temple of God; you are the habitation of the Spirit of God; therefore, know ye not that ye are the Temple of God." Here (the argument having been stated under the form of an *Enthymeme*, the minor premiss being expressed), the suppressed major premiss is a general proposition which defines the true nature of the Temple of God; and may be regarded either as being itself a new revelation, or, perhaps, merely as the record or register of earlier revelations on the subject. The minor premiss, in turn, is itself a revelation; for Christ had already declared:—"The Spirit of Truth Whom the world cannot receive. * * * He dwelleth with you, and shall be in you."—S. John, xiv. 17. The conclusion, thus deduced, becomes, in the next place, a premiss in the argument stated in the following verse:—"If any man defile the Temple of God, him shall God destroy; FOR the Temple of God **is holy,** ***which Temple ye are.***"

THE END.

www.ingramcontent.com/pod-product-compliance
Lightning Source LLC
LaVergne TN
LVHW020931110826
845150LV00004B/833

9781425553302